O9-ABH-508

Brief Contents

On the Study Site

Detailed Contents

INVESTIGATING
the SOCIAL
WORLD

THE PROCESS AND PRACTICE OF RESEARCH

Russell K. Schutt
University of Massachusetts Boston

Los Angeles | London | New Delhi
Singapore | Washington DC

Los Angeles | London | New Delhi
Singapore | Washington DC

FOR INFORMATION:

SAGE Publications, Inc.
2455 Teller Road
Thousand Oaks, California 91320
E-mail: order@sagepub.com

SAGE Publications Ltd.
1 Oliver's Yard
55 City Road
London, EC1Y 1SP
United Kingdom

SAGE Publications India Pvt. Ltd.
B 1/I 1 Mohan Cooperative Industrial Area
Mathura Road, New Delhi 110 044
India

SAGE Publications Asia-Pacific Pte. Ltd.
3 Church Street
#10-04 Samsung Hub
Singapore 049483

Acquisitions Editor: Jerry Westby
Associate Editor: Jessica Miller
Digital Content Editor: Rachael Leblond
Editorial Assitant: Laura Kirkhuff
Production Editor: Tracy Buyan
Copy Editor: Robin Gold/Forbes Mill Press
Typesetter: C&M Digitals (P) Ltd.
Proofreader: Christine Dahlin
Indexer: Maria Sosnowski
Cover Designer: Michael Dubowe
Marketing Manager: Erica DeLuca

Copyright © 2015 by SAGE Publications, Inc.

All rights reserved. No part of this book may be reproduced or utilized in any form or by any means, electronic or mechanical, including photocopying, recording, or by any information storage and retrieval system, without permission in writing from the publisher.

Printed in Canada

Library of Congress Cataloging-in-Publication Data

Schutt, Russell K.
Investigating the social world : the process and practice of research / Russell K. Schutt, University of Massachusetts Boston. — Eighth edition.

pages cm
Includes bibliographical references and index.

ISBN 978-1-4833-5067-7 (pbk.)

1. Social problems—Research. 2. Social sciences—Research. I. Title.

HN29.S34 2015
302.01′5195—dc23   2014024683

This book is printed on acid-free paper.

14 15 16 17 18 10 9 8 7 6 5 4 3 2 1

5. Sampling and Generalizability   147

10. Qualitative Methods   354

On the Study Site

About the Author

Russell K. Schutt, PhD, is Professor and Chair of Sociology at the University of Massachusetts Boston and Lecturer on Sociology in the Department of Psychiatry (Massachusetts Mental Health Center, Beth Israel Deaconess Medical Center) at the Harvard Medical School. He completed his BA, MA, and PhD degrees at the University of Illinois at Chicago and was a postdoctoral fellow in the Sociology of Social Control Training Program at Yale University. In addition to *Investigating the Social World: The Process and Practice of Research* and adaptations of that text—*Making Sense of the Social World* (with Dan Chambliss), *Research Methods in Psychology* (with Paul G. Nestor), *The Practice of Research in Criminology and Criminal Justice* and *Fundamentals of Research in Criminology and Criminal Justice* (with Ronet Bachman), *The Practice of Research in Social Work* and *Fundamentals of Social Work Research* (with Ray Engel), and *Research Methods in Education* (with Joseph Check)—he is the author of *Homelessness, Housing, and Mental Illness* and *Organization in a Changing Environment*, coeditor of *Social Neuroscience: Brain, Mind, and Society* and of *The Organizational Response to Social Problems*, and coauthor of *Responding to the Homeless: Policy and Practice*. He has authored and coauthored 50 peer-reviewed journal articles as well as many book chapters and research reports on homelessness, service preferences and satisfaction, mental health, organizations, law, and teaching research methods. His research has included a mixed-methods investigation of a public health coordinated care program, a study of community health workers and recruitment for cancer clinical trials, a mixed-methods study of a youth violence reduction program, a randomized trial of a peer support program for homeless dually diagnosed veterans, and a randomized evaluation of housing alternatives for homeless persons diagnosed with severe mental illness, with funding from the National Cancer Institute, the Veterans Health Administration, the National Institute of Mental Health, the John E. Fetzer Institute, and state agencies. His current scholarly foci are the impact of the social environment on cognitive and community functioning, the meaning of housing and service preferences, and the value of alternative organizational and occupational structures for service delivery. His prior research has also included investigation of social factors in legal decisions and admission practices and of influences on job and service satisfaction. Details are available at http://rschutt.wikispaces.umb.edu.

Preface

"Roughly nine in 10 college graduates ages 25 to 32 said that their bachelor's degree had paid off or will pay off in the future." And in the same Pew Research Center report, almost as many young adults who had borrowed money for college said their degrees would be worth it (Yen 2014:A9). Isn't it reassuring to read this as you begin yet another course—perhaps the most important one—in your college career? And are you troubled by the other side of the coin: "The economic penalties for not getting a college degree are so much stiffer now than in

| Exhibit P.1 | Rising Earnings Disparity Between Young Adults With and Without a College Degree |

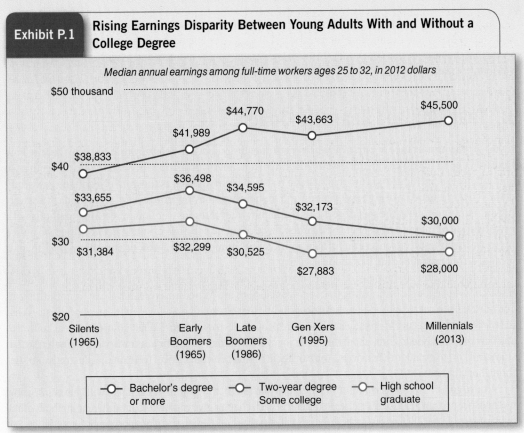

Median annual earnings among full-time workers ages 25 to 32, in 2012 dollars

Bachelor's degree or more:
- Silents (1965): $38,833
- Early Boomers (1965): $41,989
- Late Boomers (1986): $44,770
- Gen Xers (1995): $43,663
- Millennials (2013): $45,500

Two-year degree / Some college:
- Silents (1965): $33,655
- Early Boomers (1965): $36,498
- Late Boomers (1986): $34,595
- Gen Xers (1995): $32,173
- Millennials (2013): $30,000

High school graduate:
- Silents (1965): $31,384
- Early Boomers (1965): $32,299
- Late Boomers (1986): $30,525
- Gen Xers (1995): $27,883
- Millennials (2013): $28,000

Legend: ─○─ Bachelor's degree or more ─○─ Two-year degree Some college ─○─ High school graduate

Source: Pew Research Center, February 10, 2014. "The Rising Cost of Not Going to College." Pew Research Center tabulations of the 2013, 1995, 1986, 1979, and 1965 March Current Population Survey (CPS) Integrated Public Use Micro Samples. Reprinted with permission from Pew Social and Demographic Trends.

Notes: Median annual earnings are based on earnings and work status during the calendar year prior to interview and limited to 25- 32-year-olds who worked full time during the previous calendar year and reported positive earnings. "Full time" refers to those who usually worked at least 35 hours a week last year.

the past"? (Paul Taylor, as quoted in Yen 2014:A9). (See Exhibit P.1 for a picture of the trends underlying Taylor's quote.)

Do you wonder how these findings were obtained? Are you sure the information is trustworthy; that the findings are correct? If you read Hope Yen's *Boston Globe* article about this research, you would learn that these findings come from an analysis of the Census Bureau's *Current Population Survey* and a survey of 2,002 adults conducted by the Pew Research Center. But is that all you need to know to assess the trustworthiness of these findings? Do you want to know what questions were asked in the survey and how the adults were selected?

You can find answers to these questions in the full Pew report, *The Rising Cost of Not Going to College*, by Paul Taylor, Rick Fry, and Paul Oates (2014:12). But these answers will in turn raise more questions: What are "weighted" data? What is a "representative sample"? What is a "margin of sampling error"? How good are the questions asked in the Pew survey (which appear in an appendix to the report)? And what else would you like to know about the "payoff" for college? Is it the same for men and women? Does it vary by race or ethnicity?

Of course, I have only presented a little bit of the evidence in the Taylor, Fry, and Oates report and just a few of its conclusions; there are many related issues to consider and important questions about the evidence to ask. If you're interested, check out the complete report at (http://www.pewsocialtrends.org/2014/02/11/the-rising-cost-of-not-going-to-college/). In any case, this research provides a good starting point for introducing a text on research methods because it illustrates both how systematic research helps us understand pressing social questions and why we need to learn more about research methods to evaluate the results of such research.

Neither our own limited perceptions nor a few facts gleaned from even reputable sources provide us with a trustworthy basis for understanding the social world. We need systematic methods for investigating our social world that enable us to chart our course through the passions of the moment and to see beyond our own personal experience.

▣ Teaching and Learning Goals

If you see the importance of pursuing answers to questions about the social world the way that the Pew Research Center does, you can understand the importance of investigating the social world. One purpose of this book is to introduce you to social science research methods such as those involved in the Pew study of the economic benefits of higher education and to show how they improve everyday methods of answering our questions about the social world. Each chapter integrates instruction in research methods with investigation of interesting aspects of the social world, such as the use of social networking; the police response to domestic violence; and influences on crime, homelessness, work organizations, health, patterns of democratization, and likelihood of voting.

Another purpose of this book is to give you the critical skills necessary to evaluate research. Just "doing research" is not enough. Just reading that some conclusions are "based on a research study" is not sufficient. You must learn to ask many questions before concluding that research-based conclusions are appropriate. What did the researchers set out to investigate? How were people selected for study? What information was collected, and how was it analyzed? Throughout this book, you will learn what questions to ask when critiquing a research study and how to evaluate the answers. You can begin to sharpen your critical teeth on the illustrative studies throughout the book.

A third goal of this book is to train you to actually do research. Substantive examples will help you see how methods are used in practice. Exercises at the end of each chapter give you ways to try different methods alone or in a group. A checklist for research proposals will chart a course when you plan more ambitious studies. But research methods cannot be learned by rote and applied mechanically. Thus, you will learn the benefits and liabilities of each major approach to research and why employing a combination of them is often preferable. You will come to appreciate why the results of particular research studies must always be interpreted within the context of prior research and through the lens of social theory.

▣ Organization of the Book

The way the book is organized reflects my beliefs in making research methods interesting, teaching students how to critique research, and viewing specific research techniques as parts of an integrated research strategy. The text is divided into four sections. The three chapters in the first section, Foundations for Social Research, introduce the why and how of research in general. Chapter 1 shows how research has helped us understand the impact of social networking and changes in social ties. It also introduces some alternative approaches to social research, with a particular emphasis on the contrast between quantitative and qualitative research approaches. Chapter 2 illustrates the basic stages of research with a series of experiments on the police response to domestic violence, it emphasizes the role of theory in guiding research, and it describes the major strategies for research projects. Chapter 3 highlights issues of research ethics by taking you inside of Stanley Milgram's research on obedience to authority and by introducing the institutional review boards that examine the ethics of proposed research. The chapter ends by discussing the organization of research proposals.

The next three chapters, Fundamentals of Social Research, discuss how to evaluate the way researchers design their measures (Chapter 4), draw their samples (Chapter 5), and justify their statements about causal connections (Chapter 6). As you learn about these procedures, you will also read about research on substance abuse and gangs, homelessness, and the causes of violence.

In the next section, Basic Social Research Designs, Chapters 7, 8, and 9 present the primary strategies used in quantitative research: collecting data through experiments and surveys and analyzing data with statistics. The fascinating research examples in these chapters come from investigations of the causes of interpersonal confrontations, the effects of education on health, and the factors associated with voting. Chapters 10 and 11 then introduce the primary strategies used in collecting qualitative data (including participant observation, intensive interviews, and focus groups), and analyzing the results. You will learn in these two chapters about the response to disasters and the course of social interaction.

The Advanced Social Research Designs in Chapters 12 through 16 each can involve both quantitative and qualitative methodologies. Evaluation research, the focus of Chapter 12, can employ experiments, surveys, and qualitative methods to learn about the need for and the effects of social and other types of programs. This chapter begins with an overview of evaluation research on drug abuse prevention programs. Chapter 13 focuses on historical and comparative methodologies, which can use data obtained with one or more of the primary methods to study processes at regional and societal levels over time and between units; research examples focus on the process of democratization and the bases of social revolutions. This chapter also introduces content analysis, which can be used to good effect in historical and comparative research, as well as in research on issues such as gender roles, to reveal how text or pictures reflect social processes.

Chapter 14 introduces the techniques and challenges of secondary data analysis and use of "Big Data." The online availability of thousands of data sets from social science studies has helped make secondary data analysis—the use of previously collected data to investigate new research questions—the method of choice in many investigations. What is termed *big data* is generated by social interaction on the web and by many other processes that create electronic records that can be analyzed with modern computers. Chapter 15 introduces the mixed methods that combine quantitative and qualitative research techniques to improve understanding of the complexities of the social world. Chapter 16 finishes up with an overview of the process of and techniques for reporting research results, an introduction to meta-analysis—a special tool for studying prior research—and some research on ethical problems in writing.

▣ Distinctive Features of the Eighth Edition

The eighth edition of *Investigating the Social World* retains the strengths of previous editions while breaking new ground with newly popular research methods, enhanced tools for learning in the text and online, and contemporary, fascinating research findings. I have reorganized the chapters to better connect related

Berkeley, website (http://sda.berkeley.edu/archive.htm) or at the National Opinion Research Center site (www.norc.uchicago.edu/GSS+Website/).

▣ Ancillaries

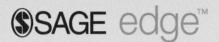

edge.sagepub.com/schutt8e

SAGE edge offers a robust online environment featuring an impressive array of tools and resources for review, study, and further exploration, keeping both instructors and students on the cutting edge of teaching and learning. SAGE edge content is open access and available on demand. Learning and teaching has never been easier!

SAGE edge for students provides a personalized approach to help students accomplish their coursework goals in an easy-to-use learning environment.

- Mobile-friendly **eFlashcards** strengthen understanding of key terms and concepts

- Mobile-friendly practice **quizzes** allow for independent assessment by students of their mastery of course material

- A customized online **action plan** includes tips and feedback on progress through the course and materials, which allows students to individualize their learning experience

- **Chapter summaries** with **learning objectives** reinforce the most important material

- **Interactive exercises** and meaningful web links facilitate student use of internet resources, further exploration of topics, and responses to critical thinking questions

- EXCLUSIVE! Access to full-text **SAGE journal articles** that have been carefully selected to support and expand on the concepts presented in each chapter

SAGE edge for instructors supports teaching by making it easy to integrate quality content and create a rich learning environment for students.

- **Test banks** provide a diverse range of pre-written options as well as the opportunity to edit any question and/or insert personalized questions to effectively assess students' progress and understanding

- **Sample course syllabi** for semester and quarter courses provide suggested models for structuring one's course

- Editable, chapter-specific **PowerPoint® slides** offer complete flexibility for creating a multimedia presentation for the course

- EXCLUSIVE! Access to full-text **SAGE journal articles** that have been carefully selected to support and expand on the concepts presented in each chapter to encourage students to think critically

- **Multimedia content** includes original SAGE videos that appeal to students with different learning styles

- **Lecture notes** summarize key concepts by chapter to ease preparation for lectures and class discussions

- A **Course cartridge** provides easy LMS integration

Acknowledgments

My thanks first to Jerry Westby, publisher and acquisitions editor extraordinaire for SAGE Publications. Jerry's consistent support and exceptional vision have made it possible for this project to flourish, and his good cheer and collegiality have even made it all rather fun. Associate Editor Jessica Miller also contributed her outstanding talents to the success of this edition and to the quality of the Careers and Research highlights. Book production was managed with great expertise and good cheer by Tracy Buyan, while the remarkable Robin Gold proved herself to be one of publishing's most conscientious and effective copy editors. Rachael Leblond artfully managed development of book ancillaries, and Erica DeLuca developed an ambitious marketing strategy. I am grateful to work with such talented staff at what has become the world's best publisher in social science.

I also am indebted to the first-rate social scientists Jerry Westby recruited to critique the seventh edition, and in turn assisted in developing the eighth edition. Their thoughtful suggestions and cogent insights have helped improve every chapter. They are

Karl Besel, Indiana University at Kokomo

Gregory Fulkerson, SUNY Oneonta

Lisa Ann Gittner, Tennessee State University

George Guay, Bridgewater State University

Amy Kroska, University of Oklahoma

Derek Lester, Texas A&M University

Roseanne Macias, California State University at Dominguez Hills

Gina Mann-Delbert, Suffolk University

Tajuana D. Massie, South Carolina State University

Peggy Walsh, Keene University

Greg Weaver, Auburn University

Reviewers for the seventh edition were

Robyn Brown, DePaul University

Jennifer Bulanda, Miami University

Jerry Daday, Western Kentucky University

Marvin Dawkins, University of Miami

Patricia Drentea, University of Alabama at Birmingham

Kenneth Fernandez, University of Nevada, Las Vegas

Elizabeth Monk-Turner, Old Dominion University

David Sanders, Angelo State University

Jimmy Kazaara Tindigarukayo, University of the West Indies

Susan Wurtzburg, University of Hawai'i

The quality of *Investigating the Social World* benefits increasingly from the wisdom and creativity of my coauthors on adaptations for other markets and disciplines, as well as from the pleasure of being part of the support group that we provide each other. My profound gratitude to my SAGE coauthors: Ronet Bachman (University of Delaware), Dan Chambliss (Hamilton College), Joe Check (University of Massachusetts Boston), Ray Engel (University of Pittsburgh), and Paul Nestor (University of Massachusetts Boston). Thanks are also due to Philip Brenner and Peter Marsden for valuable presentations about the latest in survey research at my biennial meeting with coauthors at the Harvard Faculty Club. And I continue to be grateful for advice shared at previous HFC meetings by Charles DiSogra, Karen Hacker, Sunshine Hillygus, Catherine Kohler Riessman, and Robert J. Sampson.

Whitney Gecker, one of my amazing former graduate students, provided indispensable, timely assistance for the eighth edition, checking websites, updating SPSS exercises and the SPSS appendix, identifying SAGE articles for the introductory chapter vignettes, reviewing exhibits, and developing new interactive exercises for this edition. My thanks for her exceptional dedication, consistent good humor, and impressive skills. One of my wonderful current doctoral students, Tatiana Williams-Rodriguez, reviewed the online researcher videos on the *ISW8* Study Site and drafted questions that are now included as chapter exercises.

Reviewers for the sixth edition were

Von Bakanic, College of Charleston

Marvin Dawkins, University of Miami

Carol Erbes, Old Dominion University

Kenneth E. Fernandez, University of Nevada, Las Vegas

Isaac Heacock, Indiana University, Bloomington

Edward Lascher, California State University, Sacramento

Quan Li, University of Central Florida

Steve McDonald, North Carolina State University

Kevin A. Yoder, University of North Texas

Reviewers for the fifth edition were

James David Ballard, California State University, Northridge

Carl Bankston, Tulane University

Diana Bates, The College of New Jersey

Sandy Cook-Fon, University of Nebraska at Kearny

Christopher Donoghue, William Paterson University

Tricia Mein, University of California at Santa Barbara

Jeanne Mekolichick, Radford University

Kevin Mulvey, George Washington University

Jennifer Parker-Talwar, Pennsylvania State University at Lehigh Valley

Nicholas Parsons, Washington State University

Michael J. Scavio, University of California at Irvine

Shaihid M. Shahidullah, Virginia State University

Tabitha Sharp, Texas Woman's University

John Talmage, University of North Florida

Bill Tillinghas, San Jose State University

Fourth edition reviewers were

Marina A. Adler, University of Maryland, Baltimore

Diane C. Bates, Sam Houston State University

Andrew E. Behrendt, University of Pennsylvania

Robert A. Dentler, University of Massachusetts Boston (Chapter 10)

David H. Folz, University of Tennessee

Christine A. Johnson, Oklahoma State University

Carolyn Liebler, University of Washington

Carol D. Miller, University of Wisconsin–La Crosse

Dan Olson, Indiana University South Bend

Brian J. Stults, University of Florida

John R. Warren, University of Washington

Ken Wilson, East Carolina University

Third edition reviewers were

Emmanuel N. Amadi, Mississippi Valley State University

Doug Anderson, University of Southern Maine

Robert B. Arundale, University of Alaska, Fairbanks

Hee-Je Bak, University of Wisconsin–Madison

Marit Berntson, University of Minnesota

Deborah Bhattacharayya, Wittenbert University

Karen Bradley, University of Central Missouri State

Cynthia J. Buckley, The University of Texas at Austin

J. P. Burnham, Cumberland College

Gerald Charbonneau, Madonna University

Hugh G. Clark, Texas Woman's University

Mark E. Comadena, Illinois State University

John Constantelos, Grand Valley State University

Mary T. Corrigan, Binghamton University

John Eck, University of Cincinnati

Kristin Espinosa, University of Wisconsin–Milwaukee

Kimberly Faust, Fitchburg State College

Kenneth Fidel, DePaul University

Jane Hood, University of New Mexico

Christine Johnson, Oklahoma State University

Joseph Jones, Taylor University

Sean Keenan, Utah State University

Debra Kelley, Longwood College

Kurt Kent, University of Florida

Jan Leighley, Texas A&M University

Joel Lieberman, University of Nevada, Las Vegas

Randall MacIntosh, California State University, Sacramento

Peter J. May, University of Washington

Michael McQuestion, University of Wisconsin–Madison

Bruce Mork, University of Minnesota

Jennifer R. Myhre, University of California, Davis

Zeynep Özgen, Arizona State University

Norah Peters-Davis, Beaver College

Ronald Ramke, High Point University

Adinah Raskas, University of Missouri

Akos Rona-Tas, University of California, San Diego

Therese Seibert, Keene State College

Mark A. Shibley, Southern Oregon University

Pamela J. Shoemaker, Syracuse University

Herbert L. Smith, University of Pennsylvania

Paul C. Smith, Alverno College

Glenna Spitze, University at Albany, State University of New York

Beverly L. Stiles, Midwestern State University

Carolina Tolbert, Kent State University

Tim Wadsworth, University of Washington

Charles Webb, Freed-Hardeman University

Adam Weinberg, Colgate University

Special thanks to Barbara Costello, University of Rhode Island; Nancy B. Miller, University of Akron; and Gi-Wook Shin, University of California, Los Angeles, for their contributions to the third edition.

Second edition reviewers were

Nasrin Abdolali, Long Island University, C. W. Post

Lynda Ames, State University of New York, Plattsburgh

Matthew Archibald, University of Washington

Karen Baird, Purchase College, State University of New York

Kelly Damphousse, Sam Houston State University

Ray Darville, Stephen F. Austin State University

Jana Everett, University of Colorado, Denver

Virginia S. Fink, University of Colorado, Colorado Springs

Jay Hertzog, Valdosta State University

Lin Huff-Corzine, University of Central Florida

Gary Hytrek, University of California, Los Angeles

Debra S. Kelley, Longwood College

Manfred Kuechler, Hunter College (CUNY)

Thomas Linneman, College of William & Mary

Andrew London, Kent State University

Stephanie Luce, University of Wisconsin–Madison

Ronald J. McAllister, Elizabethtown College

Kelly Moore, Barnard College, Columbia University

Kristen Myers, Northern Illinois University

Michael R. Norris, University of Texas, El Paso

Jeffrey Prager, University of California, Los Angeles

Liesl Riddle, University of Texas, Austin

Janet Ruane, Montclair State University

Josephine A. Ruggiero, Providence College

Mary Ann Schwartz, Northeastern Illinois University

Mildred A. Schwartz, University of Illinois, Chicago (Chapter 11)

Gi-Wook Shin, University of California, Los Angeles

Howard Stine, University of Washington

William J. Swart, The University of Kansas

Guang-zhen Wang, Russell Sage College

Shernaaz M. Webster, University of Nevada, Reno

Karin Wilkins, University of Texas, Austin

Keith Yanner, Central College

First edition reviewers were

Catherine Berheide, Skidmore College

Terry Besser, University of Kentucky

Lisa Callahan, Russell Sage College

Herbert L. Costner, formerly of University of Washington

Jack Dison, Arkansas State University

Sandra K. Gill, Gettysburg College

Gary Goreham, North Dakota State University

Barbara Keating, Mankato State University

Bebe Lavin, Kent State University

Scott Long, Indiana University

Elizabeth Morrissey, Frostburg State University

Chandra Muller, University of Texas

G. Nanjundappa, California State University, Fullerton

Josephine Ruggiero, Providence College

Valerie Schwebach, Rice University

Judith Stull, Temple University

Robbyn Wacker, University of Northern Colorado

Daniel S. Ward, Rice University

Greg Weiss, Roanoke College

DeeAnn Wenk, University of Oklahoma

I am also grateful for Kathy Crittenden's support on the first three editions, for the contributions of Herbert L. Costner and Richard Campbell to the first edition, and to Steve Rutter, whose vision and enthusiasm launched the whole project on a successful journey.

The interactive exercises on the website began with a series of exercises that I developed in a project at the University of Massachusetts Boston. They were expanded for the second edition by Tom Linneman and a team of graduate students he directed at the University of Washington—Mark Edwards, Lorella Palazzo, and Tim Wadsworth—and tested by Gary Hytrek and Gi-Wook Shin at the University of California, Los Angeles. My format changes in the exercises for the third edition were tested by my daughter, Julia Schutt. Diane Bates and Matthew Archibald helped revise material for instructors and Judith Richlin-Klonsky revised some examples in Chapter 9 for the third edition. Kate Russell developed a new set of exercises and made many other contributions for the seventh edition. Whitney Gecker has now added another track of exercises based on the Research That Matters articles that are also on the study site.

Reef Youngreen and Phil Kretsedemas provided helpful feedback for the seventh edition on, respectively, Chapters 3 and 4. Several former faculty, staff, and graduate students at the University of Massachusetts Boston made important contributions to earlier editions: Heather Albertson, Ra'eda Al-Zubi, Bob Dentler and students in his 1993–1994 graduate research methods class, Anne Foxx, Chris Gillespie, Tracey Newman, Megan Reynolds, Kathryn Stoeckert, and Jeffrey Xavier. Heather Johnson at Northeastern University also contributed to an earlier edition. I continue to be indebted to the many students I have had the opportunity to teach and mentor, at both the undergraduate and graduate levels. In many respects, this book could not have been so successful without the ongoing teaching experiences we have shared. I also share a profound debt to the many social scientists and service professionals with whom I have collaborated in social science research projects.

No scholarly book project can succeed without good library resources, and for these I continue to incur a profound debt to the Harvard University library staff and their extraordinary collection. I also have benefited from the resources maintained by the excellent librarians at the University of Massachusetts Boston.

Again, most important, I thank my wife, Elizabeth, for her love and support and our daughter, Julia, for the joy she brings to our lives and the good she has done in the social world.

—Russell K. Schutt

To Julia Ellen Schutt

SECTION I

Foundations for Social Research

CHAPTER 1

Science, Society, and Social Research

Journal Link
Wi-Fi Use

Online social networking services added a new dimension to the social world in the early years of the 21st century. Mark Zuckerberg started Facebook in 2004 as a service for college students like himself, but by September 30, 2013, Facebook (2013) had grown to be a global service with more than 1.19 billion users—more than one of every six people in the world and four out of every five persons in the United States (Internet World Statistics 2012; Statistic Brain 2013; U.S. Census Bureau 2013a). When we talk about our social world, social media must be part of the conversation.

And what about *your* social world? Has social networking helped you keep in touch with your friends? To make new friends? Is it changing your face-to-face interactions with other people? Are computer-mediated forms of communication enriching your social life?

Research That Matters, Questions That Count

How does wireless access to the Internet affect social life? Do people become less engaged with those around them? Will local community ties suffer? Since the development of the Internet in the 1980s, social scientists have been concerned with the impact of Internet connections on social interaction. Professor Keith Hampton at the University of Pennsylvania and Neeti Gupta at Microsoft investigated these questions by studying wireless Internet users in four coffee shops in Boston and Seattle. The researchers observed at each café for 30 hours, recording notes on the mobile device users' gender and approximate age as well as on their interaction with customers and staff. Hampton and Gupta concluded that there were two types of Internet users in the coffee shops. Some Internet users were "true mobiles" who used the coffee shop as a place to work, for temporary or specific periods, and were largely disengaged from others around them. Hampton and Gupta found that other Internet users—"placemakers"—were primarily in the coffee shops to "hang out" and were very available for unplanned discussions with others about shared interests.

1. Have you observed the same differences in interaction as Hampton and Gupta did?

2. Do you think that their conclusions would have differed if they had studied coffee shops in other cities?

3. Why do you think some Internet users were "true mobiles" and others were "placemakers"? How could you test your explanation?

4. If you wanted to conduct a study like that of Hampton and Gupta, how would you determine whether a café user was a "true mobile" or a "placemaker"?

In this chapter, you will learn about methods used to study changes in social interaction and the conclusions from some of this research. By the end of the chapter, you will have a much firmer basis for answering the questions I have posed. After you finish the chapter, test yourself by reading the 2008 *New Media & Society* article by Keith Hampton and Neeti Gupta at the *Investigating the Social World* study site and completing the related interactive exercises for Chapter 1: edge.sagepub.com/schutt8e.

Hampton, Keith N. and Neeti Gupta. 2008. "Community and Social Interaction in the Wireless City: Wi-Fi Use in Public and Semi-Public Spaces." *New Media & Society* 10(6):831–850.

Let's focus on these issues more systematically. Please answer each of the following questions by checking one of the response options:

1. Generally speaking, would you say that most people can be trusted or that you can't be too careful in dealing with people?
   ___ Most people can be trusted
   ___ You can't be too careful

2. Do you use the Internet, at least occasionally?
   ___ Use Internet
   ___ Do not use Internet

3. Did you happen to use the Internet YESTERDAY?
   ___ Yes
   ___ No

4. Counting all of your online sessions, how much time did you spend using the Internet yesterday?

    ___ Less than 15 minutes

    ___ 15 minutes to less than half hour

    ___ Half hour or more but less than an hour

    ___ More than 1 hour but less than 2 hours

    ___ 2 hours or more but less than 3 hours

    ___ 3 hours or more but less than 4 hours

    ___ 4 hours or more

5. Please tell me if you ever use the Internet to do any of the following things. Do you ever use a social networking site like Myspace, Facebook, or LinkedIn?

    ___ Yes

    ___ No

6. Have you made a friend or contact on a social networking website like Myspace, Facebook, or LinkedIn?

    ___ Yes

    ___ No

7. Do you belong to or ever work with a community group or neighborhood association that focuses on issues or problems in your community?

    ___ Yes

    ___ No

Congratulations! You have just responded to some of the questions in the SNS [Social Networking Sites] and Facebook Survey conducted by Princeton Survey Research Associates International (2010) for the Pew Research Center Internet & American Life Project. Do your responses to these questions represent some aspects of your own engagement in the social world? Do you think other questions should have been asked to give a fuller picture? Do you wonder how your classmates responded? How others in the United States or other countries responded? Did you consider whether your use of the Internet (questions 2–6) has any bearing on other aspects of your social life (questions 1 and 7)?

You probably think about your use of social media and the Internet often and have asked yourself questions like those I have just posed about its importance in your life. That's where social researchers begin, with questions about the social world and a desire to find answers to them. What makes social research different from the ordinary process of thinking about our experiences is a focus on broader questions that involve people outside our immediate experience, issues about why things happen that we may not otherwise consider, and the use of systematic research methods to answer those questions. Keith N. Hampton, Lauren Sessions Goulet, Lee Rainie, and Kirsten Purcell (2011) analyzed the responses received in the SNS and Facebook Survey and reported that 79% of U.S. adults ages 18 to 22 use the Internet and 59% use social networking services, but this usage complements their other social ties, rather than displacing them.

In this chapter, we focus on questions about Internet use, social networking services, and social ties. As we do so, I hope to convince you that the use of research methods to investigate questions about the social world results in knowledge that can be more important, more trustworthy, and more useful than can personal opinions or individual experiences. You will learn how social scientists' investigations are helpful in answering questions about social ties and the impact of the Internet on these ties. You will also learn about the challenges that researchers confront. By the chapter's end, you should know what is "scientific" in social science and appreciate how the methods of science can help us understand the problems of society.

▣ Learning About the Social World

We can get a sense of how sociologists and other social scientists investigate the social world by reviewing some questions that social researchers have asked about the Internet and social ties and the ways they have answered those questions.

1.   What percentage of Americans are connected to the Internet?

   The 2011 Current Population Survey by the U.S. Census Bureau (File 2013a) of approximately 54,000 households revealed that 75% of U.S. households had a computer at home and almost that many were connected to the Internet (File 2013a). The Pew Research Center's Internet & American Life Project 2010 survey of 2,255 adult Americans found that almost half used a social network service (Hampton et al. 2011). These percentages have increased rapidly since personal computers first came into use in the early 1980s and after the Internet became publicly available in the 1990s (see Exhibit 1.1).

Audio Link
Social Media

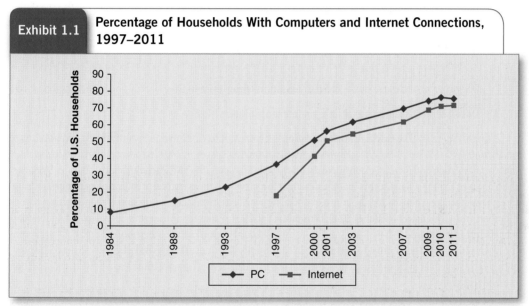

| Exhibit 1.1 | **Percentage of Households With Computers and Internet Connections, 1997–2011** |

Source: File, Thom. 2013a. "Computer and Internet Use in the United States." *Current Population Survey Reports,* P20-569. U.S. Census Bureau, Washington, DC.

2.   How does Internet use vary across social groups?

   Internet use differs dramatically between social groups. As indicated in Exhibit 1.2, Internet use in 2011 ranged from as low as 32% among those with less than a high school education to 90% among those with at least a bachelor's degree (File 2013a), although Internet use has increased for all education levels since 1997 (Strickling 2010). Internet use also increases with family income and is higher among non-Hispanic whites and Asian Americans than among Hispanic Americans and non-Hispanic black Americans (Cooper & Gallager 2004:Appendix, Table 1). Internet users younger than 30 are most likely to use social network sites (89% of those age 18 to 29), compared with those who are middle aged (78% among those age 30 to 49 and 60% of those age 50 to 64) or older (43% of those age 65 and older) (Pew Research Center 2013).

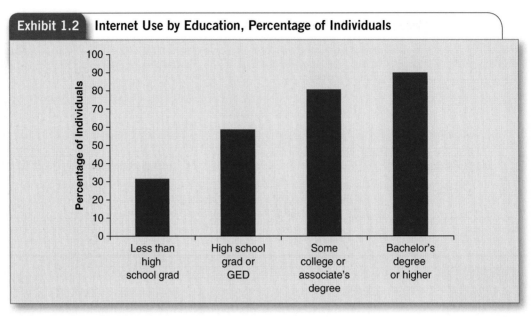

Exhibit 1.2 Internet Use by Education, Percentage of Individuals

Source: File, Thom. 2013a. "Computer and Internet Use in the United States." *Current Population Survey Reports,* P20-569. U.S. Census Bureau, Washington, DC.

3. Does Internet use interfere with the maintenance of social ties?

It doesn't seem so. The extent of social isolation—people not having anyone to confide in—did not change much from 1985 (8%) to 2008 (12%). However, results of another survey in 2004 led other researchers to conclude that social isolation had increased considerably since 1985 (Marsden 1987; McPherson, Smith-Lovin, & Brashears 2006:358 (see Exhibit 1.3). It seems that the design of the survey, changes in interpretation of a key question, and interviewer fatigue when asking the complex social network questions led to omission of some social network members from the answers (Fischer 2009; Hampton et al. 2009; Paika & Sanchagrina 2013). In fact, individuals who use the Internet tend to have larger and more diverse social networks than others do and are about as likely as those who do not use the Internet to participate in community activities. There is no better way to make the point at this early stage that even social science research projects can have errors; we must learn how to evaluate their methods carefully.

4. Does wireless access (Wi-Fi) in such public places as Starbucks decrease social interaction among customers?

As you learned in the initial example in this chapter, Hampton and Gupta (2008) observed Internet use in coffee shops with wireless access in two cities and concluded that there were two types of Wi-Fi users: some who used their Internet connection to create a secondary work office and others who used their Internet connection as a tool for meeting others in the coffee shop. What this means is that Wi-Fi was associated with less social interaction among some customers, but more interaction among others.

5. Do cell phones and e-mail tend to hinder the development of strong social ties?

Based on surveys in Norway and Denmark, Rich Ling and Gitte Stald (2010) concluded that mobile phones increase social ties among close friends and family members, whereas e-mail communication tends to decrease the intensity of our focus on close friends and family members. Other research by the Pew Center has identified positive effects of the Internet and e-mail on social ties (Boase et al. 2006).

Did your personal experiences lead you to expect different answers to these questions? You have just learned that those with more education use the Internet more than do those with less education. Does this variability lead

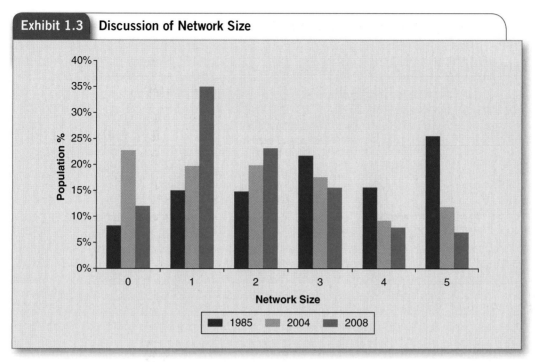

| Exhibit 1.3 | Discussion of Network Size |

Source: Hampton, Keith N, Lauren Sessions Goulet, Eun Ja Her, and Lee Rainie. November 2009. "Social Isolation and New Technology How the Internet and Mobile Phones Impact Americans' Social Networks." Washington, DC: Pew Internet & American Life Project.

you to be cautious about using your own experience as a basis for estimating the behavior of others (# 2)? Have you heard others complain about the effect of the Internet on the maintenance of social ties? Is it safe to draw general conclusions from this anecdotal evidence (# 3)? Have you been sensitive to the effects of surroundings and of mode of communication on different people (#4 and #5)?

We cannot avoid asking questions about our complex social world or trying to make sense of our position in it. Actually, the more that you begin to "think like a social scientist," the more such questions will come to mind—and that's a good thing! But as you've just seen, in our everyday reasoning about the social world, our own prior experiences and orientations can have a major influence on what we perceive and how we interpret these perceptions. As a result, one person may see a person posting a message on Facebook as being typical of what's wrong with modern society, but another person may see the same individual as helping people "get connected" with others. We need to move beyond first impressions and gut reactions to more systematic methods of investigation.

Avoiding Errors in Reasoning About the Social World

How can we avoid errors rooted in the particularities of our own backgrounds and improve our reasoning about the social world? First, let's identify the different processes involved in learning about the social world and the types of errors that can result as we reason about the social world.

When we learn about the social world, we engage in one or more of four processes: (1) "*observing*" through our five senses (seeing, hearing, feeling, tasting, or smelling); (2) *generalizing* from what we have observed to other times, places, or people; (3) *reasoning* about the connections between different things that we have observed; and (4) *reevaluating* our understanding of the social world on the basis of these processes. It is easy to make mistakes with each of these processes.

My favorite example of the errors in reasoning that occur in the nonscientific, unreflective discourse about the social world that we hear on a daily basis comes from a letter to famous advice columnist Ann Landers. The letter was written by someone who had just moved with her two cats from the city to a house in the country. In the city, she had not let her cats outside and felt guilty about confining them. When they arrived in the country, she threw her back door open. Her two cats cautiously went to the door and looked outside for a while, then returned to the living room and lay down. Her conclusion was that people shouldn't feel guilty about keeping their cats indoors—even when they have the chance, cats don't really want to play outside.

Do you see this person's errors in her approach to

- *Observing?* She observed the cats at the outside door only once.

- *Generalizing?* She observed only two cats, both of which previously were confined indoors.

- *Reasoning?* She assumed that others feel guilty about keeping their cats indoors and that cats are motivated by feelings about opportunities to play.

- *Reevaluating?* She was quick to conclude that she had no need to change her approach to the cats.

Journal Link
Social Activity and
Older Demographics

You don't have to be a scientist or use sophisticated research techniques to avoid these four errors in reasoning. If you recognize these errors for what they are and make a conscious effort to avoid them, you can improve your own reasoning about the social world. In the process, you will also be implementing the admonishments of your parents (or minister, teacher, or any other adviser) to avoid stereotyping people, to avoid jumping to conclusions, and to look at the big picture. These are the same errors that the methods of social science are designed to help us avoid.

Observing

> **Selective observation:** Choosing to look only at things that are in line with our preferences or beliefs.

One common mistake in learning about the social world is **selective observation**—choosing to look only at things that are in line with our preferences or beliefs. When we are inclined to criticize individuals or institutions, it is all too easy to notice their every failure. For example, if we are convinced in advance that all heavy Internet users are antisocial, we can find many confirming instances. But what about elderly people who serve as Internet pen pals for grade-school children? Doctors who exchange views on medical developments? Therapists who deliver online counseling? Couples who maintain their relationship when working in faraway cities? If we acknowledge only the instances that confirm our predispositions, we are victims of our own selective observation.

> **Inaccurate observation:** An observation based on faulty perceptions of empirical reality.

Our observations can also simply be inaccurate. If, after a quick glance around the computer lab, you think there are 14 students present, when there are actually 17, you have made an **inaccurate observation**. If you hear a speaker say that "for the oppressed, the flogging never really stops," when what she said was, "For the obsessed, the blogging never really stops" (Hafner 2004), you have made an inaccurate observation.

Such errors occur often in casual conversation and in everyday observation of the world around us. In fact, our perceptions do not provide a direct window onto the world around us, for what we think we have sensed is not necessarily what we have seen (or heard, smelled, felt, or tasted). Even when our senses are functioning fully, our minds have to interpret what we have sensed (Humphrey 1992). The optical illusion in Exhibit 1.4, which can be viewed as either two faces or a vase, should help you realize that perceptions involve interpretations. Different observers may perceive the same situation differently because they interpret it differently.

Generalizing

> **Overgeneralization:** Occurs when we unjustifiably conclude that what is true for some cases is true for all cases.

Overgeneralization occurs when we conclude that what we have observed or what we know to be true for some cases is true for all or most cases (Exhibit 1.5). We are always drawing conclusions about people and social processes from our own interactions with them and perceptions of them, but sometimes we forget that our experiences are limited. The social (and natural) world is, after all, a complex place. We have the ability (and inclination) to interact with just a small fraction of the individuals who inhabit the social world, especially within a limited span of time. Thanks to the Internet, social media, and the practice of "blogging" (i.e., posting personal ruminations on websites), we can easily find many examples of overgeneralization in people's thoughts about the social world. Here's one posted by a frequent blogger who was called for jury duty (http://busblog.tonypierce.com/2005/06/yesterday-i-had-to-go-to-jury-duty-to.html, posted on June 17, 2005):

> yesterday i had to go to jury duty to perform my civil duty. *unlike most people* i enjoy jury duty because i find the whole legal process fascinating, especially when its unfolding right in front of you and you get to help decide yay or nay.

| Exhibit 1.4 | An Optical Illusion |

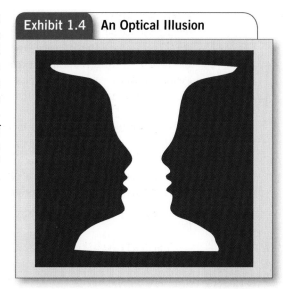

Do you know what the majority of people think about jury duty? According to a Harris Poll, 75% of Americans consider jury service to be a privilege (Grey 2005), so the blogger's generalization about "most people" is not correct. Do you ever find yourself making a quick overgeneralization like that?

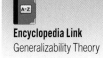

Encyclopedia Link
Generalizability Theory

| Exhibit 1.5 | The Difference Between Selective Observation and Overgeneralization |

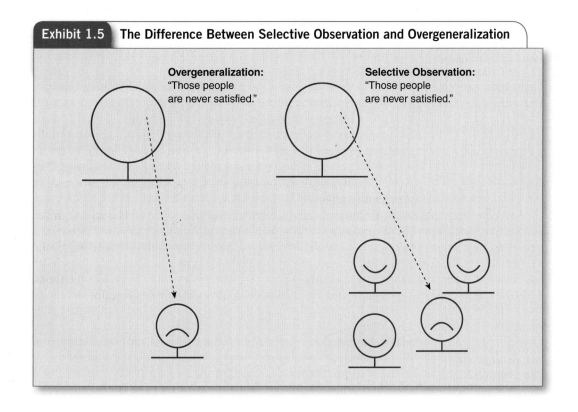

Reasoning

> **Illogical reasoning:** When we prematurely jump to conclusions or argue on the basis of invalid assumptions.

When we prematurely jump to conclusions or argue on the basis of invalid assumptions, we are using **illogical reasoning**. An Internet blogger posted a conclusion about the cause of the tsunami wave that devastated part of Indonesia in 2004 (cited in Schwartz 2005):

> Since we know that the atmosphere has become contaminated by all the atomic testing, space stuff, electronic stuff, earth pollutants, etc., is it logical to wonder if: Perhaps the "bones" of our earth where this earthquake spawned have also been affected?

Is that logical? Another blogger soon responded with an explanation of plate tectonics: "The floor of the Indian Ocean slid over part of the Pacific Ocean" (Schwartz 2005:A9). The earth's crust moves no matter what people do!

It is not always so easy to spot illogical reasoning. For example, about 72% of American households now use the Internet (File 2013a). Would it be reasonable to propose that the 28% who don't participate in the "information revolution" avoid it simply because they don't want to participate? In fact, many low-income households lack the financial resources to buy a computer or maintain an online account and so they use the Internet much less frequently; that's probably not because they don't want to use it (Rainie & Horrigan 2005:63). Conversely, an unquestioned assumption that everyone wants to connect to the Internet may overlook some important considerations; for example, 17% of nonusers of the Internet said in 2002 that the Internet has made the world a worse place, so they may not use it because they don't like what they believe to be its effects (UCLA Center for Communication Policy 2003:78). Logic that seems impeccable to one person can seem twisted to another.

Reevaluating

> **Resistance to change:** The reluctance to change our ideas in light of new information.

Resistance to change, the reluctance to reevaluate our ideas in light of new information, may occur for several reasons:

- *Ego-based commitments.* We all learn to greet with some skepticism the claims by leaders of companies, schools, agencies, and so on that people in their organization are happy, that revenues are growing, and that services are being delivered in the best possible way. We know how tempting it is to make statements about the social world that conform to our own needs rather than to the observable facts. It can also be difficult to admit that we were wrong once we have staked out a position on an issue. Barry Wellman (Boase et al. 2006:1) recounts a call from a reporter after the death of four "cyber addicts." The reporter was already committed to the explanation that computer use had caused the four deaths; now, he just wanted an appropriate quote from a computer-use expert, such as Wellman. But the interview didn't last long:

> The reporter lost interest when Wellman pointed out that other causes might be involved, that "addicts" were a low percentage of users, and that no one worries about "neighboring addicts" who chat daily in their front yards. (Boase et al. 2006:1)

- *Excessive devotion to tradition.* Some degree of devotion to tradition is necessary for the predictable functioning of society. Social life can be richer and more meaningful if it is allowed to flow along the paths charted by those who have preceded us. Some skepticism about the potential for online learning once served as a healthy antidote to unrealistic expectations of widespread student enthusiasm (Bray 1999). But too much devotion to tradition can stifle adaptation to changing circumstances. When we distort our observations or alter our reasoning so that we can maintain beliefs that "were good enough for my grandfather, so they're good enough for me," we hinder our ability to accept new findings and develop new knowledge. Of course, there was nothing "traditional" about maintaining social ties through e-mail when this first became possible in the late 20th century. Many social commentators assumed that the result of increasing communication by e-mail would be fewer social ties maintained through phone calls and personal contact. As a result, it was claimed, the social world would be impoverished. But subsequent research indicated that people who used e-mail more also kept in touch with others more in person and by phone (Benkler 2006:356; Boase et al. 2006).

Video Link
Management

- *Uncritical agreement with authority.* If we do not have the courage to evaluate critically the ideas of those in positions of authority, we will have little basis for complaint if they exercise their authority over us in ways we don't like. And, if we do not allow new discoveries to challenge our beliefs, our understanding of the social world will remain limited. Was it partly uncritical agreement with computer industry authorities that led so many to utopian visions for the future of the Internet? "Entrepreneurs saw it as a way to get rich, policy makers thought it could remake society, and business people hoped that online sales would make stock prices soar. Pundits preached the gospel of the new Internet millennium" (Wellman 2004:25).

Now take just a minute to reexamine the opinions about social ties and Internet use that you recorded earlier. Did you grasp at a simple explanation even though reality is far more complex? Did your own ego and feelings about your similarities to or differences from others influence your beliefs? Did you weigh carefully the opinions of authorities who decry the decline of "community"? Could knowledge of research methods help improve your own understanding of the social world? Do you see some of the challenges social science faces?

In the News

Research in the News

WHY DOESN'T THE INTERNET REACH EVERYONE?

As job applications, health care, movie viewing, and educational programs move online, the importance of access to high-speed Internet is increasing. More than 100 million people are being left behind. The Department of Commerce reported that only 40% of households making $25,000 or less have Internet access at home. The problem of access is highly associated with the high cost of Internet contracts, the limited competition among Internet providers, and the lack of regulatory policies.

For Further Thought

1. What else would you like to research to better understand the problem of those "left behind"?

2. How could you test the impact of lowering costs or of changing regulatory policies?

News source: Crawford, Susan P. 2011. "The New Digital Divide." *The New York Times,* December 4:A1.

▣ Science and Social Science

The scientific approach to answering questions about the natural world and the social world is designed to reduce greatly these potential sources of error in everyday reasoning. **Science** relies on logical and systematic methods to answer questions, and it does so in a way that allows others to inspect and evaluate its methods. In this way, scientific research develops a body of knowledge that is continually refined, as beliefs are rejected or confirmed on the basis of testing empirical evidence.

> **Science:** A set of logical, systematic, documented methods for investigating nature and natural processes; the knowledge produced by these investigations.

> **Social science:** The use of scientific methods to investigate individuals, societies, and social processes; the knowledge produced by these investigations.

Social science relies on scientific methods to investigate individuals, societies, and social processes. It is important to realize that when we apply scientific methods to understanding ourselves, we often engage in activities—asking questions, observing social groups, or counting people—that are similar to things we do in our everyday lives. However, social scientists develop, refine, apply, and report their understanding of the social world more systematically, or "scientifically," than Joanna Q. Public does:

Audio Link
The Internet

- Social science research methods can reduce the likelihood of overgeneralization by using systematic procedures for selecting individuals or groups to study that are representative of the individuals or groups to which we want to generalize.

- To avoid illogical reasoning, social researchers use explicit criteria for identifying causes and for determining whether these criteria are met in a particular instance.

- Social science methods can reduce the risk of selective or inaccurate observation by requiring that we measure and sample phenomena systematically.

- Because they require that we base our beliefs on evidence that can be examined and critiqued by others, scientific methods lessen the tendency to develop answers about the social world from ego-based commitments, excessive devotion to tradition, or unquestioning respect for authority.

Even as you learn to appreciate the value of social science methods, however, you shouldn't forget that *social scientists face three specific challenges:*

1. The objects of our research are people like us, so biases rooted in our personal experiences and relationships are more likely to influence our conclusions.

2. Those we study can evaluate us, even as we study them. As a result, subjects' decisions to "tell us what they think we want to hear" or, alternatively, to refuse to cooperate in our investigations can produce misleading evidence.

3. In physics or chemistry, research subjects (objects and substances) may be treated to extreme conditions and then discarded when they are no longer useful. However, social (and medical) scientists must concern themselves with the way their human subjects are treated in the course of research (much could also be said about research on animals, but this isn't the place for that).

We must never be so impressed with the use of scientific methods in investigations of the social world that we forget to evaluate carefully the quality of the resulting evidence. And we cannot ignore the need always to treat people ethically, even when that involves restrictions on the manipulations in our experiments, the questions in our surveys, or the observations in our field studies.

Pseudoscience or Science

> **Pseudoscience:** Claims presented so that they appear scientific even though they lack supporting evidence and plausibility.

We must also be on guard against our natural tendency to be impressed with knowledge that is justified with what sounds like scientific evidence, but which has not really been tested. **Pseudoscience** claims are not always easy to identify, and many people believe them (Shermer 1997:33).

Are you surprised that more than half of Americans believe in astrology, with all its charts and numbers and references to stars and planets, even though astrological predictions have been tested and found baseless (Shermer 1997:26)? Are any of your beliefs based on pseudoscience?

Motives for Social Research

Similar to you, social scientists have friends and family, observe other persons' social ties, and try to make sense of what they experience and observe. For most, that's the end of it. But for some social scientists, the quality and impact of social ties has become a major research focus. What motivates selection of this or any other particular research focus? Usually, it's one or more of the following reasons:

Research|Social Impact Link
Social Research in Practice

- *Policy motivations.* Many government agencies, elected officials, and private organizations seek better descriptions of social ties in the modern world so they can identify unmet strains in communities, deficits in organizations, or marketing opportunities. Public officials may need information for planning zoning restrictions in residential neighborhoods. Law enforcement agencies may seek to track the connections between criminal gangs and the effect of social cohesion on the crime rate. Military leaders may seek to strengthen unit cohesion. These policy guidance and program management needs can stimulate numerous research projects. As Kathleen Cooper and Nancy Victory (2002) said in their foreword to a U.S. Department of Commerce report on the Census Bureau's survey of Internet use,

> This information will be useful to a wide variety of policymakers and service providers . . . help all of us determine how we can reach Americans more effectively and take maximum advantage of the opportunities available through new information technologies. (p. iii)

- *Academic motivations.* Questions about changing social relations have stimulated much academic social science. One hundred years ago, Émile Durkheim (1951) linked social processes stemming from urbanization and industrialization to a higher rate of suicide. Fifty years ago, David Reisman (1950/1969) considered whether the growing role of the mass media, among other changes, was leading Americans to become a "lonely crowd." Similar to this earlier research, contemporary investigations of the effect of computers and the Internet are often motivated by a desire to understand influences on the strength and meaning of social bonds. Does a "virtual community" in cyberspace perform the same functions as face-to-face social relationships (Norris 2004)? The desire to understand better how the social world works is motivation enough for many social scientists (Hampton & Wellman 2001):

> It is time to move from speculation to evidence. . . . The growth of computer-mediated communication (CMC) introduces a new means of social contact with the potential to affect many aspects of personal communities. . . . This article examines . . . how this technology affected contact and support. (pp. 477, 479)

- *Personal motivations.* Some social scientists who conduct research on social ties feel that by doing so they can help improve the quality of communities, the effectiveness of organizations, or the physical and mental health of many social groups. Social scientists may become interested in social ties as a result of exposure to problems in the social world, or by watching the challenges their children face in school, or for many other reasons, including finding themselves without many friends after a career move. Exhibit 1.6 displays a photograph of Mexican immigrants living in poverty. Can you imagine a college student, in later years, developing an interest in research on poverty in other countries as a result of a study abroad experience that exposed her to such sights?

Video Link
Social Science

Types of Social Research

Whatever the motives, there are four types of social research projects. This section illustrates each type with projects from the large body of research about various aspects of social ties.

Exhibit 1.6	An Impoverished Mexican Immigrant Family

Source: © Alison Wright/Corbis.

Descriptive Research

> **Descriptive research:** Research in which social phenomena are defined and described.

Defining and describing social phenomena of interest is a part of almost any research investigation, but **descriptive research** is often the primary focus of the first research about some issue. Descriptive questions asked in research on social ties have included the following: What is the level of particular types of social ties in America (McPherson et al. 2006)? What social and cultural patterns characterize disadvantaged neighborhoods (Harding 2007)? What types of social ties do Internet users have (Nie & Erbring 2000)? Measurement (the topic of Chapter 4) and sampling (Chapter 5) are central concerns in descriptive research. Survey research (Chapter 8) is often used for descriptive purposes. Some comparative research also has a descriptive purpose (Chapter 13).

Example: Comings and goings on Facebook? Lee Rainie, Director of the Pew Internet Project, and his colleagues Aaron Smith and Maeve Duggan (2013) sought to describe the frequency with which Americans stopped using Facebook and the reasons they did so. To investigate this issue, they surveyed 1,006 American adults by phone and asked them such questions as,

> Do you ever use Facebook?

and

> Have you ever voluntarily taken a break from using Facebook for a period of several weeks or more?

They found that two thirds of American adults who use the Internet also use Facebook and that most (61%) say they have voluntarily taken a break from using Facebook at some time for at least several weeks (Rainie et al. 2013). Rainie et al. also found that one fifth of Internet users said they had once used Facebook but no longer do so, whereas almost 1 in 10 Internet users who had not used Facebook were interested in doing so. Among those who had stopped using Facebook at some point, reasons for the "break" included not having enough time, lacking interest in the site, not seeing valuable content, and disliking gossiping by their friends.

As indicated in Exhibit 1.7, Rainie et al. also found that women were more likely to report increased interest in Facebook and to expect increased use in the next year.

Exploratory Research

Exploratory research seeks to find out how people get along in the setting under question, what meanings they give to their actions, and what issues concern them. The goal is to learn "What is going on here?" and to investigate social phenomena without explicit expectations. This purpose is associated with the use of methods that capture large amounts of relatively unstructured information or that take a field of inquiry in a new direction. For example, researchers investigating social ties occurring through the Internet have had to reexamine the meaning of "community," asking whether cyberspace interactions can constitute a community that is seen as "real and essential" to participants (Fox & Roberts 1999:644). "How is identity—true or counterfeit—established in online communities?" asked Peter Kollock and Marc Smith (1999:9). How can elderly people use the Internet to manage their heart conditions better (Loader et al. 2002)? Exploratory research such as this frequently involves qualitative methods, which are the focus of Chapters 10 and 11, as well as special sections in many other chapters.

> **Exploratory research:** Seeks to find out how people get along in the setting under question, what meanings they give to their actions, and what issues concern them.

Journal Link
Mobile Communities

Example: Can Internet resources help elderly persons manage heart conditions? The Internet provides a "space where disparate individuals can find mutual solace and exchange information within a common community of interest" (Loader et al. 2002:53). It is easy to understand why these features of the Internet "space" have made it a popular medium for individuals seeking help for health problems. Too often, however, elderly persons who grew up without computers do not benefit from this potentially important resource.

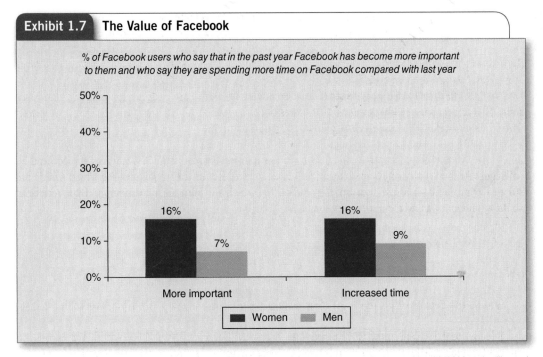

Exhibit 1.7 **The Value of Facebook**

% of Facebook users who say that in the past year Facebook has become more important to them and who say they are spending more time on Facebook compared with last year

Source: Pew Research Center's Internet & American Life Project Omnibus Survey, conducted December 13 to 16, 2012, on landline and cell phones. *N* for male Facebook users = 233. *N* for female Facebook users = 292.

British social scientists Sally Lindsay, Simon Smith, Frances Bell, and Paul Bellaby (2007) were impressed with the potential of Internet-based health resources and wondered how access to those resources might help elderly persons manage heart conditions. Lindsay and her colleagues decided to explore this question by introducing a small group of older men to computers and the Internet and then letting them discuss their experiences with using the Internet for the next 3 years. Through the Internet, participants sought support from others with similar health problems, they helped others to cope, and they learned more about their condition.

Lindsay and her colleagues read through transcripts of interviews and a guided group discussion with their participants. The researchers then identified different themes and categorized text passages in terms of the themes and their interrelations. Two researchers read each transcript and compared their classifications of themes. These two researchers also discussed their interpretations of what they learned with their coauthors as well as with two of the elderly interviewees. For example, the researchers categorized one passage as showing *how the Internet could help reduce fear about participants' heart conditions:* "There's a lot of information there. It makes you feel a lot better. It takes a lot of the fear away. It's a horrible feeling once you've had a heart attack" (Lindsay et al. 2007:103).

In general, 3 years after being introduced to the Internet, "the majority were more informed and confident about managing their health and had developed strategies for meeting their specific informational needs and making better informed decisions" (Lindsay et al. 2007:107).

The Internet provided these new users with both more knowledge and greater social support in dealing with their health problems.

Research|Social Impact Link
Exploratory Research

Explanatory Research

> **Explanatory research:** Seeks to identify causes and effects of social phenomena and to predict how one phenomenon will change or vary in response to variation in some other phenomenon.

Many consider explanation the premier goal of any science. **Explanatory research** seeks to identify the causes and effects of social phenomena and to predict how one phenomenon will change or vary in response to variation in some other phenomenon. Internet researchers adopted explanation as a goal when they began to ask such questions as "Does the Internet increase, decrease, or supplement social capital?" (Wellman et al. 2001). "Do students who meet through Internet interaction like each other more than those who meet face-to-face"? (Bargh, McKenna, & Fitzsimons 2002:41). And "how [does] the Internet affect the role and use of the traditional media?" (Nie & Erbring 2002:276). I focus on ways of identifying causal effects in Chapter 6. Explanatory research often involves experiments (see Chapter 7) or surveys (see Chapter 8), both of which are most likely to use quantitative methods.

Example: What effect does Internet use have on social relations? Jeffrey Boase, John B. Horrigan, Barry Wellman, and Lee Rainie (2006), sociologists at the University of Toronto at the time (Boase and Wellman) and researchers at the Pew Internet Project (Horrigan and Rainie), sought to understand how the Internet is affecting community life in general and the maintenance of social ties in particular. For this purpose, they analyzed data from two phone surveys, conducted in 2004 and 2005, of 4,401 Americans. The surveys included questions about Internet use, social ties, help seeking, and decision making.

Boase and his coauthors (2006) found that the Internet and e-mail help people maintain dispersed social networks and do not conflict with the maintenance of social ties in the local community involving personal or phone contact. The researchers actually found that people who have more in-person and phone connections also tend to use the Internet more. The social value of the Internet is also increased because it is used to seek help and make decisions at important times.

Other social researchers have also found that the Internet can be "a catalyst for creating and maintaining friendships and family relationships" (UCLA Center for Communication Policy 2001:8; see also Stern & Dillman 2006), despite concerns by some that using the Internet may interfere with other types of social ties (Nie & Erbring 2000).

Evaluation Research

> **Evaluation research:** Research that describes or identifies the impact of social policies and programs.

Evaluation research seeks to determine the effects of programs, policies, or other efforts to affect social patterns, whether by government agencies, private nonprofits, or for-profit businesses. This is a type of explanatory research because it deals with cause and effect, but it differs from other forms of explanatory research because evaluation research focuses on one type of cause: programs, policies, and other conscious efforts to create change (Lewis-Beck, Bryman, & Liao 2004:337). This focus raises some issues that are not relevant in other types of explanatory research. Concern regarding the potential impact of alternative policies regarding the Internet provided an impetus for new evaluation research. Chapter 12 introduces evaluation research.

Example: Does high-speed Internet access change community life? Netville's developers connected all homes in this new suburban Toronto community with a high-speed cable and appropriate devices for Internet access. Sociologists Barry Wellman and Keith Hampton (1999) used this arrangement to evaluate the impact of Internet access on social relations. They surveyed Netville residents who were connected to the Internet and compared them with residents who had not activated their computer connections. Hampton actually lived in Netville for 2 years, participating in community events and taking notes on social interaction.

It proved to be difficult to begin research in a rapidly developing community (Hampton & Wellman 1999), but a combination of household surveys and participant observation, supplemented by analysis of postings to the community e-mail list and special group discussions (focus groups), resulted in a comprehensive investigation of the role of the computer network in community social life (Hampton & Wellman 2000).

Hampton and Wellman found that Internet access increased social relations of residents ("Ego" in Exhibit 1.8) with other households, resulting in a larger and less geographically concentrated circle of friends. E-mail was used to set up face-to-face social events rather than as a substitute for them. Information about home repair and other personal and community topics and residents' service needs were exchanged over the Internet. Sensitive personal topics, however, were discussed offline. Although wired residents knew more people within Netville by name and talked to more people on a regular basis than did the nonwired residents, they were not more likely to actually visit other residents (Hampton 2003:422). Hampton and Wellman also found that being wired into the computer network enabled residents to maintain more effectively their relations with friends and relatives elsewhere. Overall, community ties were enriched and extra-community social ties were strengthened (Hampton & Wellman 2001).

IE

Interactive Exercises Link
Types of Research

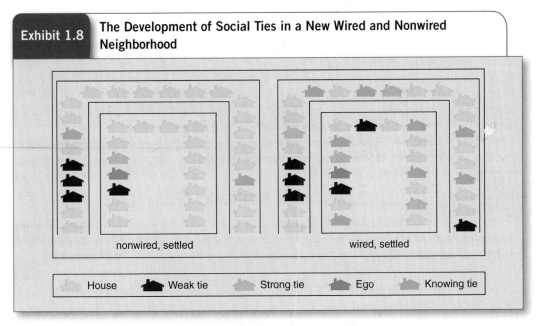

| Exhibit 1.8 | The Development of Social Ties in a New Wired and Nonwired Neighborhood |

nonwired, settled   wired, settled

House   Weak tie   Strong tie   Ego   Knowing tie

Source: Hampton and Wellman 2000. Reprinted with permission.

CAREERS AND RESEARCH

Jessica LeBlanc, Research Assistant

Jessica LeBlanc majored in sociology at the University of New Hampshire, but she didn't really know what kind of career it would lead to. Then she took an undergraduate statistics course and found she really enjoyed it. She took additional methods courses—survey research and an individual research project course—and really liked those also.

By the time she graduated, LeBlanc knew she wanted a job in social research. She looked online for research positions in marketing, health care, and other areas. She noticed an opening at the Center for Survey Research (CSR) at the University of Massachusetts in Boston and thought their work sounded fascinating. The job description said "MA preferred," but within a week she had an interview and then was hired. LeBlanc liked CSR because it was academic, had a wide range of projects, and had many that were focused on her primary interests in health.

As a Research Assistant II, LeBlanc designed survey questions, transcribed focus group audiotapes, programmed web surveys, and managed incoming data. She also conducted interviews, programmed computer-assisted telephone surveys, and helped conduct focus groups.

The knowledge that LeBlanc gained in her methods courses about research designs, statistics, question construction, and survey procedures prepared her well for her position at CSR. She has found that it's important to understand validity and reliability and the basics of statistical software. Her advice to aspiring researchers: Pay attention in your first methods class!

LeBlanc has also benefited from on-the-job training. In her first year, she learned the ins and outs of the center and social research, she completed an online course in human subjects protections, and she learned how to conduct cognitive interviews and moderate focus groups. She's also learned how to use Microsoft Access and Excel and how to program surveys delivered through computers. Overall, LeBlanc enjoys the nitty-gritty and hands-on, day-to-day management tasks.

Alternative Research Orientations

Encyclopedia Link
Qualitative Research

In addition to deciding on the type of research they will conduct, social researchers also must choose among several alternative orientations to research. Some researchers always adopt the same orientation in their research, but others vary their orientation based on the research particulars. It's also possible to combine these alternative orientations in different ways. I introduce alternative orientations in this chapter that represent answers to three important questions that must be considered when you begin a research project: (1) Will the research use primarily quantitative or qualitative methods, or some mixture? (2) Will your guiding philosophy in the research be more "positivist," with a focus on social realities, or more "constructivist," with a focus on the meanings that people create? (3) Is the goal to accumulate new knowledge (basic science) or to make a practical contribution (applied research), or to do both?

Quantitative and/or Qualitative Methods

Quantitative methods: Methods such as surveys and experiments that record variation in social life in terms of categories that vary in amount. Data that are treated as quantitative are either numbers or attributes that can be ordered by magnitude.

Did you notice the difference between the types of data used in the studies about the Internet? The primary data used in the descriptive survey about Facebook use were counts of the number of people who had particular numbers of social ties and particular kinds of social ties, as well as their age, education, and other characteristics (Rainie et al. 2013). These data were numerical, so we say that this study used **quantitative methods.** The Census Bureau survey (Strickling 2010), the Lewis research

(Lewis et al. 2008), and the Ling and Stald (2010) research also used quantitative methods—they reported their findings as percentages and other statistics that summarized the relationship between Internet usage and various aspects of social relations. In contrast, Hampton and Gupta (2008) observed Wi-Fi users in public spaces. Because the researchers recorded their actual observations and did not attempt to quantify what they were studying, we say that Hampton and Gupta (2008) used **qualitative methods.**

> **Qualitative methods:** Methods such as participant observation, intensive interviewing, and focus groups that are designed to capture social life as participants experience it rather than in categories predetermined by the researcher. These methods rely on written or spoken words or observations that do not often have a direct numerical interpretation and typically involve exploratory research questions, inductive reasoning, an orientation to social context and human subjectivity, and the meanings attached by participants to events and to their lives.

The distinction between quantitative and qualitative methods involves more than just the type of data collected. Quantitative methods are most often used when the motives for research are explanation, description, or evaluation. Exploration is more often the motive for using qualitative methods, although researchers also use these methods for descriptive, explanatory, and evaluative purposes. I highlight several other differences between quantitative and qualitative methods in the next two chapters. Chapters 10 and 11 present qualitative methods in much more detail. Chapter 3 introduces the alternative research philosophies that often lie behind the preference for quantitative or qualitative methods.

Important as it is, I don't want to place too much emphasis on the distinction between quantitative and qualitative orientations or methods. Social scientists often combine these methods to enrich their research. For example, Hampton and Wellman (2000) used surveys to generate counts of community network usage and other behaviors in Netville, but to help interpret these behaviors, they also observed social interaction and recorded spoken comments. In this way, qualitative data about social settings can be used to understand patterns in quantitative data better (Campbell & Russo 1999:141).

The use of multiple methods to study one research question is called **triangulation**. The term suggests that a researcher can get a clearer picture of the social reality being studied by viewing it from several different perspectives. Each will have some liabilities in a specific research application, and all can benefit from a combination of one or more other methods (Brewer & Hunter 1989; Sechrest & Sidani 1995).

> **Triangulation:** The use of multiple methods to study one research question; also used to mean the use of two or more different measures of the same variable.

The distinction between quantitative and qualitative data is not always sharp. Qualitative data can be converted to quantitative data when we count the frequency of particular words or phrases in a text or measure the time elapsed between different observed behaviors. Surveys that collect primarily quantitative data may also include questions asking for written responses, and these responses may be used in a qualitative, textual analysis. Qualitative researchers may test explicit explanations of social phenomena using textual or observational data. We consider a *mixed-method* strategy in more detail in Chapter 15 and we examine particular combinations of methods in most other chapters.

Positivist or Constructivist Philosophies

Your general assumptions about how the social world can best be investigated—your social research philosophy—will partly shape your investigations of the social world. Researchers with a *positivist philosophy* believe that an objective reality exists apart from the perceptions of those who observe it, and that the goal of science is to understand this reality better. This is the philosophy traditionally associated with natural science, with the expectation that there are universal laws of human behavior, and with the belief that scientists must be objective and unbiased to see reality clearly (Weber 1949:72). **Positivism** asserts that a well-designed test of a specific prediction—for example, the prediction that social ties decrease among those who use the Internet more—can move us closer to understanding actual social processes. Quantitative researchers are often guided by a positivist philosophy.

> **Positivism:** The belief, shared by most scientists, that there is a reality that exists quite apart from our own perception of it, that it can be understood through observation, and that it follows general laws.

Postpositivism: A philosophical view that modifies the positivist premise of an external, objective reality by recognizing its complexity, the limitations of human observers, and therefore the impossibility of developing more than a partial understanding of reality.

Intersubjective agreement: Agreement between scientists about the nature of reality; often upheld as a more reasonable goal for science than certainty about an objective reality.

Postpositivism is a philosophy that is closely related to positivism because it also assumes an external, objective reality, but postpositivists acknowledge the complexity of this reality and the limitations and biases of the scientists who study it (Guba & Lincoln 1994:109–111). For example, postpositivists may worry that researchers, who are heavy computer users themselves, will be biased in favor of finding positive social effects of computer use. As a result of concerns such as this, postpositivists do not think we can ever be sure that scientific methods allow us to perceive objective reality. Instead, they believe that the goal of science is to achieve **intersubjective agreement** among scientists about the nature of reality (Wallace 1983:461). We can be more confident in the community of social researchers than in any individual social scientist (Campbell & Russo 1999:144).

The positivist and postpositivist philosophies consider value considerations to be beyond the scope of science: "An empirical science cannot tell anyone what he should do—but rather what he can do—and under certain circumstances—what he wishes to do" (Weber 1949:54). The idea is that developing valid knowledge about how society *is* organized, or how we live our lives, does not tell us how society *should* be organized or how we *should* live our lives. The determination of empirical facts should be a separate process from the evaluation of these facts as satisfactory or unsatisfactory (Weber 1949:11). The idea is not to ignore value considerations, but to hold them in abeyance during the research project, until results are published.

Constructivism: Methodology based on questioning belief in an external reality; emphasizes the importance of exploring the way in which different stakeholders in a social setting construct their beliefs.

Qualitative research is often guided by the philosophy of **constructivism**. Constructivist social scientists believe that social reality is socially constructed and that the goal of social scientists is to understand what meanings people give to reality, not to determine how reality works apart from these constructions. This philosophy rejects the positivist belief that there is a concrete, objective reality that scientific methods help us understand (Lynch & Bogen 1997); instead, constructivists believe that people construct an image of reality based on their own preferences and prejudices and their interactions with others and that this is as true of scientists as it is of everyone else in the social world. This means that we can never be sure that we have understood reality properly, that "objects and events are understood by different people differently, and those perceptions are the reality—or realities—that social science should focus on" (Rubin & Rubin 1995:35).

Constructivism emphasizes that different stakeholders in a social setting construct different beliefs (Guba & Lincoln 1989:44–45). Constructivists give particular attention to the different goals of researchers and other participants in a research setting and may seek to develop a consensus among participants about how to understand the focus of inquiry (Sulkunen 2008:73): "Truth is a matter of the best-informed and most sophisticated construction on which there is consensus at a given time" (Schwandt 1994:128). **Interpretivism** is a related research philosophy that emphasizes the importance of understanding subjective meanings people give to reality without believing that reality itself is socially constructed.

Interpretivism: The belief that the subjective meanings people give to their experiences are a key focus for social science research without believing that reality itself is socially constructed.

Hermeneutic circle: Represents the dialectical process in which the researcher obtains information from multiple stakeholders in a setting, refines his or her understanding of the setting, and then tests that understanding with successive respondents.

Feminist research: Research with a focus on women's lives that often includes an orientation to personal experience, subjective orientations, the researcher's standpoint, and emotions.

Constructivist inquiry may use an interactive research process, in which a researcher begins an evaluation in some social setting by identifying the different interest groups in that setting. In a circular process known as a **hermeneutic circle** (Exhibit 1.9), the researcher interviews each respondent (R1, R2, etc.) to learn how they "construct" their thoughts and feelings about the topic of concern (C1, C2, etc.), and then gradually tries to develop a shared perspective on the problem being evaluated (Guba & Lincoln 1989:42, 180–181).

Feminist research is a term used to refer to research done by feminists (Reinharz 1992:6–7) and to a perspective on research that can involve many

Exhibit 1.9 The Hermeneutic Circle

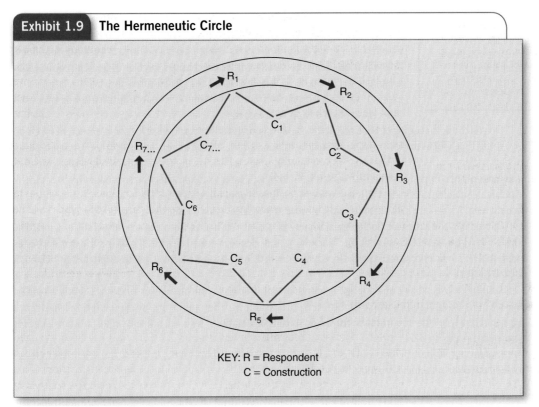

KEY: R = Respondent
C = Construction

Source: Guba and Lincoln 1989.

different methods (Reinharz 1992:240). The feminist perspective on research includes the interpretivist and constructivist elements of concern with personal experience and subjective feelings and with the researcher's position and standpoint (Hesse-Biber & Leavy 2007:4–5). Feminist researchers Sharlene Hesse-Biber and Patricia Lina Leavy (2007:139) emphasize the importance of viewing the social world as complex and multilayered, of sensitivity to the impact of social differences, of being an "insider" or an "outsider," and of being concerned with the researcher's position. African American feminist researcher Patricia Hill Collins (1991) suggests that researchers who are sensitive to their "outside" role within a social situation may have unique advantages:

> Outsiders within occupy a special place—they become different people and their difference sensitizes them to patterns that may be more difficult for established sociological insiders to see. (p. 53)

Basic Science or Applied Research

You know that social scientists seek to describe and explain how society works. McPherson et al. (2006) sought to answer questions such as, "How do social ties vary between people or societies?" and "Why do some people, groups, or societies have more social ties than others?" Other researchers have investigated the meaning people attach to social ties and the consequences of having fewer social ties. The effort to figure out what the world is like and why it works as it does—academic motivations—is the goal of **basic science** (Hammersley 2008:50).

> **Basic science:** Research conducted using the scientific method that has the goals of figuring out what the world is like and why it works as it does.

> **Applied research:** Research conducted using the scientific method that addresses immediate, practical concerns, such as determining whether one program or policy has a more desirable impact than another.

Social research may also have more immediate, practical concerns. Evaluation research like that conducted by Hampton and Wellman (1999) seeks to determine whether one program or policy has a more desirable impact than another does. This knowledge can then lead to practical changes, such as increasing community members' access to the Internet so that their possibilities for social relations will expand. Evaluation research and other social research motivated by practical concerns are termed **applied research**.

Do you think that doing applied research would be good for society as well as for social researchers? Or do you think that a focus on how to improve society might lead social researchers to distort their understanding of how society works? Whether you think you would prefer a basic or applied orientation in social research, you have lots of company. In the 19th century, sociologist Lester Frank Ward (who subsequently became the American Sociological Society's first president) endorsed applied research: "The real object of science is to benefit man. A science which fails to do this, however agreeable its study, is lifeless" (Ward 1897:xxvii).

But in 1929, the American Sociological Society President William Fielding Ogburn urged sociologists to be guided by a basic research orientation: "Sociology as a science is not interested in making the world a better place to live. . . . Science is interested directly in one thing only, to wit, discovering new knowledge" (Ogburn 1930:300–301).

Tension between basic and applied research orientations has continued ever since these early disputes. Lynn Smith-Lovin (2007), who collaborated with Miller McPherson in the "social isolation" study, has argued recently for the importance of the basic science orientation: "I would, indeed, argue for knowledge for knowledge's sake" (p. 127).

In contrast, Robert Bellah, and his *Habits of the Heart* coauthors (1985) urged social scientists to focus explicit attention on achieving a more just society:

> Social science . . . whether it admits it or not, makes assumptions about good persons and a good society and considers how far these conceptions are embodied in our actual society. . . . By probing the past as well as the present, by looking at "values" as much as at "facts," such a social science [as "public philosophy"] is able to make connections that are not obvious and to ask difficult questions. (p. 301)

Interactive Exercises
Link
Philosophies

You will encounter examples of basic and applied research throughout this book. By the time you finish *Investigating the Social World,* I know you'll have a good understanding of the difference between these orientations, but I can't predict whether you'll decide one is preferable. Maybe you'll conclude that they both have some merit.

▣ Strengths and Limitations of Social Research

Using social scientific research methods to develop answers to questions about the social world reduces the likelihood of making everyday errors in reasoning. The various projects that we have reviewed in this chapter illustrate this point:

- A clear definition of the population of interest in each study increased the researchers' ability to draw conclusions without overgeneralizing findings to groups to which they did not apply. Selection of a data set based on a broad, representative sample of the population enabled McPherson et al. (2006) to describe social ties throughout the United States rather than among some unknown set of their friends or acquaintances. The researchers' explicit recognition that persons who do not speak English were not included in their data set helps prevent overgeneralization to groups that were not actually studied (McPherson et al. 2006:356).

- The use of surveys in which each respondent was asked the same set of questions reduced the risk of selective or inaccurate observation, as did careful attention to a range of measurement issues (McPherson et al. 2006:355–356).

- The risk of illogical reasoning was reduced by carefully describing each stage of the research, clearly presenting the findings, and carefully testing the bases for cause-and-effect conclusions. For example, Ling and Stald (2010) tested to see whether age or gender, rather than cell phone use, might have increased the tightness of social group ties in Norway.

- Resistance to change was reduced by providing free computers to participants in the Internet health study (Lindsay et al. 2007:100). The publications by all the researchers help other researchers critique and learn from their findings as well as inform the general public.

Nevertheless, I would be less than honest if I implied that we enter the realm of truth and light when we conduct social research or when we rely solely on the best available social research. Research always has some limitations and some flaws (as does any human endeavor), and our findings are always subject to differing interpretations. Social research permits us to see more, to observe with fewer distortions, and to describe more clearly to others what our opinions are based on, but it will not settle all arguments. Others will always have differing opinions, and some of those others will be social scientists who have conducted their own studies and drawn different conclusions.

Although Nie and Erbring (2000) concluded that the use of the Internet diminished social relations, their study at Stanford was soon followed by the UCLA Center for Communication Policy (2001) and by others at the Pew Internet & American Life Project (Boase et al. 2006). These more recent studies also used survey research methods, but their findings suggested that the use of the Internet does *not* diminish social relations. Psychologist Robert Kraut's early research suggested that Internet use was isolating, but his own more recent research indicates more positive effects (Kraut et al. 2002). To what extent do different conclusions result from differences in research methods, from different perspectives on similar findings, from rapid changes in the population of Internet users?

It's not easy to answer such questions, so one research study often leads to another, and another, each one improving on previous research or examining a research question from a somewhat different angle. Part of becoming a good social researcher is learning that we have to evaluate critically each research study and weigh carefully the entire body of research about a research question before coming to a conclusion. And we have to keep an open mind about alternative interpretations and the possibility of new discoveries. The social phenomena we study are often complex, so we must consider this complexity when we choose methods to study social phenomena and when we interpret the results of these studies.

However, even in the areas of research that are fraught with controversy, where social scientists differ in their interpretations of the evidence, the quest for new and more sophisticated research has value. What is most important for improving understanding of the social world is not the result of any particular study but the accumulation of evidence from different studies of related issues. By designing new studies that focus on the weak points or controversial conclusions of prior research, social scientists contribute to a body of findings that gradually expands our knowledge about the social world and resolves some of the disagreements about it.

Whether you plan to conduct your own research projects, read others' research reports, or just think about and act in the social world, knowing about research methods has many benefits. This knowledge will give you greater confidence in your own opinions; improve your ability to evaluate others' opinions; and encourage you to refine your questions, answers, and methods of inquiry about the social world.

▣ Conclusions

I hope this first chapter has given you an idea of what to expect from the rest of the book. My aim is to introduce you to social research methods by describing what social scientists have learned about the social world as well as how they have learned it. The substance of social science is inevitably more interesting than its methods, but the methods become more interesting when they're linked to substantive investigations. I have focused attention in this chapter on research about social ties; in the subsequent chapters, I introduce research examples from other areas.

The eighth edition of *Investigating the Social World* is organized into four sections. The first section on Foundations for Social Research includes the introduction in Chapter 1, and then an overview of the research process in Chapter 2 and an introduction to issues in research ethics in Chapter 3. In Chapter 2, I review how social scientists select research questions for investigation, how they orient themselves to those questions with social theories, and how they review related prior research. Most of the chapter focuses on the steps involved in the overall research process and the criteria that researchers use to assess the quality of their answers to the original research questions. Several studies of domestic violence illustrate the research process in Chapter 2. Chapter 3, on research ethics, completes the foundation for our study of social research. I emphasize in this chapter and in the subsequent end-of-chapter exercises the importance of ethical treatment of human subjects in research. I also introduce in this chapter the process of writing research proposals, which I then continue in the end-of-chapter exercises throughout the book. In actual research projects, submission of a research proposal to an Institutional Review Board for the Protection of Human Subjects is often the final step in laying the foundation for a research project.

The second section, Fundamentals of Social Research, presents methods for conceptualization and measurement, sampling, and causation and other elements of research design that must be considered in any social research project. In Chapter 4, I discuss the concepts we use to think about the social world and the measures we use to collect data about those concepts. This chapter begins with the example of research on student substance abuse, but you will find throughout this chapter a range of examples from contemporary research. In Chapter 5, I use research on homelessness to exemplify the issues involved in sampling cases to study. In Chapter 6, I use research on violence to illustrate how to design research to answer such causal research questions as "What causes violence?" I also explain in this chapter the decisions that social researchers must make about two research design issues that affect our ability to draw causal conclusions: (1) whether to use groups or individuals as units of analysis and (2) whether to use a cross-sectional or longitudinal research design.

The third section, Basic Social Research Designs, introduces the three primary methods of data collection and related methods of data analysis. Experimental studies, the subject of Chapter 7, focus attention on testing causal effects and are used often by social psychologists, psychologists, and policy evaluation researchers. Survey research is the most common method of data collection in sociology, so in Chapter 8, I describe the different types of surveys and explain how researchers design survey questions. I highlight in this chapter the ways in which the Internet and cell phones are changing the nature of survey research. The next chapter on quantitative data analysis introduces the statistics used to analyze data collected with experimental and survey designs. Chapter 9 is not a substitute for an entire course in statistics, but it provides the basic tools you can use to answer most research questions. To make this chapter realistic, I walk you through an analysis of quantitative data on voting in the 2008 presidential election. You can replicate this analysis with data on the book's study site (if you have access to the SPSS statistical analysis program). You can also learn more about statistics with the SPSS exercises at the end of most chapters and with the study site's tutorials.

Qualitative methods have long been the method of choice in anthropology, but they also have a long tradition in American sociology and have become the favored method of many social researchers around the world. Chapter 10 shows how qualitative techniques can uncover aspects of the social world that we are likely to miss in experiments and surveys and can sometimes result in a different perspective on social processes. Chapter 11 then focuses on the logic and procedures of analyzing qualitative data. In these chapters, you will learn about research on disasters such as Hurricane Katrina, on work organizations, on psychological distress, on gender roles, and on classroom behavior.

The fourth section, Advanced Social Research Designs, presents research designs that can involve combinations of one or more of the basic research designs. Evaluation research, the subject of Chapter 12, is conducted to identify the impact of social programs or to clarify social processes involving such programs. Evaluation research often uses experimental methods, but survey research and qualitative methods can also be helpful in evaluation research projects. Historical and comparative methods, the subject of Chapter 13, may involve either quantitative or qualitative methods that are used to compare societies and groups at one point in time and to analyze their development over time. We will see how these different approaches have been used to learn about political change in transitional societies. I also explain the method of content analysis in this chapter; it can be used in historical and comparative research and provides another way to investigate social processes in an unobtrusive way. Chapter 14 reviews the methods of secondary data analysis and the related approach that has come to be known as "Big Data." In this chapter, you will learn how to obtain previously collected data and to investigate important social issues such as poverty dynamics.

By the time you read Chapter 15, you should be convinced of the value of ways in which different methods can help us to understand different aspects of the social world. Chapter 15 takes this basic insight a few steps further by introducing the use of "mixed methods." This increasingly popular approach to research design involves a careful plan for combining qualitative and quantitative methods in a research project.

Plan to read Chapter 16 carefully. Our research efforts are only as good as the attention given to our research reports, so my primary focus in this chapter is on writing research reports. I also present means for enhancing graphic displays to communicate quantitative results more effectively in research reports. In addition, I introduce meta-analysis—a statistical technique for assessing many research studies about a particular research question. By the end of the chapter, you should have a broader perspective on how research methods can improve understanding of the social world (as well as an appreciation for how much remains to be done).

Each chapter ends with several helpful learning tools. Lists of key terms and chapter highlights will help you review the ideas that have been discussed. Discussion questions and practice exercises will help you apply and deepen your knowledge. Special exercises guide you in developing your first research proposal, finding information on the Internet, grappling with ethical dilemmas, and conducting statistical analyses. A "careers and research" example may help you envision future job possibilities.

The study site for this book on the SAGE website provides interactive exercises and quizzes for reviewing key concepts, as well as research articles to review, websites to visit, data to analyze, and short lectures to hear. Check it out at edge.sagepub.com/schutt8e.

Key Terms

Applied research 22	Hermeneutic circle 20	Pseudoscience 12
Basic science 21	Illogical reasoning 10	Qualitative methods 19
Constructivism 20	Inaccurate observation 8	Quantitative methods 18
Descriptive research 14	Interpretivism 20	Resistance to change 10
Evaluation research 16	Intersubjective agreement 20	Science 11
Explanatory research 16	Overgeneralization 8	Selective observation 8
Exploratory research 15	Positivism 19	Social science 12
Feminist research 20	Postpositivism 20	Triangulation 19

Highlights

- Social research differs from the ordinary process of thinking about our experiences by focusing on broader questions that involve people outside our immediate experience and issues about why things happen, and by using systematic research methods to answer those questions. Four common errors in reasoning are (1) selective or inaccurate observation, (2) overgeneralization, (3) illogical reasoning, and (4) resistance to change. These errors result from the complexity of the social world, subjective processes that affect the reasoning of researchers and those they study, researchers' self-interestedness, and unquestioning acceptance of tradition or of those in positions of authority.

- Social science is the use of logical, systematic, documented methods to investigate individuals, societies, and social processes, as well as the knowledge produced by these investigations.

- Social research cannot resolve value questions or provide permanent, universally accepted answers.

- Social research can be motivated by policy guidance and program management needs, academic concerns, and personal or charitable impulses.

- Social research can be descriptive, exploratory, explanatory, or evaluative—or some combination of these.

- Quantitative and qualitative methods structure research in different ways and are differentially appropriate for diverse research situations. They may be combined in research projects.

- Positivism and postpositivism are research philosophies that emphasize the goal of understanding the real world; these philosophies guide most quantitative researchers.

- The constructivist paradigm emphasizes the importance of exploring and representing the ways in which different stakeholders in a social setting construct their beliefs. Constructivists interact with research subjects to develop a shared perspective on the issue being studied. Interpretivism is a related research philosophy that emphasizes an understanding of the meaning people attach to their experiences; it guides many qualitative researchers.

- Feminist researchers often emphasize interpretivist and constructivist perspectives in research and urge a concern with underprivileged groups.

- Basic science research focuses on expanding knowledge and providing results to other researchers. Applied research seeks to have an impact on social practice and to share results with a wide audience.

STUDENT STUDY SITE

Sharpen your skills with SAGE edge at **edge.sagepub.com/schutt8e**. **SAGE edge for students** provides a personalized approach to help you accomplish your coursework goals in an easy-to-use learning environment.

Discussion Questions

1. Select a social issue that interests you, such as Internet use or crime. List at least four of your beliefs about this phenomenon. Try to identify the sources of each of these beliefs.

2. Does the academic motivation to do the best possible job of understanding how the social world works conflict with policy or personal motivations? How could personal experiences with social isolation or with Internet use shape research motivations? In what ways might the goal of influencing policy about social relations shape a researcher's approach to this issue?

3. Pick a contemporary social issue of interest to you. Describe different approaches to research on this issue that would involve descriptive, exploratory, explanatory, and evaluative approaches.

4. Review each of the research alternatives. Do you find yourself more attracted to a quantitative or a qualitative approach? Or to doing research to contribute to basic knowledge or shape social policy? What is the basis of your preferences? Would you prefer to take a mixed-methods approach? What research questions do you think are most important to pursue to improve government policies?

5. Do you favor the positivist/postpositivist or the interpretivist/constructivist philosophy as a guide for social research? Review the related guidelines for research and explain your position.

Practice Exercises

1. Read the abstracts (initial summaries) of five articles available in the "article review matrix" on the study site. On the basis of the abstract only, classify each research project represented in the articles as primarily descriptive, exploratory, explanatory, or evaluative. Note any indications that the research focused on other types of research questions.

2. Find a report of social science research in an article in a daily newspaper. What are the motives for the research? How much information is provided about the research design? What were the major findings? What additional evidence would you like to see in the article to increase your findings in the research conclusions?

3. Review "Types of Research" from the Interactive Exercises link on the study site. To use these lessons, choose one of the four "Types of Research" exercises from the opening menu. About 10 questions are presented in each version of the lesson. After reading each question, choose one answer from the list presented. The program will evaluate your answers. If an answer is correct, the program will explain why you were right and go on to the next question. If you have made an error, the program will explain the error to you and give you another chance to respond.

4. Now, select a journal article from edge.sagepub.com/schutt8e and read its abstract. Identify the type of research (descriptive, exploratory, or evaluative) that appeared to be used. Now scan the article and decide whether the approach was quantitative or qualitative (or both) and whether it included any discussion of policy implications.

Ethics Questions

Throughout the book, we will discuss the ethical challenges that arise in social research. At the end of each chapter, you are asked to consider some questions about ethical issues related to that chapter's focus. I introduce this critical topic formally in Chapter 3, but we will begin here with some questions for you to ponder.

1. The chapter refers to research on social isolation. What would *you* do if you were interviewing elderly persons in the community and found that one was very isolated and depressed or even suicidal, apparently as a result of his or her isolation? Do you believe that social researchers have an obligation to take action in a situation like this? What if you discovered a similar problem with a child? What guidelines would you suggest for researchers?

2. Would you encourage social researchers to announce their findings in press conferences about topics such as the impact of the Internet on social ties, and to encourage relevant agencies to adopt policies aimed to lessen social isolation? Are there any advantages to studying research questions only to contribute to academic knowledge? Do you think there is a fundamental conflict between academic and policy motivations? Do social researchers have an ethical obligation to recommend policies that their research suggests would help other people?

Web Exercises

1. The research on social ties by McPherson and his colleagues was publicized in a *Washington Post* article that also included comments by other sociologists. Read the article at www.washingtonpost.com/wp-dyn/content/article/2006/06/22/AR2006062201763_pf.html and continue the commentary. Do your own experiences suggest that there is a problem with social ties in your community? Does it seem, as Wellman suggests in the *Washington Post* article, that a larger number of social ties can make up for the decline in intimate social ties that McPherson found?

2. Scan one of the publications about the Internet and society at the Berkman Center for Internet & Society website, http://cyber.law.harvard.edu. Describe one of the projects discussed: its goals, methods, and major findings. What do the researchers conclude about the impact of the Internet on

social life in the United States? Next, repeat this process with a report from the Pew Internet Project at www.pewinternet.org, or with the Digital Future report from the University of Southern California's Center for the Digital Future site, www.digitalcenter.org. What aspects of the methods, questions, or findings might explain differences in their conclusions? Do you think the researchers approached their studies with different perspectives at the outset? If so, what might these perspectives have been?

Video Interview Questions

Listen to the researcher interview for Chapter 1 at edge.sagepub.com/schutt8e.

1. What are the benefits to breaking down questions in a text-based interview structure?

Researcher Interview Link
Online Interviews

2. As Janet Salmons mentions, one can enhance his or her research by deciding carefully on the various kinds of technology to be used. What are some the considerations Salmons mentions in deciding whether to use text-based interviews or video conference calls?

SPSS Exercises

The SPSS Exercises at the end of each chapter focus on support for the death penalty. A portion of the 2012 GSS survey data is available on the study site. You will need this portion of the 2012 GSS to carry out these exercises. If you are able to use the complete version of SPSS (perhaps in your university's computer lab), download the GSS2012x file. If you are using the student version of SPSS (purchased with this text), download the GSS2012a file. You will begin your empirical investigation by thinking a bit about the topic and the data you have available for study.

1. What personal motivation might you have for studying support for the death penalty? What might motivate other people to conduct research on this topic? What policy and academic motives might be important?

2. After you download the GSS2012x or GSS2012a file and save it in a directory, open the GSS2012x or GSS2012a file containing the 2012 GSS data. In the SPSS menu, click on File, then on Open and Data, and then on the name of the data file in the directory where it is saved. How many respondents are there in this subset of the complete GSS file? (Scroll down to the bottom of the data set.) How many variables were measured? (Scroll down to the bottom of the Variable View in SPSS v. 21.)

3. What would you estimate as the level of support for capital punishment in the United States in 2012? Now for your first real research experience in this text: Describe the distribution of support for capital punishment. Obtaining the relevant data is as simple as "a, b, c, d, e."

   a. Click on Graphs.

   b. Click on Legacy Dialogs > Bar.

   c. Select "Simple" and "Summaries for groups of cases" under Data in Chart Area > Define.

   d. Place the CAPPUN variable in the box below "Category Axis:" and select "% of cases" under "Bar Represent."

   e. Click OK.

Now describe the distribution of support for capital punishment. What percentage of the population supported capital punishment in the United States in 2012?

Developing a Research Proposal

Will you develop a research proposal in this course? If so, you should begin to consider your alternatives.

1. What topic would you focus on, if you could design a social research project without any concern for costs? What are your motives for studying this topic?

2. Develop four questions that you might investigate about the topic you just selected. Each question should reflect a different research motive: description, exploration, explanation, or evaluation. Be specific.

3. Which question most interests you? Would you prefer to attempt to answer that question with quantitative or qualitative methods? Do you seek to contribute to basic science or to applied research?

CHAPTER 2

The Process and Problems of Social Research

Research That Matters, Questions That Count

The Charlotte-Mecklenburg (North Carolina) Police Department (CMPD) had been responding to reports of violence against intimate partners by arresting many of the suspects. Unfortunately, 6 months after the arrests it appeared that suspects who had been arrested were just as likely to reoffend, as were those who were simply advised to cool off. In 1995, the CMPD decided to try a different approach to domestic violence cases. Like police departments in many cities, CMPD developed a special domestic violence unit that took a comprehensive, team approach to investigating cases and assisting victims. Did this new approach reduce reoffending? With funding from the National Institute of Justice, Professors M. Lyn Exum, Jennifer L. Hartman, Paul C. Friday, and Vivian B. Lord at the University of North Carolina in Charlotte set out to answer this question. Their research design involved checking the arrest records of 891 domestic violence cases to see if suspects processed through the domestic violence unit were less likely to reoffend over a period of 18 to 30 months than were those who were processed with standard police practices. Exum and her colleagues found that 29.3% of the suspects processed by the domestic violence unit reoffended, compared with 36.9% of those processed by a standard police patrol unit.

1. Are you surprised by the lack of effect of arresting suspects?

2. Did the domestic violence unit's comprehensive approach do any better?

3. What if suspects referred to the domestic violence unit were not like those processed with standard police practices? Would this affect your answer to question 2?

4. Why do you think the domestic violence unit approach might have reduced reoffending?

In this chapter, you will learn about methods used to study the response to domestic violence and the conclusions from some of this research. By the end of the chapter, you will have a much firmer basis for answering the questions I have posed. After you finish the chapter, test yourself by reading the 2010 *Crime & Delinquency* article by Lyn Exum and her colleagues at the *Investigating the Social World* study site and completing the related interactive exercises for Chapter 2 at edge.sagepub.com/schutt8e.

Exum, M. Lyn, Jennifer L. Hartman, Paul C. Friday, and Vivian B. Lord. 2010. "Policing Domestic Violence in the Post-SARP Era: The Impact of a Domestic Violence Police Unit." *Crime & Delinquency* 20(10):1–34.

D omestic violence is a major problem in countries around the world. An international survey by the World Health Organization of 24,000 women in 10 countries estimated lifetime physical or sexual abuse ranging from a low of 15% in Japan to a high of 71% in rural Ethiopia (WHO 2005:6) (Exhibit 2.1). In a 2010 U.S. survey of 16,507 men and women sponsored by the Department of Justice and the Centers for Disease Control and Prevention, 35.6% of women and 28.5% of men said they had experienced rape, physical violence, or stalking by an intimate partner at some time in their lives (Black et al. 2011). And most partners seem to get away with the abuse: only one fifth of all rapes and one quarter of all physical assaults perpetrated against female respondents by intimates were reported to the police (Tjaden & Thoennes 2000:v).

What can be done to reduce this problem? In 1981, the Police Foundation and the Minneapolis Police Department began an experiment to determine whether arresting accused spouse abusers on the spot would deter repeat incidents. The study's results, which were widely publicized, indicated that arrests did have a deterrent effect. Partly because of this, the percentage of urban police departments that made arrest the preferred response to complaints of domestic violence rose from 10% in 1984 to 90% in 1988 (Sherman 1992:14).

Journal Link
Domestic Violence

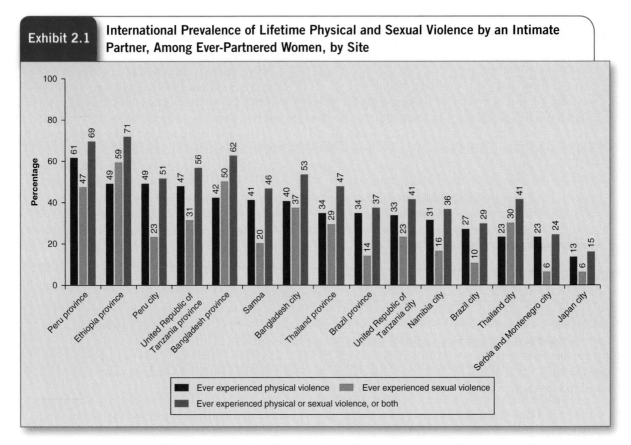

Exhibit 2.1 International Prevalence of Lifetime Physical and Sexual Violence by an Intimate Partner, Among Ever-Partnered Women, by Site

Source: World Health Organization. 2005. *Multi-country Study on Women's Health and Domestic Violence Against Women: Summary Report.*

Researchers in six other cities then conducted similar experiments to determine whether changing the location or other research procedures would result in different outcomes (Sherman 1992; Sherman & Berk 1984). Many other studies have been conducted since these original seven experiments to better understand issues involved in responding to domestic violence, including a recent 23-year follow-up to determine the long-term effects of the police intervention in the Milwaukee experiment (Sherman & Harris 2013). The Minneapolis Domestic Violence Experiment, the additional research inspired by it, and the controversies arising from it will provide good examples for our systematic overview of the social research process.

In this chapter, we shift from examining the *why* of social research to an overview of the *how*—the focus of the rest of the book. We will consider how to develop a question for social research, then how to review the existing literature about this question while connecting the question to social theory and, in many studies, formulating specific testable hypotheses (see Exhibit 2.2). We then discuss different social research strategies and standards for social research as a prelude to the details about these stages in subsequent chapters. You will find more details in Appendixes A and B about reviewing the literature. I will use the Minneapolis experiment and the related research to illustrate the different research strategies and some of the related techniques. The chapter also expands on the role of social theories in developing research questions and guiding research decisions. By the chapter's end, you should be ready to formulate a research question, critique previous studies that addressed this question, and design a general strategy for answering the question. In the next chapter, you will learn how to review ethical issues and write a research proposal.

Video Link
Advice for Researchers

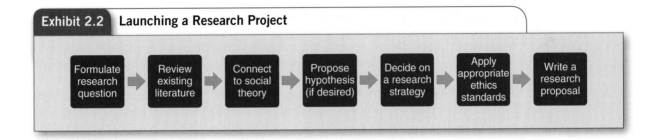

Exhibit 2.2 | **Launching a Research Project**

Formulate research question → Review existing literature → Connect to social theory → Propose hypothesis (if desired) → Decide on a research strategy → Apply appropriate ethics standards → Write a research proposal

Social Research Questions

A **social research question** is a question about the social world that one seeks to answer through the collection and analysis of firsthand, verifiable, empirical data. It is not a question about who did what to whom, but a question about people in groups, about general social processes, or about tendencies in community change such as the following: What distinguishes Internet users from other persons? Does community policing reduce the crime rate? What influences the likelihood of spouse abuse? How do people react to social isolation? So many research questions are possible that it is more of a challenge to specify what does not qualify as a social research question than to specify what does.

> **Social research question:** A question about the social world that is answered through the collection and analysis of firsthand, verifiable, empirical data.

But that doesn't mean it is easy to specify a research question. Actually, formulating a good research question can be surprisingly difficult. We can break the process into three stages: (1) identifying one or more questions for study, (2) refining the questions, and then (3) evaluating the questions.

Identifying Social Research Questions

Social research questions may emerge from your own experience—from your "personal troubles," as C. Wright Mills (1959) put it. One experience might be membership in a church, another could be victimization by crime, and yet another might be moving from a dorm to a sorority house. You may find yourself asking a question such as "In what ways do people tend to benefit from church membership?" "Does victimization change a person's trust in others?" or "How do initiation procedures influence group commitment?" What other possible research questions can you develop based on your own experiences in the social world?

Audio Link
Social Research Questions

The research literature is often the best source for research questions. Every article or book will bring new questions to mind. Even if you're not feeling too creative when you read the literature, most research articles highlight unresolved issues and end with suggestions for additional research. For example, Richard A. Berk, Alec Campbell, Ruth Klap, and Bruce Western (1992) concluded an article on four of the replications of the Minneapolis experiment on police responses to spouse abuse by suggesting, "Deterrence may be effective for a substantial segment of the offender population. . . . However, the underlying mechanisms remain obscure" (p. 706). A new study could focus on these mechanisms: Why does the arrest of offenders deter some of them from future criminal acts? Any research article in a journal in your field is likely to have comments that point toward unresolved issues.

Many social scientists find the source of their research questions in social theory. Some researchers spend much of their careers conducting research intended to refine an answer to one research question that is critical for a particular social theory. For example, you may have concluded that labeling theory can explain much social deviance, so you may ask whether labeling theory can explain how spouse abusers react to being arrested.

Finally, some research questions have very pragmatic sources. You may focus on a research question someone else posed because it seems to be to your advantage to do so. Some social scientists conduct research on specific questions posed by a funding source in what is termed an *RFP,* a request for proposals. (Sometimes the acronym RFA is used, meaning request for applications.) The six projects to test the conclusions of the Minneapolis Domestic Violence Experiment were developed in response to such a call for proposals from the National Institute of Justice. Or you may learn that the social workers in the homeless shelter where you volunteer need help with a survey to learn about client needs, which becomes the basis for another research question.

Refining Social Research Questions

It is even more challenging to focus on a problem of manageable size than it is to come up with an interesting question for research. We are often interested in much more than we can reasonably investigate with limited time and resources. In addition, researchers may worry about staking a research project (and thereby a grant or a grade) on a single problem, and so they may address several research questions at once. Also, it might seem risky to focus on a research question that may lead to results discrepant with our own cherished assumptions about the social world. The prospective commitment of time and effort for some research questions may seem overwhelming, resulting in a certain degree of paralysis.

The best way to avoid these problems is to develop the research question gradually. Don't keep hoping that the perfect research question will just spring forth from your pen. Instead, develop a list of possible research questions as you go along. At the appropriate time, look through this list for the research questions that appear more than once. Narrow your list to the most interesting, most workable candidates. Repeat this process as long as it helps improve your research question.

Evaluating Social Research Questions

In the third stage of selecting a research question, we evaluate the best candidate against the criteria for good social research questions: feasibility, given the time and resources available; social importance; and scientific relevance (King, Keohane, & Verba 1994).

Feasibility

We must be able to conduct any study within the time and resources available. If time is short, questions that involve long-term change may not be feasible. Another issue is to what people or groups we can expect to gain access. For example, observing social interaction in corporate boardrooms may be taboo. Next, we must consider whether we will have any additional resources, such as research funds or other researchers with whom to collaborate. Remember that there are severe limits on what one person can accomplish. However, we may be able to piggyback our research onto a larger research project. We also must consider the constraints we face because of our schedules, our other commitments, and our skill level.

The Minneapolis Domestic Violence Experiment shows how ambitious a social research question can be when a team of seasoned researchers secures the backing of influential groups. The project required hundreds of thousands of dollars, the collaboration of many social scientists and criminal justice personnel, and the volunteer efforts of 41 Minneapolis police officers. Of course, for this reason, the Sherman and Berk (1984) question would not be feasible for a student project. You might instead ask the question "Do students think punishment deters spouse abuse?" Or perhaps you could work out an arrangement with a local police department to study the question, "How satisfied are police officers with their treatment of domestic violence cases?"

Social Importance

Social research is not a simple undertaking, so it's hard to justify the expenditure of effort and resources unless we focus on a substantive area that is important. Besides, you need to feel motivated to carry out the study. Nonetheless, "importance" is relative, so for a class assignment, student reactions to dormitory rules or something similar might be important enough.

For most research undertakings, we should consider whether the research question is important to other people. Will an answer to the research question make a difference for society or for social relations? Again, the Minneapolis Domestic Violence Experiment is an exemplary case. But the social sciences are not wanting for important research questions. The August 2013 issue of the *American Sociological Review*—the journal that published the first academic article on the Minneapolis experiment—contained articles on environment, urbanization, leadership, migration processes, social class and lifestyle, and global social change. All these articles addressed research questions about important social issues, and all raised new questions for additional research.

Scientific Relevance

Journal Link
Culture and Theory

Every research question should be grounded in the social science literature. Whether we formulate a research question because we have been stimulated by an academic article or because we want to investigate a current social problem, we should first turn to the social science literature to find out what has already been learned about this question. You can be sure that some prior study is relevant to almost any research question you can think of.

Audio Link
Research and Change

The Minneapolis experiment was built on a substantial body of contradictory theorizing about the impact of punishment on criminality (Sherman & Berk 1984). Deterrence theory predicted that arrest would deter individuals from repeat offenses; labeling theory predicted that arrest would make repeat offenses more likely. Only one prior experimental study of this issue had been conducted with juveniles, and studies among adults had yielded inconsistent findings. Clearly, the Minneapolis researchers had good reason for another study. Any new research question should be connected in this way to past research.

回 Social Theories

Neither domestic violence nor police policies exist in a vacuum, set apart from the rest of the social world. We can understand the particular behaviors and orientations better if we consider how they reflect broader social patterns. Do abusive men keep their wives in positions of subservience? Are community members law abiding? Our answers to general questions such as these will help shape the research questions that we ask and the methods that we use.

Although everyone has general notions about "how things work," "what people are like," and so on, social scientists draw on more formal sets of general ideas—social theories—to guide their research (Collins 1994). A **theory** is a logically interrelated set of propositions that helps us make sense of many interrelated phenomena and predict behavior or attitudes that are likely to occur when certain

> **Theory:** A logically interrelated set of propositions about empirical reality.

conditions are met. Theory helps social scientists decide which questions are important to ask about the social world and which are just trivial pursuits. Theory focuses a spotlight on the particular features of the social world where we should look to get answers for these questions, how these features are related to each other, and what features can be ignored. Building and evaluating theory is therefore one of the most important objectives of social science.

Lawrence Sherman and Richard Berk's (1984) domestic violence experiment tested predictions derived from **rational choice theory**. Rational choice theory assumes that people's behavior is shaped by practical cost–benefit calculations (Coleman 1990:14). *Specific deterrence theory* applies rational choice theory to crime and punishment (Lempert & Sanders 1986:86–87). It states that arresting spouse abusers will lessen their likelihood of reoffending by increasing the costs of reoffending. Crime "doesn't pay" (as much) for these people (see Exhibit 2.3).

> **Rational choice theory:** A social theory that explains individual action with the principle that actors choose actions that maximize their gains from taking that action.

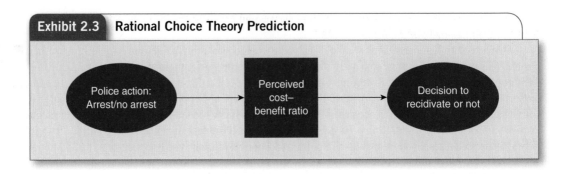

Exhibit 2.3 Rational Choice Theory Prediction

Police action:
Arrest/no arrest → Perceived cost–benefit ratio → Decision to recidivate or not

Do these concepts interest you? Do these propositions strike you as reasonable ones? If so, you might join a long list of researchers who have attempted to test, extend, and modify various aspects of rational choice theory.

Raymond Paternoster and his colleagues (1997) concluded that rational choice theory—in particular, specific deterrence theory—did not provide an adequate framework for explaining how citizens respond to arrest. Paternoster et al. turned to **procedural justice theory** for a very different prediction. *Procedural justice theory* predicts that people will obey the law from a sense of obligation that flows from seeing legal authorities as moral and legitimate (Tyler 1990). From this perspective, individuals who are arrested will be less likely to reoffend if they are treated fairly, irrespective of the outcome of their case, because fair treatment will enhance their view of legal authorities as moral and legitimate. Procedural justice theory expands our view of the punishment process by focusing attention on *how* authorities treat subjects rather than just on *what* decisions they make.

> **Procedural justice theory:** A theory that predicts that people will obey the law from a sense of obligation that flows from seeing legal authorities as moral and legitimate.

Some sociologists attempt to understand the social world by looking inward, at the meaning people attach to their interactions. These researchers focus on the symbolic nature of social interaction—how social interaction conveys meaning and promotes socialization. Herbert Blumer developed these ideas into **symbolic interaction theory** (Turner, Beeghley, & Powers 1995:460).

> **Symbolic interaction theory:** Focuses on the symbolic nature of social interaction—how social interaction conveys meaning and promotes socialization.

Labeling theory uses a symbolic interactionist approach to explain deviance as an "offender's" reaction to the application of rules and sanctions (Becker 1963:9; Scull 1988:678). Sherman and Berk (1984) recognized that a labeling process might influence offenders' responses to arrest in domestic violence cases. Once the offender is labeled as a deviant by undergoing arrest, other people treat the offender as deviant, and he or she is then more likely to act in a way that is consistent with the label *deviant*. Ironically, the act of punishment stimulates more of the very behavior that it was intended to eliminate. This theory suggests that persons arrested for domestic assault are more likely to reoffend than are those who are not punished, which is the reverse of the deterrence theory prediction.

Video Link
Rational Choice
Theory

Do you find yourself thinking of some interesting research foci when you read about this labeling theory of deviance? If so, consider developing your knowledge of symbolic interaction theory and use it as a guide in your research.

Conflict theory focuses on basic conflicts between different social groups in society and how groups attempt to exercise domination to their own benefit (Collins 1994:47). The theory has its origins in Karl Marx and Friedrich Engels' (1961:13–16) focus on social classes as the key groupings in society and their belief that conflict between social classes was not only the norm but also the "engine" of social change.

> **Conflict theory:** Identifies conflict between social groups as the primary force in society; understanding the bases and consequences of the conflict is key to understanding social processes.

Although different versions of conflict theory emphasize different bases for conflict, they focus attention on the conflicting interests of groups rather than on the individuals' concerns with maximizing their self-interest. As applied to crime, conflict theory suggests that laws and the criminal justice system are tools of the upper classes to maintain their dominance over lower classes.

Do these concepts strike a responsive chord with you? Can you think of instances when propositions of conflict theory might help explain social change?

French social theorist Émile Durkheim used a very different theory, **functionalism**, to explain crime and other forms of deviance in society. Writing during the period of rapid social change in Europe at the dawn of the 20th century, Durkheim (1984) was concerned with the strength of social bonds in society. He posited that traditional social bonds based on similarity between people were being replaced by social bonds based on interdependence between people performing different social roles. For example, urban dwellers needed farmers to grow their food, truckers to bring the crops to market, merchants to arrange the sale of the crops, butchers to prepare meat, cobblers to make shoes, and so forth. Durkheim (1966) termed social bonds based in this way on interdependence as *organic solidarity* (bringing to mind the interdependence of different organs in the body). Crime is explained by functionalists as occurring because it is functional for society to delimit the boundaries around acceptable behavior.

> **Functional theory:** A social theory that explains social patterns in terms of their consequences for society as a whole and emphasizes the interdependence of social institutions and their common interest in maintaining the social order.

As a social researcher, you may work with one of these theories, seeking to extend it, challenge it, or specify it. You may test alternative implications of the different theories against each other. If you're feeling ambitious, you may even seek to combine some aspects of the different perspectives. Maybe you'll come up with a different theoretical perspective altogether. Or you may find that you lose sight of the larger picture in the midst of a research project; after all, it is easier to focus on accumulating particular findings rather than considering how those findings fit into a more general understanding of the social world. But you'll find that in any area of research, developing an understanding of relevant theories will help you ask important questions, consider reasonable alternatives, and choose appropriate research procedures.

Interactive Exercises Link
Social Theories

Scientific Paradigms

Scientific paradigms are sets of beliefs that guide scientific work in an area, including unquestioned presuppositions, accepted theories, and exemplary research findings. In his famous book on the history of science, *The Structure of Scientific Revolutions,* Thomas S. Kuhn (1970) argued that most of the time one scientific paradigm is accepted as the prevailing wisdom in a field and that scientists test ideas that make sense within that paradigm. They are conducting what Kuhn called **normal science**. Only after a large body of contrary evidence accumulates might there be a rapid shift to a new paradigm—that is, a **scientific revolution** (Hammersley 2008:46).

> **Scientific paradigm:** A set of beliefs that guide scientific work in an area, including unquestioned presuppositions, accepted theories, and exemplary research findings.
>
> **Normal science:** The gradual, incremental research conducted by scientists within the prevailing scientific paradigm.
>
> **Scientific revolution:** The abrupt shift from one dominant scientific paradigm to an alternative paradigm that may be developed after accumulation of a large body of evidence that contradicts the prevailing paradigm.

Some refer to conflict theory, functionalist theory, and symbolic interaction theory as alternative paradigms, although this stretches the meaning of "paradigm" a bit. When we think of these theories in the context of other beliefs, however, calling them *paradigms* seems more reasonable. Symbolic interaction theory is often used in tandem with qualitative methods of investigation that are in turn guided by a constructivist research philosophy (see Chapter 1). This perspective contrasts markedly with one defined by functionalist theorizing that uses quantitative methods to test explicit hypotheses based on a positivist research philosophy. If social science overall were to shift from one of these perspectives to another, that would be a true revolution in social science. However, many social scientists draw on both of these perspectives in their research and so reject the notion that these are truly incommensurable paradigms. We also should be sensitive to the insights that can be provided by examining social phenomena from both perspectives. In research articles published in sociology journals, C. David Gartrell and John W. Gartrell (2002) found that positivism continues to be the dominant perspective in the United States, but it has become much less common in British sociology journals.

Encyclopedia Link
Paradigm

▣ Social Research Foundations

How do we find prior research and theorizing on questions of interest? You may already know some of the relevant material from prior coursework or your independent reading, but that won't be enough. You need to find reports of previous investigations that sought to answer the same research question that you want to answer, not just those that were about a similar topic. If there have been no prior studies of exactly the same research question on which you want to focus, you should seek reports from investigations of very similar research questions. Once you have located reports from prior research similar to the research that you want to conduct, you may expand your search to include investigations about related topics or studies that used similar methods.

Although it's most important when you're starting out, reviewing the literature is also important at later stages of the research process. Throughout a research project, you will uncover new issues and encounter unexpected problems; at each of these times, you should search the literature to locate prior research on these issues and to learn how others responded to similar problems. Published research that you ignored when you were seeking other research on domestic violence might become very relevant when you have to decide which questions to ask people about their attitudes toward police and other authorities.

Searching the Literature

Conducting a thorough search of the research literature and then reviewing critically what you have found lays an essential foundation for any research project. Fortunately, much of this information can be identified online, without leaving your desktop, and an increasing number of published journal articles can be downloaded directly onto your own computer (depending on your particular access privileges). But just because there's a lot available online doesn't mean that you need to find it *all*. Keep in mind that your goal is to find relevant reports of prior research investigations. The type of reports you should focus on are those that have been screened for quality through critique by other social scientists before publication. Scholarly journals, or *refereed journals* that publish *peer-reviewed articles,* manage this review process. Most often, editors of refereed journals send articles that authors submit to three or more other social scientists for anonymous review. Based on the reviewers' comments, the journal editor then decides whether to accept or reject the article, or to invite the author to "revise and resubmit." This process results in the rejection of most articles (top journals such as the *American Sociological Review* or the *American Journal of Sociology* may reject about 90% of the articles submitted), and those that are ultimately accepted for publication normally have to be revised and resubmitted first. This helps ensure a much higher-quality standard, although journals vary in the rigor of their review standards, and of course, different reviewers may be impressed by different types of articles; you thus always have to make your own judgment about article quality.

Newspaper and magazine articles may raise important issues or summarize social science research investigations, but they are not an acceptable source for understanding the research literature. The web offers much useful material, including research reports from government and other sources, sites that describe social programs, and even indexes of the published research literature. You may find copies of particular rating scales, reports from research in progress, papers that have been presented at professional conferences, and online discussions of related topics. Web search engines will also find academic journal articles that you can access directly online, although usually for a fee. Most of the published research literature will be available to you online only if you go through the website of your college or university library. The library pays a fee to companies that provide online journals so that you can retrieve this information without paying anything extra yourself. Of course, no library can afford to pay for every journal, so if you can't find a particular issue of a particular journal that you need online, you will have to order the article that you need through interlibrary loan or, if the hard copy of the journal is available, walk over to your library to read it.

As with any part of the research process, your method for searching the literature will affect the quality of your results. Your search method should include the following steps:

Specify your research question. Your research question should be neither so broad that hundreds of articles are judged relevant nor so narrow that you miss important literature. "Is informal social control effective?" is probably too broad. "Does informal social control reduce rates of burglary in my town?" is probably too narrow. "Is informal social control more effective in reducing crime rates than policing?" provides about the right level of specificity.

Identify appropriate bibliographic databases to search. Sociological Abstracts or SocINDEX may meet many of your needs, but if you are studying a question about social factors in illness, you should also search in Medline, the database for searching the medical literature. If your focus is on mental health, you'll also want to include a search in the online Psychological Abstracts database, PsycINFO, or the version that also contains the full text of articles, PsycARTICLES. Search Criminal Justice Abstracts if your topic is in the area of criminology or criminal justice, or EconLit, if your topic might be addressed in the economic literature, which indexes literature on contemporary women's issues. It will save you a lot of time if you ask a librarian to teach you the best techniques for retrieving the most relevant articles to answer your questions.

To find articles that refer to a previous publication, such as Sherman and Berk's study of the police response to domestic violence, the Social Science Citation Index (SSCI) will be helpful. SSCI is an extremely useful tool for tracing the cumulative research in an area across the social sciences. SSCI has a unique "citation searching" feature that allows you to look up articles or books, see who else has cited them in their work, and find out which articles and books have had the biggest impact in a field.

Create a tentative list of search terms. List the parts and subparts of your research question and any related issues that you think are important: "informal social control," "policing," "influences on crime rates," and perhaps "community cohesion and crime." List the authors of relevant studies. Specify the most important journals that deal with your topic.

Narrow your search. The sheer number of references you find can be a problem. For example, searching for "social capital" in December 2013 resulted in 6,086 citations in SocINDEX. Depending on the database you are working with and the purposes of your search, you may want to limit your search to English-language publications, to journal articles rather than conference papers or dissertations (both of which are more difficult to acquire), and to materials published in recent years. If your search yields too many citations, try specifying the search terms more precisely (e.g., "neighborhood social capital"). If you have not found much literature, try using more general or multiple terms (e.g., "social relations" OR "social ties"). Whatever terms you search first, don't consider your search complete until you have tried several different approaches and have seen how many articles you find. A search for "domestic violence" in SocINDEX on December 29, 2013, yielded 8,319 hits; by adding "effects" *or* "influences" as required search terms and limiting the search to peer-reviewed articles published since 2010, the number of hits dropped to 160.

Use Boolean search logic. It's often a good idea to narrow your search by requiring that abstracts contain combinations of words or phrases that include more of the specific details of your research question. Using the Boolean connector *and* allows you to do this, while using the connector *or* allows you to find abstracts containing different words that mean the same thing (see Exhibit 2.4 later in this chapter).

Use appropriate subject descriptors. Once you have found an article that you consider appropriate, look at the "descriptors" field in the citation. You can then redo your search after requiring that the articles be classified with some or all of these descriptor terms.

Check the results. Read the titles and abstracts you have found and identify the articles that appear to be most relevant. If possible, click on these article titles and generate a list of their references. See if you find more articles that are relevant to your research question but that you have missed so far. You will be surprised (I always am) at how many important articles your initial online search missed.

Locate the articles. Whatever database you use, the next step after finding your references is to obtain the articles themselves. You will probably find the full text of many articles available online, but this will be determined by what journals your library subscribes to and the period for which it pays for online access. The most recent issues of some journals may not be available online. Keep in mind that your library will not have anywhere near all the journals (and books) that you run across in your literature search, so you will have to add another step to your search: checking the "holdings" information.

If an article that appears to be important for your topic isn't available from your own library, or online, you may be able to request a copy online through your library site or by asking a member of the library staff. You can also check http://worldcat.org to see what other libraries have the journal.

Be sure to take notes on each article you read, organizing your notes into standard sections: theory, methods, findings, conclusions. In any case, write your review of the literature so that it contributes to your study in some concrete way; don't feel compelled to discuss an article just because you have read it. Be judicious. You are conducting only one study of one issue, and it will only obscure the value of your study if you try to relate it to every tangential point in related research.

Don't think of searching the literature as a one-time-only venture—something that you leave behind as you move on to your *real* research. You may encounter new questions or unanticipated problems as you conduct your research or as you burrow deeper into the literature. Searching the literature again to determine what others have found in response to these questions or what steps they have taken to resolve these problems can yield substantial improvements in your own research. There is so much literature on so many topics that it often is not possible to figure out in advance every subject for which you should search the literature, or what type of search will be most beneficial.

Another reason to make searching the literature an ongoing project is that the literature is always growing. During the course of one research study, whether it takes only one semester or several years, new findings will be published and relevant questions will be debated. Staying attuned to the literature and checking it at least when you are writing up your findings may save your study from being outdated as soon as it is finished.

Reviewing Research

Research|Social Impact Link
Ethics

Your literature review will suggest specific research questions for further investigation and research methods with which to study those questions. Sherman and Berk (1984) learned from their literature review that there had been little empirical research about the impact of arrest policies in domestic violence cases. What prior research had been conducted did not use very rigorous research designs. There was thus potential value in conducting new research using a rigorous design. Subsequent researchers questioned whether Sherman and Berk's results would be replicated in other cities and whether some of their methods could be improved. When the original results did not replicate, researchers designed more investigations to test explanations for the different findings. In this way, reviewing the literature identifies unanswered questions and contradictory evidence.

Effective review of the prior research is thus an essential step in building the foundation for new research. You must assess carefully the quality of each research study, consider the implications of each article for your own plans, and expand your thinking about your research question to account for new perspectives and alternative arguments. Through reviewing the literature and using it to extend and sharpen your own ideas and methods you become a part of the social science community. Instead of being just one individual studying an issue that interests you, you are building on an ever-growing body of knowledge that is being constructed by the community of scholars.

Sometimes you'll find that someone else has already searched the literature on your research question and discussed what they found in a special review article or book chapter. For example, Aygül Akyüz, Tülay Yavan, Gönül Şahiner, and Ayşe Kılıç (2012) published a review of the research on domestic violence and women's reproductive health in the journal *Aggression and Violent Behavior.* Most of the research articles that you find will include a short literature review on the specific focus of the research. These reviews can help a lot, but they are no substitute for searching the literature yourself, selecting the articles and other sources that are most pertinent to your research question, and then reviewing what you have found. No one but you can decide what is relevant for your research question and the research circumstances you will be facing—the setting you will study, the timing of your study, the new issues that you want to include in your study, and your specific methods. And you can't depend on any published research review for information on the most recent works. New research results about many questions appear continually in scholarly journals and books, in research reports from government agencies and other organizations, and on websites all over the world; you'll need to check for new research like this yourself.

Caveat emptor (buyer beware) is the watchword when you search the web, but the published scholarly journal literature can be identified in databases such as Sociological Abstracts, SocINDEX, and Psychological Abstracts. Because these literature databases follow a more standard format and use a careful process to decide what literature to include, they are the sources on which you should focus. This section concentrates on the procedures you should use for reviewing the articles you find in a search of the scholarly literature, but these procedures can also be applied to reviews of research monographs—books that provide more information from a research project than can be contained in a journal article.

Reviewing the literature is really a two-stage process. In the first stage, you must assess each article separately. This assessment should follow a standard format such as that represented by the "Questions to Ask About a Research Article" in Appendix A. However, you should keep in mind that you can't adequately understand a research study if you just treat it as a series of discrete steps involving a marriage of convenience among separate techniques. Any research project is an integrated whole, so you must be concerned with how each component of the research design influenced the others—for example, how the measurement approach might have affected the causal validity of the researcher's conclusions and how the sampling strategy might have altered the quality of measures.

The second stage of the review process is to assess the implications of the entire set of articles (and other materials) for the relevant aspects of your research question and procedures, and then to write an integrated review that highlights these implications. Although you can find literature reviews that consist simply of assessments of one published article after another—that never get beyond the first stage in the review process—your understanding of the literature and the quality of your own work will be much improved if you make the effort to write an integrated review.

In the next two sections, I show how you might answer many of the questions in Appendix A as I review a research article about domestic violence. I will then show how the review of a single article can be used within an integrated review of the body of prior research on this research question. Because at this early point in the text you won't be familiar with all the terminology used in the article review, you might want to read through the more elaborate article review in Appendix B later in the course.

A Single-Article Review: Formal and Informal Deterrents to Domestic Violence

Antony Pate and Edwin Hamilton at the national Police Foundation designed one of the studies funded by the U.S. Department of Justice to replicate the Minneapolis Domestic Violence Experiment. In this section, we will examine the article that resulted from that replication, which was published in the *American Sociological Review* (Pate & Hamilton 1992). The numbers in square brackets refer to the article review questions in Appendix A.

The research question. Like Sherman and Berk's (1984) original Minneapolis study, Pate and Hamilton's (1992) Metro-Dade spouse assault experiment sought to test the deterrent effect of arrest in domestic violence cases, but with an additional focus on the role of informal social control [1]. The purpose of the study was explanatory, because the goal was to explain variation in the propensity to commit spouse abuse [2]. Deterrence theory provided the theoretical framework for the study, but this framework was broadened to include the proposition by Kirk Williams and Richard Hawkins (1986) that informal sanctions such as stigma and the loss of valued relationships augment the effect of formal sanctions such as arrest [4]. Pate and Hamilton's (1992) literature review referred, appropriately, to the original Sherman and Berk (1984) research, to the other studies that attempted to replicate the original findings, and to research on informal social control [3].

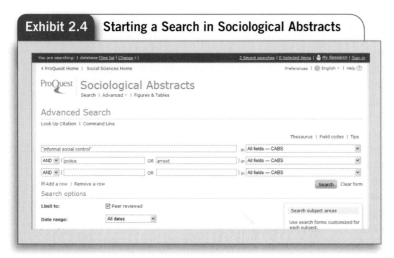

Exhibit 2.4   Starting a Search in Sociological Abstracts

Exhibit 2.4 shows what Pate and Hamilton might have entered on their computer if they searched Sociological Abstracts to find research on "informal social control" and "police" or "arrest."

There is no explicit discussion of ethical guidelines in the article, although reference is made to a more complete unpublished report [6]. Clearly, important ethical issues had to be considered, given the experimental intervention in the police response to serious assaults, but the adherence to standard criminal justice procedures suggests attention to the welfare of victims as well as to the rights of suspects. We will consider these issues in more detail later in this chapter.

The research design. Developed as a follow-up to the original Minneapolis experiment, the Metro-Dade experiment exemplifies the features of a well-designed, deductive evaluation research study [5]. It was designed systematically, with careful attention to specification of terms and clarification of assumptions, and focused on the possibility of different outcomes rather than certainty about one preferred outcome. The major concepts in the study, formal and informal deterrence, were defined clearly [9] and then measured with straightforward indicators—arrest or nonarrest for formal deterrence and marital status and employment status for informal deterrence. However, the specific measurement procedures for marital and employment status were not discussed, and no attempt was made to determine whether they captured adequately the concept of informal social control [9, 10].

Three hypotheses were stated and related to the larger theoretical framework and prior research [7]. The study design focused on the behavior of individuals [13] and collected data over time, including records indicating subsequent assault as many as 6 months after the initial arrest [14]. The project's experimental design was used appropriately to test for the causal effect of arrest on recidivism [15, 17]. The research project involved all eligible cases, rather than a sample of cases, but there were a number of eligibility criteria that narrowed the ability to generalize these results to the entire population of domestic assault cases in the Metro-Dade area or elsewhere [11]. There is a brief discussion of the 92 eligible cases that were not given the treatment to which they were assigned, but it does not clarify the reasons for the misassignment [15].

The research findings and conclusion. Pate and Hamilton's (1992) analysis of the Metro-Dade experiment was motivated by concern with the effect of social context because the replications in other cities of the original Minneapolis Domestic Violence Experiment had not had consistent results [19]. Pate and Hamilton's analysis gave strong support to the expectation that informal social control processes are important: As they had hypothesized, arrest had a deterrent effect on suspects who were employed, but not on those who were unemployed (Exhibit 2.5). However, marital status had no such effect [20]. The subsequent discussion of these findings gives no attention to the implications of the lack of support for the effect of marital status [21], but the study represents an important improvement over earlier research that had not examined informal sanctions [22]. The need for additional research is highlighted, and the importance of the findings for social policy is discussed: Pate and Hamilton suggest that their finding that arrest deters only those who have something to lose (e.g., a job) must be considered when policing policies are established [23].

Overall, the Pate and Hamilton (1992) study represents an important contribution to understanding how informal social control processes influence the effectiveness of formal sanctions such as arrest. Although the use of a population of actual spouse assault cases precluded the use of very sophisticated measures of informal social control, the experimental design of the study and the researchers' ability to interpret the results in the

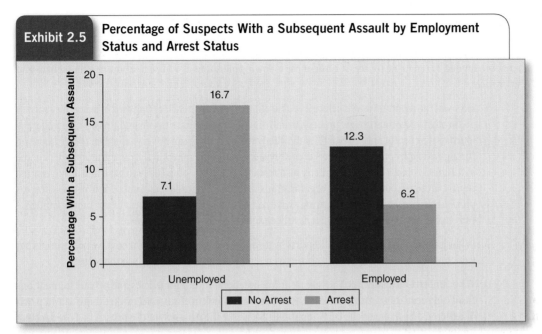

Exhibit 2.5 Percentage of Suspects With a Subsequent Assault by Employment Status and Arrest Status

Source: Pate, Antony M. and Hamilton Edwin E. 1992. "Formal and Informal Deterrents to Domestic Violence: The Dade County Spouse Assault Experiment.". *American Sociological Review* 57(October):691–697.

context of several other comparable experiments distinguish this research as exceptionally worthwhile. It is not hard to understand why these studies continue to stimulate further research and ongoing policy discussions.

An Integrated Literature Review: When Does Arrest Matter?

The goal of the second stage of the literature review process is to integrate the results of your separate article reviews and develop an overall assessment of the implications of prior research. The integrated literature review should accomplish three goals: (1) summarize prior research, (2) critique prior research, and (3) present pertinent conclusions (Hart 1998:186–187). I'll discuss each of these goals in turn.

1. *Summarize prior research.* Your summary of prior research must focus on the particular research questions that you will address, but you may also need to provide some more general background. Carolyn Hoyle and Andrew Sanders (2000:14) begin their *British Journal of Criminology* research article about mandatory arrest policies in domestic violence cases with what they term a "provocative" question: What is the point of making it a crime for men to assault their female partners and ex-partners? The researchers then review the different theories and supporting research that have justified different police policies: the "victim choice" position, the "pro-arrest" position, and the "victim empowerment" position. Finally, Hoyle and Sanders review the research on the "controlling behaviors" of men that frames the specific research question on which they focus: how victims view the value of criminal justice interventions in their own cases (Hoyle & Sanders 2000:15).

Ask yourself three questions about your summary of the literature:

a. Have you been selective? If there have been more than a few prior investigations of your research question, you will need to narrow your focus to the most relevant and highest-quality studies. Don't cite a large number of prior articles "just because they are there."

b. Is the research up-to-date? Be sure to include the most recent research, not just the "classic" studies.

c. Have you used direct quotes sparingly? To focus your literature review, you need to express the key points from prior research in your own words. Use direct quotes only when they are essential for making an important point (Pyrczak 2005:51–59).

2. *Critique prior research.* Evaluate the strengths and weaknesses of the prior research. In addition to all the points that you develop as you answer the article review questions in Appendix A, you should also select articles for review that reflect work published in peer-reviewed journals and written by credible authors who have been funded by reputable sources. Consider the following questions as you decide how much weight to give each article:

a. How was the report reviewed before its publication or release? Articles published in academic journals go through a rigorous review process, usually involving careful criticism and revision. Top refereed journals may accept only 10% of the submitted articles, so they can be very selective. Dissertations go through a lengthy process of criticism and revision by a few members of the dissertation writer's home institution. A report released directly by a research organization is likely to have had only a limited review, although some research organizations maintain a rigorous internal review process. Papers presented at professional meetings may have had little prior review. Needless to say, more confidence can be placed in research results that have been subject to a more rigorous review.

b. What is the author's reputation? Reports by an author or team of authors who have published other work on the research question should be given somewhat greater credibility at the outset.

c. Who funded and sponsored the research? Major federal funding agencies and private foundations fund only research proposals that have been evaluated carefully and ranked highly by a panel of experts. These agencies also often monitor closely the progress of the research. This does not guarantee that every such project report is good, but it goes a long way toward ensuring some worthwhile products. Conversely, research that is funded by organizations that have a preference for a particular outcome should be given particularly close scrutiny (Locke, Silverman, & Spirduso 1998:37–44).

3. *Present pertinent conclusions.* Don't leave the reader guessing about the implications of the prior research for your own investigation. Present the conclusions you draw from the research you have reviewed. As you do so, follow several simple guidelines:

a. Distinguish clearly your own opinion of prior research from the conclusions of the authors of the articles you have reviewed.

b. Make it clear when your own approach is based on the theoretical framework that you use and not on the results of prior research.

c. Acknowledge the potential limitations of any empirical research project. Don't emphasize problems in prior research that you can't avoid (Pyrczak 2005:53–56).

d. Explain how the unanswered questions raised by prior research or the limitations of methods used in prior research make it important for you to conduct your own investigation (Fink 2005:190–192).

A good example of how to conclude an integrated literature review is provided by an article based on the replication in Milwaukee of the Minneapolis Domestic Violence Experiment. For this article, Paternoster et al. (1997) sought to determine whether police officers' use of fair procedures when arresting assault suspects would lessen the rate of subsequent domestic violence. Paternoster et al. (1997) conclude that there has been a major gap in the prior literature: "Even at the end of some seven experiments and millions of dollars, then, there is a great deal of ambiguity surrounding the question of how arrest impacts future spouse assault" (p. 164). Specifically, the researchers note that each of the seven experiments focused on the effect of arrest itself, but ignored the possibility that "particular kinds of police procedure might inhibit the recurrence of spouse assault" (p. 165).

So, Paternoster and his colleagues (1997) ground their new analysis in additional literature on procedural justice and conclude that their new analysis will be "the first study to examine the effect of fairness judgments regarding a punitive criminal sanction (arrest) on serious criminal behavior (assaulting one's partner)" (p. 172).

🔲 Social Research Strategies

With a research question formulated, a review of the pertinent literature taking shape, and a theoretical framework in mind, we are ready to consider the process of conducting our research.

When we conduct social research, we are attempting to connect theory with empirical data—the evidence we obtain from the social world. Researchers may make this connection by starting with a social theory and then testing some of its implications with data. This is the process of deductive research; it is most often the strategy used in quantitative methods. Alternatively, researchers may develop a connection between social theory and data by first collecting the data and then developing a theory that explains the patterns in the data (see Exhibit 2.6). This inductive research process is more often the strategy used in qualitative methods. As you'll see, a research project can draw on both deductive and inductive strategies.

Exhibit 2.6	**The Links Between Theory and Data**

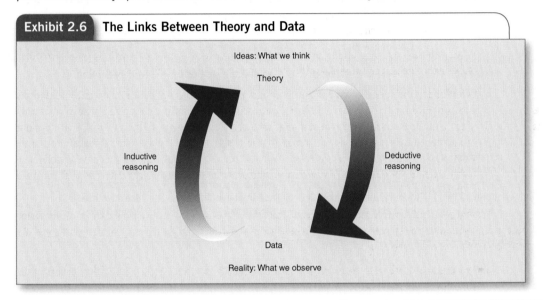

Research in the News

INVESTIGATING CHILD ABUSE DOESN'T REDUCE IT

Congress intended the 1974 Child Abuse Prevention and Treatment Act to increase documentation of and thereby reduce the prevalence of child abuse. However, a review of records of 595 high-risk children nationwide from the ages of 4 to 8 found that those children whose families were investigated were not doing any better than were those whose families were not investigated—except that mothers in investigated families had more depressive symptoms than did mothers in uninvestigated families. The services families were offered after being investigated, if any, failed to reduce the risk of future child abuse.

For Further Thought ❓

1. What might be the value of a longitudinal design with several surveys of these families?

2. Why might the conclusions have differed if this study had used an experimental design?

News source: Bakalar, Nicholas. 2010. "Child Abuse Investigations Didn't Reduce Risk, a Study Finds." *The New York Times,* October 12:D3.

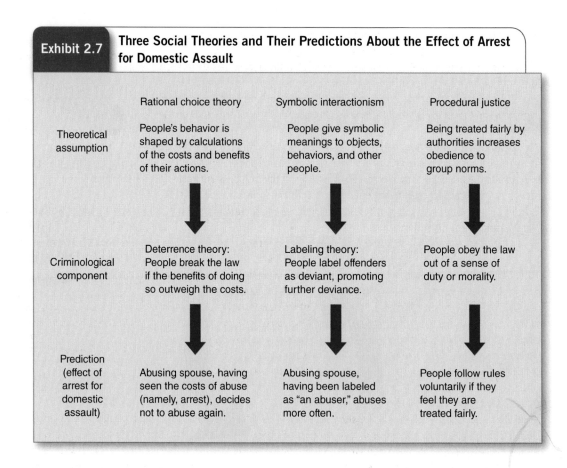

Exhibit 2.7 Three Social Theories and Their Predictions About the Effect of Arrest for Domestic Assault

Social theories do not provide the answers to the questions we pose as topics for research. Instead, social theories suggest the areas on which we should focus and the propositions that we should consider for a test. Exhibit 2.7 summarizes how the two theories that guided Sherman and Berk's (1984) research and the theory that guided Paternoster et al.'s (1997) reanalysis relate to the question of whether to arrest spouse abusers. By helping us make such connections, social theory makes us much more sensitive to the possibilities, and thus helps us design better research and draw out the implications of our results. Before, during, and after a research investigation, we need to keep thinking theoretically.

Explanatory Research

The process of conducting research designed to test explanations for social phenomena involves moving from theory to data and then back to theory. This process can be characterized with a **research circle** (Exhibit 2.8).

Deductive Research

As Exhibit 2.8 shows, in **deductive research**, a specific expectation is deduced from a general theoretical premise and then tested with data that have been collected for this purpose. We call the specific expectation deduced from the more general theory a **hypothesis**. It is the hypothesis that researchers actually test, not the

Research circle: A diagram of the elements of the research process, including theories, hypotheses, data collection, and data analysis.

Deductive research: The type of research in which a specific expectation is deduced from a general premise and is then tested.

Hypothesis: A tentative statement about empirical reality, involving a relationship between two or more variables.

Example of a hypothesis: The higher the poverty rate in a community, the higher the percentage of community residents who are homeless.

complete theory itself. A hypothesis proposes a relationship between two or more **variables**—characteristics or properties that can vary.

Variation in one variable is proposed to predict, influence, or cause variation in the other. The proposed influence is the **independent variable**; its effect or consequence is the **dependent variable**. After the researchers formulate one or more hypotheses and develop research procedures, they collect data with which to test the hypothesis.

Hypotheses can be worded in several different ways, and identifying the independent and dependent variables is sometimes difficult. When in doubt, try to rephrase the hypothesis as an *if-then* statement: "*If* the independent variable increases (or decreases), *then* the dependent variable increases (or decreases)." Exhibit 2.9 presents several hypotheses with their independent and dependent variables and their if-then equivalents.

Exhibit 2.9 demonstrates another feature of hypotheses: **direction of association**. When researchers hypothesize that one variable increases as the other variable increases, the direction of association is positive (Hypotheses 1 and 4). When one variable decreases as the other variable decreases, the direction of association is also positive (Hypothesis 3). But when one variable increases as the other decreases, or vice versa, the direction of association is negative, or inverse (Hypothesis 2). Hypothesis 5 is a special case, in which the independent variable is qualitative: It cannot be said to increase or decrease. In this case, the concept of direction of association does not apply, and the hypothesis simply states that one category of the independent variable is associated with higher values on the dependent variable.

Both explanatory and evaluative studies are types of deductive research. The original Minneapolis Domestic Violence Experiment was an evaluative study because Sherman and Berk (1984) sought to explain what sort of response by the authorities might keep a spouse abuser from repeating the offense. The researchers deduced from deterrence theory the expectation that arrest would deter domestic violence. They then collected data to test this expectation.

In both explanatory and evaluative research, the statement of expectations for the findings and the design of the research to test these expectations strengthen the confidence we can place in the test. Deductive researchers show their hand or state their expectations in advance and then design a fair test of those expectations. Then, "the chips fall where they may"—in other words, the researcher accepts the resulting data as a more or less objective picture of reality.

Domestic Violence and the Research Circle

The classic Sherman and Berk (1984) study of domestic violence provides our first example of how the research circle works. In an attempt to determine ways to prevent the recurrence of spouse abuse, the researchers repeatedly linked theory and data, developing both hypotheses and empirical generalizations.

> **Variable:** A characteristic or property that can vary (take on different values or attributes).
>
> *Example of a variable:* The degree of honesty in verbal statements.
>
> **Independent variable:** A variable that is hypothesized to cause, or lead to, variation in another variable.
>
> *Example of an independent variable:* Poverty rate.
>
> **Dependent variable:** A variable that is hypothesized to vary depending on, or under the influence of, another variable.
>
> *Example of a dependent variable:* Percentage of community residents who are homeless.

> **Direction of association:** A pattern in a relationship between two variables—the values of variables tend to change consistently in relation to change on the other variable; the direction of association can be either positive or negative.

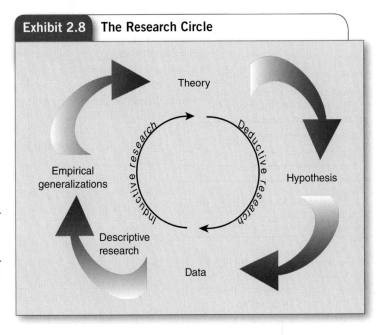

Exhibit 2.8   The Research Circle

Exhibit 2.9 Examples of Hypotheses

Original Hypothesis	Independent Variable	Dependent Variable	If-Then Hypothesis	Direction of Association
1. The greater the use of the Internet, the greater the strength of distant family ties.	Level of Internet use	Strength of distant family ties	*If* Internet use is greater, *then* the strength of distant family ties is greater.	+
2. The risk of property theft decreases as income increases.	Income	Risk of property theft	*If* income is higher, *then* the risk of property theft is less.	–
3. If years of education decrease, income decreases.	Years of education	Income	*If* years of education decrease, *then* income decreases.	+
4. Political conservatism increases with income.	Income	Political conservatism	*If* income increases, *then* political conservatism increases.	+
5. Property crime is higher in urban areas than in suburban or rural areas.	Type of community	Rate of property crime	*If* areas are urban, *then* property crime is higher compared with crime in suburban or rural areas.	NA

Interactive Exercises Link

Variables and Hypotheses

The first phase of Sherman and Berk's study was designed to test a hypothesis. According to deterrence theory, punishment will reduce recidivism, or the propensity to commit further crimes. From this theory, Sherman and Berk deduced a specific hypothesis: "Arrest for spouse abuse reduces the risk of repeat offenses." In this hypothesis, arrest is the independent variable and the risk of repeat offenses is the dependent variable (it is hypothesized to depend on arrest).

Of course, in another study, arrest might be the dependent variable in relation to some other independent variable. For example, in the hypothesis, "The greater the rate of layoffs in a community, the higher the frequency of arrest," the dependent variable is frequency of arrest. Only within the context of a hypothesis, or a relationship between variables, does it make sense to refer to one variable as dependent and the other as independent.

Sherman and Berk tested their hypothesis by setting up an experiment in which the police responded to the complaints of spouse abuse in one of three ways: (1) arresting the offender, (2) separating the spouses without making an arrest, or (3) simply warning the offender. When the researchers examined their data (police records for the persons in their experiment), they found that of those arrested for assaulting their spouse, only 13% repeated the offense, compared with a 26% recidivism rate for those who were separated from their spouse by the police without any arrest. This pattern in the data, or **empirical generalization**, was consistent with the hypothesis that the researchers deduced from deterrence theory. The theory thus received support from the experiment (see Exhibit 2.10).

> **Empirical generalization:** A statement that describes patterns found in data.

> **Replications:** Repetitions of a study using the same research methods to answer the same research question.

Because of their doubts about the generalizability of their results, Sherman, Berk, and other researchers began to journey around the research circle again, with funding from the National Institute of Justice for **replications** (repetitions) of the experiment in six more cities. These replications used the same basic research approach but with some improvements. The random assignment process was tightened in most of the cities so that police officers would be less likely to replace the assigned treatment with a treatment of their own choice. In addition, data were collected about repeat violence against other victims as well as against the original complainant. Some of the replications also examined different aspects of the arrest process, to see whether professional counseling helped and whether the length of time spent in jail after the arrest mattered at all.

By the time results were reported from five of the cities in the new study, a problem was apparent. In three of the cities—Omaha, Nebraska; Charlotte, North Carolina; and Milwaukee, Wisconsin—researchers were finding long-term increases in domestic violence incidents among arrestees. But in two—Colorado Springs, Colorado, and Dade County, Florida—the predicted deterrent effects seemed to be occurring (Sherman & Smith 1992). Sherman and his colleagues had now traversed the research circle twice in an attempt to answer the original research question, first in Minneapolis and then in six other cities. But rather than leading to more confidence in deterrence theory, the research results were questioning it. Deterrence theory

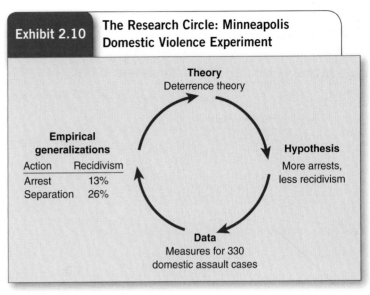

Exhibit 2.10 **The Research Circle: Minneapolis Domestic Violence Experiment**

Source: Data from Sherman and Berk 1984:267.

now seemed inadequate to explain empirical reality, at least as the researchers had measured this reality. So, the researchers began to reanalyze the follow-up data from several cities in an attempt to explain the discrepant results, thereby starting around the research circle once again (Berk et al. 1992; Pate & Hamilton 1992; Sherman & Smith 1992).

Inductive Research

In contrast to deductive research, **inductive research** begins with specific data, which are then used to develop (induce) a general explanation (a theory) to account for the data. One way to think of this process is in terms of the research circle: Rather than starting at the top of the circle with a theory, the inductive researcher starts at the bottom of the circle with data and then develops the theory. Another way to think of this process is represented in Exhibit 2.11. In deductive research, reasoning from specific premises results in a conclusion that a theory is supported, but in inductive research, the identification of similar empirical patterns results in a generalization about some social process.

> **Inductive research:** The type of research in which general conclusions are drawn from specific data.

Inductive reasoning enters into deductive research when we find unexpected patterns in the data we have collected for testing a hypothesis. We may call these patterns **anomalous findings**. When these unexpected patterns lead to new explanations, insights, or theoretical approaches, we call them **serendipitous findings**. However, the adequacy of an explanation formulated after the fact is necessarily less certain than an explanation presented before the collection of data and tested in a planned way with the data. Every phenomenon can always be explained in *some* way. Inductive explanations are thus more trustworthy if they are tested subsequently with deductive research.

> **Anomalous findings:** Unexpected patterns in data.
>
> **Serendipitous findings:** Unexpected patterns in data, which stimulate new explanations, insights, or theoretical approaches.

An inductive approach to explaining domestic violence. The domestic violence research took an inductive turn when Sherman and the other researchers began trying to make sense of the differing patterns in the data collected in the different cities. Could systematic differences in the samples or in the implementation of arrest policies explain the differing outcomes? Or was the problem an inadequacy in the theoretical basis of their research? Was deterrence theory really the best

Exhibit 2.11 Deductive and Inductive Reasoning

Deductive

Premise 1: *All unemployed spouse abusers recidivate.*

Premise 2: *Joe is an unemployed spouse abuser.*

Conclusion: **Joe will recidivate.**

Inductive

Evidence 1: *Joe, an unemployed spouse abuser, recidivated.*

Evidence 2: *Harold, an unemployed spouse abuser, recidivated.*

Evidence 3: *George, an employed spouse abuser, didn't recidivate.*

Conclusion: **All unemployed spouse abusers recidivate.**

way to explain the patterns in the data they were collecting?

As you learned in my review of the Pate and Hamilton (1992) study, the researchers had found that individuals who were married and employed were deterred from repeat offenses by arrest, but individuals who were unmarried and unemployed were actually more likely to commit repeat offenses if they were arrested. What could explain this empirical pattern? The researchers turned to control theory, which predicts that having a "stake in conformity" (resulting from inclusion in social networks at work or in the community) decreases a person's likelihood of committing crimes (Toby 1957). The implication is that people who are employed and married are more likely to be deterred by the threat of arrest than are those without such stakes in conformity. And this is indeed what the data revealed.

Now, the researchers had traversed the research circle almost three times, a process perhaps better described as a spiral (see Exhibit 2.12). The first two times, the researchers had traversed the research circle in a deductive, hypothesis-testing way. They started with theory and then deduced and tested hypotheses. The third time, they were more inductive: They started with empirical generalizations from the data they had already obtained and then turned to a new theory to account for the unexpected patterns in the data. At this point, they believed that deterrence theory made correct predictions, given certain conditions, and that another theory, control theory, might specify what these conditions were.

This last inductive step in their research made for a more complex, but also conceptually richer, picture of the impact of arrest on domestic violence. The researchers seemed to have come closer to understanding how to inhibit domestic violence. But they cautioned us that their initial question—the research problem—was still not completely answered. Employment status and marital status do not solely measure the strength of social attachments; they are also related to how much people earn and the social standing of victims in court. So, maybe social ties are not really what make arrest an effective deterrent to domestic violence. The real deterrent may be cost–benefit calculations ("If I have a higher income, jail is more costly for me") or perceptions about the actions of authorities ("If I am a married woman, judges will treat my complaint more seriously"). Additional research was needed (Berk et al. 1992).

Journal Link
Inductive and Deductive
Techniques

Exploratory Research

Qualitative research is often exploratory and, hence, inductive: The researchers begin by observing social interaction or interviewing social actors in depth and then developing an explanation for what has been found. The researchers often ask questions such as "What is going on here?" "How do people interpret these experiences?" or "Why do people do what they do?" Rather than testing a hypothesis, the researchers are trying to make sense of some social phenomenon. They may even put off formulating a research question until after they begin to collect data—the idea is to let the question emerge from the situation itself (Brewer & Hunter 1989:54–58).

Battered Women's Help Seeking

Angela Moe (2007) used exploratory research methods in her study of women's decisions to seek help after abuse experiences. Rather than interviewing women in court, Moe interviewed 19 women in a domestic

Exhibit 2.12 **The Research Spiral: Domestic Violence Experiment**

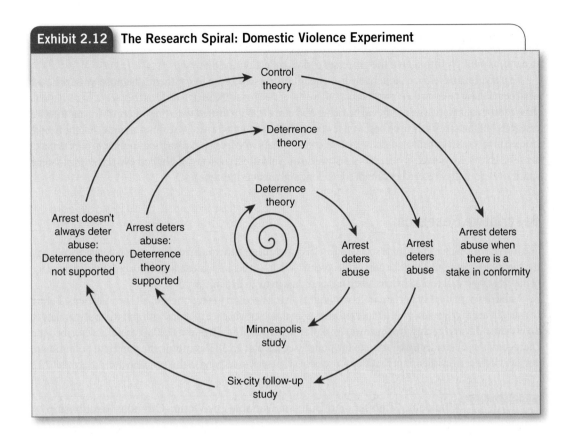

violence shelter. In interviews lasting about 1 hour each, the women were able to discuss, in their own words, what they had experienced and how they had responded. Moe then reviewed the interview transcripts carefully and identified major themes that emerged in the comments.

The following quote is from a woman who had decided not to call the police to report her experience of abuse (Moe 2007:686). We can use this type of information to identify some of the factors behind the underreporting of domestic violence incidents. Moe or other researchers might then design a survey of a larger sample to determine how frequently each basis for underreporting occurs.

I tried the last time to call the police and he ripped both the phones out of the walls. . . .

That time he sat on my upper body and had his thumbs in my eyes and he was just squeezing.

He was going, "I'll gouge your eyes out. I'll break every bone in your body. Even if they do find you alive, you won't know to tell them who did it to you because you'll be in intensive care for so long you'll forget." (Terri)

The Moe (2007) example illustrates how the research questions that serve as starting points for qualitative data analyses do not simply emerge from the setting studied, but are shaped by the investigator. As Harry Wolcott (1995) explains,

[The research question] is not embedded within the lives of those whom we study, demurely waiting to be discovered. Quite the opposite: *We instigate the problems we investigate.* There is no point in simply sitting by, passively waiting to see what a setting is going to "tell" us or hoping a problem will "emerge." (p. 156)

My focus on the importance of the research question as a tool for guiding qualitative data analyses should not obscure the iterative nature of the analytic process. The research question can change, narrow, expand, or multiply throughout the processes of data collection and analysis.

Explanations developed inductively from qualitative research can feel authentic because we have heard what people have to say in their own words, and we have tried to see the social world as they see it. Explanations derived from qualitative research will be richer and more finely textured than they often are in quantitative research, but they are likely to be based on fewer cases from a limited area. We cannot assume that the people studied in this setting are like others or that other researchers will develop explanations similar to ours to make sense of what was observed or heard. Because we do not initially set up a test of a hypothesis according to some specific rules, another researcher cannot come along and conduct the same test.

Descriptive Research

Research|Social Impact Link
Descriptive Research

You learned in Chapter 1 that some social research is purely descriptive. Such research does not involve connecting theory and data, but it is still a part of the research circle—it begins with data and proceeds only to the stage of making empirical generalizations based on those data (refer to Exhibit 2.8).

Valid description is important in its own right—it is a necessary component of all investigations. Before they began an investigation of differences in arrests for domestic violence in states with and without mandatory arrest laws, David Hirschel, Eve Buzawa, April Pattavina, and Don Faggiani (2008) carefully described the characteristics of incidents reported to the police (see Exhibit 2.13). Describing the prevalence of intimate partner violence is an important first step for societies that seek to respond to this problem (refer to Exhibit 2.1).

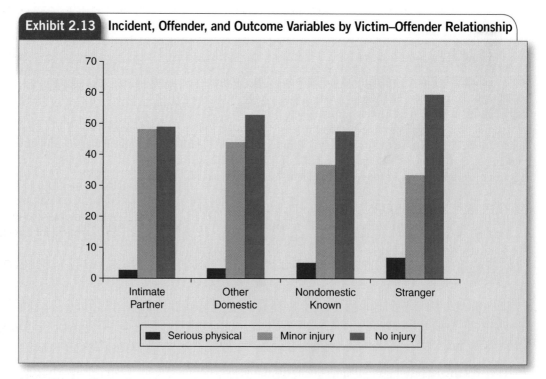

Exhibit 2.13 **Incident, Offender, and Outcome Variables by Victim–Offender Relationship**

Source: Based on Hirschel, David, Eve Buzawa, April Pattavina, and Don Faggiani. 2008. "Domestic Violence and Mandatory Arrest Laws: To What Extent Do They Influence Police Arrest Decisions?" *Journal of Criminal Law & Criminology* 98(1):255–298.

Government agencies and nonprofit organizations frequently sponsor research that is primarily descriptive: How many poor people live in this community? Is the health of the elderly improving? How frequently do convicted criminals return to crime? Simply put, good description of data is the cornerstone of the scientific research process and an essential component for understanding the social world.

Good descriptive research can also stimulate more ambitious deductive and inductive research. The Minneapolis Domestic Violence Experiment was motivated, in part, by a growing body of descriptive research indicating that spouse abuse is very common: 572,000 cases of women victimized by a violent partner each year (Buzawa & Buzawa 1996:1).

Researcher Interview Link
Randomized Research Design

CAREERS AND RESEARCH
Russell Schutt, PhD

Congratulations! You can now take the first step to becoming a social researcher and a consumer of social research, by developing a research question and deciding to begin the process of research. As a result, I hope you are beginning to see the potential for using social research methods to understand issues that matter to you, to identify policies that can help others, and to add to the body of social science knowledge.

There are many ways to develop research interests, and I'd like to share with you some of my own experiences about that. My research experience as a graduate student at the University of Illinois at Chicago and as a postdoctoral fellow at Yale University was in the sociology of organizations, occupations, and law. My interest in research in a new area, homelessness and mental health, developed gradually in subsequent years after I joined the faculty at the University of Massachusetts Boston. One day, I found in my mailbox a plea from a recent graduate for help with "computerizing the case management records" at the shelter for which she had started to work. I was scheduled to teach a graduate course in computer applications and decided to take on this effort as a class project.

With the experience my students and I gained in the project, I was able to write a proposal with a colleague for funding from a new university initiative in health research. As a result of making connections with other researchers and service providers, writing research reports for funders, reading the relevant research literature, and investigating the needs of homeless persons, I was able to write additional research proposals to study homeless persons and shelter services that were funded by the university and by local service programs. Although my proposal to the National Science Foundation with medical sociologist Mary Fennell to study organizational change in shelters was not funded, the pilot study we carried out led to an invitation to join a team of researchers at Harvard's Massachusetts Mental Health Center who were responding to a special National Institute of Mental Health request for proposals about housing and services for homeless persons with serious mental health problems.

The $13.1 million our team received from NIMH and Housing and Urban Development (HUD) allowed us to carry out a longitudinal randomized test of the value of group and independent housing using a mixed-method design that in turn led to many journal articles, some book chapters, and one book (Schutt 2011b). From the small beginning of a class project involving secondary data analysis, to cross-sectional surveys of homeless persons, shelter staff, and shelter directors, to longitudinal evaluation research and then a randomized experiment, these research projects became increasingly sophisticated and supported more significant contributions to social policy and the scholarly literature.

So be prepared to follow your interests, take advantage of opportunities, and maintain ambitious goals!

▣ Social Research Standards

> **Validity:** The state that exists when statements or conclusions about empirical reality are correct.

Social science research can improve our understanding of empirical reality—the reality we encounter firsthand. We have achieved the goal of **validity** when our conclusions about this empirical reality are correct. I look out my window and observe that it is raining—a valid observation, if my eyes and ears are to be trusted. I pick up the newspaper and read that the rate of violence may be climbing after several years of decline. I am less certain of the validity of this statement, based as it is on an interpretation of some trends in crime indicators obtained through some process that isn't explained. As you learned in this chapter, many social scientists who have studied the police response to domestic violence came to the conclusion that arrest deters violence—that there is a valid connection between this prediction of rational choice theory and the data obtained in research about these processes.

> **Measurement validity:** Exists when a measure measures what we think it measures.
>
> **Generalizability:** Exists when a conclusion holds true for the population, group, setting, or event that we say it does, given the conditions that we specify.
>
> **Causal validity (internal validity):** Exists when a conclusion that A leads to or results in B is correct.
>
> **Authenticity:** When the understanding of a social process or social setting is one that reflects fairly the various perspectives of participants in that setting.

If validity sounds desirable to you, you're a good candidate for becoming a social scientist. If you recognize that validity is often a difficult goal to achieve, you may be tough enough for social research. In any case, the goal of social science is not to come up with conclusions that people will like or conclusions that suit our own personal preferences. The goal is to figure out how and why the social world—some aspect of it—operates as it does. In *Investigating the Social World,* we are concerned with three standards for validity: (1) **measurement validity**, (2) **generalizability**, and (3) **causal validity** (also known as **internal validity**) (Hammersley 2008:43). We will learn that invalid measures, invalid generalizations, or invalid causal inferences will result in invalid conclusions. We will also focus on the standard of **authenticity**, a concern with reflecting fairly the perspectives of participants in a setting that we study.

Measurement Validity

Measurement validity is our first concern in establishing the validity of research results because without having measured what we think we measured, we really don't know what we're talking about. Measurement validity is the focus of Chapter 4. A measure is valid when it measures what we think it measures. In other words, if we seek to describe the frequency of domestic violence in families, we need to develop a valid procedure for measuring domestic violence.

The first step in achieving measurement validity is to specify clearly what it is we intend to measure. Patricia Tjaden and Nancy Thoennes (2000) identified this as one of the problems with research on domestic violence: "definitions of the term vary widely from study to study, making comparisons difficult" (p. 5). To avoid this problem, Tjaden and Thoennes (2000) presented a clear definition of what they meant by *intimate partner violence:*

> Rape, physical assault, and stalking perpetrated by current and former dates, spouses, and cohabiting partners, with cohabiting meaning living together at least some of the time as a couple. (p. 5)

Tjaden and Thoennes also provided a measure of each type of violence. For example, "'physical assault' is defined as behaviors that threaten, attempt, or actually inflict physical harm" (Tjaden & Thoennes 2000:5).

With this definition in mind, Tjaden and Thoennes (2000:6) then specified the set of questions they would use to measure intimate partner violence (the questions pertaining to physical assault):

> Not counting any incidents you have already mentioned, after you became an adult, did any other adult, male or female, ever:

—Throw something at you that could hurt?

—Push, grab, or shove you?

—Pull your hair?

—Slap or hit you?

—Kick or bite you?

—Choke or attempt to drown you?

—Hit you with some object?

—Beat you up?

—Threaten you with a gun?

—Threaten you with a knife or other weapon?

—Use a gun on you?

—Use a knife or other weapon on you?

Do you believe that answers to these questions provide a valid measure of having been physically assaulted? Do you worry that some survey respondents might not report all the assaults they have experienced? Might some respondents make up some incidents? Issues like these must be considered when we evaluate measurement validity. Suffice it to say that we must be very careful in designing our measures and in subsequently evaluating how well they have performed. Chapter 4 introduces several different ways to test measurement validity. We cannot just *assume* that measures are valid.

Generalizability

The generalizability of a study is the extent to which it can be used to inform us about persons, places, or events that were not studied. Generalizability is the focus of Chapter 5.

You have already learned in this chapter that Sherman and Berk's findings in Minneapolis about the police response to domestic violence simply did not hold up in several other cities: The initial results could not be generalized. As you know, this led to additional research to figure out what accounted for the different patterns in different cities.

If every person or community we study were like every other one, generalizations based on observations of a small number would be valid. But that's not the case. We are on solid ground if we question the generalizability of statements about research based on the results of a restricted sample of the population or in just one community or other social context.

Generalizability has two aspects. **Sample generalizability** refers to the ability to generalize from a sample, or subset, of a larger population to that population itself. This is the most common meaning of generalizability. **Cross-population generalizability** refers to the ability to generalize from findings about one group, population, or setting to other groups, populations, or settings (see Exhibit 2.14). Cross-population generalizability can also be referred to as **external validity**. (Some social scientists equate the term *external validity* to *generalizability*, but in this book, I restrict its use to the more limited notion of cross-population generalizability.)

> **Sample generalizability:** Exists when a conclusion based on a sample, or subset, of a larger population holds true for that population.
>
> **Cross-population generalizability (external validity):** Exists when findings about one group, population, or setting hold true for other groups, populations, or settings.

Sample generalizability is a key concern in survey research. Political pollsters may study a sample of likely voters, for example, and then generalize their findings to the entire population of likely voters. No one would

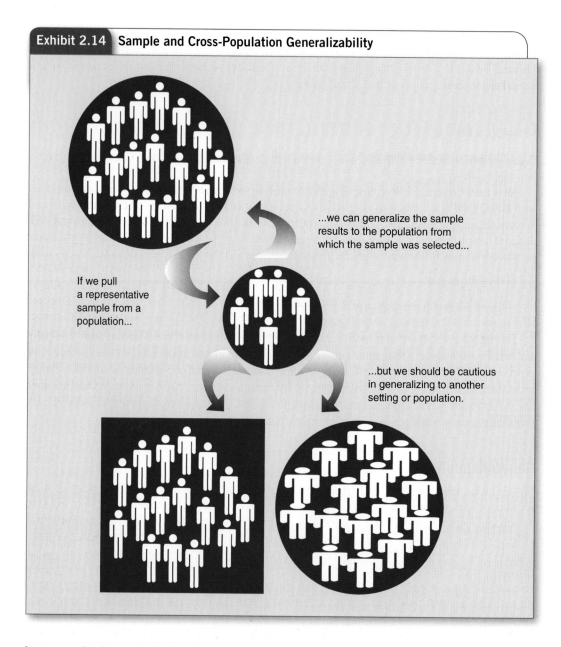

Exhibit 2.14 Sample and Cross-Population Generalizability

If we pull a representative sample from a population...

...we can generalize the sample results to the population from which the sample was selected...

...but we should be cautious in generalizing to another setting or population.

be interested in the results of political polls if they represented only the relatively tiny sample that actually was surveyed rather than the entire population. The procedures for the National Violence Against Women Survey that Tjaden and Thoennes (2000) relied on were designed to maximize sample generalizability.

Cross-population generalizability occurs to the extent that the results of a study hold true for multiple populations; these populations may not all have been sampled, or they may be represented as subgroups within the sample studied. This was the problem with Sherman and Berk's (1984) results: persons in Minneapolis who were arrested for domestic violence did not respond in the same way as persons arrested for the same crime in several other cities. The conclusions from Sherman and Berk's (1984) initial research in Minneapolis were not "externally valid."

Generalizability is a key concern in research design. We rarely have the resources to study the entire population that is of interest to us, so we have to select cases to study that will allow our findings to be generalized to the population of interest. Chapter 5 reviews alternative approaches to selecting cases so that findings can be generalized to the population from which the cases were selected. Nonetheless, because we can never be sure that our findings will hold under all conditions, we should be cautious in generalizing to populations or periods that we did not actually sample.

Causal Validity

Causal validity, also known as *internal validity,* refers to the truthfulness of an assertion that A causes B. It is the focus of Chapter 6.

Most research seeks to determine what causes what, so social scientists frequently must be concerned with causal validity. Sherman and Berk (1984) were concerned with the effect of arrest on the likelihood of recidivism by people accused of domestic violence. To test their causal hypothesis, Sherman and Berk designed their experiment so that some accused persons were arrested and others were not. Of course, it may seem heavy-handed for social scientists to influence police actions for the purpose of a research project, but this step reflects just how difficult it can be to establish causally valid understandings about the social world. Only because police officials did not know whether arrest caused spouse abusers to reduce their level of abuse were they willing to allow an experiment to test the effect of different policies. Hirschel and his collaborators (2008) used a different approach to investigate the effect of mandatory arrest laws on police decisions to arrest: They compared the rate of arrest for domestic violence incidents in jurisdictions with and without mandatory arrest laws.

Which of these two research designs gives you more confidence in the causal validity of the conclusions? Chapter 6 will give you much more understanding of how some features of a research design can help us evaluate causal propositions. However, you will also learn that the solutions are neither easy nor perfect: We always have to consider critically the validity of causal statements that we hear or read.

Authenticity

The goal of authenticity is stressed by researchers who focus attention on the subjective dimension of the social world. An authentic understanding of a social process or social setting is one that reflects fairly the various perspectives of participants in that setting (Gubrium & Holstein 1997). Authenticity is one of several different standards proposed by some as uniquely suited to qualitative research; it reflects a belief that those who study the social world should focus first and foremost on how participants view that social world, rather than on developing a unique social scientists' interpretation of that world. Rather than expecting social scientists to be able to provide a valid mirror of reality, this perspective emphasizes the need for recognizing that what is understood by participants as reality is a linguistic and social construction of reality (Kvale 2002:306).

Moe (2007) explained her basis for considering the responses of women she interviewed in the domestic violence shelter to be authentic:

> Members of marginalized groups are better positioned than members of socially dominant groups to describe the ways in which the world is organized according to the oppressions they experience. (p. 682)

Moe's (2007) assumption was that "battered women serve as experts of their own lives" (p. 682). Adding to her assessment of authenticity, Moe (2007) found that the women "exhibited a great deal of comfort through their honesty and candor" as they produced "a richly detailed and descriptive set of narratives" (p. 683). You will learn more about how authenticity can be achieved in qualitative methods in Chapters 10 and 11.

▣ Conclusions

Selecting a worthy research question does not guarantee a worthwhile research project. The simplicity of the research circle presented in this chapter belies the complexity of the social research process. In the following chapters, I focus on particular aspects of the research process. Chapter 4 examines the interrelated processes of conceptualization and measurement, arguably the most important part of research. Measurement validity is the foundation for the other two aspects of validity. Chapter 5 reviews the meaning of generalizability and the sampling strategies that help us achieve this goal. Chapter 6 introduces causal validity and illustrates different methods for achieving it. Most of the remaining chapters then introduce different approaches to data collection—experiments, surveys, participant observation and intensive interviewing, evaluation research, comparative historical research, secondary data analysis, and content analysis—that help us, in different ways, achieve results that are valid.

Of course, our answers to research questions will never be complete or entirely certain. We always need to ground our research plans and results in the literature about related research. Our approach should be guided by explicit consideration of a larger theoretical framework. When we complete a research project, we should evaluate the confidence that can be placed in our conclusions, point out how the research could be extended, and consider the implications for social theory. Recall how the elaboration of knowledge about deterrence of domestic violence required sensitivity to research difficulties, careful weighing of the evidence, identification of unanswered questions, and consideration of alternative theories.

Owning a large social science toolkit is no guarantee for making the right decisions about which tools to use and how to use them in the investigation of particular research problems, but you are now forewarned about, and thus I hope forearmed against, some of the problems that social scientists face in their work. I hope that you will return often to this chapter as you read the subsequent chapters, when you criticize the research literature, and when you design your own research projects. To be conscientious, thoughtful, and responsible—this is the mandate of every social scientist. If you formulate a feasible research problem, ask the right questions in advance, try to adhere to the research guidelines, and steer clear of the most common difficulties, you will be well along the road to fulfilling this mandate.

Key Terms

Highlights

- Research questions should be feasible (within the time and resources available), socially important, and scientifically relevant.

- A theory is a logically interrelated set of propositions that helps us make sense of many interrelated phenomena and predict behavior or attitudes that are likely to occur when certain conditions are met.

- Building social theory is a major objective of social science research. Relevant theories should be investigated before starting social research projects and they should be used to focus attention on particular research questions and to draw out the implications of research findings.

- Rational choice theory focuses attention on the rational bases for social exchange and explains most social phenomena in terms of these motives.

- Symbolic interaction theory focuses attention on the meanings that people attach to and gain from social interaction and explains most social phenomena in terms of these meanings.

- Conflict theory focuses attention on the bases of conflict between social groups and uses these conflicts to explain most social phenomena.

- Functional theory explains social patterns in terms of their consequences for society as a whole and emphasizes the interdependence of social institutions and their common interest in maintaining the social order.

- A scientific paradigm is a set of beliefs that guide most scientific work in an area. A scientific revolution occurs when the accumulation of contrary evidence leads to a shift from acceptance of one paradigm to another. Some researchers view positivism/postpositivism and interpretivism/constructivism as alternative paradigms.

- Reviewing peer reviewed journal articles that report prior research is an essential step in designing new research.

- The type of reasoning in most research can be described as primarily deductive or inductive. Research based on deductive reasoning proceeds from general ideas, deduces specific expectations from these ideas, and then tests the ideas with empirical data. Research based on inductive reasoning begins with specific data and then develops general ideas or theories to explain patterns in the data.

- It may be possible to explain unanticipated research findings after the fact, but such explanations have less credibility than those that have been tested with data collected for the purpose of the study.

- The scientific process can be represented as circular, with a path from theory to hypotheses, to data, and then to empirical generalizations. Research investigations may begin at different points along the research circle and traverse different portions of it. Deductive research begins at the point of theory, inductive research begins with data but ends with theory, and descriptive research begins with data and ends with empirical generalizations.

- Replications of a study are essential to establishing its generalizability in other situations. An ongoing line of research stemming from a particular research question should include a series of studies that, collectively, traverse the research circle multiple times.

STUDENT STUDY SITE

Sharpen your skills with SAGE edge at **edge.sagepub.com/schutt8e. SAGE edge for students** provides a personalized approach to help you accomplish your coursework goals in an easy-to-use learning environment.

Discussion Questions

1. Pick a social issue about which you think research is needed. Draft three research questions about this issue. Refine one of the questions and evaluate it in terms of the three criteria for good research questions.

2. Identify variables that are relevant to your three research questions. Now formulate three related hypotheses. Which are the independent and which are the dependent variables in these hypotheses?

3. If you were to design research about domestic violence, would you prefer an inductive approach or a deductive approach? Explain your preference. What would be the advantages and disadvantages of each approach? Consider in your answer the role of social theory, the value of searching the literature, and the goals of your research.

4. Sherman and Berk's (1984) study of the police response to domestic violence tested a prediction derived from rational choice theory. Propose hypotheses about the response to domestic violence that are consistent with conflict and symbolic interactionist theories. Which theory seems to you to provide the best framework for understanding domestic violence and how to respond to it?

5. Review my description of the research projects in the section "Types of Social Research" in Chapter 1. Can you identify the stages of each project corresponding to the points on the research circle? Did each project include each of the four stages? Which theory (or theories) seems applicable to each of these projects?

6. The research on battered women's help seeking used an exploratory research approach. Why do you think the researchers adopted this approach in these studies? Do you agree with their decision? Propose a research project that would address issues in one of these studies with a deductive approach.

7. Critique the Sherman and Berk (1984) research on the police response to domestic violence from the standpoint of measurement validity, generalizability, and causal validity. What else would you like to know about this research so you can strengthen your critique? What does consideration of the goal of authenticity add to your critique?

Practice Exercises

1. Pair up with one other student and select one of the research articles available on the book's study site, at edge.sagepub.com/schutt8e. One of you should evaluate the research article in terms of its research strategy. Be generally negative but not unreasonable in your criticisms. The other student should critique the article in the same way but from a generally positive standpoint, defending its quality. Together, write a summary of the study's strong and weak points, or conduct a debate in the class.

2. Research problems posed for explanatory studies must specify variables and hypotheses, which need to be stated properly and need to correctly imply any hypothesized causal relationship. The "Variables and Hypotheses" lessons, found in the Interactive Exercises on the study site, will help you learn how to do this.

   To use these lessons, choose one of the sets of "Variables and Hypotheses" exercises from the opening menu. About 10 hypotheses are presented in the lesson. After reading each hypothesis, name the dependent and independent variables and state the direction (positive or negative) of the relationship between them. In some of these Interactive Exercises, you must write in your own answer, so type carefully. The program will evaluate your answers. If an answer is correct, the program will present its version of the correct answer and go on to the next question. If you have made an error, the program will explain the error to you and give you another chance to respond. If your answer is unrecognizable, the program will instruct you to check your spelling and try again.

3. Now choose another article from the Learning From Journal Articles option on the study site. Read one article based on empirical research and diagram the process of research that it reports. Your diagram should have the structure of the research circle in Exhibit 2.8. How well does the process of research in this study seem to match the process symbolized in Exhibit 2.8? How much information is provided about each step in that process?

4. Review the section in this chapter on literature searching. Now choose a topic for investigation and search the social science literature for prior research on this topic. You will need to know how to use a database such as Sociological Abstracts at your own library as well as how to retrieve articles you locate (those that are available through your library). Try to narrow your search so that most of the articles you find are relevant to your topic (or broaden your search, if you don't find many relevant articles). Report your search terms and the results of your search with each term or combination of terms.

Ethics Questions

1. Sherman and Berk (1984) and those who replicated their research on the police response to domestic violence assigned persons accused of domestic violence by chance (randomly) to be arrested or not. The researchers' goal was to ensure that the people who were arrested were similar to those who were not arrested. Based on what you now know, do you feel that this random assignment procedure was ethical? Why or why not?

2. Concern with how research results are used is one of the hallmarks of ethical researchers, but deciding what form that concern should take is often difficult. You learned in this chapter about the controversy that occurred after Sherman and Berk (1984) encouraged police departments to adopt a pro-arrest policy in domestic abuse cases, based on findings from their Minneapolis study. Do you agree with the researchers' decision to suggest policy changes to police departments based on their study, in an effort to minimize domestic abuse? Several replication studies failed to confirm the Minneapolis findings. Does this influence your evaluation of what the researchers should have done after the Minneapolis study was completed?

Web Exercises

1. You can brush up on a range of social theorists at www.sociologyprofessor.com. Pick a theorist and read some of what you find. What social phenomena does this theorist focus on? What hypotheses seem consistent with his or her theorizing? Describe a hypothetical research project to test one of these hypotheses.

2. You've been assigned to write a paper on domestic violence and the law. To start, you can review relevant research on the American Bar Association's website at www.americanbar.org/groups/domestic_violence/resources/statistics.html. What does the research summarized at this site suggest about the prevalence of domestic violence, its distribution among social groups, and its causes and effects? Write your answers in a one- to two-page report.

Video Interview Questions

Listen to the researcher interview for Chapter 2 at edge.sagepub.com/schutt8e.

1. What were the research questions that I focused on in the research project about homelessness and housing?

2. Why did we use a randomized experimental design?

3. I stated that the research design was consistent with reasonable ethical standards. Do you agree? Why or why not?

4. What were the answers to the two central research questions, as I described them?

To learn more, read Schutt (2011b), *Homelessness, Housing, and Mental Illness,* and pay particular attention to my appendix on research methods! http://www.hup.harvard.edu/catalog.php?isbn=9780674051010.

SPSS Exercises

1. Formulate four research questions about support for capital punishment—one question per research purpose: (1) exploratory, (2) descriptive, (3) explanatory, and (4) evaluative. You should be able to answer two of these questions with the GSS2012x data. Highlight these two.

2. Now, to develop some foundation from the literature, check the bibliography of this book for the following articles that drew on the GSS: Adalberto Aguirre Jr. and David Baker (1993); Steven Barkan and Steven Cohn (1994); Marian Borg (1997, 1998); Mark Warr (1995); and Robert Young (1992). How have social scientists used social theory to explain support for capital punishment? What potential influences on capital punishment have been tested? What influences could you test again with the 2012 GSS?

3. State four hypotheses in which support for capital punishment (CAPPUN) is the dependent variable and another variable in the GSS2012x or GSS2012a is the independent variable. Justify each hypothesis in a sentence or two.

4. Test at least one hypothesis. Borg (1997) suggests that region might be expected to influence support for the death penalty.

Test this as follows (after opening the GSS2012x or GSS2012a file, as explained in Chapter 1, SPSS Exercise 3):

 a. Click on Analyze/Descriptive Statistics/Crosstabs.

 b. Highlight CAPPUN and click on the arrow so that it moves into the Rows box; highlight REGION and click on the arrow to move it into the Columns box.

 c. Click on Cells, click off Counts-Observed, and click on Percentages-Column.

 d. Click Continue and then OK. Inspect the table.

5. Does support for capital punishment vary by region? Scroll down to the percentage table (in which regions appear across the top) and compare the percentages in the Favor row for each region. Describe what you have found.

6. Now you can go on to test your other hypotheses in the same way, if you have the time. Because of space constraints, I can't give you more guidance, but I will warn you that there could be some problems at this point (e.g., if your independent variable has lots of values). Proceed with caution!

Developing a Research Proposal

Now you can prepare the foundation for your research proposal.

1. State a problem for research. If you have not already identified a problem for study, or if you need to evaluate whether your research problem is doable, a few suggestions should help get the ball rolling and keep it on course:

 a. Jot down questions that have puzzled you in some area having to do with people and social relations, perhaps questions that have come to mind while reading textbooks or research articles or even while hearing news stories. Don't hesitate to jot down many questions, and don't bore yourself—try to identify questions that really interest you.

 b. Now take stock of your interests, your opportunities, and the work of others. Which of your research questions no longer seem feasible or interesting? What additional research questions come to mind? Pick out a question that is of interest and seems feasible and that your other coursework suggests has been the focus of some prior research or theorizing.

 c. Write out your research question in one sentence, and elaborate on it in one paragraph. List at least three reasons why it is a good research question for you to investigate. Then present your proposal to your classmates and instructor for discussion and feedback.

2. Search the literature (and the web) on the research question you identified. Refer to the section on searching the literature for more guidance on conducting the search. Copy down at least 10 citations to articles (with abstracts from Sociological Abstracts or SocINDEX) and five websites reporting research that seems highly relevant to your research question; then look up at least five of these articles and three of the sites.

Inspect the article bibliographies and the links on the website, and identify at least one more relevant article and website from each source.

Write a brief description of each article and website you consulted and evaluate its relevance to your research question. What additions or changes to your thoughts about the research question do the sources suggest?

3. Which general theoretical perspective do you believe is most appropriate to guide your proposed research? Write two paragraphs in which you (1) summarize the major tenets of the theoretical perspective you choose and (2) explain the relevance of this perspective to your research problem.

4. Propose at least two hypotheses that pertain to your research question. Justify these hypotheses in terms of the literature you have read.

Research Ethics and Research Proposals

Journal Link
Driving While Impaired

L et's begin with a thought experiment (or a trip down memory lane, depending on your earlier exposure to this example). One spring morning as you are drinking coffee and reading the newspaper, you notice a small ad for a psychology experiment at the local university. "Earn money and learn about yourself," it says. Feeling a bit bored with your job as a high school teacher, you call and schedule an evening visit to the lab.

WE WILL PAY YOU $45 FOR ONE HOUR OF YOUR TIME

Persons Needed for a Study of Memory

Research That Matters, Questions That Count

You are driving on the highway at about 3 p.m. on a Friday when you see a police officer standing by his squad car, lights flashing. The officer motions you to pull off the road and stop in an area marked off with traffic cones. You are both relieved and surprised when someone in plain clothes working with the police officer then walks over to your car and asks if you would consent to be in a survey. You then notice two large signs that say NATIONAL ROADSIDE SURVEY and VOLUNTARY SURVEY. You are offered $10 to provide an oral fluid sample and answer a few additional questions on drug use.

This is what happened to 10,909 U.S. motorists between July 20 and December 1, 2007, at sites across the United States. Those who agreed to the oral fluid collection were also offered an additional $5 to complete a short alcohol and drug-use disorder questionnaire. Before they drove off, participants were also offered a $50 incentive for providing a blood sample. Drivers who were found to be too impaired to be able to drive safely (blood alcohol level above .05) were given a range of options, including switching with an unimpaired passenger, getting a free ride home, or spending a night in a local motel (at no expense to them). None were arrested or given citations and no crashes occurred in relation to the study. Those younger than 21 years and those who were pregnant were given informational brochures because of the special risk they face if they consume alcohol.

John H. Lacey and others from the Pacific Institute for Research and Evaluation, C. Debra Furr-Holden from Johns Hopkins University, and Amy Berning from the National Highway Traffic Safety Administration (NHTSA, which funded the study) reported the procedures for this survey in a 2011 article in the *Evaluation Review*. The survey explained that all data collected were maintained as anonymous, so no research participants could be linked to their survey.

The 2007 National Roadside Survey identified 10.5% of the drivers as using illegal drugs and 3% as having taken medications.

What is your initial reaction to these research procedures, involving collaboration with the police, diversion of drivers, and measurement of substance abuse?

1. The institute's institutional review board (IRB) reviewed all staff training and operational procedures and a human subjects protection training module was used to prepare interviewers for the roadside encounters. Do you think human subjects were protected? How about the procedures with impaired drivers?

2. What types of persons do you think should have been on the IRB at this research institute when the study was reviewed?

3. Do you think that the potential benefits of this study for improving policies about impaired driving would outweigh concerns about interference with individuals' activities?

In this chapter, you will learn about standards and procedures for the protection of human subjects in research. By the end of the chapter, you will have a much firmer basis for answering the questions I have posed. After you finish the chapter, test yourself by reading the 2011 *Evaluation Review* article at the *Investigating the Social World* study site and completing the related interactive exercises for Chapter 3 at edge.sagepub.com/schutt8e.

Lacey, John H., Tara Kelley-Baker, Robert B. Voas, Eduardo Romano, C. Debra Furr-Holden, Pedro Torres, and Amy Berning. 2011. "Alcohol- and Drug-Involved Driving in the United States: Methodology for the 2007 National Roadside Survey." *Evaluation Review* 35:319–353.

You arrive at the assigned room at the university, ready for an interesting hour or so, and are impressed immediately by the elegance of the building and the professional appearance of the personnel. In the waiting room, you see a man dressed in a lab technician's coat talking to another visitor—a middle-aged fellow dressed in casual attire. The man in the lab coat turns and introduces himself and explains that as a psychologist, he is interested in the question of whether people learn things better when they are punished for making a mistake.

He quickly convinces you that this is a very important question for which there has been no adequate answer; he then explains that his experiment on punishment and learning will help answer this question. Then he announces, "I'm going to ask one of you to be the teacher here tonight and the other one to be the learner."

"The experimenter" [as we'll refer to him from now on] says he will write either *teacher* or *learner* on small identical slips of paper and then asks both of you to draw out one. Yours says teacher.

The experimenter now says, in a matter-of-fact way, "All right. Now the first thing we'll have to do is to set the learner up so that he can get some type of punishment."

He leads you both behind a curtain, sits the learner down, attaches a wire to his left wrist, and straps both his arms to the chair so that he cannot remove the wire (see Exhibit 3.1). The wire is connected to a console with 30 switches and a large dial on the other side of the room. When you ask what the wire is for, the experimenter says he will demonstrate. He then asks you to hold the end of the wire, walks back to the control console, flips several switches, and focuses his attention on the dial. You hear a clicking noise, see the dial move, and then feel an electric shock in your hand. The shock increases and the dial registers more current when the experimenter flips the next switch on the console.

"Oh, I see," you say. "This is the punishment. Couldn't it cause injury?" The experimenter explains that the machine is calibrated so that it will not cause permanent injury, but acknowledges that when it is turned up all the way it is very, very painful and can result in severe, although momentary, discomfort.

Now you walk back to the other side of the room (so that the learner is behind the curtain) and sit before the console. The experimental procedure has four simple steps: (1) You read aloud a series of word pairs, such as *blue box, nice day, wild duck,* and so on. (2) You read one of the first words from those pairs and a set of four words, one of which contains the original paired word. For example, you might say, "blue: sky ink box lamp." (3) The learner states the word that he thinks was paired with the first word you read ("blue"). If he gives a correct response, you compliment him and move on to the next word. If he makes a mistake, you flip a switch on the console. This causes the learner to feel a shock on his wrist. (4) After each mistake, you are to flip the next

Exhibit 3.1　Learner Strapped in Chair With Electrodes

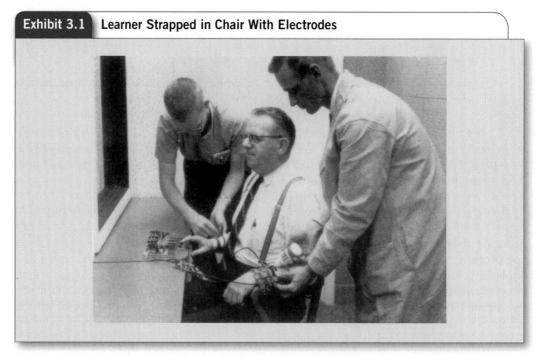

Source: From the film *OBEDIENCE.* Copyright © 1968 by Stanley Milgram, copyright renewed 1993 by Alexandra Milgram and distributed by Alexander Street Press.

switch on the console, progressing from left to right. You note that there is a label corresponding to every fifth mark on the dial, with the first mark labeled *slight shock,* the fifth mark labeled *moderate shock,* the tenth *strong shock,* and so on through *very strong shock, intense shock, extreme intensity shock,* and *danger: severe shock.*

You begin. The learner at first gives some correct answers, but then he makes a few errors. Soon you are beyond the fifth mark (moderate shock) and are moving in the direction of more and more severe shocks. You recall having heard about this experiment and so you know that as you turn the dial, the learner's responses increase in intensity from a grunt at the tenth mark (strong shock) to painful groans at higher levels, anguished cries to "get me out of here" at the extreme intensity shock levels, to a deathly silence at the highest level. You also know that as you proceed and indicate your discomfort at administering the stronger shocks, the experimenter will tell you, "The experiment requires that you continue," and occasionally, "It is absolutely essential that you continue." Now, please note on the meter in Exhibit 3.2 the most severe shock that you would agree to give to the learner.

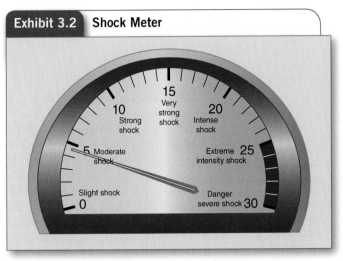

Exhibit 3.2 **Shock Meter**

Source: From the film *OBEDIENCE.* Copyright © 1968 by Stanley Milgram, copyright renewed 1993 by Alexandra Milgram and distributed by Alexander Street Press.

> **Milgram's obedience experiments:**
> Experiments begun in 1960 at Yale University by psychologist Stanley Milgram to determine the likelihood of people following orders from an authority despite their own sentiments; widely cited as helping to understand the emergence of phenomena such as Nazism and mass cults.

You may very well recognize that this thought experiment is a slightly simplified version of **Milgram's obedience experiments**, begun at Yale University in 1960. Did you know that Stanley Milgram also surveyed Yale undergraduates and asked them to indicate at what level they would terminate their "shocks"? The average (mean) maximum shock level predicted by the Yale undergraduates was 9.35, corresponding to a strong shock. Only one student predicted that he would provide a stimulus above that level, but only barely so, for he said he would stop at the very strong level. Responses were similar from nonstudent groups who were asked the same question.

What was the actual average level of shock administered by the 40 New Haven adults who volunteered for the experiment? A shock level of 24.53, or a level higher than extreme intensity shock and just short of danger: severe shock. Of Milgram's original 40 subjects, 25 (62.5%) complied with the experimenter's demands, all the way to the top of the scale (originally labeled simply as *XXX*). And lest you pass this result off as simply the result of the subjects having thought that the experiment wasn't "real," we hasten to point out that there is abundant evidence from the subjects' own observed high stress and their subsequent reports that many subjects really believed that the learner was receiving actual, hurtful shocks.

Are you surprised by the subjects' responses? By the Yale undergraduates' predictions of so many compassionate responses? By your own response? (I leave it to you to assess how accurately you predicted the response you would have given if you had been an actual subject.) Do you think the results of this experiment tell us about how people behave in the real world?

Of course, my purpose in introducing this small "experiment" is not to focus attention on the prediction of obedience to authority; instead, I want to introduce the topic of research ethics by encouraging you to think about research from the standpoint of the people who are the participants in social science research. I will refer to Milgram's (1963) famous research on obedience throughout this chapter because it is fair to say that this research ultimately had as profound an influence on the way social scientists think about research ethics as it had on the way they understand obedience to authority.

Every social scientist needs to consider how to practice his or her discipline ethically. Whenever we interact with other people as social scientists, we must give paramount importance to the rational concerns and

Video Link
Milgram's Experiment

emotional needs that will shape their responses to our actions. Ethical research practice begins here, with the recognition that our research procedures involve people who deserve as much respect for their well-being as we do for ours.

🔲 Historical Background

Concern with ethical practice in relation to people who are in some respect dependent, whether as patients or research subjects, is not a new idea. Ethical guidelines for medicine trace back to Hippocrates in 5 BC Greece (Hippocratic Oath, n.d.) and the American Medical Association (AMA) adopted the world's first formal professional ethics code in medicine in 1847 (AMA 2011). Human subjects protections issues were widely discussed during the experiments that identified the cause of yellow fever in 1900 and 1901 (http://virtualmentor.ama-assn.org/2009/04/mhst1-0904.html). Current AMA ethical principles include respecting patient rights, maintaining confidentiality, and regarding "responsibility to the patient as paramount" (AMA 2011). Yet the history of medical practice makes it clear that having an ethics code is not sufficient to ensure ethical practice, at least when there are clear incentives to do otherwise.

> **Nuremberg War Crime Trials:** The International Military Tribunal held by the victorious Allies after World War II in Nuremberg, Germany, that exposed the horrific medical experiments conducted by Nazi doctors and others in the name of "science."
>
> **Tuskegee Study of Untreated Syphilis in the Negro Male:** U.S. Public Health Service study of the "natural" course of syphilis that followed 399 low-income African American men from the 1930s to 1972, without providing them with penicillin after this was discovered as treating the illness. The study was stopped after it was exposed in 1972, resulting in an out-of-court settlement and then, in 1997, an official public apology by President Bill Clinton.

A defining event occurred in 1946, when the **Nuremberg War Crime Trials** exposed the horrific medical experiments conducted by Nazi doctors and others in the name of "science." Almost 20 years later, Milgram's research on obedience also generated controversy about participant protections (Perry 2013:37). As late as 1972, Americans learned from news reports that researchers funded by the U.S. Public Health Service had followed 399 low-income African American men in the **Tuskegee Study of Untreated Syphilis in the Negro Male** since the 1930s, collecting data to study the "natural" course of the illness (Exhibit 3.3) (http://www.tuskegee.edu/about_us/centers_of_excellence/bioethics_center/about_the_usphs_syphilis_study.aspx). At the time, there was no effective treatment for the disease, but the men were told they were being treated for "bad blood," whether they had syphilis or not. Participants received free medical exams, meals, and burial insurance but were not asked for their consent to be studied. What made this research study, known as the Tuskegee Syphilis Experiment, so shocking was that many participants were not informed of their illness and, even after penicillin was recognized as an effective treatment in 1945 and in large-scale use by 1947, the study participants were not treated. The research was only ended after the study was exposed. In 1973, congressional hearings began, and in 1974, an out-of-court settlement of $10 million was reached; it was not until 1997 that President Bill Clinton made an official apology (CDC 2009).

Audio Link
Research Ethics

These and other widely publicized abuses made it clear that formal review procedures were needed to protect research participants. The U.S. government created a National Commission for the Protection of Human Subjects of Biomedical and Behavioral Research and charged it with developing guidelines (Kitchener & Kitchener 2009:7). The commission's 1979 *Belmont Report* (Department of Health, Education, and Welfare 1979) established three basic ethical principles for the protection of human subjects:

> **Belmont Report:** Guidelines developed by the U.S. National Commission for the Protection of Human Subjects of Biomedical and Behavioral Research in 1979 for the protection of human subjects.
>
> **Respect for persons:** The ethical principle of treating persons as autonomous agents and protecting those with diminished autonomy in research involving human subjects that was included in the *Belmont Report*.

- **Respect for persons:** treating persons as autonomous agents and protecting those with diminished autonomy

- **Beneficence:** minimizing possible harms and maximizing benefits

- **Justice:** distributing benefits and risks of research fairly

| Exhibit 3.3 | **Tuskegee Syphilis Experiment** |

Source: Tuskegee Syphilis Study Administrative Records. Records of the Centers for Disease Control and Prevention. National Archives—Southeast Region (Atlanta).

The Department of Health and Human Services and the Food and Drug Administration then translated these principles into specific regulations that were adopted in 1991 as the **Federal Policy for the Protection of Human Subjects**. This policy has shaped the course of social science research ever since, and you will have to consider it as you design your own research investigations. Professional associations such as the American Sociological Association (ASA), university review boards, and ethics committees in other organizations also set standards for the treatment of human subjects by their members, employees, and students, although these standards are all designed to comply with the federal policy. This section introduces these regulations.

Beneficence: The ethical requirement of minimizing possible harms and maximizing benefits in research involving human subjects that was included in the *Belmont Report*.

Justice: The ethical principle of distributing benefits and risks of research in research involving human subjects fairly that was included in the *Belmont Report*.

Federal Policy for the Protection of Human Subjects: Specific regulations adopted in 1991 by the Department of Health and Human Services and the Food and Drug Administration that were based on the principles of the *Belmont Report*.

🔲 Ethical Principles

The ASA, like other professional social science organizations, has adopted, for practicing sociologists, ethical guidelines that are more specific than the federal regulations are. Professional organizations may also review complaints of unethical practices when asked.

The *Code of Ethics* of the ASA (1999) is summarized on the ASA website (http://www.asanet.org/about/ethics.cfm); the complete text of the code is also available at this site. The general principles articulated in the code are intended to

Code of Ethics: Professional code of the American Sociological Association for the treatment of human subjects by members, employees, and students, designed to comply with federal policy and revised in 1997.

guide professional practice in diverse settings, while some of the specific standards focus specifically on the protection of human subjects in research.

According to the general principles, sociologists should be committed in their work to high levels of competence, to practicing with integrity, and to maintaining responsibility for their actions. They must also respect the rights, dignity, and diversity of others, including research participants, as well as be socially responsible to their communities and use research to contribute to the public good. The following sections discuss the most important implications of these principles for the conduct of research, including the protection of human subjects.

Achieving Valid Results

Commitment to achieving valid results is the necessary starting point for ethical research practice. Simply put, we have no business asking people to answer questions, submit to observations, or participate in experimental procedures if we are simply seeking to verify our preexisting prejudices or convince others to take action on behalf of our personal interests. The pursuit of objective knowledge about human behavior—the goal of validity—motivates and justifies our investigations and gives us some claim to the right to influence others to participate in our research. Knowledge is the foundation of human progress as well as the basis for our expectation that we, as social scientists, can help people achieve a brighter future. If we approach our research projects objectively, setting aside our personal predilections in the service of learning a bit more about human behavior, we can honestly represent our actions as potentially contributing to the advancement of knowledge.

Encyclopedia Link
Ethical Codes

Milgram made a strong case in his 1963 article and 1974 book on the obedience experiments that he was committed to achieving valid results—to learning how and why obedience influences behavior. He tied his motivations directly to the horror of the Holocaust, to which the world's attention had been drawn once again by the capture and trial of Adolf Hitler's mastermind of that genocide, Adolf Eichmann (Perry 2013:210). In Milgram's (1963) own words,

> It has been reliably established that from 1933–45 millions of innocent persons were systematically slaughtered on command. . . . Obedience is the psychological mechanism that links individual action to political purpose. It is the dispositional cement that binds men to systems of authority . . . for many persons obedience may be a deeply ingrained behavior tendency. . . . Obedience may [also] be ennobling and educative and refer to acts of charity and kindness, as well as to destruction. (p. 371)

Milgram (1963) then explains how he devised experiments to study the process of obedience in a way that would seem realistic to the subjects and still allow "important variables to be manipulated at several points in the experiment" (p. 372). According to Milgram, every step in the experiment was carefully designed to ensure that subjects received identical stimuli and that their responses were measured carefully. The experiment's design also reflected what had become in the preceding 30 years a tradition in social psychology of laboratory experiments that used deception to create different believable conditions for participants (Perry 2013:31–35).

Milgram (1963:377) made every effort to convince readers that "the particular conditions" of his experiment created the conditions for achieving valid results. These particular conditions included the setting for the experiment at Yale University, its purported "worthy purpose" to advance knowledge about learning and memory, and the voluntary participation of the subject as well as of the learner—as far as the subject knew. Milgram then tested the importance of some of these "particular conditions" (e.g., the location at Yale) in replications of the basic experiment (Milgram 1965).

However, not all social scientists agreed that Milgram's approach could achieve valid results. Milgram's first article on the research, "Behavioral Study of Obedience," was published in 1963 in the *Journal of Abnormal and Social Psychology*. In the next year, the *American Psychologist* published a critique of the experiment's methods and ethics by the psychologist Diana Baumrind (1964). Her critique begins with a rejection of the external validity—the generalizability—of the experiment, because

The laboratory is unfamiliar as a setting and the rules of behavior ambiguous. . . . Therefore, the laboratory is not the place to study degree of obedience or suggestibility, as a function of a particular experimental condition. [And so,] the parallel between authority-subordinate relationships in Hitler's Germany and in Milgram's laboratory is unclear. (pp. 421–423)

Milgram (1964) quickly published a rejoinder in which he disagreed with (among other things) the notion that it is inappropriate to study obedience in a laboratory setting: "A subject's obedience is no less problematical because it occurs within a social institution called the psychological experiment" (p. 850).

Milgram (1974:169–178) also argued in his later book that his experiment had been replicated in other places and settings with the same results, that there was considerable evidence that the subjects had believed that they actually were administering shocks, and that the "essence" of his experimental manipulation—the request that subjects comply with a legitimate authority—was also found in the dilemma faced by people in Nazi Germany, soldiers at the My Lai massacre in Vietnam, and even the cultists who drank poison in Jonestown, Guyana, at the command of their leader, Jim Jones (Miller 1986:182–183).

Baumrind (1985) was still not convinced. In a follow-up article in *American Psychologist,* she argued that "far from illuminating real life, as he claimed, Milgram in fact appeared to have constructed a set of conditions so internally inconsistent that they could not occur in real life" (p. 171). Although Milgram died in 1984, the controversy did not. A recent review of the transcripts and interviews with many participants raises additional concerns about the experiment's validity (Perry 2013). Milgram understated the "experimenter's" efforts to get the subjects to comply, he overstated the subjects' level of obedience, he never publicized one condition in which most subjects refused to give strong shocks when the "learner" was a friend, and he didn't acknowledge that even those classified as "obedient" were looking for a way to get out of the experiment. His claim that the results were replicated in similar experiments around the world was only partially true, and it seems clear from the transcripts and interviews that the aura created by the location at Yale University and the emphasis on a contribution to "science" influenced many participants.

Do you agree with Milgram's assumption that obedience could fruitfully be studied in the laboratory? Do you find merit in Baumrind's criticism? Are you troubled by the new evidence that Milgram may have presented his evidence selectively, to make his conclusions as convincing as possible? Will your evaluation of the ethics of Milgram's experiments be influenced by your answers to these questions? Should our ethical judgments differ depending on whether we decide that a study provides valid information about important social psychological processes? Should it matter that a 2005 replication of Milgram's experiment (with less severe "shocks") for ABC TV supported Milgram's conclusions (Perry 2013:275–279)?

I can't answer these questions for you, but before you dismiss them as inappropriate when we are dealing with ethical standards for the treatment of human subjects, bear in mind that both Milgram and his strongest critic at the time, Baumrind, buttressed their ethical arguments with assertions about the validity (or invalidity) of the experimental results. It is hard to justify *any* risk for human subjects, or even *any* expenditure of time and resources, if our findings tell us nothing about human behavior.

Audio Link
Milgram's Experiment

Interactive Exercises Link
Ethical Issues

Honesty and Openness

The scientific concern with validity requires, in turn, that scientists be open in disclosing their methods and honest in presenting their findings. In contrast, research distorted by political or personal pressures to find particular outcomes or to achieve the most marketable results is unlikely to be carried out in an honest and open fashion. To assess the validity of a researcher's conclusions and the ethics of their procedures, you need to know exactly how the research was conducted. This means that articles or other reports must include a detailed methodology section, perhaps supplemented by appendixes containing the research instruments, or websites or an address where more information can be obtained.

Milgram presented his research in a way that would signal his adherence to the goal of honesty and openness. His initial 1963 article included a detailed description of study procedures, including the text of

Journal Link
Intensive Rehabilitation Supervision Program

Research|Social Impact Link
Research Ethics

the general introduction to participants, the procedures involved in the learning task—the "shock generator," the administration of the "sample shock," the shock instructions and the preliminary practice run, the standardized feedback from the "victim" and from the experimenter—and the measures used. Many more details, including pictures, were provided in Milgram's (1974) subsequent book (Exhibit 3.4).

The act of publication itself is a vital element in maintaining openness and honesty. Others can review and question study procedures and so generate an open dialogue with the researcher. Although Milgram disagreed sharply with Baumrind's criticisms of his experiments, their mutual commitment to public discourse in journals widely available to social scientists resulted in a more comprehensive presentation of study procedures and a more thoughtful discourse about research ethics. Almost 50 years later, this commentary continues to inform debates about research ethics (Cave & Holm 2003).

The latest significant publication in this open dialogue about Milgram's work actually challenges his own commitment to the standard of openness and honesty. Gina Perry's (2013) *Behind the Shock Machine: The Untold Story of the Notorious Milgram Psychology Experiments* reveals many misleading statements about participants' postexperiment debriefing, about adherence to the treatment protocol, about the extent of participants' apparent distress, and about the extent of support for his favored outcome.

Openness about research procedures and results thus goes hand in hand with honesty in research design and in research reporting. Despite this need for openness, some researchers may hesitate to disclose their procedures or results to prevent others from building on their ideas and taking some of the credit or, as may have occurred with Milgram, to make their procedures seem more acceptable or their findings more impressive. You might have heard of the long legal battle between a U.S. researcher, Robert Gallo, and a French researcher, Luc Montagnier, about how credit for discovering the AIDS virus should be allocated. Although a public dispute such as this one is unusual—even more unusual was its resolution through an agreement announced by then U.S. President Ronald Reagan and then French Prime Minister Jacques Chirac (Altman 1987)—concerns with priority of discovery are common. Scientists are like other people in their desire to be first. Enforcing standards of honesty and encouraging openness about research are the best solutions to these problems (as exemplified by the chronology of discovery that Gallo and Montagnier jointly developed as part of the agreement).

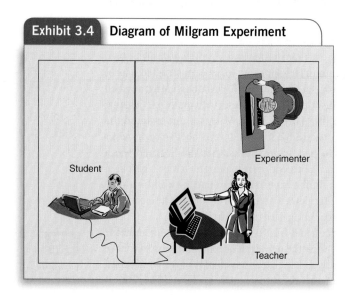

| Exhibit 3.4 | Diagram of Milgram Experiment |

Source: Northern Illinois University Department of Psychology, http://www3.niu.edu/acad/psych/Millis/History/2004/milgram2.gif

Conflict of interest: When a researcher has a significant financial stake in the design or outcome of his or her own research.

Conflicts of interest may occur when a researcher has a significant financial stake in the design or outcome of the research. Receiving speaking fees, consulting fees, patents or royalties, and other financial benefits as a result of the way in which a research project is designed or the results that it obtains creates a pressure to distort decisions and findings in one's (financial) favor. Both federal research funding agencies and journal editors require disclosure of possible conflicts of interest so that others can scrutinize the extent to which these conflicts may have lessened researchers' honesty and openness (Fisher & Anushko 2008:96–97). Unfortunately, experimental research suggests that disclosure does not reduce trust in advice from people who have disclosed a conflict of interest (Humphries 2011:K3). In fact, researchers can be unduly motivated by concerns about their publication records and career prospects even without explicit financial inducements.

Protecting Research Participants

Several standards concerning the treatment of human subjects are emphasized in federal regulations and the ethical guidelines adopted by many professional social science organizations:

- Research should cause no harm to subjects.

- Participation in research should be voluntary, and therefore subjects must give their informed consent to participate in the research and researchers must disclose their identity.

- Researchers should avoid deception, except in limited circumstances.

- Anonymity or confidentiality must be maintained for individual research participants unless it is voluntarily and explicitly waived.

- Consider the uses of a research project so that its benefits outweigh any foreseeable risks.

Each of these standards became a focus of debate about Milgram's experiments, so we will return frequently to that debate to keep our discussion realistic. We will also refer frequently to the ASA code to keep our treatment current. You will soon realize that there is no simple answer to the question: What is (or isn't) ethical research practice? The issues are just too complicated and the relevant principles too subject to different interpretations. But, I do promise that by the time you finish this chapter, you will be aware of the major issues in research ethics and be able to make informed, defensible decisions about the ethical conduct of social science research.

Journal Link
Written Consent

Avoid Harming Research Participants

Although this standard may seem straightforward, it can be difficult to interpret in specific cases and harder yet to define in a way agreeable to all social scientists. Does it mean that subjects should not be harmed psychologically as well as physically at all? That they should feel no anxiety or distress whatsoever during the study or only after their involvement ends? Should the possibility of any harm, no matter how remote, deter research?

Before we address these questions with respect to Milgram's experiments, a verbatim transcript of one session will give you an idea of what participants experienced (Milgram 1965:67):

150 volts delivered.	You want me to keep going?
165 volts delivered.	That guy is hollering in there. There's a lot of them here. He's liable to have a heart condition. You want me to go on?
180 volts delivered.	He can't stand it! I'm not going to kill that man in there! You hear him hollering? He's hollering. He can't stand it. . . . I mean who is going to take responsibility if anything happens to that gentleman? *[The experimenter accepts responsibility.]* All right.
195 volts delivered.	You see he's hollering. Hear that. Gee, I don't know. *[The experimenter says: "The experiment requires that you go on."]* I know it does, sir, but I mean—hugh—he don't know what he's in for. He's up to 195 volts.
210 volts delivered.	
225 volts delivered.	
240 volts delivered.	

This experimental manipulation generated "extraordinary tension" (Milgram 1963:377):

> Subjects were observed to sweat, tremble, stutter, bite their lips, groan and dig their fingernails into their flesh. . . . Full-blown, uncontrollable seizures were observed for 3 subjects. One . . . seizure so violently convulsive that it was necessary to call a halt to the experiment [for that individual]. (p. 375)

An observer (behind a one-way mirror) reported, "I observed a mature and initially poised businessman enter the laboratory smiling and confident. Within 20 minutes he was reduced to a twitching, stuttering wreck, who was rapidly approaching a point of nervous collapse" (Milgram 1963:377).

From critic Baumrind's (1964:422) perspective, this emotional disturbance in subjects was "potentially harmful because it could easily effect an alteration in the subject's self-image or ability to trust adult authorities in the future." Milgram (1964) quickly countered,

> Momentary excitement is not the same as harm. As the experiment progressed there was no indication of injurious effects in the subjects; and as the subjects themselves strongly endorsed the experiment, the judgment I made was to continue the experiment. (p. 849)

When Milgram (1964:849) surveyed participants in a follow-up, 83.7% endorsed the statement that they were "very glad" or "glad" "to have been in the experiment," 15.1% were "neither sorry nor glad," and just 1.3% were "sorry" or "very sorry" to have participated (p. 849). Interviews by a psychiatrist a year later found no evidence "of any traumatic reactions" (p. 849)—although he did not disclose that of 780 initial participants, only 140 were invited for an interview and only 32 of those accepted the invitation (Perry 2013:217). After these later revelations, Milgram's (1977:21) subsequent argument that "the central moral justification for allowing my experiment is that it was judged acceptable by those who took part in it" rings hollow.

Milgram (1963) also reported that he attempted to minimize harm to subjects with postexperimental procedures "to assure that the subject would leave the laboratory in a state of well being" (p. 374). He said that a friendly reconciliation was arranged between the subject and the victim, and an effort was made to reduce any tensions that arose as a result of the experiment, but it turns out that his "dehoaxing" was normally very brief and did not disclose the deception to most participants. Most participants did not receive a letter informing them of the nature of the experiment until almost a year had passed (Milgram 1964:849; Perry 2013:72, 84).

Baumrind (1964:422) was unconvinced even without knowing of these later revelations: "It would be interesting to know what sort of procedures could dissipate the type of emotional disturbance just described [citing Milgram 1964]."

In a later article, Baumrind (1985:168) dismissed the value of the self-reported "lack of harm" of subjects who had been willing to participate in the experiment—although noting that still 16% did *not* endorse the statement that they were "glad" they had participated in the experiment. Baumrind (1985:169) also argued that research indicates most introductory psychology students (and some students in other social sciences) who have participated in a deception experiment report a decreased trust in authorities as a result—a tangible harm in itself.

Many social scientists, ethicists, and others concluded that Milgram's procedures had not harmed the subjects and so were justified for the knowledge they produced, but others sided with Baumrind's criticisms (Miller 1986:88–138; Perry 2013:269). Perry's (2013:77–78) recent investigation found even more evidence of psychological harm, including feelings of shame that had persisted since the experiment. The experimental records also reveal that debriefing never occurred for some participants and was very limited for almost all (Perry 2013:76–84). Most were not told after the experiment that the shocks were fake; the usual "dehoaxing" consisted of the "learner" reassuring the "teacher" that the shocks he had received were not harmful.

What is your opinion of the possibility for harm at this point? Does Milgram's debriefing process relieve your concerns? Are you as persuaded by the subjects' own endorsement of the experiment as was Milgram?

What about possible harm to the subjects of the famous prison simulation study at Stanford University (Haney, Banks, & Zimbardo 1973)? The study was designed to investigate the impact of social position on behavior—specifically, the impact of being either a guard or a prisoner in a prison, a "total institution." The researchers selected apparently stable and mature young male volunteers and asked them to sign a

Video Link
Zimbardo's Prison
Experiment

contract to work for 2 weeks as a guard or a prisoner in a simulated prison. Within the first 2 days after the prisoners were incarcerated by the "guards" in a makeshift basement prison, the prisoners began to be passive and disorganized, while the guards became "sadistic"—verbally and physically aggressive (Exhibit 3.5). Five "prisoners" were soon released for depression, uncontrollable crying, fits of rage, and, in one case, a psychosomatic rash. Instead of letting things continue for 2 weeks as planned, Philip Zimbardo and his colleagues terminated the experiment after 6 days to avoid harming the subjects.

Through discussions in special postexperiment encounter sessions, feelings of stress among the participants who played the role of prisoner seemed to be relieved; follow-up during the next year indicated no lasting negative effects on the participants and some benefits in the form of greater insight.

Would you ban such experiments because of the potential for harm to subjects? Does the fact that Zimbardo's and Milgram's experiments seemed to yield significant insights into the effect of a social situation on human behavior—insights that could be used to improve prisons or perhaps lessen the likelihood of another holocaust—make any difference (Reynolds 1979:133–139)? Do you believe that this benefit outweighs the foreseeable risks?

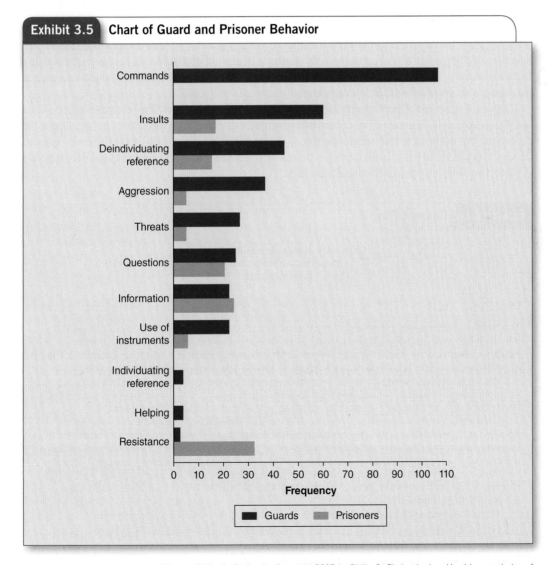

Exhibit 3.5 **Chart of Guard and Prisoner Behavior**

Source: Adapted from *The Lucifer Effect* by Philip G. Zimbardo. Copyright 2007 by Philip G. Zimbardo, Inc. Used by permission of Random House, Inc., and Random House Group Ltd.

> **Zimbardo's prison simulation study:** Famous prison simulation study at Stanford University by psychologist Philip Zimbardo designed to investigate the impact of social position on behavior—specifically, the impact of being either a guard or a prisoner in a "total institution"; widely cited as demonstrating the likelihood of emergence of sadistic behavior in guards.

Well-intentioned researchers may also fail to foresee all the potential problems. Milgram (1974:27–31) reported that he and his colleagues were surprised by the subjects' willingness to carry out such severe shocks. In **Zimbardo's prison simulation study**, all the participants signed consent forms, but how could they have been fully informed in advance? The researchers themselves did not realize that the study participants would experience so much stress so quickly, that some prisoners would have to be released for severe negative reactions within the first few days, or that even those who were not severely stressed would soon be begging to be released from the mock prison. If this risk was not foreseeable, was it acceptable for the researchers to presume in advance that the benefits would outweigh the risks? And are you concerned, like Arthur Miller (1986), that real harm "could result from *not doing* research on destructive obedience" (p. 138) and other troubling human behaviors?

Obtain Informed Consent

The requirement of informed consent is also more difficult to define than it first appears. To be informed, consent must be given by the persons who are competent to consent, have consented voluntarily, are fully informed about the research and know who is conducting the research, and have comprehended what they have been told (Reynolds 1979). Yet you probably realize, as Baumrind (1985) did, that because of the inability to communicate perfectly, "full disclosure of everything that could possibly affect a given subject's decision to participate is not possible, and therefore cannot be ethically required" (p. 165).

Obtaining informed consent creates additional challenges for researchers. The researcher's actions and body language should help convey his or her verbal assurance that consent is voluntary. The language of the consent form must be clear and understandable to the research participants and yet sufficiently long and detailed to explain what will actually happen in the research. Consent Forms A (Exhibit 3.6) and B (Exhibit 3.7) illustrate two different approaches to these trade-offs.

Research|Social Impact Link
Informed Consent

Exhibit 3.6   Consent Form A

University of Massachusetts Boston
Department of Sociology
(617) 287-6250

Dear _____:

The health of students and their use of alcohol and drugs are important concerns for every college and university. The enclosed survey is about these issues at UMass/Boston. It is sponsored by University Health Services and the PRIDE Program (Prevention, Resources, Information, and Drug Education). The questionnaire was developed by graduate students in Applied Sociology, Nursing, and Gerontology.

You were selected for the survey with a scientific, random procedure. Now it is important that you return the questionnaire so that we can obtain an unbiased description of the undergraduate student body. Health Services can then use the results to guide campus education and prevention programs.

The survey requires only about 20 minutes to complete. Participation is completely voluntary and anonymous. No one will be able to link your survey responses to you. In any case, your standing at the University will not be affected whether or not you choose to participate. Just be sure to return the enclosed postcard after you mail the questionnaire so that we know we do not have to contact you again.

Please return the survey by November 15th. If you have any questions or comments, call the PRIDE program at 287-5680 or Professor Schutt at 287-6250. Also call the PRIDE program if you would like a summary of our final report.

Thank you in advance for your assistance.

Russell K. Schutt, PhD
Professor and Chair

| Exhibit 3.7 | Consent Form B |

**Research Consent Form for Social
and Behavioral Research**

Dana-Farber/Harvard Cancer Center

BIDMC/BWH/CH/DFCI/MGH/Partners Network Affiliates   OPRS 11-05

Protocol Title: ASSESSING COMMUNITY HEALTH WORKERS' ATTITUDES AND KNOWLEDGE ABOUT
EDUCATING COMMUNITIES ABOUT CANCER CLINICAL TRIALS

DF/HCC Principal Research Investigator / Institution: Dr. Russell Schutt, PhD / Beth Israel Deaconess
Medical Center and Univ. of Massachusetts, Boston

DF/HCC Site-Responsible Research Investigator(s) / Institution(s): Lidia Schapira, MD / Massachusetts
General Hospital

Interview Consent Form

A. INTRODUCTION

We are inviting you to take part in a research study. Research is a way of gaining new knowledge. A person
who participates in a research study is called a "subject." This research study is evaluating whether community
health workers might be willing and able to educate communities about the pros and cons of participating in
research studies.

It is expected that about 10 people will take part in this research study.

An institution that is supporting a research study either by giving money or supplying something that is
important for the research is called the "sponsor." The sponsor of this protocol is National Cancer Institute
and is providing money for the research study.

This research consent form explains why this research study is being done, what is involved in participating
in the research study, the possible risks and benefits of the research study, alternatives to participation, and
your rights as a research subject. The decision to participate is yours. If you decide to participate, please
sign and date at the end of the form. We will give you a copy so that you can refer to it while you are involved
in this research study.

If you decide to participate in this research study, certain questions will be asked of you to see if you are
eligible to be in the research study. The research study has certain requirements that must be met. If the
questions show that you can be in the research study, you will be able to answer the interview questions.

If the questions show that you cannot be in the research study, you will not be able to participate in this
research study.

Page 1 of 6

| DFCI Protocol Number: 06-085 | Date DFCI IRB Approved this Consent Form: January 16, 2007 |
| Date Posted for Use: January 16, 2007 | Date DFCI IRB Approval Expires: August 13, 2007 |

(Continued)

Exhibit 3.7   Continued

**Research Consent Form for Social and
   Behavioral Research**

Dana-Farber/Harvard Cancer Center

BIDMC/BWH/CH/DFCI/MGH/Partners Network Affiliates   OPRS 11-05

We encourage you to take some time to think this over and to discuss it with other people and to ask questions now and at any time in the future.

B. <u>WHY IS THIS RESEARCH STUDY BEING DONE?</u>

Deaths from cancer in general and for some specific cancers are higher for black people compared to white people, for poor persons compared to nonpoor persons, and for rural residents compared to non-rural residents. There are many reasons for higher death rates between different subpopulations. One important area for changing this is to have more persons from minority groups participate in research about cancer. The process of enrolling minority populations into clinical trials is difficult and does not generally address the needs of their communities. One potential way to increase particpation in research is to use community health workers to help educate communities about research and about how to make sure that researchers are ethical. We want to know whether community health workers think this is a good strategy and how to best carry it out.

C. <u>WHAT OTHER OPTIONS ARE THERE?</u>

Taking part in this research study is voluntary. Instead of being in this research study, you have the following option:

- Decide not to participate in this research study.

D. <u>WHAT IS INVOLVED IN THE RESEARCH STUDY?</u>

<u>**Before the research starts (screening):**</u> After signing this consent form, you will be asked to answer some questions about where you work and the type of community health work you do to find out if you can be in the research study.

If the answers show that you are eligible to participate in the research study, you will be eligible to participate in the research study. If you do not meet the eligibility criteria, you will not be able to participate in this research study.

<u>**After the screening procedures confirm that you are eligible to participate in the research study:**</u> You will participate in an interview by answering questions from a questionnaire. The interview will take about 90 minutes. If there are questions you prefer not to answer we can skip those questions. The questions are about the type of work you do and your opinions about participating in research. If you agree, the interview will be taped and then transcribed. Your name and no other information about you will be associated with the tape or the transcript. Only the research team will be able to listen to the tapes.

Page 2 of 6

DFCI Protocol Number: <u>06-085</u>	Date DFCI IRB Approved this Consent Form: <u>January 16, 2007</u>
Date Posted for Use: <u>January 16, 2007</u>	Date DFCI IRB Approval Expires: <u>August 13, 2007</u>

**Research Consent Form for Social and
    Behavioral Research**

Dana-Farber/Harvard Cancer Center

BIDMC/BWH/CH/DFCI/MGH/Partners Network Affiliates   OPRS 11-05

Immediately following the interview, you will have the opportunity to have the tape erased if you wish to withdraw your consent to taping or participation in this study. You will receive $30.00 for completing this interview.

After the interview is completed: Once you finish the interview there are no additional interventions.

...

N. <u>DOCUMENTATION OF CONSENT</u>

My signature below indicates my willingness to participate in this research study and my understanding that I can withdraw at any time.

_____   _____
Signature of Subject   Date
or Legally Authorized Representative

_____   _____
Person obtaining consent   Date

To be completed by person obtaining consent:

The consent discussion was initiated on _____ (date) at _____ (time.)

☐ A copy of this signed consent form was given to the subject or legally authorized representative.

For Adult Subjects

☐ The subject is an adult and provided consent to participate.

☐ The subject is an adult who lacks capacity to provide consent and his/her legally authorized
    representative:

   ☐ gave permission for the adult subject to participate

   ☐ did not give permission for the adult subject to participate

Page 6 of 6

DFCI Protocol Number: <u>06-085</u>	Date DFCI IRB Approved this Consent Form: <u>January 16, 2007</u>
Date Posted for Use: <u>January 16, 2007</u>	Date DFCI IRB Approval Expires: <u>August 13, 2007</u>

Consent Form A was approved by my university IRB for a mailed survey about substance abuse among undergraduate students. It is brief and to the point.

Consent Form B reflects the requirements of an academic hospital's IRB (I have only included a portion of the six-page form). Because the hospital is used to reviewing research proposals involving drugs and other treatment interventions with hospital patients, it requires a very detailed and lengthy explanation of procedures and related issues, even for a simple interview study such as mine with Dr. Schapira. You can probably imagine that the requirement that prospective participants sign such lengthy consent forms can reduce their willingness to participate in research and perhaps influence their responses if they do agree to participate (Larson 1993:114).

As in Milgram's study, experimental researchers whose research design requires some type of subject deception try to get around this problem by withholding some information before the experiment begins, but then debriefing subjects at the end. In a **debriefing**, the researcher explains to the subjects what happened in the experiment and why, and then responds to their questions. A carefully designed debriefing procedure can help the research participants learn from the experimental research and grapple constructively with feelings elicited by the realization that they were deceived (Sieber 1992:39–41). However, even though debriefing can be viewed as a substitute, in some cases, for securing fully informed consent before the experiment, debriefed subjects who disclose the nature of the experiment to other participants can contaminate subsequent results (Adair, Dushenko, & Lindsay 1985). Apparently for this reason, Milgram provided little information in his "debriefing" to participants in most of his experiments. It was only in the last two months of his study that he began to provide more information, while still asking participants not to reveal the true nature of the experimental procedures until after the study was completely over (Perry 2013:76, 84). Unfortunately, if the debriefing process is delayed, the ability to lessen any harm resulting from the deception is also reduced.

> **Debriefing:** A researcher's informing subjects after an experiment about the experiment's purposes and methods and evaluating subjects' personal reactions to the experiment.

For a study of the social background of men who engage in homosexual behavior in public facilities, Laud Humphreys (1970) decided that truly informed consent would be impossible to obtain. Instead, he first served as a lookout—a "watch queen"—for men who were entering a public bathroom in a city park with the intention of having sex. In a number of cases, he then left the bathroom and copied the license plate numbers of the cars driven by the men. One year later, he visited the homes of the men and interviewed them as part of a larger study of social issues. Humphreys changed his appearance so that the men did not recognize him. In *Tearoom Trade*, his book on this research, Humphreys concluded that the men who engaged in what were viewed as deviant acts were, for the most part, married, suburban men whose families were unaware of their sexual practices. But debate has continued ever since about Humphreys's failure to tell the men what he was really doing in the bathroom or why he had come to their homes for the interview. He was criticized by many, including some faculty members at the University of Washington who urged that his doctoral degree be withheld. However, many other professors and some members of the gay community praised Humphreys for helping normalize conceptions of homosexuality (Miller 1986:135).

> **Tearoom Trade:** Study by sociologist Laud Humphreys of men who engage in homosexual behavior in public facilities, including subsequent later interviews in their homes after recording their license plate numbers; widely cited in discussions of the need for informed consent to research.

If you were to serve on your university's IRB, would you allow this research to be conducted? Can students who are asked to participate in research by their professor be considered able to give informed consent? Do you consider *informed consent* to be meaningful if the true purpose or nature of an experimental manipulation is not revealed?

The process and even possibility of obtaining informed consent must consider the capacity of prospective participants to give informed consent. Children cannot legally give consent to participate in research; instead, they must in most circumstances be given the opportunity to give or withhold their *assent* to participate in research, usually by a verbal response to an explanation of the research. In addition, a child's legal guardian must give written informed consent to have the child participate in research (Sieber 1992). There are also special protections for other populations who are likely to be vulnerable to coercion—prisoners, pregnant women, persons with mental disabilities, and educationally or economically disadvantaged persons. Would you allow research on prisoners, whose ability to give informed consent can be questioned? What special protections do you think would be appropriate?

Obtaining informed consent also becomes more challenging in collectivist communities in which leaders or the whole group are accustomed to making decisions for individual members. In such settings, usually in non-Western cultures, researchers may have to develop a relationship with the community before individuals can be engaged in research (Bledsoe & Hopson 2009:397–398).

Subject payments create another complication for achieving the goal of informed consent. Although payments to research participants can be a reasonable way to compensate them for their time and effort, payments also serve as an inducement to participate. If the payment is a significant amount in relation to the participants' normal income, it could lead people to set aside their reservations about participating in a project—even though they may harbor those reservations (Fisher & Anushko 2008:104–105).

Avoid Deception in Research, Except in Limited Circumstances

Deception occurs when subjects are misled about research procedures to determine how they would react to the treatment if they were not research subjects. Deception is a critical component of many social psychology experiments, partly because of the difficulty of simulating real-world stresses and dilemmas in a laboratory setting. The goal is to get subjects "to accept as true what is false or to give a false impression" (Korn 1997:4). In Milgram's (1964) experiment, for example, deception seemed necessary because the subjects could not be permitted to administer real electric

> **Deception:** Used in social experiments to create more "realistic" treatments in which the true purpose of the research is not disclosed to participants, often within the confines of a laboratory.

shocks to the "stooge," yet it would not have made sense to order the subjects to do something that they didn't find to be so troubling. Milgram (1992:187–188) insisted that the deception was absolutely essential, although the experimental records indicate that some participants figured out the deception (Perry 2013:128–129).

The results of many other social psychological experiments would be worthless if subjects understood what was really happening to them while the experiment was in progress. The real question: Is this sufficient justification to allow the use of deception?

Gary Marshall and Philip Zimbardo (1979:971–972) sought to determine the physiological basis of emotion by injecting student volunteers with adrenaline, so that their heart rates and sweating would increase, and then placing them in a room with a student "stooge" who acted silly. The students were told that they were being injected with a vitamin supplement to test its effect on visual acuity (Korn 1997:2–3). Jane Allyn Piliavin and Irving Piliavin (1972:355–356) staged fake seizures on subway trains to study helpfulness (Korn 1997:3–4). If you were a member of your university's IRB, would you vote to allow such deceptive practices in research? What about less dramatic instances of deception in laboratory experiments with students like yourself?

Do you believe that deception itself is the problem? Elliot Aronson and Judson Mills's (1959) study of the severity of initiation to groups is a good example of experimental research that does not pose greater-than-everyday risks to subjects, but still uses deception. This study was conducted at an all-women's college in the 1950s. The student volunteers who were randomly assigned to the "severe initiation" experimental condition had to read a list of embarrassing words. I think it's fair to say that even in the 1950s, reading a list of potentially embarrassing words in a laboratory setting and listening to a taped discussion were unlikely to increase the risks to which students are exposed in their everyday lives. Moreover, the researchers informed the subjects that they would be expected to talk about sex and could decline to participate in the experiment if this requirement would bother them. None dropped out.

To further ensure that no psychological harm was caused, Aronson and Mills (1959) explained the true nature of the experiment to the subjects after the experiment. The subjects did not seem perturbed: "None of the Ss [subjects] expressed any resentment or annoyance at having been misled. In fact, the majority were intrigued by the experiment, and several returned at the end of the academic quarter to ascertain the result" (p. 179).

Are you satisfied that this procedure caused no harm? Do you react differently to Aronson and Mills's debriefing than you did to Milgram's debriefing? The minimal deception in the Aronson and Mills experiment, coupled with the lack of any ascertainable risk to subjects plus a debriefing, satisfies the ethical standards for research of most social scientists and IRBs, even today.

What scientific, educational, or applied value would make deception justifiable, even if there is some potential for harm? Who determines whether a nondeceptive intervention is "equally effective"? (Miller 1986:103). Baumrind (1985:167) suggested that personal "introspection" would have been sufficient to test Milgram's hypothesis and has argued subsequently that intentional deception in research violates the ethical principles of self-determination, protection of others, and maintenance of trust between people, and so can never be justified. How much risk, discomfort, or unpleasantness might be seen as affecting willingness to participate? When should a postexperimental "attempt to correct any misconception" caused by deception be deemed sufficient?

Can you see why an IRB, representing a range of perspectives, is an important tool for making reasonable, ethical research decisions when confronted with such ambiguity? Exhibit 3.8 shows a portion of the complex flowchart developed by the U.S. Department of Health and Human Services to help researchers decide what type of review will be needed for their research plans. Any research involving deception requires formal human subjects review.

Maintain Privacy and Confidentiality

Maintaining privacy and confidentiality is another key ethical standard for protecting research participants, and the researcher's commitment to that standard should be included in the informed consent agreement (Sieber 1992). Procedures to protect each subject's privacy—such as locking records and creating special identifying codes—must be created to minimize the risk of access by unauthorized persons. However, statements about confidentiality should be realistic: Laws allow research records to be subpoenaed and may require reporting of child abuse; a researcher may feel compelled to release information if a health- or life-threatening situation arises and participants need to be alerted. Also, the standard of confidentiality does not apply to observation in public places and information available in public records.

> **Certificate of Confidentiality:** A certificate issued to a researcher by the National Institutes of Health that ensures the right to protect information obtained about high-risk populations or behaviors—except child abuse or neglect—from legal subpoenas.
>
> **Health Insurance Portability and Accountability Act (HIPAA):** A congressional act passed in 1996 that creates stringent regulations for the protection of health care data.

There is one exception to some of these constraints: The National Institutes of Health (NIH) can issue a **Certificate of Confidentiality** to protect researchers from being legally required to disclose confidential information. This is intended to help researchers overcome the reluctance of individuals engaged in illegal behavior to sign a consent form or to risk exposure of their illegal activities (Sharma 2009:426). Researchers who are focusing on high-risk populations or behaviors, such as crime, substance abuse, sexual activity, or genetic information, can request such a certificate. Suspicions of child abuse or neglect must still be reported, and in some states, researchers may still be required to report such crimes as elder abuse (Arwood & Panicker 2007).

The **Health Insurance Portability and Accountability Act (HIPAA)** passed by Congress in 1996 created more stringent regulations for the protection of health care data. As implemented by the U.S. Department of Health and Human Services in 2000 (revised in 2002), the HIPAA Final Privacy Rule applies to oral, written, and electronic information that "relates to the past, present or future physical or mental health or condition of an individual." The HIPAA rule requires that researchers have valid authorization for any use or disclosure of "protected health information" (PHI) from a health care provider. Waivers of authorization can be granted in special circumstances (Cava, Cushman, & Goodman 2007).

Consider Uses of Research So That Benefits Outweigh Risks

Scientists must also consider the uses to which their research is put. Although many scientists believe that personal values should be left outside the laboratory, some feel that it is proper—even necessary—for scientists to concern themselves with the way their research is used.

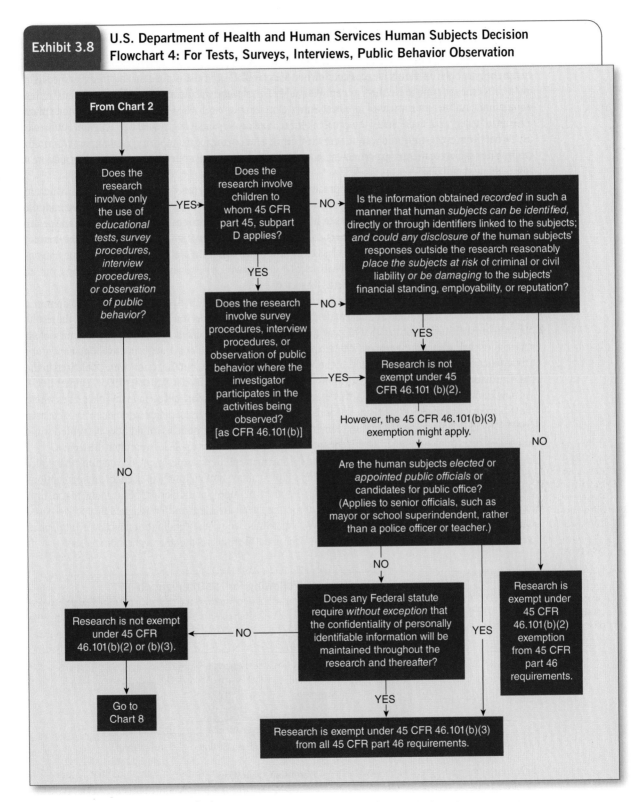

Exhibit 3.8 U.S. Department of Health and Human Services Human Subjects Decision Flowchart 4: For Tests, Surveys, Interviews, Public Behavior Observation

Source: Department of Health and Human Services.

Milgram made it clear that he was concerned about the phenomenon of obedience precisely because of its implications for people's welfare. As you have already learned, his first article (Milgram 1963) highlighted the atrocities committed under the Nazis by citizens and soldiers who were "just following orders." In his more comprehensive book on the obedience experiments (Milgram 1974), he also argued that his findings shed light on the atrocities committed in the Vietnam War at My Lai, slavery, the destruction of the American Indian population, and the internment of Japanese Americans during World War II. Milgram makes no explicit attempt to "tell us what to do" about this problem. In fact, as a dispassionate social scientist, Milgram (1974) tells us, "What the present study [did was] to give the dilemma [of obedience to authority] contemporary form by treating it as subject matter for experimental inquiry, and with the aim of understanding rather than judging it from a moral standpoint" (p. xi).

Yet it is impossible to ignore the very practical implications of Milgram's investigations, which Milgram took pains to emphasize. His research highlighted the extent of obedience to authority and identified multiple factors that could be manipulated to lessen blind obedience (e.g., encouraging dissent by just one group member, removing the subject from direct contact with the authority figure, and increasing the contact between the subject and the victim). It is less clear how much Milgram's laboratory manipulation can tell us about obedience in the very different historical events to which he generalized his conclusions, but its conclusions still have potentially great benefits for society.

The evaluation research by Lawrence Sherman and Richard Berk (1984) on police response to domestic violence provides an interesting cautionary tale about the uses of science. As you recall from Chapter 2, the results of this field experiment indicated that those who were arrested were less likely to subsequently commit violent acts against their partners. Sherman (1993) explicitly cautioned police departments not to adopt mandatory arrest policies based solely on the results of the Minneapolis experiment, but the results were publicized in the mass media and encouraged many jurisdictions to change their policies (Binder & Meeker 1993; Lempert 1989). We now know that the original finding of a deterrent effect of arrest did not hold up in many other cities where the experiment was repeated, so it is not clear that the initial changes in arrest policy were beneficial. Sherman (1992:150–153) later suggested that implementing mandatory arrest policies might have prevented some subsequent cases of spouse abuse, but this does not change the fact that these policies were often ineffective.

Given the mixed findings from the replications of Sherman and Berk's experiment, do you think that police policy should be changed in light of JoAnn Miller's (2003) analysis of victims' experiences and perceptions concerning their safety after the mandatory arrest experiment in Dade County, Florida? Miller found that victims reported experiencing less violence after their abuser had been arrested (and/or assigned to a police-based counseling program called Safe Streets) (Exhibit 3.9). Should this Dade County finding be publicized in the popular press, so it could be used to improve police policies? What about the results of the other replication studies?

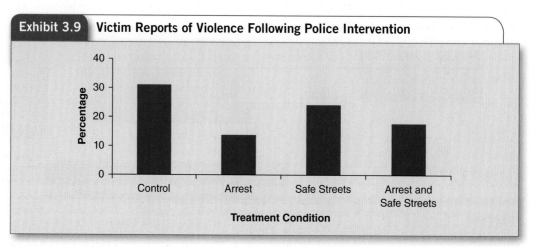

Exhibit 3.9   Victim Reports of Violence Following Police Intervention

Source: Miller, JoAnn. 2003. "An Arresting Experiment: Domestic Violence Victim Experiences and Perceptions." *Journal of Interpersonal Violence* 18:695–716. Based on table 1.

Social scientists who conduct research on behalf of specific organizations may face additional difficulties when the organization, instead of the researcher, controls the final report and the publicity it receives. If organizational leaders decide that particular research results are unwelcome, the researcher's desire to have the findings used appropriately and reported fully can conflict with contractual obligations. Researchers can often anticipate such dilemmas in advance and resolve them when the contract for research is negotiated—or they may simply decline a particular research opportunity altogether. But, often, such problems come up only after a report has been drafted, or the problems are ignored by a researcher who needs to have a job or needs to maintain particular personal relationships. These possibilities cannot be avoided entirely, but because of them, it is always important to acknowledge the source of research funding in reports and to consider carefully the sources of funding for research reports written by others.

The potential of withholding a beneficial treatment from some subjects also is a cause for ethical concern. The Sherman and Berk (1984) experiment required the random assignment of subjects to treatment conditions and thus had the potential of causing harm to the victims of domestic violence whose batterers were not arrested. The justification for the study design, however, is quite persuasive: The researchers didn't know before the experiment which response to a domestic violence complaint would be most likely to deter future incidents (Sherman 1992). The experiment provided what seemed at first to be clear evidence about the value of arrest, so it can be argued that the benefits outweighed the risks.

▣ The Institutional Review Board

Federal regulations require that every institution that seeks federal funding for biomedical or behavioral research on human subjects have an **institutional review board (IRB)** that reviews research proposals involving human subjects—including data about living individuals. According to federal regulations [45 CFR 46.102(d)], research is "a systematic investigation . . . designed to develop or contribute to generalizable knowledge," and according to the Department of Health and Human Services (DHHS) [45 CFR 46.102 (f)], a human subject is "a living individual about whom an investigator (whether professional or student) conducting research obtains data through intervention or interaction with the individual or just identifiable private information." The IRB determines whether a planned activity is research or involves human subjects.

> **Institutional review board (IRB):** A group of organizational and community representatives required by federal law to review the ethical issues in all proposed research that is federally funded, involves human subjects, or has any potential for harm to human subjects.

IRBs at universities and other agencies apply ethical standards that are set by federal regulations but can be expanded or specified by the institution's IRB and involve all research at the institution irrespective of the funding source (Sieber 1992:5, 10). The IRB has the authority to require changes in a research protocol or to refuse to approve a research protocol if it deems human subjects protections inadequate. Consent forms must include contact information for the IRB, and the IRB has the authority to terminate a research project that violates the procedures the IRB approved or that otherwise creates risks for human subjects. The **Office for Protection From Research Risks, National Institutes of Health** monitors IRBs, with the exception of research involving drugs (which is the responsibility of the federal Food and Drug Administration).

> **Office for Protection From Research Risks, National Institutes of Health:** The office in the U.S. Department of Health and Human Services (DHHS) that provides leadership and supervision about the protection of the rights, welfare, and well-being of subjects involved in research conducted or supported by HHS, including monitoring IRBs.

To promote adequate review of ethical issues, the regulations require that IRBs include at least five members, with at least one nonscientist and one from outside the institution (Speiglman & Spear 2009:124). The IRB must also include members from both sexes, diverse backgrounds, and multiple professions. When research is reviewed concerning vulnerable populations, such as prisoners, the IRB must include a member having experience with and knowledge about that vulnerable population. Sensitivity to community attitudes and training in human subjects protection procedures is also required (Selwitz, Epley, & Erickson 2013).

Every member of an institution with an IRB—including faculty, students, and staff at a college or university—must submit a proposal to their IRB before conducting research with identifiable people. The IRB proposal must include research instruments and consent forms, as applicable, as well as enough detail about the research design to convince the IRB members that the potential benefits of the research outweigh any risks (Speiglman & Spear 2009:124). Most IRBs also require that researchers complete a training program about human subjects, usually the Collaborative Institutional Training Initiative (CITI) at the University of Miami (https://www.citiprogram.org/). CITI training is divided into topical modules ranging from history, ethical principles, and informed consent to vulnerable populations, Internet-based research, educational research, and records-based research. Each IRB determines which CITI training modules researchers at its institution must complete.

Research in the News

WHAT WOULD AN IRB SAY?

Former New York City Mayor Michael Bloomberg and his health commissioner Thomas Frieden unilaterally moved New Yorkers to a lower salt diet. While numerous research experiments have attempted to find a relationship between low salt diets and improved health, there have been no conclusive results. But New York City administrators required restaurants to impose a cap on salt intake.

For Further Thought

1. Is it ethical to base public policies on ambiguous research results? What about if the results are definitive? Should these restaurants be using informed consent forms?
2. Could you imagine a real social experiment in New York restaurants to test the value of lowering salt in foods? What steps might an IRB require?

News Source: Tierney, John. 2009. "Public Policy That Makes Test Subjects of Us All." *The New York Times,* April 7: D1.

Researcher Interview Link
Institutional Review Boards

Although the IRB is the responsible authority within the institution, many research proposals do not have to be reviewed by the full board (Hicks 2013). Some proposals, including many developed by social scientists, may be exempt from review because they involve very low perceived risk: research about educational procedures in an educational setting, a survey that does not collect information that could be harmful to respondents if it were disclosed, or analysis of existing records that are not individually identifiable. However, the decision of whether a research project is *exempt* from IRB review must be made by an official designated by the institution to screen applications—typically one or more representatives of the IRB.

Many research proposals that do not meet the criteria for exemption but still pose only minimal risk to human subjects may be given an *expedited* review by IRB representatives (often an IRB administrator and the IRB chair), rather than being sent to a hearing at a meeting of the full IRB. According to the regulations (DHHS 2009),

1. Research activities that (1) present no more than minimal risk to human subjects, and (2) involve only procedures listed in one or more of the following categories, may be reviewed by the IRB through the expedited review procedure authorized by 45 CFR 46.110 and 21 CFR 56.110. The activities listed should not be deemed to be of minimal risk simply because they are included on this list. Inclusion on this list merely means that the activity is eligible for review through the expedited review procedure when the specific circumstances of the proposed research involve no more than minimal risk to human subjects.

2. The categories in this list apply regardless of the age of subjects, except as noted.

    a. The expedited review procedure may not be used where identification of the subjects or their responses would reasonably place them at risk of criminal or civil liability or be damaging to the subjects' financial standing, employability, insurability, reputation, or be stigmatizing, unless reasonable and appropriate protections will be implemented so that risks related to invasion of privacy and breach of confidentiality are no greater than minimal.

    b. The expedited review procedure may not be used for classified research involving human subjects.

    c. IRBs are reminded that the standard requirements for informed consent (or its waiver, alteration, or exception) apply regardless of the type of review—expedited or convened—used by the IRB.

    d. Categories one (1) through seven (7) pertain to both initial and continuing IRB review.

The categories of research that can be considered for expedited review include collection of biological specimens and some medical data for research purposes by noninvasive means; collection of data from voice, video, digital, or image recordings made for research purposes; and research on individual or group characteristics or behavior (including, but not limited to, research on perception, cognition, motivation, identity, language, communication, cultural beliefs or practices, and social behavior) or research employing survey, interview, oral history, focus group, program evaluation, human factors evaluation, or quality assurance methodologies (DHHS 2009).

Many projects must be reviewed before the full IRB (Speiglman & Spear 2009:125–126). An IRB must ensure that several specific standards are met by research projects that it reviews either on an expedited basis or in a full board review (Hicks 2013):

1. Risks to subjects are minimized: (i) By using procedures that are consistent with sound research design and that do not unnecessarily expose subjects to risk, and (ii) whenever appropriate, by using procedures already being performed on the subjects for diagnostic or treatment purposes.

2. Risks to subjects are reasonable in relation to anticipated benefits, if any, to subjects, and the importance of the knowledge that may reasonably be expected to result. In evaluating risks and benefits, the IRB should consider only those risks and benefits that may result from the research (as distinguished from risks and benefits of therapies subjects would receive even if not participating in the research). The IRB should not consider possible long-range effects of applying knowledge gained in the research (for example, the possible effects of the research on public policy) as among those research risks that fall within the purview of its responsibility.

3. Selection of subjects is equitable. In making this assessment the IRB should consider the purposes of the research and the setting in which the research will be conducted and should be particularly cognizant of the special problems of research involving vulnerable populations, such as children, prisoners, pregnant women, mentally disabled persons, or economically or educationally disadvantaged persons.

4. Informed consent will be sought from each prospective subject or the subject's legally authorized representative, in accordance with, and to the extent required by §46.116.

5. Informed consent will be appropriately documented, in accordance with, and to the extent required by §46.117.

6. When appropriate, the research plan makes adequate provision for monitoring the data collected to ensure the safety of subjects.

7. When appropriate, there are adequate provisions to protect the privacy of subjects and to maintain the confidentiality of data.

In addition, when some or all of the subjects are likely to be vulnerable to coercion or undue influence, such as children, prisoners, pregnant women, mentally disabled persons, or economically or educationally disadvantaged persons, additional safeguards have been included in the study to protect the rights and welfare of these subjects.

The IRB may also serve as the privacy board that ensures researchers' compliance with the HIPAA. In this capacity, the IRB responds to requests for waivers or alterations of the authorization requirement under the privacy rule for uses and disclosures of protected health information (PHI) in research. Researchers seeking to collect or use existing HIPAA data must provide additional information to the IRB about their plans for using the health information.

A proposed research project that does not meet these standards will have to be revised to increase human subjects protections or it will be rejected.

CAREERS AND RESEARCH

Kristen Kenny, Research Compliance Specialist

Kristen Kenny comes from a long line of musicians and artists and was the first in her family to graduate from college. Kenny majored in filmmaking and performance art at the Massachusetts College of Art and soon started working on small films and in theater doing everything from set design, hair, and make-up to costume design and acting. The arts have their fair share of interesting characters; this was the beginning of Kenny's training in dealing with a variety of difficult personalities and learning how to listen and how to react.

After years of working a variety of jobs in the entertainment field, Kenny found herself working as a receptionist in the music industry, a hotbed of difficult personalities, contracts, and negotiations. Within a year, Kenny had been promoted to assistant talent buyer for small clubs and festivals in the Boston area. This job helped Kenny develop the skill of reading dense contract documents and being able to identify what contractual clause language stays and what gets deleted. Eventually the music industry started to wane and Kenny was laid off, but a friend at a local hospital who was in dire need of someone who could interpret volumes of documents and deal with bold personalities asked her to apply for a job as their IRB administrator. Kenny had no idea what an IRB was, but she attended trainings and conferences to learn the IRB trade. Three years later, Kenny was asked to join the Office of Research and Sponsored Programs at the University of Massachusetts Boston as the IRB administrator.

Now, as a research compliance specialist II, Kenny maintains the IRB and other regulatory units and has developed a training curriculum and program for the Office of Research and Sponsored Programs. And if you look hard enough you can find her clothing and fabric designs on eBay, Etsy, and her own website.

🔲 Social Research Proposals

Now that you have an overview of the research process and a basic understanding of IRB requirements, it is time to introduce the process of writing a research proposal. A research proposal is the launching pad for a formal research project, and it serves the very important function of forcing a researcher to set out a problem statement and a research plan—to think through the details of what you are trying to accomplish and how you will go about that—as well as to think through procedures for the protection of human subjects. So whether you must write a proposal for a professor, a thesis committee, an organization seeking practical advice, or a government agency that funds basic research, you should approach the requirement as a key step toward achieving your goals. Just writing down your ideas will help you see how they can be improved, and almost any feedback will help you refine your plans.

Each chapter in this book includes a section, "Developing a Research Proposal," with exercises that guide you through the process of proposal writing. This section introduces the process of proposal writing as well as these special end-of-chapter exercises. It also provides a schematic overview of the entire research process. You will want to return to this section frequently so you will remember "where you are" in the research process as you learn about particular methods in the remaining chapters.

Research proposals often have five sections (Locke, Spirduso, & Silverman 2000:8–34):

- *An introductory statement of the research problem,* in which you clarify what it is that you are interested in studying

- *A literature review,* in which you explain how your problems and plans build on what has already been reported in the literature on this topic

- *A methodological plan,* detailing just how you will respond to the particular mix of opportunities and constraints you face

- *An ethics statement,* identifying human subjects issues in the research and how you will respond to them in an ethical fashion

- *A statement of limitations,* reviewing the potential weaknesses of the proposed research design and presenting plans for minimizing their consequences

You will also need to include a budget and project timeline, unless you are working within the framework of a class project.

When you develop a research proposal, it will help to ask yourself a series of questions such as those in Exhibit 3.10; see also Gregory Herek (1995). It is easy to omit important details and to avoid being self-critical while rushing to put a proposal together. However, it is even more painful to have a proposal rejected (or to receive a low grade). It is better to make sure the proposal covers what it should and confronts the tough issues that reviewers (or your professor) will be sure to consider.

The series of questions in Exhibit 3.10 can serve as a map to subsequent chapters in this book and as a checklist of decisions that must be made throughout any research project. The questions are organized in five sections, each concluding with a checkpoint at which you should consider whether to proceed with the research as planned, modify the plans, or stop the project altogether. The sequential ordering of these questions obscures a bit the way in which they should be answered: not as single questions, one at a time, but as a unit—first as five separate stages and then as a whole. Feel free to change your answers to earlier questions on the basis of your answers to later questions.

We will learn how to apply the decision checklist with an example from a proposal focused on a public health care coordination program. At this early point in your study of research methods, you may not recognize all the terms in this checklist. Don't let that bother you now because my goal is just to give you a quick overview of the decision-making process. Your knowledge of these terms and your understanding of the decisions will increase as you complete each chapter. Your decision-making skills will also improve if you complete the "Developing a Research Proposal" exercises at the end of each chapter.

Case Study: Evaluating a Public Health Program

Exhibit 3.11 provides excerpts from the research proposal I submitted to our IRB as part of an evaluation of a public health program for low-income residents funded by the U.S. Centers for Disease Control and the Massachusetts Department of Public Health (DPH) (Schutt 2011a). Appendixes included consent forms, research instruments, and the bibliography.

As you can see from the excerpts, I proposed to evaluate a care coordination program for low-income uninsured and underinsured Massachusetts residents (before universal health care). The proposal included

Exhibit 3.10 Decisions in Research

Problem Formulation (Chapters 1–3)

1. Developing a research question
2. Assessing researchability of the problem
3. Consulting prior research
4. Relating to social theory
5. Choosing an approach: Deductive? Inductive? Descriptive?
6. Reviewing research guidelines and ethical standards

Checkpoint 1
Alternatives:

- Continue as planned.
- Modify the plan.
- Stop. Abandon the plan.

Research Validity (Chapters 4–6)

7. Establishing measurement validity:

   - How should concepts be defined?
   - What measures are available and what measures must be developed?
   - How can reliability and validity be assessed?
   - Is authenticity an important goal and how can it be assessed?

8. Establishing generalizability:

   - Was a representative sample used?
   - Are the findings applicable to particular subgroups?
   - Does the population sampled correspond to the population of interest?

9. Establishing causality:

   - What is the possibility of experimental or statistical controls?
   - How to assess the causal mechanism?
   - What is the causal context?

10. Determining the data required: Longitudinal or cross-sectional?
11. Determining the units of analysis: Individuals or groups?
12. Determining the major possible sources of causal invalidity

Checkpoint 2
Alternatives:

- Continue as planned.
- Modify the plan.
- Stop. Abandon the plan.

Research Design (Chapters 7, 8, 10, 12–15)

13. Choosing a research design and procedures: Experimental? Survey? Participant observation? Historical, comparative? Evaluation research? Secondary data analysis? Mixed methods?
14. Specifying the research plan: Type of surveys, observations, etc.
15. Determining secondary analysis and availability of suitable data sets
16. Choosing a causal approach: Idiographic or nomothetic?
17. Assessing human subjects protections

Checkpoint 3
Alternatives:

- Continue as planned.
- Modify the plan.
- Stop. Abandon the plan.

Data Analysis (Chapters 9, 11)

18. Choosing an analytic approach:

- Identifying statistics and graphs for describing data
- Identifying relationships between variables
- Deciding about statistical controls
- Testing for interaction effects
- Evaluating inferences from sample data to the population
- Developing a qualitative analysis approach

Checkpoint 4
Alternatives:

- Continue as planned.
- Modify the plan.
- Stop. Abandon the plan.

Reporting Research (Chapter 16)

19. Clarifying research goals and prior research findings
20. Identifying the intended audience
21. Developing tables and charts
22. Organizing the text
23. Reviewing research limitations

Checkpoint 5
Alternatives:
- Complete the research!
- Modify the plan.
- Stop. Abandon the plan.

a lengthy literature review, a description of the population and the sampling procedure, measures to be used in the survey, and the methods for conducting phone interviews as well as in-person interviews with a subset of the sample. Required sections for the IRB also included a statement of risks and benefits, procedures for obtaining informed consent, and means for maintaining confidentiality. A HIPAA compliance statement was included because of the collection of health-related data.

Let's review the issues identified in Exhibit 3.10 as they relate to the public health proposal. The research question concerned the effectiveness of a care coordination program involving the use of patient navigators—an evaluation research question [Question 1]. This problem certainly was suitable for social research, and it was one that was feasible with the money DPH had committed [2]. Prior research demonstrated clearly that the program had potential but also that this approach had not previously been studied [3]. The treatment approach was connected to theories about health care disparities [4] and, given prior work and uncertainties in this area, mixed methods involving both a deductive, hypothesis-testing approach and an inductive, exploratory approach was called for [5]. I argued to the IRB that our plan protected human subjects and took each research guideline into account [6]. So it seemed reasonable to continue to develop the proposal (Checkpoint 1).

Exhibit 3.11 An IRB Proposal for a Program Evaluation

Evaluation of the Coordinated Care Program

Rationale

Inadequate personal resources, knowledge, and service opportunities limit the access of low income and minority populations to health care services. . . . four types of barriers to effective service delivery in interviews with Latina women . . . additional systemic barriers of provider bias and poor quality of care. Many public health agencies have adopted programs designed to overcome these barriers and thus to reduce disparities in health care services and, ultimately, outcomes.

The Massachusetts Department of Public Health began a Coordinated Care Program in 2006 in order to improve identification of health needs among low income uninsured and underinsured residents and to increase the effectiveness of health services for this population. . . .

The purpose . . . is to investigate patient experience with the program, including subjective outcomes of the program and the bases of these outcomes. . . .

Program Background

Congress funded the National Breast and Cervical Cancer Early Detection Program (Breast and Cervical Cancer Mortality Prevention Act of 1990) to improve the rate of screening, testing and referral to treatment for low income uninsured and underinsured women at risk of breast and cervical cancer . . .

Patient navigation is designed to overcome barriers to treatment, while coordinated care is intended to improve treatment benefits, so the combination of both elements in one program should improve treatment outcomes.

The first patient navigation program appeared to reduce average stage at diagnosis among cancer patients. . . .

Care coordination is an important property of health care systems as well as a key aspect of patients' experience of health care. . . .

The emphases on coordinated care and on patient navigation may not always be complementary. . . . Programs offering patient navigation and care coordination have not typically been combined together due to their different disease foci: cancer for patient navigation and chronic illness for care coordination. The MA CCP program thus provides a unique opportunity to study the effect of combining these two different types of programs and examining their value for a very diverse and historically underserved population.

HIPAA Compliance Information

. . . No information about health conditions will be reported in a way that could be linked to any particular client.

Methodology

. . . Data will be collected with a statewide phone survey of a representative sample and through in-person interviews with a small number of clients at six of the 17 program delivery sites.

The phone survey is to result in a total sample of 400 interviews. One thousand clients will be sent an informational letter about the survey, indicating that they may receive a call. Cases will be selected randomly from the initial sampling frame and called to determine study eligibility. Phone calls will be repeated up to 20 times in order to make contact. Questions S0-S4 (in the attached questionnaire) will serve as the screening questions. . . . The phone survey instrument will be translated into Spanish and Portuguese. . . .

Questions in the phone survey instrument are designed to identify relation to the health center and patient navigator, ethnic and linguistic background and some other sociodemographic characteristics, current health status, including levels of depression and anxiety, use of health services, perceived barriers to the use of health services, and satisfaction with health services. . . .

A sample of 30 clients will be selected for more intensive interviews about program experience and orientations. . . . For those clients who consent, the in-person interviews will be recorded and transcribed. The resulting textual data will be coded and analyzed with the assistance of qualitative analysis software . . .

Human Participants Information

Participant Data

The client database maintained by the Massachusetts Care Coordination Program identifies . . . active clients. . . .

Risks and Benefits

Participation in the Client Survey involves a minimal risk of loss of confidentiality. In addition, the probability and magnitude of harm or discomfort anticipated from responding to the Client Survey items is no greater than what would ordinarily be encountered in daily life, that is, minimal risk. Although the only direct benefit to survey participants is the opportunity to express their perceptions of and satisfaction with . . . case management, the information gained may be helpful to case managers and other health care providers. The societal benefit is having objective data on which to base effective models of case management. The potential benefits of the proposed survey outweigh the minimal risk for individual survey participants.

Informed Consent and Confidentiality

The . . . phone survey interviewer will inform the clients that the survey is voluntary and explain procedures to be followed (the respondent can stop at any time; can skip any question she does not want to answer). The script for the telephone interview is in the Appendix. [P]hone interviewers and other staff adhere to strict confidentiality requirements. Identifying information will be used only for client contact and no personal identifiers will be maintained in the phone survey database. The phone survey ID numbers will be stored in a locked file with a list that links them to an identifier in the DPH CCP healthcare database. This linked list will allow subsequent matching in Stage III of data from the phone survey with data from CCP records about health outcomes. Signed consent forms for client in-person interviews will be stored in a locked cabinet. A list linking identification numbers and names of staff who were interviewed will be available only to the Principal Investigator. All in-person interviews will be taped and transcribed and records will also be stored in a locked cabinet and on password-protected computers. . . . Consent forms will include consent for the interview, consent for taping, and consent for follow-up.

Measures were to include structured survey questions to measure many variables and open-ended questions to allow exploration of barriers to care [7]. Use of a representative sample of the population of program recipients would increase the generalizability of the findings, although I was limited to interviews in English, Spanish, and Portuguese even though we knew there were a small number of recipients who spoke other languages [8]. The problem was well suited to a survey design [9] and could be adequately addressed with cross-sectional data [10], involving individuals [11]. The design left several sources of causal invalidity, including the possibility that persons who received the most services from patient navigators were those who had more resources and so were more healthy [12]. It seemed that I would be able to meet basic criteria for validity (Checkpoint 2).

A survey design was preferable because this was to be a study of a statewide population, but I did include a qualitative component so that I could explore orientations [13, 14]. Because the effectiveness of the program strategy had not been studied before in this type of population, I could not propose doing a secondary data analysis or meta-analysis [15]. I sought only to investigate causation from a *nomothetic* perspective, without attempting to show how the particular experiences of each participant may have led to their outcome [16]. The study design was low-risk and included voluntary participation; the research design seemed ethical [17] (Checkpoint 3). Standard statistical tests were proposed as well as some analysis of qualitative data [18] (Checkpoint 4). My goal was to use the research as the basis for several academic articles, as well as a report to the agency [19, 20]. I had reviewed the research literature carefully [21], but as is typical in most research proposals, I did not develop the research reporting plans any further [22, 23] (Checkpoint 5).

Discussion Questions

1. Should social scientists be permitted to conduct replications of Milgram's obedience experiments? Zimbardo's prison simulation? Can you justify such research as permissible within the current ASA ethical standards? If not, do you believe that these standards should be altered to permit Milgram-type research?

2. How do you evaluate the current ASA ethical code? Is it too strict or too lenient, or just about right? Are the enforcement provisions adequate? What provisions could be strengthened?

3. Why does unethical research occur? Is it inherent in science? Does it reflect "human nature"? What makes ethical research more or less likely?

4. Does debriefing solve the problem of subject deception? How much must researchers reveal after the experiment is over as well as before it begins?

5. What policy would you recommend that researchers such as Sherman and Berk (1984) follow in reporting the results of their research? Should social scientists try to correct misinformation in the popular press about their research or should they just focus on what is published in academic journals? Should researchers speak to audiences such as police conventions to influence policies related to their research results?

Practice Exercises

1. Pair up with one other student and read the article by John Lacey and others, or another from the Research That Matters vignettes in the preceding two chapters. One of you should criticize the research in terms of its adherence to each of the ethical principles for research on human subjects, as well as for the authors' apparent honesty, openness, and consideration of social consequences. Be generally negative but not unreasonable in your criticisms. The other one of you should critique the article in the same way but from a generally positive standpoint, defending its adherence to the five guidelines, but without ignoring the study's weak points. Together, write a summary of the study's strong and weak points, or conduct a debate in the class.

2. Investigate the standards and operations of your university's IRB. Review the IRB website, record the composition of the IRB (if indicated), and outline the steps that faculty and students must take to secure IRB approval for human subjects research. In your own words, distinguish the types of research that can be exempted from review, that qualify for expedited review, and that require review by the full board. If possible, identify another student or a faculty member who has had a proposal reviewed by the IRB. Ask them to describe their experience and how they feel about it. Would you recommend any changes in IRB procedures?

3. Choose one of the four "Ethical Issues" lessons from the opening menu for the Interactive Exercises. Review issues in ethical practice by reading the vignettes and entering your answers when requested. You have two chances to answer each question.

4. Also from the book's study site, at edge.sagepub.com/schuttisw8e, choose the Learning From Journal Articles option. Read one article based on research involving human subjects. What ethical issues did the research pose and how were they resolved? Does it seem that subjects were appropriately protected?

Ethics Questions

1. Lacey and his collaborators in the National Roadside Survey (2011), described in the Research That Matters vignette, conducted a purely descriptive study of the prevalence of impaired driving. What if they had sought to test the impact of conducting such traffic stops on the subsequent likelihood of drivers drinking (or drugging) and driving? If this had been their goal, they might have proposed conducting the traffic stops at randomly determined locations, while

conducting surveys without a test for impaired driving at other randomly determined locations as their control condition. They could then have followed up a year later to see if those in the traffic stop group were less likely to have been arrested for DUI. The results of such a study could help devise more effective policies for reducing driving under the influence. Do you think an IRB should approve a study like this with a randomized design? Why or why not?

2. Milgram's research on obedience to authority has been used to explain the behavior of soldiers charged with intentionally harming civilians during armed conflicts, both on the battlefield and when guarding prisoners of war. Do you think social scientists can use experiments such as Milgram's to learn about ethical behavior in the social world in general? What about in situations of armed conflict? Consider in your answers Perry's discoveries about aspects of Milgram's research that he did not disclose.

Web Exercises

1. The Collaborative Institutional Training Initiative (CITI) offers an extensive online training course in the basics of human subjects protections issues. Go to the public access CITI site at www.citiprogram.org/rcrpage.asp?affiliation=100 and complete the course in social and behavioral research. Write a short summary of what you have learned.

2. The U.S. Department of Health and Human Services maintains extensive resources concerning the protection of human subjects in research. Read several documents that you find on its website, www.hhs.gov/ohrp, and write a short report about them.

3. Read the entire ASA *Code of Ethics* at the website of the ASA Ethics Office, www.asanet.org/images/asa/docs/pdf/CodeofEthics.pdf. Discuss the difference between the aspirational goals and the enforceable rules.

Video Interview Questions

Listen to the researcher interview for Chapter 3 at edge.sagepub.com/schutt8e.

1. What are the key issues that an institutional review board (IRB) evaluates in a research proposal?

2. What are some challenges that an IRB faces? How does Dr. Nestor suggest that these challenges can be resolved?

SPSS Exercises

1. Consider three variables in the GSS2012 survey: helpblk, income06, and owngun. Review the corresponding variable labels in the "Variable View" in the GSS2012x or GSS2012a file so that you know what questions were used to measure these variables. Are there any ethical issues involved in asking these questions? Do you imagine that some respondents would be more likely to give untruthful answers to these questions? Explain your answers.

2. Imagine that you are invited by a friend of a friend to speak to members of a fundamentalist church about the implications of the latest General Social Survey for persons of faith. Suppose that you believe in "a woman's right to choose" and in "free speech." Examine the cross-tabulation between fundamentalist beliefs and support for the right to abortion after a rape and support for allowing an anti-religionist to speak (Analyze→ Descriptive Statistics→ Crosstabs→ (Rows=abrape, spkath; Columns=fund; Cells/Percentages=columns). How will the relationship between fundamentalist beliefs and these political attitudes affect your speech? Why or why not?

CHAPTER 4

Conceptualization and Measurement

Research That Matters, Questions That Count

Youth gangs have been active in the United States for more than a century. It is therefore no surprise that U.S. sociologists, criminologists, and other social scientists have conducted many studies of youth gangs. The same cannot be said about China. There has been much less evidence of youth gangs and little research has been conducted about them. Only in recent years, as China has rapidly industrialized and urbanized, have social scientists begun to focus attention on Chinese youth gangs.

Vincent Webb, Ling Ren, Jihong "Solomon" Zhao, Ni "Phil" He, and Ineke Haen Marshall decided to study the prevalence of youth gangs in contemporary China, but they realized that the term *youth gang* has not been used in the same way in the two countries. In China, youth gangs have been defined strictly in terms used in the Chinese legal code, whereas in the United States, the term is used in a broader way that encompasses groups that are not primarily involved in crime. Webb et al.'s research design involved asking youth in both China and the United States identical questions about their involvement in gangs. The researchers found a much lower rate of reported gang connections in China, but they also discovered that the Chinese word they were using for "gang" did not have the same negative connotation as did the English word.

"The use of the almost identical survey instrument in the two very different cultural settings makes it possible to compare youth gangs and related behaviors" (Webb et al. 2011:233). But they also concluded, "The Chinese students did not fully understand the concept of gang in the way it is understood in the West due to the cultural and political differences." In China, answers to the question "Do you consider your group of friends a gang?" meant something different than they meant in the United States (p. 234).

1. How would you define the concept of *youth gang*?

2. What questions would you ask in a youth survey to determine whether respondents are gang members?

3. What would you suggest doing to assess whether answers to the survey questions mean what you think they mean?

4. What advantages and disadvantages do you see to comparing research results between countries that differ in culture and language?

In this chapter, you will learn about concepts and measures used in studies of substance abuse, youth gangs, and other social phenomena. By the end of the chapter, you will understand why defining concepts and developing measures are critical steps in research and you will have a much firmer basis for answering the questions I have posed. After you finish the chapter, test yourself by reading the 2011 *International Criminal Justice Review* article by Webb and his colleagues at the *Investigating the Social World* study site and completing the related interactive exercises for Chapter 4 at edge.sagepub.com/schutt8e.

Webb, Vincent J., Ling Ren, Jihong "Solomon" Zhao, Ni "Phil" He, and Ineke Haen Marshall. 2011. "A Comparative Study of Youth Gangs in China and the United States: Definition, Offending, and Victimization." *International Criminal Justice Review* 21:225–242.

Substance abuse is a social problem of remarkable proportions, both on and off campus. About 18 million Americans have an alcohol use disorder (Grant et al. 2004; Hasin et al. 2007; NIAAA 2013), and about 80,000 die every year from alcohol-related causes (NIAAA 2013). Workplace alcohol use occurs among 15% of the U.S. workforce, and illicit drug use occurs among 3% (Frone 2008). While in college, 4 out of 10 students binge drink (Wechsler et al. 2002), and about 1 out of 3 could be diagnosed as alcohol abusers (Knight et al. 2002). Drinking is a factor in at least half of on-campus sexual assaults (Abbey 2002). Among all American males 12 years of age or older in 2010, about 11% had used an illicit drug and 10% had

Journal Link
Youth Gangs

drunk at least five drinks on at least five occasions within a one-month period; the corresponding figures for female Americans are 7% and 3% (NCHS 2013:193–194). All told, the annual costs of prevention and treatment for alcohol and drug abuse exceed $340 billion in the United States (Miller & Hendrie 2008). Across the globe, alcohol misuse results in about 2.5 million deaths annually (WHO 2013).

Whether your goal is to learn how society works, to deliver useful services, to design effective social policies, or simply to try to protect yourself and your peers, at some point you might decide to read some of the research literature on substance abuse. Perhaps you will even attempt to design your own study of it. Every time you begin to review or design relevant research, you will have to answer two questions: (1) What is meant by *substance abuse* in this research? (the conceptualization issue) and (2) How was substance abuse measured? (the operationalization issue). Both types of questions must be answered when we evaluate prior research, and both types of questions must be kept in the forefront when we design new research. Only when we conclude that a study used valid measures of its key concepts can we have some hope that its conclusions are valid.

In this chapter, I first address the issue of conceptualization, using substance abuse and other concepts as examples. I then focus on measurement, reviewing first how indicators of substance abuse and several other concepts have been constructed using such operations as questions, observations, and less direct and obtrusive measures. Next I discuss the different possible levels of measurement and methods for assessing the validity and reliability of measures. The final topic is to consider the unique insights that qualitative methods can add to the measurement process. By the chapter's end, you should have a good understanding of measurement, the first of the three legs on which a research project's validity rests.

▣ Concepts

Although the drinking statistics sound scary, we need to be clear about what they mean before we march off to a Temperance Society meeting. What, after all, is binge drinking? The definition that Henry Wechsler et al. (2002) used is "heavy episodic drinking"; more specifically, "we defined binge drinking as the consumption of at least 5 drinks in a row for men or 4 drinks in a row for women during the 2 weeks before completion of the questionnaire" (p. 205).

Is this what you call *binge drinking?* This definition is widely accepted among social researchers, so when they use the term they can understand each other. However, the National Institute on Alcoholism and Alcohol Abuse (College Alcohol Study 2008) provides a more precise definition: "A pattern of drinking alcohol that brings blood alcohol concentration to 0.08 grams percent or above." Most researchers consider the so-called 5/4 definition (5 drinks for men; 4 for women) to be a reasonable approximation to this more precise definition. We can't say that only one definition of *binge drinking* is "correct," or even that one is "better." What we can say is that we need to specify what we mean when we use the term. We also have to be

> **Concept:** A mental image that summarizes a set of similar observations, feelings, or ideas.

sure that others know what definition we are using. And of course, the definition has to be useful for our purposes: A definition based solely on blood alcohol concentration will not be useful if we are not taking blood measures.

We call binge drinking a **concept**—a mental image that summarizes a set of similar observations, feelings, or ideas. To make that concept useful in research (and even in ordinary discourse), we have to define it. Many concepts are used in everyday discourse without consistent definition, sometimes definitions of concepts are themselves the object of intense debate, and the meanings of concepts may change over time. For example, when we read a *New York Times* article (Stille 2000) announcing a rise in the "social health" of the United States, after a precipitous decline in the 1970s and 1980s, we don't know whether we should feel relieved or disinterested. In fact, the authorities on the subject didn't even agree about what the term *social health* meant: lessening of social and economic inequalities (Marc Miringoff) or clear moral values (William J. Bennett). Most agreed that social health has to do with "things that are not measured in the gross national product" and that it is "a more subtle and more meaningful way of measuring what's important to [people]" (Stille 2000:A19), but the sparks flew over whose **conceptualization** of social health would prevail.

Prejudice is an interesting example of a concept whose meaning has changed over time. As Harvard psychologist Gordon Allport (1954) pointed out, during the 1950s many people conceptualized prejudice as referring to "faulty generalizations" about other groups. The idea was that these cognitive "errors in reasoning" could be improved with better education. But by the end of the 1960s, this one-size-fits-all concept was replaced with more specific terms such as *racism, sexism,* and *anti-Semitism* that were conceptualized as referring to negative dispositions about specific groups that "ran too deep to be accessible to cursory introspection" (Nunberg 2002:WK3). The *isms* were conceived as both more serious and less easily acknowledged than prejudice.

> **Conceptualization:** The process of specifying what we mean by a term. In deductive research, conceptualization helps translate portions of an abstract theory into specific variables that can be used in testable hypotheses. In inductive research, conceptualization is an important part of the process used to make sense of related observations.

Concepts such as social health, prejudice, and even binge drinking require an explicit definition before they are used in research because we cannot be certain that all readers will share a particular definition or that the current meaning of the concept is the same as it was when previous research was published. It is especially important to define clearly concepts that are abstract or unfamiliar. When we refer to concepts such as *social control, anomie,* or *social health,* we cannot count on others knowing exactly what we mean. Even experts may disagree about the meaning of frequently used concepts if they have based their conceptualizations on different theories. That's okay. The point is not that there can only be one definition of a concept but that we have to specify clearly what we mean when we use a concept, and we must expect others to do the same.

Conceptualization in Practice

If we are to do an adequate job of conceptualizing, we must do more than just think up some definition, any definition, for our concepts (Goertz 2006). We have to turn to social theory and prior research to review appropriate definitions. We need to identify what we think is important about the phenomenon that interests us. We should understand how the definition we choose fits within the theoretical framework guiding the research, and what assumptions underlie this framework. We may decide the concept has several dimensions, or subconcepts, that should be distinguished.

Substance Abuse

What observations or images should we associate with the concept *substance abuse?* Someone leaning against a building with a liquor bottle, barely able to speak coherently? College students drinking heavily at a party? Someone in an Alcoholics Anonymous group drinking one beer? A 10-year-old boy drinking a small glass of wine in an alley? A 10-year-old boy drinking a small glass of wine at the dinner table in France? Do all these images share something in common that we should define as substance abuse for the purposes of a particular research study? Do only some of them share something in common? Should we consider the cultural differences? Social situations? Physical tolerance for alcohol? Individual standards?

Many researchers now use the definition of *substance abuse* contained in the American Psychiatric Association's (2000) *Diagnostic and Statistical Manual of Mental Disorders, Text Revision (DSM-IV-TR):* "a maladaptive pattern of substance use manifested by recurrent and significant adverse consequences related to the repeated use of substances . . . must have occurred repeatedly during the same 12-month period or been persistent" (*DSM-IV-TR:* Substance Abuse Features section, p. 198). But, despite its popularity among professionals, we cannot judge the *DSM-IV-TR* definition of substance abuse as "correct" or "incorrect." Each researcher has the right to conceptualize as he or she sees fit. However, we can say that the *DSM-IV-TR* definition of substance abuse is useful, partly because it has been widely adopted. It is also stated in a clear and precise language that minimizes differences in interpretation and maximizes understanding.

This clarity should not prevent us from recognizing that the definition reflects a particular theoretical orientation. *DSM-IV-TR* applies a medical *disease model* to mental illness (which is conceptualized, in *DSM-IV-TR,* to include substance abuse). This theoretical model emphasizes behavioral and biological criteria instead of the social expectations that are emphasized in a social model of substance abuse. How we conceptualize reflects how we theorize.

Just as we can connect concepts to theory, we also can connect them to other concepts. What this means is that the definition of any one concept rests on a shared understanding of the other terms used in the definition. So if our audience does not already have a shared understanding of terms such as *significant adverse consequences* and *repeated use,* we must also define these terms before we are finished with the process of defining substance abuse.

Youth Gangs

Do you have a clear image in mind when you hear the term *youth gangs*? Although this is quite an ordinary term, social scientists' attempts to define precisely the concept, youth gang, have not yet succeeded: "Neither gang researchers nor law enforcement agencies can agree on a common definition . . . and a concerted national effort . . . failed to reach a consensus" (Howell 2003:75). You learned at the start of this chapter that the term has a different meaning in China. Exhibit 4.1 lists a few of the many alternative definitions of youth gangs.

What is the basis of this conceptual difficulty? Researcher James Howell (2003:27–28) suggests that defining the term *youth gangs* has been difficult for four reasons:

1. Youth gangs are not particularly cohesive.

2. Individual gangs change their focus over time.

3. Many have a "hodgepodge of features," with diverse members and unclear rules.

4. There are many incorrect but popular myths about youth gangs.

Exhibit 4.1 **Alternative Definitions of Youth Gangs**

The term gang tends to designate collectivities that are marginal members of mainstream society, loosely organized, and without a clear, social purpose. (Ball & Curry 1995:227)

The gang is an interstitial group (between childhood and maturity) originally formed spontaneously, and then integrated through conflict. (Thrasher 1927:18)

[A gang is] any denotable adolescent group of youngsters who (a) are generally perceived as a distinct aggregation by others in the neighborhood, (b) recognize themselves as a denotable group (almost invariably with a group name), and (c) have been involved in a sufficient number of delinquent incidents to call forth a consistently negative response from neighborhood residents and/or law enforcement agencies. (Klein 1971:13)

A youth gang is a self-formed association of peers united by mutual interests with identifiable leadership and internal organization who act collectively or as individuals to achieve specific purposes, including the conduct of illegal activity and control of a particular territory, facility, or enterprise. (Miller 1992:21)

[A gang is] an age-graded peer group that exhibits some permanence, engages in criminal activity, and has some symbolic representation of membership. (Decker & Van Winkle 1996:31)

[A gang is] a self-identified group of kids who act corporately, at least sometimes, and violently, at least sometimes. (Kennedy, Piehl, & Braga 1996:158)

A Criminal Street Gang is any ongoing organization, association, or group of three or more persons, whether formal or informal, having as one of its primary activities the commission of criminal acts. (Street Terrorism Enforcement and Prevention Act, 1988, California Penal Code sec. 186.22[f])

Source: Based on Howell 2003:76.

In addition, youth gangs are only one type of social group, and it is important to define *youth gangs* in a way that distinguishes them from these other types of groups, for example, childhood play groups, youth subculture groups, delinquent groups, and adult criminal organizations. You can think of *social group* as a broader concept that has multiple dimensions, one of which is youth gangs. In the same way, you can think of *substance abuse* as a concept with three dimensions: alcohol abuse, drug abuse, and polysubstance abuse. Whenever you define a concept, you need to consider whether the concept is unidimensional or multidimensional. If it is multidimensional, your job of conceptualization is not complete until you have specified the related subconcepts that belong under the umbrella of the larger concept (see Exhibit 4.2).

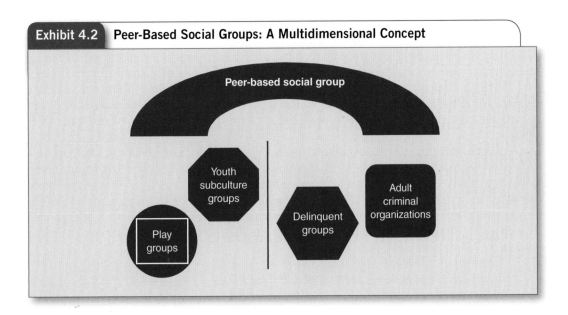

Exhibit 4.2 **Peer-Based Social Groups: A Multidimensional Concept**

Poverty

Decisions about how to define a concept reflect the theoretical framework that guides the researchers. For example, the concept *poverty* has always been somewhat controversial, because different conceptualizations of poverty lead to different estimates of its prevalence and different social policies for responding to it.

Most of the statistics that you see in the newspapers about the poverty rate in the United States reflect a conception of poverty that was formalized by Mollie Orshansky of the Social Security Administration in 1965 and subsequently adopted by the federal government and many researchers (Putnam 1977). She defined *poverty* in terms of what is called an *absolute* standard, based on the amount of money required to purchase an emergency diet that is estimated to be nutritionally adequate for about 2 months. The idea is that people are truly poor if they can just barely purchase the food they need and other essential goods. This poverty standard is adjusted for household size and composition (number of children and adults), and the minimal amount of money needed for food is multiplied by three because a 1955 survey indicated that poor families spend about one third of their incomes on food (Orshansky 1977).

Does this sound straightforward? As is often the case with important concepts, the meaning of an absolute poverty standard has been the focus of a vigorous debate (Eckholm 2006:A8). Although the traditional definition of absolute poverty only accounts for a family's cash income, some argue that noncash benefits that low-income people can receive, such as food stamps, housing subsidies, and tax rebates, should be added to cash income before the level of poverty is calculated. Douglas Besharov of the American Enterprise Institute terms this approach "a much needed corrective" (Eckholm 2006:A8). But some social scientists have proposed increasing the absolute standard for poverty so that it reflects what a low-income family must spend to maintain a "socially acceptable standard of living" that allows for a telephone, house repairs, and decent clothes (Uchitelle 1999). A new "Multidimensional Poverty Index" (MPI) to aid international comparisons considers absolute deprivations in health, education, and living standards (Alkire et al. 2011). Others argue that the persistence of poverty should be considered, so someone who is poor for no more than a year, for example, is distinguished from someone who is poor for many years (Walker, Tomlinson, & Williams 2010:367–368). Any change in the definition of poverty will change eligibility for government benefits such as food stamps and Medicaid, so the feelings about this concept run deep.

Some social scientists disagree altogether with the absolute standard and have instead urged adoption of a *relative* poverty standard (see Exhibit 4.3). They identify the poor as those in the lowest fifth or tenth of the income distribution or as those having some fraction of the average income. The idea behind this relative conception is that poverty should be defined in terms of what is normal in a given society at a particular time. "For example, while a car may be a luxury in some poor countries, in a country where most families own cars and public transportation is inadequate, a car is a basic necessity for finding and commuting to work" (Mayrl et al. 2004:10). This relative conception of poverty has largely been accepted in Europe (Walker et al. 2010:356). Using such a relative conception, the Luxembourg Income Study (LIS) has found considerable variation in poverty rates between 31 developed countries (see Exhibit 4.4), with the United States ranking 24th (Raphael 2013).

Some social scientists prefer yet another conception of poverty. With the *subjective* approach, *poverty* is defined as what people think would be the minimal income they need to make ends meet. Of course, many have argued that this approach is influenced too much by the different standards that people use to estimate what they "need" (Ruggles 1990:20–23). There is a parallel debate about the concept of "subjective well-being," which is now measured annually with responses (on a 10-point scale) to four questions in the United Kingdom by its Office of National Statistics (Venkatapuram 2013). The four questions are (Venkatapuram 2013:9):

1. Overall, how satisfied are you with your life nowadays?

2. Overall, to what extent do you feel the things you do in your life are worthwhile?

3. Overall, how happy did you feel yesterday?

4. Overall, how anxious did you feel yesterday?

Which do you think is a more reasonable approach to defining poverty: some type of absolute standard, a relative standard, or a subjective standard? Be careful here: Conceptualization has consequences! Research using the standard absolute concept of poverty indicated that the percentage of Americans in poverty declined by 1.7% in the 1990s, but use of a relative concept of poverty led to the conclusion that poverty increased by 2.7% (Mayrl et al. 2004:10). No matter which conceptualization we decide to adopt, our understanding of the concept of poverty will be sharpened after we consider these alternative definitions.

Trust

Take a look at Exhibit 4.5. It's a picture used by Pamela Paxton to illustrate the concept of *trust*. Do you see what it is about the picture that represents trust in other people? Have you ever thought about trust when you have left cash on a restaurant table and then walked away? Paxton (2005) defines the concept of trust with examples: "We trust others when we take a chance, yielding them some control over our money, secrets, safety, or other things we value" (p. 40).

She then distinguishes trust in people from trust in institutions. According to the survey data she reports, trust in people has been declining in the United States since the early 1960s, but there has not been an overall change in trust in institutions (Paxton 2005:41–44).

Exhibit 4.3   **Absolute, Relative, and Subjective Poverty Standards**

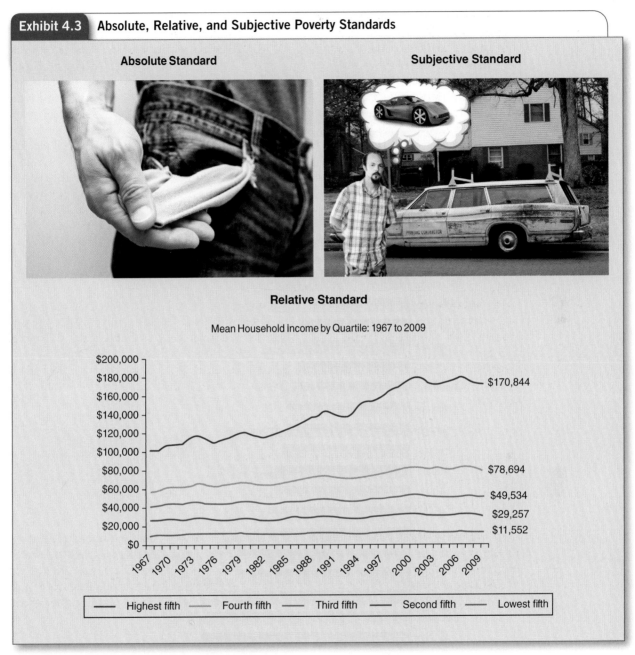

Absolute Standard

Subjective Standard

Relative Standard

Mean Household Income by Quartile: 1967 to 2009

— Highest fifth — Fourth fifth — Third fifth — Second fifth — Lowest fifth

Source: Based on Giovanni Vecchi, Universita di Roma "Tor Vergata," Poverty Lines. Bosnia and Herzegovina Poverty Analysis Workshop, September 17–21, 2007.

🔲 From Concepts to Indicators

Identifying the concepts we will study, specifying dimensions of these concepts, and defining their meaning only begin the process of connecting our ideas to concrete observations. If we are to conduct empirical research involving a concept, we must be able to distinguish it in the world around us and determine how it

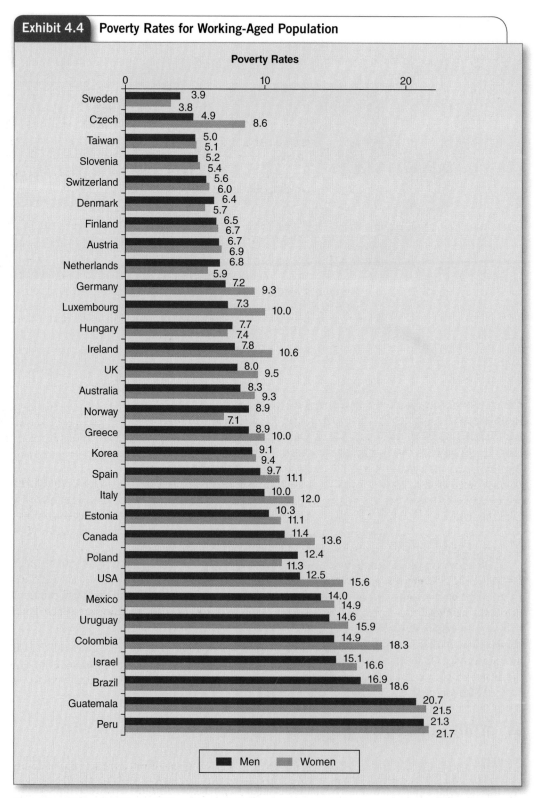

Exhibit 4.4 Poverty Rates for Working-Aged Population

Poverty Rates

Country	Men	Women
Sweden	3.9	3.8
Czech	4.9	8.6
Taiwan	5.0	5.1
Slovenia	5.2	5.4
Switzerland	5.6	6.0
Denmark	6.4	5.7
Finland	6.5	6.7
Austria	6.7	6.9
Netherlands	6.8	5.9
Germany	7.2	9.3
Luxembourg	7.3	10.0
Hungary	7.7	7.4
Ireland	7.8	10.6
UK	8.0	9.5
Australia	8.3	9.3
Norway	8.9	7.1
Greece	8.9	10.0
Korea	9.1	9.4
Spain	9.7	11.1
Italy	10.0	12.0
Estonia	10.3	11.1
Canada	11.4	13.6
Poland	12.4	11.3
USA	12.5	15.6
Mexico	14.0	14.9
Uruguay	14.6	15.9
Colombia	14.9	18.3
Israel	15.1	16.6
Brazil	16.9	18.6
Guatemala	20.7	21.5
Peru	21.3	21.7

Legend: ■ Men ■ Women

Source: Raphael, Dennis. 2013. "The Politics of Poverty: Definitions and Explanations." *Social Alternatives* 32:5–11. Figure 1. Reprinted with permission.

Research in the News

WHAT IS YOUR RACE?

In the 2010 census, 18 million Latinos checked "other" as their race after already checking HIspanic or Latino as their ethnicity. Census researchers and other social science researchers say the measurement error stems from fundamentally different concepts of race and ethnicity. Census data on race affects the makeup of voting districts for minority groups. The Census Bureau continues to alter its line of questioning, and critics argue for a new way of thinking.

For Further Thought

1. Is the conceptual distinction between race and ethnicity meaningful? Should it be maintained in the census and social science research?

2. Which approach would you recommend? Should social science researchers change their definitions of concepts to reflect popular usage or should they try to operationalize concepts so that respondents interpret them as desired by the researchers?

News source: Navarro, Mireya. 2012. "For Many Latinos, Racial Identity Is More Culture Than Color." *The New York Times,* January 14:A9.

---

may change over time or differ between persons or locations. **Operationalization** involves connecting concepts to measurement operations. You can think of it as the empirical counterpart of the process of conceptualization. When we conceptualize, we specify what we mean by a term (see Exhibit 4.6). When we operationalize, we identify specific measurements we will take to indicate that concept in empirical reality. Operationalization is the critical research step for those who identify with a positivist or postpositivist research philosophy (see Chapter 1): Through operationalization, researchers link the abstract ideas (concepts) in our heads to concrete indicators in the real world. Researchers also find that the process of figuring out how to measure a concept helps improve their understanding of what the concept means (Bartholomew 2010:457). Improving conceptualization and improving operationalization go hand in hand.

> **Operationalization:** The process of specifying the measures that will indicate the value of cases on a variable.

Exhibit 4.6 illustrates conceptualization and operationalization by using the concept of *social control,* which Donald Black (1984) defines as "all of the processes by which people define and respond to deviant behavior" (p. xi). What observations can indicate this conceptualization of social control? Billboards that condemn drunk driving? Proportion of persons arrested in a community? Average length of sentences for crimes? Types of bystander reactions to public intoxication? Gossiping among neighbors? Some combination of these? Should we distinguish formal social control such as laws and police actions from informal types of social control such as social stigma? If we are to conduct research on the concept of social control, we must identify empirical **indicators** that are pertinent to our theoretical concerns.

> **Indicator:** The question or other operation used to indicate the value of cases on a variable.

Abstract and Concrete Concepts

Concepts vary in their level of abstraction, and this, in turn, affects how readily we can specify the indicators pertaining to the concept. We may not think twice before we move from a conceptual definition of *age* as time elapsed since birth to the concrete indicator "years since birth." Binge drinking is also a relatively concrete concept, but it requires a bit more thought (see Exhibit 4.7). As you've seen, most researchers define *binge drinking*

Research|Social Impact Link
Variables

conceptually as heavy episodic drinking and operationally as drinking five or more drinks in a row (for men) (Wechsler et al. 2002:205). That's pretty straightforward, although we still need to specify the questions that will be used to determine the frequency of drinking.

An abstract concept such as *social status* may have a clear role in social theory but a variety of meanings in different social settings. Indicators that pertain to social status may include level of esteem in a group, extent of influence over others, level of income and education, or number of friends. It is very important to specify what we mean by an abstract concept such as social status in a particular study and to choose appropriate indicators to represent this meaning.

You have already learned in Chapter 2 that variables are phenomena that vary (and I hope you have practiced using the language of variables and hypotheses with the interactive exercises on the book's website). Where do variables fit in the continuum from concepts to operational indicators that is represented in Exhibit 4.6? Think of it this way: Usually, the term *variable* is used to refer to some specific aspect of a concept that varies, and for which we then have to select even more concrete indicators. For example, research on the *concept* of social support might focus on the *variable* level of perceived support, and we might then select as our *indicator* the responses to a series of statements about social support, such as this one from S. Cohen et al.'s (1985) social support index, the "Interpersonal Support Evaluation List": "If I needed a quick emergency loan of $100, there is someone I could get it from" (p. 93). Identifying the variables we will measure is a necessary step on the road to developing our specific measurement procedures. I give more examples in the next section.

The term *variable* is sometimes used interchangeably with the term *indicator,* however, so that you might find "crime rate" or "importance of extrinsic rewards" being termed as either variables or indicators. Sometimes the term *variable* is used to refer to phenomena that are more abstract, such as "alienation" or "social capital." You might hear one researcher referring to *social support* as one of the important concepts in a study, another referring to it as a variable that was measured, and another calling it an indicator of group cohesion. The important thing to keep in mind is that we need to define clearly the concepts we use and then develop specific procedures for identifying variation in the variables related to these concepts.

Exhibit 4.5 | Picturing Trust

Source: Adam Henerey.

Exhibit 4.6 | Conceptualization and Operationalization of Social Control

Concept	Definition	Types	Possible Operational Indicators
Social control	The normative aspect of social life[a]	Law	Legal rules; punishments; police stops
		Etiquette	Handbooks
		Customs	Gossip; aphorisms
		Bureaucracy	Official conduct rules; promotion procedures
		Psychiatric treatment	Rules for dangerousness; competency hearings

[a]Specifically, "the definition of deviant behavior and the response to it" (Black 1984:2).

Source: Based on Black, Donald. 1976. *The Behavior of Law.* New York: Academic Press.

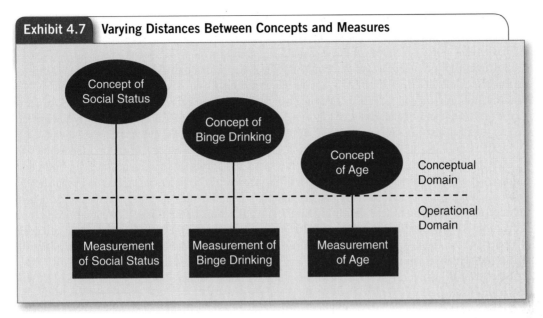

Exhibit 4.7   Varying Distances Between Concepts and Measures

Source: Adapted from Viswanathan 2005:7.

Bear in mind that concepts don't necessarily vary. For example, gender may be an important concept in a study of influences on binge drinking, but it isn't a variable in a study of members of a fraternity. When we explain excessive drinking in the fraternity, we might attach great importance to the all-male fraternity subculture. However, because gender doesn't vary in this setting, we won't be able to study differences in binge drinking between male and female students. So, gender will be a **constant**, not a variable, in this study (unless we expand our sample to include members of both sororities and fraternities, or perhaps the general student population).

> **Constant:** A number that has a fixed value in a given situation; a characteristic or value that does not change.

How do we know what concepts to consider and then which variables to include in a study? It's very tempting, and all too common, to try simply to measure everything by including in a study every variable we can think of that might have something to do with our research question. This haphazard approach will inevitably result in the collection of some data that are useless and the failure to collect some data that are important. Instead, a careful researcher will examine relevant theories to identify key concepts, review prior research to learn how useful different indicators have been, and assess the resources available for measuring adequately variables in the specific setting to be studied.

Operationalizing the Concept of Race

Race is an important concept in social research. In research applications as in everyday life, the concept of race is often treated as if it is an obvious distinction of several categories based on physical appearance (in turn related to ancestry). But in fact, what people mean by the concept of *race* has varied over time and differs between countries. These inconsistencies only become clear when we examine how the concept of race has been operationalized in specific questions.

Repeated changes in questions about race in the decennial U.S. Census reflect social and political pressures (Snipp 2003:565–567). Race was not assessed directly in the censuses of 1790, 1800, or 1810, but slaves and American Indians were distinguished from others. In 1820, 1830, and 1840, *color* was distinguished; then, as racial consciousness heightened before the Civil War, the 1850 census added the category of *Mulatto* to identify people of mixed-race parentage. In response to concerns with increasing immigration, *Chinese* and *Indian* (Asian) persons were distinguished in 1860 and then *Japanese* was added to the list in 1870. In the 1890 census,

Octoroons and *Quadroons* were distinguished as different categories of Mulatto. The infamous 1896 U.S. Supreme Court decision, *Plessy v. Ferguson,* reflected the victory of "Jim Crow" legislation in the South and defined as black any person who had as much as one black ancestor. (Homer Plessy was a Louisiana shoemaker whose skin was white, but he was told he could not ride in the "whites only" section of the train because he had one black ancestor.) By 1920, the U.S. Census reflected this absolute distinction between persons judged black and white by dropping the distinctions involving mixed-race ancestry. In 1930 and 1940, *Mexican* was distinguished, but in 1950 political pressure led to dropping this category as an ethnic minority and instead treating Mexicans as *white* (Snipp 2003:568–569).

By the late 1950s, the civil rights movement began to influence the concept of race as used by the U.S. Census. In 1960, the census shifted from assessing race on the basis of physical appearance to self-identification (Snipp 2003:569–570). As one result, the number of people identified as American Indians rose dramatically. More important, this shift reflected a change in thinking about the concept of race as reflecting primarily physical appearance and instead indicating cultural identification. In the 1970s, the Federal Interagency Committee on Education (FICE) established an ad hoc committee that led the 1980 U.S. Census (and all federal agencies) to use a five-category distinction: (1) American Indians and Alaska Natives, (2) Asians and Pacific Islanders, (3) non-Hispanic blacks, (4) non-Hispanic whites, and (5) Hispanics (Snipp 2003:572–574). In that census, Spanish/Hispanic origin or descent was asked as a question distinct from the question about race (U.S. Census Bureau 1981:3).

But the new concept of race reflected in these five categories only led to new complaints. Some parents in "mixed-race" marriages insisted that they should be able to classify their children as multiracial (Snipp 2003:575–576)—in opposition to some civil rights leaders concerned with diluting the numbers of Americans designated as black (Holmes 2001b:WK 1). The chair of the Census Bureau's Hispanic advisory committee complained, "We don't fit into the categories that the Anglos want us to fit in" (Swarns 2004:A18). Sociologist Orlando Patterson (1997) and many others argued that the concept of ethnicity was more meaningful than race. As a result of these and other complaints, a new federal task force developed a new approach that allowed respondents to designate themselves as being of more than one race. The resulting question about race reflected these changes as well as increasing distinctions within what had been the Asians and Pacific Islanders category (Exhibit 4.8). An official census report after the 2010 census also included this caveat about the definition:

> The race categories included in the census questionnaire generally reflect a social definition of race recognized in this country and are not an attempt to define race biologically, anthropologically, or genetically. In addition, it is recognized that the categories of the race question include race and national origin or sociocultural groups. (Humes, Jones, & Ramirez 2011:2).

With this new procedure in the 2010 U.S. Census, 36.7% of the country's 50.5 million Latinos classified themselves as "some other race"—neither white nor black; they wrote in such terms as *Mayan, Tejano,* and *mestizo* to indicate their own preferred self-identification, using terms that focused on what social scientists term *ethnic* rather than on racial differences. In that same census, 3% of Americans identified themselves as multiracial (Humes et al. 2011). But this does not solve the problem of defining the concept of race. When David Harris and Jeremiah Sim (2002) analyzed responses in a national study of youths, they found that racial self-classification can vary with social context: 6.8% of youths classified themselves as multiracial when asked at school, but only 3.6% did so when asked at home. Even the presence of a parent during the in-home interview had an effect: Youths were less likely to self-identify as multiracial, rather than monoracial, in the presence of a parent. As already mentioned, more than a third of those who identified themselves as Hispanic declined to also classify themselves as white or black and instead checked "some other race." Some Arab American groups have now also asked for a special category (Vega 2014:A16).

The concept of race also varies internationally, so any research involving persons in or from other countries may need to use a different definition of race. For example, Darryl Fears, former director of the Brazilian American Cultural Institute (in Washington, D.C.), explains how social conventions differ in Brazil: "In this

Video Link
Operationalization

Exhibit 4.8	The U.S. Census Bureau Ethnicity and Race Questions

→ **NOTE: Please answer BOTH Question 8 about Hispanic origin and Question 9 about race. For this census, Hispanic origins are not races.**

8. Is Person 1 of Hispanic, Latino, or Spanish origin?

☐ **No,** not of Hispanic, Latino, or Spanish origin
☐ Yes, Mexican, Mexican Am., Chicano
☐ Yes, Puerto Rican
☐ Yes, Cuban
☐ Yes, another Hispanic, Latino, or Spanish origin — *Print origin, for example, Argentinean, Colombian, Dominican, Nicaraguan, Salvadoran, Spaniard, and so on.* ↗

[   ]

9. What is Person 1's race? *Mark* ⊠ *one or more boxes.*

☐ White
☐ Black, African Am., or Negro
☐ American Indian or Alaska Native — *Print name of enrolled or principal tribe.* ↗

[   ]

☐ Asian Indian   ☐ Japanese   ☐ Native Hawaiian
☐ Chinese   ☐ Korean   ☐ Guamanian or Chamorro
☐ Filipino   ☐ Vietnamese   ☐ Samoan
☐ Other Asian — *Print race, for example, Hmong, Laotian, Thai, Pakistani, Cambodian, and so on.* ↗   ☐ Other Pacific Islander — *Print race, for example, Fijian, Tongan, and so on.* ↗

[   ]

☐ Some other race — *Print race.* ↗

[   ]

→ **If more people were counted in Question 1, continue with Person 2.**

Source: U.S. Census Bureau, 2010 Census Questionnaire.

country, if you are not quite white, then you are black." But in Brazil, "If you are not quite black, then you are white" (Fears 2002:A3). In Mexico, the primary ethnic distinction is between indigenous and nonindigenous residents, without a clear system of categorization based on skin color. Nonetheless, survey research indicates a marked preference for whiter skin and "profound social stratification by skin color" (Villarreal 2010:671). The conception and operationalization of race, then, varies with place.

Operationalizing the Concept of Intimate Partner Violence

Congressional hearings from 1990 to 1994 made it clear to members of the U.S. Congress that violence against women is a widespread problem, but raised "concerns that current crime statistics do not provide a full assessment of the problem" (Larence 2006:1). The concerns resulted from the discovery that there was little consistency across agencies in the operationalization of intimate partner violence. Congress thus mandated a study by the Government Accountability Office (GAO) to review the concept and the ways it has been operationalized and to suggest a consistent approach.

The GAO (U.S. GAO 2006) soon realized that sometimes intimate partner violence was measured in terms of *incidence*—"the number of separate times a crime is committed against individuals during a specific time period" and sometimes in terms of *prevalence*—"the unique number of individuals who were victimized during a specific time period" (p. 26). The GAO concluded that both approaches to measuring intimate partner violence should be collected. The GAO (2006:31) also found inconsistency in the inclusion of perpetrator intentionality: The Centers for Disease Control and Prevention (CDC) required that the violence be intentional, whereas the questions used to measure intimate partner violence in the Victimization of Children and Youth Survey did not address intentionality. As a result, the GAO (2006) concluded,

> Without comparable information, including both reported and unreported incidents, it is not possible to combine prevalence estimates from national data collection efforts, and these efforts likely underestimate the prevalence of these categories of crime. Policy formulation and resource allocation could therefore be misdirected. (p. 42)

Assistant Secretary of Health and Human Services Vincent J. Ventimiglia reviewed the GAO report and wrote a letter to the GAO concurring with its conclusions and promising to help the Department of Justice to resolve this problem in operationalization. As Ventimiglia observed,

> Although definitions may be similar, if different operationalizations and measures are used, the result could be that survey questions will be different and, if so, prevalence estimates could not be combined across those studies. (cited in Larence 2006:53)

Although the process of achieving consistency in operationalizing intimate partner violence will not be completed quickly, the operational definition of *intimate partner violence* in the National Violence Against Women survey provides a good example of a useful approach:

> Intimate partner violence . . . includes rape, physical assault, and stalking perpetrated by current and former dates, spouses, and cohabiting partners, with cohabiting meaning living together at least some of the time as a couple. Both same-sex and opposite-sex cohabitants are included in the definition. (Tjaden & Thoennes 2000:5)

Operationalizing Social Network Position

The concept of a social network has an intuitive appeal for sociological analysis because it focuses attention on the relationships between people that are the foundation of larger social structures (Scott 2013:5). Since Émile Durkheim's study of forms of solidarity, sociologists have been concerned with the nature of ties between people, how they differ between groups and societies, and how they affect social behavior. Social network analyses begin by operationalizing aspects of social network position. For example, in their Teenage Health in Schools study of 3,146 adolescents in nine schools in western Scotland, Michael Pearson and his colleagues (2006) distinguished a number of sociometric positions. They distinguished some adolescents as participating in large or small groups, some who were isolated or participated in only a relationship dyad, and some as peripheral to others (Pearson et al. 2006:522). Exhibit 4.9 shows how some of these sociometric differences could be represented in diagrams, as well as how egalitarian and more hierarchical groups could be distinguished. A diagram like this can almost let you "feel the pain" of the adolescents who are peripheral or isolated compared with those who are involved in interlinked connections to their peers in social groups. In this way, social network analysis helps to understand individuals within their social context.

Adolescents' sociometric position could be distinguished in their schools as involving membership in large or small groups, being peripheral to existing groups, or being less socially connected in positions labeled as "tree," "dyad," or "isolate." Pearson and his colleagues (2006:524) also operationalized the concept of social network position with measures of popularity—the number of other youth who listed a student as a

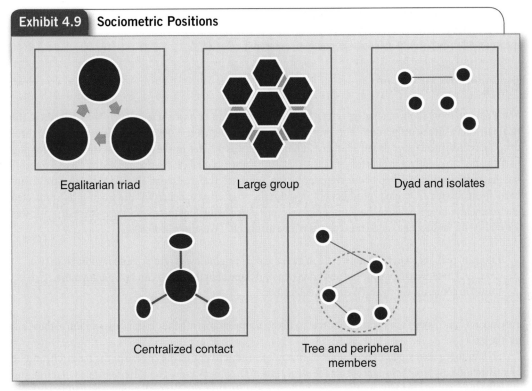

Exhibit 4.9 **Sociometric Positions**

Egalitarian triad   Large group   Dyad and isolates

Centralized contact   Tree and peripheral members

Source: Based on Pearson, Michael, Helen Sweeting, Patrick West, Robert Young, Jacki Gordon, and Katrina Turner. 2006. "Adolescent Substance Use in Different Social and Peer Contexts: A Social Network Analysis." *Drugs: Education, Prevention and Policy* 13:519–536.

friend—and expansiveness—the number of other youth with whom a student said they were best friends. One important finding was that youth in large groups were least likely to smoke or use drugs (Pearson et al. 2006:532). In another study of youth social networks, Susan Ennett and her colleagues (2006) also found that youth who were more embedded in school social networks were less likely to abuse substances.

Other aspects of the concept of social network position that have been operationalized in research include frequency—the number of contacts; strength—feelings that the tie is intimate, special, and mutual and that frequent interactions are desirable; multiplexity—multiple-role relations between two individuals; similarity—the correspondence of ego and alter characteristics; and source—whether the alter to whom ego is tied is a friend, kin, staff, or other (Walker, Wasserman, & Wellman 1993; Wasserman & Faust, 1994). Several of these social network position indicators are associated with better mental health (Wellman & Wortley 1990).

From Observations to Concepts

Qualitative research projects usually take an inductive approach to the process of conceptualization. In an inductive approach, concepts emerge from the process of thinking about what has been observed, compared with the deductive approach that I have just described, in which we develop concepts on the basis of theory and then decide what should be observed to indicate that concept. So instead of deciding in advance which concepts are important for a study, what these concepts mean, and how they should be measured, if you take an inductive approach, you will begin by recording verbatim what you hear in intensive interviews or see during observational sessions. You will then review this material to identify important concepts and their meaning for participants. At this point, you may also identify relevant variables and develop procedures for indicating variation between participants and settings or variation over time. As your understanding of the participants and social processes develops, you may refine your concepts and modify your indicators. The sharp boundaries in quantitative research between developing measures, collecting data with those measures, and evaluating the measures often do not exist in inductive, qualitative research.

Being "In" and "Out"

You will learn more about qualitative research in Chapter 9, but an example here will help you understand the qualitative measurement approach. For several months, Darin Weinberg (2000) observed participants in three drug abuse treatment programs in Southern California. He was puzzled by the drug abuse treatment program participants' apparently contradictory beliefs—that drug abuse is a medical disease marked by "loss of control" but that participation in a therapeutic community can be an effective treatment. He discovered that treatment participants shared an "ecology of addiction" in which they conceived of being "in" the program as a protected environment, whereas being in the community was considered being "out there" in a place where drug use was inevitable—in "a space one's addiction compelled one to inhabit" (Weinberg 2000:609).

> I'm doin' real, real bad right now. . . . I'm havin' trouble right now staying clean for more than two days. . . . I hate myself for goin' out and I don't know if there's anything that can save me anymore. . . . I think I'm gonna die out there. (Weinberg 2000:609)

Participants contrasted their conscientiousness while in the program with the personal dissolution of those out in "the life."

So Weinberg developed the concepts of *in* and *out* inductively, in the course of the research, and he identified indicators of these concepts at the same time in the observational text. He continued to refine and evaluate the concepts throughout the research. Conceptualization, operationalization, and validation were ongoing and interrelated processes. We'll study this process in more detail in Chapter 10.

Diversity

Qualitative research techniques may also be used to explore the meaning of a concept. For example, everybody uses the term *diversity*, but Joyce Bell and Douglas Hartmann (2007) designed a qualitative interview project to find out "what are Americans really saying about diversity? How do they understand and experience it?" In 166 interviews, the researchers uncovered a complex pattern. Most respondents initially gave optimistic interpretations of diversity: It "makes life more fun" or "more exciting" (Bell & Hartmann 2007:899). However, many respondents went on to add a more pessimistic view: "If you have too much diversity, then you have to change the Constitution, you have to take down the Statue of Liberty, you have to take down those things that set this country up as it is" (Bell & Hartmann 2007:901).

Bell and Hartmann (2007:911) concluded that the term *diversity* is often used to avoid considering the implications of social inequality—that the concept of diversity supports "happy talk" that obscures social divisions. So their understanding of the concept of diversity changed as a result of the evidence they collected. What is *your* concept of diversity?

> **Measurement:** The process of linking abstract concepts to empirical indicants.

🔲 Measurement

The deductive researcher proceeds from defining concepts in the abstract (conceptualizing) to identifying variables to measure, and finally to developing specific measurement procedures. **Measurement** is the "process of linking abstract concepts to empirical indicants" (Carmines & Zeller 1979:10). The goal is to achieve measurement validity, so the measures, or indicators, must actually measure the variables they are intended to measure.

Exhibit 4.10 represents the operationalization process in three studies. The first researcher defines her concept, binge drinking, and chooses one variable—frequency of heavy episodic drinking—to represent it. This variable is then measured with responses to a single question, or indicator: "How often within the past 2 weeks did you consume five or more drinks containing alcohol in a row?" Because "heavy" drinking is defined differently for men and women (relative to their different metabolism), the question is phrased in terms of "four or more drinks" for women. The second researcher defines her concept, poverty, as having two aspects or dimensions: subjective poverty and absolute poverty. Subjective poverty is measured with responses to a survey question: "Would you say you are poor?" Absolute poverty is measured by comparing family income to the poverty threshold. The third researcher decides that her concept, socioeconomic status, is defined by a position on three measured variables: income, education, and occupational prestige.

Social researchers have many options for operationalizing concepts. Measures can be based on activities as diverse as asking people questions, reading judicial opinions, observing social interactions, coding words in books, checking census data tapes, enumerating the contents of trash receptacles, or drawing urine and blood samples. Experimental researchers may operationalize a concept by manipulating its value. For example, to operationalize the concept of *exposure to antidrinking messages,* some subjects may listen to a talk about binge drinking while others do not. I will focus here on the operations of asking questions, observing behavior, using unobtrusive means of measuring people's behavior and attitudes, and using published data.

The variables and particular measurement operations chosen for a study should be consistent with the research question. If we ask the evaluative research question "Are self-help groups more effective than hospital-based treatments in reducing drinking among substance abusers?," we may operationalize "form of treatment" in terms of participation in these two types of treatments. However, if we are attempting to answer the explanatory research question "What influences the success of substance abuse treatment?," we should probably consider what it is about these treatment alternatives that is associated with successful abstinence. Prior theory

Researcher Interview Link
Measurement

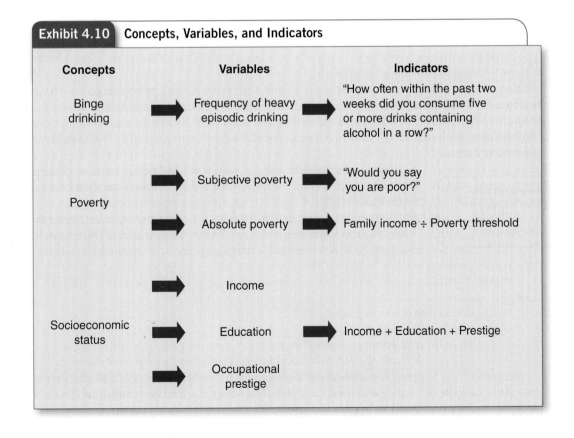

Exhibit 4.10 Concepts, Variables, and Indicators

and research suggest that some of the important variables that differ between these treatment approaches are level of peer support, beliefs about the causes of alcoholism, and financial investment in the treatment.

Time and resource limitations must also be considered when we select variables and devise measurement operations. For many sociohistorical questions (e.g., "How has the poverty rate varied since 1950?"), census data or other published counts must be used. However, a historical question about the types of social bonds among combat troops in 20th-century wars probably requires retrospective interviews with surviving veterans. The validity of the data is lessened by the unavailability of many veterans from World War I and by problems of recall, but direct observation of their behavior during the war is certainly not an option.

Constructing Questions

Asking people questions is the most common and probably the most versatile operation for measuring social variables. Most concepts about individuals can be defined in such a way that measurement with one or more questions becomes an option. We associate questions with survey research, but questions are also often the basis of measures used in social experiments and in qualitative research. In this section, I introduce some options for writing single questions; in Chapter 8, I explain why single questions can be inadequate measures of some concepts, and then I examine measurement approaches that rely on multiple questions to measure a concept.

Of course, even though questions are, in principle, a straightforward and efficient means to measure individual characteristics, facts about events, level of knowledge, and opinions of any sort, they can easily result in misleading or inappropriate answers. Memories and perceptions of the events about which we might like to ask can be limited, and some respondents may intentionally give misleading answers. For these reasons, all questions proposed for a study must be screened carefully for their adherence to basic guidelines and then tested and revised until the researcher feels some confidence that they will be clear to the intended respondents and likely to measure the intended concept (Fowler 1995). Alternative measurement approaches will be needed when such confidence cannot be achieved.

Specific guidelines for reviewing survey questions are presented in Chapter 8; here, my focus is on the different types of questions used in social research.

Measuring variables with single questions is very popular. Public opinion polls based on answers to single questions are reported frequently in newspaper articles and TV newscasts: "Do you favor or oppose U.S. policy . . . ?" "If you had to vote today, for which candidate would you vote?" Social science surveys also rely on single questions to measure many variables: "Overall, how satisfied are you with your job?" "How would you rate your current health?"

> **Closed-ended (fixed-choice) question:** A survey question that provides preformatted response choices for the respondent to circle or check.

Single questions can be designed with or without explicit response choices. The question that follows is a **closed-ended (fixed-choice) question** because respondents are offered explicit responses from which to choose. It has been selected from the Core Alcohol and Drug Survey distributed by the Core Institute, Southern Illinois University, for the Fund for the Improvement of Postsecondary Education (FIPSE) Core Analysis Grantee Group (Presley, Meilman, & Lyerla 1994):

Compared to other campuses with which you are familiar, this campus's use of alcohol is . . . (Mark one)

_____ Greater than other campuses

_____ Less than other campuses

_____ About the same as other campuses

Most surveys of a large number of people contain primarily fixed-choice questions, which are easy to process with computers and analyze with statistics. With fixed-choice questions, respondents are also more likely to answer the questions that the researcher really wants them to answer. Including response choices reduces ambiguity and makes it easier for respondents to answer. However, fixed-response choices can obscure what people really think if the choices do not match the range of possible responses to the question; many studies show that some respondents will choose response choices that do not apply to them simply to give some sort of answer (Peterson 2000:39).

Most important, response choices should be **mutually exclusive** and **exhaustive**, so that every respondent can find one and only one choice that applies to him or her (unless the question is of the "Check all that apply" format). To make response choices exhaustive, researchers may need to offer at least one option with room for ambiguity. For example, a questionnaire asking college students to indicate their school status should not use freshman, sophomore, junior, senior, and graduate student as the only response choices. Most campuses also have students in a "special" category, so you might add "Other (please specify)" to the five fixed responses to this question. If respondents do not find a response option that corresponds to their answer to the question, they may skip the question entirely or choose a response option that does not indicate what they are really thinking.

Mutually exclusive: A question's response choices are mutually exclusive when every case can be classified as having only one attribute (or value).

Exhaustive: A question's response choices are exhaustive when they cover all possible responses.

Open-ended questions, questions without explicit response choices, to which respondents write in their answers, are preferable when the range of responses cannot adequately be anticipated—namely, questions that have not previously been used in surveys and questions that are asked of new groups. Open-ended questions can also lessen confusion about the meaning of responses involving complex concepts. The next question is an open-ended version of the earlier fixed-choice question:

Open-ended question: A survey question to which the respondent replies in his or her own words, either by writing or by talking.

> How would you say alcohol use on this campus compares with that on other campuses?

In qualitative research, open-ended questions are often used to explore the meaning respondents give to abstract concepts. *Mental illness,* for example, is a complex concept that tends to have different meanings for different people. In a survey I conducted in homeless shelters, I asked the staff members whether they believed that people at the shelter had become homeless because of mental illness (Schutt 1992). When given fixed-response choices, 47% chose "Agree" or "Strongly agree." However, when these same staff members were interviewed in depth, with open-ended questions, it became clear that the meaning of these responses varied among staff members. Some believed that mental illness caused homelessness by making people vulnerable in the face of bad luck and insufficient resources:

> Mental illness [is the cause]. Just watching them, my heart goes out to them. Whatever the circumstances were that were in their lives that led them to the streets and being homeless I see it as very sad. . . . Maybe the resources weren't there for them, or maybe they didn't have the capabilities to know when the resources were there. It is misfortune. (Schutt 1992:7)

Other staff believed that mental illness caused people to reject housing opportunities:

> I believe because of their mental illness that's why they are homeless. So for them to say I would rather live on the street than live in a house and have to pay rent, I mean that to me indicates that they are mentally ill. (Schutt 1992:7)

Just like fixed-choice questions, open-ended questions should be reviewed carefully for clarity before they are used. For example, if respondents are just asked, "When did you move to Boston?" they might respond with a wide range of answers: "In 1944." "After I had my first child." "When I was 10." "Twenty years ago." Such answers would be very hard to compile. A careful review should identify potential ambiguity. To avoid it, rephrase the question to guide the answer in a certain direction, such as "In what year did you move to Boston?" or provide explicit response choices (Center for Survey Research 1987).

The decision to use closed-ended or open-ended questions can have important consequences for the information reported. Leaving an attitude or behavior off a fixed set of response choices is likely to mean that it is not reported, even if an "other" category is provided. However, any attitude or behavior is less likely to be reported if it must be volunteered in response to an open-ended question (Schwarz 2010:48).

Making Observations

Observations can be used to measure characteristics of individuals, events, and places. The observations may be the primary form of measurement in a study, or they may supplement measures obtained through questioning.

Direct observations can be used as indicators of some concepts. For example, Albert Reiss (1971a) studied police interaction with the public by riding in police squad cars, observing police–citizen interactions, and recording their characteristics on a form. Notations on the form indicated variables such as how many police–citizen contacts occurred, who initiated the contacts, how compliant citizens were with police directives, and whether police expressed hostility toward the citizens.

Using a different approach, psychologists Dore Butler and Florence Geis (1990) studied unconscious biases and stereotypes that they thought might hinder the advancement of women and minorities in work organizations. In one experiment, discussion groups of male and female students were observed from behind one-way mirrors as group leaders presented identical talks to each group. The trained observers (who were not told what the study was about) rated the number of frowns, furrowed brows, smiles, and nods of approval as the group leaders spoke. (The leaders themselves did not know what the study was about.) Group participants made disapproving expressions, such as frowns, more often when the group leader was a woman than when the leader was a man. To make matters worse, the more the women talked, the less attention they were given. Butler and Geis concluded that there was indeed a basis for discrimination in these unconscious biases..

Psychologists Joshua Correll, Bernadette Park, Charles Judd, and Bernd Wittenbrink (2002) used an even more creative approach to measure unconscious biases that could influence behavior despite an absence of conscious prejudice. Their approach focused on measuring reaction times to controlled observations. Correll et al. (2002) constructed a test in which individuals played a video game that required them to make a split-second decision of whether to shoot an image of a person who was holding what was a gun in some pictures and a nonlethal object such as a camera, cell phone, or bottle in others. In this ambiguous situation, white respondents were somewhat more likely to shoot a black man holding a nonlethal object than they were to shoot a white man holding a nonlethal object.

Observations may also supplement data collected in an interview study. This approach was used in a study of homeless persons participating in the Center for Mental Health Services' Access to Community Care and Effective Services and Supports (ACCESS) program. After a 47-question interview, interviewers were asked to record observations that would help indicate whether the respondent was suffering from a major mental illness. For example, the interviewers indicated, on a rating scale from 0 to 4, the degree to which the homeless participants appeared to be responding, during the interview, to voices or noises that others couldn't hear or to other private experiences (U.S. Department of Health and Human Services 1995).

Many interviews contain at least a few observational questions. Clinical studies often request a *global*, or holistic, interviewer rating of clients, based on observations and responses to questions throughout the interview. One such instrument is called the Global Assessment of Functioning Scale (American Psychiatric Association 1994).

Direct observation is often the method of choice for measuring behavior in natural settings, as long as it is possible to make the requisite observations. Direct observation avoids the problems of poor recall and self-serving distortions that can occur with answers to survey questions. It also allows measurement in a context that is more natural than an interview. But observations can be distorted, too. Observers do not see or hear everything, and what they do see is filtered by their own senses and perspectives. Disagreements about crowd size among protestors, police, and journalists are notorious, even though there is a good method of estimating crowd size based on the "carrying capacity" of public spaces (McPhail & McCarthy 2004). When the goal is to observe behavior, measurement can be distorted because the presence of an observer may cause people to act differently than the way they would otherwise (Emerson 1983). I discuss these issues in more depth in Chapters 10 and 11, but it is important to consider them whenever you read about observational measures.

Collecting Unobtrusive Measures

Unobtrusive measures allow us to collect data about individuals or groups without their direct knowledge or participation. In their classic book (now revised), Eugene Webb and his colleagues (2000) identified four types of unobtrusive measures: physical trace evidence, archives (available data), simple observation, and contrived observation (using hidden recording hardware or manipulation to elicit a response). We have already considered observational data and we will consider available data (from "archives") in the next section, so I focus here on the other approaches suggested by Webb et al. (2000).

> **Unobtrusive measure:** A measurement based on physical traces or other data that are collected without the knowledge or participation of the individuals or groups that generated the data.

The physical traces of past behavior are one type of unobtrusive measure that is most useful when the behavior of interest cannot be directly observed (perhaps because it is hidden or occurred in the past) and has not been recorded in a source of available data. To measure the prevalence of drinking in college dorms or fraternity houses, we might count the number of empty bottles of alcoholic beverages in the surrounding dumpsters. Student interest in the college courses they are taking might be measured by counting the number of times that books left on reserve as optional reading are checked out or by the number of class handouts left in trash barrels outside a lecture hall. Webb and his colleagues (2000:37) suggested measuring the interest in museum exhibits by the frequency with which tiles in front of the exhibits needed to be replaced. Social variables can also be measured by observing clothing, hair length, or people's reactions to such stimuli as dropped letters or jaywalkers.

You can probably see that care must be taken to develop trace measures that are useful for comparative purposes. For instance, comparison of the number of empty bottles in dumpsters outside different dorms can be misleading; at the very least, you would need to account for the number of residents in the dorms, the time since the last trash collection, and the accessibility of each dumpster to passersby. Counts of usage of books on reserve will only be useful if you consider how many copies of the books are on reserve for the course, how many students are enrolled in the course, and whether reserve reading is required. Measures of tile erosion in the museum must account for the nearness of each exhibit to doors, other popular exhibits, and so on (Webb et al. 2000:47–48).

Using Available Data

Government reports are rich and readily accessible sources of social science data. Organizations ranging from nonprofit service groups to private businesses also compile a wealth of figures that may be available to some social scientists for some purposes. In addition, the data collected in many social science surveys are archived and made available for researchers who were not involved in the original survey project.

Before we assume that available data will be useful, we must consider how appropriate they are for our concepts of interest. We may conclude that some other measure would provide a better fit with a concept or that a particular concept simply cannot be adequately operationalized with the available data. For example, law enforcement and health statistics provide several community-level indicators of substance abuse (Gruenewald et al. 1997). Statistics on arrests for the sale and possession of drugs, drunk driving arrests, and liquor law violations (such as sales to minors) can usually be obtained on an annual basis, and often quarterly, from local police departments or state crime information centers. Health-related indicators of substance abuse at the community level include single-vehicle fatal crashes, the rate of mortality from alcohol or drug abuse, and the use of alcohol and drug treatment services.

Indicators such as these cannot be compared across communities or over time without reviewing carefully how they were constructed. The level of alcohol in the blood that is legally required to establish intoxication can vary among communities, creating the appearance of different rates of substance abuse even though drinking and driving practices may be identical. Enforcement practices can vary among police jurisdictions and over time (Gruenewald et al. 1997:14).

We also cannot assume that available data are accurate, even when they appear to measure the concept in which we are interested in a way that is consistent across communities. "Official" counts of homeless persons have been notoriously unreliable because of the difficulty in locating homeless persons on the streets, and government agencies have, at times, resorted to "guesstimates" by service providers (Rossi 1989). Even available data for such seemingly straightforward measures as counts of organizations can contain a surprising amount of error. For example, a 1990 national church directory reported 128 churches in a midwestern U.S. county; an intensive search in that county in 1992 located 172 churches (Hadaway, Marler, & Chaves 1993:744). Perhaps 30% or 40% of death certificates identify incorrectly the cause of death (Altman 1998).

Government statistics that are generated through a central agency such as the U.S. Census Bureau are often of high quality, but caution is warranted when using official data collected by local levels of government. For example, the Uniform Crime Reports (UCR) program administered by the Federal Bureau of Investigation (FBI) imposes standard classification criteria, with explicit guidelines and regular training at the local level, but data are still inconsistent for many crimes. Consider only a few of the many sources of inconsistency between jurisdictions: Variation in the classification of forcible rape cases due to differences in what is considered to be "carnal knowledge of a female"; different decisions about what is considered "more than necessary force" in the definition of "strong-arm" robberies; whether offenses in which threats were made but no physical injury occurred are classified as aggravated or simple assaults (Mosher, Miethe, & Phillips 2002:66). A new National Incident-Based Reporting System (NIBRS) corrects some of the problems with the UCR, but it requires much more training and documentation and has not yet been widely used (Mosher et al. 2002:70).

In some cases, problems with an available indicator can be lessened by selecting a more precise indicator. For example, the number of single-vehicle nighttime crashes, whether fatal or not, is a more specific indicator of the frequency of drinking and driving than is just the number of single-vehicle fatal accidents (Gruenewald et al. 1997:40–41). Focusing on a different level of aggregation may also improve data quality, because procedures for data collection may differ between cities, counties, states, and so on (Gruenewald et al. 1997:40–41). Only after factors such as legal standards, enforcement practices, and measurement procedures have been accounted for do comparisons between communities become credible.

Coding Content

Unobtrusive measures can also be created from diverse forms of media such as newspaper archives or magazine articles, TV or radio talk shows, legal opinions, historical documents, personal letters, or e-mail messages. Qualitative researchers may read and evaluate text, as Sally Lindsay and her colleagues (2007) did in their study of computer-mediated social support for people with diabetes (see Chapter 1). Quantitative researchers use content analysis to measure aspects of media such as the frequency of use of particular words or ideas or the consistency with which authors convey a particular message in their stories. An investigation of the drinking climate on campuses might include a count of the amount of space devoted to ads for alcoholic beverages in a sample of issues of the student newspaper. Campus publications also might be coded to indicate the number of times that statements discouraging substance abuse appear. With this tool, you could measure the frequency of articles reporting substance abuse–related crimes, the degree of approval of drinking expressed in TV shows or songs, or the relationship between region of the country and the amount of space devoted in the print media to drug usage.

Taking Pictures

Photographs record individual characteristics and social events, so they can become an important tool for investigating the social world. In recent years, photography has become a much more common part of the social world, as cameras embedded in cell phones and the use of websites and social media encourage taking and sharing photos.

Sociologists and other social scientists are increasingly using photos as indicators of peoples' orientations in other times and places, as clues to the perspectives of the photographers themselves (Tinkler 2013:15).

Exhibit 4.11 displays a photo of two Ukrainian women embroidering traditional Ukrainian Easter towels, but they are doing so while sitting on a park bench in Italy where they are domestic live-in workers. Olena Fedyuk (2012) included the picture in her analysis of photos exchanged by Ukrainian domestic workers in Italy with their family members who remained in Ukraine. Fedyuk concludes that pictures like these help convey the reassuring message to their families that these women are still focused on their home country and family and are not engaged in Italian social life.

Combining Measurement Operations

Asking questions, making observations, using unobtrusive indicators, including available data or coding content, and taking pictures are interrelated measurement tools, each of which may include or be supplemented by the others. From people's answers to survey questions, the U.S. Census Bureau develops widely consulted census reports containing available data on people, firms, and geographic units in the United States. Data from employee surveys may be supplemented by information available in company records. Interviewers may record observations about those whom they question. Researchers may use insights gleaned from questioning participants to make sense of the social interaction they have observed. Unobtrusive indicators can be used to evaluate the honesty of survey respondents.

The available resources and opportunities often determine the choice of a particular measurement method, but measurement is improved if this choice also accounts for the particular concept or concepts to be measured. Responses to questions such as "How socially engaged were you at the party?" or "How many days did you use sick leave last year?" are unlikely to provide information as valid as, respectively, direct observation or company

| Exhibit 4.11 | **Ukrainian Domestic Workers** |

Source: Photo from Oksana Pronyuk. From Fedyuk, Olena. 2012. "Images of Transnational Motherhood: The Role of Photographs in Measuring Time and Maintaining Connections Between Ukraine and Italy." *Journal of Ethnic and Migration Studies* 38:279–300.

records. However, observations at social gatherings may not answer our questions about why some people do not participate; we may have to ask people. Or, if no record is kept of sick leaves in a company, we may have to ask direct questions.

Questioning can be a particularly poor approach for measuring behaviors that are very socially desirable, such as voting or attending church, or that are socially stigmatized or illegal, such as abusing alcohol or drugs. The tendency of people to answer questions in socially approved ways was demonstrated in a study of church attendance in the United States (Hadaway et al. 1993). More than 40% of adult Americans say in surveys that they attend church weekly—a percentage much higher than in Canada, Australia, or Europe. However, a comparison of observed church attendance with self-reported attendance suggested that the actual rate of church attendance was much lower (see Exhibit 4.12). Always consider the possibility of measurement error when only one type of operation has been used. Of course, it is much easier to recognize this possibility than it is to determine the extent of error resulting from a particular measurement procedure. Refer to the February 1998 issue of the *American Sociological Review* for a fascinating exchange of views and evidence on the subject of measuring church attendance.

Triangulation

Encyclopedia Link
Triangulation

Triangulation—the use of two or more different measures of the same variable—can strengthen measurement considerably (Brewer & Hunter 1989:17). When we achieve similar results with different measures of the same variable, particularly when they are based on such different methods as survey questions and field-based observations, we can be more confident in the validity of each measure. If results diverge with different measures, it may indicate that one or more of these measures are influenced by more measurement error than we can tolerate.

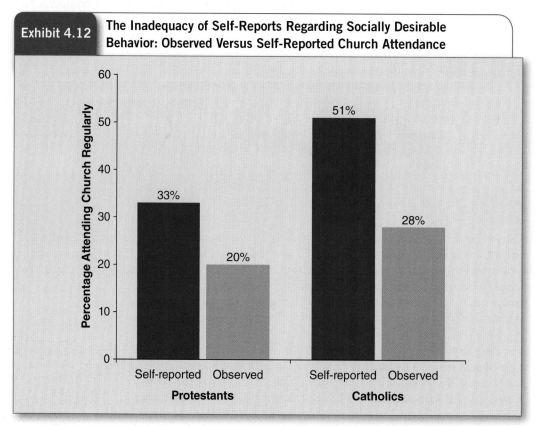

| Exhibit 4.12 | **The Inadequacy of Self-Reports Regarding Socially Desirable Behavior: Observed Versus Self-Reported Church Attendance** |

Source: Data from Hadaway, C. Kirk, Penny Long Marker, and Mark Chaves.1993. "What the Polls Don't Show: A Closer Look at U.S. Church Attendance." *American Sociological Review* 58(6):741–752.

Divergence between measures could also indicate that they actually operationalize different concepts. An interesting example of this interpretation of divergent results comes from research on crime. Official crime statistics only indicate those crimes that are reported to and recorded by the police; when surveys are used to measure crimes with self-reports of victims, many "personal annoyances" are included as if they were crimes (Levine 1976).

CAREERS AND RESEARCH

Dana Hunt, PhD, Principal Scientist

In the study site video for this chapter, Dana Hunt discusses two of the many lessons she has learned about measurement in a decades-long career in social research. Hunt received her BA in sociology from Hood College in Maryland and then earned her PhD in sociology at the University of Pennsylvania. After teaching at Hood for several years, she took an applied research position at National Development and Research Institutes (NDRI) in New York City. NDRI's description on its website gives you an idea of what drew the attention of a talented young social scientist.

Founded in 1967, NDRI is a nonprofit research and educational organization dedicated to advancing scientific knowledge in the areas of drug and alcohol abuse, treatment, and recovery; HIV, AIDS and HCV [Hepatitis C Virus]; therapeutic communities; youth at risk; and related areas of public health, mental health, criminal justice, urban problems, prevention, and epidemiology.

Hunt moved from New York to the Boston area in 1990, where she is now a principal scientist at Abt Associates, Inc. in Cambridge. Abt's website description conveys the scope of the research projects the company directs.

Abt Associates applies scientific research, consulting, and technical assistance expertise on a wide range of issues in social, economic, and health policy; international development; clinical trials; and registries. One of the largest for-profit government and business research and consulting firms in the world, Abt Associates delivers practical, measurable, high-value-added results.

Two of Hunt's major research projects in recent years are the nationwide Arrestee Drug Abuse Monitoring Program for the Office of National Drug Control Policy and an 11-city study of HIV prevention and treatment for the Substance Abuse and Mental Health Services Administration.

▣ Levels of Measurement

Can you name the variables represented in Exhibit 4.12? One variable is "religion"; it is represented by only two attributes, or categories, in Exhibit 4.12—Protestant and Catholic—but you know that there many others. One religion is not "more religion" than another; they are different in kind, not amount. Another variable represented in Exhibit 4.12 is "frequency of church attendance"; of course frequencies *do* differ in amount. We can say that religion and frequency of church attendance differ in their level of measurement.

When we know a variable's **level of measurement**, we understand more about how cases vary on that variable and so appreciate more fully what we have measured. Level of measurement also has important implications for the type of statistics that can be used with the variable, as you will learn in Chapter 14. There are four levels of measurement: (1) nominal, (2) ordinal, (3) interval, and (4) ratio. For most purposes, variables measured at the interval and ratio levels are treated in the same way, so I will sometimes refer to these two levels together as *interval–ratio*. Exhibit 4.13 depicts the differences between these four levels.

> **Level of measurement:** The mathematical precision with which the values of a variable can be expressed. The nominal level of measurement, which is qualitative, has no mathematical interpretation; the quantitative levels of measurement—ordinal, interval, and ratio—are progressively more precise mathematically.

Exhibit 4.13 Levels of Measurement

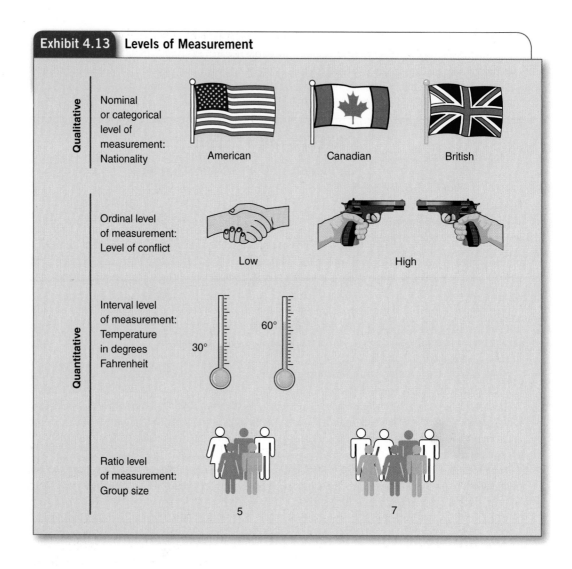

Journal Link
Nominal Variables

IE
Interactive Exercises Link
Levels of Measurement

> **Nominal level of measurement:**
> Variables whose values have no mathematical interpretation; they vary in kind or quality, but not in amount.

Nominal Level of Measurement

The **nominal level of measurement** identifies variables whose values have no mathematical interpretation; they vary in kind or quality but not in amount (they may also be called *categorical* or *qualitative variables*). It is conventional to refer to the values of nominal variables as *attributes* instead of values. *State* (referring to the United States) is one example. The variable has 50 attributes (or categories or qualities). We might indicate the specific states with numbers, so that California might be represented by the value 1, Oregon with the value 2, and so on, but these numbers do not tell us anything about the difference between the states except that they are different. California is not one unit less of *state* than Oregon is, nor is Oregon twice as much *state*. Nationality, occupation, religious affiliation, and region of the country are also measured at the nominal level. A person may be Spanish or Portuguese, but one nationality does not represent more nationality than another—just a different nationality (see Exhibit 4.13). A person may be a doctor or a truck driver, but one does not represent three units more occupation than the other. Of course, more people may identify themselves as of one nationality than another, or one occupation may have a higher average income than another, but these are comparisons involving variables other than *nationality* or *occupation per se*.

Although the attributes of categorical variables do not have a mathematical meaning, they must be assigned to cases with great care. The attributes we use to measure, or to categorize, cases must be mutually exclusive and exhaustive:

- A variable's attributes or values are mutually exclusive if every case can have only one attribute.

- A variable's attributes or values are exhaustive when every case can be classified into one of the categories.

When a variable's attributes are mutually exclusive and exhaustive, every case corresponds to one, and only one, attribute.

I know this sounds pretty straightforward, and in many cases it is. However, what we think of as mutually exclusive and exhaustive categories may really be so only because of social convention; when these conventions change, or if they differ between the societies in a multicountry study, appropriate classification at the nominal level can become much more complicated. You learned of complexities such as this in the earlier discussion of the history of measuring race.

Issues similar to these highlight the importance of informed selection of concepts, careful conceptualization of what we mean by a term, and systematic operationalization of the procedures for indicating the attributes of actual cases. The debate regarding the concept of race also reminds us of the value of qualitative research that seeks to learn about the meaning that people give to terms, without requiring that respondents use predetermined categories.

Ordinal Level of Measurement

The first of the three quantitative levels is the **ordinal level of measurement**. At this level, the numbers assigned to cases specify only the order of the cases, permitting *greater than* and *less than* distinctions. The properties of variables measured at the ordinal level are illustrated in Exhibit 4.13 by the contrast between the levels of conflict in two groups. The first group, symbolized by two people shaking hands, has a low level of conflict. The second group, symbolized by two persons pointing guns at each other, has a high level of conflict. To measure conflict, we would put the groups "in order" by assigning the number 1 to the low-conflict group and the number 2 to the high-conflict group. The numbers thus indicate only the relative position or order of the cases. Although low level of conflict is represented by the number 1, it is not one less unit of conflict than high level of conflict, which is represented by the number 2.

> **Ordinal level of measurement:** A measurement of a variable in which the numbers indicating a variable's values specify only the order of the cases, permitting *greater than* and *less than* distinctions.

The Favorable Attitudes Toward Antisocial Behavior Scale measures attitudes toward antisocial behavior among high school students with a series of questions that each involves an ordinal distinction (see Exhibit 4.14). The response choices to each question range from "very wrong" to "not wrong at all"; there's no particular quantity of "wrongness" that these distinctions reflect, but the idea is that a student who responds that it is "not wrong at all" to a question about taking a handgun to school has a more favorable attitude toward antisocial behavior than does a student who says it is "a little bit wrong," which is in turn more favorable than those who respond "wrong" or "very wrong."

As with nominal variables, the different values of a variable measured at the ordinal level must be mutually exclusive and exhaustive. They must cover the range of observed values and allow each case to be assigned no more than one value. Often, questions that use an ordinal level of measurement simply ask respondents to rate their response to some question or statement along a continuum of, for example, strength of agreement, level of importance, or relative frequency. Like variables measured at the nominal level, variables measured at the ordinal level in this way classify cases in discrete categories and so are termed **discrete measures**.

> **Discrete measure:** A measure that classifies cases in distinct categories.

| Exhibit 4.14 | Example of Ordinal Measures: Favorable Attitudes Toward Antisocial Behavior Scale |

1. How wrong do you think it is for someone your age to take a handgun to school?

| Very wrong | Wrong | A little bit wrong | Not wrong at all |

2. How wrong do you think it is for someone your age to steal anything worth more than $5?

| Very wrong | Wrong | A little bit wrong | Not wrong at all |

3. How wrong do you think it is for someone your age to pick a fight with someone?

| Very wrong | Wrong | A little bit wrong | Not wrong at all |

4. How wrong do you think it is for someone your age to attack someone with the idea of seriously hurting them?

| Very wrong | Wrong | A little bit wrong | Not wrong at all |

5. How wrong do you think it is for someone your age to stay away from school all day when their parents think they are at school?

| Very wrong | Wrong | A little bit wrong | Not wrong at all |

Sources: Lewis, Chandra, Gwen Hyatt, Keith Lafortune, and Jennifer Lembach. 2010. *History of the Use of Risk and Protective Factors in Washington State's Healthy Youth Survey.* Portland, OR: RMC Research Corporation. Retrieved May 11, 2014, from https://www.askhys.net/library/Old/RPHistory.pdf, page 26. See also Arthur, Michael W., John S. Briney, J. David Hawkins, Robert D. Abbott, Blair L. Brooke-Weiss, and Richard F. Catalano. 2007. "Measuring Risk and Protection in Communities Using the Communities That Care Youth Survey." *Evaluation and Program Planning* 30:197–211.

> **Index:** The sum or average of responses to a set of questions about a concept.

A series of similar questions may be used instead of one question to measure the same concept. The set of questions in the Favorable Attitudes Toward Antisocial Behavior Scale in Exhibit 4.14 is a good example. In such a multi-item **index,** or *scale*; numbers are assigned to reflect the order of the responses (such as 1 for "very wrong," 2 for "wrong," 3 for "a little bit wrong," and 4 for "not wrong at all"); these responses are then summed or averaged to create the index score. One person's responses to the five questions in Exhibit 4.14 could thus range from 5 (meaning they said each behavior is "very wrong") to 20 (meaning they said each behavior is "not wrong at all"). However, even though these are numeric scores, they still reflect an ordinal level of measurement because the responses they are based on involve only ordinal distinctions.

Interval Level of Measurement

> **Interval level of measurement:** A measurement of a variable in which the numbers indicating a variable's values represent fixed measurement units but have no absolute, or fixed, zero point.

The numbers indicating the values of a variable at the **interval level of measurement** represent fixed measurement units but have no absolute, or fixed, zero point. This level of measurement is represented in Exhibit 4.13 by the difference between two Fahrenheit temperatures. Although 60 degrees is 30 degrees hotter than 30 degrees, 60, in this case, is not twice as hot as 30. Why not? Because "heat" does not begin at 0 degrees on the Fahrenheit scale.

An interval-level measure is created by a scale that has fixed measurement units but no absolute, or fixed, zero point. The numbers can, therefore, be added and subtracted, but ratios are not meaningful. Again, the values must be mutually exclusive and exhaustive. There are few true interval-level measures in the social sciences, but cross-disciplinary investigations such as those that examine the linkage between climate and social life or historical change in social organization may involve interval measures such as temperature or calendar year.

Many social scientists use indexes created by combining responses to a series of variables measured at the ordinal level as if they were interval-level measures. You have already seen an example of such a multi-item index in Exhibit 4.14. Scores on scales that are standardized in a distribution can also be treated as measured at the interval level. For example, the so-called Intelligence Quotient, or IQ score, is standardized so that a score of 100 indicates that a person is in the middle of the distribution, and each score above and below 100 indicates fixed points on the distribution of IQ scores in the population. A score of 114 would represent a score higher than that of 84% of the population.

Ratio Level of Measurement

The numbers indicating the values of a variable at the **ratio level of measurement** represent fixed measuring units and an absolute zero point (zero means absolutely no amount of whatever the variable indicates). For example, the following question was used on the National Minority SA/HIV Prevention Initiative Youth Questionnaire to measure number of days during the past 30 days that the respondent drank at least one alcoholic beverage. We can easily calculate the number of days that separate any response from any other response (except for the missing value of "don't know").

> **Ratio level of measurement:** A measurement of a variable in which the numbers indicating a variable's values represent fixed measuring units and an absolute zero point.

During the past 30 days, on how many days did you drink one or more drinks of an alcoholic beverage?

☐ 0 days	☐ 12 days	☐ 24 days
☐ 1 day	☐ 13 days	☐ 25 days
☐ 2 days	☐ 14 days	☐ 26 days
☐ 3 days	☐ 15 days	☐ 27 days
☐ 4 days	☐ 16 days	☐ 28 days
☐ 5 days	☐ 17 days	☐ 29 days
☐ 6 days	☐ 18 days	☐ 30 days
☐ 7 days	☐ 19 days	☐ Don't know
☐ 8 days	☐ 20 days	or can't say
☐ 9 days	☐ 21 days	
☐ 10 days	☐ 22 days	
☐ 11 days	☐ 23 days	

Exhibit 4.13 also displays an example of a variable measured at the ratio level. The number of people in the first group is five, and the number in the second group is seven. The ratio of the two groups' sizes is then 1.4, a number that mirrors the relationship between the sizes of the groups. Note that there does not actually have to be any group with a size of zero; what is important is that the numbering scheme begins at an absolute zero—in this case, the absence of any people.

For most statistical analyses in social science research, the interval and ratio levels of measurement can be treated as equivalent. In addition to having numerical values, both the interval and ratio levels also involve **continuous measures**: The numbers indicating the values of variables are points on a continuum, not discrete categories. But despite these similarities, there is an important difference between variables measured at the interval and ratio levels. On a ratio scale, 10 is 2 points higher than 8 and is also 2 *times* greater than 5—the numbers can be compared in a ratio. Ratio numbers can be added and subtracted, and because the numbers begin at an absolute zero point, they can be multiplied and divided (so ratios can be formed between the numbers). For example, people's ages can be represented by values ranging from 0 years (or some fraction of a year) to 120 or more. A person who is 30 years old is 15 years older than someone who is 15 years old (30 – 15 = 15) and is twice as old as that person (30/15 = 2). Of course, the numbers also are mutually exclusive and exhaustive, so that every case can be assigned one and only one value.

> **Continuous measure:** A measure with numbers indicating the values of variables as points on a continuum.

It's tempting to accept the numbers that represent the values of a variable measured at the ratio level at face value, but the precision of the numbers can't make us certain about their accuracy. Income data provided in the

U.S. Census is often incomplete (Scott 2001); the unemployment rate doesn't account for people who have given up looking for work (Zitner 1996); and the Consumer Price Index (CPI) does not reflect the types of goods that many groups of consumers buy (Uchitelle 1997). In each of these cases, we have to be sure that the measures that we use reflect adequately the concepts that we intend.

The Special Case of Dichotomies

Dichotomies, variables having only two values, are a special case from the standpoint of levels of measurement. The values or attributes of a variable such as gender clearly vary in kind or quality but not in amount. Thus, the variable is categorical—measured at the nominal level. Yet we can also think of the variable as indicating the presence of the attribute *female* (or *male*) or not. Viewed in this way, there is an inherent order: A female has more of the female attribute (it is present) than a male (the attribute is not present). It's also possible to think

> **Dichotomy:** Variable having only two values.

of a **dichotomy** as representing an interval level of measurement because there is an equal interval between the two attributes. So what do you answer to the test question, "What is the level of measurement of *gender*?" "Nominal," of course, but you'll find that when a statistical procedure requires that variables be quantitative, a dichotomy can be perfectly acceptable.

Comparison of Levels of Measurement

Exhibit 4.15 summarizes the types of comparisons that can be made with different levels of measurement, as well as the mathematical operations that are legitimate. Each higher level of measurement allows a more precise mathematical comparison to be made between the value measured at that level compared with those measured at lower levels. However, each comparison between cases measured at lower levels can also be made about cases measured at the higher levels. Thus, all four levels of measurement allow researchers to assign different values to different cases. All three quantitative measures allow researchers to rank cases in order.

Researchers choose the levels of measurement in the process of operationalizing variables; the level of measurement is not inherent in the variable itself. Many variables can be measured at different levels, with different procedures. For example, the Core Alcohol and Drug Survey (Core Institute 1994) identifies binge drinking by asking students, "Think back over the last two weeks. How many times have you had five or more

Exhibit 4.15   Properties of Levels of Measurement

Level of Measurement	Possible Statements: Age of two individuals: Sara (24) and Bill (12)	Quality of Level	Appropriate Math Operations
Nominal	Adults (Over 18) Adolescent (Under 18)	Different from	= (≠)
Ordinal	Sara is older than Bill; Bill is younger than Sara.	Greater than	> (<)
Interval	Sara is 12 years older than Bill; Bill is 12 years younger than Sara	A year is a year is a year	+ (−)
Ratio	Bill is ½ Sara's age; or Sara is twice Bill's age	Absolute zero	X (÷)

Source: Adapted from material provided by Tajuana D. Massie, assistant professor, social sciences, South Carolina State University.

drinks at a sitting?" You might be ready to classify this as a ratio-level measure, but this would be true only if responses are recorded as the actual number of "times." Instead, the Core Survey treats this as a closed-ended question, and students are asked to indicate their answer by checking "None," "Once," "Twice," "3 to 5 times," "6 to 9 times," or "10 or more times." Use of these categories makes the level of measurement ordinal. The distance between any two cases cannot be clearly determined. A student with a response in the "6 to 9 times" category could have binged just one more time than a student who responded "3 to 5 times." You just can't tell.

It is usually a good idea to try to measure variables at the highest level of measurement possible. The more information available, the more ways we have to compare cases. We also have more possibilities for statistical analysis with quantitative than with qualitative variables. Thus, if doing so does not distort the meaning of the concept that is to be measured, measure at the highest level possible. Even if your primary concern is only to compare teenagers with young adults, measure age in years rather than in categories; you can always combine the ages later into categories corresponding to teenager and young adult.

Be aware, however, that other considerations may preclude measurement at a higher level. For example, many people are very reluctant to report their exact incomes, even in anonymous questionnaires. So asking respondents to report their income in categories (such as less than $10,000, $10,000–$19,999, $20,000–$29,999) will result in more responses, and thus more valid data, than will asking respondents for their income in dollars.

Often, researchers treat variables measured at the interval and ratio levels as comparable. They then refer to this as the **interval–ratio level of measurement**. You will learn in Chapter 14 that different statistical procedures are used for variables with fixed measurement units, but it usually doesn't matter whether there is an absolute zero point.

> **Interval–ratio level of measurement:**
> A measurement of a variable in which the numbers indicating a variable's values represent fixed measurement units but may not have an absolute, or fixed, zero point.

Evaluating Measures

Do the operations developed to measure our variables actually do so—are they valid? If we have weighed our measurement options, carefully constructed our questions and observational procedures, and selected sensibly from the available data indicators, we should be on the right track. But we cannot have much confidence in a measure until we have empirically evaluated its validity. What good is our measure if it doesn't measure what we think it does? If our measurement procedure is invalid, we might as well go back to the starting block and try again. As a part of evaluating the validity of our measures, we must also evaluate their reliability, because reliability (consistency) is a prerequisite for measurement validity.

Research|Social Impact Link
Reliability and Validity

Measurement Validity

In Chapter 2, you learned that measurement validity refers to the extent to which measures indicate what they are intended to measure. More technically, a valid measure of a concept is one that is closely related to other apparently valid measures of the concept and to the known or supposed correlates of that concept, but that is not related to measures of unrelated concepts, irrespective of the methods used for the other different measures (Brewer & Hunter 1989:134).

When a measure "misses the mark"—when it is not valid—our measurement procedure has been affected by measurement error. Measurement error has two sources:

1. *Idiosyncratic (or "random") errors* are errors that affect individuals or cases in unique ways that are unlikely to be repeated in just the same way (Viswanathan 2005:289). Individuals make **idiosyncratic errors** when they don't understand a question, when some unique feelings are triggered by the wording of a question, or when they are feeling out of sorts because of some recent events. Idiosyncratic errors

> **Idiosyncratic, or random, errors:**
> Errors that affect individuals or other cases in unique ways that are unlikely to be repeated in just the same way.

may arise in observational research when the observer is distracted or misperceives an event. In coding content, an idiosyncratic error may be made in recording a numerical code or in skipping a page or web screen. Some idiosyncratic error is unavoidable with any measurement procedure, although it is important to reduce their size as much as possible. However, because such errors are idiosyncratic, or random, they are as likely to be above as below the true value of the measure; this means that idiosyncratic errors should not bias the measure in one direction.

2. *Systematic errors* occur when responses are affected by factors that are not what the instrument is intended to measure. For example, individuals who like to please others by giving socially desirable responses may have a tendency to say that they "agree" with the statements, simply because they try to avoid saying they "disagree" with anyone. Systematic errors may also arise when the same measure is used across cultures that differ in their understanding of the concepts underlying the measures (Church 2010:152–153). In addition, questions that are unclear may be misinterpreted by most respondents, while **unbalanced response choices** may lead most respondents to give positive rather than negative responses. For example, if respondents are asked the question with the unbalanced response choices in Exhibit 4.16, they are more likely to respond that gun ownership is wrong than if they are asked the question with the **balanced response choices** (Viswanathan 2005:142–148).

> **Unbalanced response choices:** A fixed-choice survey question has a different number of positive and negative response choices.
>
> **Balanced response choices:** An equal number of responses to a fixed-choice survey question express positive and negative choices in comparable language.

Systematic errors can do much more damage to measurement validity than idiosyncratic errors can because they will lead to the average value of the indicator being higher or lower than the phenomenon that it is measuring. For example, if a political poll uses questions that generate agreement bias, a politician may believe that voters agree with her position much more than they actually do.

The social scientist must try to reduce measurement errors and then to evaluate the extent to which the resulting measures are valid. The extent to which measurement validity has been achieved can be assessed with four different approaches: (1) face validation, (2) content validation, (3) criterion validation, and (4) construct validation. The methods of criterion and construct validation also include subtypes.

Audio Link
Measurement Validity

Exhibit 4.16 Balanced and Unbalanced Response Choices

Unbalanced response choices

How wrong do you think it is for someone who is not a hunter to own a gun?

- Very wrong
- Wrong
- A little bit wrong
- Not wrong at all

Balanced response choices

Some people think it is wrong for someone who is not a hunter to own a gun, and some people think it is a good idea to own a gun. Do you think it is very wrong, wrong, neither right nor wrong, right, or very right for someone who is not a hunter to own a gun?

- Very wrong
- Wrong
- Neither right nor wrong
- Right
- Very right

Face Validity

Researchers apply the term **face validity** to the confidence gained from careful review of a measure to see if it seems appropriate "on its face." More precisely, we can say that a measure is face valid if it obviously pertains to the meaning of the concept being measured more than to other concepts (Brewer & Hunter 1989:131). For example, a count of the number of drinks people had consumed in the past week would be a face-valid measure of their alcohol consumption. But speaking of "face" validity, what would you think about assessing the competence of political candidates by how mature their faces look? It turns out that people are less likely to vote for candidates with more "baby-faced" features, such as rounded features and large eyes, irrespective of the candidates' records (Cook 2005). It's an unconscious bias, and, of course, it's not one that we would use as a basis for assessing competence in a social science study!

> **Face validity:** The type of validity that exists when an inspection of items used to measure a concept suggests that they are appropriate "on their face."

Although every measure should be inspected in this way, face validation in itself does not provide convincing evidence of measurement validity. The question "How much beer or wine did you have to drink last week?" looks valid on its face as a measure of frequency of drinking, but people who drink heavily tend to underreport the amount they drink. So the question would be an invalid measure, at least in a study of heavy drinkers.

Content Validity

Content validity establishes that the measure covers the full range of the concept's meaning. To determine that range of meaning, the researcher may solicit the opinions of experts and review literature that identifies the different aspects, or dimensions, of the concept.

> **Content validity:** The type of validity that exists when the full range of a concept's meaning is covered by the measure.

An example of a measure that covers a wide range of meaning is the Michigan Alcoholism Screening Test (MAST). The MAST includes 24 questions representing the following subscales: recognition of alcohol problems by self and others; legal, social, and work problems; help seeking; marital and family difficulties; and liver pathology (Skinner & Sheu 1982). Many experts familiar with the direct consequences of substance abuse agree that these dimensions capture the full range of possibilities. Thus, the MAST is believed to be valid from the standpoint of content validity.

Journal Link
Content Analysis

Criterion Validity

When people drink an alcoholic beverage, the alcohol is absorbed into their blood and then gradually metabolized (broken down into other chemicals) in their livers (National Institute on Alcohol Abuse and Alcoholism [NIAAA] 1997). The alcohol that remains in their blood at any point, unmetabolized, impairs both thinking and behavior (NIAAA 1994). As more alcohol is ingested, cognitive and behavioral consequences multiply. The bases for these biological processes can be identified with direct measures of alcohol concentration in the blood, urine, or breath. Questions about the quantity and frequency of drinking can be viewed as attempts to measure indirectly what biochemical tests measure directly.

Criterion validity is established when the scores obtained on one measure can be accurately compared with those obtained with a more direct or already validated measure of the same phenomenon (the criterion). A measure of blood–alcohol concentration or a urine test could serve as the criterion for validating a self-report measure of drinking, as long as the questions we ask about drinking refer to the same time period. Chemical analysis of hair samples can reveal unacknowledged drug use (Mieczkowski 1997). Friends' or relatives' observations of a person's substance use also could serve, in some limited circumstances, as a criterion for validating self-report substance use measures.

> **Criterion validity:** The type of validity that is established by comparing the scores obtained on the measure being validated with those obtained with a more direct or already validated measure of the same phenomenon (the criterion).

Criterion–validation studies of self-report substance abuse measures have yielded inconsistent results. Self-reports of drug use agreed with urinalysis results for about 85% of the drug users who volunteered for a health study in several cities (Weatherby et al. 1994). However, the posttreatment drinking behavior self-reported by 100 male alcoholics was substantially less than the drinking behavior observed by the alcoholics' friends or relatives (Watson et al. 1984). College students' reports of drinking are suspect too: A standard question to measure alcohol use is to ask respondents how many glasses they consume when they do drink. A criterion–validation study of this approach measured how much of the drink students poured when they had what they considered to be a "standard" drink (White et al. 2003). The students consistently overestimated how much fluid goes into a standard drink.

Inconsistent findings about the validity of a measure can occur because of differences in the adequacy of a measure across settings and populations. We cannot simply assume that a measure that was validated in one study is also valid in another setting or with a different population. The validity of even established measures has to be tested when they are used in a different context (Viswanathan 2005:297).

Concurrent validity: The type of validity that exists when scores on a measure are closely related to scores on a criterion measured at the same time.

Predictive validity: The type of validity that exists when a measure predicts scores on a criterion measured in the future.

The criterion that researchers select can be measured either at the same time as the variable to be validated or after that time. **Concurrent validity** exists when a measure yields scores that are closely related to scores on a criterion measured at the same time. A store might validate a question-based test of sales ability by administering it to sales personnel who are already employed and then comparing their test scores with their sales performance. Or a measure of walking speed based on mental counting might be validated concurrently with a stopwatch. **Predictive validity** is the ability of a measure to predict scores on a criterion measured in the future. For example, a store might administer a test of sales ability to new sales personnel and then validate the measure by comparing these test scores with the criterion—the subsequent sales performance of the new personnel.

An attempt at criterion validation is well worth the effort because it greatly increases confidence that the standard is measuring what was intended. However, for many concepts of interest to social scientists, no other variable can reasonably be considered a criterion. If we are measuring feelings or beliefs or other subjective states, such as feelings of loneliness, what *direct* indicator could serve as a criterion? Even with variables for which a reasonable criterion exists, the researcher may not be able to gain access to the criterion—as would be the case with a tax return or employer document that we might wish we could use as a criterion for self-reported income.

Construct validity: The type of validity that is established by showing that a measure is related to other measures as specified in a theory.

Construct Validity

Measurement validity can also be established by showing that a measure is related to a variety of other measures as specified in a theory. This validation approach, known as **construct validity**, is commonly used in social research when no clear criterion exists for validation purposes. For example, in one study of the validity of the Addiction Severity Index (ASI), A. Thomas McLellan and his associates (1985) compared subject scores on the ASI with a number of indicators that they felt, from prior research, should be related to substance abuse: medical problems, employment problems, legal problems, family problems, and psychiatric problems. The researchers could not use a criterion validation approach because they did not have a more direct measure of abuse, such as laboratory test scores or observer reports. However, their extensive research on the subject had given them confidence that these sorts of problems were all related to substance abuse, and, indeed, they found that individuals with higher ASI ratings tended to have more problems in each of these areas.

Convergent validity: An approach to construct validation; the type of validity achieved when one measure of a concept is associated with different types of measures of the same concept.

Discriminant validity: An approach to construct validation; the scores on the measure to be validated are compared with scores on another measure of the same variable and to scores on variables that measure different but related concepts. Discriminant validity is achieved if the measure to be validated is related most strongly to its comparison measure and less so to the measures of other concepts.

Two other approaches to construct validation are convergent validation and discriminant validation. **Convergent validity** is achieved when one measure of a concept is associated with different types of measures of the same concept (this relies on the same type of logic as measurement triangulation). **Discriminant validity** is a complementary approach to construct validation. In this approach, scores on the measure to be validated are compared with scores on measures of different but related concepts. Discriminant validity is achieved if the measure to be validated is not associated strongly with the measures of different concepts. McLellan et al. (1985) found that the ASI passed the tests of convergent and discriminant validity: The ASI's measures of alcohol and drug problems were related more strongly to other measures of alcohol and drug problems than they were to measures of legal problems, family problems, medical problems, and the like.

The distinction between criterion validation and construct validation is not always clear. Opinions can differ about whether a particular indicator is indeed a criterion for the concept that is to be measured. For example, if you need to validate a question-based measure of sales ability for applicants to a sales position, few would object to using actual sales performance as a criterion. But what if you want to validate a question-based measure of the amount of social support that people receive from their friends? Could friends' reports of the amount of support they provided serve as a criterion for validating the amount of support that people say they have received? Are verbal accounts of the amount of support provided adequate? What about observation of social support that people receive? Even if you could observe people in the act of counseling or otherwise supporting their friends, can observers be sure that the interaction is indeed supportive, or that they have observed all the relevant interactions? There isn't really a criterion here, only related concepts that could be used in a construct validation strategy. Even biochemical measures of substance abuse are questionable as criteria for validating self-reported substance use. Urine test results can be altered by ingesting certain substances, and blood tests vary in their sensitivity to the presence of drugs over a particular period.

What both construct validation and criterion validation have in common is the comparison of scores on one measure with the scores on other measures that are predicted to be related. It is not so important that researchers agree that a particular comparison measure is a criterion rather than a related construct. But it is very important to think critically about the quality of the comparison measure and whether it actually represents a different view of the same phenomenon. For example, correspondence between scores on two different self-report measures of alcohol use is a much weaker indicator of measurement validity than is the correspondence of a self-report measure with an observer-based measure of substance use.

Measurement Reliability

Reliability means that a measurement procedure yields consistent scores when the phenomenon being measured is not changing (or that the measured scores change in direct correspondence to actual changes in the phenomenon). If a measure is reliable, it is affected less by random error, or chance variation, than if it is unreliable. Reliability is a prerequisite for measurement validity: We cannot really measure a phenomenon if the measure we are using gives inconsistent results. Actually, because it is usually easier to assess reliability than validity, you are more likely to see an evaluation of measurement reliability in a research report than an evaluation of measurement validity.

> **Reliability:** A measurement procedure yields consistent scores when the phenomenon being measured is not changing.

Problems in reliability can occur when inconsistent measurements are obtained after the same phenomenon is measured multiple times, with multiple indicators, or by multiple observers. For example, a test of your knowledge of research methods would be unreliable if every time you took it, you received a different score even though your knowledge of research methods had not changed in the interim, not even as a result of taking the test more than once. This is test–retest reliability. A measure also would be unreliable if slightly different versions of it resulted in markedly different responses (it would not achieve alternate-forms reliability). Similarly, an index composed of questions to measure knowledge of research methods would be unreliable if respondents' answers to each question were totally independent of their answers to the others. By contrast, the index has interitem reliability if the component items are closely related. Finally, an assessment of the level of conflict in social groups would be unreliable if ratings of the level of conflict by two observers were not related to each other (it would then lack interobserver reliability).

Test–retest reliability: A measurement showing that measures of a phenomenon at two points in time are highly correlated, if the phenomenon has not changed, or has changed only as much as the measures have changed.

Intrarater (or intraobserver) reliability: Consistency of ratings by an observer of an unchanging phenomenon at two or more points in time.

Multiple Times: Test–Retest and Alternative Forms

When researchers measure a phenomenon that does not change between two points separated by an interval of time, the degree to which the two measurements are related to each other is the **test–retest reliability** of the measure. If you take a test of your math ability and then retake the test 2 months later, the test is performing reliably if you receive a similar score both times—presuming that nothing happened during the 2 months to change your math ability. Of course, if events between the test and the retest have changed the variable being measured, then the difference between the test and retest scores should reflect that change.

When ratings by an observer, rather than ratings by the subjects themselves, are being assessed at two or more points in time, test–retest reliability is termed **intrarater (or intraobserver) reliability**.

If an observer's ratings of individuals' drinking behavior in bars are similar at two or more points in time, and the behavior has not changed, the observer's ratings of drinking behavior are reliable.

One example of how evidence about test–retest reliability may be developed is a study by Linda Sobell and her associates (1988) of alcohol abusers' past drinking behavior (using the Lifetime Drinking History Questionnaire) and life changes (using the Recent Life Changes Questionnaire). All 69 subjects in the study were patients in an addiction treatment program. They had not been drinking before the interview (determined by a breath test). The two questionnaires were administered by different interviewers about 2 or 3 weeks apart, both times asking the subjects to recall events 8 years before the interviews. Reliability was high: 92% of the subjects reported the same life events both times, and at least 81% of the subjects were classified consistently at both the interviews as having had an alcohol problem or not. When asked about their inconsistent answers, subjects reported that in the earlier interview they had simply dated an event incorrectly, misunderstood the question, evaluated the importance of an event differently, or forgotten an event. Answers to past drinking questions were less reliable when they were very specific, apparently because the questions exceeded the subjects' capacities to remember accurately.

Alternate-forms reliability: A procedure for testing the reliability of responses to survey questions in which subjects' answers are compared after the subjects have been asked slightly different versions of the questions or when randomly selected halves of the sample have been administered slightly different versions of the questions.

Researchers test **alternate-forms reliability** by comparing the subjects' answers with slightly different versions of the survey questions (Litwin 1995:13–21). A researcher may reverse the order of the response choices in an index or modify the question wording in minor ways and then re-administer that index to the subjects. If the two sets of responses are not too different, alternate-forms reliability is established.

Multiple Indicators: Interitem and Split-Half

Interitem reliability: An approach that calculates reliability based on the correlation among multiple items used to measure a single concept; also known as internal consistency.

Cronbach's alpha: A statistic commonly used to measure interitem reliability.

Reliability measure: Statistics that summarize the consistency among a set of measures; Cronbach's alpha is the most common measure of the reliability of a set of items included in an index.

When researchers use multiple items to measure a single concept, they must be concerned with **interitem reliability** (or internal consistency). For example, if we are to have confidence that a set of questions (such as those in Exhibit 4.17) reliably measures depression, the answers to these questions should be highly associated with one another. The stronger the association between the individual items and the more items included, the higher the reliability of the index. **Cronbach's alpha** is a **reliability measure** commonly used to measure interitem reliability. Of course, interitem reliability cannot be computed if only one question is used to measure a concept. For this reason, it is much better to use a multi-item index to measure an important concept (Viswanathan 2005:298–299).

Donald Hawkins, Paul Amato, and Valarie King (2007:1007) used the "CES-D" index to measure depression in their study of adolescent well-being and obtained a high level of interitem reliability. They measured "negative outlook" with a similar set of questions (Exhibit 4.17), but the interitem reliability of this set was lower. Read

Exhibit 4.17	Examples of Indexes: Short Form of the Center for Epidemiologic Studies (CES-D) and "Negative Outlook" Index

At any time during the past week . . . (Circle one response on each line)	Never	Some of the Time	Most of the Time
a. Was your appetite so poor that you did not feel like eating?	1	2	3
b. Did you feel so tired and worn out that you could not enjoy anything?	1	2	3
c. Did you feel depressed?	1	2	3
d. Did you feel unhappy about the way your life is going?	1	2	3
e. Did you feel discouraged and worried about your future?	1	2	3
f. Did you feel lonely?	1	2	3

Negative outlook

How often was each of these things true during the past week? (Circle one response on each line)	A Lot, Most, or All of the Time	Sometimes	Never or Rarely
a. You felt that you were just as good as other people.	0	1	2
b. You felt hopeful about the future.	0	1	2
c. You were happy.	0	1	2
d. You enjoyed life.	0	1	2

Source: Hawkins, Daniel N. Paul R. Amato, and Valarie King. 2007. "Nonresident Father Involvement and Adolescent Well-Being: Father Effects or Child Effects?" *American Sociological Review* 72:990.

through the two sets of questions. Do the sets seem to cover what you think of as being depressed and having a negative outlook? If so, they seem to be *content valid* to you.

A related test of reliability is the **split-half reliability** approach. After a set of survey questions intended to form an index is administered, the researcher divides the questions into half by distinguishing even- and odd-numbered questions, flipping a coin, or using some other random procedure. Scores are then computed for these two sets of questions. The researchers then compare the scores for the two halves and check the relation between the subjects' scores on them. If scores on the two halves are similar and highly related to each other (so that people who score high on one half also score high on the other half, etc.), then the measure's split-half reliability is established.

> **Split-half reliability:** Reliability achieved when responses to the same questions by two randomly selected halves of a sample are about the same.

Multiple Observers: Interobserver and Intercoder

When researchers use more than one observer to rate the same people, events, or places, **interobserver reliability** is their goal. If observers are using the same

> **Interobserver reliability:** When similar measurements are obtained by different observers rating the same persons, events, or places.

instrument to rate the same thing, their ratings should be very similar. If they are similar, we can have much more confidence that the ratings reflect the phenomenon being assessed rather than the orientations of the observers.

Assessing interobserver reliability is most important when the rating task is complex. Consider a measure of neighborhood disorder, the African American Health Neighborhood Assessment Scale (AAH NAS), which is shown in Exhibit 4.18. The rating task seems straightforward, with clear descriptions of the block characteristics that are rated to produce an overall neighborhood score. However, the judgments that the rater must make while using this scale are very complex. They are affected by a wide range of subject characteristics, attitudes, and behaviors as well as by the rater's reactions. As a result, although interobserver agreement on the AAH NAS can be sufficient to achieve a reasonable level of reliability, achieving reliable ratings required careful training of the raters. Qualitative researchers confront the same issue when multiple observers attempt to observe similar phenomena in different settings or at different times. We return to this issue in the qualitative research chapters.

> **Intercoder reliability:** When the same codes are entered by different coders who are recording the same data.

It is also important to establish an adequate level of **intercoder reliability** when data are transferred from their original form, whether observations or interviews, into structured codes or simply into a data entry program or spreadsheet. There can be weak links in data processing, so the consistency of coders should be tested.

Ways to Improve Reliability and Validity

Interactive Exercises Link
Valid and Reliable Measures

Whatever the concept measured or the validation method used, no measure is without some error, nor can we expect it to be valid for all times and places. For example, the reliability and validity of self-report measures of substance abuse vary with factors such as whether the respondents are sober or intoxicated at the time of the interview, whether the measure refers to recent or lifetime abuse, and whether the respondents see their responses as affecting their chances of receiving housing, treatment, or some other desired outcome (Babor, Stephens, & Marlatt 1987). In addition, persons with severe mental illness are, in general, less likely to respond accurately (Corse, Hirschinger, & Zanis 1995). We should always be on the lookout for ways in which we can improve the reliability and validity of the measures we use.

Remember that a reliable measure is not necessarily a valid measure, as Exhibit 4.19 illustrates. This discrepancy is a common flaw of self-report measures of substance abuse. Most respondents answer the multiple questions in self-report indexes of substance abuse in a consistent way, so the indexes are reliable. However, a number of respondents will not admit to drinking, even though they drink a lot. Their answers to the questions are consistent, but they are consistently misleading. As a result, some indexes based on self-report are reliable but invalid. Such indexes are not useful and should be improved or discarded. Unfortunately, many measures are judged to be worthwhile on the basis of only a reliability test.

Video Link
Validity vs. Reliability

The reliability and validity of measures in any study must be tested after the fact to assess the quality of the information obtained. But then, if it turns out that a measure cannot be considered reliable and valid, little can be done to save the study. Hence, it is supremely important to select, in the first place, measures that are likely to be reliable and valid. Don't just choose the first measure you find or can think of: Consider the different strengths of different measures and their appropriateness to your study. Conduct a pretest in which you use the measure with a small sample, and check its reliability. Provide careful training to ensure a consistent approach if interviewers or observers will administer the measures. In most cases, however, the best strategy is to use measures that have been used before and whose reliability and validity have been established in other contexts. But the selection of tried and true measures still does not absolve researchers from the responsibility of testing the reliability and validity of the measure in their own studies.

When the population studied or the measurement context differs from that in previous research, instrument reliability and validity may be affected. So the researchers must take pains with the design of their study. For example, test–retest reliability has proved to be better for several standard measures used to assess substance use among homeless persons when the interview was conducted in a protected setting and when the measures focused on factual information and referred to a recent time interval (Drake, McHugo, &

Biesanz 1995). Subjects who were younger, female, recently homeless, and less severely afflicted with psychiatric problems were also more likely to give reliable answers.

| Exhibit 4.18 | The Challenge of Interobserver Reliability: African American Health Seven-Item Neighborhood Assessment Scale (AAH NAS) |

The first 3 questions refer to the full block and street on which the respondent lives.

1. Volume of traffic
   0. No Traffic
   1. Light (occasional cars)
   2. Moderate
   3. Heavy (steady stream of cars)

2. Condition of the street
   0. Under construction
   1. Very poor (many sizeable cracks, potholes, or broken curbs)
   2. Fair
   3. Moderately good (no sizeable cracks, potholes, or broken curbs)
   4. Very good

3. How noisy is the street?
   0. Very quiet – easy to hear almost anything
   1. Fairly quiet – can hear people walking by talking, though you may not understand them
   2. Somewhat noisy – voices are not audible unless very near
   3. Very noisy – difficult to hear a person talking near to you

Items 4 through 7 are answered based on observations of the side of the street on the block where the respondent lives (block face).

4. Are empty beer or liquor bottles in street, yard, or alley present?
   1. Yes
   0. No

5. Are there cigarette or cigar butts or discarded cigarette packages on the sidewalk or in the gutters?
   1. Yes
   0. No

6. Is there garbage, litter, or broken glass in the street or on the sidewalks?
   0. None
   1. Light (some visible)
   2. Moderate
   3. Heavy (visible along most or all of street)

7. In general, how would you rate the condition of most of the residential units in the block face?
   0. Very well kept/good condition – attractive for its type
   1. Moderately well kept condition
   2. Fair condition (peeling paint, needs repair)
   3. Poor/Badly deteriorated condition

Source: Andresen E., T. K. Malmstrom, F. D. Wolinsky, M. Schootman, J. P. Miller, and D. K. Miller. 2008. "Rating Neighborhoods for Older Adult Health: Results from the African American Health Study." *BMC Public Health* 8:35. doi:10.1186/1471-2458-8-35.

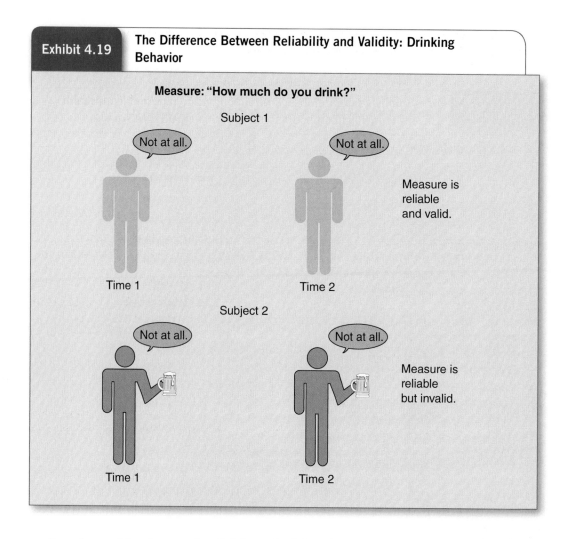

Exhibit 4.19 **The Difference Between Reliability and Validity: Drinking Behavior**

It may be possible to improve the reliability and validity of measures in a study that already has been conducted if multiple measures were used. For example, in our study of housing for homeless mentally ill persons, funded by the National Institute of Mental Health, we assessed substance abuse with several different sets of direct questions as well as with reports from subjects' case managers and others (Goldfinger et al. 1996). We found that the observational reports were often inconsistent with self-reports and that different self-report measures were not always in agreement; hence, the measures were not valid. A more valid measure was initial reports of lifetime substance abuse problems, which identified all those who subsequently abused substances during the project. We concluded that the lifetime measure was a valid way to identify persons at risk for substance abuse problems. No single measure was adequate to identify substance abusers at a particular point in time during the project. Instead, we constructed a composite of observer and self-report measures that seemed to be a valid indicator of substance abuse over 6-month periods.

If the research focuses on previously unmeasured concepts, new measures will have to be devised. Researchers can use one of three strategies to improve the likelihood that new question-based measures will be reliable and valid (Fowler 1995):

Engage potential respondents in group discussions about the questions to be included in the survey. This strategy allows researchers to check for consistent understanding of terms and to hear the range of events or experiences that people will report.

Conduct cognitive interviews. Ask people a test question, then probe with follow-up questions about how they understood the question and what their answer meant.

Audiotape test interviews during the pretest phase of a survey. The researchers then review these audiotapes and systematically code them to identify problems in question wording or delivery. (pp. 104–129)

In these ways, qualitative methods help improve the validity of the fixed-response questions used in quantitative surveys.

▣ Conclusions

Remember always that measurement validity is a necessary foundation for social research. Gathering data without careful conceptualization or conscientious efforts to operationalize key concepts often is a wasted effort.

The difficulties of achieving valid measurement vary with the concept being operationalized and the circumstances of the particular study. The examples in this chapter of difficulties in achieving valid measures of substance abuse should sensitize you to the need for caution. However, don't let these difficulties discourage you: Substance abuse is a relatively difficult concept to operationalize because it involves behavior that is socially stigmatized and often illegal. Most other concepts in social research present fewer difficulties. But even substance abuse can be measured adequately with a proper research design.

Planning ahead is the key to achieving valid measurement in your own research; careful evaluation is the key to sound decisions about the validity of measures in others' research. Statistical tests can help determine whether a given measure is valid after data have been collected, but if it appears after the fact that a measure is invalid, little can be done to correct the situation. If you cannot tell how key concepts were operationalized when you read a research report, don't trust the findings. And if a researcher does not indicate the results of tests used to establish the reliability and validity of key measures, remain skeptical.

Key Terms

Alternate-forms reliability   136
Balanced response choices   132
Closed-ended (fixed-choice)
   question   118
Concept   102
Conceptualization   103
Concurrent validity   134
Constant   111
Construct validity   134
Content validity   133
Continuous measure   129
Convergent validity   134
Criterion validity   133
Cronbach's alpha   136
Dichotomy   130

Discrete measure   127
Discriminant validity   134
Exhaustive   119
Face validity   133
Idiosyncratic, or random, errors   131
Index   128
Indicator   109
Intercoder reliability   138
Interitem reliability   136
Interobserver reliability   137
Interval level of measurement   128
Interval–ratio level of
   measurement   131
Intrarater (or intraobserver)
   reliability   136

Level of measurement   125
Measurement   116
Mutually exclusive   119
Nominal level of measurement   126
Open-ended question   119
Operationalization   109
Ordinal level of measurement   127
Predictive validity   134
Ratio level of measurement   129
Reliability   135
Reliability measure   136
Split-half reliability   137
Test–retest reliability   136
Unbalanced response choices   132
Unobtrusive measure   121

Highlights

- Conceptualization plays a critical role in research. In deductive research, conceptualization guides the operationalization of specific variables; in inductive research, it guides efforts to make sense of related observations.

- Concepts may refer to either constant or variable phenomena. Concepts that refer to variable phenomena may be quite similar to the actual variables used in a study, or they may be much more abstract.

- Concepts are operationalized in research by one or more indicators, or measures, which may derive from observation, self-report, available records or statistics, books and other written documents, clinical indicators, pictures, discarded materials, or some combination of these.

- Single-question measures may be closed-ended, with fixed-response choices, or open-ended, with fixed-response choices and an option to write another response.

- Indexes and scales measure a concept by combining answers to several questions and thus reducing idiosyncratic error variation. Several issues should be explored with every intended index: Does each question actually measure the same concept? Does combining items in an index obscure important relationships between individual questions and other variables? Is the index multidimensional?

- Level of measurement indicates the type of information obtained about a variable and the type of statistics that can be used to describe its variation. The four levels of measurement can be ordered by the complexity of the mathematical operations they permit: nominal (least complex), ordinal, interval, ratio (most complex). The measurement level of a variable is determined by how the variable is operationalized. Dichotomies, a special case, may be treated as measured at the nominal, ordinal, or interval level.

- The validity of measures should always be tested. There are four basic approaches: (1) face validation, (2) content validation, (3) criterion validation (either predictive or concurrent), and (4) construct validation (convergent or discriminant validity). Criterion validation provides the strongest evidence of measurement validity, but there often is no criterion to use in validating social science measures.

- Measurement reliability is a prerequisite for measurement validity, although reliable measures are not necessarily valid. Reliability can be assessed through a test–retest procedure, by interitem consistency, through a comparison of responses to alternate forms of the test, or by consistency among observers.

STUDENT STUDY SITE

Sharpen your skills with SAGE edge at **edge.sagepub.com/schutt8e. SAGE edge for students** provides a personalized approach to help you accomplish your coursework goals in an easy-to-use learning environment.

Discussion Questions

1. What does trust mean to you? Is the picture in this chapter "worth a thousand words" about trust, or is something missing? Identify two examples of "trust in action" and explain how they represent *your* concept of trust. Now develop a short definition of trust (without checking a dictionary). Compare your definition with those of your classmates and what you find in a dictionary. Can you improve your definition based on some feedback?

2. What questions would you ask to measure level of trust among students? How about feelings of being "in" or "out" with regard to a group? Write five questions for an index and suggest response choices for each. How would you validate this measure using a construct validation approach? Can you think of a criterion validation procedure for your measure?

3. If you were given a questionnaire right now that asked you about your use of alcohol and illicit drugs in the past year, would you disclose the details fully? How do you think others would respond? What if the questionnaire was anonymous? What if there was a confidential ID number on the questionnaire so that the researcher could keep track of who responded? What criterion validation procedure would you suggest for assessing measurement validity?

4. The questions in Exhibit 4.20 are selected from my survey of shelter staff (Schutt & Fennell 1992). First, identify the level of measurement for each question. Then, rewrite each question so that it measures the same variable but at a different level.

For example, you might change the question that measures seniority at the ratio level (in years, months, and days) to one that measures seniority at the ordinal level (in categories). Or you might change a variable measured at the ordinal level, such as highest grade in school completed, to one measured at the ratio level. For the variables measured at the nominal level, try to identify at least two underlying quantitative dimensions of variation, and write questions to measure variation along these dimensions. For example, you might change the question asking, "What is your current job title?" to two questions that ask about the pay in their current job and the extent to which their job is satisfying.

What are the advantages and disadvantages of phrasing each question at one level of measurement rather than another? Do you see any limitations on the types of questions for which levels of measurement can be changed?

Exhibit 4.20 **Selected Shelter Staff Survey Questions**

1. What is your current job title? _____

2. What is your current employment status?
   Paid, full-time _____ 1
   Paid, part-time (less than 30 hours per week) _____ 2

3. When did you start your current position? _____ / _____ / _____
                                              Month   Day   Year

4. In the past month, how often did you help guests deal with each of the following types of problems? (Circle one response on each line.)

	Very often						Never
Job training/placement	1	2	3	4	5	6	7
Lack of food or bed	1	2	3	4	5	6	7
Drinking problems	1	2	3	4	5	6	7

5. How likely is it that you will leave this shelter within the next year?
   Very likely _____ 1
   Moderately _____ 2
   Not very likely _____ 3
   Not likely at all _____ 4

6. What is the highest grade in school you have completed at this time?
   First through eighth grade _____ 1
   Some high school _____ 2
   High school diploma _____ 3
   Some college _____ 4
   College degree _____ 5
   Some graduate work _____ 6
   Graduate degree _____ 7

7. Are you a veteran?
   Yes _____ 1
   No _____ 2

Source: Based on Schutt 1992: 7–10, 15, 16. Results reported in Schutt, R. K., & M. L. Fennell. 1992. "Shelter Staff Satisfaction With Services, the Service Network and Their Jobs." *Current Research on Occupations and Professions* 7:177–200.

Practice Exercises

1. Now it's time to try your hand at operationalization with survey-based measures. Formulate a few fixed-choice questions to measure variables pertaining to the concepts you researched for the discussion questions, such as feelings of trust or perceptions of the level of substance abuse in your community. Arrange to interview one or two other students with the questions you have developed. Ask one fixed-choice question at a time, record your interviewee's answer, and then probe for additional comments and clarifications. Your goal is to discover how respondents understand the meaning of the concept you used in the question and what additional issues shape their response to it.

   When you have finished the interviews, analyze your experience: Did the interviewees interpret the fixed-choice questions and response choices as you intended? Did you learn more about the concepts you were working on? Should your conceptual definition be refined? Should the questions be rewritten, or would more fixed-choice questions be necessary to capture adequately the variation among respondents?

2. Now, try index construction. You might begin with some of the questions you wrote for Practice Exercise 1. Try to write about four or five fixed-choice questions that each measure the same concept. Write each question so that it has the same response choices. Now, conduct a literature search to identify an index that another researcher used to measure your concept or a similar concept. Compare your index to the published index. Which seems preferable to you? Why?

3. Develop a plan for evaluating the validity of a measure. Your instructor will give you a copy of a questionnaire actually used in a study. Pick one question, and define the concept that you believe it is intended to measure. Then develop a construct validation strategy involving other measures in the questionnaire that you think should be related to the question of interest—if it measures what you think it measures.

4. What are some of the research questions you could attempt to answer with the available statistical data? Visit your library and ask for an introduction to the government documents collection. Inspect the volumes from the U.S. Census Bureau that report population characteristics by city and state. List five questions you could explore with such data. Identify six variables implied by these research questions that you could operationalize with the available data. What are the three factors that might influence variation in these measures, other than the phenomenon of interest? (Hint: Consider how the data are collected.)

5. One quick and easy way to check your understanding of the levels of measurement, reliability, and validity is with the interactive exercises on the study site. First, select one of the "Levels of Measurement" options from the Interactive Exercises link on the main menu, and then read the review information at the start of the lesson. You will then be presented with about 10 variables and response choices and asked to identify the level of measurement for each one. If you make a mistake, the program will give a brief explanation about the level of measurement. After you have reviewed one to four of these lessons, repeat the process with one or more of the "Valid and Reliable Measures" lessons.

6. Go to the book's study site and review the Methods section of two of the research articles that you find at edge.sagepub.com/schutt8e. Write a short summary of the concepts and measures used in these studies. Which article provides clearer definitions of the major concepts? Does either article discuss possible weaknesses in measurement procedures?

Ethics Questions

1. The ethical guidelines for social research require that subjects give their *informed consent* before participating in an interview. How "informed" do you think subjects have to be? If you are interviewing people to learn about substance abuse and its impact on other aspects of health, is it okay to just tell respondents in advance that you are conducting a study of health issues? What if you plan to inquire about victimization experiences? Explain your reasoning.

2. Some Homeland Security practices as well as inadvertent releases of web searching records have raised new concerns about the use of unobtrusive measures of behavior and attitudes. If all identifying information is removed, do you think social scientists should be able to study the extent of prostitution in different cities by analyzing police records? How about how much alcohol different types of people use by linking deidentified credit card records to store purchases?

Web Exercises

1. How would you define *alcoholism*? Write a brief definition. Based on this conceptualization, describe a method of measurement that would be valid for a study of alcoholism (alcoholism as you define it). Now go to the American Council for Drug Education (ACDE) and read some of their facts about alcohol at www.niaaa.nih.gov/alcohol-health/overview-alcohol-consumption/alcohol-use-disorders. Is this information consistent with your definition?

   What are the "facts" about alcoholism presented by the National Council on Alcohol and Drug Dependence (NCADD) at www.ncadd.org? How is alcoholism conceptualized? Based on this conceptualizing, give an example of one method that would be a valid measurement in a study of alcoholism.

   Now look at some of the other related links accessible from the ACDE and NCADD websites. What are some of the different conceptualizations of alcoholism that you find? How does the chosen conceptualization affect one's choice of methods of measurement?

2. What are the latest findings about student substance abuse from the Harvard School of Public Health? Check out http://archive.sph.harvard.edu/cas/AllIndex.html and write a brief report.

3. A list of different measures of substance abuse is available at a site maintained by the National Institute on Alcoholism and Alcohol Abuse, www.niaaa.nih.gov/research/guidelines-and-resources/recommended-alcohol-questions. There is lengthy discussion of the various self-report instruments for alcohol problem screening among adults at http://pubs.niaaa.nih.gov/publications/AssessingAlcohol/selfreport.htm (Connors & Volk 2004). Read the Connors and Volk article, and pick two of the instruments they discuss (Connors & Volk 2004:27–32). What concept of substance abuse is reflected in each measure? Is either measure multidimensional? What do you think the relative advantages of each measure might be? What evidence is provided about their reliability and validity? What other test of validity would you suggest?

Video Interview Questions

Listen to the researcher interview for Chapter 4 at edge.sagepub.com/schutt8e.

1. What problems does Dana Hunt identify with questions designed to measure frequency of substance abuse and aggressive feelings"?

2. What could be done to overcome these problems?

SPSS Exercises

1. View the variable information for the variables *AGE, CHILDS, PARTYID3, SOCBAR, RACE,* and *INCOME06.* Click on the "variable list" icon or choose Utilities/Variables from the menu. Choose *PARTYID,* then *SOCBAR.* At which levels (nominal/categorical, ordinal, interval, ratio) are each of these variables measured? (By the way, DK means "Don't Know," NA means "No Answer," and NAP means "Not Applicable.")

2. Review the actual questions used to measure four of the variables in Question 1 or in your hypotheses in Chapter 2's

   SPSS exercise (Question 3). You can find most GSS questions at the following website: www.norc.org/GSS+Website/Browse+GSS+Variables. Name the variable that you believe each question measures. Discuss the face validity and content validity of each question as a measure of its corresponding variable. Explain why you conclude that each measure is valid or not.

3. CONGOV is part of an index involving the following question: How much confidence do you have in

   a. Executive branch of the federal government

Research That Matters, Questions That Count

Young adults who are homeless face a number of barriers to gaining housing and maintaining community connections. Lack of a job is one of the greatest such barriers, but little is known about how many homeless young adults are able to obtain a job and what distinguishes them from others who remain unemployed. Kristin Ferguson at the University of California, San Diego, and social scientists at other universities, Kimberly Bender, Sanna Thompson, Elaine Maccio, and David Pollio (2012) designed a research project to investigate this issue.

Ferguson and her collaborators (2012:389–390) decided to interview homeless young adults in five U.S. cities in different regions. The researchers secured the cooperation of multiservice, nonprofit organizations that provide comprehensive services to homeless youth and then approached youth in these agencies and on the streets—accompanied by agency outreach staff. The researchers first told potential participants about the project and then asked whether they were 18 to 24 years old and had been away from home for at least 2 weeks in the previous month. The potential participants who indicated they were interested and eligible for the study were then offered the opportunity to sign a consent form.

One of the survey findings was that young adults in three of the five cities differed in their employment status and sources of income generation. For example, homeless young adults in Los Angeles were more likely to be employed than others were, and Austin young adults were significantly more likely to receive their income from panhandling (Ferguson et al. 2012:400).

1. What other research questions would interest you in a study of this population?

2. How confident are you that the differences found between the youth surveyed in the five cities reflect the actual differences on average between all the homeless youth in these cities? Explain your reasoning.

3. Presuming the researchers did not have the time or money to interview all the homeless youth, is there anything they could have done in selecting youth that would have made you more confident in their findings? Be as specific as possible.

4. How would you go about selecting students to survey at your school if you wanted to describe accurately the social backgrounds of the entire student body?

In this chapter, you will learn about procedures for selecting samples from larger populations. By the end of the chapter, you will understand why drawing a representative sample is very important and often very difficult, particularly in studies of hard-to-reach groups such as homeless youth. You will also learn strategies for identifying people to interview intensively when representing a larger population is not the key goal. After you finish the chapter, test yourself by reading the 2012 *Youth & Society* article by Kristin Ferguson and her colleagues at the *Investigating the Social World* study site and completing the related interactive exercises for Chapter 5 at edge.sagepub.com/schutt8e.

Ferguson, Kristin M., Kimberly Bender, Sanna J. Thompson, Elaine M. Maccio, and David Pollio. 2012. "Employment Status and Income Generation Among Homeless Young Adults: Results From a Five-City, Mixed-Methods Study." *Youth & Society* 44:385–407.

It is a sad story with an all-too-uncommon happy—although uncertain—ending. Together with one other such story and comments by several service staff, the article provides a persuasive rationale for the new housing program. However, we don't know whether the two participants interviewed for the story are like most program participants, most homeless persons in New York, or most homeless persons throughout the United States—or whether they are just two people who caught the eye of this one reporter. In other words, we don't know how generalizable their stories are, and if we don't have confidence in generalizability, then the validity of this account of how the program participants became homeless is suspect. Because we don't know whether their situation is widely shared or unique, we cannot really judge what the account tells us about the social world.

In this chapter, you will learn about sampling methods, the procedures that primarily determine the generalizability of research findings. I first review the rationale for using sampling in social research and consider two circumstances when sampling is not necessary. The chapter then turns to specific sampling methods and when they are most appropriate, using examples from research on homelessness. This section is followed by a section on sampling distributions, which introduces you to the logic of statistical inference—that is, how to determine how likely it is that our sample statistics represent the population from which the sample was drawn. By the chapter's end, you should understand which questions you need to ask to evaluate the generalizability of a study as well as what choices you need to make when designing a sampling strategy. You should also realize that it is just as important to select the "right" people or objects to study as it is to ask participants the right questions.

Video Link
History of Sampling

🔲 Sample Planning

You have encountered the problem of generalizability in each of the studies you have read about in this book. For example, Keith Hampton and Barry Wellman (1999) discussed their findings in Netville as though they could be generalized to residents of other communities; Norman Nie and Lutz Erbring (2000) generalized their Internet survey findings to the entire U.S. adult population; and Stanley Milgram's (1963) findings about obedience to authority were generalized to the entire world. Whether we are designing a sampling strategy or evaluating someone else's findings, we have to understand how and why researchers decide to sample and what the consequences of these decisions are for the generalizability of the study's findings.

The Purpose of Sampling

Have you ever met, or seen, a homeless person like "Mr. Scott"? Perhaps you have encountered many, or know some people who have been homeless. Did you ever wonder if other homeless persons are like those you have encountered yourself? Have you found yourself drawing conclusions about persons who are homeless based on those you have met? Just like the reporter, you know that you shouldn't conclude that all homeless persons are like those you have encountered yourself, but you also know that you can't hope to learn about every homeless person, even in your own city or town.

The purpose of sampling is to generate a set of individuals or other entities that give us a valid picture of all such individuals, or other entities. That is, a sample is a subset of the larger set of individuals or other entities in which we are interested. If we have done a good job of sampling, we will be able to generalize what we have learned from the subset to the larger set from which it was selected.

As researchers, we call the set of individuals or other entities to which we want to be able to generalize our findings the **population**. For example, a city government may want to describe the city's entire adult homeless population. If, as is usually the case, the government does not have the time or resources to survey all homeless individuals in the city, it may fund a survey of a subset of these individuals. This subset of the population of interest is a **sample**. The individual members of this sample are called **elements**, or elementary units.

> **Population:** The entire set of individuals or other entities to which study findings are to be generalized.
>
> **Sample:** A subset of a population that is used to study the population as a whole.
>
> **Elements:** The individual members of the population whose characteristics are to be measured.

Define Sample Components and the Population

In many studies, we sample directly from the elements in the population of interest. We may survey a sample of the entire population of students in a school, based on a list obtained from the registrar's office. This list, from which the elements of the population are selected, is termed the **sampling frame**. The students who are selected and interviewed from that list are the elements.

> **Sampling frame:** A list of all elements or other units containing the elements in a population.

In some studies, the entities that can be reached easily are not the same as the elements from which we want information, but they include those elements. For example, we may have a list of households but not a list of the entire population of a town, even though the adults are the elements that we actually want to sample. In this situation, we could draw a sample of households so that we can identify the adult individuals in these households. The households are termed **enumeration units**, and the adults in the households are the elements (Levy & Lemeshow 1999:13–14).

> **Enumeration units:** Units that contain one or more elements and that are listed in a sampling frame.

Sometimes, the individuals or other entities from which we collect information are not actually the elements in our study. For example, a researcher might sample schools for a survey about educational practices and then interview a sample of teachers in each sampled school to obtain the information about educational practices. Both the schools and the teachers are termed **sampling units**, because we sample from both (Levy & Lemeshow 1999:22). The schools are selected in the first stage of the sample, so they are the *primary sampling units* (in this case, they are also the elements in the study). The teachers are *secondary sampling units* (but they are not elements because they are used to provide information about the entire school) (see Exhibit 5.1).

> **Sampling units:** Units listed at each stage of a multistage sampling design.

It is important to know exactly what population a sample can represent when you select or evaluate sample components. In a survey of "adult Americans," the general population may reasonably be construed as all residents of the United States who are at least 21 years old. But always be alert to ways in which the population may have been narrowed by the sample selection procedures. For example, perhaps only English-speaking residents of the United States were surveyed. The population for a study is the aggregation of elements that we actually focus on and sample from, not some larger aggregation that we really wish we could have studied.

Some populations, such as the homeless, are not identified by a simple criterion such as a geographic boundary or an organizational membership. Clear definition of such a population is difficult but quite necessary. Anyone should be able to determine just what population was actually studied. However, studies of homeless persons in the early 1980s "did not propose definitions, did not use screening questions to be sure that the people they interviewed were indeed homeless, and did not make major efforts to cover the universe of homeless people" (Burt 1996:15). (Perhaps just homeless persons in one shelter were studied.) The result was a "collection of studies that could not be compared" (Burt 1996:15). Several studies of homeless persons in urban areas addressed the problem by employing a more explicit definition of the population: "people who had no home or permanent place to stay of their own (meaning they rented or owned it themselves) and no regular arrangement to stay at someone else's place" (Burt 1996:18).

Even this more explicit definition still leaves some questions unanswered: What is a "regular arrangement"? How permanent does a "permanent place" have to be? In a study of homeless persons in Chicago, Michael Sosin, Paul Colson, and Susan Grossman (1988) answered these questions in their definition of the population of interest:

> We define the homeless as: those current[ly] residing for at least one day but for less than fourteen with a friend or relative, not paying rent, and not sure that the length of stay will surpass fourteen days; those currently residing in a shelter, whether overnight or transitional; those currently without normal, acceptable shelter arrangements and thus sleeping on the street, in doorways, in abandoned buildings, in cars, in subway or bus stations, in alleys, and so forth; those residing in a treatment center for the indigent who have lived at the facility for less than 90 days and who claim that they have no place to go, when released. (p. 22)

Journal Link
Symbolic Boundaries

This definition reflects accurately Sosin et al.'s concept of homelessness and allows researchers in other locations or at other times to develop procedures for studying a comparable population. The more complete and explicit the definition is of the population from which a sample was selected, the more precise our generalizations can be.

Exhibit 5.1 Sample Components in a Two-Stage Study

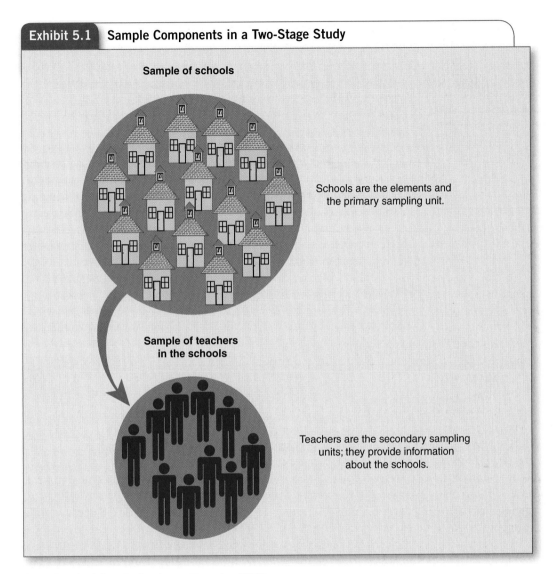

Sample of schools

Schools are the elements and the primary sampling unit.

Sample of teachers in the schools

Teachers are the secondary sampling units; they provide information about the schools.

Source: Based on information from Levy and Lemeshow (1999).

Evaluate Generalizability

Once we have defined clearly the population from which we will sample, we need to determine the scope of the generalizations we will make from our sample. Do you recall from Chapter 2 the two different meanings of generalizability?

Can the findings from a sample of the population be generalized to the population from which the sample was selected? Did Miller McPherson, Lynn Smith-Lovin, and Matthew Brashears' (2006) findings about social ties apply to the United States, Rich Ling and Gitte Stald's (2010) to all of Norway and Denmark, or Henry Wechsler and colleagues' (2002) study of binge drinking to all U.S. college students? This type of generalizability was defined as *sample generalizability* in Chapter 2.

Can the findings from a study of one population be generalized to another, somewhat different population? Are mobile phone users in Norway and Denmark similar to those in other Scandinavian countries? In other

European countries? Throughout the world? Are students similar to full-time employees, housewives, or other groups in their drinking patterns? Do findings from a laboratory study about obedience to authority at an elite northeastern U.S. college in the 1960s differ from those that would be obtained today at a commuter college in the Midwest? What is the generalizability of the results from a survey of homeless persons in one city? This type of generalizability question was defined as *cross-population generalizability* in Chapter 2.

> **Sampling error:** Any difference between the characteristics of a sample and the characteristics of a population; the larger the sampling error, the less representative the sample.

This chapter focuses attention primarily on the problem of sample generalizability: Can findings from a sample be generalized to the population from which the sample was drawn? This is really the most basic question to ask about a sample, and social research methods provide many tools with which to address it.

Sample generalizability depends on sample quality, which is determined by the amount of **sampling error**—the difference between the characteristics of a sample and the characteristics of the population from which it was selected. The larger the sampling error, the less representative the sample—and thus the less generalizable the findings. To assess sample quality when you are planning or evaluating a study, ask yourself these questions:

- From what population were the cases selected?

- What method was used to select cases from this population?

- Do the cases that were studied represent, in the aggregate, the population from which they were selected?

Research in the News

WHAT ARE BEST PRACTICES FOR SAMPLING VULNERABLE POPULATIONS?

In the 1950s, Perry Hudson studied the effectiveness of early prostate screening in reducing cancer. He sampled 1,200 alcoholic homeless men from the flophouses of Lower Manhattan. His research was funded and supported by the National Institutes of Health, but he did not properly inform participants of the risks associated with prostate screening. Many men who participated endured a painful prostate biopsy and no medical follow-up if they screened positive for cancer. Robert Aronowitz, a medical historian, looks back at this ethical tragedy as "a convenient population" used in the name of science.

For Further Thought

1. Since this time, research standards have been changed to protect vulnerable populations. In what types of circumstances do you think that it is ethical to draw samples for research from prisoners, patients, students, and other "captive" populations that are convenient to study?

2. Should samples of large populations exclude persons who suffer from mental illness, addiction, extreme poverty, limited literacy, or other conditions that might make them less likely to make a fully informed decision about participation in research? Are there any risks with such exclusions?

News source: Kolata, Gina. 2013. "Decades Later, Condemnation for a Skid Row Cancer Study." *The New York Times,* October 18:A1.

Cross-population generalizability involves quite different considerations. Researchers are engaging in cross-population generalizability when they project their findings onto groups or populations much larger than, or simply different from, those they have actually studied. The population to which generalizations are made in this way can be termed the **target population**—a set of elements larger than or different from the population that was sampled and to which the researcher would like to generalize any study findings. When we generalize findings to target populations, we must be somewhat speculative. We must carefully consider the validity of claims that the findings can be applied to other groups, geographic areas, cultures, or times.

> **Target population:** A set of elements larger than or different from the population sampled and to which the researcher would like to generalize study findings.

Because the validity of cross-population generalizations cannot be tested empirically, except by conducting more research in other settings, I do not focus much attention on this problem here. But I return to the problem of cross-population generalizability in Chapter 7, which addresses experimental research, and in Chapter 13, which discusses methods for studying different societies.

Assess the Diversity of the Population

Sampling is unnecessary if all the units in the population are identical. Physicists don't need to select a representative sample of atomic particles to learn about basic physical processes. They can study a single atomic particle because it is identical to every other particle of its type. Similarly, biologists don't need to sample a particular type of plant to determine whether a given chemical has toxic effects on that particular type. The idea is "If you've seen one, you've seen 'em all."

What about people? Certainly, all people are not identical (nor are other animals, in many respects). Nonetheless, if we are studying physical or psychological processes that are the same among all people, sampling is not needed to achieve generalizable findings. Psychologists and social psychologists often conduct experiments on college students to learn about processes that they think are identical across individuals. They believe that most people would have the same reactions as the college students if they experienced the same experimental conditions. Field researchers who observe group processes in a small community sometimes make the same assumption.

There is a potential problem with this assumption, however: There's no way to know for sure if the processes being studied are identical across all people. In fact, experiments can give different results depending on the type of people who are studied or the conditions for the experiment. Milgram's (1965) classic experiments on obedience to authority, which you studied in Chapter 3, illustrate this point very well. You remember that the original Milgram experiments tested the willingness of male volunteers in New Haven, Connecticut, to comply with the instructions of an authority figure to give "electric shocks" to someone else, even when these shocks seemed to harm the person receiving them. In most cases, the volunteers complied. Milgram concluded that people are very obedient to authority.

Were these results generalizable to all men, to men in the United States, or to men in New Haven? The initial experiment was repeated many times to assess the generalizability of the findings. Similar results were obtained in many replications of the Milgram experiments—that is, when the experimental conditions and subjects were similar to those Milgram studied. Other studies showed that some groups were less likely to react so obediently. Given certain conditions, such as another "subject" in the room who refused to administer the shocks, subjects were likely to resist authority.

So, what do the initial experimental results tell us about how people will react to an authoritarian movement in the real world, when conditions are not so carefully controlled? In the real social world, people may be less likely to react obediently as well. Other individuals may argue against obedience to a particular leader's commands, or people may see on TV the consequences of their actions. But alternatively, people in the real world may be even more obedient to authority than were the experimental subjects, for example, when they get swept up in mobs or are captivated by ideological fervor. Milgram's initial research and the many replications of it give us great insight into human behavior partly because they help identify the types of people and conditions to which the initial findings (lack of resistance to authority) can be generalized. But generalizing the results of single experiments is always risky because such research often studies a small number of people who are not selected to represent any particular population.

But what if your goal is not to learn about individuals, but about the culture or subculture in a society or group? The logic of sampling does not apply if the goal is to learn about culture that is shared across individuals:

> When people all provide the same information, it is redundant to ask a question over and over. Only enough people need to be surveyed to eliminate the possibility of errors and to allow for those who might diverge from the norm. (Heise 2010:15)

If you are trying to describe a group or society's culture, you may choose individuals for the survey based on their knowledge of the culture, not as representatives of a population of individuals (Heise 2010:16). In this situation, what is important about the individuals surveyed is what they have in common, not their diversity.

Representative sample: A sample that "looks like" the population from which it was selected in all respects that are potentially relevant to the study. The distribution of characteristics among the elements of a representative sample is the same as the distribution of those characteristics among the total population. In an unrepresentative sample, some characteristics are overrepresented or underrepresented.

Keep these exceptions in mind, but the main point is that social scientists rarely can skirt the problem of demonstrating the generalizability of their findings. If a small sample has been studied in an experiment or a field research project, the study should be replicated in different settings or, preferably, with a **representative sample** of the population to which generalizations are sought (see Exhibit 5.2). The social world and the people in it are just too diverse to be considered *identical units* in most respects. Social psychological experiments and small field studies have produced good social science, but they need to be replicated in other settings, with other subjects, to claim any generalizability. Even when we believe that we have uncovered basic social processes in a laboratory experiment or field observation, we should be very concerned with seeking confirmation in other samples and in other research.

Consider a Census

Census: Research in which information is obtained through responses from or information about all available members of an entire population.

In some circumstances, it may be feasible to skirt the issue of generalizability by conducting a **census**—studying the entire population of interest—rather than drawing a sample. This is what the federal government tries to do every 10 years with the U.S. Census. Censuses also include studies of all the employees (or students) in small organizations, studies comparing all 50 states, and studies of the entire population of a particular type of organization in some area. However, in comparison with the U.S. Census and similar efforts in other countries, states, and cities, the population that is studied in these other censuses is relatively small.

The reason that social scientists don't often attempt to collect data from all the members of some large population is simply that doing so would be too expensive and time-consuming—and they can do almost as well with a sample. Some social scientists conduct research with data from the U.S. Census, but the government collects the data and our tax dollars pay for the effort to get one person in about 134 million households to answer 10 questions. To conduct the 2010 census, the U.S. Census Bureau spent more than $5.5 billion and hired 3.8 million people (U.S. Census Bureau 2010a, 2010b).

Even if the population of interest for a survey is a small town of 20,000 or students in a university of 10,000, researchers will have to sample. The costs of surveying "just" thousands of individuals exceed by far the budgets for most research projects. In fact, not even the U.S. Census Bureau can afford to have everyone answer all the questions that should be covered in the census. So it draws a sample. Every household

Exhibit 5.2 Representative and Unrepresentative Samples

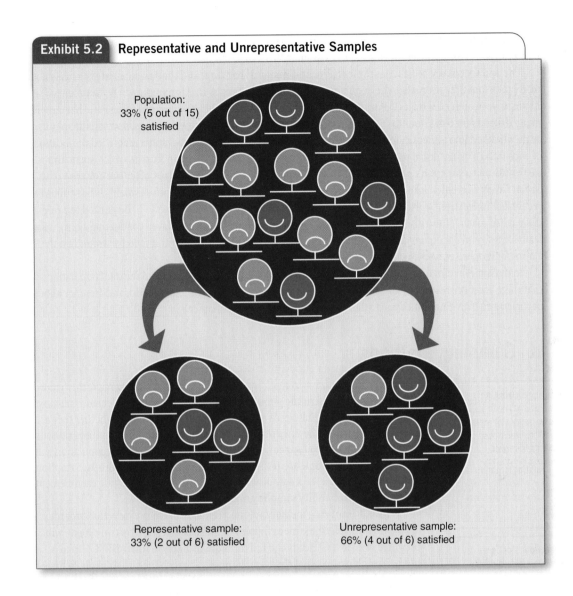

Population:
33% (5 out of 15)
satisfied

Representative sample:
33% (2 out of 6) satisfied

Unrepresentative sample:
66% (4 out of 6) satisfied

must complete a short version of the census (it had 10 basic questions in 2010), but a sample of 3 million households is sent a long form (with about 60 questions) every year (U.S. Census Bureau 2010d). This more detailed sample survey was launched in 2005 as the American Community Survey and replaces what formerly was a long form of the census that was administered to one sixth of the population at the same time as the regular census.

The fact that it is hard to get people to complete a survey is another reason why survey research can be costly. Even the U.S. Census Bureau (1999) must make multiple efforts to increase the rate of response despite the federal law requiring all citizens to complete their census questionnaire. Almost three quarters (72%) of the U.S. population returned their 2010 census questionnaire through the mail (costing 42 cents per envelope) (U.S. Census Bureau 2010a, 2010c). However, 565,000 temporary workers and as many as six follow-ups were required to contact the rest of the households that did not respond by mail, at a cost of $57 per nonrespondent (U.S. Census Bureau 2010a, 2010c). Even after all that, we know from the 2000 U.S. Census that some groups are still likely to be underrepresented (Armas 2002; Holmes 2001a), including minority groups (Kershaw 2000), impoverished cities (Zielbauer 2000), well-to-do individuals in gated communities and luxury buildings (Langford 2000), and even college students (Abel 2000). The number of persons missed in the 2000 census was estimated to be between 3.2 and 6.4 million (U.S. Census Bureau 2001).

The average survey project has far less legal and financial backing, and thus an adequate census is not likely to be possible. Consider the problems of conducting a census in Afghanistan. The first census in 23 years was conducted by its Central Statistics Office in 2003 and 2004, interrupted by snow that cut off many districts for 6 or 7 months. Teams of census takers carried tents, sleeping bags, and satellite phones as they trekked into remote mountainous provinces. An accompanying cartographer identified the location of each village using global positioning systems (GPS) (Gall 2003:A4). Even in Russia, which spent almost $200 million to survey its population of about 145 million, resource shortages after the collapse of the Soviet Union prevented an adequate census (Myers 2002). In Vladivostok, "Many residents, angry about a recent rise in electricity prices, refused to take part. Residents on Russian Island . . . boycotted to protest dilapidated roads" (Tavernise 2002:A13). In Iraq, dominant groups may have delayed conducting a census for fear that it would document gains in population among disadvantaged groups and thereby strengthen their claims for more resources (Myers 2010:A10).

In most survey situations, it is much better to survey only a limited number from the total population so that there are more resources for follow-up procedures that can overcome reluctance or indifference about participation. (I give more attention to the problem of nonresponse in Chapter 8.)

🔲 Sampling Methods

Probability sampling method: A sampling method that relies on a random, or chance, selection method so that the probability of selection of population elements is known.

Nonprobability sampling method: Sampling method in which the probability of selection of population elements is unknown.

Probability of selection: The likelihood that an element will be selected from the population for inclusion in the sample. In a census of all elements of a population, the probability that any particular element will be selected is 1.0. If half the elements in the population are sampled on the basis of chance (say, by tossing a coin), the probability of selection for each element is one half, or .5. As the size of the sample as a proportion of the population decreases, so does the probability of selection.

Random sampling: A method of sampling that relies on a random, or chance, selection method so that every element of the sampling frame has a known probability of being selected.

We can now study more systematically the features of samples that make them more or less likely to represent the population from which they are selected. The most important distinction that needs to be made about the samples is whether they are based on a probability or a nonprobability sampling method. Sampling methods that allow us to know in advance how likely it is that any element of a population will be selected for the sample are termed **probability sampling methods**. Sampling methods that do not let us know in advance the likelihood of selecting each element are termed **nonprobability sampling methods**.

Probability sampling methods rely on a random, or chance, selection procedure, which is, in principle, the same as flipping a coin to decide which of two people "wins" and which one "loses." Heads and tails are equally likely to turn up in a coin toss, so both persons have an equal chance of winning. That chance, their **probability of selection**, is 1 out of 2, or .5.

Flipping a coin is a fair way to select one of two people because the selection process harbors no systematic bias. You might win or lose the coin toss, but you know that the outcome was due simply to chance, not to bias. For the same reason, a roll of a six-sided die is a fair way to choose one of six possible outcomes (the odds of selection are 1 out of 6, or .17). Dealing out a hand after shuffling a deck of cards is a fair way to allocate sets of cards in a poker game (the odds of each person getting a particular outcome, such as a full house or a flush, are the same). Similarly, state lotteries use a random process to select winning numbers. Thus, the odds of winning a lottery, the probability of selection, are known, even though they are very much smaller (perhaps 1 out of 1 million) than the odds of winning a coin toss.

There is a natural tendency to confuse the concept of **random sampling**, in which cases are selected only on the basis of chance, with a haphazard method of sampling. On first impression, "leaving things up to chance" seems to imply not exerting any control over the sampling method. But to ensure that nothing but chance influences the selection of cases, the researcher must proceed very methodically, leaving nothing to chance except the selection of the cases themselves. The researcher must follow carefully controlled procedures if a purely random process is to occur. When reading about sampling methods, do not assume that a random sample was obtained just because the researcher used a random selection method at some point in the sampling process. Look for those two particular problems: selecting elements from an incomplete list of the total population and failing to obtain an adequate response rate.

If the sampling frame is incomplete, a sample selected randomly from that list will not really be a random sample of the population. You should always consider the adequacy of the sampling frame. Even for a simple population such as a university's student body, the registrar's list is likely to be at least a bit out-of-date at any given time. For example, some students will have dropped out, but their status will not yet be officially recorded. Although you may judge the amount of error introduced in this particular situation to be negligible, the problems are greatly compounded for a larger population. The sampling frame for a city, state, or nation is always likely to be incomplete because of constant migration into and out of the area. Even unavoidable omissions from the sampling frame can bias a sample against particular groups within the population.

An inclusive sampling frame may still yield systematic bias if many sample members cannot be contacted or refuse to participate. Nonresponse is a major hazard in survey research because **nonrespondents** are likely to differ systematically from those who take the time to participate. You should not assume that findings from a randomly selected sample will be generalizable to the population from which the sample was selected if the rate of nonresponse is considerable (certainly not if it is much above 30%).

> **Nonrespondents:** People or other entities who do not participate in a study although they are selected for the sample.

Probability Sampling Methods

Probability sampling methods are those in which the probability of selection is known and is not zero (so there is some chance of selecting each element). These methods randomly select elements and therefore have no **systematic bias**; nothing but chance determines which elements are included in the sample. This feature of probability samples makes them much more desirable than nonprobability samples when the goal is to generalize to a larger population.

> **Systematic bias:** Overrepresentation or underrepresentation of some population characteristics in a sample resulting from the method used to select the sample; a sample shaped by systematic sampling error is a biased sample.

Although a random sample has no systematic bias, it will certainly have some sampling error resulting from chance. The probability of selecting a head is .5 in a single toss of a coin and in 20, 30, or however many tosses of a coin you like. But it is perfectly possible to toss a coin twice and get a head both times. The random "sample" of the two sides of the coin is selected in an unbiased fashion, but it still is unrepresentative. Imagine selecting randomly a sample of 10 people from a population comprising 50 men and 50 women. Just by chance, can't you imagine finding that these 10 people include 7 women and only 3 men? Fortunately, we can determine mathematically the likely degree of sampling error in an estimate based on a random sample (as we'll discuss later in this chapter)—assuming that the sample's randomness has not been destroyed by a high rate of nonresponse or by poor control over the selection process.

In general, both the size of the sample and the homogeneity (sameness) of the population affect the degree of error as a result of chance; the proportion of the population that the sample represents does not. To elaborate,

- *The larger the sample, the more confidence we can have in the sample's representativeness.* If we randomly pick 5 people to represent the entire population of our city, our sample is unlikely to be very representative of the entire population in age, gender, race, attitudes, and so on. But if we randomly pick 100 people, the odds of having a representative sample are much better; with a random sample of 1,000, the odds become very good indeed.

- *The more homogeneous the population, the more confidence we can have in the representativeness of a sample of any particular size.* Let's say we plan to draw samples of 50 from each of two communities to estimate mean family income. One community is quite diverse, with family incomes varying from $12,000 to $85,000. In the other, more homogeneous community, family incomes are concentrated in a narrow range, from $41,000 to $64,000. The estimated mean family income based on the sample from the homogeneous community is more likely to be representative than is the estimate based on the sample from the more heterogeneous community. With less variation to represent, fewer cases are needed to represent the homogeneous community.

- *The fraction of the total population that a sample contains does not affect the sample's representativeness unless that fraction is large.* We can regard any sampling fraction less than 2% with about the same degree of confidence (Sudman 1976:184). Actually, sample representativeness is not likely to increase much until the sampling fraction is quite a bit higher. Other things being equal, a sample of 1,000 from a population of 1 million (with a sampling fraction of 0.001, or 0.1%) is much better than a sample of 100 from a population of 10,000 (although the sampling fraction for this smaller sample is 0.01, or 1%, which is 10 times higher). The size of the samples is what makes representativeness more likely, not the proportion of the whole that the sample represents.

Polls to predict presidential election outcomes illustrate both the value of random sampling and the problems that it cannot overcome. In most presidential elections pollsters have predicted accurately the outcomes of the actual votes by using random sampling and phone interviewing to learn for which candidate the likely voters intend to vote. Exhibit 5.3 shows how close these sample-based predictions have been in the last 14 contests. The exceptions were the 1980 and 1992 elections, when third-party candidates had an unpredicted effect. Otherwise, the small discrepancies between the votes predicted through random sampling and the actual votes can be attributed to random error.

The Gallup poll did not do quite as well in predicting the results of the 2008 and 2012 presidential elections as some other major polling organizations did. The final 2008 Gallup prediction was that Barack Obama would win with 55% to John McCain's 44% (Gallup 2011). The race turned out a bit closer, with Obama winning by

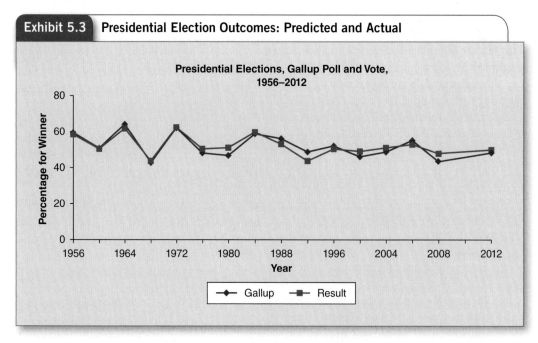

Exhibit 5.3 Presidential Election Outcomes: Predicted and Actual

Sources: Gallup. 2011. *Election Polls—Accuracy Record in Presidential Elections;* Panagopoulos, Costas. 2008. "Poll Accuracy in the 2008 Presidential Election"; Jones, Jeffrey. 2012. "Gender Gap in 2012 Vote Is Largest in Gallup's History."

53% to McCain's 46%, with other polling organizations closer to the final mark (the Rasmussen and Pew polls were exactly on target) (Panagopoulos 2008). In 2012, Gallup predicted that Mitt Romney would win by a percentage point, when the reverse occurred. In 2004, the final Gallup prediction of 49% for George W. Bush was within 2 percentage points of his winning total of 51% (actually, 50.77%); the "error" is partially the result of the 1% of votes cast for third-party candidate Ralph Nader. The results of different polls can vary slightly because of differences in how the pollsters estimate who will actually vote, but the overall rate of accuracy is consistently impressive.

Nevertheless, election polls have produced some major errors in prediction. The reasons for these errors illustrate some of the ways in which unintentional systematic bias can influence sample results. In 1936, a *Literary Digest* poll predicted that Alfred M. Landon would defeat President Franklin Delano Roosevelt in a landslide, but instead Roosevelt took 63% of the popular vote. The problem? The *Digest* mailed out 10 million mock ballots to people listed in telephone directories, automobile registration records, voter lists, and so on. But in 1936, during the Great Depression, only relatively wealthy people had phones and cars, and they were more likely to be Republican. Furthermore, only 2,376,523 completed ballots were returned, and a response rate of only 24% leaves much room for error. Of course, this poll was not designed as a random sample, so the appearance of systematic bias is not surprising. Gallup predicted the 1936 election results accurately with a more systematically selected sample of just 3,000 that avoided so much bias (although they did not yet use random sampling) (Bainbridge 1989:43–44).

In 1948, pollsters mistakenly predicted that Thomas E. Dewey would beat Harry S. Truman, based on the sampling method that George Gallup had used successfully since 1934. The problem was that pollsters stopped collecting data several weeks before the election, and in those weeks, many people changed their minds (Kenney 1987). The sample was systematically biased by underrepresenting shifts in voter sentiment just before the election. This experience convinced Gallup to use only random sampling methods (as well as to continue polling until the election).

The fast-paced 2008 presidential primary elections were also challenging for the pollsters, primarily among Democratic Party voters. In the early New Hampshire primary, polls successfully predicted Republican John McCain's winning margin of 5.5% (the polls were off by only 0.2%, on average). However, all the polls predicted that Barack Obama would win New Hampshire's Democratic primary by a margin of about 8 percentage points, but he lost to Hillary Clinton by 12 points (47% to 35%). In a careful review of different explanations that have been proposed for that failure, the president of the Pew Research Center, Andrew Kohut (2008:A27), concluded that the problem was that voters who are poorer, less well educated, and white and who tend to refuse to respond to surveys tend to be less favorable to blacks than do other voters. These voters, who were unrepresented in the polls, were more likely to favor Clinton over Obama.

Because they do not disproportionately exclude or include particular groups within the population, random samples that are successfully implemented avoid systematic bias in the selection process. However, when some types of people are more likely to refuse to participate in surveys or are less likely to be available for interviews, systematic bias can still creep into the sampling process. In addition, random error will still influence the specific results obtained from any random sample.

The likely amount of random error will also vary with the specific type of random sampling method used, as I explain in the next sections. The four most common methods for drawing random samples are (1) simple random sampling, (2) systematic random sampling, (3) stratified random sampling, and (4) cluster sampling.

Research|Social Impact Link
Samples and Resources

Simple Random Sampling

Simple random sampling requires some procedure that generates numbers or otherwise identifies cases strictly on the basis of chance. As you know, flipping a coin or rolling a die can be used to identify cases strictly on the basis of chance,

> **Simple random sampling:** A method of sampling in which every sample element is selected only on the basis of chance, through a random process.

> **Random number table:** A table containing lists of numbers that are ordered solely on the basis of chance; it is used for drawing a random sample.

but these procedures are not very efficient tools for drawing a sample. A **random number table**, such as the one in Appendix C, simplifies the process considerably. The researcher numbers all the elements in the sampling frame and then uses a systematic procedure for picking corresponding numbers from the random number table. (Practice Exercise 1 at the end of this chapter explains the process step by step.) Alternatively, a researcher may use a lottery procedure. Each case number is written on a small card, and then the cards are mixed up and the sample is selected from the cards.

When a large sample must be generated, these procedures are very cumbersome. Fortunately, a computer program can easily generate a random sample of any size. The researcher must first number all the elements to be sampled (the sampling frame) and then run the computer program to generate a random selection of the numbers within the desired range. The elements represented by these numbers are the sample.

> **Random digit dialing:** The random dialing by a machine of numbers within designated phone prefixes, which creates a random sample for phone surveys.

Organizations that conduct phone surveys often draw random samples using another automated procedure, called **random digit dialing.** A machine dials random numbers within the phone prefixes corresponding to the area in which the survey is to be conducted. Random digit dialing is particularly useful when a sampling frame is not available. The researcher simply replaces any inappropriate number (e.g., those that are no longer in service or that are for businesses) with the next randomly generated phone number.

Researcher Interview Link
Phone Survey Research

As the fraction of the population that has only cell phones has increased (40% in 2013), it has become essential to explicitly sample cell phone numbers as well as landline phone numbers (McGeeney & Keeter 2014). Those who use cell phones only tend to be younger, more male, more single, more likely to be black or Hispanic, and less likely to vote compared with those who have a landline phone. As a result, failing to include cell phone numbers in a phone survey can introduce bias (Christian et al. 2010). In fact, in a 2008 presidential election survey, those who use only cell phones were less likely to be registered voters than were landline users but were considerably more favorable to Obama than landline users (Keeter 2008) (Exhibit 5.4).

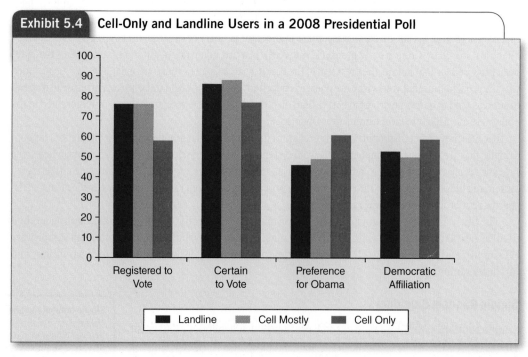

Exhibit 5.4 | **Cell-Only and Landline Users in a 2008 Presidential Poll**

Source: Based on "Cell Phones and the 2008 Vote: An Update." Keeter, Scott, Michael Dimock, and Leah Christian. Pew Center for the People & the Press, September 23, 2008.

The probability of selection in a true simple random sample is equal for each element. If a sample of 500 is selected from a population of 17,000 (i.e., a sampling frame of 17,000), then the probability of selection for each element is 500 to 17,000, or .03. Every element has an equal chance of being selected, just like the odds in a toss of a coin (1 to 2) or a roll of a die (1 to 6). Thus, simple random sampling is an *equal probability of selection method*, or EPSEM.

Simple random sampling can be done either with or without replacement sampling. In **replacement sampling**, each element is returned to the sampling frame after it is selected so that it may be sampled again. In sampling without replacement, each element selected for the sample is then excluded from the sampling frame. In practice, it makes no difference whether sampled elements are replaced after selection as long as the population is large and the sample is to contain only a small fraction of the population. Random sampling with replacement is, in fact, rarely used.

> **Replacement sampling:** A method of sampling in which sample elements are returned to the sampling frame after being selected, so they may be sampled again. Random samples may be selected with or without replacement.

In a study involving simple random sampling, Bruce Link and his associates (1996) used random digit dialing to contact adult household members in the continental United States for an investigation of public attitudes and beliefs about homeless people. Of the potential interviewees, 63% responded. The sample actually obtained was not exactly comparable with the population sampled: Compared with U.S. Census figures, the sample overrepresented women, people age 25 to 54, married people, and those with more than a high school education; it underrepresented Latinos.

How does this sample strike you? Let's assess sample quality using the questions posed earlier in the chapter:

- *From what population were the cases selected?* There is a clearly defined population: the adult residents of the continental United States (who live in households with phones).

- *What method was used to select cases from this population?* The case selection method is a random selection procedure, and there are no systematic biases in the sampling.

- *Do the cases that were studied represent, in the aggregate, the population from which they were selected?* The findings will very likely represent the population sampled because there were no biases in the sampling and a very large number of cases were selected. However, 37% of those selected for interviews could not be contacted or chose not to respond. This rate of nonresponse seems to create a small bias in the sample for several characteristics.

We must also consider the issue of cross-population generalizability: Do findings from this sample have implications for any larger group beyond the population from which the sample was selected? Because a representative sample of the entire U.S. adult population was drawn, this question has to do with cross-national generalizations. Link and his colleagues (1996) don't make any such generalizations. There's no telling what might occur in other countries with different histories of homelessness and different social policies.

Systematic Random Sampling

Systematic random sampling is a variant of simple random sampling. The first element is selected randomly from a list or from sequential files, and then every *n*th element is selected. This is a convenient method for drawing a random sample when the population elements are arranged sequentially. It is particularly efficient when the elements are not actually printed (i.e., there is no sampling frame) but instead are represented by folders in filing cabinets.

> **Systematic random sampling:** A method of sampling in which sample elements are selected from a list or from sequential files, with every *n*th element being selected after the first element is selected randomly within the first interval.

Systematic random sampling requires the following three steps:

> **Sampling interval:** The number of cases from one sampled case to another in a systematic random sample.

1. The total number of cases in the population is divided by the number of cases required for the sample. This division yields the sampling interval, the number of cases from one sampled case to another. If 50 cases are to be selected out of 1,000, the **sampling interval** is 20; every 20th case is selected.

2. A number from 1 to 20 (or whatever the sampling interval is) is selected randomly. This number identifies the first case to be sampled, counting from the first case on the list or in the files.

3. After the first case is selected, every *n*th case is selected for the sample, where *n* is the sampling interval. If the sampling interval is not a whole number, the size of the sampling interval is varied systematically to yield the proper number of cases for the sample. For example, if the sampling interval is 30.5, the sampling interval alternates between 30 and 31. In almost all sampling situations, systematic random sampling yields what is essentially a simple random sample. The exception is a situation in which the sequence of elements is affected by **periodicity**—that is, the sequence varies in some regular, periodic pattern. For example, the houses in a new development with the same number of houses in each block (e.g., 8) may be listed by block, starting with the house in the northwest corner of each block and continuing clockwise. If the sampling interval is 8, the same as the periodic pattern, all the cases selected will be in the same position (see Exhibit 5.5). But in reality, periodicity and the sampling interval are rarely the same.

> **Periodicity:** A sequence of elements (in a list to be sampled) that varies in some regular, periodic pattern.

Exhibit 5.5 The Effect of Periodicity on Systematic Random Sampling

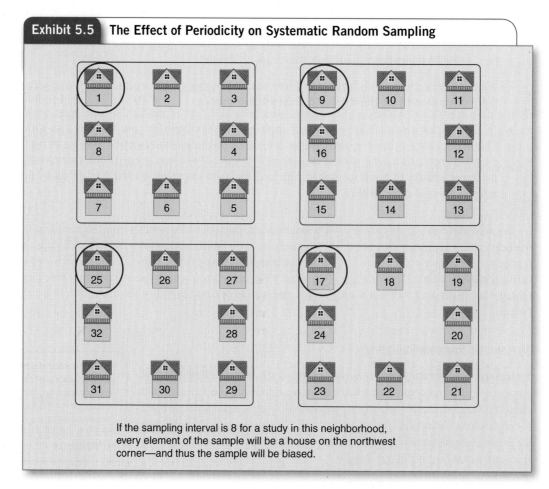

If the sampling interval is 8 for a study in this neighborhood, every element of the sample will be a house on the northwest corner—and thus the sample will be biased.

Stratified Random Sampling

Although all probability sampling methods use random sampling, some add steps to the sampling process to make sampling more efficient or easier. **Stratified random sampling** uses information known about the total population before sampling to make the sampling process more efficient. First, all elements in the population (i.e., in the sampling frame) are distinguished according to their value on some relevant characteristic. This characteristic might be year in school in a study of students,

> **Stratified random sampling:** A method of sampling in which sample elements are selected separately from population strata that are identified in advance by the researcher.

marital status in a study of family relations, or average property value in a study of towns. That characteristic forms the sampling strata, but of course you can only use this approach if you know the value of all elements in the population on this characteristic before you draw the sample. Next, elements are sampled randomly from within these strata. For example, race may be the basis for distinguishing individuals in some population of interest. Within each racial category, individuals are then sampled randomly. Of course, using this method requires more information before sampling than is the case with simple random sampling. It must be possible to categorize each element in one and only one stratum, and the size of each stratum in the population must be known.

This method is more efficient than drawing a simple random sample because it ensures appropriate representation of elements across strata. Imagine that you plan to draw a sample of 500 from the population of a large company to study the experiences of different ethnic groups. You know from company records that the workforce is 15% black, 10% Hispanic, 5% Asian, and 70% white. If you drew a simple random sample, you might end up with somewhat disproportionate numbers of each group. But if you created sampling strata based on race and ethnicity, you could randomly select cases from each stratum: 75 blacks (15% of the sample), 50 Hispanics (10%), 25 Asians (5%), and 350 whites (70%). By using **proportionate stratified sampling**, you would eliminate any possibility of sampling error in the sample's distribution of ethnicity. Each stratum would be represented exactly in proportion to its size in the population from which the sample was drawn (see Exhibit 5.6).

> **Proportionate stratified sampling:** Sampling method in which elements are selected from strata in exact proportion to their representation in the population.

This is the strategy Brenda Booth et al. (2002) used in a study of homeless adults in two Los Angeles county sites with large homeless populations. Specifically, Booth et al. (2002:432) selected subjects at random from homeless shelters, from meal facilities, and from literally homeless populations on the streets. Respondents were sampled proportionately to their numbers in the downtown and Westside areas, as determined by a one-night enumeration. They were also sampled proportionately to their distribution across three nested sampling strata: the population using shelter beds, the population using meal facilities, and the unsheltered population using neither.

In **disproportionate stratified sampling**, the proportion of each stratum that is included in the sample is intentionally varied from what it is in the population. In the case of the company sample stratified by ethnicity, you might select equal numbers of cases from each racial or ethnic group: 125 blacks (25% of the sample), 125 Hispanics (25%), 125 Asians (25%), and 125 whites (25%). In this type of sample, the probability of selection of every case is known but unequal between strata. You know what the

> **Disproportionate stratified sampling:** Sampling in which elements are selected from strata in different proportions from those that appear in the population.

proportions are in the population, and so you can easily adjust your combined sample statistics to reflect these true proportions. For instance, if you want to combine the ethnic groups and estimate the average income of the total population, you would have to *weight* each case in the sample. The weight is a number you multiply by the value of each case based on the stratum it is in. For example, you would multiply the incomes of all blacks in the sample by 0.6 (75/125), the incomes of all Hispanics by 0.4 (50/125), and so on. Weighting in this way reduces the influence of the oversampled strata and increases the influence of the undersampled strata to what they would have been if pure probability sampling had been used.

Booth et al. (2002:432) included one element of *dis*proportionate random sampling in their otherwise proportionate random sampling strategy for homeless persons in Los Angeles: The researchers oversampled women so that women composed 26% of the sample compared with their actual percentage of 16% in the

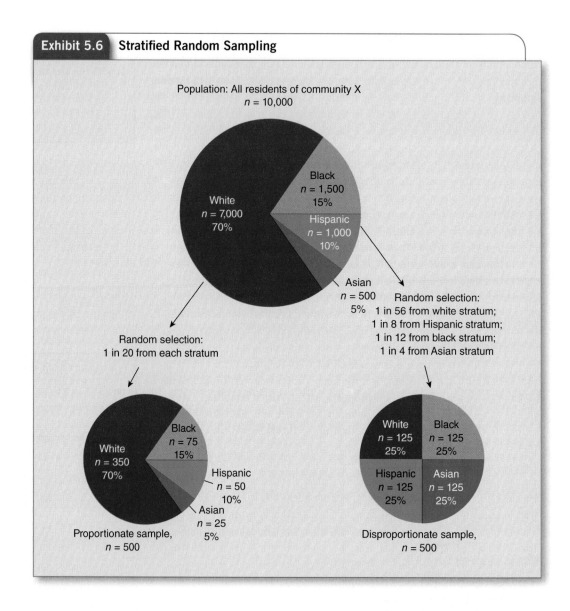

Exhibit 5.6 Stratified Random Sampling

Population: All residents of community X
n = 10,000

White
n = 7,000
70%

Black
n = 1,500
15%

Hispanic
n = 1,000
10%

Asian
n = 500
5%

Random selection:
1 in 56 from white stratum;
1 in 8 from Hispanic stratum;
1 in 12 from black stratum;
1 in 4 from Asian stratum

Random selection:
1 in 20 from each stratum

White
n = 350
70%

Black
n = 75
15%

Hispanic
n = 50
10%

Asian
n = 25
5%

Proportionate sample,
n = 500

White
n = 125
25%

Black
n = 125
25%

Hispanic
n = 125
25%

Asian
n = 125
25%

Disproportionate sample,
n = 500

homeless population. Why would anyone select a sample that is so unrepresentative in the first place? The most common reason is to ensure that cases from smaller strata are included in the sample in sufficient numbers to allow separate statistical estimates and to facilitate comparisons between strata. Remember that one of the determinants of sample quality is sample size. The same is true for subgroups within samples. If a key concern in a research project is to describe and compare the incomes of people from different racial and ethnic groups, then it is important that the researchers base the mean income of each group on enough cases to be a valid representation. If few members of a particular minority group are in the population, they need to be oversampled. Such disproportionate sampling may also result in a more efficient sampling design if the costs of data collection differ markedly between the strata or if the variability (heterogeneity) of the strata differs.

Weighting is also sometimes used to reduce the lack of representativeness of a sample that occurs because of nonresponse. On finding that the obtained sample does not represent the population for some known characteristics such as, perhaps, gender or education, the researcher weights the cases in the sample so that the sample has the same proportions of men and women, or high school graduates and college graduates, as the complete population (see Exhibit 5.7). Keep in mind, though, that this procedure does not solve the problems caused by an unrepresentative sample because you still don't know what the sample composition should have been relative to the other variables in your study; all you have done is to reduce the sample's unrepresentativeness relative to the variables used in weighting. This may, in turn, make it more likely that the sample is representative of the population relative to other characteristics, but you don't really know.

Cluster Sampling

Cluster sampling is useful when a sampling frame of elements is not available, as often is the case for large populations spread out across a wide geographic area or among many different organizations. A **cluster** is a naturally occurring, mixed aggregate of elements of the population, with each element appearing in one, and only one, cluster. Schools could serve as clusters for sampling students, blocks could serve as clusters for sampling city residents, counties could serve as clusters for sampling the general population, and businesses could serve as clusters for sampling employees.

> **Cluster sampling:** Sampling in which elements are selected in two or more stages, with the first stage being the random selection of naturally occurring clusters and the last stage being the random selection of elements within clusters.
>
> **Cluster:** A naturally occurring, mixed aggregate of elements of the population.

Drawing a cluster sample is, at least, a two-stage procedure. First, the researcher draws a random sample of clusters. A list of clusters should be much easier to obtain than a list of all the individuals in each cluster in the population. Next, the researcher draws a random sample of elements within each selected cluster. Because only a fraction of the total clusters are involved, obtaining the sampling frame at this stage should be much easier.

In a cluster sample of city residents, for example, blocks could be the first-stage clusters. A research assistant could walk around each selected block and record the addresses of all occupied dwelling units. Or, in a cluster sample of students, a researcher could contact the schools selected in the first stage and make arrangements with the registrar to obtain lists of students at each school. Cluster samples often involve multiple stages (see Exhibit 5.8), with clusters within clusters, as when a national sample of individuals might involve first sampling states, then geographic units within those states, then dwellings within those units, and finally, individuals

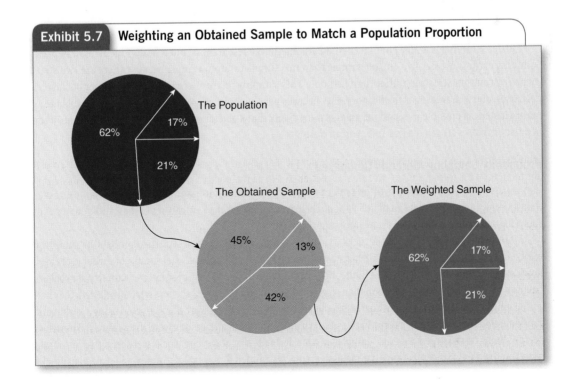

Exhibit 5.7 **Weighting an Obtained Sample to Match a Population Proportion**

The Population

62% 17% 21%

The Obtained Sample

45% 13% 42%

The Weighted Sample

62% 17% 21%

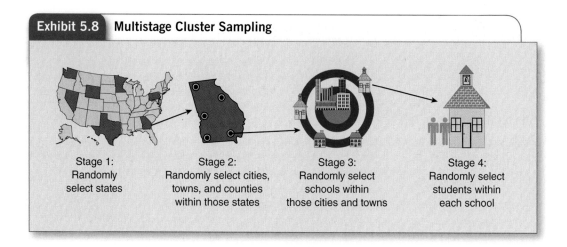

Exhibit 5.8 **Multistage Cluster Sampling**

Stage 1:
Randomly
select states

Stage 2:
Randomly select cities,
towns, and counties
within those states

Stage 3:
Randomly select
schools within
those cities and towns

Stage 4:
Randomly select
students within
each school

within the dwellings. In multistage cluster sampling, the clusters at the first stage of sampling are termed the *primary sampling units* (Levy & Lemeshow 1999:228).

How many clusters should be selected, and how many individuals within each cluster should be selected? As a general rule, the sample will be more similar to the entire population if the researcher selects as many clusters as possible—even though this will mean the selection of fewer individuals within each cluster. Unfortunately, this strategy also maximizes the cost of the sample for studies using in-person interviews. The more clusters a researcher selects, the more time and money will have to be spent traveling to the different clusters to reach the individuals for interviews.

The calculation of how many clusters to sample and how many individuals are within the clusters is also affected by the degree of similarity of individuals within clusters: The more similar the individuals are within the clusters, the fewer the number of individuals needed to represent each cluster. So if you set out to draw a cluster sample, be sure to consider how similar individuals are within the clusters as well as how many clusters you can afford to include in your sample.

Cluster sampling is a very popular method among survey researchers, but it has one general drawback: Sampling error is greater in a cluster sample than in a simple random sample because there are two steps involving random selection rather than just one. This sampling error increases as the number of clusters decreases, and it decreases as the homogeneity of cases per cluster increases. In sum, it's better to include as many clusters as possible in a sample, and it's more likely that a cluster sample will be representative of the population if cases are relatively similar within clusters.

Probability Sampling Methods Compared

Can you now see why researchers often prefer to draw a stratified random sample or a cluster sample rather than a simple random sample? Exhibit 5.9 should help you remember the key features of these different types of sampling and to determine when each is most appropriate.

Many professionally designed surveys use combinations of clusters and stratified probability sampling methods. For example, Peter Rossi (1989) drew a disproportionate stratified cluster sample of shelter users for a homelessness study in Chicago (see Exhibit 5.10). The shelter sample was stratified by size, with smaller shelters having a smaller likelihood of selection than larger shelters. In fact, the larger shelters were all selected; they had a probability of selection of 1.0. Within the selected shelters, shelter users were then sampled using a systematic random selection procedure (except in the small shelters, in which all persons were interviewed). Homeless persons living on the streets were also sampled randomly. In the first stage, city blocks were classified into strata based on the likely concentration of homeless persons (estimated by several knowledgeable groups). Blocks

Exhibit 5.9   Features of Probability Sampling Methods

Feature	Simple	Systematic	Stratified	Cluster
Unbiased selection of cases	Yes	Yes	Yes	Yes
Sampling frame required	Yes	No	Yes	No
Ensures representation of key strata	No	No	Yes	No
Uses natural grouping of cases	No	No	No	Yes
Reduces sampling costs	No	No	No	Yes
Sampling error compared with simple random sample	–	Same	Lower	Higher

were then picked randomly within these strata and, on the survey night between 1 a.m. and 6 a.m., teams of interviewers screened each person found outside on that block for his or her homeless status. Persons identified as homeless were then interviewed (and given $5 for their time). The rate of response for two different samples (fall and winter) in the shelters and on the streets was between 73% and 83%.

How would we evaluate the Chicago homeless sample, using the sample evaluation questions?

- *From what population were the cases selected?* The population was clearly defined for each cluster.

Exhibit 5.10   Chicago Shelter Universe and Shelter Samples, Fall and Winter Surveys

A. Shelter Universe and Samples

	Fall	Winter
Eligible shelters in universe	28	45
Universe bed capacities	1,573	2,001
Shelters drawn in sample	22	27

B. Details of Winter Shelter Sample

Shelter Size Classification	Number in Universe	Number in Sample	Occupant Sampling Ratio
Large (37 or more beds)	17	17	0.25
Medium (18–33 beds)	12	6	0.50
Small (under 18 beds)	16	4	1.00

Source: Rossi, Peter H. 1989. *Down and Out in America: The Origins of Homelessness.* Reprinted with permission from the University of Chicago Press.

Audio Link
Sampling Methods and
Trends

- *What method was used to select cases from this population?* The random selection method was carefully described.

- *Do the cases that were studied represent, in the aggregate, the population from which they were selected?* The unbiased selection procedures make us reasonably confident in the representativeness of the sample, although we know little about the nonrespondents and therefore may justifiably worry that some types of homeless persons were missed.

Cross-population generalization seems to be reasonable with this sample because it seems likely that the findings reflect general processes involving homeless persons. Rossi (1989) clearly thought so because his book's title refers to homelessness in America, not just in Chicago.

Nonprobability Sampling Methods

Nonprobability sampling methods are often used in qualitative research; they also are used in quantitative studies when researchers are unable to use probability selection methods. In qualitative research, a focus on one setting or a very small sample allows a more intensive portrait of activities and actors, but it also limits field researchers' ability to generalize and lowers the confidence that others can place in these generalizations. The use of nonprobability sampling methods in quantitative research too often reflects a lack of concern with generalizability or a lack of understanding of the importance of probability-based sampling.

There are four common nonprobability sampling methods: (1) availability sampling, (2) quota sampling, (3) purposive sampling, and (4) snowball sampling. Because these methods do not use a random selection procedure, we cannot expect a sample selected with any of these methods to yield a representative sample. They should not be used in quantitative studies if a probability-based method is feasible. Nonetheless, these methods are useful when random sampling is not possible, when a research question calls for an intensive investigation of a small population, or when a researcher is performing a preliminary, exploratory study.

Availability Sampling

Availability sampling: Sampling in which elements are selected on the basis of convenience.

Elements are selected for **availability sampling** because they're available or easy to find. Thus, this sampling method is also known as haphazard, accidental, or convenience sampling. There are many ways to select elements for an availability sample: Standing on street corners and talking to whoever walks by, asking questions of employees who have time to talk when they pick up their paychecks at a personnel office, or approaching particular individuals at opportune times while observing activities in a social setting. You may find yourself interviewing available students at campus hangouts as part of a course assignment. To study sexual risk-taking among homeless youth in Minneapolis, Linda Halcón and Alan Lifson (2004:73) hired experienced street youth outreach workers who approached youth known or suspected to be homeless and asked if they would be willing to take part in a 20- to 30-minute interview. The interviewers then conducted the 44-question interview, after which they gave respondents some risk reduction and referral information and a $20 voucher.

A participant observation study of a group may require no more sophisticated approach. When Philippe Bourgois, Mark Lettiere, and James Quesada (1997) studied homeless heroin addicts in San Francisco, they immersed themselves in a community of addicts living in a public park. These addicts became the availability sample.

An availability sample is often appropriate in social research—for example, when a field researcher is exploring a new setting and trying to get some sense of the prevailing attitudes or when a survey researcher conducts a preliminary test of a new set of questions.

Audio Link
Convenience Sampling

Now, answer the sample evaluation questions in relation to the street youth interviews by Halcón and Lifson. If your answers are something like "The population was unknown," "The method for selecting cases was haphazard," and "The cases studied do not represent the population," you're right! There is no clearly definable population from which the respondents were drawn, and no systematic technique was used to select the respondents from a list of the population. There certainly is not much likelihood in such an availability sample that the interviewees represent the distribution of sentiment among all homeless youth in the Minneapolis area, or of impoverished teenagers generally, or of whatever we imagine the relevant population is in a particular study.

In a similar vein, perhaps person-in-the-street comments to news reporters suggest something about what homeless persons think, or maybe they don't; we can't really be sure. But let's give reporters their due: If they just want to have a few quotes to make their story more appealing, nothing is wrong with their sampling method. However, their approach gives us no basis for thinking that we have an overview of community sentiment. The people who happen to be available in any situation are unlikely to be just like those who are unavailable. We can't be at all certain that what we learn can be generalized with any confidence to a larger population of concern.

Availability sampling often masquerades as a more rigorous form of research. Popular magazines periodically survey their readers by printing a questionnaire for readers to fill out and mail in. A follow-up article then appears in the magazine under a title such as "What You Think About Intimacy in Marriage." If the magazine's circulation is large, a large sample can be achieved in this way. The problem is that usually only a tiny fraction of readers return the questionnaire, and these respondents are probably unlike other readers who did not have the interest or time to participate. So the survey is based on an availability sample. Even though the follow-up article may be interesting, we have no basis for thinking that the results describe the readership as a whole—much less the population at large.

Do you see now why availability sampling differs so much from random sampling methods, which require that "nothing but chance" affects the actual selection of cases? What makes availability sampling "haphazard" is precisely that a great many things other than chance can affect the selection of cases, ranging from the prejudices of the research staff to the work schedules of potential respondents. To truly leave the selection of cases up to chance, we have to design the selection process very carefully so that other factors are not influential. There's nothing haphazard about selecting cases randomly.

Interactive Exercises Link
Identifying Sampling Techniques

CAREERS AND RESEARCH

Ross Koppel, PhD, Sociologist

Sociologist Ross Koppel received his PhD at Temple University in Philadelphia. In 1985 he founded the Social Research Corporation and since has served as SRC's president. His work has had major impacts across society. One of his most famous projects was developed in response to a lawsuit against the Boston public transit system's (MBTA) treatment of people with disabilities. He constructed a unique sampling design that had people in wheelchairs or walkers (accompanied by hidden, trained observers) ride buses on representative routes. Thousands of hours of observations were recorded. The case was won resoundingly and became the model for the U.S. Department of Justice.

His more recent work focuses on healthcare IT, where he has published over 40 medical journal articles in 5 years and has become a major force for patient safety and better healthcare.

Professor Koppel has taught and directed research at the University of Pennsylvania since 1991. In 2010 he received the American Sociological Association Distinguished Career Award for the Practice of Sociology, and in 2012 he was elected as a Fellow to the American College of Medical Informatics. In 2013 he was appointed a Senior Fellow of the Leonard Davis Institute for Health Economics (Wharton School).

Quota Sampling

> **Quota sampling:** A nonprobability sampling method in which elements are selected to ensure that the sample represents certain characteristics in proportion to their prevalence in the population.

Quota sampling is intended to overcome the most obvious flaw of availability sampling—that the sample will just consist of whoever or whatever is available, without any concern for its similarity to the population of interest. The distinguishing feature of a quota sample is that quotas are set to ensure that the sample represents certain characteristics in proportion to their prevalence in the population.

Suppose that you want to sample adult residents of a town in a study of support for a tax increase to improve the town's schools. You know from the town's annual report what the proportions of town residents are in gender, race, age, and number of children. You think that each of these characteristics might influence support for new school taxes, so you want to be sure that the sample includes men, women, whites, blacks, Hispanics, Asians, older people, younger people, big families, small families, and childless families in proportion to their numbers in the town population.

This is where quotas come in. Let's say that 48% of the town's adult residents are men and 52% are women, and that 60% are employed, 5% are unemployed, and 35% are out of the labor force. These percentages and the percentages corresponding to the other characteristics become the quotas for the sample. If you plan to include 500 residents in your sample, 240 must be men (48% of 500), 260 must be women, 300 must be employed, and so on.

Characteristic	Population	Quota	Calculation
Sex			
Men	48%	240	(.48*500)
Women	52%	260	(.52*500)
Employment Status			
Employed	60%	300	(.60*500)
Unemployed	5%	25	(.05*500)
Out of Labor Force	35%	175	(.35*500)
Total Sample Size	**500**		

You may even set more refined quotas, such as certain numbers of employed women, employed men, unemployed men, and so on. With the quota list in hand, you (or your research staff) can now go out into the community looking for the right number of people in each quota category. You may go door to door, bar to bar, or just stand on a street corner until you have surveyed 240 men, 260 women, and so on.

The problem is that even when we know that a quota sample is representative of the particular characteristics for which quotas have been set, we have no way of knowing if the sample is representative for any other characteristics. In Exhibit 5.11, for example, quotas have been set for gender only. Under these circumstances, it's no surprise that the sample is representative of the population only for gender, not race. Interviewers are only human; they may avoid potential respondents with menacing dogs in the front yard, or they could seek out respondents who are physically attractive or who look like they'd be easy to interview. Realistically, researchers can set quotas for only a small fraction of the characteristics relevant to a study, so a quota sample is really not much better than an availability sample (although following careful, consistent procedures for selecting cases within the quota limits always helps).

This last point leads me to another limitation of quota sampling: You must know the characteristics of the entire population to set the right quotas. In most cases, researchers know what the population looks like relative to no more than a few of the characteristics relevant to their concerns—and in some cases, they have no such information on the entire population.

If you're now feeling skeptical of quota sampling, you've gotten the drift of my remarks. Nonetheless, in some situations, establishing quotas can add rigor to sampling procedures. It's almost always better to maximize possibilities for comparison in research, and quota sampling techniques can help qualitative researchers do this. For instance, Doug Timmer, Stanley Eitzen, and Kathryn Talley (1993:7) interviewed homeless persons in several cities and other

Exhibit 5.11 Quota Sampling

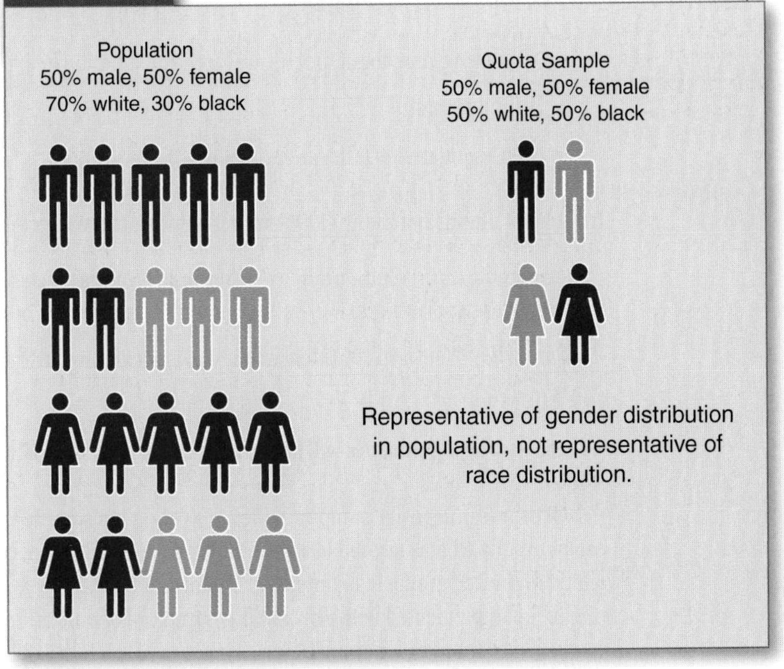

Population
50% male, 50% female
70% white, 30% black

Quota Sample
50% male, 50% female
50% white, 50% black

Representative of gender distribution in population, not representative of race distribution.

locations for their book on the sources of homelessness. Persons who were available were interviewed, but the researchers paid some attention to generating a diverse sample. They interviewed 20 homeless men who lived on the streets without shelter and 20 mothers who were found in family shelters. About half of those whom the researchers selected in the street sample were black, and about half were white. Although the researchers did not use quotas to try to match the distribution of characteristics among the total homeless population, their informal quotas helped ensure some diversity in key characteristics.

Does quota sampling remind you of stratified sampling? It's easy to understand why because they both select sample members partly on the basis of one or more key characteristics. Exhibit 5.12 summarizes the differences between quota sampling and stratified random sampling. The key difference, of course, is quota sampling's lack of random selection.

Exhibit 5.12 Comparison of Stratified and Quota Sampling Methods

Feature	Stratified	Quota
Unbiased (random) selection of cases	Yes	No
Sampling frame required	Yes	No
Ensures representation of key strata	Yes	Yes

Purposive Sampling

In **purposive sampling**, each sample element is selected for a purpose, usually because of the unique position of the sample elements. Purposive sampling may involve studying the entire population of some limited group (directors of shelters for homeless adults) or a subset of a population (mid-level managers with a reputation for efficiency). Or a purposive sample may be a *key informant survey*, which targets individuals who are particularly knowledgeable about the issues under investigation.

Purposive sampling: A nonprobability sampling method in which elements are selected for a purpose, usually because of their unique position.

Herbert Rubin and Irene Rubin (1995) suggest three guidelines for selecting informants when designing any purposive sampling strategy. Informants should be

- Knowledgeable about the cultural arena or situation or experience being studied
- Willing to talk
- Represent[ative of] the range of points of view (p. 66)

In addition, Rubin and Rubin (1995) suggest continuing to select interviewees until you can pass two tests:

Completeness: What you hear provides an overall sense of the meaning of a concept, theme, or process. (p. 72)

Saturation: You gain confidence that you are learning little that is new from subsequent interview[s]. (p. 73)

Adhering to these guidelines will help ensure that a purposive sample adequately represents the setting or issues studied.

Of course, purposive sampling does not produce a sample that represents some larger population, but it can be exactly what is needed in a case study of an organization, community, or some other clearly defined and relatively limited group. In an intensive organizational case study, a purposive sample of organizational leaders might be complemented with a probability sample of organizational members. Before designing her probability samples of hospital patients and homeless persons, Dee Roth (1990:146–147) interviewed a purposive sample of 164 key informants from organizations that had contact with homeless people in each of the counties she studied.

Snowball Sampling

Snowball sampling: A method of sampling in which sample elements are selected as they are identified by successive informants or interviewees.

Snowball sampling is useful for hard-to-reach or hard-to-identify populations for which there is no sampling frame, but the members of which are somewhat interconnected (at least some members of the population know each other). It can be used to sample members of groups such as drug dealers, prostitutes, practicing criminals, participants in Alcoholics Anonymous groups, gang leaders, informal organizational leaders, and homeless persons. It may also be used for charting the relationships between members of some group (a sociometric study), for exploring the population of interest before developing a formal sampling plan, and for developing what becomes a census of informal leaders of small organizations or communities. However, researchers using snowball sampling normally cannot be confident that their sample represents the total population of interest, so generalizations must be tentative.

Rob Rosenthal (1994) used snowball sampling to study homeless persons living in Santa Barbara, California:

I began this process by attending a meeting of homeless people I had heard about through my housing advocate contacts. . . . One homeless woman . . . invited me to . . . where she promised to introduce me around. Thus a process of snowballing began. I gained entree to a group through people I knew, came to know others, and through them gained entree to new circles. (pp. 178, 180)

One problem with this technique is that the initial contacts may shape the entire sample and foreclose access to some members of the population of interest:

Sat around with [my contact] at the Tree. Other people come by, are friendly, but some regulars, especially the tougher men, don't sit with her. Am I making a mistake by tying myself too closely to her? She lectures them a lot. (Rosenthal 1994:181)

More systematic versions of snowball sampling can reduce the potential for bias. For example, *respondent-driven sampling* gives financial incentives to respondents to recruit diverse peers (Heckathorn 1997). Limitations on the number of incentives that any one respondent can receive increase the sample's diversity. Targeted incentives can steer the sample to include specific subgroups. When the sampling is repeated through several waves, with new respondents bringing in more peers, the composition of the sample converges on a more representative mix of characteristics than would occur with uncontrolled snowball sampling. Exhibit 5.13 shows how the sample spreads out through successive recruitment waves to an increasingly diverse pool (Heckathorn 1997:178). Exhibit 5.14 shows that even if the starting point were all white persons, respondent-driven sampling would result in an appropriate ethnic mix from an ethnically diverse population (Heckathorn 2002:17).

Lessons About Sample Quality

Some lessons are implicit in my evaluations of the samples in this chapter:

- We can't evaluate the quality of a sample if we don't know what population it is supposed to represent. If the population is unspecified because the researchers were never clear about the population they were trying to sample, then we can safely conclude that the sample itself is no good.

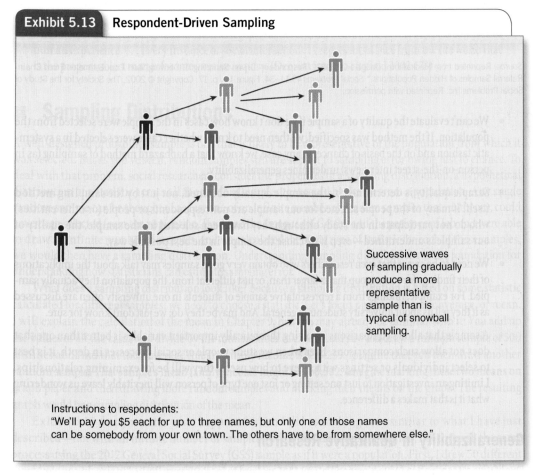

| Exhibit 5.13 | Respondent-Driven Sampling |

Successive waves of sampling gradually produce a more representative sample than is typical of snowball sampling.

Instructions to respondents:
"We'll pay you $5 each for up to three names, but only one of those names can be somebody from your own town. The others have to be from somewhere else."

Source: Based on Heckathorn (1997):178.

CHAPTER 6

Research Design and Causation

Journal Link
Economic Causes
of Crime

Identifying causes—figuring out why things happen—is the goal of most social science research. Unfortunately, valid explanations of the causes of social phenomena do not come easily. Why did the number and rate of homicides rise in the early 1990s and then begin a sustained drop that has continued in the 2000s, even during the 2008–2010 recession, to a level last seen in 1968 (Smith & Cooper 2013) (Exhibit 6.1)? Arizona State University criminologist Scott Decker points to the low levels of crime committed by illegal immigrants to explain the falling crime rate in his state (Archibold 2010), and sociologist

Research That Matters, Questions That Count

Since 2005, youth unemployment in the United Kingdom has been increasing, but "youth offending is in sharp and sustained decline" (Fergusson 2013:31). This pattern contradicts a popular theory that economic distress causes crime, and it reverses the pattern of increased youth crime during the previous recession in the early 1990s. Ross Fergusson (2013:52) at the UK's Open University was puzzled by these findings and decided to conduct an extensive review of prior research to better understand these "puzzling paradoxical and potentially contradictory issues" about the causes of youth crime.

Fergusson found that findings in previous research about the unemployment–crime association varied with the type of crime measured, the ages of youth studied, and the use of aggregate or individual data. He also considered evidence about the effect of new UK justice system programs for youth but remained unconvinced that these new programs had been responsible for declining crime despite rising unemployment. He concluded that the criminogenic effects of unemployment could be delayed or that they could be displaced by a turn toward mass protests.

1. What do you believe causes youth crime? Does the continuing decline in youth crime despite increased youth unemployment make sense to you?

2. Fergusson focuses on changes over time at the national level. What do you think are the advantages and disadvantages of investigating the causes of youth crime with national-level data?

3. What evidence about youth unemployment and crime would lead you to conclude that more unemployment causes more crime?

4. Fergusson considers the possible effect of the new UK Youth Justice Board program on reducing youth crime. How would you design a study to test whether a new social program reduced crime?

In this chapter, you will learn about the implications of research design features for causal analyses. By the end of the chapter, you will understand why testing causal hypotheses can be difficult and how to design research to strengthen causal conclusions. After you finish the chapter, test yourself by reading the 2013 *Youth Justice* article by Ross Fergusson at the *Investigating the Social World* study site and completing the related interactive exercises for Chapter 6 at edge .sagepub.com/schutt8e.

Fergusson, Ross. 2013. "Risk, Responsibilities and Rights: Reassessing the 'Economic Causes of Crime' Thesis in a Recession." *Youth Justice* 13(1):31–56.

Robert J. Sampson (2008:29) draws attention to the rising level of immigration through the 1990s to help explain the national decline in the crime rate. Criminal justice advocates in Texas point to the state's investment in community treatment and diversion programs (Grissom 2011). Police officials in New York City point to the effectiveness of CompStat, the city's computer program that indicates to the police where crimes are clustering (Dewan 2004a:A25; Dewan 2004b:A1; Kaplan 2002:A3), but other New Yorkers credit the increase in the ranks of New York's police officers because of its Safe Streets, Safe Cities program (Rashbaum 2002). Yet another possible explanation in New York City is the declining level of crack cocaine use (Dewan 2004b:C16). But then should we worry about the increasing number of drug arrests nationally (Bureau of Justice Statistics 2011) and a rise in abuse of prescription drugs (Goodnough 2010)? For cautionary lessons, should we look to Japan, where the crime rate rose sharply after being historically very low (Onishi 2003)? To explain changes in the rate of serious crime, we must design our research strategies carefully.

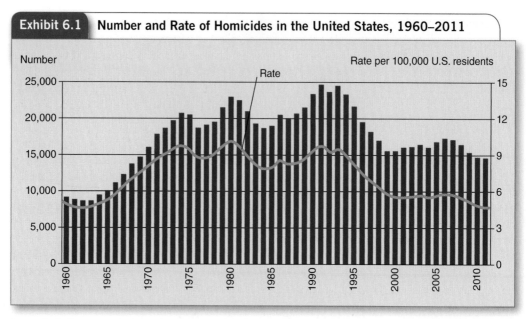

Exhibit 6.1 **Number and Rate of Homicides in the United States, 1960–2011**

Source: Smith, Erica L. and Alexia Cooper. 2013. *Homicide in the U.S. Known to Law Enforcement, 2011*. Washington, DC: Bureau of Justice Statistics, U.S. Department of Justice.

🔲 Research Design Alternatives

Video Link
Planning Your
Social Research

I begin this chapter by discussing three key elements of research design: the design's units of analysis, its use of cross-sectional or longitudinal data, and whether its methods are primarily quantitative or qualitative. Whenever we design research, we must decide whether to use individuals or groups as our units of analysis and whether to collect data at one or several points in time. The decisions that we make about these design elements will affect our ability to draw causal conclusions in our analysis. Whether the design is primarily quantitative or qualitative in its methods also affects the type of causal explanation that can be developed: Quantitative projects lead to nomothetic causal explanations, whereas qualitative projects that have a causal focus can lead to idiographic explanations. After reviewing these three key design elements, I will also review the criteria for achieving explanations that are causally valid from a nomothetic perspective. By the end of the chapter, you should have a good grasp of the different meanings of causation and be able to ask the right questions to determine whether causal inferences are likely to be valid. You also may have a better answer about the causes of crime and violence.

Units of Analysis

Units of analysis: The level of social life on which a research question is focused, such as individuals, groups, towns, or nations.

In nonexperimental research designs, we can be misled about the existence of an association between two variables when we do not know to what **units of analysis** the measures in our study refer—that is, the level of social life on which the research question is focused, such as individuals, groups, towns, or nations. I first discuss this important concept before explaining how it can affect causal conclusions.

Individual and Group

In most sociological and psychological studies, the units of analysis are individuals. The researcher may collect survey data from individuals, analyze the data, and then report on, say, how many individuals felt socially isolated and whether substance abuse by individuals was related to their feelings of social isolation.

The units of analysis may instead be groups of some sort, such as families, schools, work organizations, towns, states, or countries. For example, a researcher may collect data from town and police records on the number of accidents in which a driver was intoxicated and the presence or absence of a server liability law in the town. (These laws make those who serve liquor liable for accidents caused by those to whom they served liquor.) The researcher can then analyze the relationship between server liability laws and the frequency of accidents caused by drunk driving (perhaps also taking into account the town's population). Because the data describe the town, towns are the units of analysis.

In some studies, groups are the units of analysis, but data are collected from individuals. For example, in their study of influences on violent crime in Chicago neighborhoods, Robert Sampson, Stephen Raudenbush, and Felton Earls (1997:919) hypothesized that efficacy would influence neighborhood crime rates. *Collective efficacy* was defined conceptually as a characteristic of the neighborhood: the extent to which residents were likely to help other residents and were trusted by other residents. However, Sampson et al. measured this variable in a survey of individuals. The responses of individual residents about their perceptions of their neighbors' helpfulness and trustworthiness were averaged together to create a collective efficacy score for each neighborhood. This neighborhood measure of collective efficacy was used to explain variation in the rate of violent crime between neighborhoods. The data were collected from individuals and were about individuals, but they were combined (aggregated) to describe neighborhoods. The units of analysis were thus groups (neighborhoods).

In a study such as that of Sampson et al. (1997), we can distinguish the concept of units of analysis from the **units of observation**. Data were collected from individuals, the units of observation in this study, and then the data were aggregated and analyzed at the group level. In most studies, the units of observation and the units of analysis are the same. For example, Yili Xu, Mora Fiedler, and Karl Flaming

> **Units of observation:** The cases about which measures actually are obtained in a sample.

Research in the News

HOW TO REDUCE CRIME

Social science researchers are looking at New York City's decline in crime and incarceration rates to find the answer to "what works?" Researchers are trying to pull apart a number of possible explanations, from demographic shifts to policing strategies. Experiments reviewed by Anthony A. Braga, Andrew V. Papachristos, and David M. Hureau suggest that "hot-spot" policing may be the solution to reducing crime and incarceration. Hot-spot policing involves concentrating extra policing resources in narrowly defined areas with high rates of crime and then being very aggressive in issuing tickets and making arrests. However, there is as yet no consensus about how to implement this strategy.

For Further Thought

1. Which theory of crime would predict that hot-spot policing would be effective in reducing crime? (see chapter 2)

2. Pose a research question that would extend research on hot-spot policing.

News source: Tierney, John. 2013. "Prison Population Can Shrink When Police Crowd the Streets." *The New York Times,* January 26:A1.

(2005), in collaboration with the Colorado Springs Police Department, surveyed a stratified random sample of 904 residents to test whether their sense of collective efficacy and other characteristics would predict their perceptions of crime, fear of crime, and satisfaction with police. Their data were collected from individuals and analyzed at the individual level. They concluded that collective efficacy was not as important as in Sampson et al.'s (1997) study.

The important point is to know what the units of observation are and what the level of analysis is, and then to evaluate whether the conclusions are appropriate to these study features. A conclusion that "crime increases with joblessness" could imply either that individuals who lose their jobs are more likely to commit a crime or that a community with a high unemployment rate is likely to have a high crime rate—or both. Whether we are drawing conclusions from data we collected or interpreting others' conclusions, it is important to be clear about which relationship is being referred to.

We also have to know what the units of analysis are to interpret statistics appropriately. Measures of association tend to be stronger for group-level than for individual-level data because measurement errors at the individual level tend to cancel out at the group level (Bridges & Weis 1989:29–31).

The Ecological Fallacy and Reductionism

Researchers should make sure that their causal conclusions reflect the units of analysis in their study. Conclusions about processes at the individual level should be based on individual-level data; conclusions about group-level processes should be based on data collected about groups. When this rule is violated, we can often be misled about the existence of an association between two variables.

> **Ecological fallacy:** An error in reasoning in which incorrect conclusions about individual-level processes are drawn from group-level data.

A researcher who draws conclusions about individual-level processes from group-level data could be making what is termed an **ecological fallacy** (see Exhibit 6.2). The conclusions may or may not be correct, but we must recognize the fact that group-level data do not necessarily reflect solely individual-level processes. For example, a researcher may examine factory records and find that the higher the percentage of unskilled workers in factories, the higher the rate of employee sabotage in those factories. But the researcher would commit an ecological fallacy if he or she then concluded that individual unskilled factory workers are more likely to engage in sabotage. This conclusion is about an individual-level causal process (the relationship between the occupation and criminal propensities of individuals), even though the data describe groups (factories). It could actually be that white-collar workers are the ones more likely to commit sabotage in factories with more unskilled workers, perhaps because the white-collar workers feel they won't be suspected in these settings.

> **Reductionist fallacy (reductionism):** An error in reasoning that occurs when incorrect conclusions about group-level processes are based on individual-level data; also known as an individualist fallacy.

Conversely, when data about individuals are used to make inferences about group-level processes, a problem occurs that can be thought of as the mirror image of the ecological fallacy: the **reductionist fallacy**, also known as *reductionism,* or the *individualist fallacy* (see Exhibit 6.2). For example, a reductionist explanation of individual violence would focus on biological factors, such as genes or hormones, rather than on the community's level of social control. Similarly, a reductionist explanation of behavior problems in grade school classrooms would focus on the children's personalities, rather than on classroom structure, teacher behavior, or the surrounding neighborhood.

> **Emergence:** The appearance of phenomena at a group level that cannot be explained by the properties of individuals within the group; emergence implies phenomena that are more than "the sum of their parts."

There is, of course, nothing inherently wrong with considering biological, psychological, or other factors that affect individuals when explaining behavior in social contexts (Sayer 2003). The key issue is whether there are properties of groups or other aggregates that are more than "the sum of their parts." If there are such "higher level properties," we can speak of "**emergence**" at the group level and we need to be careful to avoid a reductionist fallacy.

Exhibit 6.2	Errors in Causal Conclusions

		You make conclusions about	
		Groups	**Individuals**
You collect data from	**Groups**	More homogeneous groups tend to have stronger social bonds.	Groups with a higher average age are more conservative, so older people are more conservative. *Possible Ecological Fallacy*
	Individuals	Students who socialize more have lower grades, so schools with more social engagement will have poorer student performance. *Possible Reductionist Fallacy*	Older people tend to be more conservative.

The fact that errors in causal reasoning can be made in this way should not deter you from conducting research with group-level data nor make you unduly critical of researchers who make inferences about individuals on the basis of group-level data. When considered broadly, many research questions point to relationships that could be manifested in many ways and on many levels. Sampson's (1987) study of urban violence is a case in point. His analysis involved only aggregate data about cities, and he explained his research approach as partly a response to the failure of other researchers to examine this problem at the structural, aggregate level. Moreover, Sampson argued that the rates of joblessness and family disruption in communities influence community social processes, not just individuals who are unemployed or who grew up without two parents. Yet Sampson suggested that the experience of joblessness and poverty is what tends to reduce the propensity of individual men to marry and that the experience of growing up in a home without two parents, in turn, increases the propensity of individual juveniles to commit crimes. These conclusions about individual behavior seem consistent with the patterns Sampson found in his aggregate, city-level data, so it seems unlikely that he committed an ecological fallacy when he proposed them.

The solution is to know what the units of analysis and units of observation were in a study and to consider these in weighing the credibility of the researcher's conclusions. The goal is not to reject out of hand conclusions that refer to a level of analysis different from what was actually studied. Instead, the goal is to consider the likelihood that an ecological fallacy or a reductionist fallacy has been made when estimating the causal validity of the conclusions.

IE

Interactive Exercises
Link
Units of Analysis

Cross-Sectional and Longitudinal Designs

Do you want to describe or understand social phenomena in the present? If you want to assess support for a candidate a month before a local election, you would need to collect your data at that time. If you want to describe the level of violence in Canadian communities, your focus might be on the current year. If the focus of your investigation is on the present or some other specific limited period, your research design will be cross-sectional. In **cross-sectional research designs**, all data are collected at one point in time. However, if you want to track changes in support for a candidate during the entire campaign period, or describe variation during the last decades in the level of violence in Canadian communities, you will need to collect data from the entire period you are investigating. In **longitudinal research designs**, data are collected at two or more points in time.

> **Cross-sectional research design:** A study in which data are collected at only one point in time.
>
> **Longitudinal research design:** A study in which data are collected that can be ordered in time; also defined as research in which data are collected at two or more points in time.

> **Time order:** A criterion for establishing a causal relation between two variables; the variation in the presumed cause (the independent variable) must occur before the variation in the presumed effect (the dependent variable).

Therefore, the research question determines whether a researcher needs to collect cross-sectional or longitudinal data. If the research question only concerns the here and now, there is no need for longitudinal data. However, it is also important to recognize that any research question involving a causal analysis—about what causes what—creates an issue about change over time. Identifying the **time order** of effects—what happened first, and so on—is critical for developing a causal analysis, but can be an insurmountable problem with a cross-sectional design. In longitudinal research designs, identification of the time order of effects can be quite straightforward.

Journal Link
Natural Experiment

Cross-Sectional Designs

Much of the research you have encountered so far in this text—the observations of computer use in Chapter 1, the surveys of binge drinking in Chapter 4 and of homeless persons in Chapter 5—has been cross-sectional. Although each of these studies took some time to carry out, researchers measured the actions, attitudes, and characteristics of respondents at only one point in time.

Sampson and Raudenbush (1999) used an ambitious cross-sectional design to investigate the effect of visible public social and physical disorder on the crime rate in Chicago neighborhoods. Their theoretical framework focused on the concept of informal social control: the ability of residents to regulate social activity in their neighborhoods through their collective efforts according to desired principles. The researchers believed that informal social control would vary between neighborhoods, and they hypothesized that the strength of informal social control would explain variation in crime rates rather than just the visible sign of disorder. Sampson and Raudenbush contrasted this prediction with the "broken windows" theory: the belief that signs of disorder themselves cause crime. In the theory Sampson and Raudenbush proposed, both visible disorder and crime were consequences of low levels of informal social control (measured with an index of collective efficacy). One did not cause the other (Exhibit 6.3).

Sampson and Raudenbush (1999) measured visible disorder through direct observation: Trained observers rode slowly around every street in 196 Chicago census tracts. Sampson and Raudenbush also conducted a survey of residents and examined police records. Both survey responses and police records were used to measure crime levels. The level of neighborhood informal social control and other variables were measured with the average

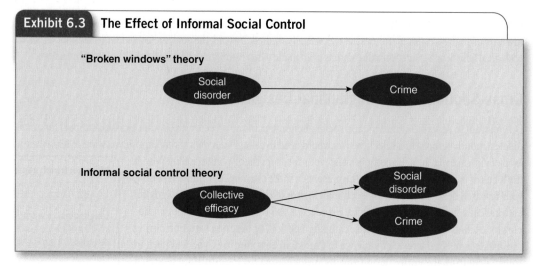

Exhibit 6.3 The Effect of Informal Social Control

Source: Based on Sampson and Raudenbush (1999).

resident responses to several survey questions. Both the crime rate and the level of social and physical disorder varied between neighborhoods in relation to the level of informal social control. Informal social control (collective efficacy) was a much more important factor in the neighborhood crime rate than was visible social and physical disorder, measured at the same time (Exhibit 6.4).

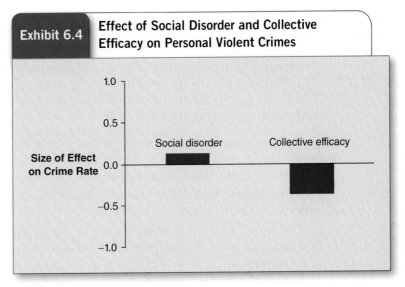

Exhibit 6.4 — Effect of Social Disorder and Collective Efficacy on Personal Violent Crimes

Source: Based on Sampson and Raudenbush (1999).

But note that we are left with a difficult question about the relations Sampson and Raudenbush identified between the variables they measured. Did neighborhoods that developed higher levels of informal social control then experience reductions in crime, or was it the other way around: Did neighborhoods that experienced a drop in crime then develop higher levels of informal social control? After all, if you are afraid to leave your apartment because you fear crime, you can't do a very good job of keeping an eye on things or attending community meetings. Maybe the crime reduction made residents feel safe to engage in more informal social control efforts, rather than just calling the police. Because of uncertainty like this, it is almost always better to use a longitudinal research design to answer questions about causal effects, rather than a cross-sectional research design.

There are four special circumstances in which we can be more confident in drawing conclusions about time order—and hence conclusions about causality—on the basis of cross-sectional data. Because in these special circumstances the data can be ordered in time, they might even be thought of as longitudinal designs (Campbell 1992). These four special circumstances are as follows:

1. *The independent variable is fixed at some point before the variation in the dependent variable.* So-called demographic variables that are determined at birth—such as sex, race, and age—are fixed in this way. So are variables such as education and marital status, if we know when the value of cases on these variables was established and if we know that the value of cases on the dependent variable was set some time afterward. For example, say we hypothesize that education influences the type of job individuals have. If we know that respondents completed their education before taking their current jobs, we would satisfy the time order requirement even if we were to measure education at the same time we measure the type of job. However, if some respondents possibly went back to school as a benefit of their current jobs, the time order requirement would not be satisfied.

2. *We believe that respondents can give us reliable reports of what happened to them or what they thought at some earlier point in time.* Julie Horney, D. Wayne Osgood, and Ineke Haen Marshall (1995) provide an interesting example of the use of such retrospective data. The researchers wanted to identify how criminal activity varies in response to changes in life circumstances. They interviewed 658 newly convicted male offenders sentenced to a Nebraska state prison. In a 45- to 90-minute interview, Horney et al. recorded each inmate's report of his life circumstances and of his criminal activities for the preceding 2 to 3 years. The researchers then found that criminal involvement was related strongly to adverse changes in life circumstances, such as marital separation or drug use. Retrospective data are often inadequate for measuring variation in past feelings, events, or behaviors, however,

because we may have difficulty recalling what we have felt or what has happened in the past and what we do recall is likely to be influenced by what we feel in the present (Elliott, Holland, & Thomson 2008:229). For example, retrospective reports by both adult alcoholics and their parents appear to overestimate greatly the frequency of childhood problems (Vaillant 1995). People cannot report reliably the frequency and timing of many past events, from hospitalization to hours worked. However, retrospective data tend to be reliable when it concerns major, persistent experiences in the past, such as what type of school someone went to or how a person's family was structured (Campbell 1992).

3. *Our measures are based on the records that contain information on cases in earlier periods.* Government, agency, and organizational records are excellent sources of time-ordered data after the fact. However, sloppy record keeping and changes in data collection policies can lead to inconsistencies, which must be considered. Another weakness of such archival data is that they usually contain measures of only a fraction of the variables that we think are important.

4. *We know that the value of the dependent variable was similar for all cases before the treatment.* For example, we may hypothesize that a training program (independent variable) improves the English-speaking abilities (dependent variable) of a group of recent immigrants. If we know that none of the immigrants could speak English before enrolling in the training program, we can be confident that any subsequent variation in their ability to speak English did not precede exposure to the training program. This is one way that traditional experiments establish time order: Two or more equivalent groups are formed before exposing one of them to some treatment.

Longitudinal Designs

In longitudinal research, data are collected that can be ordered in time. By measuring the value of cases on an independent variable and a dependent variable at different times, the researcher can determine whether variation in the independent variable precedes variation in the dependent variable.

In some longitudinal designs, the same sample (or panel) is followed over time; in other designs, sample members are rotated or completely replaced. The population from which the sample is selected may be defined broadly, as when a longitudinal survey of the general population is conducted. Or the population may be defined narrowly, as when the members of a specific age group are sampled at multiple points in time. The frequency of follow-up measurement can vary, ranging from a before-and-after design with just the one follow-up to studies in which various indicators are measured every month for many years.

Certainly, it is more difficult to collect data at two or more points in time than at one time. Quite frequently researchers simply cannot, or are unwilling to, delay completion of a study for even 1 year to collect follow-up data. But think of the many research questions that really should involve a much longer follow-up period: What is the impact of job training on subsequent employment? How effective is a school-based program in improving parenting skills? Under what conditions do traumatic experiences in childhood result in mental illness? It is safe to say that we will never have enough longitudinal data to answer many important research questions. Nonetheless, the value of longitudinal data is so great that every effort should be made to develop longitudinal research designs when they are appropriate for the research question asked. The following discussion of the three major types of longitudinal designs will give you a sense of the possibilities (see Exhibit 6.5).

> **Repeated cross-sectional design (trend study):** A type of longitudinal study in which data are collected at two or more points in time from different samples of the same population.

Repeated cross-sectional designs (trend studies). Studies that use a **repeated cross-sectional design**, also known as *trend studies,* have become fixtures of the political arena around election time. Particularly in presidential election years, we have all become accustomed to reading weekly, even daily, reports on the percentage of the population that supports each candidate. Similar

Exhibit 6.5 Three Types of Longitudinal Design

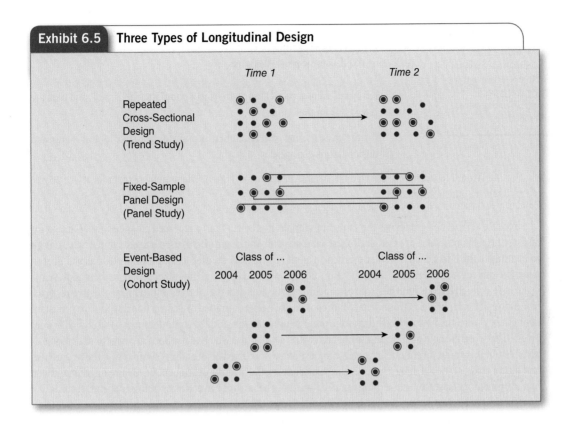

polls are conducted to track sentiment on many other social issues. For example, a 1993 poll reported that 52% of adult Americans supported a ban on the possession of handguns, compared with 41% in a similar poll conducted in 1991. According to pollster Louis Harris, this increase indicated a "sea change" in public attitudes (cited in Barringer 1993). Another researcher said, "It shows that people are responding to their experience [of an increase in handgun-related killings]" (cited in Barringer 1993:A14).

Repeated cross-sectional surveys are conducted as follows:

1. A sample is drawn from a population at Time 1, and data are collected from the sample.

2. As time passes, some people leave the population and others enter it.

3. At Time 2, a different sample is drawn from this population.

These features make the repeated cross-sectional design appropriate when the goal is to determine whether a population has changed over time. Has racial tolerance increased among Americans in the past 20 years? Are employers more likely to pay maternity benefits today than they were in the 1950s? These questions concern the changes in the population as a whole, not just the changes in individuals within the population. We want to know whether racial tolerance increased in society, not whether this change was due to migration that brought more racially tolerant people into the country or to individual U.S. citizens becoming more tolerant. We are asking whether employers overall are more likely to pay maternity benefits today than they were yesterday, not whether any such increase was due to recalcitrant employers going out of business or to individual employers changing their maternity benefits. When we do need to know whether individuals in the population changed, we must turn to a panel design.

> **Fixed-sample panel design (panel study):** A type of longitudinal study in which data are collected from the same individuals—the panel—at two or more points in time. In another type of panel design, panel members who leave are replaced with new members.

Fixed-sample panel designs (panel studies). Panel designs *allow* us to identify changes in individuals, groups, or whatever we are studying. This is the process for conducting **fixed-sample panel designs**:

1. A sample (called a panel) is drawn from a population at Time 1, and data are collected from the sample.

2. As time passes, some panel members become unavailable for follow-up, and the population changes.

3. At Time 2, data are collected from the same people as at Time 1 (the panel)—except for those people who cannot be located.

Because a panel design follows the same individuals, it is better than a repeated cross-sectional design for testing causal hypotheses. For example, Robert Sampson and John Laub (1990) used a fixed-sample panel design to investigate the effect of childhood deviance on adult crime. They studied a sample of white males in Boston when the subjects were between 10 and 17 years old and followed up when the subjects were in their adult years. Data were collected from multiple sources, including the subjects themselves and criminal justice records. Sampson and Laub (1990:614) found that children who had been committed to a correctional school for persistent delinquency were much more likely than were other children in the study to commit crimes as adults: 61% were arrested between the ages of 25 and 32, compared with 14% of those who had not been in correctional schools as juveniles. In this study, juvenile delinquency unquestionably occurred before adult criminality. If the researchers had used a cross-sectional design to study the past of adults, the juvenile delinquency measure might have been biased by memory lapses, by self-serving recollections about behavior as juveniles, or by loss of agency records.

Christopher Schreck, Eric Steward, and Bonnie Fisher (2006) wanted to identify predictors of adolescent victimization and wondered if the cross-sectional studies that had been conducted about victimization might have provided misleading results. Specifically, they suspected that adolescents with lower levels of self-control might be more prone to victimization and so needed to collect or find longitudinal data in which self-control was measured before experiences of victimization. The theoretical model they proposed to test included several other concepts that criminologists have identified as related to delinquency and that also might be influenced by levels of self-control: having delinquent peers, engaging in more delinquency, and being less attached to parents and school (Exhibit 6.6). Schreck et al. analyzed data available from a panel study of delinquency and found that low self-control at an earlier time made it more likely that adolescents would subsequently experience victimization, even accounting for other influences. The researchers' use of a panel design allowed them to be more confident that the self-control–victimization relationship was causal than if they had used a cross-sectional design.

Researcher Interview Link
Longitudinal Research

Despite their value in establishing time order of effects, panel studies are a challenge to implement successfully, so they often are not even attempted. There are two major difficulties:

1. *Expense and attrition.* It can be difficult, and very expensive, to keep track of individuals over a long period, and inevitably the proportion of panel members who can be located for follow-up will decline over time. Panel studies often lose more than one quarter of their members through attrition (Miller 1991:170), and those who are lost were often not necessarily like those who remain in the panel. As a result, a high rate of subject attrition may mean that the follow-up sample will no longer be representative of the population from which it was drawn and may no longer provide a sound basis for estimating change. Subjects who were lost to follow-up may have been those who changed the most, or the least, over time. For example, between 5% and 66% of subjects are lost in substance abuse prevention studies, and the dropouts typically had begun the study with higher rates of tobacco and marijuana use (Snow, Tebes, & Arthur 1992:804).

It does help to compare the baseline characteristics of those who are interviewed at follow-up with characteristics of those lost to follow-up. If these two groups of panel members were not very different at baseline, it is less likely that changes had anything to do with characteristics of the missing panel members.

> **Exhibit 6.6   Schreck et al.'s (2006) Explanatory Model of Adolescent Victimization**

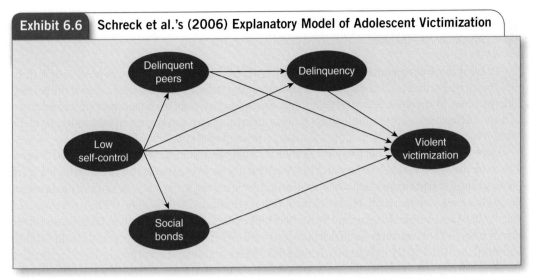

Source: Schreck, Christopher J., Eric A. Steward, and Bonnie S. Fisher. 2006. "Self-Control, Victimization, and Their Influence on Risky Lifestyles: A Longitudinal Analysis Using Panel Data." *Journal of Quantitative Criminology* 22:319–340. Copyright © 2006, Springer Science + Business Media, Inc. Reprinted with permission.

Even better, subject attrition can be reduced substantially if sufficient staff can be used to keep track of panel members. In their panel study, Sampson and Laub (1990) lost only 12% of the juveniles in the original sample (8% if you do not count those who had died).

2. *Subject fatigue.* Panel members may grow weary of repeated interviews and drop out of the study, or they may become so used to answering the standard questions in the survey that they start giving stock answers rather than actually thinking about their current feelings or actions (Campbell 1992). This problem is called **subject fatigue.** Fortunately, subjects do not often seem to become fatigued in this way, particularly if the research staff have maintained positive relations with the subjects. For example, at the end of an 18-month-long experimental study of housing alternatives for persons with mental illness who had been homeless, only 3 or 4 individuals (out of 93 who could still be located) refused to participate in the fourth and final round of interviews. The interviews took a total of about 5 hours to complete, and participants received about $50 for their time (Schutt, Goldfinger, & Penk 1997).

> **Subject fatigue:** Problems caused by panel members growing weary of repeated interviews and dropping out of a study or becoming so used to answering the standard questions in the survey that they start giving stock or thoughtless answers.

Because panel studies are so useful, social researchers have developed increasingly effective techniques for keeping track of individuals and overcoming subject fatigue. But when resources do not permit use of these techniques to maintain an adequate panel, repeated cross-sectional designs usually can be employed at a cost that is not a great deal higher than that of a one-time-only cross-sectional study. The payoff in explanatory power should be well worth the cost.

Event-based designs (cohort studies). In an **event-based design**, often called a *cohort study,* the follow-up samples (at one or more times) are selected from the same **cohort**—people who all have experienced a similar event or a common starting point. Examples include the following:

> **Event-based design (cohort study):** A type of longitudinal study in which data are collected at two or more points in time from individuals in a cohort.
>
> **Cohort:** Individuals or groups with a common starting point. Examples include college class of 1997, people who graduated from high school in the 1980s, General Motors employees who started work between the years 1990 and 2000, and people who were born in the late 1940s or the 1950s (the baby boom generation).

- *Birth cohorts*—those who share a common period of birth (those born in the 1940s, 1950s, 1960s, etc.)

- *Seniority cohorts*—those who have worked at the same place for about 5 years, about 10 years, and so on

- *School cohorts*—freshmen, sophomores, juniors, and seniors

An event-based design can be a type of repeated cross-sectional design or a type of panel design. In an event-based repeated cross-sectional design, separate samples are drawn from the same cohort at two or more different times. In an event-based panel design, the same individuals from the same cohort are studied at two or more different times. Comparing findings between different cohorts can help reveal the importance of the social or cultural context that the different cohorts experienced (Elliott et al. 2008:230).

Event-based research can improve identification of causal effects compared with cross-sectional designs. We can see this value of event-based research in a comparison between two studies that estimated the impact of public and private schooling on high school students' achievement test scores, only one of which used a cohort design. In a cross-sectional study, James Coleman, Thomas Hoffer, and Sally Kilgore (1982:68–69) compared standardized achievement test scores of high school sophomores and seniors in public, Catholic, and other private schools. The researchers found that test scores were higher in the private high schools (both Catholic and other) than in the public high schools. But was this difference a causal effect of private schooling? Perhaps the parents of higher-performing children were choosing to send them to private rather than to public schools. In other words, the higher achievement levels of private-sector students might have been in place before they started high school and not have developed as a consequence of their high school education.

The researchers tried to reduce the impact of this problem by statistically controlling for a range of family background variables: family income, parents' education, race, number of siblings, number of rooms in the home, number of parents present, mother working, and other indicators of a family orientation to education. But some critics pointed out that even with all these controls for family background, the cross-sectional study did not ensure that the students had been comparable in achievement when they started high school.

Coleman and Hoffer (1987) thus went back to the high schools and studied the test scores of the former sophomores 2 years later, when they were seniors; in other words, the researchers used an event-based panel design (a cohort study). This time they found that the verbal and math achievement test scores of the Catholic school students had increased more over the 2 years than was the case for the public school students (it was not clear whether the scores of the other private school students had increased). Irrespective of students' initial achievement test scores, the Catholic schools seemed to "do more" for their students than did the public schools. This finding continued to be true even when the dropouts were studied, too. The researchers' causal conclusion rested on much stronger ground because they used a cohort study design.

Quantitative or Qualitative Causal Explanations

A cause is an explanation for some characteristic, attitude, or behavior of groups, individuals, or other entities (such as families, organizations, or cities) or for events. Most social scientists seek causal explanations that reflect tests of the types of hypotheses with which you are familiar (see Chapter 3): The independent variable is the presumed cause, and the dependent variable is the potential effect. For example, the study by Sampson and Raudenbush (2001) tested whether disorder in urban neighborhoods (the independent variable) leads to crime (the dependent variable). (As you know, they concluded that it didn't, at least not directly.) This type of causal explanation is termed *nomothetic*.

A different type of cause is the focus of some qualitative research (Chapter 10), some historical and comparative research (Chapter 13), and our everyday conversations about causes. In this type of causal explanation, termed *idiographic*, individual events or the behaviors of individuals are explained with a series of related, prior events. For example, you might explain a particular crime as resulting from several incidents in the life of the perpetrator that resulted in a tendency toward violence, coupled with stress resulting from a failed marriage and a chance meeting.

Quantitative (Nomothetic) Causal Explanations

A **nomothetic causal explanation** is one involving the belief that variation in an independent variable will be followed by variation in the dependent variable, when all other things are equal (*ceteris paribus*). Researchers who claim a **causal effect** from a **nomothetic perspective** have concluded that the value of cases on the dependent variable differs from what their value would have been in the absence of variation in the independent variable. For instance, researchers might claim that the likelihood of committing violent crimes is higher for individuals who were abused as children than it would be if these same individuals had not been abused as children. Or researchers might claim that the likelihood of committing violent crimes is higher for individuals exposed to media violence than it would be if these same individuals had not been exposed to media violence. The situation as it would have been in the absence of variation in the independent variable is termed the **counterfactual** (see Exhibit 6.7).

Of course, the fundamental difficulty with this perspective is that we never really know what would have happened at the same time to the same people (or groups, cities, etc.) if the independent variable had not varied—because it did (Shrout 2011:4–5). We can't rerun real-life scenarios (King, Keohane, & Verba 1994). We could observe the aggressiveness of people's behavior before and after they were exposed to media violence. But this comparison involves an earlier time, when, by definition, the people and their circumstances were not exactly the same.

> **Nomothetic causal explanation:** An explanation that identifies common influences on a number of cases or events.
>
> ***Ceteris paribus:*** Latin phrase meaning "other things being equal."
>
> **Causal effect (nomothetic perspective):** When variation in one phenomenon, an independent variable, leads to or results, on average, in variation in another phenomenon, the dependent variable.
>
> *Example of a nomothetic causal effect:* Individuals arrested for domestic assault tend to commit fewer subsequent assaults than do similar individuals who are accused in the same circumstances but not arrested.
>
> **Counterfactual:** The situation that would have occurred if the subjects who were exposed to the treatment actually were not exposed, but otherwise had had identical experiences to those they underwent during the experiment.

Exhibit 6.7	The Counterfactual in Causal Research

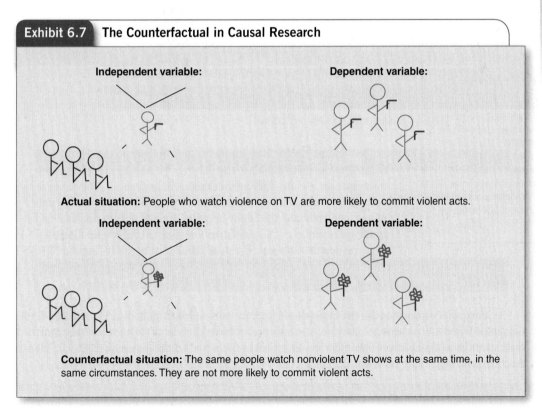

Actual situation: People who watch violence on TV are more likely to commit violent acts.

Counterfactual situation: The same people watch nonviolent TV shows at the same time, in the same circumstances. They are not more likely to commit violent acts.

Journal Link
Causal Relationships: Delinquency

But we do not need to give up hope! Far from it. We can design research to create conditions that are comparable indeed, so that we can confidently assert our conclusions *ceteris paribus*—other things being equal. We can examine the impact on the dependent variable of variation in the independent variable alone, even though we will not be able to compare the same people at the same time in exactly the same circumstances, except for the variation in the independent variable. And by knowing the ideal standard of comparability (the counterfactual), we can improve our research designs and strengthen our causal conclusions even when we cannot come so close to living up to the meaning of *ceteris paribus*.

Quantitative researchers seek to test nomothetic causal explanations with either experimental or nonexperimental research designs. However, the way in which experimental and nonexperimental designs attempt to identify causes differs quite a bit. It is very hard to meet some of the criteria for achieving valid nomothetic causal explanations using a nonexperimental design. Most of the rest of this chapter is devoted to a review of these causal criteria and a discussion of how experimental and nonexperimental designs can help establish them.

Qualitative (Idiographic) Causal Explanations

The other meaning of the term *cause* is one that we have in mind very often in everyday speech. This is **idiographic causal explanation**: the concrete, individual sequence of events, thoughts, or actions that resulted in a particular outcome for a particular individual or that led to a particular event (Hage & Meeker 1988). An idiographic explanation also may be termed an *individualist* or a *historicist* explanation.

A **causal effect** from an **idiographic perspective** includes statements of initial conditions and then relates a series of events at different times that led to the outcome, or causal effect. This narrative or story is the critical element in an idiographic explanation, which may therefore be classified as narrative reasoning (Richardson 1995:200–201). Idiographic explanations focus on particular social actors, in particular social places, at particular social times (Abbott 1992). Idiographic explanations are also typically very concerned with context—with understanding the particular outcome as part of a larger set of interrelated circumstances. Idiographic explanations can thus be termed *holistic*.

Elijah Anderson's (1990) field research in a poor urban community produced a narrative account of how drug addiction can result in a downward slide into residential instability and crime:

> **Idiographic causal explanation:** An explanation that identifies the concrete, individual sequence of events, thoughts, or actions that resulted in a particular outcome for a particular individual or that led to a particular event; may be termed an *individualist* or *historicist* explanation.
>
> **Causal effect (idiographic perspective):** When a series of concrete events, thoughts, or actions results in a particular event or individual outcome.
>
> *Example of an idiographic causal effect:* An individual is neglected by her parents but has a supportive grandparent. She comes to distrust others, has trouble in school, is unable to keep a job, and eventually becomes homeless. She subsequently develops a supportive relationship with a shelter case manager, who helps her find a job and regain her housing (based on Hirsch 1989).

> When addicts deplete their resources, they may go to those closest to them, drawing them into their schemes. . . . The family may put up with the person for a while. They provide money if they can. . . . They come to realize that the person is on drugs. . . . Slowly the reality sets in more and more completely, and the family becomes drained of both financial and emotional resources. . . . Close relatives lose faith and begin to see the person as untrustworthy and weak. Eventually the addict begins to "mess up" in a variety of ways, taking furniture from the house [and] anything of value. . . . Relatives and friends begin to see the person . . . as "out there" in the streets. . . . One deviant act leads to another. (pp. 86–87)

An idiographic explanation can also be developed from the narration of an individual. For example, Carole Cain interviewed AA (Alcoholics Anonymous) members about their experiences to learn how they construct their identities as alcoholics. In one interview, excerpted by Catherine Kohler Riessman (2008:71), "Hank" describes some of his experiences with drinking:

> One morning he found he could not get up even after several drinks. . . . When he did get up, he found AA, although he cannot remember how he knew where to go. . . . From the morning when he contacted

AA, he did not drink again for over five years. . . . Life improved, he got himself in better shape and got back together with his wife. After several years, the marriage broke up again, and in anger with his wife, he went back to drinking for another five years.

An idiographic explanation such as Anderson's or Cain's pays close attention to time order and causal mechanisms. Nonetheless, it is difficult to make a convincing case that one particular causal narrative should be chosen over an alternative narrative (Abbott 1992). Does low self-esteem result in vulnerability to the appeals of drug dealers, or does a chance drug encounter precipitate a slide in self-esteem? Did drinking lead Hank to go to AA, or did he start drinking more because he knew it would push him to go to AA? Did his drinking start again because his marriage broke up, or did his orientation lead his wife to leave and to his renewed drinking? The prudent causal analyst remains open to alternative explanations.

Idiographic explanation is deterministic, focusing on what caused a particular event to occur or what caused a particular case to change. As in nomothetic explanations, idiographic causal explanations can involve counterfactuals, by trying to identify what would have happened if a different circumstance had occurred. But unlike in nomothetic explanations, in idiographic explanations, the notion of a probabilistic relationship, an average effect, does not really apply. A deterministic cause has an effect in the case under consideration.

CAREERS AND RESEARCH

John Laub, PhD, Distinguished University Professor

John H. Laub is Distinguished University Professor in the Department of Criminology and Criminal Justice at the University of Maryland, College Park, and served from 2010 to 2013 as the director of the National Institute of Justice in the U.S. Department of Justice. These achievements and his many awards (including, with Robert J. Sampson, the 2011 Stockholm Prize in Criminology) rest on a foundation of decades of research, much of it with Harvard sociologist Robert Sampson, on crime across the life course and other key issues in criminology. Laub received his BA in criminal justice from the University of Illinois at Chicago and his MA and PhD in criminal justice from the State University of New York at Albany.

The National Institute of Justice (NIJ) mission is to enhance the administration of justice and public safety for the U.S. Department of Justice by advancing scientific research, development, and evaluation. As NIJ Director, Laub emphasized programs to improve the dissemination of research findings into new criminal justice policies and to develop new ambitious research projects involving partnerships with other agencies. One of these projects was designed to test a program developed in Hawai'i that was designed to improve outcomes for probationers. The "Honest Opportunity Probation with Enforcement" (or HOPE) program had shown promise for reducing rearrests, drug use, and skipped appointments for probationers in Hawai'i, so Laub partnered with the Bureau of Justice Assistance to evaluate the program with randomized experiments in four other sites.

Laub also developed new criminal justice policy recommendations based on his research on life course criminology with Sampson. Laub and Sampson's research indicated that incarceration does not itself *reduce* the risk of further reoffending after release, but that it does reduce the likelihood of securing employment, and this in turn *increases* the risk of reoffending. As NIJ director, Laub therefore encouraged reconsideration of the value of lengthy prison terms.

Laub and Sampson received the "Stockholm Prize" in 2011—the equivalent in criminology of the Nobel Prize. A former NIJ director (Stewart 2011) highlighted at that time the impact of the research of Laub and Sampson on criminal justice policy: "Research of this caliber is becoming a valued part of the national, regional and local public policy discussion."

Laub, John H. 2012. "Presidential Plenary Address—Strengthening Science to Promote Justice and Public Safety." ACJS Annual Conference, March 15. Retrieved June 11, 2014, from http://www.nij.gov/about/speeches/pages/acjs-march-2012.aspx

Stewart, James K. 2011. "John Laub and Robert Sampson Awarded Stockholm Prize." Retrieved June 11, 2014, from http://www.nij.gov/about/director/Pages/stockholm-prize.aspx

▣ Criteria and Cautions for Nomothetic Causal Explanations

How the research is designed influences our ability to draw causal conclusions. In this section, I introduce the features that need to be considered in a research design to evaluate how well it can support nomothetic causal conclusions.

Three criteria must be considered when deciding whether a causal connection exists. When a research design leaves one or more of the criteria unmet, we may have some important doubts about causal assertions that the researcher may have made. These three criteria are generally considered the most important bases for identifying a nomothetic causal effect: (1) empirical association, (2) appropriate time order, and (3) nonspuriousness (Hammersley 2008:43). The features of experimental research designs are particularly well suited to meeting these criteria and for testing nomothetic causal explanations. However, we must also consider the degree to which these criteria are met when evaluating nonexperimental research that is designed to test causal hypotheses.

Two other issues that I introduce as "cautions" in this chapter are a bit different. They are not necessary for establishing that a causal connection exists, but they help us understand it better. If we have not identified a causal mechanism, the first caution, we do not understand fully *why* a causal connection exists. The second caution is to specify the context in which a causal effect occurs because by understanding *when* or *under what conditions* the causal effect occurs, we will understand better what that effect *is*. Providing information about both mechanism and context can considerably strengthen causal explanations (Hammersley 2008:44–45).

In the following subsections, I will indicate how researchers attempt to meet the three criteria and address the two cautions with both experimental and nonexperimental designs. Illustrations of experimental design features will use a 2002 study by M. Lyn Exum on the effect of intoxication and anger on aggressive intentions. Most illustrations of nonexperimental design features will be based on the study by Sampson and Raudenbush (1999) of neighborhood social control, which I have already introduced.

Exum (2002) and her assistants recruited 84 male students of legal drinking age at a mid-Atlantic university, using classroom announcements and fliers (women were not included because it was not possible for them to be screened for pregnancy before participation, as required by federal guidelines). Students who were interested in participating were given some background information that included the explanation that the study was about alcohol and cognitive skills. All participants were scheduled for individual appointments. When they arrived for the experiment, they completed a mood questionnaire and engaged in a meaningless video game. Those who were randomly assigned to the Alcohol condition were then given 1.5 ounces of 50% ethanol (vodka) per 40 pounds of body weight in orange juice (those in the No Alcohol condition just drank orange juice).

The other part of the experimental manipulation involved inducing anger among a randomly selected half of the participants. This was accomplished by the experimenter, who falsely accused the selected students of having come to the experiment 30 minutes late, informing them that as a consequence of their tardiness, they would not be paid as much for their time, and then loudly saying "bullshit" when the students protested. After these manipulations, the students read a fictional scenario involving the student and another man in a conflict about a girlfriend. The students were asked to rate how likely they would be to physically assault the other man, and what percentage of other male students they believed would do so (see Exhibit 6.8).

The students in the Alcohol condition (who were intoxicated) and had also been angered predicted that more students would react with physical aggression to the events depicted in the scenario (see Exhibit 6.9). The students in the four experimental conditions did not differ in their reports of their own likely aggressiveness, but Exum suggested this could be a result of the well-established phenomenon of *self-enhancement bias*—the tendency to evaluate oneself more positively than others. She concluded that she found mixed support for her hypothesis that alcohol increases violent decision making among persons who are angry.

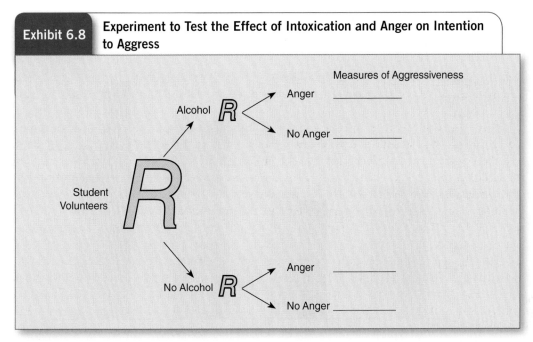

| Exhibit 6.8 | **Experiment to Test the Effect of Intoxication and Anger on Intention to Aggress** |

Source: Exum, M. Lyn. 2002. "The Application and Robustness of the Rational Choice Perspective in the Study of Intoxicated and Angry Intentions to Aggress." *Criminology* 40:933–966. Reprinted with permission from the American Society of Criminology.

Was this causal conclusion justified? How confident can we be in its internal validity? Do you think that college students' reactions in a controlled setting with a fixed amount of alcohol are likely to be generalized to other people and settings? Does it help to know that Exum carefully confirmed that the students in the Alcohol condition were indeed intoxicated and that those in the Anger condition were indeed angry when they read the scenario? What about the causal conclusion by Sampson and Raudenbush (1999) that social and physical disorder does not directly cause neighborhood crime? Were you convinced? In the next sections, I will show how well the features of the research designs used by Exum and by Sampson and Raudenbush meet the criteria for nomothetic causal explanation, and thus determine the confidence we can place in their causal conclusions. I will also identify those features of a *true experiment* that make this research design particularly well suited to testing nomothetic causal hypotheses.

Association

We say that there was an **association** between aggressive intentions and intoxication (for angry students) in Exum's (2002) experiment because the level of aggressive intentions varied according to whether students were intoxicated. An empirical (or observed) association between the independent and dependent variables is the first criterion for identifying a nomothetic causal effect.

> **Association:** A criterion for establishing a nomothetic causal relationship between two variables: Variation in one variable is related to variation in another variable.

We can determine whether an association exists between the independent and dependent variables in a true experiment because there are two or more groups that differ in their value on the independent variable. One group receives some "treatment," such as reading a cathartic message, that manipulates the value of the independent variable. This group is termed the *experimental group*. In a simple experiment, there may be one other group that does not receive the treatment; it is termed the *control group*. The Exum study compared four groups created with two independent variables; other experiments may compare only two groups that differ

Video Link
Control Groups and
Social Experiments

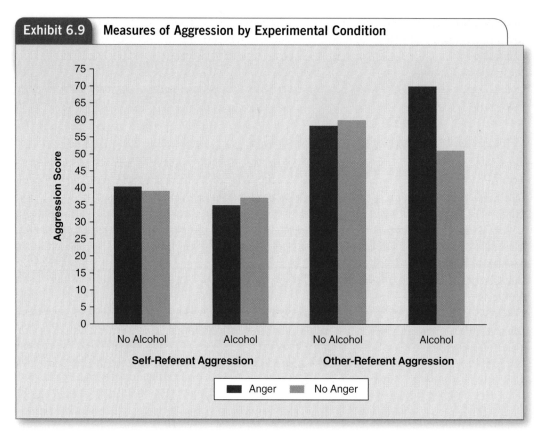

Exhibit 6.9 Measures of Aggression by Experimental Condition

Source: Adapted from Exum, M. Lyn. 2002. "The Application and Robustness of the Rational Choice Perspective in the Study of Intoxicated and Angry Intentions to Aggress." *Criminology* 40:933–966. Reprinted with permission from the American Society of Criminology.

in one independent variable, or more groups that represent multiple values of the independent variable or combinations of the values of more than two independent variables.

In nonexperimental research, the test for an association between the independent and dependent variables is like that used in experimental research—seeing whether values of cases that differ on the independent variable tend to differ in the dependent variable. The difference with nonexperimental research designs is that the independent variable is not a treatment to which the researcher assigns some individuals. In their nonexperimental study of neighborhood crime, Sampson and Raudenbush (1999) studied the association between the independent variable (level of social and physical disorder) and the crime rate, but they did not assign individuals to live in neighborhoods with low or high levels of disorder.

Time Order

Association is a necessary criterion for establishing a causal effect, but it is not sufficient. We must also ensure that the variation in the dependent variable occurred after the variation in the independent variable. This is the criterion of time order. Our research design determines our ability to determine time order.

Experimental Designs

In a true experiment, the researcher determines the time order. Exum (2002) first had some students drink alcohol and some experience the anger-producing manipulation and then measured their level of aggressive intentions. If we find an association between intoxication or anger and aggressiveness outside of an experimental situation, the criterion of time order may not be met. People who are more inclined to interpersonal aggression may be more likely than others to drink to the point of intoxication or to be angered by others in the first place. This would result in an association between intoxication and aggressive intentions, but the association would reflect the influence of being an aggressive person on drinking behavior rather than the other way around.

Nonexperimental Designs

You have already learned that nonexperimental research designs can be either cross-sectional or longitudinal. Because cross-sectional designs do not establish the time order of effects, their conclusions about causation must be more tentative. For example, although Sampson and Raudenbush (1999) found that lower rates of crime were associated with more informal social control (collective efficacy), their cross-sectional design could not establish directly that the variation in the crime rate occurred after variation in informal social control. Maybe it was a high crime rate that led residents to stop trying to exert much control over deviant activities in the neighborhood. It is difficult to discount such a possibility when only cross-sectional data are available, even though we can diagram hypothetical relations between the variables as if they are ordered in time (see Exhibit 6.10, panel 1).

In contrast, Sampson and Laub's (1990) longitudinal study of the effects of childhood deviance (antisocial behavior) on adult crime provided strong evidence of appropriate time order. Data on juvenile delinquency were collected when subjects were between 10 and 17 years old, so there's no question that the delinquency occurred before the job and marital experiences and then the adult criminality and other troublesome behaviors with which it was associated (see Exhibit 6.10, panel 2).

Encyclopedia Link
Spurious Relationship

Nonspuriousness

Nonspuriousness is another essential criterion for establishing the existence of a causal effect of an independent variable on a dependent variable; in some respects, it is the most important criterion. We say that a relationship between two variables is not spurious when it is not caused by variation in a third variable. Have you heard the old adage "Correlation does not prove causation"? It is meant to remind us that an

> **Nonspuriousness:** A criterion for establishing a causal relation between two variables; when a relationship between two variables is not caused by variation in a third variable.

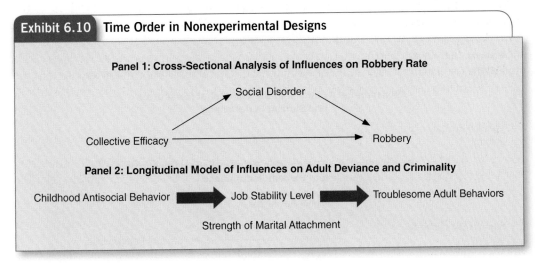

Exhibit 6.10 Time Order in Nonexperimental Designs

Panel 1: Cross-Sectional Analysis of Influences on Robbery Rate

Social Disorder

Collective Efficacy — Robbery

Panel 2: Longitudinal Model of Influences on Adult Deviance and Criminality

Childhood Antisocial Behavior → Job Stability Level → Troublesome Adult Behaviors

Strength of Marital Attachment

Sources: Based on Sampson and Raudenbush (1999); Sampson and Laub (1990).

> **Spurious relationship:** A relationship between two variables that is caused by variation in a third variable.

association between two variables might be caused by something other than an effect of the presumed independent variable on the dependent variable—that is, it might be a **spurious relationship**. If we measure children's shoe sizes and their academic knowledge, for example, we will find a positive association. However, the association results from the fact that older children have larger feet as well as more academic knowledge. Shoe size does not cause knowledge, or vice versa.

> **Extraneous variable:** A variable that influences both the independent and dependent variables, creating a spurious association between them that disappears when the extraneous variable is controlled.

Do storks bring babies? If you believe that correlation proves causation, then you might think so. The more storks that appear in certain districts in Holland, the more babies are born. But the association in Holland between number of storks and number of babies is spurious. In fact, both the number of storks and the birthrate are higher in rural districts than in urban districts. The rural or urban character of the districts (the **extraneous variable**) causes variation in the other two variables.

If you think this point is obvious, consider a social science example. Do schools with more resources produce better student outcomes? Before you answer the question, consider the fact that parents with more education and higher income tend to live in neighborhoods that spend more on their schools. These parents also are more likely to have books in the home and provide other advantages for their children. Do the parents cause variation in both school resources and student performance? If so, there would be an association between school resources and student performance that was at least partially spurious (Exhibit 6.11).

Randomization

> **Randomization:** The random assignment of cases, as by the toss of a coin.

A true experiment like Brad Bushman, Roy Baumeister, and Angela Stack's (1999) study of catharsis uses a technique called **randomization** to reduce the risk of spuriousness. Students in Bushman's experiment were asked to select a message to read by drawing a random number out of a bag. That is, the students were assigned randomly to a treatment condition. If students were assigned to only two groups, a coin toss could have been used (see Exhibit 6.12).

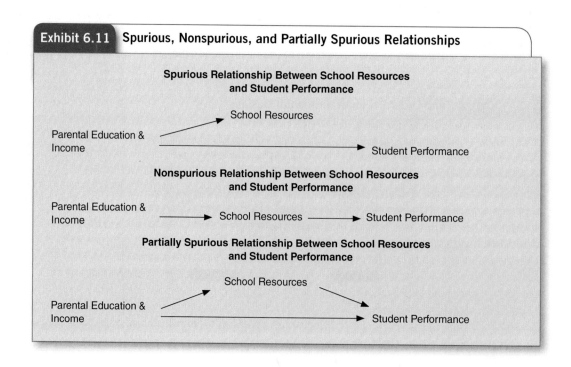

Exhibit 6.11   Spurious, Nonspurious, and Partially Spurious Relationships

Spurious Relationship Between School Resources
and Student Performance

Parental Education & Income → School Resources
Parental Education & Income → Student Performance

Nonspurious Relationship Between School Resources
and Student Performance

Parental Education & Income → School Resources → Student Performance

Partially Spurious Relationship Between School Resources
and Student Performance

School Resources
Parental Education & Income → School Resources → Student Performance
Parental Education & Income → Student Performance

Exhibit 6.12 Random Assignment to One of Two Groups

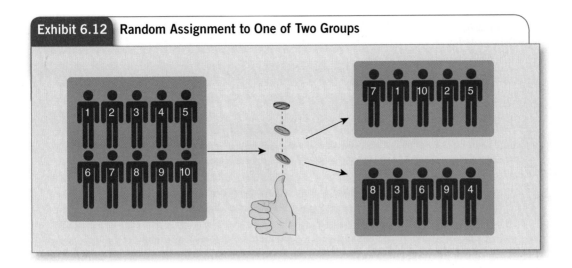

Random assignment ensures that neither the students' aggressiveness nor any of their other characteristics or attitudes could influence which of the messages they read. As a result, the different groups are likely to be equivalent in all respects at the outset of the experiment. The greater the number of cases assigned randomly to the groups, the more likely that the groups will be equivalent in all respects. Whatever the preexisting sources of variation among the students, these could not explain why the group that read the procatharsis message became more aggressive, whereas the others didn't.

> **Random assignment:** A procedure by which each experimental subject is placed in a group randomly.

Statistical Control

A nonexperimental study such as Sampson and Raudenbush's (1999) cannot use random assignment to comparison groups to minimize the risk of spurious effects. Even if we wanted to, we couldn't randomly assign people to live in neighborhoods with different levels of informal social control. Instead, nonexperimental researchers commonly use an alternative approach to try to achieve the criterion of nonspuriousness. The technique of **statistical control** allows researchers to determine whether the relationship between the independent and dependent variables still occurs while we hold constant the values of other variables. If it does, the relationship could not be caused by variation in these other variables.

Sampson and Raudenbush designed their study, in part, to determine whether the apparent effect of visible disorder on crime—the "broken windows" thesis—was spurious because of the effect of informal social control (see Exhibit 6.3). Exhibit 6.13 shows how statistical control was used to test this possibility. The data for all neighborhoods show that neighborhoods with much visible disorder had higher crime rates than did those with less visible disorder. However, when we examine the relationship between visible disorder and neighborhood crime rate separately for neighborhoods with high and low levels of informal social control (i.e., when we statistically control for social control level), we see that the crime rate no longer varies with visible disorder. Therefore, we must conclude that the apparent effect of broken windows was spurious because of the level of informal social control. Neighborhoods with low levels of social control were more likely to have high levels of visible social and physical disorder, and they were also more likely to have a high crime rate, but the visible disorder itself did not alter the crime rate.

> **Statistical control:** A method in which one variable is held constant so that the relationship between two (or more) other variables can be assessed without the influence of variation in the control variable.
>
> *Example:* In a different study, Sampson (1987) found a relationship between rates of family disruption and violent crime. He then classified cities by their level of joblessness (the control variable) and found that same relationship between the rates of family disruption and violent crime among cities with different levels of joblessness. Thus, the rate of joblessness could not have caused the association between family disruption and violent crime.

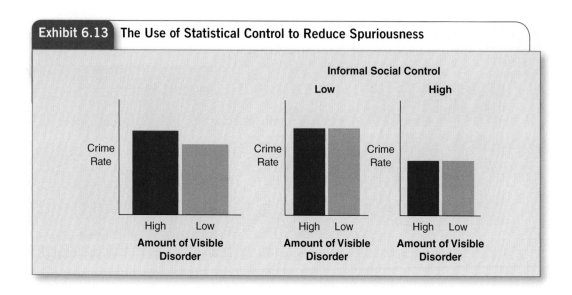

Exhibit 6.13 The Use of Statistical Control to Reduce Spuriousness

We can strengthen our understanding of nomothetic causal connections, and increase the likelihood of drawing causally valid conclusions, by considering two cautions: the need to investigate causal mechanism and the need to consider the causal context. These two cautions are emphasized in the definition of idiographic causal explanation, with its attention to the sequence of events and the context in which they happen, but here I will limit my discussion to research oriented toward nomothetic causal explanations.

Mechanism

> **Mechanism:** A discernible process that creates a causal connection between two variables.
>
> **Mediator:** A variable involved in a causal mechanism (intervening variable).

A causal **mechanism** is some process that creates the connection between variation in an independent variable and the variation in the dependent variable the independent variable is hypothesized to cause (Cook & Campbell 1979:35; Marini & Singer 1988). Many social scientists (and scientists in other fields) argue that no nomothetic causal explanation is adequate until a causal mechanism is identified (Costner 1989; Hedström & Swedberg 1998). In statistical analysis, variables that involve a mechanism are termed "**mediators**."

Research|Social Impact Link
The Placebo Effect

Research|Social Impact Link
Spurious Correlations

Our confidence in causal conclusions based on nonexperimental research increases with identification of a causal mechanism (Shrout 2011:15–16). Such mechanisms help us understand how variation in the independent variable results in variation in the dependent variable. For example, in a study that reanalyzed data from Sheldon Glueck and Eleanor Glueck's (1950) pathbreaking study of juvenile delinquency, Sampson and Laub (1994) found that children who grew up with structural disadvantages such as family poverty and geographic mobility were more likely to become juvenile delinquents. Why did this occur? Sampson and Laub's (1994) analysis indicated that these structural disadvantages led to lower levels of informal social control in the family (less parent–child attachment, less maternal supervision, and more erratic or harsh discipline). In turn, lower levels of informal social control resulted in a higher probability of delinquency (Exhibit 6.14). Informal social control thus intervened in the relationship between structural disadvantage and juvenile delinquency.

In their study of deterrence of spouse abuse (introduced in Chapter 2), Lawrence Sherman and Richard Berk (1984) designed follow-up experiments to test or control several causal mechanisms that they wondered about after their first experiment: Did recidivism decrease for those who were arrested for spouse abuse *because* of the exemplary work of the arresting officers? Did recidivism increase for arrestees *because* they experienced more

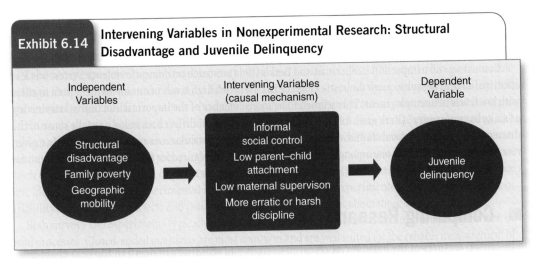

Exhibit 6.14 Intervening Variables in Nonexperimental Research: Structural Disadvantage and Juvenile Delinquency

Source: Based on Sampson and Raudenbush (1999).

stressors with their spouses as time passed? Investigating these and other possible causal mechanisms enriched Sherman and Berk's eventual explanation of how arrest influences recidivism.

Of course, you might ask why structural disadvantage tends to result in lower levels of family social control or how family social control influences delinquency. You could then conduct research to identify the mechanisms that link, for example, family social control and juvenile delinquency. (Perhaps the children feel they're not cared for, so they become less concerned with conforming to social expectations.) This process could go on and on. The point is that identification of a mechanism through which the independent variable influences the dependent variable increases our confidence in the conclusion that a causal connection does indeed exist. However, identification of a causal mechanism—one or more mediating variables—in turn requires concern for the same causal criteria that we consider when testing the original relationship, including time order and nonspuriousness (Shrout 2011:15–21).

Context

Do the causal processes in which we are interested vary across neighborhoods? Among organizations? Across regions? Over time? For different types of people? When relationships between variables differ across geographic units such as counties or across other social settings, researchers say there is a **contextual effect**. Identification of the **context** in which a causal relationship occurs can help us understand that relationship. The changes in the crime rate with which we began this chapter differed for blacks and whites, for youth and adults, and in urban and rural areas (Ousey & Lee 2004:359–360). These contextual effects suggest that single-factor explanations about these changes are incorrect (Rosenfeld 2004:89). In statistical analysis, variables that identify contexts for the effects of other variables are termed **moderators.**

> **Contextual effects:** Variation in relationships of dependent with independent variables between geographic units or other social settings.
>
> **Context:** A set of interrelated circumstances that alters a relationship between other variables or social processes.
>
> **Moderator:** A variable that identifies a context for the effect of other variables.

Sampson and Laub (1993) found support for a contextual effect in their study of 538,000 juvenile justice cases in 322 U.S. counties: In counties having a relatively large underclass and poverty concentrated among minorities, juvenile cases were more likely to be treated harshly. These relationships occurred for both African American and white juveniles, but were particularly strong for African Americans. The results of this research suggest the importance of considering social context when examining criminal justice processes (see also Dannefer & Schutt 1982; Schutt & Dannefer 1988).

When you read the results of a social scientific study, you should now be able to evaluate critically the validity of the study's findings. If you plan to engage in social research, you should now be able to plan an approach that will lead to valid findings. And with a good understanding of three dimensions of validity (measurement validity, generalizability, and causal validity) under your belt, and with sensitivity also to the goal of *authenticity,* you are ready to focus on the major methods of data collection used by social scientists.

Key Terms

Association   203
Causal effect (idiographic
    perspective)   200
Causal effect (nomothetic
    perspective)   199
Ceteris paribus   199
Cohort   197
Context   209
Contextual effects   209
Counterfactual   200
Cross-sectional research design   191
Ecological fallacy   190

Emergence   190
Event-based design (cohort study)   197
Extraneous variable   206
Fixed-sample panel design
    (panel study)   196
Idiographic causal explanation   200
Longitudinal research design   191
Mechanism   208
Mediator   208
Moderator   209
Nomothetic causal explanation   199
Nonspuriousness   205

Random assignment   207
Randomization   206
Reductionist fallacy
    (reductionism)   190
Repeated cross-sectional design
    (trend study)   194
Spurious relationship   206
Statistical control   207
Subject fatigue   197
Time order   192
Units of analysis   188
Units of observation   189

Highlights

- We do not fully understand the variables in a study until we know to which units of analysis—what level of social life—they refer.

- Invalid conclusions about causality may occur when relationships between variables measured at the group level are assumed to apply at the individual level (the ecological fallacy) and when relationships between variables measured at the level of individuals are assumed to apply at the group level (the reductionist fallacy). Nonetheless, many research questions point to relationships at multiple levels and so may profitably be investigated at multiple units of analysis.

- Longitudinal designs are usually preferable to cross-sectional designs for establishing the time order of effects. Longitudinal designs vary in whether the same people are measured at different times, how the population of interest is defined, and how frequently follow-up measurements are taken. Fixed-sample panel designs provide the strongest test for the time order of effects, but they can be difficult to carry out successfully because of their expense as well as subject attrition and fatigue.

- Causation can be defined in either nomothetic or idiographic terms. Nomothetic causal explanations deal with effects on average. Idiographic causal explanations deal with the sequence of events that led to a particular outcome.

- The concept of nomothetic causal explanation relies on a comparison. The value of cases on the dependent variable is measured after they have been exposed to variation in an independent variable. This measurement is compared with what the value of cases on the dependent variable would have been if they had not been exposed to the variation in the independent variable (the counterfactual). The validity of nomothetic causal conclusions rests on how closely the comparison group comes to the ideal counterfactual.

- From a nomothetic perspective, three criteria are generally viewed as necessary for identifying a causal relationship: (1) association between the variables, (2) proper time order, and (3) nonspuriousness of the association. In addition, the basis for concluding that a causal relationship exists is strengthened by the identification of a causal mechanism and the context for the relationship.

- Association between two variables is in itself insufficient evidence of a causal relationship. This point is commonly made with the expression, "Correlation does not prove causation."

- Experiments use random assignment to make comparison groups as similar as possible at the outset of an experiment to reduce the risk of spurious effects resulting from extraneous variables.

- Nonexperimental designs use statistical controls to reduce the risk of spuriousness. A variable is controlled when it is held constant so that the association between the independent and dependent variables can be assessed without being influenced by the control variable.

- Ethical and practical constraints often preclude the use of experimental designs.

- Idiographic causal explanations can be difficult to identify because the starting and ending points of particular events and the determination of which events act as causes in particular sequences may be ambiguous.

STUDENT STUDY SITE

Sharpen your skills with SAGE edge at **edge.sagepub.com/schutt8e. SAGE edge for students** provides a personalized approach to help you accomplish your coursework goals in an easy-to-use learning environment.

Discussion Questions

1. There's a lot of "sound and fury" in the social science literature about units of analysis and levels of explanation. Some social researchers may call another a *reductionist* if the latter explains a problem such as substance abuse as caused by "lack of self-control." The idea is that the behavior requires consideration of social structure—a group level of analysis rather than an individual level of analysis. Another researcher may be said to commit an *ecological fallacy* if she assumes that group-level characteristics explain behavior at the individual level (such as saying that "immigrants are more likely to commit crime" because the *neighborhoods* with higher proportions of immigrants have higher crime rates). Do you favor causal explanations at the individual or the group (or social structural) level? If you were forced to mark on a scale from 0 to 100 the percentage of crime that results from problems with individuals rather than from problems with the settings in which they live, where would you make your mark? Explain your decision.

2. Researchers often try to figure out how people have changed over time by conducting a cross-sectional survey of people of different ages. The idea is that if people who are in their 60s tend to be happier than people who are in their 20s, it is because people tend to "become happier" as they age. But maybe people who are in their 60s now were just as happy when they were in their 20s, and people in their 20s now will be just as unhappy when they are in their 60s. (That's called a *cohort effect.*) We can't be sure unless we conduct a panel or cohort study (survey the same people at different ages). What, in your experience, are the major differences between the generations today in social attitudes and behaviors? Which would you attribute to changes as people age, and which to differences between cohorts in what they have experienced (such as common orientations among baby boomers)? Explain your reasoning.

3. The chapter begins with some alternative explanations for recent changes in the crime rate. Which of the explanations make the most sense to you? Why? How could you learn more about the effect on crime of one of the "causes" you have identified in a laboratory experiment? What type of study could you conduct in the community to assess its causal impact?

4. This chapter discusses both experimental and nonexperimental approaches to identifying causes. What are the advantages and disadvantages of both approaches for achieving each of the five criteria identified for causal explanations?

5. Construct an idiographic causal explanation for a recent historical or a personal event. For example, what was the sequence of events that led to the outcome of the 2012 U.S. presidential election? What was the sequence of events that led to the Russian takeover of the Crimean region in Ukraine?

catharsis (Chapter 6) did not have a pretest, nor did Sherman and Berk's (1984) experimental study of the police response to domestic violence (Chapter 2).

Let's examine how well true experiments meet the criteria for identifying a nomothetic cause that were identified in Chapter 6:

Association between the hypothesized independent and dependent variables. As you have seen, experiments can provide unambiguous evidence of association by comparing the distribution of the dependent variable (or its average value) between the experimental and comparison groups.

Time order of effects of one variable on the others. Unquestionably, arrest for spouse abuse preceded recidivism in the Sherman and Berk (1984) study (described in Chapter 2), and the "confrontations" in the Czopp et al. (2006) study preceded the differential changes in prejudicial attitudes between the experimental and comparison groups. In true experiments, randomization to the experimental and comparison groups equates the groups at the start of the experiment, so time order can be established by comparing posttest scores between the groups. However, experimental researchers include a pretest when possible so that equivalence of the groups at baseline can be confirmed and the amount of change can be compared between the experimental and comparison groups.

Nonspurious relationships between variables. Nonspuriousness is difficult—some would say impossible—to establish in nonexperimental designs. The random assignment of subjects to experimental and comparison groups is what makes true experiments such powerful designs for testing causal hypotheses. Randomization controls for the host of possible extraneous influences that can create misleading, spurious relationships in both experimental and nonexperimental data. If we determine that a design has used randomization successfully, we can be much more confident in the resulting causal conclusions.

Mechanism that creates the causal effect. The features of a true experiment do not in themselves allow identification of causal mechanisms; as a result, there can be some ambiguity about how the independent variable influenced the dependent variable and the resulting causal conclusions (Bloom 2008:128). However, Czopp et al. (2006:798) investigated possible mechanisms linking confrontation to change in prejudicial attitudes in their experiment. One finding from this investigation was that the confrontations led to a more negative self-appraisal, which in turn led to decreased expression of prejudice.

Context in which change occurs. Control over conditions is more feasible in many experimental designs than it is in nonexperimental designs. Czopp et al. (2006) allowed their student subjects to communicate with the "other student" collaborator only through a computer to maintain control over conditions. The researchers didn't want the student subjects to notice something about the "other student" that might not have to do with their manipulation about confrontation. In another version of the experiment, Czopp and colleagues compared the responses of student subjects with "other students" who were said to be black and white (and found that the race of the confederate did not matter) (pp. 791–794). Bear in mind that it is often difficult to control conditions in experiments conducted outside of a laboratory setting; later in this chapter, you will see how the lack of control over experimental conditions can threaten internal validity.

Research|Social Impact Link
Social Science Research Today

🔲 Quasi-Experiments

Often, testing a hypothesis with a true experimental design is not feasible with the desired participants and in the desired setting. Such a test may be too costly or take too long to carry out, it may not be ethical to randomly assign subjects to the different conditions, or it may be too late to do so. In these situations, researchers may instead use *quasi-experimental* designs that retain several components of experimental design but do not randomly assign participants to different conditions.

A **quasi-experimental design** is one in which the comparison group is predetermined to be comparable with the treatment group in critical ways, such as being eligible for the same services or being in the same school cohort (Rossi & Freeman 1989:313). These research designs are *quasi*-experimental because subjects are not randomly assigned to the comparison and experimental groups. As a result, we cannot be as confident in the comparability of the groups as in true experimental designs. Nonetheless, to term a research design quasi-experimental, we have to be sure that the comparison groups meet specific criteria that help lessen the possibility of preexisting differences between groups.

I discuss here the two major types of quasi-experimental designs—nonequivalent control group designs and before-and-after designs—as well as a nonexperimental design that can be very similar to nonequivalent control group designs (other types can be found in Cook & Campbell 1979; Mohr 1992):

> **Quasi-experimental design:** A research design in which there is a comparison group that is comparable to the experimental group in critical ways, but subjects are not randomly assigned to the comparison and experimental groups.

1. **Nonequivalent control group designs** have experimental and comparison groups that are designated before the treatment occurs and are not created by random assignment.

2. **Ex post facto control group designs** have experimental and comparison groups that are not designated before the treatment occurs and are not created by random assignment, so that participants may select themselves to be in a group. This ability to chose the desired type of group actually makes this design nonexperimental rather than quasi-experimental, but it is often confused with the nonequivalent control group design.

3. **Before-and-after designs** have a pretest and posttest but no comparison group. In other words, the subjects exposed to the treatment serve, at an earlier time, as their own controls.

> **Nonequivalent control group design:** A quasi-experimental design in which experimental and comparison groups are designated before the treatment occurs but are not created by random assignment.
>
> **Ex post facto control group design:** A nonexperimental design in which comparison groups are selected after the treatment, program, or other variation in the independent variable has occurred, but when the participants were able to choose the group in which they participated. Often confused with a quasi-experimental design.
>
> **Before-and-after design:** A quasi-experimental design consisting of several before-after comparisons involving the same variables but no comparison group.

Nonequivalent Control Group Designs

This is the most common type of quasi-experimental design, also called a *differences-in-differences* design. In it, a comparison group is selected to be as comparable as possible to the treatment group. Two selection methods can be used: aggregate matching and individual matching.

Aggregate Matching

Once research moves outside of laboratories on college campuses and samples of available students, it becomes much harder to control what people do and what type of experiences they will have. When random assignment is not possible, an alternative approach to testing the effect of some treatment or other experience can be to find a comparison group that matches the treatment group in many ways but differs in exposure to the treatment. For example, a sociologist who hypothesizes that the experience of a disaster increases social solidarity might identify two towns that are similar in population characteristics but where one experienced an unexpected disaster. If the population in the two towns has similar distributions on key variables such as age, gender, income, and so on, but they differ after the disaster in their feelings of social solidarity, the sociologist might conclude that a higher level of solidarity in the affected town resulted from the disaster. However, it is important in a nonequivalent control group design that individuals have not been able to choose whether to join the group that had one experience or the other. If many people moved from the stricken town to the unaffected town right after the disaster, higher levels of postdisaster solidarity among residents in the stricken town could reflect the departure of people with feelings of low solidarity from that town, rather than the effect of the disaster on increasing feelings of solidarity.

Audio Link
Audience Research

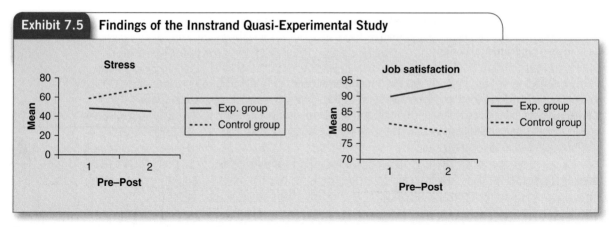

Exhibit 7.5 Findings of the Innstrand Quasi-Experimental Study

Source: Innstrand, Siw Tone, Geir Arild Espries, and Reidar Mykletun. 2004. "Job Stress, Burnout and Job Satisfaction: An Intervention Study of Staff Working With People With Intellectual Disabilities." *Journal of Applied Research in Intellectual Disabilities* 17:119–126. Copyright © 2004, John Wiley & Sons. Reprinted with permission.

Siw Tone Innstrand, Geir Arild Espries, and Reidar Mykletun (2004) used a nonequivalent control group design with aggregate matching to study the effect of a new program in Norway to reduce stress among staff working with people with intellectual disabilities. The researchers chose two Norwegian municipalities that offered the same type of community residential care and used similar staff. The two municipalities were in different locations and had no formal communication with each other.

When their research began, Innstrand and colleagues asked staff in both municipalities to complete an anonymous survey that measured their stress, job satisfaction, and other outcomes. This was their pretest. The researchers then implemented the stress reduction program in one municipality. This was their experimental treatment. Ten months later, they again distributed their survey. This was their posttest. Two of their primary findings appear in Exhibit 7.5: Levels of stress declined in the experimental group and increased in the control group, and job satisfaction increased in the experimental group and declined in the control group. It seemed that the program had at least some of the effects that Innstrand and colleagues predicted.

Ruth Wageman (1995) used a more complicated quasi-experimental design to investigate how the organization of work tasks and rewards affected work team functioning (Exhibit 7.6). Her research question was whether it was preferable to organize work tasks and work rewards in a way that stressed team interdependence or

Exhibit 7.6 Quasi-Experimental Designs

Nonequivalent control group design (Wageman 1995)				
Experimental Group:		O_1	X_a	O_2
Comparison Group 1:		O_2	X_b	O_2
Comparison Group 2:		O_3	X_c	O_2
		Pretest	**Treatment**	**Posttest**
Team interdependence	Group	Team performance	Interdependent tasks	Team performance
	Hybrid	Team performance	Mixed tasks	Team performance
	Individual	Team performance	Individual tasks	Team performance

individual autonomy. More than 800 Xerox service technicians in 152 teams participated in the research. District managers were able to choose which intervention they would implement in their work team. This means that even though the work teams were not randomized to the different conditions, the team participants themselves were not able to choose which conditions to work in. Thus, this design met the definition of a nonequivalent control group quasi-experiment. One month before the intervention, Wageman collected survey data and company records about group performance. These measures were repeated 4 months after the intervention began.

Surprisingly, team performance improved more when management stressed either interdependence or autonomy than when they used a hybrid model in which team members worked part of the time as an interdependent team and part of the time as autonomous individuals (Exhibit 7.7).

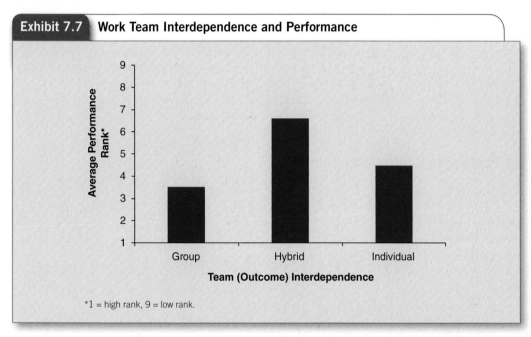

Exhibit 7.7   Work Team Interdependence and Performance

*1 = high rank, 9 = low rank.

Source: Reprinted from "Interdependence and Group Effectiveness" by Ruth Wageman. P. 170 in *Administrative Science Quarterly,* vol. 40, pp. 145–180, March 1995. Published by SAGE Publications on behalf of Johnson Graduate School of Management, Cornell University.

Nonequivalent control group designs based on aggregate matching should always be considered when the goal is to compare effects of treatments or other experiences and a true experiment is not feasible. However, it is important to recognize that simply comparing outcome measures in two groups that offer different programs is not in itself a quasi-experiment. If individuals can choose which group to join, partly on the basis of what programs they offer, then the groups will differ in preference for the treatment as well as in having had the treatment. When such selection bias is possible, the design is nonexperimental rather than quasi-experimental. More generally, the validity of this design depends on the adequacy of matching of the comparison group with the treatment group (Cook & Wong 2008:151).

Individual Matching

In individual matching, individual cases in the treatment group are matched with similar individuals in the comparison group. In some situations, this can create a comparison group that is very similar to the experimental group, as when children in Head Start were matched with their siblings to estimate the effect of participation in Head Start (Currie & Thomas 1995:341). However, in many studies, it is not possible to match in this way on the most important variables. Simply matching on the basis of such readily available characteristics as gender or age will be of little value if these sociodemographic characteristics are not related to propensity to participate in the treatment group or extent of response to treatment (Cook & Wong 2008:153).

It is important to realize that variables chosen for matching affect the quality of a nonequivalent comparison group design (Cook & Wong 2008:154–155). Matching with comparison groups comprising twins, siblings, members of the same organization, or others who are very similar will often be the best choice.

The quality of a nonequivalent comparison group design can also be improved by inclusion of several other features (Cook & Wong 2008:154–155):

- A pretest in both groups, so that the starting point for the groups can be compared

- Identical procedures to measure outcomes in the two groups (same measure, same time of assessment)

- Several outcome measures reflecting the same overall causal hypothesis

- Investigating the process of selection into the two groups and controlling for the elements of this process that can be measured

Audio Link
Sibling Effect Research

Quasi-experimental designs with these features can result in estimates of effects that are very similar to those that have been obtained with a randomized design (Cook & Wong 2008:159).

Ex Post Facto Control Group Designs

The ex post facto control group design is similar to the nonequivalent control group design and is often confused with it, but it does not meet as well the criteria for quasi-experimental designs. This design has experimental and comparison groups that are not created by random assignment, but unlike nonequivalent control group designs, individuals may decide themselves whether to enter the "treatment" or control group. As a result, in ex post facto (after the fact) designs, the people who join the treatment group may differ because of

Exhibit 7.8 Ex Post Facto Control Group Design

Self-managing work teams (Cohen & Ledford 1994)			
Experimental Group	**O**$_1$	**X**	**O**$_2$
Comparison Group	**O**$_1$		**O**$_2$
Experimental group	Pretest: Measures of satisfaction and productivity	Self-managing work team	Posttest: Measures of satisfaction and productivity
Comparison group	Pretest: Measures of satisfaction and productivity	Traditionally managed work team	Posttest: Measures of satisfaction and productivity
Key:			
O = Observation (pretest or posttest) X = Experimental treatment			

Source: Based on Cohen and Ledford (1994).

what attracted them to the group initially, rather than because of their experience in the group. However, in some studies, we may conclude that the treatment and control groups are so similar at the outset that causal effects can be tested (Rossi & Freeman 1989:343–344).

Susan Cohen and Gerald Ledford (1994) studied the effectiveness of self-managing teams in a telecommunications company with an ex post facto design (Exhibit 7.8). They compared work teams they rated as self-managing with those they found to be traditionally managed (meaning that a manager was responsible for the team's decisions). Cohen and Ledford found that the self-reported quality of work life was higher in the self-managed groups than in the traditionally managed groups.

What distinguishes this study design from a quasi-experimental design like the one Wageman (1995) used to study work teams is the fact that the teams themselves and their managers had some influence on how they were managed. As the researchers noted, "If the groups which were already high performers were the ones selected to be self-managing teams, then the findings could be due to a selection bias rather than any effects of self-management" (Cohen & Ledford 1994:34). Thus, preexisting characteristics of employees and managers or their team composition might have influenced which "treatment" they received, as well as the outcomes achieved. This leaves us less certain about the effect of the treatment itself.

Before-and-After Designs

The common feature of before-and-after designs is the absence of a comparison group. Because all cases are exposed to the experimental treatment, the basis for comparison is provided by comparing the pretreatment with the posttreatment measures. These designs are thus useful for studies of interventions that are experienced by virtually every case in some population, including total coverage programs such as Social Security or studies of the effect of a new management strategy in a single organization. The simplest type of before-and-after design is the fixed-sample panel design, with one pretest and one posttest (see Chapter 6).

> **Multiple group before-and-after design:** A type of quasi-experimental design in which several before-and-after comparisons are made involving the same independent and dependent variables but different groups.

David Phillips's (1982) study of the effect of TV soap opera suicides on the number of actual suicides in the United States illustrates a more powerful **multiple group before-and-after design**. In this design, several before-and-after comparisons are made involving the same variables but with different groups. Phillips identified 13 soap opera suicides in 1977 and then recorded the U.S. suicide rate in the weeks before and following each TV story. Because several suicides occurred in adjacent weeks, the analysis proceeded as if there had been 9 soap opera suicides. In effect, the researcher had 9 different before-and-after studies, one for each suicide story occurring in a unique week. In 8 of these 9 comparisons, deaths from suicide increased from the week before each soap opera suicide to the week after (see Exhibit 7.9).

Another type of before-and-after design involves multiple pretest and posttest observations of the same group. These may be **repeated measures panel designs**, which include several pretest and posttest observations, and **time series designs**, which include many (preferably 30 or more) such observations in both pretest and posttest periods. Repeated measures panel designs are stronger than simple before-and-after panel designs because they allow the researcher to study the process by which an intervention or treatment has an impact over time.

> **Repeated measures panel design:** A quasi-experimental design consisting of several pretest and posttest observations of the same group.
>
> **Time series design:** A quasi-experimental design consisting of many pretest and posttest observations of the same group over an extended period.

In a time series design, the trend in the dependent variable until the date of the intervention or event whose effect is being studied is compared with the trend in the dependent variable after the intervention. A substantial disparity between the preintervention trend and the postintervention trend is evidence that the intervention or event had an impact (Rossi & Freeman 1989:260–261, 358–363).

Time series designs are particularly useful for studies of the impact of new laws or social programs that affect everyone and that are readily assessed by some ongoing measurement. For example, Paul A. Nakonezny, Rebecca

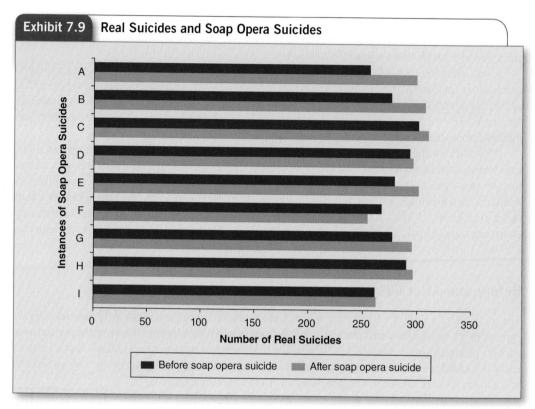

Exhibit 7.9 Real Suicides and Soap Opera Suicides

Source: Adapted from Phillips (1982):1347. Reprinted with permission from the University of Chicago Press.

Reddick, and Joseph Lee Rodgers (2004) used a time series design to identify the impact of the Oklahoma City terrorist bombing in April 1995 on the divorce rate in Oklahoma. They hypothesized that people would be more likely to feel a need for support in the aftermath of such a terrifying event and thus be less likely to divorce. Nakonezny et al. first calculated the average rate of change in divorce rates in Oklahoma's 77 counties in the 10 years before the bombing and then projected these rates forward to the 5 years after the bombing. As they hypothesized, they found that the actual divorce rate in the first years after the bombing was lower than the prebombing trend would have predicted, but this effect diminished to nothing by the year 2000 (see Exhibit 7.10).

The most powerful type of quasi-experimental design that can be considered a before-and-after design is the **regression–discontinuity design**. This type of design can be used if participants are assigned to treatment solely based on a cutoff score on some **assignment variable**. Students may be admitted to a special intensive course based on a test score, or persons may become eligible for a housing voucher based on their income. In these two situations, test score and personal income are assignment variables.

Researchers using a regression–discontinuity design plot the relationship (the regression line) between scores on the assignment variable and the outcome of interest for those who did not enter the treatment as well as for those who did enter the treatment. If there is a jump in the regression line at the cutoff score, it indicates an effect of the treatment. For example, Sarah Kuck Jalbert, William Rhodes, Christopher Flygare, and Michael Kane (2010) studied the effect of reduced caseload size and intensive supervision on probation outcomes, using a regression–discontinuity design. Probationers were assigned to this program if they exceeded a certain value

Regression–discontinuity design: A quasi-experimental design in which individuals are assigned to a treatment and a comparison group solely on the basis of a cutoff score on some assignment variable, and then treatment effects are identified by a discontinuity in the regression line that displays the relation between the outcome and the assignment variable at the cutoff score.

Assignment variable: The variable used to specify a cutoff score for eligibility for some treatment in a regression–discontinuity design.

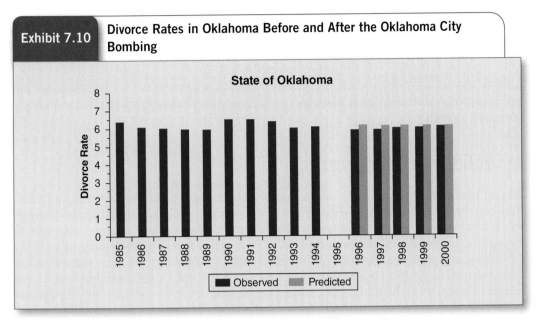

| Exhibit 7.10 | Divorce Rates in Oklahoma Before and After the Oklahoma City Bombing |

Source: Nakonezny et al. 2004. "Did Divorces Decline After the Oklahoma City Bombing?" *Journal of Marriage and Family*, 66:90–100. Copyright © 2004, John Wiley & Sons. Reprinted with permission.

on a recidivism risk score. Jalbert and her colleagues found that at the point for probationers with risk scores near the cutoff score for program participation, recidivism dropped by 25.5% after 6 months for those who were admitted to the program.

Summary: Causality in Quasi-Experiments

Let's now examine how well quasi-experiments meet the criteria for identifying a nomothetic cause and the two additional challenges for such identification that were identified in Chapter 6.

Association between the hypothesized independent and dependent variables. Quasi-experiments can provide evidence of association between the independent and dependent variables that is as unambiguous as that provided by a true experiment.

Time order of effects of one variable on the others. This is a strength of the various quasi-experimental before-and-after designs, but we cannot be as sure of correctly identifying the time order of effects with nonequivalent control group designs because we cannot be certain that some features of the groups did not attract individuals to them who differed at the outset. This is a much greater problem with ex post facto control group designs.

Nonspurious relationships between variables. We cannot entirely meet this challenge with a quasi-experimental design because we cannot be certain of ruling out all potentially extraneous influences with either nonequivalent control group designs or before-and-after designs. Nonetheless, it is important to note that the criteria for these designs do give us considerable confidence that most extraneous influences could not have occurred. Ex post facto control group designs give us much less confidence about the occurrence of extraneous influences because of the likelihood of self-selection into the groups. This is why most researchers do not consider ex post facto control group designs to be "quasi"-experimental.

Mechanism that creates the causal effect. The features of quasi-experiments and ex post facto designs do not in themselves allow identification of causal mechanisms; however, the repeated measures design does provide a means for testing hypotheses about the causal mechanism.

Context in which change occurs. The quasi-experimental designs that involve multiple groups can provide a great deal of information about the importance of context, as long as the researcher measures contextual variables.

🔳 Validity in Experiments

Like any research design, experimental designs must be evaluated for their ability to yield valid conclusions. True experiments are particularly well suited for producing valid conclusions about causality (internal validity), but they are likely to fare less well in achieving generalizability. Quasi-experiments may provide more generalizable results than true experiments do, but they are more prone to problems of internal invalidity (although some quasi-experimental designs allow the researcher to rule out almost as many potential sources of internal invalidity as does a true experiment). It is important to distinguish nonequivalent control group designs from ex post facto designs when evaluating internal validity, given the problem of self-selection in ex post facto designs. Measurement validity is also a central concern, but experimental design does not in itself offer any special tools or particular advantages or disadvantages in measurement. In this section, you will learn more about the ways in which experiments help (or don't help) resolve potential problems of internal validity and generalizability (Campbell & Stanley 1966).

Causal (Internal) Validity

Encyclopedia Link
Internal Validity

An experiment's ability to yield valid conclusions about causal effects is determined by the comparability of its experimental and comparison groups. First, of course, a comparison group must be created. Second, this comparison group must be so similar to the experimental group or groups that it can show in the posttest what the experimental group would have been like if it had not received the experimental treatment—if the independent variable had not varied. You now know that randomization is used to create a comparison group that is identical to the experimental group at the start of the experiment—with a certain margin of error that occurs with a process of random assignment. For this reason, a true experiment—a design with random assignment—is prone to fewer sources of internal invalidity than a quasi-experiment is.

Several sources of internal invalidity are considerably reduced by a research design that has a comparison group, but others are likely to occur unless a true experimental design with random assignment is used.

Sources of Internal Invalidity Reduced by a Comparison Group

The types of problem that can largely be eliminated by having a comparison group as well as a treatment group are those that arise during the study period itself (Campbell & Stanley 1966:8). Something unanticipated may happen (an effect of "history"), the pretest may have an unanticipated effect on subsequent posttests ("testing"), or the measurement instrument itself may perform differently a second time ("instrumentation"). Also, the participants themselves may change over time ("maturation") or simply decline to their normal levels of performance ("regression effects"). Each of these potential sources of internal invalidity is explained in more detail:

> **History effect:** A source of causal invalidity that occurs when events external to the study influence posttest scores; also called an effect of **external events.**

1. *History:* **External events** during the experiment (things that happen outside the experiment) can change subjects' outcome scores. Examples are newsworthy events that have to do with the focus of an experiment and major disasters to which subjects are exposed. This problem is often referred to as a **history effect**—that is, history during the experiment.

It is important to realize that features of how the treatment is delivered can result in an effect of history, or external events, when there is a comparison, including in true and quasi-experimental designs. For example, in an experiment in which subjects go to a special location for a treatment, something in that location unrelated to the treatment might influence these subjects. Experimental and comparison group subjects in Richard Price, Michelle Van Ryn, and Amiram Vinokur's (1992) study of job search services differed in whether they attended the special seminars, so external events could have happened to subjects in the experimental group that might not have happened to those in the control group. Perhaps program participants witnessed a robbery outside the seminar building one day, and their orientations changed as a result. External events are a major concern in evaluation studies that compare programs in different cities or states (Hunt 1985:276–277).

IE

Interactive Exercises Link
Sources of Internal Invalidity

2. *Testing:* Taking the pretest can in itself influence posttest scores. Subjects may learn something or be sensitized to an issue by the pretest and, as a result, respond differently the next time they are asked the same questions on the posttest.

3. *Instrumentation:* If the instrument used to measure the dependent variable changes in performance between the pretest and posttest, the result is termed a problem of instrumentation. For example, observers rating the behavior of students in a classroom may grow accustomed to the level of disruptions and therefore rate the same behavior as more appropriate in the posttest than they did in the pretest. This is similar to the problem of testing, except that it may be possible to reduce the effect of instrumentation by increasing control over the measurement instrument.

4. *Maturation:* Changes in outcome scores during experiments that involve a lengthy treatment period may result from maturation. Subjects may age, gain experience, or grow in knowledge, all as part of a natural maturational experience, and thus respond differently on the posttest than on the pretest.

5. *Regression:* People experience cyclical or episodic changes that result in different posttest scores, a phenomenon known as a **regression effect**. Subjects who are chosen for a study because they received very low scores on a test may show improvement in the posttest, on average, simply because some of the low scorers were having a bad day. Conversely, individuals selected for an experiment because they are suffering from tooth decay will not show improvement in the posttest because a decaying tooth is not likely to improve in the natural course of things. It is hard, in many cases, to know whether a phenomenon is subject to naturally occurring fluctuations, so the possibility of regression effects should be considered whenever subjects are selected because of their extremely high or low values on the outcome variable (Mohr 1992:56, 71–79).

> **Regression effect:** A source of causal invalidity that occurs when subjects who are chosen for a study because of their extreme scores on the dependent variable become less extreme on the posttest because of natural cyclical or episodic change in the variable.

History, testing, maturation, instrumentation, and regression effects could explain any change over time in most of the before-and-after designs because these designs do not have a comparison group. Repeated measures panel studies and time series designs are better in this regard because they allow the researcher to trace the pattern of change or stability in the dependent variable until and after the treatment. However, it is much more desirable to have a comparison group that, like the treatment group, will also be affected by these sources of internal invalidity and so can control for them. Of course, these factors are not a problem in true experiments because those have an experimental group and the comparison group.

Sources of Internal Invalidity Reduced by Randomization

You have already learned that the purpose of randomization, or random assignment to the experimental and comparison groups, is to equate the two or more groups at the start of the experiment. The goal is to eliminate the effect of **selection bias**.

> **Selection bias:** A source of internal (causal) invalidity that occurs when characteristics of experimental and comparison group subjects differ in any way that influences the outcome.

6. *Selection bias:* The composition of the experimental and comparison groups in a true experiment is unlikely to be affected by selection bias. Randomization equates the groups' characteristics, although with some possibility for error due to chance. The likelihood of difference due to chance can be identified with appropriate statistics.

When subjects are not assigned randomly to treatment and comparison groups, as in non-equivalent control group designs, the threat of selection bias is very great. Even if the researcher selects a comparison group that matches the treatment group on important variables, there is no guarantee that the groups were similar initially in the dependent variable or in some other characteristic that ultimately influences posttest scores. However, a pretest helps the researchers determine and control for selection bias. Because most variables that might influence outcome scores will also have influenced scores on the pretest, statistically controlling for the pretest scores also controls many of the unmeasured variables that might have influenced the posttest scores. The potential for selection bias is much greater with an ex post facto control group design because participants have the ability to select the group they enter based on the treatment they expect to receive.

Sources of Internal Invalidity That Require Attention While the Experiment Is in Progress

Even in a research design that involves a comparison group and random assignment, whether or not there is a pretest, the experimental and comparison groups can become different over time because of changes in group membership, interaction between members of the experimental and comparison groups, or effects that are related to the treatment but are not the treatment itself.

> **Differential attrition (mortality):** A problem that occurs in experiments when comparison groups become different because subjects are more likely to drop out of one of the groups for various reasons.

7. *Differential attrition:* This problem occurs when the groups become different after the experiment begins because more participants drop out of one of the groups than out of the other(s) for various reasons. **Differential attrition** is not a likely problem in a laboratory experiment that occurs in one session, such as Czopp et al.'s (2006) experiment with college students, but some experiments continue over time. Subjects who experience the experimental condition may become more motivated than comparison subjects are to continue in the experiment and so be less likely to drop out.

You have already learned in Chapter 6 that attrition can be a major problem in longitudinal designs, whether these are simple panel studies or quasi-experimental repeated measures designs. When many subjects have left a panel between the pretest and posttest (or between any repeated measures in the study), a comparison of the average differences between subjects at the start and end of the study period may mislead us to think that the subjects have changed, when what actually happened is that subjects who had dropped out of the study were different from those who remained in it. For example, people with less education and who are not married have been less likely to continue in the large ongoing Panel Study of Income Dynamics (Lillard & Panis 1998:442). Statistical adjustments can reduce the effects of panel attrition, but it is always important to compare the characteristics of study dropouts and those who remain for follow-up.

> **Intent-to-treat analysis:** When analysis of the effect of a treatment on outcomes in an experimental design compares outcomes for all those who were assigned to the treatment group with outcomes for all those who were assigned to the control group, whether or not participants remained in the treatment group.

When the independent variable in an experimental study is a treatment or an exposure to something over time, bias caused by differential attrition can be reduced by using **intent-to-treat analysis**. In this type of analysis, outcomes are compared between all participants who started in the experimental group—those who were intended to receive the treatment—and all participants who started in the control group, whether or not any of these participants left the study before the treatment was fully delivered (Shrout 2011:7). Of course, an intent-to-treat analysis is likely to reduce the researcher's estimate of the treatment effect because some participants will not have received the full treatment, but it provides a more realistic estimate of effects that are likely to occur if the treatment is administered to persons who can leave before the experiment is over (Bloom 2008:120).

8. *Contamination:* When the comparison group in an experiment is in some way affected by, or affects, the treatment group, there is a problem with **contamination**. Contamination is not ruled out by the basic features of experimental and quasi-experimental designs, but careful inspection of the research design can determine how much it is likely to be a problem in a particular experiment. This problem basically arises from the failure to control adequately the conditions of the experiment. If the experiment is conducted in a laboratory, if members of the experimental group and the comparison group have no contact while the study is in progress, and if the treatment is relatively brief, contamination is not likely to be a problem. To the degree that these conditions are not met, the likelihood of contamination will increase. For example, contamination was a potential problem in a field-based study by Price et al. (1992) about the effects of a job search training program on the risk of depression among newly unemployed persons. Because the members of both the experimental group (who received the training) and the control group (who did not receive the training) used the same unemployment offices, they could have talked to each other about their experiences while the study was in progress.

> **Contamination:** A source of causal invalidity that occurs when either the experimental or the comparison group is aware of the other group and is influenced in the posttest as a result.

9. *Compensatory rivalry:* A problem related to contamination, also termed the **John Henry effect**, can occur when comparison group members are aware that they are being denied some advantages and, in response, increase their efforts to compensate for this denial (Cook & Campbell 1979:55).

10. *Demoralization:* This problem involves the opposite reaction to compensatory rivalry; that is, comparison group participants discover that they are being denied some treatments they believe are valuable and as a result they feel demoralized and perform worse than expected. Both **compensatory rivalry** and **demoralization** thus distort the impact of the experimental treatment.

> **Compensatory rivalry (John Henry effect):** A type of contamination in experimental and quasi-experimental designs that occurs when control group members are aware that they are being denied some advantages and increase their efforts by way of compensation.
>
> **Demoralization:** A type of contamination in experimental and quasi-experimental designs that occurs when control group members feel they have been left out of some valuable treatment and perform worse as a result.

11. *Expectancies of experimental staff:* Change among experimental subjects may result from the positive expectations of the experimental staff who are delivering the treatment rather than from the treatment itself. **Expectancies of experimental staff** may alter the experimental results if staff—even well-trained staff—convey their enthusiasm for an experimental program to the subjects in subtle ways. This is a special concern in evaluation research, when program staff and researchers may be biased in favor of the program for which they work and eager to believe that their work is helping clients. Such positive staff expectations thus create a self-fulfilling prophecy. However, in experiments on the effects of treatments such as medical drugs, **double-blind procedures** can be used: Staff delivering the treatments do not know which subjects are getting the treatment and which are receiving a placebo, something that looks like the treatment but has no effect.

> **Expectancies of experimental staff:** A source of treatment misidentification in experiments and quasi-experiments that occurs when change among experimental subjects results from the positive expectancies of the staff who are delivering the treatment rather than from the treatment itself; also called a *self-fulfilling prophecy.*
>
> **Double-blind procedure:** An experimental method in which neither the subjects nor the staff delivering experimental treatments know which subjects are getting the treatment and which are receiving a placebo.

12. *Placebo effect:* Treatment misidentification may occur when subjects receive a treatment that they consider likely to be beneficial and improve because of that expectation rather than because of the

> **Placebo effect:** A source of treatment misidentification that can occur when subjects receive a fake "treatment" they think is beneficial and improve because of that expectation even though they did not receive the actual treatment or received a treatment that had no real effect.

treatment itself. In medical research, where the **placebo effect** often results from a chemically inert substance that looks like the experimental drug but actually has no direct physiological effect, some research has indicated that the placebo effect itself produces positive health effects in many patients suffering from relatively mild medical problems (Goleman 1993a:C3). It is not clear that these improvements are really any greater than what the patients would have experienced without the placebo (Hrobjartsson & Gotzsche 2001). In any case, it is possible for placebo effects to occur in social science research also, so, when possible, experimental researchers can reduce this threat to internal validity by treating the comparison group with something that seems similar to what the experimental group receives. You read earlier about the short feedback that Czopp et al. (2006:795) had their "control" subjects receive to give them an experience similar to the "confrontation" feedback that the experimental subjects received.

13. *Hawthorne effect:* Members of the treatment group may change relative to the dependent variable because their participation in the study makes them feel special. This problem can occur when treatment group members compare their situation with that of members of the control group, who are not receiving the treatment; in this situation, it would be a type of contamination effect. But experimental group members might feel special simply because they are in the experiment. This is termed a **Hawthorne effect**, after a famous productivity experiment at the Hawthorne electric plant outside Chicago. As the story has been told, the workers worked harder no matter what physical or economic conditions the researchers changed to influence productivity; the motivation for the harder work simply seemed to be that the workers felt special because of being in the experiment (Whyte 1955:34).

> **Hawthorne effect:** A type of contamination in research designs that occurs when members of the treatment group change relative to the dependent variable because their participation in the study makes them feel special.

Let me quickly add that a careful review of the actual Hawthorne results shows that there wasn't really a clear effect of participating in that experiment (Jones 1992). The Hawthorne effect was itself mostly a matter of misinterpretation and hype. But we can never ignore the possibility that participation in an experiment may itself change participants' orientations and behavior. This is a particular concern in evaluation research when program clients know that the research findings may affect the chances for further program funding.

Generalizability

The need for generalizable findings can be thought of as the Achilles heel of true experimental design. The design components that are essential for a true experiment and that minimize the threats to causal validity make it more difficult to achieve sample generalizability (being able to apply the findings to some clearly defined larger population) and cross-population generalizability (generalizing across subgroups and to other populations and settings). Nonetheless, no one conducts experiments just to find out how freshman psychology students react to confrontation (or some other experimental "treatment") at your university. Experimental researchers are seeking to learn about general processes, so we have to worry about the generalizability of their results.

> **Journal Link**
> Validity of Cross-Cultural Social Studies

Sample Generalizability

Subjects who can be recruited for a laboratory experiment, randomly assigned to a group, and kept under carefully controlled conditions for the study's duration are unlikely to be a representative sample of any large population of interest to social scientists. Can they be expected to react to the experimental treatment in the same way as members of the larger population? The generalizability of the treatment and of the setting for the experiment also must be considered (Cook & Campbell 1979:73–74). The more artificial the experimental arrangements are, the greater the problem will be (Campbell & Stanley 1966:20–21).

A researcher can take steps both before and after an experiment to increase a study's generalizability. Conducting a field experiment, such as Sherman and Berk's (1984) study of arrest in actual domestic violence incidents, is likely to yield more generalizable findings than are laboratory experiments, for which subjects must volunteer. In some field experiments, participants can even be selected randomly from the population of interest, and, thus, the researchers can achieve results generalizable to that population. For example, some studies of the effects of income supports on the work behavior of poor persons have randomly sampled persons within particular states before randomly assigning them to experimental and comparison groups. When random selection is not feasible, the researchers may be able to increase generalizability by selecting several different experimental sites that offer marked contrasts on key variables (Cook & Campbell 1979:76–77).

Factorial Surveys

Factorial surveys embed the features of true experiments into a survey design to maximize generalizability. In the most common type of factorial survey, respondents are asked for their likely responses to one or more vignettes about hypothetical situations. The content of these vignettes is varied randomly among survey respondents to create "treatment groups" that differ in particular variables reflected in the vignettes.

> **Factorial survey:** A survey in which randomly selected subsets of respondents are asked different questions, or are asked to respond to different vignettes, to determine the causal effect of the variables represented by these differences.

Greet Van Hoye and Filip Lievens (2003) used a factorial survey design to test the effect of job applicants' sexual orientation on ratings of their hirability by professionals who make personnel decisions. Van Hoye and Lievens first identified 252 actual selection professionals—people involved daily in personnel selection and recruitment—from consulting firms and company human resource departments. The researchers mailed to each of these professionals a packet with four items: (1) a *letter* inviting their participation in the study, (2) a *job posting* that described a company and a particular job opening in that company, (3) a *candidate profile* that described someone ostensibly seeking that job, and (4) a *response form* on which the selection professionals could rate the candidate's hirability.

The experimental component of the survey was created by varying the candidate profiles. Van Hoye and Lievens created nine different candidate profiles. Each profile used very similar language to describe a candidate's gender (they were all male), age, nationality, family situation, education, professional experience, and personality. However, the family situations were varied to distinguish candidates as heterosexual, homosexual, or "possibly homosexual"—single and older than 30. Other characteristics were varied to distinguish candidates who were "poor," "moderate," and "excellent" matches to the job opening. An example of a profile for a homosexual male who was a "good" candidate for the job included the following language:

1. Personal Data

   Name: Peter Verschaeve

   Gender: Male

   Age: 33 years

   Family situation: Living together with John Vermeulen, fashion designer

2. Educational and Professional Experience

   1990–1993: PUC Diepenbeek—MBA, Marketing Major

   1991–now; Human Resources manager of an electronics manufacturer

3. Personality

   Peter Verschaeve is self-assured and assertive. He interacts with others in a friendly and warm manner. (Van Hoye & Lievens 2003:27)

The combination of three different descriptions of family situation and three different levels of candidate quality resulted in nine different candidate profiles. Each selection professional was randomly assigned to receive one of these nine candidate profiles. As a result, there was no relationship between who a particular selection professional was and the type of candidate profile he or she received.

The results of the study appear in Exhibit 7.11. The average hirability ratings did not differ between candidates who were gay, heterosexual, or single, but hirability increased in direct relation to candidate quality. Van Hoye and Lievens (2003:26) concluded that selection professionals based their evaluations of written candidate profiles on candidate quality, not on their sexual orientation—at least in Flanders, Belgium.

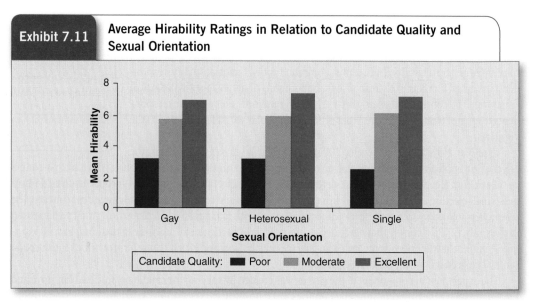

Exhibit 7.11 **Average Hirability Ratings in Relation to Candidate Quality and Sexual Orientation**

Source: Van Hoye, Greet and Filip Lievens. 2003. "The Effects of Sexual Orientation on Hirability Ratings: An Experimental Study." *Journal of Business and Psychology* 18:15–30. Copyright © 2003, Human Science Press, Inc. Reprinted with permission from Springer.

Because Van Hoye and Lievens surveyed real selection professionals at their actual workplaces, we can feel more comfortable with the generalizability of their results than if they had just recruited college students for an experiment in a laboratory. However, there is still an important limitation to the generalizability of factorial surveys such as this: A factorial survey research design indicates only what respondents say they would do in situations that have been described to them. If the selection professionals had to make a recommendation for hiring to an actual employer, we cannot be sure that they would act in the same way. So factorial surveys do not completely resolve the problems caused by the difficulty of conducting true experiments with representative samples. Nonetheless, by combining some of the advantages of experimental and survey designs, factorial surveys can provide stronger tests of causal hypotheses than can other surveys and more generalizable findings than can experiments.

External Validity

Researchers are often interested in determining whether treatment effects identified in an experiment hold true for subgroups of subjects and across different populations, times, or settings. Of course, determining that a relationship between the treatment and the outcome variable holds true for certain subgroups does not establish that the relationship also holds true for these subgroups in the larger population, but it suggests that the relationship might be externally valid.

We have already seen examples of how the existence of treatment effects in particular subgroups of experimental subjects can help us predict the cross-population generalizability of the findings. For example, Sherman and Berk's (1984) research (see Chapter 2) found that arrest did not deter subsequent domestic violence for unemployed individuals; arrest also failed to deter subsequent violence in communities with high levels of unemployment. Price et al. (1992) found that intensive job search assistance reduced depression among individuals who were at high risk for it because of other psychosocial characteristics; however, the intervention did not influence the rate of depression among individuals at low risk for depression. This is an important interaction effect that limits the generalizability of the treatment, even if Price et al.'s sample was representative of the population of unemployed persons.

Interaction of Testing and Treatment

A variant on the problem of external validity occurs when the experimental treatment has an effect only when particular conditions created by the experiment occur. One such problem occurs when the treatment has an effect only if subjects have had the pretest. The pretest sensitizes the subjects to some issue, so that when they are exposed to the treatment, they react in a way that differs from how they would have reacted had they not taken the pretest. In other words, testing and treatment interact to produce the outcome. For example, answering questions in a pretest about racial prejudice may sensitize subjects so that when exposed to the experimental treatment, seeing a film about prejudice, their attitudes are different from what they would have been otherwise. In this situation, the treatment truly had an effect, but it would not have had an effect had it been provided without the sensitizing pretest. This possibility can be evaluated with the Solomon four-group design described earlier (see Exhibit 7.12).

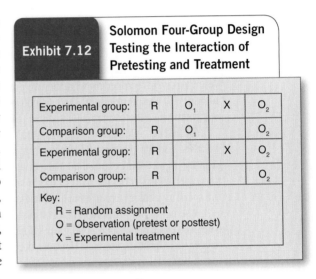

Exhibit 7.12 Solomon Four-Group Design Testing the Interaction of Pretesting and Treatment

Experimental group:	R	O_1	X	O_2
Comparison group:	R	O_1		O_2
Experimental group:	R		X	O_2
Comparison group:	R			O_2

Key:
R = Random assignment
O = Observation (pretest or posttest)
X = Experimental treatment

As you can see, no single procedure establishes the external validity of experimental results. Ultimately, we must base our evaluation of external validity on the success of replications taking place at different times and places and using different forms of the treatment.

There is always an implicit trade-off in experimental design between maximizing causal validity and generalizability. The more the assignment to treatments is randomized and all experimental conditions are controlled, the less likely it is that the research subjects and setting will be representative of the larger population. College students are easy to recruit and assign to artificial but controlled manipulations, but both practical and ethical concerns preclude this approach with many groups and with respect to many treatments. However, although we need to be skeptical about the generalizability of the results of a single experimental test of a hypothesis, the body of findings accumulated from many experimental tests with different people in different settings can provide a solid basis for generalization (Campbell & Russo 1999:143).

▣ Ethical Issues in Experimental Research

Social science experiments can raise difficult ethical issues. You have already read in Chapter 3 that Philip Zimbardo (2004:34) ended his Stanford prison experiment after only 6 days, rather than after the planned 2 weeks, because of the psychological harm that seemed to result from the unexpectedly sadistic behavior of some of the "guards." Although Zimbardo's follow-up research convinced him that there had been no lasting harm to subjects, concern about the potential for harm would preclude many such experiments today.

Nonetheless, experimental research continues because of the need for very good evidence about cause–effect relationships to inform social theory as well as social policy. The particular strength of randomized experiments for answering causal questions means that they can potentially prevent confusion in social theory and avoid wasting time and resources on ineffective social programs (Mark & Gamble 2009:203).

Two ethical issues are of special importance in experimental research designs. Deception is an essential part of many experimental designs, despite the ethical standard of subjects' informed consents. As a result, contentious debate continues about the interpretation of this standard. In addition, experimental evaluations of social programs pose ethical dilemmas because they require researchers to withhold possibly beneficial treatment from some of the subjects just on the basis of chance (Boruch 1997). In this section, I give special attention to the problems of deception and the distribution of benefits in experimental research.

Journal Link
Ethics in Fieldwork

Deception

Deception is used in social experiments to create more "realistic" treatments, often within the confines of a laboratory. You learned in Chapter 3 about Milgram's (1965) use of deception in his classic study of obedience to authority. Volunteers were recruited for what they were told was a study of the learning process, not a study of "obedience to authority." The experimenter told the volunteers that they were administering electric shocks to a "student" in the next room, when there were actually neither students nor shocks. Most subjects seemed to believe the deception.

You learned in Chapter 3 that Milgram's description of dehoaxing inflated the consistency with which it was used and the amount of deception that was revealed. You also learned that the dehoaxing increased the negative impact of the experimental experience for some participants. You may therefore be reassured to know that experiments by Davide Barrera and Brent Simpson (2012) found that students' experience of being deceived in a social psychology experiment did not affect their subsequent behavior toward others.

Whether or not you believe that you could be deceived in this way, you are not likely to be invited to participate in an experiment such as Milgram's. Current federal regulations preclude deception in research that might trigger such upsetting feelings. However, deception such as that used by Czopp and his colleagues (2006) is still routine in social psychology laboratories. Deceiving students that they were working with another student whom they could not see was essential to their manipulation of interpersonal confrontation. In this experiment, as in many others, the results would be worthless if subjects understood what was really happening to them. The real question is "Is this sufficient justification to allow the use of deception?"

The American Sociological Association's (ASA) *Code of Ethics and Policies and Procedures of the ASA Committee on Professional Ethics* (1999) does not discuss experimentation explicitly, but it does highlight the ethical dilemma posed by deceptive research:

> 12.05 Use of Deception in Research: (a) Sociologists do not use deceptive techniques (1) unless they have determined that their use will not be harmful to research participants; is justified by the study's prospective scientific, educational, or applied value; and that equally effective alternative procedures that do not use deception are not feasible, and (2) unless they have obtained the approval of institutional review boards or, in the absence of such boards, with another authoritative body with expertise on the ethics of research. (b) Sociologists never deceive research participants about significant aspects of the research that would affect their willingness to participate, such as physical risks, discomfort, or unpleasant emotional experiences. (c) When deception is an integral feature of the design and conduct of research, sociologists attempt to correct any misconception that research participants may have no longer than at the conclusion of the research. (p. 16)

Thus, the ASA approach is to allow deception when it is unlikely to cause harm, is necessary for the research, and is followed by adequate explanation after the experiment is over.

David Willer and Henry A. Walker (2007:"Debriefing") pay particular attention to debriefing after deception in their book about experimental research. They argue that every experiment involving deception should be followed immediately for each participant with dehoaxing, in which the deception is explained, and then by desensitization, in which all the participants' questions are answered to their satisfaction and those participants who still feel aggrieved are directed to a university authority to file a complaint or to a counselor for help with their feelings. This is sound advice.

Selective Distribution of Benefits

Field experiments conducted to evaluate social programs also can involve issues of informed consent (Hunt 1985:275–276). One ethical issue that is somewhat unique to field experiments is the **selective distribution of benefits**: How much are subjects harmed by the way treatments are distributed in the experiment? For example, Sherman and Berk's (1984) experiment, and its successors, required police to make arrests in domestic violence cases largely on the basis of a random process. When arrests were not made, did the subjects' abused spouses suffer? Price et al. (1992) randomly assigned unemployed individuals who had volunteered for job search help to an intensive program. Were the unemployed volunteers assigned to the comparison group at a big disadvantage?

> **Selective distribution of benefits:** An ethical issue about how much researchers can influence the benefits subjects receive as part of the treatment being studied in a field experiment.

Is it ethical to give some potentially advantageous or disadvantageous treatment to people on a random basis? Random distribution of benefits is justified when the researchers do not know whether some treatment actually is beneficial or not—and, of course, it is the goal of the experiment to find out (Mark & Gamble 2009:205). Chance is as reasonable a basis for distributing the treatment as any other. Also, if insufficient resources are available to fully fund a benefit for every eligible person, distribution of the benefit on the basis of chance to equally needy persons is ethically defensible (Boruch 1997:66–67).

The extent to which participation was voluntary varied in the field studies discussed in this chapter. Potential participants in the Price et al. (1992) study of job search training for unemployed persons signed a detailed consent form in which they agreed to participate in a study involving random assignment to one of the two types of job search help. However, researchers only accepted into the study persons who expressed equal preference for the job search seminar and the mailed job materials used for the control group.

Thus, Price et al. (1992) avoided the problem of not acceding to subjects' preferences. It, therefore, doesn't seem at all unethical that the researchers gave treatment to only some of the subjects. As it turned out, subjects did benefit from the experimental treatment (the workshops). Now that the study has been conducted, government bodies will have a basis for expecting that tax dollars spent on job search workshops for the unemployed will have a beneficial impact. If this knowledge results in more such programs, the benefit of the experiment will have been considerable, indeed.

Unlike the subjects in the Price et al. (1992) study, individuals who were the subjects of domestic violence complaints in the Sherman and Berk (1984) study had no choice about being arrested or receiving a warning, nor were they aware that they were in a research study.

Perhaps it seems unreasonable to let a random procedure determine how police resolve cases of domestic violence. And, indeed, it would be unreasonable if this procedure were a regular police practice. The Sherman and Berk (1984) experiment and its successors do pass ethical muster, however, when seen for what they were: a way of learning how to increase the effectiveness of police responses to this all-too-common crime (Mark & Gamble 2009:205). The initial Sherman and Berk findings encouraged police departments to make many more arrests for these crimes, and the follow-up studies resulted in a better understanding of when arrests are not likely to be effective. The implications of this research may be complex and difficult to implement, but the research provides a much stronger factual basis for policy development.

Researcher Interview Link
Experimental Design

▣ Conclusions

True experiments play two critical roles in social science research. First, they are the best research design for testing nomothetic causal hypotheses. Even when conditions preclude use of a true experimental design, many research designs can be improved by adding some experimental components. Second, true experiments also provide a comparison point for evaluating the ability of other research designs to achieve causally valid results.

Research That Matters, Questions That Count

Functional limitations caused by aging are associated with more psychological distress, whereas being married is associated with less psychological distress. But does marriage reduce the adverse effects of functional limitations? Alex Bierman at the University of Calgary sought to answer this question with data collected in the Aging, Status, and Sense of Control survey (ASOC) by the Survey Research Laboratory at the University of Illinois at Urbana-Champaign. ASOC used a longitudinal panel design that attempted to survey the same respondents in 1995, 1998, and 2001. There were 966 respondents aged 60 and older in the first wave and 907 who participated in all three waves.

The ASOC measured psychological distress with responses to seven questions that make up a version of the Center for Epidemiological Studies Depression Scale. These questions ask about the number of times in the previous week the respondent had trouble getting to sleep, felt that everything was an effort, felt they couldn't get going, etc. Functional limitations were measured with respondents' ratings of the difficulty they experience with such common tasks as climbing stairs, kneeling, and shopping. Bierman's analysis of the ASOC data indicated that married respondents tended to feel less psychological distress in relation to functional limitations they experienced than did unmarried respondents. This "protective effect" of marriage was stronger for men than for women.

1. Do the CES-D questions make sense to you as indicators of psychological distress? Everyone has feelings like this at some times, but do you think that the range of such feelings experienced could be used to indicate variation over a range from feeling good to feeling distressed? Explain your reasoning.

2. Bierman sought to determine whether marriage mitigates the effects of functional limitations on psychological distress. What would be the advantages and disadvantages of conducting a survey about these issues using in-person interviews, a self-administered paper questionnaire, a phone survey, or a survey on the web?

3. Thinking of the preceding chapter, can you imagine any way to study this effect of marriage using an experimental design?

In this chapter, you will learn how to write survey questions and how to design survey projects. You will also learn more about the ASOC. By the end of the chapter, you will know about the major challenges involved in survey research and how they can be reduced by adhering to guidelines for writing questions and using survey designs that match a survey's purpose. After you finish the chapter, test yourself by reading the 2012 *Society and Mental Health* article by Alex Bierman at the *Investigating the Social World* study site and completing the related interactive exercises for Chapter 8 at edge .sagepub.com/schutt8e.

Bierman, Alex. 2012. "Functional Limitations and Psychological Distress: Marital Status as Moderator." *Society and Mental Health* 2(1):35–52.

"Education forms a unique dimension of social status, with qualities that make it especially important to health." John Mirowsky and Catherine Ross (2003:1) make this claim at the start of *Education, Social Status, and Health* and then present evidence to support it throughout the book. Most of their evidence comes from two surveys. In this chapter, we will focus on one of them, the Aging, Status, and the Sense of Control (ASOC) survey that was funded by the National Institute on Aging.

I begin this chapter with a brief review of the reasons for using survey methods, but I will then focus attention on the Mirowsky and Ross ASOC survey and use it to illustrate some key features of survey research. Next, I will discuss guidelines for writing survey questions—a concern in every type of survey research. I will then explain the major steps in questionnaire design and discuss the features of five types of surveys, highlighting the unique problems attending each one and suggesting some possible solutions. I will give particular attention to the ways in which new means of communication such as cell phones and the Internet have been changing

Journal Link
Psychological Distress

survey research since the first ASOC survey in 1995 (there have been two more, in 1998 and 2001). I discuss ethics issues in the final section. By the chapter's end, you should be well on your way to becoming an informed consumer of survey reports and a knowledgeable developer of survey designs. As you read the chapter, I also hope that you will occasionally reflect on how education influences social status and health.

Survey Research in the Social Sciences

Survey research involves the collection of information from a sample of individuals through their responses to questions. Mirowsky and Ross (2003) turned to survey research for their study of education, social status, and health because it is an efficient method for systematically collecting data from a broad spectrum of individuals and social settings. As you probably have observed, a great many social scientists—as well as newspaper editors, political pundits, government agencies, and marketing gurus—make the same methodological choice. In fact, surveys have become a multibillion-dollar industry in the United States that shapes what we read in the newspapers, see on TV, and find in government reports (Converse 1984; Tourangeau 2004:776).

> **Survey research:** Research in which information is obtained from a sample of individuals through their responses to questions about themselves or others.

Attractions of Survey Research

Survey research owes its popularity to three features: versatility, efficiency, and generalizability. Each of these features is changing as a result of new technologies.

Versatility

First, survey methods are versatile. Although a survey is not the ideal method for testing all hypotheses or learning about every social process, a well-designed survey can enhance our understanding of just about any social issue. Mirowsky and Ross's (2003) survey covered a range of topics about work and health, and there is hardly any other topic of interest to social scientists that has not been studied at some time with survey methods. Politicians campaigning for election use surveys, as do businesses marketing a product, governments assessing community needs, agencies monitoring program effectiveness, and lawyers seeking to buttress claims of discrimination or select favorable juries.

Audio Link
U.S. Census Surveys

Computer technology has made surveys even more versatile. Computers can be programmed so that different types of respondents are asked different questions. Short videos or pictures can be presented to respondents on a computer screen. An interviewer may give respondents a laptop on which to record their answers to sensitive personal questions, such as about illegal activities, so that not even the interviewer will know what they said (Tourangeau 2004:788–794).

Efficiency

Surveys also are popular because data can be collected from many people at relatively low cost and, depending on the survey design, relatively quickly. John Mirowsky and Catherine Ross (2003:207) contracted with the Survey Research Laboratory (SRL) of the University of Illinois for their 25-minute 2003 telephone survey of 2,495 adult Americans. SRL estimated that the survey would incur direct costs of $183,000—that's $73.35 per respondent—and take as long as 1 year to complete. Both this cost and the length of time required were relatively high because SRL made special efforts to track down respondents from the first wave of interviews in 1995. One-shot telephone interviews can cost as little as $30 per subject (Ross 1990). Large mailed surveys cost even less, about $10 to $15 per potential respondent, although the costs can increase greatly when intensive follow-up efforts are made. Surveys of the general population using personal interviews are much more expensive, with costs ranging from about $100 per potential respondent, for studies in a limited geographical area, to

$300 or more when lengthy travel or repeat visits are needed to connect with respondents (F. Fowler, personal communication, January 7, 1998; see also Dillman 1982; Groves & Kahn 1979). Surveys through the web have become the quickest way to gather survey data, but there are problems with this method that I will soon discuss.

Surveys are efficient because many variables can be measured without substantially increasing the time or cost. Mailed questionnaires can include as many as 10 pages of questions before respondents begin to balk. In-person interviews can be much longer. For example, the 2012 General Social Survey (GSS) had three versions in English and Spanish that measured 799 variables for the 1,794 cases that were newly interviewed in that year, and totaled 234 pages—although many sections applied only to particular respondents (National Opinion Research Center [NORC] 2014). The upper limit for phone surveys seems to be about 45 minutes.

Of course, these efficiencies can be attained only in a place with a reliable communications infrastructure (Labaw 1980:xiii–xiv). A reliable postal service, which is required for mail surveys, generally has been available in the United States—although residents of the Bronx, New York, have complained that delivery of local first-class mail often takes 2 weeks or more, almost ruling out mail surveys (Purdy 1994). The British postal service, the Royal Mail, has been accused of even worse performance: a "total shambles," with mail abandoned in some cases and purposely misdelivered in other cases (Lyall 2004:A4). Phone surveys have been very effective in countries such as the United States, where 96% of households have phones (Tourangeau 2004:777). Also important to efficiency are the many survey research organizations—about 120 academic and nonprofit organizations in the United States—that provide trained staff and proper equipment (Survey Research Laboratory 2008).

Research|Social Impact
Link
Survey Methods and Results

Modern information technology has been a mixed blessing for survey efficiency. The Internet makes it easier to survey some populations, but it leaves out important segments. Caller ID and answering machines make it easy to screen out unwanted calls, but these tools also make it harder to reach people in phone surveys. In addition, as discussed in Chapter 5, a growing number of people use only cell phones. As a result, after a long decline to below 5% in 2001, the percentage of U.S. households without landline telephones climbed to 29% by 2011, and then to 40% by 2013 (Christian et al. 2010; McGeeney & Keeter 2014). U.S. Census Bureau 2013b) (see Exhibit 8.1). Survey researchers must spend more time and money to reach potential respondents (Tourangeau 2004:781–782).

Generalizability

Survey methods lend themselves to probability sampling from large populations. Thus, survey research is very appealing when sample generalizability is a central research goal. In fact, survey research is often the only means available for developing a representative picture of the attitudes and characteristics of a large population.

Surveys are also the method of choice when cross-population generalizability is a key concern, because they allow a range of social contexts and subgroups to be sampled. The consistency of relationships can then be examined across the various subgroups. An ambitious Internet-based international survey sponsored by the National Geographic Society (2000) was completed by 80,012 individuals from 178 countries and territories.

Unfortunately (for survey researchers), the new technologies that are lowering the overall rate of response to phone surveys are also making it more difficult to obtain generalizable samples. Although in the United States, only 14% of households in 2013 didn't have access to the Internet at home or work, in these households persons tend to be elderly, poor, and have no more than a high school education compared to those who are "connected" (de Leeuw 2008:321; Pew Research Center 2014; Tourangeau 2004:792; U.S. Census Bureau 2013b).

Those who rely exclusively on cell phones tend to be younger and poorer than are those who also have landline phones. In addition, cell phone–only households are more likely in some states and regions than others and they are more likely to be Hispanic, compared with households with landlines (AAPOR 2014b).

Another challenge in survey research is the growing foreign-born population in the United States, 13% in 2012, requires foreign-language versions of survey forms; survey results cannot be generalized to the entire population (Grieco et al. 2012:2; Tourangeau 2004:783).

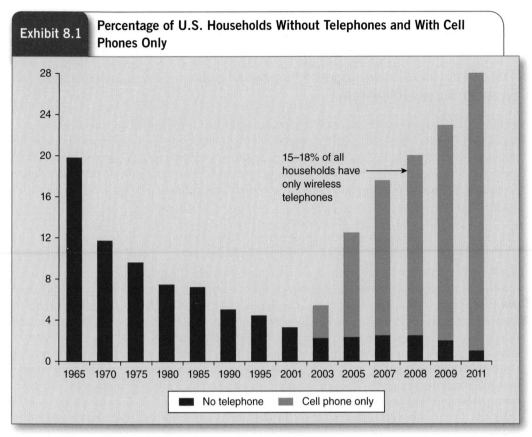

| Exhibit 8.1 | Percentage of U.S. Households Without Telephones and With Cell Phones Only |

15–18% of all households have only wireless telephones

No telephone   Cell phone only

Sources: Adapted from Link, Michael. 2008. "Solving the Problems Cell Phones Create for Survey Research." Presentation to the Harvard Program on Survey Research Spring Conference, New Technologies and Survey Research. Cambridge, MA: Institute of Quantitative Social Science, Harvard University, May 9; Christian, Leah, Scott Keeter, Kristen Purcell, and Aaron Smith. 2010. "Assessing the Cell Phone Challenge to Survey Research in 2010." Washington, DC: Pew Research Center for the People & the Press and Pew Internet & American Life Project.

The Omnibus Survey "Kitchen Say Survey"

An omnibus survey shows just how versatile, efficient, and generalizable a survey can be. An **omnibus survey** covers a range of topics of interest to different social scientists, in contrast to the typical survey that is directed at a specific research question. The omnibus survey has multiple sponsors or is designed to generate data useful to a broad segment of the social science community rather than to answer a particular research question. It is usually directed to a sample of some general population, so the questions, about a range of different issues, are appropriate to at least some sample members.

> **Omnibus survey:** A survey that covers a range of topics of interest to different social scientists.

One of sociology's most successful omnibus surveys is the GSS of the National Opinion Research Center at the University of Chicago. It is an extensive interview administered biennially to a probability sample of at least 3,000 Americans (4,820 in 2012), with a wide range of questions and topic areas chosen by a board of overseers. Some questions are asked of only a randomly selected subset of respondents. This **split-ballot design** allows more questions without increasing the survey's cost. It also facilitates experiments on the effect of question wording: Different forms of the same question are included in the split-ballot subsets. The GSS is widely available to universities, instructors, and

> **Split-ballot design:** Unique questions or other modifications in a survey administered to randomly selected subsets of the total survey sample, so that more questions can be included in the entire survey or so that responses to different question versions can be compared.

students (Davis & Smith 1992; National Opinion Research Center 2011), as are many other survey data sets archived by the Inter-University Consortium for Political and Social Research (ICPSR) (more details about the ICPSR are in Chapter 13). Mirowsky and Ross contributed their survey data set to the ICPSR.

Errors in Survey Research

It might be said that surveys are too easy to conduct. Organizations and individuals often decide that a survey will help solve some important problem because it seems so easy to write up some questions and distribute them. But without careful attention to sampling, measurement, and overall survey design, the effort is likely to be a flop. Such flops are too common for comfort, so the responsible survey researcher must take the time to design surveys properly and to convince sponsoring organizations that this time is worth the effort (Turner & Martin 1984:68).

For a survey to succeed, it must minimize four types of error (Groves 1989:vi, 10–12): (1) poor measurement, (2) nonresponse, (3) inadequate coverage of the population, and (4) sampling error.

Poor measurement. Measurement error was a key concern in Chapter 4, but there is much more to be learned about how to minimize these errors of observation in the survey process. The theory of *satisficing* can help us understand the problem. It takes effort to answer survey questions carefully: Respondents have to figure out what each question means, then recall relevant information, and finally decide which answer is most appropriate. Survey respondents *satisfice* when they reduce the effort required to answer a question by interpreting questions superficially and giving what they think will be an acceptable answer (Krosnick 1999:547–548). Presenting clear and interesting questions in a well-organized questionnaire will help reduce measurement error by encouraging respondents to answer questions carefully and to take seriously the request to participate in the survey. Tailoring questions to the specific population surveyed is also important. In particular, persons with less education are more likely to satisfice in response to more challenging questions (Holbrook, Green, & Krosnick 2003; Narayan & Krosnick 1996).

Errors in measurement also arise when respondents are unwilling to disclose their feelings and behaviors, unable to remember past events, and misunderstand survey questions. What people say they can do—such as ability to carry out various tasks—is not necessarily consistent with what they are able to do (Schutt 2011b:88). What people report that they have done is not necessarily what they have actually done (Brenner 2012). Careful assessment of survey question quality is thus an essential step in survey design. The next section focuses on how to write good survey questions.

Nonresponse. Nonresponse is a major and growing problem in survey research, although it is a problem that varies between particular survey designs. Social exchange theory can help us understand why nonresponse rates have been growing in the United States and Western Europe since the early 1950s (Dillman 2000:14–15; Groves & Couper 1998:155–189; Tourangeau 2004:782). According to social exchange theory, a well-designed survey effort will maximize the social rewards for survey participation and minimize its costs, as well as establish trust that the rewards will outweigh the costs (Blau 1964). The perceived benefits of survey participation have declined with decreasing levels of civic engagement and with longer work hours (Groves, Singer, & Corning 2000; Krosnick 1999:539–540). Perceived costs have increased with the widespread use of telemarketing and the ability of many people to screen out calls from unknown parties with answering machines and caller ID. In addition, recipients pay for time on cell phone calls, so the ratio of costs to benefits worsens for surveys attempting to reach persons using cell phones (Nagourney 2002). We will review more specifics about nonresponse in this chapter's sections on particular survey methods.

Inadequate coverage of the population. A poor sampling frame can invalidate the results of an otherwise well-designed survey. We considered the importance of a good sampling frame in Chapter 5; in this chapter, I will discuss special coverage problems related to each of the particular survey methods.

Sampling error. The process of random sampling can result in differences between the characteristics of the sample members and the population simply on the basis of chance. I introduced this as a topic in Chapter 5. You will learn how to calculate sampling error in Chapter 9.

It is most important to maintain a realistic perspective on the nature of surveys to avoid making unrealistic assumptions about the validity of survey results. Although surveys provide an efficient means for investigating a wide range of issues in large and diverse populations, the data they provide is necessarily influenced by these four sources of error. Survey researchers must make every effort to minimize each one. Only through learning more about different survey features and survey research alternatives can we prepare to weigh the advantages and disadvantages of survey research in particular circumstances and thus assess the value of a survey design in relation to a specific research question.

▣ Writing Survey Questions

Questions are the centerpiece of survey research. Because the way they are worded can have a great effect on the way they are answered, selecting good questions is the single most important concern for survey researchers. All hope for achieving measurement validity is lost unless the questions in a survey are clear and convey the intended meaning to respondents.

Interactive Exercises
Link
Survey Research

You may be thinking that you ask people questions all the time and have no trouble understanding the answers you receive, but can't you also think of times when you've been confused in casual conversation by misleading or misunderstood questions? Now, consider just a few of the differences between everyday conversations and standardized surveys that make writing survey questions much more difficult:

- Survey questions must be asked of many people, not just one.

- The same survey question must be used with each person, not tailored to the specifics of a given conversation.

- Survey questions must be understood in the same way by people who differ in many ways.

- You will not be able to rephrase a survey question if someone doesn't understand it because that would result in a different question for that person.

- Survey respondents don't know you and so can't be expected to share the nuances of expression that help you and your friends and family to communicate.

Writing questions for a particular survey might begin with a brainstorming session or a review of previous surveys. Then, whatever questions are being considered must be systematically evaluated and refined. Although most professionally prepared surveys contain previously used questions as well as some new ones, every question that is considered for inclusion must be reviewed carefully for its clarity and ability to convey the intended meaning. Questions that were clear and meaningful to one population may not be so to another. Nor can you simply assume that a question used in a previously published study was carefully evaluated.

Adherence to a few basic principles will go a long way toward ensuring clear and meaningful questions. Each of these principles summarizes a great deal of research, although none of them should be viewed as an inflexible mandate (Alwin & Krosnick 1991). As you will learn in the next section, every question must be considered relative to the other questions in a survey. Moreover, every survey has its own unique requirements and constraints; sometimes violating one principle is necessary to achieve others.

Make the Questionnaire Attractive

An attractive questionnaire is more likely to be completed and less likely to confuse either the respondent or, in an interview, the interviewer. An attractive questionnaire also should increase the likelihood that different respondents interpret the same questions in the same way.

Printing a multipage questionnaire in booklet form usually results in the most attractive and simple-to-use questionnaire. Printing on both sides of folded-over legal-size paper (8½" by 14") is a good approach, although pages can be printed on one side only and stapled in the corner if finances are very tight (Dillman 2000:80–86). An attractive questionnaire does not look cramped; plenty of white space—more between questions than within question components—makes the questionnaire appear easy to complete. Response choices are distinguished clearly and consistently, perhaps by formatting them with light print (while questions are formatted with dark print) and keeping them in the middle of the pages. Response choices are listed vertically rather than horizontally across the page.

The proper path through the questionnaire for each respondent is identified with arrows or other graphics and judicious use of spacing and other aspects of layout. Respondents should not be confused about where to go next after they are told to skip a question. Instructions should help route respondents through skip patterns, and such skip patterns should be used infrequently. Instructions should also explain how each type of question is to be answered (e.g., by circling a number or writing a response) in a neutral way that isn't likely to influence responses. Some distinctive formatting should be used to identify instructions.

The visual design of a questionnaire has more subtle effects on how respondents answer questions. Seemingly minor differences, such as whether responses are grouped under headings or just listed, whether separate response choices are provided or just the instruction to write in a response from a list of choices, and how much space there is between response choices can all affect the distribution of responses to a question (Dillman & Christian 2005:43–48).

Exhibit 8.8 contains portions of the questionnaire Ross (1990) used in a previous phone survey about aging and health. This page illustrates three of the features that I have just reviewed: (1) numeric designation of response choices, (2) clear instructions, and (3) an attractive, open layout. Because this questionnaire was read over the phone, rather than being self-administered, there was no need for more explicit instructions about the matrix question (Question 49) or for a more distinctive format for the response choices (Questions 45 and 48). A questionnaire designed to be self-administered also should include these additional features.

Consider Translation

Should the survey be translated into one or more languages? In the 21st century, no survey plan in the United States or many other countries can be considered complete until this issue has been considered. In the United States in 2006, 15.3% of persons aged 18 years and older were foreign born (Pew Hispanic Center 2008:Table 1) and more than half of these adults said that they did not speak English very well (Pew Hispanic Center 2008:Table 20). Depending on the specific region or group that is surveyed, these proportions can be much higher and can include persons fluent in various languages (with Spanish being the most common). Although English becomes the primary language spoken by almost all children of immigrants, many first-generation immigrants are not fluent in English (Hakimzadeh & Cohn 2007:i; Pew Hispanic Center 2008:Table 21). As a result, they can only be included in a survey if it is translated into their native language.

When immigrants are a sizable portion of a population, omitting them from a survey can result in a misleading description of the population. Foreign-born persons in the United States tend to be younger than native-born persons and their average income is lower (Pew Hispanic Center 2008:Tables 8a, 29). They also are more likely to be married, to be in a household with five or more family members, and to have less than a high school education (Pew Hispanic Center 2008:Tables 13, 18, 22). However, none of these differences are true for all immigrant groups. In particular, persons from South and East Asia and the Middle East tend to have more education and higher incomes than do persons born in the United States (Pew Hispanic Center 2008:Tables 22, 29).

So, survey researchers find increasingly that they must translate their questionnaires into one or more languages to represent the population of interest. This does not simply mean picking up a bilingual dictionary, clicking "translate" in a web browser, or hiring a translator to translate the questions and response choices word for word. Such a literal translation may not result in statements that are interpreted in the same way to non-English speakers. The U.S. Census Bureau's (2006) guidelines for translation designate the literal translation as only one step in the process. What is needed is to achieve some equivalence of the concepts in different cultures (Church 2010:154–159). The U.S. Census Bureau and the World Health Organization (n.d.) recommend that questionnaires be translated by a team that includes trained translators, persons who are specialists in the subject matter of the survey, persons with expertise in questionnaire design, and experts with several of these skills who can review the translation and supervise a pretest (Pan & de la Puente 2005).

A properly translated questionnaire will be

- *Reliable:* conveys the intended meaning of the original text

- *Fluent:* reads well and makes sense in the target language

- *Appropriate:* the style, tone, and function are appropriately transferred

Needless to say, this translation process adds cost and complexity to survey design.

▣ Organizing Surveys

There are five basic social science survey designs: (1) mailed, (2) group-administered, (3) phone, (4) in-person, and (5) electronic. Survey researchers can also combine elements of two or more of these basic designs in mixed-mode surveys. Exhibit 8.9 summarizes the typical features of the five basic survey designs.

Manner of administration. The five survey designs differ in the manner in which the questionnaire is administered (see Exhibit 8.9). Mailed, group, and **electronic surveys** are completed by the respondents themselves. During phone and in-person interviews, the researcher or a staff person asks the questions and records the respondent's answers. However, new *mixed-mode* surveys break down these distinctions. For example, in *audio computer-assisted self-interviewing* (or *audio-CASI*), the interviewer gives the respondent a laptop and a headset (Tourangeau 2004:790–791). The respondent reads the questions on the computer screen, hears the questions in the headset, and responds by choosing answers on the computer screen.

> **Electronic survey:** A survey that is sent and answered by computer, either through e-mail or on the web.

Exhibit 8.9	Typical Features of the Five Survey Designs

Design	Manner of Administration	Setting	Questionnaire Structure	Cost
Mailed survey	Self	Individual	Mostly structured	Low to moderate
Group survey	Self	Group	Mostly structured	Very low
Phone survey	Professional	Individual	Structured	Moderate
In-person interview	Professional	Individual	Structured or unstructured	High
Electronic survey	Self	Individual	Mostly structured	Low

- *Interesting:* The statement should interest the respondent in the contents of the questionnaire. Never make the mistake of assuming that what is of interest to you will also interest your respondents. Try to put yourself in their shoes before composing the statement, and then test your appeal with a variety of potential respondents.

- *Responsible:* Reassure the respondent that the information you obtain will be treated confidentially, and include a phone number to call if the respondent has any questions or would like a summary of the final report. Point out that the respondent's participation is completely voluntary (Dillman 1978:165–172).

Exhibit 8.10 is an example of a cover letter for a questionnaire.

Other steps are necessary to maximize the response rate (Fowler 1988:99–106; Mangione 1995:79–82; Miller 1991:144):

- It is particularly important, in self-administered surveys, that the individual questions are clear and understandable to all the respondents because no interviewers will be on hand to clarify the meaning of the questions or to probe for additional details.

Exhibit 8.10	Sample Questionnaire Cover Letter

University of Massachusetts Boston
Department of Sociology

Jane Doe
AIDS Coordinator
Shattuck Shelter

Dear Jane:

AIDS is an increasing concern for homeless people and for homeless shelters. The enclosed survey is about the AIDS problem and related issues confronting shelters. It is sponsored by the Life Lines AIDS Prevention Project for the Homeless—a program of the Massachusetts Department of Public Health.

As an AIDS coordinator/shelter director, you have learned about homeless persons' problems and about implementing programs in response to those problems. The Life Lines Project needs to learn from your experience. Your answers to the questions in the enclosed survey will improve substantially the base of information for improving AIDS prevention programs.

Questions in the survey focus on AIDS prevention activities and on related aspects of shelter operations. It should take about 30 minutes to answer all the questions.

Every shelter AIDS coordinator (or shelter director) in Massachusetts is being asked to complete the survey. And every response is vital to the success of the survey: The survey report must represent the full range of experiences.

You may be assured of complete confidentiality. No one outside of the university will have access to the questionnaire you return. (The ID number on the survey will permit us to check with nonrespondents to see if they need a replacement survey or other information.) All information presented in the report to Life Lines will be in aggregate form, with the exception of a list of the number, gender, and family status of each shelter's guests.

Please mail the survey back to us by Monday, June 4, and feel free to call if you have any questions.

Thank you for your assistance.

Yours sincerely,

Russell K. Schutt   *Stephanie Howard*

Russell K. Schutt, PhD   Stephanie Howard

Project Director   Project Assistant

- Use no more than a few open-ended questions because respondents are likely to be put off by the idea of having to write out answers.

- Write an identifying number on the questionnaire so you can determine whom the nonrespondents are. This is essential for follow-up efforts. Of course, the identification must be explained in the cover letter.

- Enclose a token incentive with the survey. A $2 or $5 bill seems to be the best incentive. It is both a reward for the respondent and an indication of your trust that the respondent will carry out his or her end of the "bargain." The response rate to mailed surveys increases by 19 percentage points, on average, in response to such an incentive (Church 1993). Offering a large monetary reward or some type of lottery ticket only for those who return their questionnaire is actually less effective, apparently because it does not indicate trust in the respondent (Dillman 2000:167–170).

- Include a stamped, self-addressed return envelope with each copy of the questionnaire. This reduces the cost for responding. The stamp helps personalize the exchange and is another indication of trust in the respondent (who could use the stamp for something else). Using a stamp rather than metered postage on the mail-out envelope does not seem to influence the response rate, but it is very important to use first class rather than bulk rate postage (Dillman 2000:171–174).

- Consider presurvey publicity efforts. A vigorous advertising campaign increased considerably the response to the 2000 Census mailed questionnaire; the results were particularly successful among minority groups, who had been targeted because of low response rates in the 1990 Census (Holmes 2000).

If Dillman's procedures are followed, and the guidelines for cover letters and questionnaire design also are adhered to, the response rate is almost certain to approach 70%. One review of studies using Dillman's method to survey the general population indicates that the average response to a first mailing will be about 24%; the response rate will rise to 42% after the postcard follow-up, to 50% after the first replacement questionnaire, and to 72% after a second replacement questionnaire is sent by certified mail (Dillman et al. 1974).

The response rate may be higher with particular populations surveyed on topics of interest to them, and it may be lower with surveys of populations that do not have much interest in the topic. When a survey has many nonrespondents, getting some ideas about their characteristics, by comparing late respondents with early respondents, can help determine the likelihood of bias resulting from the low rate of response. If those who returned their questionnaires at an early stage are more educated or more interested in the topic of the questionnaire, the sample may be biased; if the respondents are not more educated or more interested than nonrespondents, the sample will be more credible.

If resources did not permit phone calls to all nonrespondents, a random sample of nonrespondents can be selected and contacted by phone or interviewed in person. It should be possible to secure responses from a substantial majority of these nonrespondents in this way. With appropriate weighting, these new respondents can then be added to the sample of respondents to the initial mailed questionnaire, resulting in a more representative total sample (for more details, see Levy & Lemeshow 1999:398–402).

Related to the threat of nonresponse in mailed surveys is the hazard of incomplete response. Some respondents may skip some questions or just stop answering questions at some point in the questionnaire. Fortunately, this problem does not occur often with well-designed questionnaires. Potential respondents who have decided to participate in the survey usually complete it. But there are many exceptions to this observation because questions that are poorly written, too complex, or about sensitive personal issues simply turn off some respondents. The revision or elimination of such questions during the design phase should minimize the problem. When it does not, it may make sense to impute values for the missing data (in effect, estimate the values of missing data). One imputation procedure would be to substitute the mean (arithmetic average) value of a variable for those cases that have a missing value on the variable (Levy & Lemeshow 1999:404–416).

Group-Administered Surveys

Group-administered survey: A survey that is completed by individual respondents who are assembled in a group.

A **group-administered survey** is completed by individual respondents assembled in a group. The response rate is not usually a major concern in surveys that are distributed and collected in a group setting because most group members will participate. The real difficulty with this method is that it is seldom feasible because it requires what might be called a captive audience. With the exception of students, employees, members of the armed forces, and some institutionalized populations, most populations cannot be sampled in such a setting.

Whoever is responsible for administering the survey to the group must be careful to minimize comments that might bias answers or that could vary between different groups in the same survey (Dillman 2000:253–256). A standard introductory statement should be read to the group that expresses appreciation for their participation, describes the steps of the survey, and emphasizes (in classroom surveys) that the survey is not the same as a test. A cover letter like the one used in mailed surveys also should be distributed with the questionnaires. To emphasize confidentiality, respondents should be given an envelope in which to seal their questionnaires after they are completed.

Another issue of special concern with group-administered surveys is the possibility that respondents will feel coerced to participate and, as a result, will be less likely to answer questions honestly. Also, because administering a survey in this way requires approval of the powers that be—and this sponsorship is made quite obvious by the fact that the survey is conducted on the organization's premises—respondents may infer that the researcher is not at all independent of the sponsor. No complete solution to this problem exists, but it helps to make an introductory statement emphasizing the researcher's independence and giving participants a chance to ask questions about the survey. The sponsor should also understand the need to keep a low profile and to allow the researcher both control over the data and autonomy in report writing. Participation in group-administered surveys of grade school and high school students can be reduced because of the requirement of parental permission, but here the group context can be used to the researcher's advantage. Jane Onoye, Deborah Goebert, and Stephanie Nishimura (2012) at the University of Hawai'i at Manoa found that offering a class a reward such as a pizza if a high rate of participation was achieved led to more parental consent forms being returned than when students were offered a $5 gift card for participating.

Telephone Surveys

Phone survey: A survey in which interviewers question respondents over the phone and then record their answers.

In a **phone survey**, interviewers question respondents over the phone and then record respondents' answers. Phone interviewing became a very popular method of conducting surveys in the United States because almost all families had phones by the latter part of the 20th century. But two matters may undermine the validity of a phone survey: not reaching the proper sampling units and not getting enough complete responses to make the results generalizable.

Reaching Sample Units

Research|Social Impact Link

Sample Units

There are three different ways of obtaining a sampling frame of telephone exchanges or numbers: (1) Phone directories provide a useful frame for local studies; (2) a nationwide list of area code or exchange numbers can be obtained from a commercial firm (random digit dialing is used to fill in the last four digits); and (3) commercial firms can provide files based on local directories from around the nation. There are coverage errors with each of these frames: 10% to 15% of directory listings will turn out not to still be valid residential numbers; more than 35% of U.S. households with phones have numbers that are unlisted in directories, and the percentage is as high as 60% in some communities; and less than 25% of the area codes and exchanges in the one national comprehensive list (available from Bell Core Research, Inc.) refer to residential units (Levy & Lemeshow 1999:455–460). In planning a survey, researchers must consider the advantages and disadvantages of these methods for a particular study and develop means to compensate for the weaknesses of the specific method chosen.

Most telephone surveys use random digit dialing at some point in the sampling process (Lavrakas 1987). A machine calls random phone numbers within the designated exchanges, whether or not the numbers are published. When the machine reaches an inappropriate household (such as a business in a survey that is directed to the general population), the phone number is simply replaced with another. Most survey research organizations use special methods (some version of the Mitofsky–Waksberg method) to identify sets of phone numbers that are likely to include working numbers and so make the random digit dialing more efficient (Tourangeau 2004:778–780).

The University of Illinois SRL used this approach to draw the original sample for Mirowsky and Ross's study of education, social status, and health (Mirowsky 1999). Because the research had a particular focus on health problems related to aging, the researchers used a stratified sampling procedure and oversampled older Americans:

> The survey of Aging, Status, and the Sense of Control (ASOC) is a national telephone probability sample of United States households. A first wave of interviews was completed at the beginning of 1995. Respondents were selected using a prescreened random-digit dialing method that increases the hit rate and decreases standard errors compared with the standard Mitofsky–Waksberg method while producing a sample with the same demographic profile (Lund & Wright 1994; Waksberg 1978). The ASOC survey has two subsamples, designed to produce an 80 percent oversample of persons aged 60 or older. The general sample draws from all households; the oversample draws only from households with one or more seniors. In the general sample the adult (18 or older) with the most recent birthday was selected as respondent. In the oversample the senior (60 or older) with the most recent birthday was selected. For practical reasons the survey was limited to English-speaking adults. Up to 10 callbacks were made to select and contact a respondent, and up to 10 to complete the interview once contact was made. (p. 34)

Journal Link
Telephone Surveys

For the third wave of interviews in 2000–2001, SRL planned an intensive effort to contact the original members of the Wave I sample (Mirowsky 1999):

> Attempts will be made to contact and interview all wave 1 respondents, whether or not they were in wave 2, except for individuals who made it clear they did not want to be contacted in the future. A number of new strategies for maximizing follow-up will be tried (Smith 1995; Lyberg & Dean 1992):
>
> (1) Using tested optimal time-of-day/day-of-week callback sequences, lengthening the period of time over which calls are made, and trying a final sequence of five calls three months after an initial sequence of calls fails to make contact; (2) Giving interviewers additional training on establishing rapport and interacting flexibly; (3) Sending advance letters on letterhead to all baseline respondents that include the survey laboratory phone number that will appear on caller ID, an 800 number to call for additional information about the study, several lines of tailored motivational text, and the location of a web page with information about the study, including the e-mail address and phone number of the project coordinator; (4) Sending a letter after first refusal, signed by the investigator, explaining the study and the importance of participation, and giving an 800 number to call if they decide to participate; (5) Attempting to find respondents not at the original phone number by using directory assistance, the Equifax database, and six web database programs and search engines; (6) Interviewing persons other than the respondent who answer the phone or persons previously identified by the respondent as likely to know their whereabouts, to locate the respondent or identify a likely reason for noncontact (e.g., passed away, moved to a nursing home, too sick to participate, retired and moved away). (pp. 34–35)

However households are contacted, the interviewers must ask a series of questions at the start of the survey to ensure that they are speaking to the appropriate member of the household. Exhibit 8.11 displays a portion of the instructions that the SRL used to select the appropriate respondent for Mirowsky and Ross's phone survey about education and health. This example shows how appropriate and inappropriate households can be distinguished in a phone survey, so that the interviewer is guided to the correct respondent.

Exhibit 8.11 **Phone Interview Procedure for Respondent Designation**

868 Aging, Status, and the Sense of Control
Informant Questionnaire

Introduction and Selection of Respondent or Informant

[Not shown to interviewer, this is a check item]

[if contact attempts less than 15, the interviewer will go to >h101<.

Interviewers will only make a total of 20 attempts]

[if contact attempts greater than 15, the interviewer will go to >h102<]

YOU ARE CALLING [RNAM].

May I speak with [RNAM]?

<1> YES, CONNECTED TO RESPONDENT

<2> NOT AVAILABLE

<3> NEVER ABLE TO INTERVIEW—TOO HARD OF HEARING, PERMANENTLY ILL, OR FOR SOME OTHER REASON

<4> NO ONE THERE BY THAT NAME, OR NO LONGER LIVE THERE

<5> LANGUAGE PROBLEM

<6> DECEASED

<7> OTHER

<8> CHILD, NO ADULTS AVAILABLE

<9> REFUSED

[if <1> go to expl] (Respondents go to main study questionnaire)

[if <2-9> go to wh02]

IF RESPONDENT IS NOT AVAILABLE AFTER SEVERAL ATTEMPTS OR YOU ARE UNABLE TO COMPLETE THE INTERVIEW WITH RESPONDENT, ATTEMPT TO UPDATE RESPONDENT'S ADDRESS AND TELEPHONE INFORMATION WITH AN INFORMANT.

(Introduction for a respondent)

My name is [Interviewer name] and I am calling from the University of Illinois. Approximately 2 years ago you participated in a telephone interview regarding health and different experiences pertaining to sense of control. We are calling to complete a follow-up survey that will take about 30 minutes.

<1> YES, RESPONDENT IS AVAILABLE

<3> RESPONDENT PREFERS CALLBACK—SET UP APPOINTMENT

<4> NEVER ABLE TO INTERVIEW—TOO HARD OF HEARING, PERMANENTLY ILL, OR FOR SOME OTHER REASON

<5> DUPLICATE

<6> LANGUAGE PROBLEM

<7> OTHER

<9> REFUSED

(Introduction for an informant)

My name is [Interviewer name] and I am calling from the University of Illinois. Approximately 2 years ago [RNAM] participated in a telephone interview regarding health and different experiences pertaining to sense of control. We are calling to complete a follow-up survey with [RNAM]. Since [RNAM] is not available we would like to update (his or her) telephone and address information.

<1> INFORMANT IS AVAILABLE

<3> INFORMANT PREFERS CALLBACK—SET UP APPOINTMENT

<4> NEVER ABLE TO INTERVIEW—TOO HARD OF HEARING, PERMANENTLY ILL, OR FOR
   SOME OTHER REASON

<5> DUPLICATE

<6> LANGUAGE PROBLEM

<7> OTHER

<9> REFUSED

. . .

YOU WILL VERIFY THE SPELLING OF THE RESPONDENT'S NAME AND ADDRESS.

Because this study is about how people may change during their lives, we may want to call [RNAM] again in a few years. I'd like to verify the information we have about [RNAM]. First, I would like to ask you about the spelling of [RNAM]'s name.

<1> PROCEED [go to U1b]

<9> REFUSED [go to U4]

   Is [RNAM]'s first name spelled [R First Name]?

<1> Yes

<2> No [go to U2]

<7> NO CODED RESPONSE APPLICABLE

<8> DON'T KNOW

<9> REFUSED

. . .

Can [fill RNAM] still be reached at this phone number?

<1> Yes
<2> No
   >U22<

What is the (correct) phone number to reach [fill RNAM]?

RECORD WHO YOU COMPLETED THE INTERVIEW WITH.

DID YOU SPEAK TO THE RESPONDENT OR INFORMANT? (DO NOT ASK.)

<1> RESPONDENT

<2> INFORMANT

<8> DON'T KNOW

Source: Ross (1990:7).

Maximizing Response to Phone Surveys

Four issues require special attention in phone surveys. First, because people often are not home, multiple callbacks will be needed for many sample members. Those with more money and education are more likely to be away from home; such persons are more likely to vote Republican, so the results of political polls can be seriously biased if few callback attempts are made (Kohut 1988).

This problem has been compounded in recent years by social changes that are lowering the response rate in phone surveys (Tourangeau 2004:781–783) (see Exhibit 8.12). The Pew Research Center reports a decline in the response rate based on all those sampled from 36% in 1997 to only 9% in 2012 (Kohut et al. 2012).

The number of callbacks needed to reach respondents by telephone has increased greatly in the past 20 years, with increasing numbers of single-person households, dual-earner families, and out-of-home activities. Survey research organizations have increased the usual number of phone contact attempts from between 4 to 8 to 20. The growth of telemarketing has created another problem for telephone survey researchers: Individuals have become

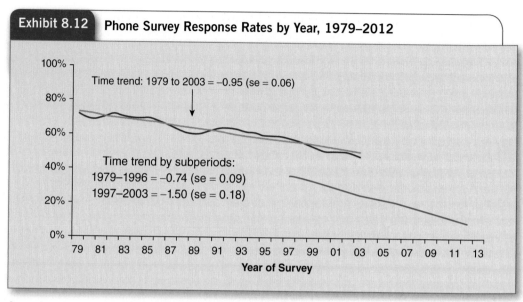

Exhibit 8.12 Phone Survey Response Rates by Year, 1979–2012

Time trend: 1979 to 2003 = –0.95 (se = 0.06)

Time trend by subperiods:
1979–1996 = –0.74 (se = 0.09)
1997–2003 = –1.50 (se = 0.18)

Year of Survey

Source: Adapted from Curtin, Richard, Stanley Presser, and Eleanor Singer. "Changes in Telephone Survey Nonresponse Over the Past Quarter Century." *Public Opinion Quarterly,* 69:87–98. Copyright © 2005, Oxford University Press, on behalf of the American Association for Public Opinion Research. Reprinted with permission.

more accustomed to "just say no" to calls from unknown individuals and organizations or to simply use their answering machines to screen out unwanted calls (Dillman 2000:8, 28). Cell phone users are also harder (and more costly) to contact in phone surveys because their numbers are not in published directories. Households with a cell phone but no landline tend to be younger, so the rate of phone survey participation is declining among those 18 to 34 years of age (Keeter 2008) (Exhibit 8.13).

The second issue researchers using phone surveys must cope with are difficulties because of the impersonal nature of phone contact. Visual aids cannot be used, so the interviewer must be able to convey verbally all information about response choices and skip patterns. Instructions to the interviewer must clarify how to ask each question, and response choices must be short. The SRL developed the instructions shown in Exhibit 8.14 to clarify procedures for asking and coding a series of questions that Ross (1990) used in another survey to measure symptoms of stress within households.

Third, interviewers must be prepared for distractions because the respondent likely will be interrupted by other household members. Sprinkling interesting questions throughout the questionnaire may help maintain respondent interest. In general, rapport between the interviewer and the respondent is likely to be lower with phone surveys than with in-person interviews, and so respondents may tire and refuse to answer all the questions (Miller 1991:166). Distractions are a special problem when respondents are called on a cell phone because they could be driving, in a restaurant or other crowded area, at work, or otherwise involved in activities that make responding difficult and that would not occur in a survey using a landline in the home (AAPOR 2014).

The fourth special consideration for phone surveys is that careful interviewer training is essential. This is how one survey research organization describes its training:

In preparation for data collection, survey interviewers are required to attend a two-part training session. The first part covers general interviewing procedures and techniques as related to the proposed survey. The second entails in-depth training and practice for the survey. This training includes instructions on relevant subject matter, a question-by-question review of the survey instrument and various forms of role-playing and practice interviewing with supervisors and other interviewers. (J. E. Blair, personal communication to C. E. Ross, April 10, 1989)

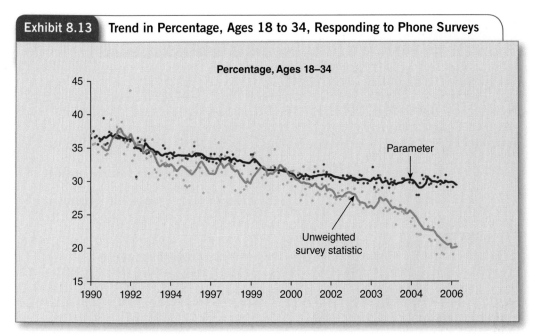

Exhibit 8.13 Trend in Percentage, Ages 18 to 34, Responding to Phone Surveys

Source: Pew Research Studies, Keeter (2008).

Procedures can be standardized more effectively, quality control maintained, and processing speed maximized when phone interviewers use **computer-assisted telephone interviews (CATI)**:

> The interviewing will be conducted using "CATI" (Computer-Assisted Telephone Interviewing). . . . The questionnaire is "programmed" into the computer, along with relevant skip patterns throughout the instrument. Only legal entries are allowed. The system incorporates the tasks of interviewing, data entry, and some data cleaning. (J. E. Blair, personal communication to C. E. Ross, April 10, 1989)

Computerized **interactive voice response (IVR)** survey technology allows even greater control over interviewer–respondent interaction. In an IVR survey, respondents receive automated calls and answer questions by pressing numbers on their touch-tone phones or speaking numbers that are interpreted by computerized voice recognition software. These surveys can also record verbal responses to open-ended questions for later transcription. Although they present some difficulties when many answer choices must be used or skip patterns must be followed, IVR surveys have been used successfully with short questionnaires and when respondents are highly motivated to participate (Dillman 2000:402–411). When these conditions are not met, potential respondents may be put off by the impersonality of this computer-driven approach.

Phone surveying had for decades been the method of choice for relatively short surveys of the general population. Response rates in phone surveys traditionally tended to be very high—often above 80%—because few individuals would hang up on a polite caller or suddenly stop answering questions (at least within the first 30 minutes or so). Mirowsky and Ross (2003:207) achieved a response rate of 71.6% for people who could be contacted in their Wave I survey in 1995. However, phone surveying is not a panacea and it should no longer be considered the best method to use for general purpose surveys. You have already learned of the dramatic decline in phone survey response rates, although this can be somewhat mitigated by extra effort. In a recent

> **Computer-assisted telephone interview (CATI):** A telephone interview in which a questionnaire is programmed into a computer, along with relevant skip patterns, and only valid entries are allowed; incorporates the tasks of interviewing, data entry, and some data cleaning.

> **Interactive voice response (IVR):** A survey in which respondents receive automated calls and answer questions by pressing numbers on their touch-tone phones or speaking numbers that are interpreted by computerized voice recognition software.

Exhibit 8.14 | **Sample Interviewer Instructions**

Question:

41. On how many of the past 7 days have you . . .
    Number of days
    a. Worried a lot about little things? _____
    b. Felt tense or anxious? _____

Instructions for interviewers:

Q41 For the series of "On how many of the past 7 days," make sure the <u>respondent</u> gives the numerical answer. If he/she responds with a vague answer like "not too often" or "just a few times," ask <u>again</u> "On how many of the past 7 days would you say?" Do <u>NOT</u> lead the respondent with a number (e.g., "Would that be 2 or 3?"). If R says "all of them," verify that the answer is "7."

Question:

45. In the past 12 months about how many times have you gone on a diet to lose weight?

Never	0
Once	1
Twice	2
Three times or more	3
Always on a diet	4

Instructions for interviews:

Q45 Notice that this question ends with a question mark. That means that you are <u>not</u> to read the answer categories. Rather, wait for R to respond and circle the appropriate number.

Source: Ross (1990).

---

phone survey of low-income women in a public health program (Schutt & Fawcett 2005), the University of Massachusetts Center for Survey Research (CSR) achieved a 55.1% response rate from all eligible sampled clients after a protocol that included as many as 30 contact attempts, although the response rate rose to 72.9 when it was calculated as a percentage of clients whom CSR was able to locate (Roman 2005:7). Response rates can be much lower in populations that are young, less educated, and poor. Those who do respond are more likely to be engaged in civic issues than those who do not respond, so estimates of related attitudes and behaviors in phone surveys can be quite biased (Kohut et al. 2012).

In-Person Interviews

> **In-person interview:** A survey in which an interviewer questions respondents face-to-face and records their answers.

What is unique to the **in-person interview**, compared with the other survey designs, is the face-to-face social interaction between interviewer and respondent. If money is no object, in-person interviewing is often the best survey design.

In-person interviewing has several advantages: Response rates are higher than with any other survey design; questionnaires can be much longer than with mailed or phone surveys; the questionnaire can be complex, with both open-ended and closed-ended questions and frequent branching patterns; the order in which questions are read and answered can be controlled by the interviewer; the physical and social circumstances of the interview can be monitored; and respondents' interpretations of questions can be probed and clarified.

But researchers must be alert to some special hazards resulting from the presence of an interviewer. Respondents should experience the interview process as a personalized interaction with an interviewer who is very interested in the respondent's experiences and opinions. At the same time, however, every respondent should have the same interview experience—asked the same questions in the same way by the same type of person, who reacts similarly to the answers (de Leeuw 2008:318). Therein lies the researcher's challenge—to plan an interview process that will be personal and engaging and yet consistent and nonreactive (and to hire interviewers who can carry out this plan). Careful training and supervision are essential because small differences in intonation or emphasis on particular words can alter respondents' interpretations of questions' meaning (Groves 1989:404–406; Peterson 2000:24). Without a personalized approach, the rate of response will be lower and answers will be less thoughtful—and potentially less valid. Without a consistent approach, information obtained from different respondents will not be comparable—less reliable and less valid.

Balancing Rapport and Control

Adherence to some basic guidelines for interacting with respondents can help interviewers maintain an appropriate balance between personalization and standardization:

- Project a professional image in the interview: that of someone who is sympathetic to the respondent but nonetheless has a job to do.

- Establish rapport at the outset by explaining what the interview is about and how it will work and by reading the consent form. Ask the respondent if he or she has any questions or concerns, and respond to these honestly and fully. Emphasize that everything the respondent says is confidential.

- During the interview, ask questions from a distance that is close but not intimate. Stay focused on the respondent and make sure that your posture conveys interest. Maintain eye contact, respond with appropriate facial expressions, and speak in a conversational tone of voice.

- Be sure to maintain a consistent approach; deliver each question as written and in the same tone of voice. Listen empathetically, but avoid self-expression or loaded reactions.

- Repeat questions if the respondent is confused. Use nondirective probes—such as "Can you tell me more about that?"—for open-ended questions.

As with phone interviewing, computers can be used to increase control of the in-person interview. In a **computer-assisted personal interviewing (CAPI)** project, interviewers carry a laptop computer that is programmed to display the interview questions and to process the responses that the interviewer types in, as well as to check that these responses fall within allowed ranges (Tourangeau 2004:790–791). Interviewers seem to like CAPI, and the data obtained are comparable in quality to data obtained in a noncomputerized interview (Shepherd et al. 1996). A CAPI approach also makes it easier for the researcher to develop skip patterns and experiment with different types of questions for different respondents without increasing the risk of interviewer mistakes (Couper et al. 1998).

> **Computer-assisted personal interview (CAPI):** A personal interview in which the laptop computer is used to display interview questions and to process responses that the interviewer types in, as well as to check that these responses fall within allowed ranges.

The presence of an interviewer may make it more difficult for respondents to give honest answers to questions about socially undesirable behaviors such as drug use, sexual activity, and not voting (Schaeffer & Presser 2003:75). CAPI is valued for this reason because respondents can enter their answers directly in the laptop without the interviewer knowing what their response is. Alternatively, interviewers can simply hand respondents a separate self-administered questionnaire containing the more sensitive questions. After answering these questions, the respondent seals the separate questionnaire in an envelope so that the interviewer does not know the answers. When this approach was used for the GSS questions about sexual activity, about 21% of men and 13% of women who were married or had been married admitted to having cheated on a spouse ("Survey on Adultery" 1993:A20). The degree of rapport becomes a special challenge when survey questions concern issues related to such demographic characteristics as race or gender (Groves 1989). If the interviewer and respondent are similar on the characteristics at issue, the responses to these questions may differ from those that would be given if the interviewer and respondent differ on these characteristics. For example, a white respondent may not disclose feelings of racial prejudice to a black interviewer that he would admit to a white interviewer.

Although in-person interview procedures are typically designed with the expectation that the interview will involve only the interviewer and the respondent, one or more other household members are often within earshot. In a mental health survey in Los Angeles, for example, almost half the interviews were conducted in the presence of another person (Pollner & Adams 1994). It is reasonable to worry that this third-party presence will influence responses about sensitive subjects—even more so because the likelihood of a third party being present may correspond with other subject characteristics. For example, in the Los Angeles survey, another person was present in 36% of the interviews with Anglos, in 47% of the interviews with African Americans, and in 59% of the interviews with Hispanics. However, there is no consistent evidence that respondents change their answers because of the presence of another person. Analysis of this problem with the Los Angeles study found very little difference in reports of mental illness symptoms between respondents who were alone and those who were in the presence of others.

Maximizing Response to Interviews

Even if the right balance has been struck between maintaining control over interviews and achieving good rapport with respondents, in-person interviews still can be problematic. Because of the difficulty of finding all the members of a sample, response rates may suffer. Exhibit 8.15 displays the breakdown of nonrespondents to the 1990 GSS. Of the total original sample of 2,165, only 86% (1,857) were determined to be valid selections of dwelling units with potentially eligible respondents. Among these potentially eligible respondents, the response

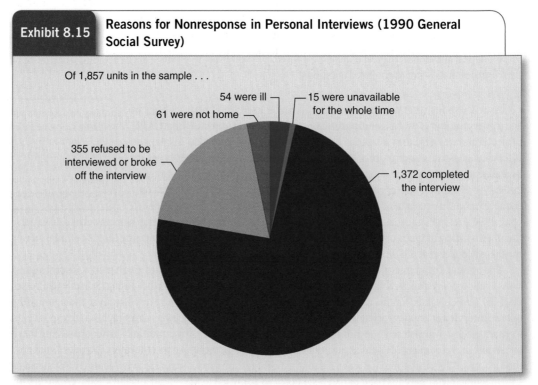

| Exhibit 8.15 | **Reasons for Nonresponse in Personal Interviews (1990 General Social Survey)** |

Of 1,857 units in the sample . . .

54 were ill

15 were unavailable for the whole time

61 were not home

355 refused to be interviewed or broke off the interview

1,372 completed the interview

Source: Data from Davis and Smith (1992):54XX.

rate was 74%. The GSS is a well-designed survey using carefully trained and supervised interviewers, so this response rate indicates the difficulty of securing respondents from a sample of the general population even when everything is done "by the book."

Several factors affect the response rate in interview studies. Contact rates tend to be lower in central cities partly because of difficulties in finding people at home and gaining access to high-rise apartments and partly because of interviewer reluctance to visit some areas at night, when people are more likely to be home (Fowler 1988:45–60). Single-person households also are more difficult to reach, whereas households with young children or elderly adults tend to be easier to contact (Groves & Couper 1998:119–154).

Refusal rates vary with some respondents' characteristics. People with less education participate somewhat less in surveys of political issues (perhaps because they are less aware of current political issues). Less education is also associated with higher rates of "Don't know" responses (Groves 1989). High-income persons tend to participate less in surveys about income and economic behavior (perhaps because they are suspicious about why others want to know about their situation). Unusual strains and disillusionment in a society can also undermine the general credibility of research efforts and the ability of interviewers to achieve an acceptable response rate. These problems can be lessened with an advance letter introducing the survey project and by multiple contact attempts throughout the day and evening, but they cannot entirely be avoided (Fowler 1988:52–53; Groves & Couper 1998). Encouraging interviewers to tailor their response when potential respondents express reservations about participating during the initial conversation can also lead to lower rates of refusal: Making small talk to increase rapport and delaying asking a potential respondent to participate may reduce the likelihood of a refusal after someone first expresses uncertainty about participating (Maynard, Freese, & Schaeffer 2010:810).

Electronic Surveys

Widespread use of e-mail and the Internet, increasingly with high-speed connections and often through smartphones, creates new opportunities for survey researchers. Surveys can be e-mailed to respondents and returned in the same way; they can be posted on a website, and they can even be designed for completion on a smartphone. I will focus in this section on the currently most popular electronic survey approach, web surveys, to illustrate both the advantages and the limitations of these approaches.

Web surveys have become an increasingly useful survey method for two reasons: growth in the fraction of the population using the Internet and technological advances that make web survey design relatively easy. Many specific populations have very high rates of Internet use, so a web survey can be a good option for groups

> **Web survey:** A survey that is accessed and responded to on the World Wide Web.

such as professionals, middle-class communities, members of organizations, and, of course, college students. Because of the Internet's global reach, web surveys also make it possible to conduct large, international surveys. However, coverage remains a major problem with many populations (Tourangeau et al. 2012). About one quarter of U.S. households are not connected to the Internet (File 2013b), so it is not yet possible to survey directly a representative sample of the U.S. population on the web—and given a plateau in the rate of Internet connections, this coverage problem may persist for the near future (Couper & Miller 2008:832). Rates of Internet usage are much lower in other parts of the world, with a worldwide average of 34.3% and rates as low as 15.6% in Africa and 27.5% averaged across all of Asia (see Exhibit 8.16; Internet World Statistics 2012). Households without Internet access also tend to be older, poorer, and less educated than do those that are connected, so web surveys of the general population can result in seriously biased estimates (File 2013b; Pew Research Center 2013). Coverage problems can be compounded in web surveys because of much lower rates of survey completion: It is just too easy to stop working on a web survey—much easier than it is to break off interaction with an interviewer (Tourangeau et al. 2012).

The extent to which the population of interest is connected to the web is the most important consideration when deciding whether to conduct a survey through the web. Other considerations that may increase the attractiveness of a web survey include the need for a large sample, for rapid turnaround, for collecting sensitive

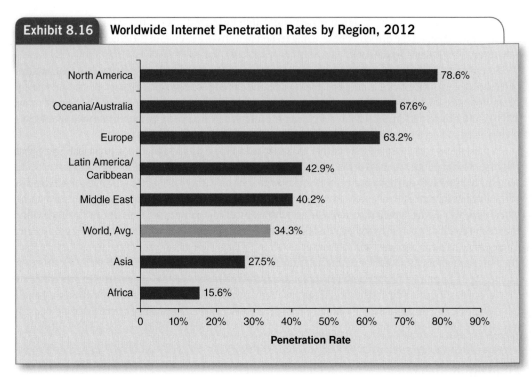

Exhibit 8.16   Worldwide Internet Penetration Rates by Region, 2012

Region	Penetration Rate
North America	78.6%
Oceania/Australia	67.6%
Europe	63.2%
Latin America/Caribbean	42.9%
Middle East	40.2%
World, Avg.	34.3%
Asia	27.5%
Africa	15.6%

Source: Internet World Stats, www.internetworldstats.com/stats.htm. Copyright © 2012, Miniwatts Marketing Group. Reprinted with permission.

information that might be embarrassing to acknowledge in person, the availability of an e-mail list of the population, and the extent to which the interactive and multimedia features will enhance interest in the survey (Sue & Ritter 2012:10–11). Jennie Connor, Andrew Gray, and Kypros Kypri (2010) achieved a 63% response rate with a web survey about substance use that began with an initial e-mail invitation to a representative sample of undergraduate students at six New Zealand campuses.

There are several different approaches to engaging people in web surveys, each with unique advantages and disadvantages and somewhat different effects on the coverage problem. Many web surveys begin with an e-mail message to potential respondents that contains a direct "hotlink" to the survey website (Gaiser & Schreiner 2009:70). It is important that such e-mail invitations include a catchy phrase in the subject line as well as attractive and clear text in the message itself (Sue & Ritter 2012:110–114). This approach is particularly useful when a defined population with known e-mail addresses is to be surveyed. The researcher can then send e-mail invitations to a representative sample without difficulty. To ensure that the appropriate people respond to a web survey, researchers may require that respondents enter a personal identification number (PIN) to gain access to the web survey (Dillman 2000:378; Sue & Ritter 2012:103–104). Connor, Gray, and Kypri (2010:488) used this approach in their survey of New Zealand undergraduates:

> Selected students received a letter which invited them to participate in an internet-based survey as part of the Tertiary Student Health Project, and provided a web address for the survey form. Details of the recruitment and data collection methods have been described in detail previously. Data were collected via a confidential online computerised survey that was completed at a time and place of the respondent's choice.

However, lists of unique e-mail addresses for the members of defined populations generally do not exist outside of organizational settings. Many people have more than one e-mail address, and often there is no apparent link between an e-mail address and the name or location of the person to whom it is assigned. As a result, there is no available method for drawing a random sample of e-mail addresses for people from any general population, even if the focus is only on those with Internet access (Dillman 2007:449).

Web surveys that use volunteer samples may instead be linked to a website that is used by the intended population and everyone who visits that site is invited to complete the survey. This was the approach used in the international web survey sponsored by the National Geographic Society in 2000 (Witte, Amoroso, & Howard 2000). However, although this approach can generate a very large number of respondents (50,000 persons completed Survey 2000), the resulting sample will necessarily reflect the type of people who visit that website (middle class, young North Americans, in Survey 2000) and thus be a biased representation of the larger population (Couper 2000:486–487; Dillman 2000:355). Some control over the resulting sample can be maintained by requiring participants to meet certain inclusion criteria (Selm & Jankowski 2006:440).

Coverage bias can also be a problem with web surveys that are designed for a population with high levels of Internet use. If the topic of the survey leads some people to be more likely to respond on the web, the resulting sample can be very unrepresentative. William Wells, Michael Cavanaugh, Jeffrey Bouffard, and Matt Nobles (2012:461) identified this problem in a comparison of attitudes of students responding to a web survey about gun violence with students at the same university who responded to the same survey administered in classes. Here is their e-mail survey introduction to potential respondents:

> Recently, in response to shootings on university campuses like Virginia Tech and Northern Illinois University, several state legislatures (South Dakota, Texas, Washington) have begun debating whether to change rules banning students and employees from carrying concealed weapons on campus. This is an important public safety issue and the faculty in . . . are interested in knowing how people on this campus feel about it.

Students who responded to the web survey were much more likely to support the right to carry concealed weapons on campus than were those who responded in the classroom survey. In general, having a more extreme attitude motivated people to participate.

Some web surveys are designed to reduce coverage bias by providing computers and Internet connections to those who do not have them. This design-based recruitment method begins by contacting people by phone and providing those who agree to participate with whatever equipment they lack. This approach considerably increases the cost of the survey, so it is normally used as part of creating the panel of respondents who agree to be contacted for multiple surveys over time. The start-up costs can then be spread across many surveys. Gfk Knowledge Networks is a company that received funding from the U.S. National Science Foundation to create such a web survey panel. CentER Data in the Netherlands also uses this panel approach (Couper & Miller 2008:832–833). Another approach to reducing coverage bias in web surveys is to recruit a volunteer panel of Internet users and then weight the resulting sample to make it comparable to the general population in such demographics as gender, race, age, and education. This is the method adopted by many market research organizations (Couper & Miller 2008:832–833); although response rates to volunteer samples are very low and the participants are often unlike the general population, it appears that weighting can reduce coverage bias by 30% to 60% (Tourangeau et al. 2012).

Of course, coverage bias is not as important when a convenience sample will suffice for an exploratory survey about some topic. Audrey Freshman (2012:41) used a web survey of a convenience sample to study symptoms of posttraumatic stress disorder (PTSD) among victims of the Bernie Madoff financial scandal.

> This convenience, nonprobability sample was solicited via direct link to the study placed in online Madoff survivor support groups and comment sections of newspapers and blogs dealing with the event. The study announcement encouraged victims to forward the link to other former investors who might be interested in responding to the survey, thereby creating a snowball effect. The link led directly to a study description and enabled respondents to give informed consent prior to study participation. Participants were assured of anonymity of their responses and were instructed how to proceed in the event of increased feelings of distress as a result of study material. The survey was presumed to take approximately five to 10 minutes to complete. (p. 41)

Although a majority of respondents met clinical criteria for a diagnosis of PTSD, there is no way to know if this sample represents the larger population of Madoff's victims.

In contrast to problems of coverage, web surveys have some unique advantages for increasing measurement validity (Selm & Jankowski 2006; Tourangeau et al. 2012). Questionnaires completed on the web can elicit more honest reports about socially undesirable behavior or experiences, including illicit behavior and victimization in the general population and failing course grades among college students, when compared with results with phone interviews (Kreuter, Presser, & Tourangeau 2008; Parks, Pardi, & Bradizza 2006). Onoye and colleagues (2012) found that conducting a survey on the web increased self-reports of substance use compared with a paper-and-pencil survey. Web surveys are relatively easy to complete because respondents simply click on response boxes and the survey can be programmed to move respondents easily through sets of questions, not presenting questions that do not apply to the respondent, thus leading to higher rates of item completion (Kreuter et al. 2008).

Use of the visual, interactive web medium can also help. Pictures, sounds, and animation can be used as a focus of particular questions and graphic and typographic variation can be used to enhance visual survey appeal (see Exhibit 8.17). Definitions of terms can also "pop up" when respondents scroll over them (Dillman 2007:458–459). In these ways, a skilled web programmer can generate a survey layout with many attractive features that make it more likely that respondents will give their answers—and have a clear understanding of the question (Smyth et al. 2004:4–5). Responses can quickly be checked to make sure they fall within the allowable range. Because answers are recorded directly in the researcher's database, data entry errors are almost eliminated and results can be reported quickly. By taking advantage of these features, Titus Schleyer and Jane Forrest (2000:420) achieved a 74% response rate in a survey of dental professionals who were already Internet users.

Despite some clear advantages of some types of web surveys, researchers who use this method must be aware of some important disadvantages. Coverage bias is the single biggest problem with web surveys of the general population and of segments of the population without a high level of Internet access, and none of the different web survey methods fully overcome this problem. Weighting web survey panels of Internet users by demographic and other characteristics does not result in similar responses on many questions with those that are obtained from a mailed survey to a sample of the larger population (Rookey, Hanway, & Dillman 2008). Although providing Internet access to all who agree to participate in a web survey panel reduces coverage bias, many potential respondents do not agree to participate in such surveys: The rate of agreement to participate was 57% in one Knowledge Networks survey and just 41.5% in a survey of students at the University of Michigan (Couper 2000:485–489). Only about one third of Internet users contacted in phone surveys agree to provide an e-mail address for a web survey and then only one third of those actually complete the survey (Couper 2000:488). Web surveys that take more than 15 minutes are too long for most respondents (de Leeuw 2008:322). Surveys by phone continue to elicit higher rates of response (Kreuter et al. 2008). Some researchers have found that when people are sent a mailed survey that also provides a link to a web survey alternative, they overwhelmingly choose the paper survey (Couper 2000:488).

Despite their advantages for measurement, visual and other highlights that are possible in web surveys should be used with caution to avoid unintended effects on interpretation of questions and response choices (Tourangeau et al. 2012). For example, respondents tend to believe that a response in the middle is the typical response, that responses near each other are related, and that things that look alike are similar. Even minor visual cues can make a difference in responses. In one survey, 5% of respondents shifted their response when one response was given more space relative to others.

Surveys are also now being conducted through social media such as Facebook, on smartphones, and via text messages (Sue & Ritter 2012:119–122). Research continues into the ways that the design of web surveys can influence rates of initial response, the likelihood of completing the survey, and the validity of the responses (Couper, Traugott, & Lamias 2001; Kreuter et al. 2008; Porter & Whitcomb 2003; Tourangeau et al. 2012). At this point, there is reason enough to consider the option of a web survey for many investigations, but proceed with caution and consider carefully their strengths and weaknesses when designing a web survey of any type and when analyzing findings from it.

> **Mixed-mode survey:** A survey that is conducted by more than one method, allowing the strengths of one survey design to compensate for the weaknesses of another and maximizing the likelihood of securing data from different types of respondents; for example, nonrespondents in a mailed survey may be interviewed in person or over the phone.

Mixed-Mode Surveys

Survey researchers increasingly are combining different survey designs to improve the overall participation rate and to take advantage of the unique strengths of different methods. **Mixed-mode surveys** allow the strengths of one survey design to compensate for the weaknesses of another, and they can maximize the likelihood of securing

Exhibit 8.17   **Survey Monkey Web Survey Example**

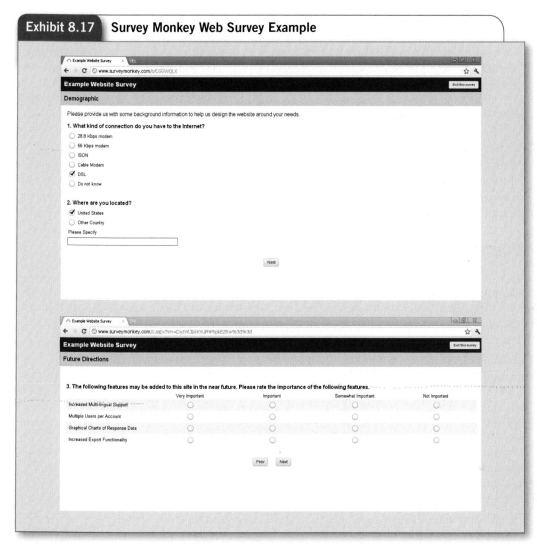

Source: Survey Monkey.

data from different types of respondents (Dillman 2007:451–453; Selm & Jankowski 2006). For example, a survey may be sent electronically to sample members who have e-mail addresses and mailed to those who don't. Phone reminders may be used to encourage responses to web or paper surveys, or a letter of introduction may be sent in advance of calls in a phone survey (Guterbock 2008). Alternatively, nonrespondents in a mailed survey may be interviewed in person or over the phone. In one comparative study, the response rate to a telephone survey rose from 43% to 80% when it was followed by a mailed questionnaire (Dillman 2007:456). Kristen Olson, Jolene Smyth, and Heather Wood (2012) at the University of Nebraska–Lincoln found that providing a survey in the mode that potential respondents preferred—either phone, mailed, or web—increased the overall rate of participation by a small amount. As noted previously, an interviewer may also mix modes by using a self-administered questionnaire to present sensitive questions to a respondent in an in-person interview.

The mixed-mode approach is not a perfect solution. Rebecca Medway and Jenna Fulton (2012) reviewed surveys that gave the option of responding to either a mailed questionnaire or a web questionnaire and found that this reduced the response rate compared with using only a mailed questionnaire. Perhaps the need to choose between the modes or the delay in deciding to start the web survey led some potential respondents not to bother.

Respondents to the same question may give different answers because of the survey mode, rather than because they actually have different opinions. For example, when equivalent samples were asked by phone or mail, "Is the gasoline shortage real or artificial?" many more phone respondents than mail respondents answered that it was "very real" (Peterson 2000:24). Respondents to phone survey questions tend to endorse more extreme responses to scalar questions (which range from more to less) than do respondents to mail or web surveys (Dillman 2007:456–457). Responses may also differ between questions—one third of the questions in one survey—when asked in web and phone survey modes, even with comparable samples (Rookey et al. 2008:974). When responses differ by survey mode, there is often no way to know which responses are more accurate, although it appears that web surveys are likely to result in more admissions of socially undesirable experiences (Kreuter et al. 2008; Peterson 2000:24). Use of the same question structures, response choices, and skip instructions across modes substantially reduces the likelihood of mode effects, as does using a small number of response choices for each question (Dillman 2000:232–240; Dillman & Christian 2005), but web survey researchers are only beginning to identify the effect of visual appearance on the response to questions (Dillman 2007:472–487).

A Comparison of Survey Designs

Video Link
Survey Design

Which survey design should be used when? Group-administered surveys are similar, in most respects, to mailed surveys, except that they require the unusual circumstance of having access to the sample in a group setting. We therefore don't need to consider this survey design by itself; what applies to mailed surveys applies to group-administered survey designs, with the exception of sampling issues. The features of mixed-mode surveys depend on the survey types that are being combined. Thus, we can focus our comparison on the four survey designs that involve the use of a questionnaire with individuals sampled from a larger population: (1) mailed surveys, (2) phone surveys, (3) in-person surveys, and (4) electronic surveys. Exhibit 8.18 summarizes their strong and weak points.

The most important consideration in comparing the advantages and disadvantages of the four methods is the likely response rate they will generate. Mailed surveys must be considered the least preferred survey design from a sampling standpoint, although declining rates of response to phone surveys are changing this comparison.

Contracting with an established survey research organization for a phone survey is often the best alternative to a mailed survey. The persistent follow-up attempts that are necessary to secure an adequate response rate are much easier over the phone than in person. But, as explained earlier, the process requires an increasing number of callbacks to many households and rates of response have been declining. Current federal law prohibits automated dialing of cell phone numbers, so it is very costly to include the growing number of cell phone–only individuals in a phone survey.

In-person surveys are preferable in the possible length and complexity of the questionnaire itself, as well as with respect to the researcher's ability to monitor conditions while the questionnaire is completed. Mailed surveys often are preferable for asking sensitive questions, although this problem can be lessened in an interview by giving respondents a separate sheet to fill out or a laptop in which to enter their answers. Although interviewers may themselves distort results, either by changing the wording of questions or by failing to record answers properly, survey research organizations can reduce this risk through careful interviewer training and monitoring. Some survey supervisors will have interviews tape recorded so that they can review the dialogue between interviewer and respondents and provide feedback to the interviewers to help improve their performance. Some survey organizations have also switched to having in-person interviews completed entirely by the respondents on a laptop as they listen to prerecorded questions.

A phone survey limits the length and complexity of the questionnaire but offers the possibility of very carefully monitoring interviewers (Dillman 1978; Fowler 1988:61–73):

Video Link
Accuracy of Surveys

> Supervisors in [one organization's] Telephone Centers work closely with the interviewers, monitor their work, and maintain records of their performance in relation to the time schedule, the quality of their work, and help detect and correct any mistakes in completed interviews prior to data reduction and processing. (J. E. Blair, personal communication to C. E. Ross, April 10, 1989)

Exhibit 8.18 Advantages and Disadvantages of the Four Survey Designs

Characteristics of Design	Mail Survey	Phone Survey	In-Person Survey	Web Survey
Representative sample				
Opportunity for inclusion is known				
For completely listed populations	High	High	High	Medium
For incompletely listed populations	Medium	Medium	High	Low
Selection within sampling units is controlled (e.g., specific family members must respond)	Medium	High	High	Low
Respondents are likely to be located				
If samples are heterogeneous	Medium	Medium	High	Low
If samples are homogeneous and specialized	High	High	High	High
Questionnaire construction and question design				
Allowable length of questionnaire	Medium	Medium	High	Medium
Ability to include				
Complex questions	Medium	Low	High	High
Open questions	Low	High	High	Medium
Screening questions	Low	High	High	High
Tedious, boring questions	Low	High	High	Low
Ability to control question sequence	Low	High	High	High
Ability to ensure questionnaire completion	Medium	High	High	Low
Distortion of answers				
Odds of avoiding social desirability bias	High	Medium	Low	High
Odds of avoiding interviewer distortion	High	Medium	Low	High
Odds of avoiding contamination by others	Medium	High	Medium	Medium
Administrative goals				
Odds of meeting personnel requirements	High	High	Low	Medium
Odds of implementing quickly	Low	High	Low	High
Odds of keeping costs low	High	Medium	Low	High

Source: Adapted from Dillman (1978):74–75. *Mail and Telephone Surveys: The Total Design Method.* Reprinted by permission of John Wiley & Sons, Inc.

Quantitative Data Analysis

This chapter introduces several common statistics used in social research and highlights the factors that must be considered when using and interpreting statistics. Think of it as a review of fundamental social statistics, if you have already studied them, or as an introductory overview, if you have not. Two preliminary sections lay the foundation for studying statistics. In the first, I discuss the role of statistics in the research process, returning to themes and techniques with which you are already familiar. In the second preliminary section, I outline the process of preparing data for statistical analysis. In the rest of the chapter, I explain how to describe the distribution of single variables and the relationship between variables. Along

Research That Matters, Questions That Count

Why do some urban youth grow up to become regular voters in elections, but others do not? Could rates of voting be improved with education programs targeted to youth before they are eligible to vote? Alison K. Cohen and Benjamin W. Chaffee sought to investigate the first question in a study that they hoped would lay the groundwork for programs that would attempt to answer the second question. Their research involved an analysis of survey data collected at the beginning of the school year from youth in Providence, Rhode Island, and Boston, Massachusetts.

Questionnaires were distributed by classroom teachers but completed by youth who signed an informed consent form on an anonymous basis. Questions were designed to measure civic knowledge, attitudes, and behaviors, as well as likelihood of voting and various academic and social characteristics.

1. What variables do you hypothesize would be related to youth self-reports of likelihood of voting? Explain your reasoning.

2. Draw a diagram that shows, with arrows, how you think each variable you mentioned is related to likelihood of voting (for example, GPA → likelihood of voting). Think about how you might improve your diagram as you read Chapter 9.

In this chapter, you will learn the basic statistical tools used to describe variation in variables and the relations between them, as well as some of the findings about influences on voting. By the end of the chapter, you will understand the primary steps involved in the analysis of quantitative data and some of the potential pitfalls in such analyses. After you finish the chapter, test yourself by reading the 2012 *Education, Citizenship and Social Justice* article by Alison Cohen and Benjamin Chaffee at the *Investigating the Social World* study site and completing the related interactive exercises for Chapter 9 at edge.sagepub.com/schutt8e.

Cohen, Alison K. and Benjamin W. Chaffee. 2012. "The Relationship Between Adolescents' Civic Knowledge, Civic Attitude, and Civic Behavior and Their Self-Reported Future Likelihood of Voting." *Education, Citizenship and Social Justice* 8(1):43–57.

the way, I address ethical issues related to data analysis. This chapter will have been successful if it encourages you to use statistics responsibly, to evaluate statistics critically, and to seek opportunities for extending your statistical knowledge.

Although many colleges and universities offer social statistics in a separate course, and for good reason (there's a *lot* to learn), I don't want you to think of this chapter as something that deals with a different topic than the rest of this book. Data analysis is an integral component of research methods, and it's important that any proposal for quantitative research include a plan for the data analysis that will follow data collection. You have to anticipate your data analysis needs if you expect your research design to secure the requisite data.

Journal Link
Youth and Voting

🔲 Introducing Statistics

Statistics play a key role in achieving valid research results—in measurement, causal validity, and generalizability. Some statistics are useful primarily to describe the results of measuring single variables and to construct and evaluate multi-item scales. These statistics include frequency distributions, graphs, measures of central tendency and variation, and reliability tests. Other statistics are useful primarily in achieving causal validity, by helping us describe the association between variables and control for, or otherwise account for, other variables. Cross-tabulation is the technique for measuring association and controlling other variables that is introduced

Descriptive statistics: Statistics used to describe the distribution of and relationship between variables.

in this chapter. All these statistics are termed **descriptive statistics** because they are used to describe the distribution of, and relationship between, variables.

You have already learned in Chapter 5 that it is possible to estimate the degree of confidence that can be placed in generalization from a sample to the population from which the sample was selected. The statistics used in making these estimates are termed *inferential statistics*. In this chapter, I introduce the use of inferential statistics for testing hypotheses involving sample data.

Social theory and the results of prior research should guide our statistical choices, as they guide the choice of other research methods. There are so many particular statistics and so many ways for them to be used in data analysis that even the best statistician can be lost in a sea of numbers if he or she does not use prior research and theorizing to develop a coherent analysis plan. It is also important to choose statistics that are appropriate to the level of measurement of the variables to be analyzed. As you learned in Chapter 4, numbers used to represent the values of variables may not actually signify different quantities, meaning that many statistical techniques will be inapplicable for some variables.

Case Study: The Likelihood of Voting

In this chapter, I use for examples data from the 2012 General Social Survey (GSS) (National Opinion Research Center 2014) on voting and the variables associated with it, and I will focus on a research question about political participation: What influences the likelihood of voting? Prior research on voting in both national and local settings provides a great deal of support for one hypothesis: The likelihood of voting increases with social status (Manza, Brooks, & Sauder 2005:208; Milbrath & Goel 1977:92–95; Salisbury 1975:326; Verba & Nie 1972:892). Research suggests that social status influences the likelihood of voting through the intervening variable of perceived political efficacy, or the feeling that one's vote matters (see Exhibit 9.1). But some research findings on political participation are inconsistent with the social status–voting hypothesis. For example, African Americans participate in politics at higher rates than do white Americans of similar social status—at least when there is an African American candidate for whom to vote (Manza et al. 2005:209; Verba & Nie 1972; Verba, Nie, & Kim 1978). This discrepant finding suggests that the impact of social status on voting and other forms of political participation varies with the social characteristics of potential participants.

The rate of voting of 57.5% in the 2012 presidential election reversed a pattern of increasing turnout since 1996 that had reached a highpoint of 62.3% in the election of Barack Obama in 2008 (Exhibit 9.2) (Gans 2008; Liptak 2012). Participation among African Americans continued to increase and for the first time in 2012 surpassed the participation rate for white non-Hispanic Americans, although turnout remained much lower among Hispanics and Asian Americans. Turnout dropped somewhat among young people in the 2012 presidential election compared with the historic high reached in the 2008 election (CIRCLE 2013).

If we are guided by prior research, a test of the hypothesis that likelihood of voting increases with social status should also account for political efficacy and some social characteristics, such as race. We can find

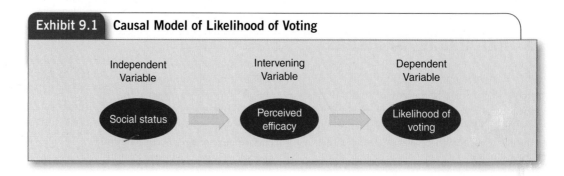

Exhibit 9.1 Causal Model of Likelihood of Voting

Independent Variable → Social status

Intervening Variable → Perceived efficacy

Dependent Variable → Likelihood of voting

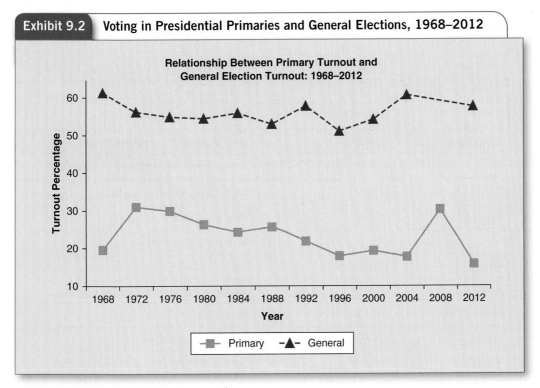

Exhibit 9.2 Voting in Presidential Primaries and General Elections, 1968–2012

Source: Center for the Study of the American Electorate, American University, Preliminary Primary Turnout Report.

indicators for each of these variables, except political efficacy, in the 2012 GSS (see Exhibit 9.3). We will substitute the variable *interpersonal trust* for political efficacy. I will use these variables to illustrate particular statistics throughout this chapter, drawing on complete 2012 GSS data. You can replicate my analysis with the 2012x GSS dataset that is posted on the study site for this book.

▣ Preparing Data for Analysis

My analysis of voting in this chapter is an example of secondary data analysis, which you will learn about in Chapter 14. Using secondary data in this way has a major advantage: The researcher doesn't have to secure the funds and spend the time required to collect his or own data. But there are also disadvantages: If you did not design the study yourself, it is unlikely that all the variables that you think should have been included actually were included and were measured in the way that you prefer. In addition, the sample may not represent just the population in which you are interested, and the study design may be only partially appropriate to your research question. For example, because it is a survey of individuals, the GSS lacks measures of political context (such as the dominant party in an area). Because the survey sample is selected only from the United States and because the questions concern just one presidential election, we will not be able to address directly the larger issues of political context that are represented in cross-national and longitudinal research (for more on cross-national and longitudinal research, see Verba et al. 1978).

Researcher Interview Link
GSS

If you conduct your own survey or experiment, your quantitative data must be prepared in a format suitable for computer entry. Several options are available. Questionnaires or other **data entry** forms can be designed for scanning or direct computer entry (see Exhibit 9.4). **Coding** of all responses should be done before data entry

> **Data entry:** The process of typing (word processing) or otherwise transferring data on survey or other instruments into a computer file.
>
> **Coding:** The process of assigning a unique numerical code to each response to survey questions.

Exhibit 9.3	List of GSS 2012 Variables for Analysis of Voting

Variable[a]	SPSS Variable Name	Description
Family income	INCOME06	Family income (in categories)
	INCOMEFAM06	Family income (in approximate dollars)
Education	EDUCR	Years of education completed (6 categories)
	EDUC4	Years of education completed (4 categories)
	EDUC3	Years of education (3 categories)
Age	AGE4	Years old (4 categories)
	AGER	Years old (in decades)
Gender	SEX	Sex
Marital status	MARITAL	Married, never married, widowed, divorced
Race	RACED	White, minority
Politics	PARTYID3	Political party affiliation
Voting	VOTE08	Voted in 2008 presidential election (yes/no)
Political views	POLVIEW3	Liberal, moderate, conservative
Interpersonal trust	TRUSTD	Believe other people can be trusted

a. Some variables recoded.

Source: General Social Survey, National Opinion Research Center 2012.

by assigning each a unique numerical value. Once the computer database software is programmed to recognize the response codes, the forms can be fed through a scanner and the data will then be entered directly into the database. If responses or other forms of data have been entered on nonscannable paper forms, a computer data entry program should be used that will allow the data to be entered into the databases by clicking on boxes corresponding to the response codes. Alternatively, if a data entry program is not used, responses can be typed directly into a computer database. If data entry is to be done this way, the questionnaires or other forms should be precoded. **Precoding** means that a number represents every response choice, and respondents are instructed to indicate their response to a question by checking a number. It will then be easier to type in the strings of numbers than to type in the responses themselves.

> **Precoding:** A number represents every response choice to a survey question, and respondents are instructed to indicate their response to a question by checking a number.

> **Data cleaning:** The process of checking data for errors after the data have been entered in a computer file.

Whatever data entry method is used, the data must be checked carefully for errors—a process called **data cleaning**. The first step in data cleaning is to check responses before they are entered into the database to make sure that one and only one valid answer code has been clearly circled or checked for each question (unless multiple responses are allowed or a skip pattern was specified). Written answers can be assigned their own numerical codes. The next step in data cleaning is to make sure that no invalid codes have been entered. Invalid codes are codes that fall outside the range of allowable values for a given variable and those that represent impossible combinations of responses to two or more questions. (For example, if a respondent says that he or she

Exhibit 9.4 Form for Direct Data Entry

OMB Control No: 6691-0001
Expiration Date: 04/30/07

Bureau of Economic Analysis
Customer Satisfaction Survey

1. Which data products do you use?

(On a scale of 1–5, please circle the appropriate answer.)

	Frequently (every week)	Often (every month)	Infrequently	Rarely	Never	Don't know or not applicable
GENERAL DATA PRODUCTS						
Survey of Current Business	5	4	3	2	1	N/A
CD-ROMs	5	4	3	2	1	N/A
BEA Web Site (www.bea.gov)	5	4	3	2	1	N/A
STAT-USA Web Site (www.stat-usa.gov)	5	4	3	2	1	N/A
Telephone Access to Staff	5	4	3	2	1	N/A
E-Mail Access to Staff	5	4	3	2	1	N/A
INDUSTRY DATA PRODUCTS						
Gross Product by Industry	5	4	3	2	1	N/A
Input-Output Tables	5	4	3	2	1	N/A
Satellite Accounts	5	4	3	2	1	N/A
INTERNATIONAL DATA PRODUCTS						
U.S. International Transactions . . . . (Balance of Payments)	5	4	3	2	1	N/A
U.S. Exports and Imports of Private Services . .	5	4	3	2	1	N/A
U.S. Direct Investment Abroad	5	4	3	2	1	N/A
Foreign Direct Investment in the United States . .	5	4	3	2	1	N/A
U.S. International Investment Position	5	4	3	2	1	N/A
NATIONAL DATA PRODUCTS						
National Income and Product Accounts (GDP)	5	4	3	2	1	N/A
NIPA Underlying Detail Data	5	4	3	2	1	N/A
Capital Stock (Wealth) and Investment . . . . by Industry	5	4	3	2	1	N/A
REGIONAL DATA PRODUCTS						
State Personal Income	5	4	3	2	1	N/A
Local Area Personal Income	5	4	3	2	1	N/A
Gross State Product by Industry	5	4	3	2	1	N/A
RIMS II Regional Multipliers	5	4	3	2	1	N/A

Source: U.S. Bureau of Economic Analysis (2004):14.

did not vote in an election, a response to a subsequent question indicating whom that person voted for would be invalid.) Most survey research organizations now use a database management program to control data entry. The program prompts the data entry clerk for each response code, checks the code to ensure that it represents a valid response for that variable, and saves the response code in the data file. This process reduces sharply the possibility of data entry errors.

If data are typed into a text file or entered directly through the data sheet of a statistics program, a computer program must be written to "define the data." A data definition program identifies the variables that are coded in each column or range of columns, attaches meaningful labels to the codes, and distinguishes values representing missing data. The procedures for doing so vary with the specific statistical package used. I used the Statistical Package for the Social Sciences (SPSS) for the analysis in this chapter; you will find examples of SPSS commands for defining and analyzing data in Appendix D (on the study site at edge.sagepub.com/schutt8e). More information on using SPSS is contained in SPSS manuals and in the SAGE Publications volume *Using IBM SPSS Statistics for Social Statistics and Research Methods,* 3rd edition, by William E. Wagner III (2011).

Research|Social Impact Link
Quantitative Data Analysis

▣ Displaying Univariate Distributions

The first step in data analysis is usually to display the variation in each variable of interest. For many descriptive purposes, the analysis may go no further. Graphs and frequency distributions are the two most popular approaches; both allow the analyst to display the distribution of cases across the categories of a variable. Graphs have the advantage of providing a picture that is easier to comprehend, although frequency distributions are preferable when exact numbers of cases having particular values must be reported and when many distributions must be displayed in a compact form.

> **Central tendency:** The most common value (for variables measured at the nominal level) or the value around which cases tend to center (for a quantitative variable).
>
> **Variability:** The extent to which cases are spread out through the distribution or clustered in just one location.
>
> **Skewness:** The extent to which cases are clustered more at one or the other end of the distribution of a quantitative variable rather than in a symmetric pattern around its center. Skew can be positive (a right skew), with the number of cases tapering off in the positive direction, or negative (a left skew), with the number of cases tapering off in the negative direction.

Whichever type of display is used, the primary concern of the data analyst is to display accurately the distribution's shape, that is, to show how cases are distributed across the values of the variable. Three features of shape are important: **central tendency, variability**, and **skewness** (lack of symmetry). All three features can be represented in a graph or in a frequency distribution.

These features of a distribution's shape can be interpreted in several different ways, and they are not all appropriate for describing every variable. In fact, all three features of a distribution can be distorted if graphs, frequency distributions, or summary statistics are used inappropriately.

A variable's level of measurement is the most important determinant of the appropriateness of particular statistics. For example, we cannot talk about the skewness (lack of symmetry) of a variable measured at the nominal level. If the values of a variable cannot be ordered from lowest or highest—if the ordering of the values is arbitrary—we cannot say that the distribution is not symmetric because we could just reorder the values to make the distribution more (or less) symmetric. Some measures of central tendency and variability are also inappropriate for variables measured at the nominal level.

The distinction between variables measured at the ordinal level and those measured at the interval or ratio level should also be considered when selecting statistics for use, but social researchers differ in just how much importance they attach to this distinction. Many social researchers think of ordinal variables as imperfectly measured interval-level variables and believe that, in most circumstances, statistics developed for interval-level variables also provide useful summaries for ordinal variables. Other social researchers believe that variation in ordinal variables will often be distorted by statistics that assume an interval level of measurement. We will touch on some of the details in the following sections on particular statistical techniques.

Encyclopedia Link
Measures of Central Tendency

We will now examine graphs and frequency distributions that illustrate these three features of shape. Summary statistics used to measure specific aspects of central tendency and variability are presented in a separate section. There is a summary statistic for the measurement of skewness, but it is used only rarely in published research reports and will not be presented here.

Graphs

A picture often is worth some unmeasurable quantity of words. Even for the uninitiated, graphs can be easy to read, and they highlight a distribution's shape. They are useful particularly for exploring data because they show the full range of variation and identify data anomalies that might be in need of further study. And good, professional-looking graphs can now be produced relatively easily with software available for personal computers. There are many types of graphs, but the most common and most useful are bar charts, histograms, and frequency polygons. Each has two axes, the vertical axis (the *y*-axis) and the horizontal axis (the *x*-axis), and labels to identify the variables and the values, with tick marks showing where each indicated value falls along the axis.

A **bar chart** contains solid bars separated by spaces. It is a good tool for displaying the distribution of variables measured at the nominal level because there is, in effect, a gap between each of the categories. The bar chart of marital status in Exhibit 9.5 indicates that almost half of adult Americans were married at the time of the survey. Smaller percentages were divorced, separated, widowed, and more than one quarter had never married. The most common value in the distribution is married, so this would be the distribution's central tendency. There is a moderate amount of variability in the distribution because the half that are not married are spread across the categories of widowed, divorced, separated, and never married. Because marital status is not a quantitative variable, the order in which the categories are presented is arbitrary, and so skewness is not relevant.

> **Bar chart:** A graphic for qualitative variables in which the variable's distribution is displayed with solid bars separated by spaces.

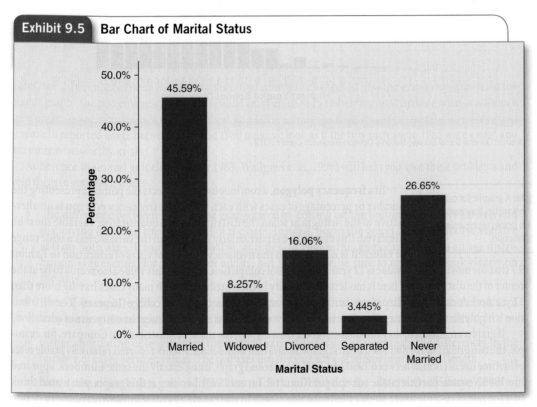

| Exhibit 9.5 | Bar Chart of Marital Status |

Source: General Social Survey, National Opinion Research Center 2012.

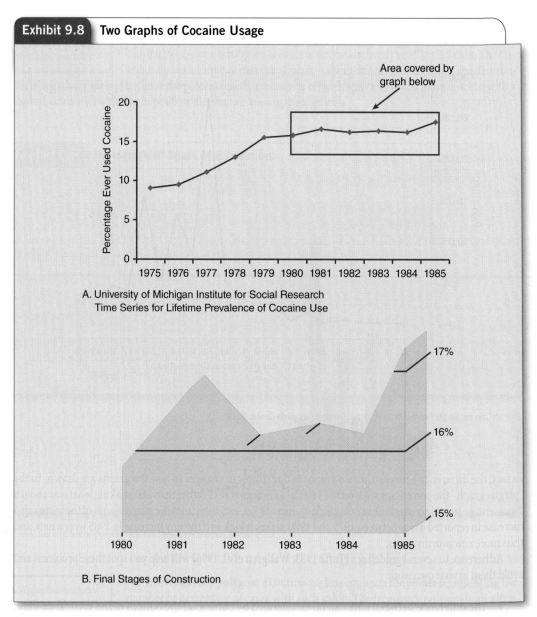

Exhibit 9.8 Two Graphs of Cocaine Usage

A. University of Michigan Institute for Social Research Time Series for Lifetime Prevalence of Cocaine Use

B. Final Stages of Construction

Source: Adapted from Orcutt and Turner (1993). Copyright 1993 by the Society for the Study of Social Problems. Reprinted by permission.

Frequency Distributions

Frequency distribution: Numerical display showing the number of cases, and usually the percentage of cases (the relative frequencies), corresponding to each value or group of values of a variable.

Base number (N): The total number of cases in a distribution.

A **frequency distribution** displays the number of cases, percentage (the relative frequencies) of cases, or both corresponding to each of a variable's values or group of values. The components of the frequency distribution should be clearly labeled, with a title, a stub (labels for the values of the variable), a caption (identifying whether the distribution includes frequencies, percentages, or both), and perhaps the number of missing cases. If percentages, rather than frequencies, are presented (sometimes both are included), the total number of cases in the distribution (the **base number N**) should be indicated (see Exhibit 9.9).

Ungrouped Data

Constructing and reading frequency distributions for variables with few values is not difficult. The frequency distribution of voting in Exhibit 9.9, for example, shows that 72.9% of the respondents eligible to vote said they voted, and 27.1% reported they did not vote. The total number of respondents to this question was 1,789, although 1,974 actually were interviewed. The rest were ineligible to vote, said they did not know whether they had voted or not, or gave no answer.

Political ideology was measured with a question having seven response choices, resulting in a longer but still relatively simple frequency distribution (see Exhibit 9.10). The most common response was moderate, with 38.0% of the sample that responded choosing this label to represent their political ideology. The distribution has a symmetric shape, although with somewhat more respondents identifying themselves as conservative rather than liberal.

If you compare Exhibits 9.10 and 9.6, you can see that a frequency distribution (Exhibit 9.10) can provide more precise information than a graph (Exhibit 9.6) about the number and percentage of cases in a variable's categories. Often, however, it is easier to see the shape of a distribution when it is graphed. When the goal of a presentation is to convey a general sense of a variable's distribution, particularly when the presentation is to an audience that is not trained in statistics, the advantages of a graph outweigh those of a frequency distribution.

Grouped Data

Many frequency distributions (and graphs) require grouping of some values after the data are collected. There are two reasons for grouping:

1. There are more than 15 to 20 values to begin with, a number too large to be displayed in an easily readable table.

2. The distribution of the variable will be clearer or more meaningful if some of the values are combined.

Exhibit 9.9 Frequency Distribution of Voting in the 2008 Presidential Election

Value	Frequency	Valid Percentage
Voted	1304	72.9%
Did not vote	485	27.1%
Ineligible	159	
Don't know	22	
No answer	4	
Total %		100.0%
N	1974	(1789)

Source: General Social Survey, National Opinion Research Center 2012.

Exhibit 9.10 Frequency Distribution of Political Views

Value	Frequency	Valid Percentage
Extremely liberal	81	4.3%
Liberal	244	13.0%
Slightly liberal	208	11.1%
Moderate	713	38.0%
Slightly conservative	268	14.3%
Conservative	292	15.6%
Extremely conservative	68	3.6%
Missing	100	
Total	1974	100.0% (1874)

Source: General Social Survey, National Opinion Research Center 2012.

Inspection of Exhibit 9.11 should clarify these reasons. In the first distribution, which is only a portion of the entire ungrouped GSS age distribution, it is very difficult to discern any shape, much less the central tendency. In the second distribution, age is grouped in the familiar 10-year intervals (except for the first, abbreviated category), and the distribution's shape is immediately clear.

the same median income but still be very different in their social character because of the shape of their income distributions. As illustrated in Exhibit 9.17, Town A is a homogeneous middle-class community; Town B is very heterogeneous; and Town C has a polarized, bimodal income distribution, with mostly very poor and very rich people and few in between. However, all three towns have the same median income.

Exhibit 9.17   **Distributions Differing in Variability but Not Central Tendency**

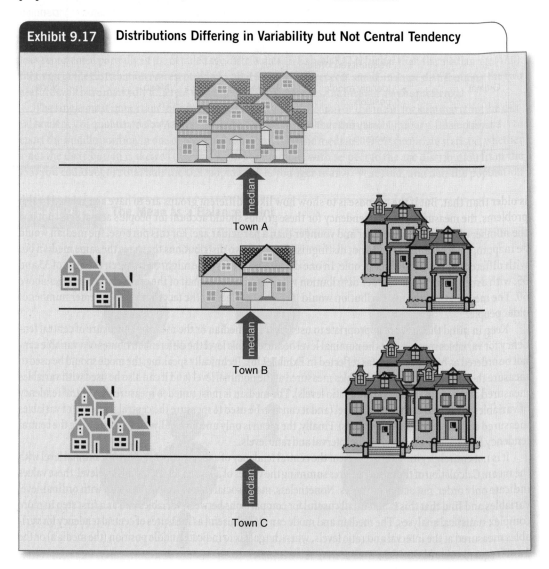

The way to capture these differences is with statistical measures of variation. Four popular measures of variation are the range, the interquartile range, the variance, and the standard deviation (which is the most popular measure of variability). To calculate each of these measures, the variable must be at the interval or ratio level (but many would argue that, like the mean, they can be used with ordinal-level measures, too). Statistical measures of variation are used infrequently with variables measured at the nominal level, so these measures will not be presented here.

It's important to realize that measures of variability are summary statistics that capture only part of what we need to be concerned with about the distribution of a variable. In particular, they do not tell us about the extent to which a distribution is skewed, which we've seen is very important for interpreting measures of central tendency. Researchers usually evaluate the skewness of distributions just by eyeballing them.

Range

The **range** is a simple measure of variation, calculated as the highest value in a distribution minus the lowest value:

> **Range:** The true upper limit in a distribution minus the true lower limit (or the highest rounded value minus the lowest rounded value, plus one).

$$\text{Range} = \text{Highest value} - \text{Lowest value}$$

It often is important to report the range of a distribution to identify the whole range of possible values that might be encountered. However, because the range can be drastically altered by just one exceptionally high or low value (termed an **outlier**), it does not do an adequate job of summarizing the extent of variability in a distribution.

> **Outlier:** An exceptionally high or low value in a distribution.

Interquartile Range

A version of the range statistic, the **interquartile range**, avoids the problem created by outliers. **Quartiles** are the points in a distribution corresponding to the first 25% of the cases, the first 50% of the cases, and the first 75% of the cases. You already know how to determine the second quartile, corresponding to the point in the distribution covering half of the cases—it is another name for the median. The first and third quartiles are determined in the same way but by finding the points corresponding to 25% and 75% of the cases, respectively. The interquartile range is the difference between the first quartile and the third quartile.

> **Interquartile range:** The range in a distribution between the end of the first quartile and the beginning of the third quartile.
>
> **Quartiles:** The points in a distribution corresponding to the first 25% of the cases, the first 50% of the cases, and the first 75% of the cases.

We can use the distribution of age for an example. If you add up the percentages corresponding to each value of age (ungrouped) in Exhibit 9.11, you'll find that you reach the first quartile (25% of the cases) at the age value of 33. If you were to continue, you would find that age 61 corresponds to the third quartile—the point where you have covered 75% of the cases. So the interquartile range for age, in the GSS 2012 data, is 28:

$$\text{Third quartile} - \text{First quartile} = \text{Interquartile range}$$

$$61 - 33 = 28$$

Variance

The **variance** is the average squared deviation of each case from the mean, so it accounts for the amount by which each case differs from the mean. An example of how to calculate the variance, using the following formula, appears in Exhibit 9.18:

> **Variance:** A statistic that measures the variability of a distribution as the average squared deviation of each case from the mean.

$$\sigma^2 = \frac{\sum (Y_i - \bar{Y}_i)^2}{N}$$

Symbol key: $\bar{Y}$ = mean; N = number of cases; Σ = sum over all cases; Y_i = value of variable Y for case i; σ^2 = variance.

You can see in Exhibit 9.18 two examples of summing over all cases, the operation represented by the Greek letter Σ in the formula ($\bar{Y} = 24.27$).

The variance is used in many other statistics, although it is more conventional to measure variability with the closely related standard deviation than with the variance.

Research|Social Impact Link

Variance

Exhibit 9.18	Calculation of the Variance		
Case #	**Score (Y_i)**	**$Y_i - \bar{Y}$**	**$(Y_i - \bar{Y})^2$**
1	21	−3.27	10.69
2	30	5.73	32.83
3	15	−9.27	85.93
4	18	−6.27	39.31
5	25	0.73	0.53
6	32	7.73	59.75
7	19	−5.27	27.77
8	21	−3.27	10.69
9	23	−1.27	1.61
10	37	12.73	162.05
11	26	1.73	2.99
			434.15

Standard Deviation

> **Standard deviation:** The square root of the average squared deviation of each case from the mean.

The **standard deviation** is simply the square root of the variance. It is the square root of the average squared deviation of each case from the mean:

$$\sigma^2 = \sqrt{\frac{\sum (Y_i - \overline{Y_i})^2}{N}}$$

Symbol key: $\bar{Y}$ = mean; N = number of cases; Σ = sum over all cases; Y_i = value of variable Y for case i; $\sqrt{\ }$ = square root; σ = standard deviation.

When the standard deviation is calculated from sample data, the denominator is supposed to be $N - 1$, rather than N, an adjustment that has no discernible effect when the number of cases is reasonably large. You also should note that the use of *squared* deviations in the formula accentuates the impact of relatively large deviations because squaring a large number makes that number count much more.

The standard deviation has mathematical properties that increase its value for statisticians. You already learned about the **normal distribution** in Chapter 5. A normal distribution is a distribution that results from chance variation around a mean. It is symmetric and tapers off in a characteristic shape from its mean. If a variable is normally distributed, 68% of the cases will lie between plus and minus 1 standard deviation from the distribution's mean, and 95% of the cases will lie between plus and minus 1.96 standard deviations from the mean (see Exhibit 9.19).

> **Normal distribution:** A symmetric, bell-shaped distribution that results from chance variation around a central value.

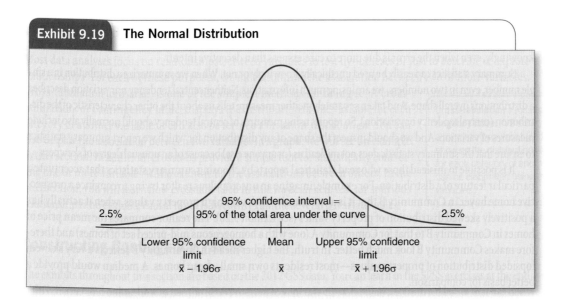

Exhibit 9.19 The Normal Distribution

95% confidence interval =
95% of the total area under the curve

2.5%   2.5%

Lower 95% confidence   Mean   Upper 95% confidence
limit   limit
x̄ − 1.96σ   x̄   x̄ + 1.96σ

This correspondence of the standard deviation to the normal distribution enables us to infer how confident we can be that the mean (or some other statistic) of a population sampled randomly is within a certain range of the sample mean. This is the logic behind calculating confidence limits around the mean. You learned in Chapter 5 that confidence limits indicate how confident we can be, based on our random sample, that the value of some statistic in the population falls within a particular range. (The actual value in the population is the *population parameter*.) Now that you know how to compute the standard deviation, it is just a short additional step to computation of the confidence limits around a mean. There are just four more steps:

Audio Link
Normal Distribution

1. Calculate the standard error. This is the estimated value of the standard deviation of the sampling distribution from which your sample was selected. $SE = \sigma/\sqrt{(n-1)}$. In words, divide the standard of the sample by the square root of the number of cases in the sample minus one.

2. Decide on the degree of confidence that you want to have that the population parameter falls within the confidence interval you compute. It is conventional to calculate the 95%, 99%, or even the 99.9% confidence limits around the mean. Most often, the 95% confidence limits are used, so I will show the calculation for this estimate.

3. Multiply the value of the SE × 1.96. This is because 95% of the area under the normal curve falls within ±1.96 standard deviation units of the mean.

4. Add and subtract the number calculated in (3) from the sample mean. The resulting numbers are the upper and lower confidence limits.

If you had conducted these steps for age with the 2012 GSS data, you would now be able to report, "Based on the GSS 2012 sample, I can be 95% confident that the true mean age in the population is between 47.4 and 49.0." When you read in media reports about polling results that the "margin of error" was ±3 points, you'll now know that the pollster was simply providing 95% confidence limits for the statistic.

▣ Analyzing Data Ethically: How Not to Lie With Statistics

Using statistics ethically means first and foremost being honest and open. Findings should be reported honestly, and the researcher should be open about the thinking that guided his or her decision to use particular statistics.

Exhibit 9.24 Cross-Tabulation of Voting in 2008 by Age (Row Percentages)

Age	Voting			
	Yes (%)	No (%)	Total (%)	(n)
20–29	56.8%	43.2%	100.0%	(234)
30–39	66.6%	33.4%	100.0%	(359)
40–49	71.9%	28.1%	100.0%	(338)
50–59	71.8%	28.2%	100.0%	(316)
60–69	84.0%	16.0%	100.0%	(282)
70–79	86.0%	14.0%	100.0%	(164)
80 or older	90.2%	9.8%	100.0%	(92)

Source: General Social Survey, National Opinion Research Center 2012.

Exhibit 9.25 Race by Region of the United States

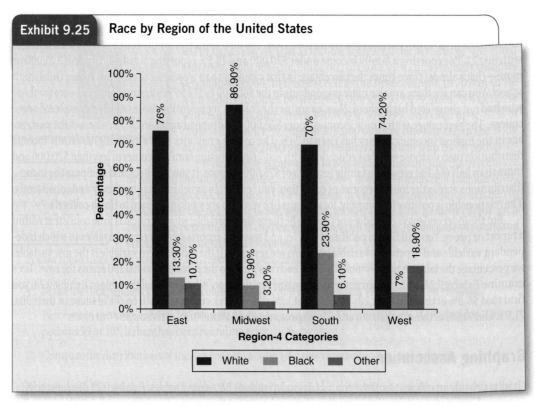

Source: General Social Survey, National Opinion Research Center 2012.

Another good example of the use of graphs to show relationships is provided by a graph that combines data from the FBI Uniform Crime Reports and the General Social Survey (Egan 2012). Exhibit 9.26 shows how the rate of violent crime, the murder rate, and fear of walking alone at night in the neighborhood have varied over time: The violent crime and murder rates rose in the 1960s (the GSS question was first asked in 1972) and the violent crime rate continued to rise into the early 1990s, although the murder rate—its much less common component—was more variable. Then both crime rates fell through 2010. The fear of walking alone remained relatively constant during the 1970s and 1980s, but then dropped early in the 2000s, although it seems to have leveled off by 2005. Because the three rates displayed in this graph are measured at the interval–ratio level, the graph can represent the variation over time with continuous lines.

Exhibit 9.26   Violence in America, 1960–2010

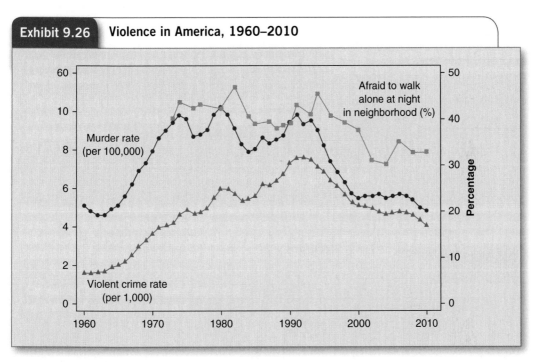

Source: General Social Survey, National Opinion Research Center 2012.

Describing Association

A cross-tabulation table reveals four aspects of the association between two variables:

- *Existence.* Do the percentage distributions vary at all between categories of the independent variable?

- *Strength.* How much do the percentage distributions vary between categories of the independent variable? In most analyses, the analyst would not pay much attention to differences of less than 10 percentage points between categories of the independent variable.

- *Direction.* For quantitative variables, do values on the dependent variable tend to increase or decrease with an increase in value on the independent variable?

- *Pattern.* For quantitative variables, are changes in the percentage distribution of the dependent variable fairly regular (simply increasing or decreasing), or do they vary (perhaps increasing, then decreasing, or perhaps gradually increasing, then rapidly increasing)?

Monotonic: A pattern of association in which the value of cases on one variable increases or decreases fairly regularly across the categories of another variable.

Looking back at Exhibit 9.23, an association exists; it is moderately strong (the difference in percentages between those who voted in the first and last column is 31.3 percentage points); and the direction of association between likelihood of voting and family income is positive. The pattern in this table is close to what is termed **monotonic**. In a monotonic relationship, the value of cases consistently increases (or decreases) on one variable as the value of cases increases on the other variable. The relationship in the table that we will examine in Exhibit 9.34, involving income and education, is also monotonic.

Monotonic is often defined a bit less strictly, with the idea being that as the values of cases on one variable increase (or decrease), the values of cases on the other variable tend to increase (or decrease), and at least do not change direction. This describes the relationship between voting and income: The likelihood of voting increases as family income increases, although the increase levels off in the middle two categories, with the result that the association is not strictly monotonic. There is also a moderately strong positive association between age and voting in Exhibit 9.24, with likelihood of voting rising 33.4 percentage points between the age categories of 20–29 and 80 or older. However, the pattern of this relationship is **curvilinear** rather than monotonic: The increase in voting with age occurs largely from those in their 20s to those in their 30s, before leveling off and then rising again for people 60 and older.

Curvilinear: Any pattern of association between two quantitative variables that does not involve a regular increase or decrease.

The relationship between the measure of trust and voting appears in Exhibit 9.27. There is an association, and in the direction I hypothesized: 84.2% of those who believe that people can be trusted or that "it depends" voted, compared with 67% of those who believe that people cannot be trusted. Because both variables are dichotomies, there can be no pattern to the association beyond the difference between the two percentages. (Comparing the column percentages in either the first or the second row gives the same picture.)

Exhibit 9.27	Voting in 2008 by Interpersonal Trust	
People Can Be Trusted		
Voting	**Can Trust**	**Cannot Trust**
Voted	84.2%	67.0%
Did not vote	15.8%	33.0%
Total	100.0%	100.0%
(n)	(449)	(763)

Source: General Social Survey, National Opinion Research Center 2012.

Exhibit 9.28, by contrast, gives less evidence of an association between gender and voting. The difference between the percentage of men and women who voted is 4 percentage points.

Evaluating Association

You will find when you read research reports and journal articles that social scientists usually make decisions about the existence and strength of association on the basis of more statistics than just a cross-tabulation table.

Exhibit 9.28	Voting in 2008 by Gender	

	Gender	
Voting	**Male**	**Female**
Voted	70.7%	74.7%
Did not vote	29.3%	25.3%
Total	100.0%	100.0%
(n)	(798)	(991)

Source: General Social Survey, National Opinion Research Center 2012.

A **measure of association** is a type of descriptive statistic used to summarize the strength of an association. There are many measures of association, some of which are appropriate for variables measured at particular levels. One popular measure of association in cross-tabular analyses with variables measured at the ordinal level is **gamma**. As with many measures of association, the possible values of gamma vary from –1, meaning the variables are perfectly associated in an inverse direction; to 0, meaning there is no association of the type that gamma measures; to +1, meaning there is a perfect positive association of the type that gamma measures.

Exhibit 9.29 provides a rough guide to interpreting the value of a measure of association like gamma that can range from 0 to –1 and +1. For example, if the value of gamma is –.23, we could say that there is a *weak negative relationship* between the two variables. If the value of gamma is +.61, we could say that there is a *strong positive relationship* between the two variables. A value of 0 always means that there is no relationship (although this really means there is no relationship that this particular statistic can identify). This "rough guide" to interpretation must be modified for some particular measures of association, and your interpretations must consider the results of previous research and the particular methods you used to collect your data. For now, however, this rough guide will get you further along in your statistical interpretations.

> **Measure of association:** A type of descriptive statistic that summarizes the strength of an association.
>
> **Gamma:** A measure of association that is sometimes used in cross-tabular analysis.

Exhibit 9.29	A Guide to Interpreting Strong and Weak Relationships

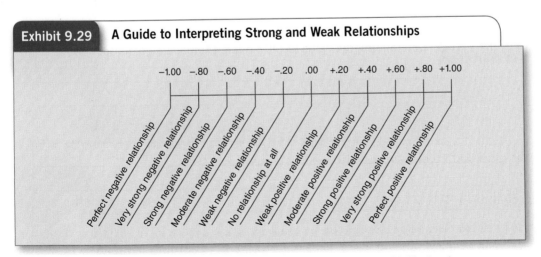

Source: Frankfort-Nachmias and Leon-Guerrero (2006:230). Reprinted with permission from SAGE Publications, Inc.

Inferential statistics are used in deciding whether it is likely that an association exists in the larger population from which the sample was drawn. Even when the association between two variables is consistent with the researcher's hypothesis, it is possible that the association was just caused by the vagaries of sampling on a random basis (of course, the problem is even worse if the sample is not random). It is conventional in statistics to avoid concluding that an association exists in the population from which the sample was drawn unless the probability that the association was due to chance is less than 5%. In other words, a statistician normally will not conclude that an association exists between two variables unless he or she can be at least 95% confident that the association was not due to chance. This is the same type of logic that you learned about earlier in this chapter, which introduced the concept of 95% confidence limits for the mean. Estimation of the probability that an association is not due to chance will be based on one of several inferential statistics, **chi-square** being the one used in most cross-tabular analyses. The probability is customarily reported in a summary form such as $p < .05$, which can be translated as "The probability that the association was due to chance is less than 5 out of 100 (5%)."

> **Chi-square:** An inferential statistic used to test hypotheses about relationships between two or more variables in a cross-tabulation.

The tables in Exhibit 9.30 and 9.31 will help you understand the meaning of chi-square, without getting into the details of how it is calculated. Let's propose, as our "null hypothesis," that trust in other people has no association with family income. In that case, trust in people would be the same percentage for all columns in the table—the same as for the overall sample across all four income categories (36.6%). So if there were no association, we would expect on the basis of chance that 36.6% of the 286 people with family income below $20,000 (the first column) will say they can trust other people or that "it depends." Because 36.6% of 286 equals 104.6 that is the number of people we would "expect" to be trusting and of low income if only chance factors were at work. This is the *expected count* and it differs from the *actual count* of 54, leaving a *residual* of –50.6. This process is repeated with respect to each cell of the table. The larger the deviations of the expected from the observed counts in the various table cells, the less likely it is that the association is due only to chance. Chi-square is calculated with a formula that combines the residuals in each cell. SPSS then compares the value of chi-square to a table that indicates how likely it is in a table of the given size that this value could have been obtained on the basis of chance, given the "degrees of freedom" (*df*) in the table [(the number of rows – 1) * (the number of columns – 1)]. In the crosstab of family income and trust, the value of chi-square was 84.8 and the probability that a chi-square value of this magnitude was obtained on the basis of chance was less than 1 in 1,000 ($p < .001$). We could therefore feel confident that an association between these two variables exists in the U.S. adult population as a whole.

> **Statistical significance:** The mathematical likelihood that an association is due to chance, judged by a criterion set by the analyst (often that the probability is less than 5 out of 100 or $p < .05$).

When the analyst feels reasonably confident (at least 95% confident) that an association was not due to chance, it is said that the association is statistically significant. **Statistical significance** means that an association is not likely to result

---

Exhibit 9.30 | **Determining the Value of Chi-Square (Actual/Expected Counts)**

People Can Be Trusted	Family Income				
	<$20,000	**$20,000–$39,999**	**$40,000–$74,999**	**$75,000+**	**Total**
Can trust or depends	54/104.6	80/99.1	119/103.8	181/126.5	434
Cannot trust	232/181.4	191/171.9	165/180.2	165/219.5	753
(n)	(286)	(271)	(284)	(346)	(1187)

$X^2 = 84.8$, df = 3, $p < .001$.

Source: Based on output from General Social Survey, National Opinion Research Center 2012.

Exhibit 9.31	Cross-Tabulation of Interpersonal Trust by Income

	Family Income			
People Can Be Trusted	**<$20,000**	**$20,000–$39,999**	**$40,000–$74,999**	**$75,000+**
Can trust or depends	18.9%	29.5%	41.9%	52.3%
Cannot trust	81.1%	70.5%	58.1%	47.7%
Total	100%	100%	100%	100%
(n)	(286)	(271)	(284)	(346)

Source: General Social Survey, National Opinion Research Center 2012.

from chance, according to some criterion set by the analyst. Convention (and the desire to avoid concluding that an association exists in the population when it doesn't) dictates that the criterion be a probability less than 5%.

But statistical significance is not everything. You may remember from Chapter 5 that sampling error decreases as sample size increases. For this same reason, an association is less likely to appear on the basis of chance in a larger sample than in a smaller sample. In a table with more than 1,000 cases, such as those involving the full 2012 GSS sample, the odds of a chance association are often very low indeed. For example, with our table based on 1,614 cases, the probability that the association between income and voting (Exhibit 9.23) was due to chance was less than 1 in 1,000 ($p < .001$)! The association in that table was only moderate, as indicated by a gamma of .43. Even weak associations can be statistically significant with such a large random sample, which means that the analyst must be careful not to assume that just because a statistically significant association exists, it is therefore important. In a large sample, an association may be statistically significant but still be too weak to be substantively significant. All this boils down to another reason for evaluating carefully both the existence and the strength of an association.

Controlling for a Third Variable

Cross-tabulation can also be used to study the relationship between two variables while controlling for other variables. We will focus our attention on controlling for a third variable in this section, but I will say a bit about controlling for more variables at the section's end. We will examine three different uses for three-variable cross-tabulation: (1) identifying an intervening variable, (2) testing a relationship for spuriousness, and (3) specifying the conditions for a relationship. Each type of three-variable crosstab helps strengthen our understanding of the "focal relationship" involving our dependent and independent variables (Aneshensel 2002). Testing a relationship for possible spuriousness helps meet the nonspuriousness criterion for causality; identifying an intervening variable can help chart the causal mechanism by which variation in the independent variable influences variation in the dependent variable; and specifying the conditions when a relationship occurs can help improve our understanding of the nature of that relationship.

All three uses for three-variable cross-tabulation are aspects of **elaboration analysis**: the process of introducing control variables into a bivariate relationship to better understand the relationship (Davis 1985; Rosenberg 1968). We will examine the gamma and chi-square statistics for each table in this analysis.

Journal Link
Controlling for a Third Variable: Guilt and Distress

Elaboration analysis: The process of introducing a third variable into an analysis to better understand—to elaborate—the bivariate (two-variable) relationship under consideration. Additional control variables also can be introduced.

Intervening Variables

We will first complete our test of one of the implications of the causal model of voting in Exhibit 9.1: that trust (or efficacy) intervenes in the relationship between social status and voting. You already have seen that both income (one of our social status indicators) and trust in people are associated with the likelihood of voting. Both relationships are predicted by the model: so far, so good. You can also see in Exhibit 9.31 that trust is related to income: Higher income is associated positively with the belief that people can be trusted (gamma = .41; $p < .001$). Another prediction of the model is confirmed. But to determine whether the trust variable is an intervening variable in this relationship, we must determine whether it explains (transmits) the influence of income on trust. We therefore examine the relationship between income and voting while controlling for the respondent's belief that people can be trusted.

According to the causal model, income (social status) influences voting (political participation) by influencing trust in people (our substitute for efficacy), which, in turn, influences voting. We can evaluate this possibility by reading the two subtables in Exhibit 9.32. **Subtables** such as those in Exhibit 9.32 describe the relationship between two variables within the discrete categories of one or more other control variables. The control variable in Exhibit 9.32 is trust in people, and the first subtable is the income-voting crosstab for only those respondents who believe that people can be trusted or that "it depends." The second subtable is for those respondents who believe that people can't be trusted. They are called subtables because together they make up the table in Exhibit 9.23. If trust in ordinary people intervened in the income-voting relationship, the effect of controlling for this third variable would be to eliminate, or at least substantially reduce, this relationship—the distribution of voting would be the same for every income category in both subtables in Exhibit 9.32.

Journal Link
Controlling for a
Third Variable:
Career Outcomes

Subtables: Tables describing the relationship between two variables within the discrete categories of one or more other control variables.

Exhibit 9.32	Voting in 2008 by Family Income by Interpersonal Trust

	Family Income			
Voting	**<$20,000**	**$20,000–$39,999**	**$40,000–$74,999**	**$75,000+**
People Can Be Trusted or It Depends				
Voted	58.3%	77.6.%	87.7%	91.0%
Did not vote	41.7%	22.4%	12.3%	9.0%
Total	100%	100%	100%	100%
(n)	(48)	(76)	(114)	(167)
People Cannot Be Trusted				
Voted	52.2%	68.4%	74.5%	82.8%
Did not vote	47.8%	31.6%	25.5%	17.2%
Total	100%	100%	100%	100%
(n)	(135)	(178)	(157)	(151)

Source: General Social Survey, National Opinion Research Center 2012.

A quick inspection of the subtables in Exhibit 9.32 reveals that trust in people does not intervene in the relationship between income and voting. There is only a modest difference in the strength of the income-voting association in the subtables (as reflected in the value of gamma, which is .475 in the first subtable and .385 in the second). In both subtables, the likelihood that respondents voted rose with their incomes. Of course, this finding does not necessarily mean that the causal model was wrong. This one measure is a measure of trust in people, which is not the same as the widely studied concept of political efficacy; a better measure, from a different survey, might function as an intervening variable. But for now, we should be less confident in the model.

Extraneous Variables

Another reason for introducing a third variable into a bivariate relationship is to see whether that relationship is spurious because of the influence of an extraneous variable (see Chapter 6)—a variable that influences both the independent and dependent variables, creating an association between them that disappears when the extraneous variable is controlled. Ruling out possible extraneous variables will help strengthen considerably the conclusion that the relationship between the independent and dependent variables is causal, particularly if all the variables that seem to have the potential for creating a spurious relationship can be controlled.

One variable that might create a spurious relationship between income and voting is education. You have already seen that the likelihood of voting increases with income. Is it not possible, though, that this association is spurious because of the effect of education? Education, after all, is associated with both income and voting, and we might surmise that it is what students learn in school about civic responsibility that increases voting, not income itself. Exhibit 9.33 diagrams this possibility, and Exhibit 9.34 shows the bivariate associations between education and voting, and education and income. As the model in Exhibit 9.33 predicts, education is associated with both income and voting. So far, so good. If education actually does create a spurious relationship between income and voting, there should be no association between income and voting after controlling for education. Because we are using crosstabs, this means there should be no association in any of the income-voting subtables for any value of education.

The trivariate cross-tabulation in Exhibit 9.35 shows that the relationship between voting and income is not spurious because of the effect of education; if it were, an association between voting and family income wouldn't appear in any of the subtables—somewhat like the first subtable, in which gamma is only .01.

The association between family income and voting is higher in the other three subtables in Exhibit 9.35, for respondents with a high school, some college, or a college education. The strength of that association as measured by gamma is .26 for those with a high school education and .29 for those with some college, and it is

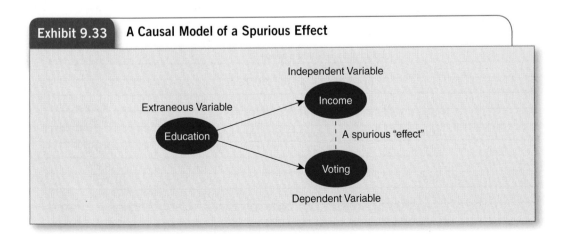

Exhibit 9.33   **A Causal Model of a Spurious Effect**

Exhibit 9.34 Voting in 2008 by Education and Income by Education

Voting by Education				
Education				
Voting	**Grade School**	**High School Graduate**	**Some College**	**College Graduate**
Voted	39.8%	69.7%	76.8%	87.2%
Did not vote	60.2%	30.3%	23.2%	12.8%
Total	100%	100%	100%	100%
(n)	(251)	(495)	(478)	(564)
Family Income by Education				
Education				
Family Income	**Less Than High School**	**High School Graduate**	**Some College**	**College Graduate or Grad School**
<$20,000	51.9%	27.3%	22.1%	7.6%
$20,000–$39,999	17.6%	27.1%	27.9%	13.7%
$40,000–$74,999	13.8%	27.1%	26.0%	24.6%
$75,000+	8.7%	18.5%	24.0%	54.1%
Total	100%	100%	100%	100%
(n)	(268)	(480)	(470)	(540)

Source: General Social Survey, National Opinion Research Center 2012.

Exhibit 9.35 Voting in 2008 by Income and Education

	Family Income			
Voting	**<$20,000**	**$20,000–$39,999**	**$40,000–$74,999**	**$75,000+**
Education = < High school				
Voted	39.8%	38.1%	42.4%	33.3%
Did not vote	60.2%	61.9%	57.6%	66.7%
Total	100%	100%	100%	100%
(n)	(113)	(63)	(33)	(12)
Education = High school graduate				
Voted	57.1%	74.4%	73.0%	80.2%
Did not vote	42.9%	25.6%	27.0%	19.8%
Total	100%	100%	100%	100%
(n)	(119)	(121)	(122)	(81)
Education = Some college				
Voted	67.0%	75.8%	73.3%	90.4%
Did not vote	33.0%	24.2%	26.7%	9.6%
Total	100%	100%	100%	100%
(n)	(91)	(124)	(116)	(104)
Education = College graduate or graduate school				
Voted	71.8%	82.4%	85.8%	90.2%
Did not vote	28.2%	17.6%	14.2%	9.8%
Total	100%	100%	100%	100%
(n)	(39)	(74)	(127)	(275)

Source: General Social Survey, National Opinion Research Center 2012.

.30 among college graduates. So our hypothesis—that income as a social status indicator leads to higher rates of voting—does not appear to be spurious because of the effect of education. The next section elaborates on the more complex pattern that we found.

Specification

By adding a third variable to an evaluation of a bivariate relationship, the data analyst can also specify the conditions under which the bivariate relationship occurs. A **specification** occurs when the association between the independent and dependent variables varies across the categories of one or more other control variables. This is what we just found in Exhibit 9.35: There is no association between income and voting for those with less than a high school education, but there is a moderate association for the higher educational categories.

> **Specification:** A type of relationship involving three or more variables in which the association between the independent and dependent variables varies across the categories of one or more other control variables.

The subtables in Exhibit 9.36 allow an evaluation of whether race specifies the effect of income on voting, as suggested by previous research. The percentages who voted in each of the family income categories vary less among African Americans (gamma = .21) and respondents who identify themselves as members of other minority groups (gamma = .14) than among whites (gamma = .50). Race, therefore, does appear to specify the association between income and voting: The likelihood of African American and other minority respondents having voted varies much less with their family income than it does among whites. The lower rate of voting among members of other minority groups is itself of interest; investigation of the reason for this would make for an interesting contribution to the literature. Is it because members of other minority groups are more likely

---

Exhibit 9.36 Voting in 2008 by Income and Race

Voting	Family Income			
	<$20,000	$20,000–$39,999	$40,000–$74,999	$75,000+
Race = White				
Voted	51.6%	68.1%	77.71%	89.4%
Did not vote	48.4%	31.9%	22.3%	10.6%
Total	100%	100%	100%	100%
(n)	(246)	(282)	(305)	(395)
Race = African American				
Voted	78.4%	86.8%	81.5%	92.7%
Did not vote	21.6%	13.2%	18.5%	7.3%
Total	100%	100%	100%	100%
(n)	(74)	(76)	(54)	(41)
Race = Other minority				
Voted	40.5%	45.8%	41.0%	55.6%
Did not vote	59.5%	54.2%	59.0%	44.4%
Total	100%	100%	100%	100%
(n)	(42)	(24)	(39)	(36)

Source: General Social Survey, National Opinion Research Center 2012.

(2007:174) used qualitative methods to study loss and bereavement in war-torn Tigray, Ethiopia, because preliminary information indicated that people in this culture adjusted to loss in a very different way than do people in Western societies.

An orientation to social context, to the interconnections between social phenomena rather than to their discrete features. The context of concern may be a program or organization, a community, or a broader social context. This feature of qualitative research is evident in Elif Kale-Lostuvali's (2007) description of Gölcük, a Turkish town, after the İzmit earthquake:

> For the first few months, the majority of the population lived in tents located either in tent cities or near partially damaged homes. Around mid-December, eligible survivors began to move into prefabricated houses built on empty hills around the center of the town. Many survivors had lost their jobs because of the earthquake. . . . Hence, daily life revolved around finding out about forms of provision. (p. 752)

A focus on human subjectivity, on the meanings that participants attach to events and that people give to their lives. "Through life stories, people 'account for their lives.' . . . The themes people create are the means by which they interpret and evaluate their life experiences and attempt to integrate these experiences to form a self-concept" (Kaufman 1986:24–25). You can see this emphasis in an excerpt from an interview Nordanger (2007) conducted with a Tigrayan woman who had lost her property and all her nine children in the preceding decades of war in Ethiopia:

> My name is the same. I was Mrs. NN, and now I am Mrs. NN. But I am not like the former. The former Mrs. NN had everything at hand, and was highly respected by others. People came to me for advice and help. But the recent Mrs. NN is considered like a half person. Though she does not go out for begging, she has the lifestyle of a beggar, so she is considered to be a beggar. (p. 179)

Use of idiographic rather than nomothetic causal explanation. With its focus on particular actors and situations and the processes that connect them, qualitative research tends to identify causes as particular events embedded within an unfolding, interconnected action sequence (Maxwell 2005). The language of variables and hypotheses appears only rarely in the qualitative literature. Havidán Rodríguez, Joseph Trainor, and Enrico Quarantelli (2006) include in their analysis of "emergent and prosocial behavior following Hurricane Katrina" the following sequence of events in New Orleans hospitals:

> The floodwaters from the levee breaks created a new kind of crisis. Basements with stored food, water, and fuel, as well as morgues, were inundated. . . . As emergency generators ran out of fuel, the water, sewage, and air-conditioning systems failed. Patients who died in the hospitals had to be temporarily stored in stairwells. Eventually, waste of all kinds was strewn almost everywhere. The rising temperatures made most diagnostic equipment inoperable. . . . Regular hospital procedures simply stopped, but personnel improvised to try to provide at least minimum health care. For instance, physicians, nurses, and volunteers fanned patients to keep them cool, sometimes using manually operated devices to keep them breathing. (pp. 89–90)

> **Adaptive research design:** A research design that develops as the research progresses.

Adaptive research design, in which the design develops as the research progresses.

Each component of the design may need to be reconsidered or modified in response to new developments or to changes in some other component. . . . The activities of collecting and analyzing data, developing and modifying theory, elaborating or refocusing the research questions, and identifying and eliminating validity threats are usually all going on more or less simultaneously, each influencing all of the others. (Maxwell 2005:2–3)

You can see this adaptive quality in Kale-Lostuvali's (2007) description of his qualitative research work as he studied state–citizen encounters in the aftermath of the İzmit earthquake:

> I made my initial trip to Gölcük at the beginning of October 1999, six weeks after the earthquake. From then until the end of July 2000, I made two to three daylong trips per month, spending a total of 25 days in Gölcük. During these trips, I spent time mainly in the Gölcük Crisis Center, the administrative offices of two major tent cities, and two major prefab areas observing interactions. . . . As I got to know some of the state agents and survivors better, I began to hear their responses after specific interactions and their views of the provision and distribution process in general. In addition, I often walked around and spoke with many people in tent cities, in prefab areas, and in the center of the town. Sometimes, people I met in this way invited me to their homes and offices. (p. 752)

Ultimately, Kale-Lostuvali (2007:752) reported conversations with approximately 100 people, in-depth interviews with 30 carefully selected people, and many observational notes.

Sensitivity to the subjective role of the researcher **(reflexivity)**. Qualitative researchers recognize that their perspective on social phenomena will reflect in part their own background and current situation. Who the researcher is and "where he or she is coming from" can affect what the research "finds." Some qualitative researchers believe that the goal of developing a purely "objective" view of the social world is impossible, but they discuss in their publications their own feelings about what they have studied so that others can consider how these feelings affected their findings. You can imagine how anthropology graduate student Hannah Gill (2004) had to consider her feelings when she encountered crime in the community she was studying in the Dominican Republic:

> **Reflexivity:** Sensitivity of and adaptation by the researcher to his or her influence in the research setting.

> On the second day I found myself flattened under a car to avoid getting shot by a woman seeking revenge for her husband's murder in the town market, and on the third I was sprinting away from a knife fight at a local hangout. (p. 2)

Rather than leaving, Gill assessed the danger, realized that although she stood out in the community as a "young, white American graduate student," she "was not a target and with necessary precautions, I would be relatively safe." She decided to use her experiences as "a constructive experience" that would give her insight into how people respond to risk.

Sociologist Barrie Thorne (1993) shared with readers her subjective reactions as she observed girls on a school playground:

> I felt closer to the girls not only through memories of my own past, but also because I knew more about their gender-typed interactions. I had once played games like jump rope and statue buyer, but I had never ridden a skateboard and had barely tried sports like basketball and soccer. . . . Were my moments of remembering, the times when I felt like a ten-year-old girl, a source of distortion or insight? (p. 26)

William Miller and Benjamin Crabtree (1999a) captured the entire process of qualitative research in a simple diagram (Exhibit 10.2). In this diagram, qualitative research begins with the qualitative researcher reflecting on the setting and his or her relation to it and interpretations of it. The researcher then describes the goals and means for the research. This description is followed by sampling and collecting data, describing the data, and organizing those data. Thus, the *gathering process* and the *analysis process* proceed together, with repeated

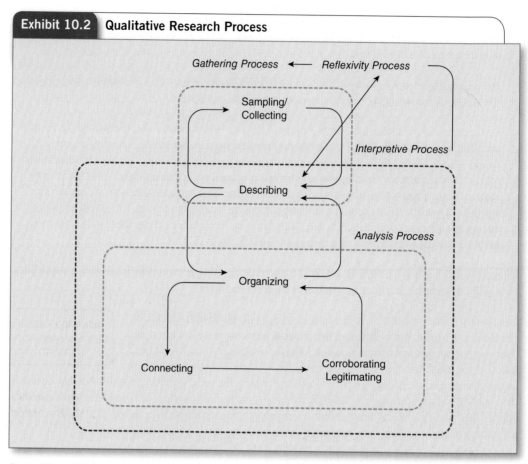

Exhibit 10.2 **Qualitative Research Process**

Source: Miller and Crabtree (1999a:16). Reprinted with permission from SAGE Publications, Inc.

description and analysis of data as they are collected and reflexive attention to the researcher's engagement in the process. As the data are organized, connections are identified between different data segments, and efforts are made to corroborate the credibility of these connections. This *interpretive process* begins to emerge in a written account that represents what has been done and how the data have been interpreted. Each of these steps in the research process informs the others and is repeated throughout the research process.

Basics of Qualitative Research

Research/Social Impact Link
Qualitative Methods

You can understand better how these different features make qualitative methods so distinct by learning the basics of specific qualitative methods and some of the insights those methods produced in leading studies. I will illustrate in this section the way in which qualitative research can produce insights about whole settings and cultures by presenting the basics of case study research and ethnographic research. I will also show how these approaches can be applied to research about social interaction on the Internet through the method of netnography. I will then introduce the three qualitative methods that will be the focus of the rest of the chapter: participant observation, intensive interviewing, and focus groups.

The Case Study

Qualitative research projects often have the goal of developing an understanding of an entire slice of the social world, not just discrete parts of it. What was the larger social context in New Orleans after Hurricane Katrina

(Rodríguez et al. 2006:87)? What was Chicago like during the 1995 Heat Wave, when thousands were hospitalized and more than 700 died of heat-related causes (Klinenberg 2002:1–9)? Sociologist Kai Erikson sent me the following verbal "picture" of New Orleans, as he observed it during a research trip a few days after Katrina:

> The carnage stretches out almost endlessly: more than a hundred thousand [crumpled] homes, at least fifty thousand [flattened] automobiles, the whole mass being covered by a crust of grey mud, dried as hard as fired clay by the sun. It was the silence of it, the emptiness of it; that is the story.

Questions and images such as these reflect a concern with developing a **case study**. Case study is not so much a single method as it is a way of thinking about what a qualitative research project can, or perhaps should, focus on. The case may be an organization, community, social group, family, or even an individual; as far as the qualitative researcher is concerned, it must be understood in its entirety. The idea is that the social world really functions as an integrated whole; social researchers therefore need to develop "deep understanding of particular instances of phenomena" (Mabry 2008:214). By contrast, from this perspective, the quantitative research focus on variables and hypotheses mistakenly "slices and dices" reality in a way that obscures how the social world actually functions.

> **Case study:** A setting or group that the analyst treats as an integrated social unit that must be studied holistically and in its particularity.

Educational researcher Robert Stake (1995) presents the logic of the case study approach thus:

> Case study is the study of the particularity and complexity of a single case, coming to understand its activity within important circumstances. . . . The qualitative researcher emphasizes episodes of nuance, the sequentiality of happenings in context, the wholeness of the individual. (pp. xi–xii)

Central to much qualitative case study research is the goal of creating a **thick description** of the setting studied—a description that provides a sense of what it is like to experience that setting from the standpoint of the natural actors in that setting (Geertz 1973). Stake's (1995) description of "a case within a case," a student in a school he studied, illustrates how a thick description gives a feel of the place and persons within it:

> **Thick description:** A rich description that conveys a sense of what it is like from the standpoint of the natural actors in that setting.

> At 8:30 a.m. on Thursday morning. Adam shows up at the cafeteria door. Breakfast is being served but Adam doesn't go in. The woman giving out meal chits has her hands on him, seems to be sparring with him, verbally. And then he disappears. Adam is one of five siblings, all arrive at school in the morning with less than usual parent attention. Short, with a beautifully sculpted head . . . Adam is a person of notice.

> At 8:55 he climbs the stairs to the third floor with other upper graders, turning to block the girls behind them and thus a string of others. Adam manages to keep the girls off balance until Ms. Crain . . . spots him and gets traffic moving again. Mr. Garson . . . notices Adam, has a few quiet words with him before a paternal shove toward the room. (p. 150)

You will learn in the next sections how qualitative methodologists design research that can generate such thick descriptions of particular cases.

Ethnography

Ethnography is the study of a culture or cultures that a group of people share (Van Maanen 1995:4). As a method, it is usually meant to refer to the process by which a single investigator immerses himself or herself in a group for a long time (often one or more years), gradually establishing trust and experiencing the social world as do the participants (Madden 2010:16). Ethnographic research can be called *naturalistic*, because it seeks to describe and understand the natural social world as it is, in all its

> **Ethnography:** The study of a culture or cultures that some group of people shares, using participant observation over an extended period.

richness and detail. This goal is best achieved when an ethnographer is fluent in the local language and spends enough time in the setting to know how people live, what they say about themselves and what they actually do, and what they value (Armstrong 2008:55).

Anthropological field research has traditionally been ethnographic, and much sociological fieldwork shares these same characteristics. But there are no particular methodological techniques associated with ethnography, other than just "being there." The analytic process relies on the thoroughness and insight of the researcher to "tell us like it is" in the setting, as he or she experienced it.

Code of the Street, Elijah Anderson's (1999) award-winning study of Philadelphia's inner city, captures the flavor of this approach:

> My primary aim in this work is to render ethnographically the social and cultural dynamics of the interpersonal violence that is currently undermining the quality of life of too many urban neighborhoods. . . . How do the people of the setting perceive their situation? What assumptions do they bring to their decision making? (pp. 10–11)

Like most traditional ethnographers, Anderson (1999) describes his concern with being "as objective as possible" and using his training as other ethnographers do, "to look for and to recognize underlying assumptions, their own and those of their subjects, and to try to override the former and uncover the latter" (p. 11). A rich description of life in the inner city emerges as Anderson's work develops. Although we often do not "hear" the residents speak, we feel the community's pain in Anderson's (1999) description of "the aftermath of death":

> When a young life is cut down, almost everyone goes into mourning. The first thing that happens is that a crowd gathers about the site of the shooting or the incident. The police then arrive, drawing more of a crowd. Since such a death often occurs close to the victim's house, his mother or his close relatives and friends may be on the scene of the killing. When they arrive, the women and girls often wail and moan, crying out their grief for all to hear, while the young men simply look on, in studied silence. . . . Soon the ambulance arrives. (p. 138)

Anderson (1999) uses this description as a foundation on which he develops key concepts, such as "code of the street":

> The "code of the street" is not the goal or product of any individual's action but is the fabric of everyday life, a vivid and pressing milieu within which all local residents must shape their personal routines, income strategies, and orientations to schooling, as well as their mating, parenting, and neighbor relations. (p. 326)

Anderson's report on his related Jelly's Bar study illustrates how his understanding deepened as he became more socially integrated into the group. He thus became more successful at "blending the local knowledge one has learned with what we already know sociologically about such settings" (Anderson 2003:236):

> I engaged the denizens of the corner and wrote detailed field notes about my experiences, and from time to time I looked for patterns and relationships in my notes. In this way, an understanding of the setting came to me in time, especially as I participated more fully in the life of the corner and wrote my field notes about my experiences; as my notes accumulated and as I reviewed them occasionally and supplemented them with conceptual memos to myself, their meanings became more clear, while even more questions emerged. (Anderson 2003:224)

A good ethnography like Anderson's is only possible when the ethnographer learns the subtleties of expression used in a group and the multiple meanings that can be given to statements or acts (Armstrong 2008:60–62). Good ethnographies also include some reflection by the researcher on the influence his or her own background has had on research plans, as well as on the impact of the research in the setting (Madden 2010:22–23).

Video Link
Ethnography

Researcher Interview Link
Ethnographic Research

Journal Link
Ethnography

CAREERS AND RESEARCH

Patrick J. Carr, PhD, Director, Program in Criminal Justice

Patrick J. Carr is the Program Director of the Program in Criminal Justice, as well as associate professor of sociology at Rutgers University; furthermore, he is an associate member of the MacArthur Foundation's Research Network on Transitions to Adulthood. He earned his PhD in sociology from the University of Chicago in 1998, and his master's degree in sociology from University College Dublin in 1990. His research interests include communities and crime, informal social control, youth violence, and the transition to adulthood.

Carr and his wife, Maria Kefalas (Saint Joseph's University), are founders of the Philadelphia Youth Solutions Project (www.pysp.org), which "offers a safe space for Philadelphia's young people to explain their views and emotions about the danger and violence that consumes so much of their daily lives, to ask questions of themselves and the people charged with running [Philadelphia], and to have a serious conversation with teachers, parents, city officials, community leaders, state legislators, reporters, politicians, and anyone else who wants to know what is going on in the city to move forward on solutions inspired by the youth perspective." The Philadelphia Youth Solutions Project is a venue for Philadelphia's young people to offer their own expert advice on how to transform the city based on their experiences and perspectives.

Carr and Kefalas are ethnographic researchers who seek to understand people's experiences through participating in their lives and interviewing them in depth. In another project, they investigated the experiences of young adults growing up in a small midwestern town by living in the town and sharing in community experiences. Their subsequent book was *Hollowing Out the Middle: The Rural Brain Drain and What It Means for America* (2009).

Netnography

Communities can refer not only to people in a common physical location, but also to relationships that develop online. Online communities may be formed by persons with similar interests or backgrounds, perhaps to create new social relationships that location or schedules did not permit, or to supplement relationships that emerge in the course of work or school or other ongoing social activities. Like communities of people who interact face-to-face, online communities can develop a culture and become sources of identification and attachment (Kozinets 2010:14–15). And like physical communities, researchers can study online communities through immersion in the group for an extended period. **Netnography**, also termed *cyberethnography* and *virtual ethnography* (James & Busher 2009:34–35), is the use of ethnographic methods to study online communities.

Video Link
Netnography

> **Netnography:** The use of ethnographic methods to study online communities; also termed *cyberethnography* and *virtual ethnography.*

In some respects, netnography is similar to traditional ethnography. The researcher prepares to enter the field by becoming familiar with online communities and their language and customs, formulating an exploratory research question about social processes or orientations in that setting, selecting an appropriate community to study. Unlike in-person ethnographies, netnographies can focus on communities whose members are physically distant and dispersed. The selected community should be relevant to the research question, involve frequent communication among actively engaged members, and have a number of participants who, as a result, generate a rich body of textual data (Kozinets 2010:89).

The netnographer's self-introduction should be clear and friendly. Robert Kozinets (2010:93) provides the following example written about the online discussion space, alt.coffee:

> I've been lurking here for a while, studying online coffee culture on alt.coffee, learning a lot, and enjoying it very much . . . I just wanted to pop out of lurker status to let you know I am here . . . I will be wanting to quote some of the great posts that have appeared here, and I will contact the individuals by personal e-mail who posted them to ask their permission to quote them. I also will be making the document on coffee culture available to any interested members of the newsgroup for their perusal and comments—to make sure I get things right.

A netnographer must keep both observational and reflective field notes, but unlike a traditional ethnographer can return to review the original data—the posted text—long after it was produced. The data can then be coded, annotated with the researcher's interpretations, checked against new data to evaluate the persistence of social patterns, and used to develop a theory that is grounded in the data.

It is now time to get into the specifics. The specifics of qualitative methods can best be understood by reviewing the three distinctive qualitative research techniques: **participant observation, intensive (in-depth) interviewing**, and **focus groups**. Participant observation and intensive interviewing are often used in the same project, whereas focus groups combine some elements of these two approaches into a unique data-collection strategy. These techniques often can be used to enrich experiments and surveys. Qualitative methods can also be used in the study of textual or other documents as well as in historical and comparative research, but we will leave these research techniques for other chapters.

▣ Participant Observation

Participant observation, termed *fieldwork* in anthropology and representing the core method of ethnographic research, was used by Rodríguez and his colleagues (2006) to study the aftermath of Hurricane Katrina, by Nordanger (2007) to study the effects of trauma in Ethiopia, and by Kale-Lostuvali (2007) to study the aftermath of the İzmit earthquake. Participant observation is a qualitative method in which natural social processes are studied as they happen (in "the field" rather than in the laboratory) and left relatively undisturbed. This is the classic field research method—a means for seeing the social world as the research subjects see it, in its totality, and for understanding subjects' interpretations of that world (Wolcott 1995:66). By observing people and interacting with them during their normal activities, participant observers seek to avoid the artificiality of experimental design and the unnatural structured questioning of survey research (Koegel 1987:8). This method encourages consideration of the context in which social interaction occurs, of the complex and interconnected nature of social relations, and of the sequencing of events (Bogdewic 1999:49).

The term *participant observer* actually refers to several different specific roles that a qualitative researcher can adopt (see Exhibit 10.3). As a **covert observer**, a researcher observes others without participating in social interaction and does not self-identify as a researcher.

This role is often adopted for studies in public places where there is nothing unusual about someone sitting and observing others. However, in many settings, a qualitative researcher will function as a **complete observer**, who does not participate in group activities and is publicly defined as a researcher. These two relatively passive roles contrast with the role of a researcher who participates actively in the setting. A qualitative researcher is a **complete participant** (also known as a *covert participant*) when she acts just like other group members and does not disclose her research role. If she publicly acknowledges being a researcher but nonetheless participates in group activities, she can be termed an *overt participant*, or true **participant observer**.

Participant observation: A qualitative method for gathering data that involves developing a sustained relationship with people while they go about their normal activities.

Intensive (in-depth) interviewing: A qualitative method that involves open-ended, relatively unstructured questioning in which the interviewer seeks in-depth information on the interviewee's feeling, experiences, and perceptions (Lofland & Lofland 1984:12).

Focus groups: A qualitative method that involves unstructured group interviews in which the focus group leader actively encourages discussion among participants on the topics of interest.

Covert observer: A role in participant observation in which the researcher does not participate in group activities and is not publicly defined as a researcher.

Complete (or overt) observer: A role in participant observation in which the researcher does not participate in group activities and is publicly defined as a researcher.

Complete (or covert) participant: A role in field research in which the researcher does not reveal his or her identity as a researcher to those who are observed while participating.

Participant observer: A researcher who gathers data through participating and observing in a setting where he or she develops a sustained relationship with people while they go about their normal activities. The term *participant observer* is often used to refer to a continuum of possible roles, from complete observation, in which the researcher does not participate along with others in group activities, to complete participation, in which the researcher participates without publicly acknowledging being an observer.

Choosing a Role

The first concern of every participant observer is to decide what balance to strike between observing and participating and whether to reveal one's role as a researcher. These decisions must take into account the specifics of the social situation being studied, the researcher's own background and personality, the larger sociopolitical context, and ethical concerns. Which balance of participating and observing is most appropriate also changes during most projects, and often many times. Moreover, the researcher's ability to maintain either a covert or an overt role will many times be challenged.

Covert Observation

In both observational roles, researchers try to see things as they happen, without actively participating in these events. Although there is no fixed formula to guide the observational process, observers try to identify the who, what, when, where, why, and how of the activities in the setting. Their observations will usually become more focused over time, as the observer develops a sense of the important categories of people and activities and gradually develops a theory that accounts for what is observed (Bogdewic 1999:54–56).

In social settings involving many people, in which observing while standing or sitting does not attract attention, covert observation is possible and is unlikely to have much effect on social processes. You may not even want to call this "covert" observation because your activities as an observer may be no different from those of others who are simply observing others to pass the time. However, when you take notes, when you systematically check out the different areas of a public space or different people in a crowd, when you arrive and leave at particular times to do your observing, you are acting differently in important respects from others in the setting. Moreover, when you write up what you have observed and, possibly, publish it, you have taken something unique from the people in that setting. If you adopt the role of a covert observer, you should always remember to evaluate how your actions in the setting and your purposes for being there may affect the actions of others and your own interpretations.

Overt Observation

When a researcher announces her role as a research observer, her presence is much more

Exhibit 10.3 The Participant Observation Continuum

To study an activist group, you could take the role of a covert observer.

> I can see who is protesting. I wonder whether their behavior will suggest why?

You could take the role of an overt observer:

> Hello, I am a researcher. Tell me, why do you participate in these activities?

You could take the role of a participant and observer:

> Hello, I am a researcher and an activist. Tell me, why do you participate in these activities?

You could take the role of a covert participant:

> I wonder if I am blending in?

> **Reactive effects:** The changes in individual or group behavior that result from being observed or otherwise studied.

likely to alter the social situation being observed. This is the problem of **reactive effects**. It is not "natural" in most social situations for someone to be present who will record his or her observations for research and publication purposes, and so individuals may alter their behavior. The overt, or complete, observer is even more likely to have an impact when the social setting involves few people or if observing is unlike the usual activities in the setting. Observable differences between the observer and those being observed also increase the likelihood of reactive effects. For example, some children observed in the research by Thorne (1993:16–17) treated her as a teacher when she was observing them in a school playground and so asked her to resolve disputes. No matter how much she tried to remain aloof, she still appeared to children as an adult authority figure and so experienced pressure to participate (Thorne 1993:20). However, in most situations, even overt observers find that their presence seems to be ignored by participants after a while and to have no discernible impact on social processes.

Overt Participation (Participant Observer)

> **Field researcher:** A researcher who uses qualitative methods to conduct research in the field.

Most **field researchers** adopt a role that involves some active participation in the setting. Usually, they inform at least some group members of their research interests, but then they participate in enough group activities to develop rapport with members and to gain a direct sense of what group members experience. This is not an easy balancing act.

> The key to participant observation as a fieldwork strategy is to take seriously the challenge it poses to participate more, and to play the role of the aloof observer less. Do not think of yourself as someone who needs to wear a white lab coat and carry a clipboard to learn about how humans go about their everyday lives. (Wolcott 1995:100)

Nordanger (2007) described how, accompanied by a knowledgeable Tigrayan research assistant, he developed rapport with community members in Tigray, Ethiopia:

> Much time was spent at places where people gathered, such as markets, "sewa houses" (houses for homebrewed millet beer: sewa), cafés, and bars, and for the entire study period most invitations for a drink or to go to people's homes for *injerra* (the sour pancake that is their staple food) and coffee ceremonies were welcomed. The fact that the research topic garnered interest and engagement made access to relevant information easy. Numerous informal interviews derived from these settings, where the researcher discussed his interests with people. (p. 176)

Participating and observing have two clear ethical advantages as well. Because group members know the researcher's real role in the group, they can choose to keep some information or attitudes hidden. By the same token, the researcher can decline to participate in unethical or dangerous activities without fear of exposing his or her identity.

Most field researchers who opt for disclosure get the feeling that, after they have become known and at least somewhat trusted figures in the group, their presence does not have any palpable effect on members' actions. The major influences on individual actions and attitudes are past experiences, personality, group structure, and so on, so the argument goes, and these continue to exert their influence even when an outside observer is present. The participant observer can then be ethical about identity disclosure and still observe the natural social world. In practice, however, it can be difficult to maintain a fully open research role in a setting in which new people come and go, often without providing appropriate occasions during which the researcher can disclose his or her identity.

Of course, the argument that the researcher's role can be disclosed without affecting the social process under investigation is less persuasive when the behavior to be observed is illegal or stigmatized, so that participants have reasons to fear the consequences of disclosure to any outsider. Konstantin Belousov and his

Research in the News

CAN TAPING INTERVIEWS CAPTURE A TREND?

Sociologist Eric Klinenberg used qualitative interviewing to debunk assumptions about individuals who live alone. Klinenberg interviewed 300 people living alone over a 10-year period. What did he find? People who live alone are more social and less isolated. Intensive interviewing revealed older individuals expressing a desire for independence and single living. Economics greatly affect the ability to live alone, and cultures all over the globe are seeing an increase in solo living.

For Further Thought

1. Why might Klinenberg have used qualitative interviewing in this research rather than a quantitative survey? Explain why qualitative interviewing may have been more suited to identifying this misconception.

2. How could you design a study to explore this issue in different cultures? What interpretations could other cultures have of living alone?

News source: Klinenberg, Eric. 2012. "One's A Crowd." *The New York Times,* February 5:SR4.

colleagues (2007) provide a dramatic example of this problem from their fieldwork on regulatory enforcement in the Russian shipping industry. In a setting normally closed to outsiders and linked to organized crime, the permission of a port official was required. However, this official was murdered shortly after the research began. After that "our presence was now barely tolerated, and to be avoided at all costs. . . . explanations became short and respondents clearly wished to get rid of us as soon as possible" (pp. 164–165).

Even when researchers maintain a public identity as researchers, ethical dilemmas arising from participation in the group activities do not go away. In fact, researchers may have to "prove themselves" to the group members by joining in some of their questionable activities. For example, police officers gave John Van Maanen (1982) a nonstandard and technically prohibited pistol to carry on police patrols. Harold Pepinsky (1980) witnessed police harassment of a citizen but did not intervene when the citizen was arrested. Trying to strengthen his ties with a local political figure in his study of a poor Boston community he called Cornerville, William Foote Whyte (1955) illegally voted multiple times in a local election.

Experienced participant observers try to lessen some of the problems of identity disclosure by evaluating both their effect on others in the setting and the effect of others on the observers writing about these effects throughout the time they are in the field and while they analyze their data. They also are sure, while in the field, to preserve some physical space and regular time when they can concentrate on their research and schedule occasional meetings with other researchers to review the fieldwork. Participant observers modify their role as circumstances seem to require, perhaps not always disclosing their research role at casual social gatherings or group outings, but being sure to inform new members of it.

Covert Participation

To lessen the potential for reactive effects and to gain entry to otherwise inaccessible settings, some field researchers have adopted the role of covert participants, keeping their research secret and trying their best to act similar to other participants in a social setting or group. Laud Humphreys (1970) took the role of a covert participant when he served as a "watch queen" so that he could learn about the men engaging in homosexual acts in a public restroom. Randall Alfred (1976) joined a group of Satanists to investigate the group members and their interaction. Erving Goffman (1961) worked as a state hospital assistant while studying the treatment of psychiatric patients.

Although the role of a covert participant lessens some of the reactive effects encountered by the complete observer, covert participants confront other problems:

- *Covert participants cannot take notes openly or use any obvious recording devices.* They must write up notes based solely on their memory and must do so at times when it is natural for them to be away from the group members.

- *Covert participants cannot ask questions that will arouse suspicion.* Thus, they often have trouble clarifying the meaning of other participants' attitudes or actions.

- *The role of a covert participant is difficult to play successfully.* Covert participants will not know how the regular participants would act in every situation in which the researchers find themselves. Regular participants have entered the situation from different social backgrounds and with goals different from that of the researchers. Researchers' spontaneous reactions to every event are unlikely to be consistent with those of the regular participants (Mitchell 1993). Suspicion that researchers are not "one of us" may then have reactive effects, obviating the value of complete participation (Erikson 1967). In his study of the Satanists, for example, Alfred (1976) pretended to be a regular group participant until he completed his research, at which time he informed the group leader of his covert role. Rather than act surprised, the leader told Alfred that he had long considered Alfred to be "strange," not similar to the other people—and we will never know for sure how Alfred's observations were affected.

- *Covert participants need to keep up the act at all times while in the setting under study.* Researchers may experience enormous psychological strain, particularly in situations where they are expected to choose sides in intragroup conflict or to participate in criminal or other acts. Of course, some covert observers may become so wrapped up in the role they are playing that they adopt not only just the mannerisms but also the perspectives and goals of the regular participants—that is, they "go native." At this point, they abandon research goals and cease to evaluate critically what they are observing.

Video Link
Participant Observation

Ethical issues have been at the forefront of debate over the strategy of covert participation. Erikson (1967) argued that covert participation is, by its very nature, unethical and should not be allowed except in public settings. Erikson points out that covert researchers cannot anticipate the unintended consequences of their actions for research subjects. If other people suspect the identity of the researcher or if the researcher contributes to or impedes group action, the consequences can be adverse. In addition, other social scientists are harmed either when covert research is disclosed during the research or on its publication because distrust of social scientists increases and access to research opportunities may decrease.

However, a total ban on covert participation would "kill many a project stone dead" (Punch 1994:90). Studies of unusual religious or sexual practices and of institutional malpractice would rarely be possible. "The crux of the matter is that some deception, passive or active, enables you to get at data not obtainable by other means" (Punch 1994:91). Richard Mitchell Jr. (1993) presents the argument of some researchers that the social world "is presumed to be shot through with misinformation, evasion, lies, and fronts at every level, and research in kind—secret, covert, concealed, and disguised—is necessary and appropriate" (p. 30). Therefore, some field researchers argue that covert participation is legitimate in some of the settings. If the researcher maintains the confidentiality of others, keeps commitments to others, and does not directly lie to others, some degree of deception may be justified in exchange for the knowledge gained (Punch 1994:90).

Entering the Field

Entering the field, the setting under investigation, is a critical stage in a participant observation project because it can shape many subsequent experiences. Some background work is necessary before entering the field—at least enough to develop a clear understanding of what the research questions are likely to be and to review one's personal stance toward the people and problems that are likely to be encountered. With participant observation, researchers must also learn in advance how participants dress and what their typical activities are to avoid being caught completely unaware. Finding a participant who can make introductions is often critical (Rossman & Rallis 1998:102–103), and formal permission may be needed in an organization's setting (Bogdewic 1999:51–53). It may take weeks or even months before entry is possible.

Timothy Diamond (1992) applied to work as an assistant to conduct research as a participant observer in a nursing home. His first effort failed miserably:

> My first job interview. . . . The administrator of the home had agreed to see me on [the recommendation of two current assistants]. The administrator . . . probed suspiciously, "Now why would a white guy want to work for these kinds of wages?" . . . He continued without pause, "Besides, I couldn't hire you if I wanted to. You're not certified." That, he quickly concluded, was the end of our interview, and he showed me to the door. (pp. 8–9)

After taking a course and receiving his certificate, Diamond was able to enter the role of nursing assistant as others did.

Many field researchers avoid systematic study and extensive reading about a setting for fear that it will bias their first impressions, but entering without any sense of the social norms can lead to a disaster. Whyte came close to such a disaster when he despaired of making any social contacts in Cornerville and decided to try an unconventional entry approach (i.e., unconventional for a field researcher). In *Street Corner Society,* Whyte (1955) describes what happened when he went to a hotel bar in search of women to talk to:

> I looked around me again and now noticed a threesome: one man and two women. It occurred to me that here was a maldistribution of females which I might be able to rectify. I approached the group and opened with something like this: "Pardon me. Would you mind if I joined you?" There was a moment of silence while the man stared at me. He then offered to throw me downstairs. I assured him that this would not be necessary and demonstrated as much by walking right out of there without any assistance. (p. 289)

Whyte needed a **gatekeeper** who could grant him access to the setting; he finally found one in "Doc" (Rossman & Rallis 1998:108–111). A helpful social worker at the local settlement house introduced Whyte to this respected leader, who agreed to help:

> **Gatekeeper:** A person in a field setting who can grant researchers access to the setting.

> Well, any nights you want to see anything, I'll take you around. I can take you to the joints—gambling joints—I can take you around to the street corners. Just remember that you're my friend. That's all they need to know [so they won't bother you]. (Whyte 1955:291)

You have already learned that Nordanger (2007:176) relied on a gatekeeper to help him gain access to local people in Tigray, Ethiopia.

When participant observing involves public figures who are used to reporters and researchers, a more direct approach may secure entry into the field. Richard Fenno (1978:257) used this direct approach in his study of members of the U.S. Congress: He simply wrote and asked permission to observe selected members of the Congress at work. He received only two refusals, attributing this high rate of subject cooperation to such

Research That Matters, Questions That Count

The Sexual Experiences Survey (SES) is used on many college campuses to assess the severity of sexual victimization, but researchers have found that it does not differentiate well between situations of unwanted sexual contact and attempted rape. Jenny Rinehart and Elizabeth Yeater (2011:927) at the University of New Mexico designed a project to develop "a deeper qualitative understanding of the details of the event, as well as the context surrounding it."

As part of a larger study of dating experiences at a West Coast university, Rinehart and Yeater analyzed written narratives provided by 78 women who had indicated some experience with sexual victimization on the SES. The authors and an undergraduate research assistant read each of the narratives and identified eight different themes and contexts, such as "relationship with the perpetrator" and "woman's relationship with the perpetrator." Next, they developed specific codes to make distinctions within each of the themes and contexts, such as "friend," "boss," or "stranger" within the "relationship" theme.

Here is an incident in one narrative that Rinehart and Yeater (2011:934) coded as involving unwanted sexual contact with a friend:

> I went out on a date with a guy (he was 24) and we had a good time. He invited me into his apartment after to "hang out" for a little while longer. He tried pressuring me into kissing him at first, even though I didn't want to. Then he wrestled me (playfully to him, but annoyingly and unwanted to me). I repeatedly asked him to get off of me, and eventually he did. I kissed him once.

Their analysis of these narratives made it clear that incidents that received the same SES severity rating often differed considerably when the particulars were examined.

1. According to the authors, "Grouping disparate events into the same category for ease of analysis or description may actually hinder researchers from truly understanding sexual victimization" (p. 939). Do you think that structured surveys can be refined to make the important distinctions, or should resarchers shift more often to qualitative interviews when investigating the social world?

2. Do you think that it would be preferable to just analyze the narratives as text, rather than coding them into categories? Why or why not?

In this chapter, you will learn the language and techniques of qualitative data analysis, as well as a bit about research on victimization. By the end of the chapter, you will understand the distinctive elements of qualitative data analysis and how it differs from quantitative data analysis. After you finish the chapter, you can test yourself by reading the 2011 *Violence Against Women* article by Rinehart and Yeater at the *Investigating the Social World* study site and by completing the related interactive exercises for Chapter 11 at edge.sagepub.com/schutt8e.

Rinehart, Jenny K. and Elizabeth A. Yeater. 2011. "A Qualitative Analysis of Sexual Victimization Narratives." *Violence Against Women* 17(7):925–943.

Journal Link
Sexual Victimization
Qualitative Study

Unfortunately, this statement was not made by a soap opera actor but by a real student writing an in-class essay about conflicts in which he had participated. But then you already knew that such conflicts are common in many high schools, so perhaps it will be reassuring to know that this statement was elicited by a team of social scientists who were studying conflicts in high schools to better understand their origins and to inform prevention policies.

The first difference between qualitative and quantitative data analysis is that the data to be analyzed are text, rather than numbers, at least when the analysis first begins. Does it trouble you to learn that there are no variables and hypotheses in this qualitative analysis by Morrill et al. (2000)? This, too, is another difference between the typical qualitative and quantitative approaches to analysis, although there are some exceptions.

In this chapter, I present the features that most qualitative data analyses share, and I will illustrate these features with research on youth conflict and on being homeless. You will quickly learn that there is no one way to analyze textual data. To quote Michael Quinn Patton (2002), "Qualitative analysis transforms data into findings. No formula exists for that transformation. Guidance, yes. But no recipe. Direction can and will be offered, but the final destination remains unique for each inquirer, known only when—and if—arrived at" (p. 432).

I will discuss some of the different types of qualitative data analysis before focusing on computer programs for qualitative data analysis; you will see that these increasingly popular programs are blurring the distinctions between quantitative and qualitative approaches to textual analysis.

▣ Features of Qualitative Data Analysis

The distinctive features of qualitative data collection methods that you studied in Chapter 10 are also reflected in the methods used to analyze those data. The focus on text—on qualitative data rather than on numbers—is the most important feature of qualitative analysis. The "text" that qualitative researchers analyze is most often transcripts of interviews or notes from participant observation sessions, but *text* can also refer to pictures or other images that the researcher examines.

What can the qualitative data analyst learn from a text? Here qualitative analysts may have two different goals. Some view analysis of a text as a way to understand what participants "really" thought, felt, or did in some situation or at some point in time. The text becomes a way to get "behind the numbers" that are recorded in a quantitative analysis to see the richness of real social experience. Other qualitative researchers have adopted a hermeneutic perspective on texts—that is, a perspective that views a text as an interpretation that can never be judged true or false. The text is only one possible interpretation among many (Patton 2002:114).

From a hermeneutic perspective, then, the meaning of a text is negotiated among a community of interpreters, and to the extent that some agreement is reached about meaning at a particular time and place, that meaning is based on consensual community validation.

A hermeneutic researcher is thus constructing a "reality" with his or her interpretations of a text provided by the subjects of research; other researchers, with different backgrounds, could come to markedly different conclusions.

You can see in this discussion about text that qualitative and quantitative data analyses also differ in the priority given to the prior views of the researcher and to those of the subjects of the research. Qualitative data analysts seek to describe their textual data in ways that capture the setting or people who produced this text on their own terms rather than in terms of predefined measures and hypotheses. What this means is that qualitative data analysis tends to be inductive—the analyst identifies important categories in the data, as well as patterns and relationships, through a process of discovery. There are often no predefined measures or hypotheses. Anthropologists term this an **emic focus**, which means representing the setting in terms of the participants and their viewpoint, rather than an **etic focus**, in which the setting and its participants are represented in terms that the researcher brings to the study.

> **Emic focus:** Representing a setting with the participants' terms and from their viewpoint.
>
> **Etic focus:** Representing a setting with the researchers' terms and from their viewpoint.

Good qualitative data analyses also are distinguished by their focus on the interrelated aspects of the setting, group, or person under investigation—the case—rather than breaking the whole into separate parts. The whole is always understood to be greater than the sum of its parts, and so the social context of events, thoughts, and actions becomes essential for interpretation. Within this framework, it doesn't really make sense to focus on two variables out of an interacting set of influences and test the relationship between just those two.

Qualitative data analysis is an iterative and reflexive process that begins as data are being collected rather than after data collection has ceased (Stake 1995). Next to her field notes or interview transcripts, the qualitative analyst jots down ideas about the meaning of the text and how it might relate to other issues. This process of reading through the data and interpreting them continues throughout the project. The analyst adjusts the data collection process itself when it begins to appear that additional concepts need to be investigated or new relationships explored. This process is termed **progressive focusing** (Parlett & Hamilton 1976).

> **Progressive focusing:** The process by which a qualitative analyst interacts with the data and gradually refines his or her focus.

We emphasize placing an interpreter in the field to observe the workings of the case, one who records objectively what is happening but simultaneously examines its meaning and redirects observation to refine or substantiate those meanings. Initial research questions may be modified or even replaced in mid-study by the case researcher. The aim is to thoroughly understand [the case]. If early questions are not working, if new issues become apparent, the design is changed. (Stake 1995:9)

Elijah Anderson (2003) describes the progressive focusing process in his memoir about his study of Jelly's Bar.

Throughout the study, I also wrote conceptual memos to myself to help sort out my findings. Usually no more than a page long, they represented theoretical insights that emerged from my engagement with the data in my field notes. As I gained tenable hypotheses and propositions, I began to listen and observe selectively, focusing on those events that I thought might bring me alive to my research interests and concerns. This method of dealing with the information I was receiving amounted to a kind of a dialogue with the data, sifting out ideas, weighing new notions against the reality with which I was faced there on the streets and back at my desk. (pp. 235–236)

Carrying out this process successfully is more likely if the analyst reviews a few basic guidelines when he or she starts the process of analyzing qualitative data (Miller & Crabtree 1999b:142–143):

- Know yourself, your biases, and preconceptions.
- Know your question.
- Seek creative abundance. Consult others and keep looking for alternative interpretations.
- Be flexible.
- Exhaust the data. Try to account for all the data in the texts, then publicly acknowledge the unexplained and remember the next principle.
- Celebrate anomalies. They are the windows to insight.
- Get critical feedback. The solo analyst is a great danger to self and others.
- Be explicit. Share the details with yourself, your team members, and your audiences.

Qualitative Data Analysis as an Art

If you find yourself longing for the certainty of predefined measures and deductively derived hypotheses, you are beginning to understand the difference between setting out to analyze data quantitatively and planning to do so with a qualitative approach in mind. Or maybe you are now appreciating better the contrast between the positivist and constructivist research philosophies that I summarized in Chapter 1. When it comes right down to it, the process of qualitative data analysis is even described by some as involving as much "art" as science—as a "dance," in the words of William Miller and Benjamin Crabtree (1999b) (Exhibit 11.1):

> Interpretation is a complex and dynamic craft, with as much creative artistry as technical exactitude, and it requires an abundance of patient plodding, fortitude, and discipline. There are many changing rhythms; multiple steps; moments of jubilation, revelation, and exasperation. . . . The dance of interpretation is a dance for two, but those two are often multiple and frequently changing, and there is always an audience, even if it is not always visible. Two dancers are the interpreters and the texts. (pp. 138–139)

Miller and Crabtree (1999b) identify three different modes of reading the text within the dance of qualitative data analysis:

1. When the researcher reads the text literally, she is focused on its literal content and form, so the text "leads" the dance.

2. When the researcher reads the text reflexively, she focuses on how her own orientation shapes her interpretations and focus. Now, the researcher leads the dance.

3. When the researcher reads the text interpretively, she tries to construct her own interpretation of what the text means.

Exhibit 11.1 **Dance of Qualitative Analysis**

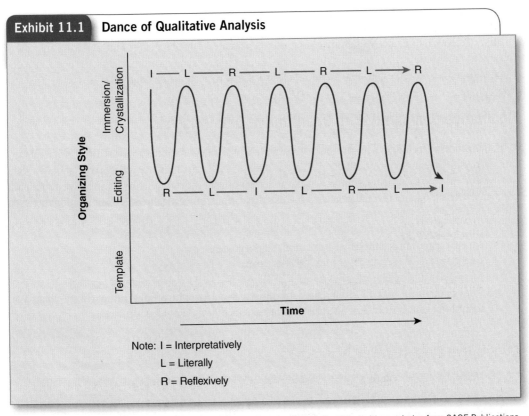

Note: I = Interpretatively
L = Literally
R = Reflexively

Source: Miller and Crabtree (1999b:139, Figure 7.1, based on Addison 1999). Reprinted with permission from SAGE Publications, Inc.

Sherry Turkle's (2011) book *Alone Together: Why We Expect More From Technology and Less From Each Other* provides many examples of this analytic dance, although of course in the published book we are no longer able to see that dance in terms of her original notes. She often describes what she observed in classrooms. Here's an example of such a *literal* focus, reflecting her experience in MIT's Media Lab at the start of the mobile computing revolution:

> In the summer of 1996, I met with seven young researchers at the MIT Media Lab who carried computers and radio transmitters in their backpacks and keyboards in their pockets. . . . They called themselves "cyborgs" and were always wirelessly connected to the Internet, always online, free from desks and cables. (Turkle 2011:151)

Such literal reports are interspersed with *interpretive* comments about the meaning of her observations:

> The cyborgs were a new kind of nomad, wandering in and out of the physical real. . . . The multiplicity of worlds before them set them apart; they could be with you, but they were always somewhere else as well. (Turkle 2011:152)

And several times in each chapter, Turkle (2011) makes *reflexive* comments on her own reactions:

> I don't like the feeling of always being on call. But now, with a daughter studying abroad who expects to reach me when she wants to reach me, I am grateful to be tethered to her through the Net. . . . Even these small things allow me to identify with the cyborgs' claims of an enhanced experience. Tethered to the Internet, the cyborgs felt like more than they could be without it. Like most people, I experience a pint-sized version of such pleasures. (p. 153)

In this artful way, the qualitative data analyst reports on her notes from observing or interviewing, interprets those notes, and considers how she reacts to the notes. These processes emerge from reading the notes and continue while she is editing the notes and deciding how to organize them, in an ongoing cycle.

Qualitative Compared With Quantitative Data Analysis

With this process in mind, let's review the many ways in which qualitative data analysis differs from quantitative analysis (Denzin & Lincoln 2000:8–10; Patton 2002:13–14). Each difference reflects the qualitative data analysts' orientation to in-depth, comprehensive understanding in which the analyst is an active participant compared with the quantitative data analyst's role as a dispassionate investigator of specific relations between discrete variables:

- A focus on meanings rather than on quantifiable phenomena
- Collection of many data on a few cases rather than few data on many cases
- Study in depth and detail, without predetermined categories or directions, rather than emphasis on analyses and categories determined in advance
- Conception of the researcher as an "instrument," rather than as the designer of objective instruments to measure particular variables
- Sensitivity to context rather than seeking universal generalizations
- Attention to the impact of the researcher's and others' values on the course of the analysis rather than presuming the possibility of value-free inquiry
- A goal of rich descriptions of the world rather than measurement of specific variables

The focus of qualitative data analysis on meaning and in-depth study also makes it a valuable supplement to analyses of quantitative data. Qualitative data can provide information about the quality of standardized case records and quantitative survey measures, as well as offer some insight into the meaning of particular fixed responses.

For example, Renee Anspach (1991) wondered about the use of standard surveys to study the effectiveness of mental health systems. Instead of drawing a large sample and asking a set of closed-ended questions, Anspach used snowball sampling techniques to select some administrators, case managers, clients, and family members in four community mental health systems, and then asked these respondents a series of open-ended questions. When asked whether their programs were effective, the interviewees were likely to respond in the affirmative. Their comments in response to other questions, however, pointed to many program failings. Anspach concluded that the respondents simply wanted the interviewer (and others) to believe in the program's effectiveness, for several reasons: Administrators wanted to maintain funding and employee morale; case managers wanted to ensure cooperation by talking up the program with clients and their families; and case managers also preferred to deflect blame for problems to clients, families, or system constraints.

You'll also want to keep in mind features of qualitative data analysis that are shared with those of quantitative data analysis. Both qualitative and quantitative data analysis can involve making distinctions about textual data. You also know that textual data can be transposed to quantitative data through a process of categorization and counting. Some qualitative analysts also share with quantitative researchers a positivist goal of describing better the world as it "really" is, although others have adopted a postmodern goal of trying to understand how different people see and make sense of the world, without believing that there is any "correct" description.

▣ Techniques of Qualitative Data Analysis

Five different techniques are shared by most approaches to qualitative data analysis:

1. Documentation of the data and the process of data collection

2. Organization/categorization/condensation of the data into concepts

3. Examination and display of relationships between concepts

4. Corroboration/legitimization of conclusions, by evaluating alternative explanations, disconfirming evidence, and searching for negative cases

5. Reflection on the researcher's role

Some researchers suggest different steps, or add additional steps, such as developing propositions that reflect the relationships found and making connections with extant theories (see Miles, Huberman, & Saldaña 2014:Chap. 1). Exhibit 11.2 highlights the key techniques and emphasizes the reciprocal relations between them. In qualitative data analysis, condensation of data into concepts may lead to some conclusions and to a particular form of display of relationships between concepts, but the conclusions may then lead to some changes in conceptualization and display, in an iterative process.

The analysis of qualitative research notes begins in the field, at the time of observation, interviewing, or both, as the researcher identifies problems and concepts that appear likely to help in understanding the situation. Simply reading the notes or transcripts is an important step in the analytic process. Researchers should make frequent notes in the margins to identify important statements and to propose ways of coding the data: "husband–wife conflict," perhaps, or "tension-reduction strategy."

An interim stage may consist of listing the concepts reflected in the notes and diagramming the relationships between concepts (Maxwell 2005:97–99). In large projects, weekly team meetings are an important part of this process. Susan Miller (1999) described this process in her study of neighborhood police officers (NPOs).

Video Link
Data Analysis

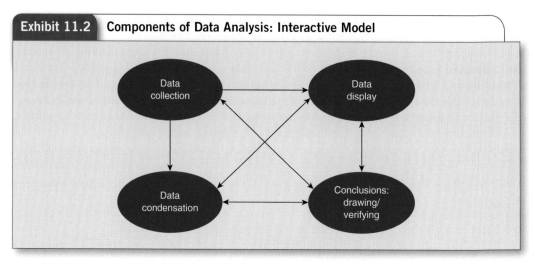

Exhibit 11.2 **Components of Data Analysis: Interactive Model**

Source: Miles, Huberman, and Soldaña (2014:Chap. 1). Reprinted with permission from SAGE Publications, Inc.

Her research team met both to go over their field notes and to resolve points of confusion, as well as to dialogue with other skilled researchers who helped identify emerging concepts:

> The fieldwork team met weekly to talk about situations that were unclear and to troubleshoot any problems. We also made use of peer-debriefing techniques. Here, multiple colleagues, who were familiar with qualitative data analysis but not involved in our research, participated in preliminary analysis of our findings. (p. 233)

This process continues throughout the project and should assist in refining concepts during the report-writing phase, long after data collection has ceased. Let's examine each of the stages of qualitative research in more detail.

Documentation

The data for a qualitative study most often are notes jotted down in the field or during an interview—from which the original comments, observations, and feelings are reconstructed—or text transcribed from audio-tapes. "The basic data are these observations and conversations, the actual words of people reproduced to the best of my ability from the field notes" (Diamond 1992:7). What to do with all this material? Many field research projects have slowed to a halt because a novice researcher becomes overwhelmed by the quantity of information that has been collected. A 1-hour interview can generate 20 to 25 pages of single-spaced text (Kvale 1996:169). Analysis is less daunting, however, if the researcher maintains a disciplined transcription schedule.

> Usually, I wrote these notes immediately after spending time in the setting or the next day. Through the exercise of writing up my field notes, with attention to "who" the speakers and actors were, I became aware of the nature of certain social relationships and their positional arrangements within the peer group. (Anderson 2003:235)

You can see the analysis already emerging from this simple process of taking notes.

The first formal analytical step is documentation. The various contacts, interviews, written documents, and whatever it is that preserves a record of what happened all need to be saved and listed. Documentation is critical to qualitative research for several reasons: It is essential for keeping track of what will be a rapidly growing volume of notes, tapes, and documents; it provides a way of developing and outlining the analytic process; and it encourages ongoing conceptualizing and strategizing about the text.

Matthew Miles and A. Michael Huberman (1994:53) provide a good example of a contact summary form that was used to keep track of observational sessions in a qualitative study of a new school curriculum (Exhibit 11.3).

Organization/Categorization/Condensation

Identifying and refining important concepts so that they can be organized and categorized is a key part of the iterative process of qualitative research. Sometimes, conceptual organization begins with a simple observation that is interpreted directly, "pulled apart," and then put back together more meaningfully. Robert Stake (1995) provides an example:

> When Adam ran a push broom into the feet of the children nearby, I jumped to conclusions about his interactions with other children: aggressive, teasing, arresting. Of course, just a few minutes earlier I had seen him block the children climbing the steps in a similar moment of smiling bombast. So I was aggregating, and testing my unrealized hypotheses about what kind of kid he was, not postponing my interpreting. . . . My disposition was to keep my eyes on him. (p. 74)

The focus in this conceptualization "on the fly" is to provide a detailed description of what was observed and a sense of why that was important.

More often, analytic insights are tested against new observations, the initial statement of problems and concepts is refined, the researcher then collects more data, interacts with the data again, and the process continues. Anderson (2003) recounts how his conceptualization of social stratification at Jelly's Bar developed over a long period:

> I could see the social pyramid, how certain guys would group themselves and say in effect, "I'm here and you're there." . . . I made sense of these crowds [initially] as the "respectables," the "nonrespectables," and the "near-respectables." . . . Inside, such nonrespectables might sit on the crates, but if a respectable came along and wanted to sit there, the lower-status person would have to move. (pp. 225–226)

But this initial conceptualization changed with experience, as Anderson realized that the participants themselves used other terms to differentiate social status: *winehead, hoodlum,* and *regular* (Anderson 2003:230). What did they mean by these terms? The regulars basically valued "decency." They associated decency with conventionality but also with "working for a living," or having a "visible means of support" (Anderson 2003:231). In this way, Anderson progressively refined his concept as he gained experience in the setting.

Howard Becker (1958) provides another excellent illustration of this iterative process of conceptual organization in his study of medical students:

> When we first heard medical students apply the term "crock" to patients, we made an effort to learn precisely what they meant by it. We found, through interviewing students about cases both they and the observer had seen, that the term referred in a derogatory way to patients with many subjective symptoms but no discernible physical pathology. Subsequent observations indicated that this usage was a regular feature of student behavior and thus that we should attempt to incorporate this fact into our model of student-patient behavior. The derogatory character of the term suggested in particular that we investigate the reasons students disliked these patients. We found that this dislike was related to what we discovered to be the students' perspective on medical school: the view that they were in school to get experience in recognizing and treating those common diseases most likely to be encountered in general

Encyclopedia Link
Coding Data

Exhibit 11.3   Example of a Contact Summary Form

Contact type: _____   Site: Tindale

Visit _____ X _____

Phone _____   Contact date: 11/28-29/79

                    (with whom)   Today's date: 12/28/79

                                                         Written by: BLT

1. What were the main issues or themes that struck you in this contact?

   Interplay between highly prescriptive, "teacher-proof" curriculum that is top-down imposed and the actual writing of the curriculum by the teachers themselves.

   Split between the "watchdogs" (administrators) and the "house masters" (dept. chairs & teachers) vis à vis job foci.

   District curric, coord'r as decision maker re school's acceptance of research relationship.

2. Summarize the information you got (or failed to get) on each of the target questions you had for this contact.

Question	Information
History of dev. of innov'n teachers	Conceptualized by Curric., Coord'r, English Chairman & Assoc. Chairman; written by teachers in summer; revised by following summer with field testing data
School's org'l structure	Principal & admin'rs responsible for discipline; dept chairs are educ'l leaders
Demographics emphasis	Racial conflicts in late 60's; 60% black stud. pop.; heavy on discipline & on keeping out non-district students slipping in from Chicago
Teachers' response to innov'n	Rigid, structured, etc. at first; now, they say they like it/ NEEDS EXPLORATION
Research access	Very good; only restriction: teachers not required to cooperate

3. Anything else that struck you as salient, interesting, illuminating or important in this contact?

   Thoroughness of the innov'n's development and training.

   Its embeddedness in the district's curriculum, as planned and executed by the district curriculum coordinator.

   The initial resistance to its high prescriptiveness (as reported by users) as contrasted with their current acceptance and approval of it (again, as reported by users).

4. What new (or remaining) target questions do you have in considering the next contact with this site?

   How do users really perceive the innov'n? If they do indeed embrace it, what accounts for the change from early resistance?

   Nature and amount of networking among users of innov'n.

   Information on "stubborn" math teachers whose ideas weren't heard initially—who are they? Situation particulars? Resolution?

   Follow-up on English teacher Reilly's "fall from the chairmanship."

   Follow a team through a day of rotation, planning, etc.

   CONCERN: The consequences of eating school cafeteria food two days per week for the next four or five months . . .

                                                                                       Stop

Source: Miles and Huberman (1994:10, Figure 4.1). Reprinted with permission from SAGE Publications, Inc.

practice. "Crocks," presumably having no disease, could furnish no such experience. We were thus led to specify connections between the student-patient relationship and the student's view of the purpose of this professional education. Questions concerning the genesis of this perspective led to discoveries about the organization of the student body and communication among students, phenomena which we had been assigning to another [segment of the larger theoretical model being developed]. Since "crocks" were also disliked because they gave the student no opportunity to assume medical responsibility, we were able to connect this aspect of the student-patient relationship with still another tentative model of the value system and hierarchical organization of the school, in which medical responsibility plays an important role. (p. 658)

This excerpt shows how the researcher first was alerted to a concept by observations in the field, then refined his understanding of this concept by investigating its meaning. By observing the concept's frequency of use, he came to realize its importance. Then he incorporated the concept into an explanatory model of student–patient relationships.

A well-designed chart, or **matrix**, can facilitate the coding and categorization process. Exhibit 11.4 shows an example of a coding form designed by Miles and Huberman (1994:93–95) to represent the extent to which teachers and teachers' aides ("users") and administrators at a school gave evidence of various supporting conditions that indicate preparedness for a new reading program. The matrix condenses data into simple categories, reflects further analysis of the data to identify degree of support, and provides a multidimensional summary that will facilitate subsequent, more intensive analysis. Direct quotes still impart some of the flavor of the original text.

> **Matrix:** A form on which can be recorded systematically particular features of multiple cases or instances that a qualitative data analyst needs to examine.

Exhibit 11.4 **Example of Checklist Matrix**

Presence of Supporting Conditions		
Condition	**For Users**	**For Administrators**
Commitment	*Strong*—"wanted to make it work."	*Weak* at building level. Prime movers in central office committed; others not.
Understanding	*"Basic"* ("felt I could do it, but I just wasn't sure how.") for teacher. *Absent* for aide ("didn't understand how we were going to get all this.")	*Absent* at building level and among staff. *Basic* for 2 prime movers ("got all the help we needed from developer.") *Absent* for other central office staff.
Materials	*Inadequate:* ordered late, puzzling ("different from anything I ever used"), discarded.	NA
Front-end training	*"Sketchy"* for teacher ("it all happened so quickly"); no demo class. *None* for aide ("totally unprepared. I had to learn along with the children.")	Prime movers in central office had training at developer site; none for others.

(Continued)

Exhibit 11.4 (Continued)

Presence of Supporting Conditions		
Condition	**For Users**	**For Administrators**
Skills	*Weak-adequate* for teacher. *"None"* for aide.	One prime mover (Robeson) skilled in substance; others unskilled.
Ongoing inservice	*None*, except for monthly committee meeting; no substitute funds.	*None*
Planning, coordination time	*None*: both users on other tasks during day; lab tightly scheduled, no free time.	*None*
Provisions for debugging	*None* systematized; spontaneous work done by users during summer.	*None*
School admin. support	*Adequate*	NA
Central admin. support	*Very strong* on part of prime movers.	Building admin. only acting on basis of central office commitment.
Relevant prior experience	*Strong* and useful in both cases: had done individualized instruction, worked with low achievers. But aide had no diagnostic experience.	*Present* and useful in central office, esp. Robeson (specialist).

Source: Miles and Huberman (1994:10, Table 5.2). Reprinted with permission from SAGE Publications, Inc.

Examination and Display of Relationships

Examining relationships is the centerpiece of the analytic process because it allows the researcher to move from simple descriptions of the people and settings to explanations of why things happened as they did with those people in those settings. The process of examining relationships can be captured in a matrix that shows how different concepts are connected, or perhaps what causes are linked with what effects.

Exhibit 11.5 displays a matrix used to capture the relationship between the extent to which stakeholders in a new program had something important at stake in the program and the researcher's estimate of their favorability toward the program. Each cell of the matrix was to be filled in with a summary of an illustrative case study. In other matrix analyses, quotes might be included in the cells to represent the opinions of these different stakeholders, or the number of cases of each type might appear in the cells. The possibilities are almost endless. Keeping this approach in mind will generate many fruitful ideas for structuring a qualitative data analysis.

Exhibit 11.5 Coding Form for Relationships: Stakeholders' Stakes

	Favorable	Neutral or Unknown	Antagonistic
High			
Moderate			
Low			

Source: Patton (2002).

The simple relationships that are identified with a matrix like that shown in Exhibit 11.5 can be examined and then extended to create a more complex causal model. Such a model represents the multiple relationships between the constructs identified in a qualitative analysis as important for explaining some outcome. A great deal of analysis must precede the construction of such a model, with careful attention to identification of important variables and the evidence that suggests connections between them. Exhibit 11.6 provides an example of these connections from a study of the implementation of a school program.

Research|Social Impact Link
Examining Relationships

Corroboration/Legitimization of Conclusions

No set standards exist for evaluating the validity, or *authenticity,* of conclusions in a qualitative study, but the need to carefully consider the evidence and methods on which conclusions are based is just as great as with other types of research. Individual items of information can be assessed in terms of at least three criteria (Becker 1958):

1. *How credible was the informant?* Were statements made by someone with whom the researcher had a relationship of trust or by someone the researcher had just met? Did the informant have reason to lie? If the statements do not seem to be trustworthy as indicators of actual events, can they at least be used to help understand the informant's perspective?

2. *Were statements made in response to the researcher's questions, or were they spontaneous?* Spontaneous statements are more likely to indicate what would have been said had the researcher not been present.

Journal Link
Qualitative Research

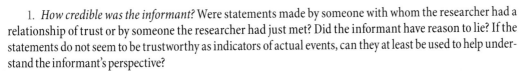

Exhibit 11.6 **Example of a Causal Network Model**

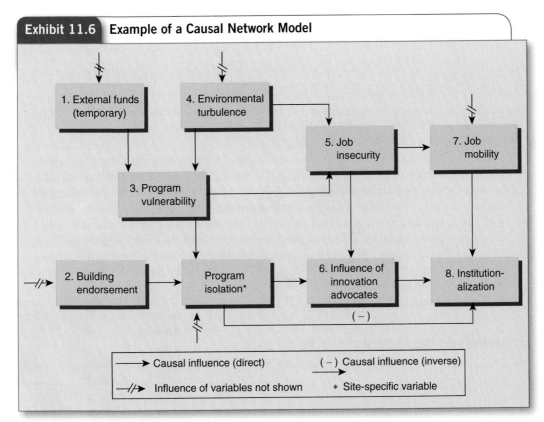

Source: Miles and Huberman (1994:10, Figure 6.5). Reprinted with permission from SAGE Publications, Inc.

3. *How does the presence or absence of the researcher or the researcher's informant influence the actions and statements of other group members?* Reactivity to being observed can never be ruled out as a possible explanation for some directly observed social phenomenon. However, if the researcher carefully compares what the informant says goes on when the researcher is not present, what the researcher observes directly, and what other group members say about their normal practices, the extent of reactivity can be assessed to some extent (pp. 654–656).

> **Tacit knowledge:** In field research, a credible sense of understanding of social processes that reflects the researcher's awareness of participants' actions as well as their words, and of what they fail to state, feel deeply, and take for granted.

A qualitative researcher's conclusions should also be assessed by his or her ability to provide a credible explanation for some aspect of social life. That explanation should capture group members' **tacit knowledge** of the social processes that were observed, not just their verbal statements about these processes. Tacit knowledge—"the largely unarticulated, contextual understanding that is often manifested in nods, silences, humor, and naughty nuances"—is reflected in participants' actions as well as their words and in what they fail to state but nonetheless feel deeply and even take for granted (Altheide & Johnson 1994:492–493). These features are evident in William Foote Whyte's (1955) analysis of Cornerville social patterns:

> The corner-gang structure arises out of the habitual association of the members over a long period of time. The nuclei of most gangs can be traced back to early boyhood. . . . Home plays a very small role in the group activities of the corner boy. . . . The life of the corner boy proceeds along regular and narrowly circumscribed channels. . . . Out of [social interaction within the group] arises a system of mutual obligations which is fundamental to group cohesion. . . . The code of the corner boy requires him to help his friends when he can and to refrain from doing anything to harm them. When life in the group runs smoothly, the obligations binding members to one another are not explicitly recognized. (pp. 255–257)

Comparing conclusions from a qualitative research project to those obtained by other researchers while conducting similar projects can also increase confidence in their authenticity. Miller's (1999) study of NPOs (non-profit organizations) found striking parallels in the ways they defined their masculinity to processes reported in research about males in nursing and other traditionally female jobs:

> In part, male NPOs construct an exaggerated masculinity so that they are not seen as feminine as they carry out the social-work functions of policing. Related to this is the almost defiant expression of heterosexuality, so that the men's sexual orientation can never truly be doubted even if their gender roles are contested. Male patrol officers' language—such as their use of terms like "pansy police" to connote neighborhood police officers—served to affirm their own heterosexuality. . . . In addition, the male officers, but not the women, deliberately wove their heterosexual status into conversations, explicitly mentioning their female domestic partner or spouse and their children. This finding is consistent with research conducted in the occupational field. The studies reveal that men in female-dominated occupations, such as teachers, librarians, and pediatricians, over-reference their heterosexual status to ensure that others will not think they are gay. (p. 222)

Reflection on the Researcher's Role

Encyclopedia Link
Reflexivity

Confidence in the conclusions from a field research study is also strengthened by an honest and informative account about how the researcher interacted with subjects in the field, what problems he or she encountered, and how these problems were or were not resolved. Such a "natural history" of the development of the evidence enables others to evaluate the findings and reflects the constructivist philosophy that guides many qualitative researchers (see Chapter 1). Such an account is important primarily because of the evolving and variable nature of field research: To an important extent, the researcher "makes up" the method in the context of a particular investigation rather than applying standard procedures that are specified before the investigation begins.

Barrie Thorne (1993) provides a good example of this final element of the analysis:

> Many of my observations concern the workings of gender categories in social life. For example, I trace the evocation of gender in the organization of everyday interactions, and the shift from boys and girls as loose aggregations to "the boys" and "the girls" as self-aware, gender-based groups. In writing about these processes, I discovered that different angles of vision lurk within seemingly simple choices of language. How, for example, should one describe a group of children? A phrase like "six girls and three boys were chasing by the tires" already assumes the relevance of gender. An alternative description of the same event—"nine fourth-graders were chasing by the tires"—emphasizes age and downplays gender. Although I found no tidy solutions, I have tried to be thoughtful about such choices. . . . After several months of observing at Oceanside, I realized that my field notes were peppered with the words "child" and "children," but that the children themselves rarely used the term. "What do they call themselves?" I badgered in an entry in my field notes. The answer it turned out, is that children use the same practices as adults. They refer to one another by using given names ("Sally," "Jack") or language specific to a given context ("that guy on first base"). They rarely have occasion to use age-generic terms. But when pressed to locate themselves in an age-based way, my informants used "kids" rather than "children." (pp. 8–9)

Qualitative data analysts, more often than quantitative researchers, display real sensitivity to how a social situation or process is interpreted from a particular background and set of values and not simply based on the situation itself (Altheide & Johnson 1994). Researchers are only human, after all, and must rely on their own senses and process all information through their own minds. By reporting how and why they think they did what they did, they can help others determine whether, or how, the researchers' perspectives influenced their conclusions. "There should be clear 'tracks' indicating the attempt [to show the hand of the ethnographer] has been made" (Altheide & Johnson 1994:493).

Interactive Exercises Link
Qualitative Data Analysis

Anderson's (2003) memoir about the Jelly's Bar research illustrates the type of "tracks" that an ethnographer makes as well as how the researcher can describe those tracks. Anderson acknowledges that his tracks began as a child:

> While growing up in the segregated black community of South Bend, from an early age, I was curious about the goings-on in the neighborhood, particularly the streets and more particularly the corner taverns where my uncles and my dad would go to hang out and drink. . . . Hence, my selection of a field setting was a matter of my background, intuition, reason, and a little bit of luck. (pp. 217–218)

After starting to observe at Jelly's, Anderson's (2003) tracks led to Herman:

> After spending a couple of weeks at Jelly's, I met Herman. I felt that our meeting marked an important step. We would come to know each other well . . . something of an informal leader at Jelly's. . . . We were becoming friends. . . . He seemed to genuinely like me, and he was one person I could feel comfortable with. (pp. 218–219)

So we learn that Anderson's observations were to be shaped, in part, by Herman's perspective, but we also find out that Anderson maintained some engagement with fellow students. This contact outside the bar helped shape his analysis: "By relating my experiences to my fellow students, I began to develop a coherent perspective, or a 'story' of the place that complemented the accounts I had detailed in my accumulating field notes" (Anderson 2003:220).

In this way, Anderson explains that the outcome of his analysis of qualitative data resulted, in part, from the way in which he "played his role" as a researcher and participant, not just from the setting itself.

▣ Alternatives in Qualitative Data Analysis

The qualitative data analyst can choose from many interesting alternative approaches. Of course, the research question under investigation should shape the selection of an analytic approach, but the researcher's preferences and experiences also will inevitably have an important influence on the method chosen. The alternative approaches I present here—ethnomethodology, conversation analysis, narrative analysis, grounded theory, qualitative comparative analysis, and case-oriented understanding—give you a good sense of the different possibilities (Patton 2002).

> **Ethnomethodology:** A qualitative research method focused on the way that participants in a social setting create and sustain a sense of reality.

Ethnomethodology

Ethnomethodology focuses on the way that participants construct the social world in which they live—how they "create reality"—rather than on describing the social world itself. Actually, ethnomethodologists do not necessarily believe that we can find an objective reality; rather, the way that participants come to create and sustain a sense of reality is of interest. In the words of Jaber Gubrium and James Holstein (1997), in ethnomethodology, compared with the naturalistic orientation of ethnography (see Chapter 10),

> The focus shifts from the scenic features of everyday life onto the ways through which the world comes to be experienced as real, concrete, factual, and "out there." An interest in members' methods of constituting their world supersedes the naturalistic project of describing members' worlds as they know them. (p. 41)

Unlike the ethnographic analyst, who seeks to describe the social world as the participants see it, the ethnomethodological analyst seeks to maintain some distance from that world. The ethnomethodologist views a code of conduct like that described by Anderson (2003) at Jelly's not as a description of a real normative force that constrains social action, but as the way that people in the setting create a sense of order and social structure (Gubrium & Holstein 1997:44–45). The ethnomethodologist focuses on how reality is constructed, not on what it is.

Sociologist Harold Garfinkel (1967) developed ethnomethodology in the 1960s and first applied it to the study of gender. Focusing on a teenage male-to-female transsexual whom he termed "Agnes," he described her "social achievement of gender" as

> the tasks of securing and guaranteeing for herself the ascribed rights and obligations of an adult female by the acquisition and use of skills and capacities, the efficacious display of female appearances and performances, and the mobilizing of appropriate feelings and purposes. (p. 134)

The ethnomethodological focus on how the meaning of gender and other categories are socially constructed leads to a concern with verbal interaction. In recent years, this concern has led ethnomethodologists and others to develop a more formal approach, called *conversation analysis*.

Research|Social Impact Link
Ethnographic Research

Conversation Analysis

Conversation analysis is a specific qualitative method for analyzing the sequential organization and details of conversation. Like ethnomethodology, from which it developed, conversation analysis focuses on how reality is constructed, rather than on what it is. From this perspective, detailed analysis of conversational interaction

Research in the News

WHAT'S IN A MESSAGE?

In response to the large number of military suicides, Attivio Inc. and military suicide experts are creating a qualitative coding scheme and searching through social media posts. Facebook and Twitter posts hold valuable information about a person's well-being; researchers are creating a way to analyze millions of posts. The program is called the Durkheim Project and aims to prevent suicides by systematically identifying at-risk soldiers or veterans.

In the News

For Further Thought

1. What are the advantages and disadvantages that you see in using Facebook and Twitter posts to determine a person's well-being?

2. How do you think that analyzing online social interaction would compare as a research method to analyzing social interaction in person, through interviews or observations? Which approach would be preferable in identifying at-risk soldiers or veterans?

News source: Weintraub, Karen. 2013. "Monitoring Social Media to Cut the Military Suicide Rate." *The New York Times,* July 22:B5.

is important because conversation is "sociological bedrock": "a form of social organization through which the work of . . . institutions such as the economy, the polity, the family, socialization, etc." is accomplished (Schegloff 1996:4).

> It is through conversation that we conduct the ordinary affairs of our lives. Our relationships with one another, and our sense of who we are to one another is generated, manifest, maintained, and managed in and through our conversations, whether face-to-face, on the telephone, or even by other electronic means. (Drew 2005:74)

Three premises guide conversation analysis (Gubrium & Holstein 2000:492):

1. Interaction is sequentially organized, and talk can be analyzed in terms of the process of social interaction rather than in terms of motives or social status.

2. Talk, as a process of social interaction, is contextually oriented—it is both shaped by interaction and creates the social context of that interaction.

3. These processes are involved in all social interaction, so no interactive details are irrelevant to understanding it.

Consider these premises as you read the following excerpt from Elizabeth Stokoe's (2006:479–480) analysis of the relevance of gender categories to "talk-in-interaction." The dialogue is between four first-year British psychology students who must write up a description of some photographs of people (Exhibit 11.7). Stokoe incorporates stills from the video recording of the interaction into her analysis of both the talk and embodied conduct in interaction. In typical conversation analysis style, the text is broken up into brief segments that capture shifts in meaning, changes in the speaker, pauses, nonspeech utterances and nonverbal actions, and emphases.

narratives as a whole, rather than of the different elements within them. The coding strategy revolves around reading the stories and classifying them into general patterns.

For example, Morrill and his colleagues (2000:534) read through 254 conflict narratives written by the ninth graders they studied and found four different types of stories:

1. *Action tales,* in which the author represents himself or herself and others as acting within the parameters of taken-for-granted assumptions about what is expected for particular roles among peers.

2. *Expressive tales,* in which the author focuses on strong, negative emotional responses to someone who has wronged him or her.

3. *Moral tales,* in which the author recounts explicit norms that shaped his or her behavior in the story and influenced the behavior of others.

4. *Rational tales,* in which the author represents himself or herself as a rational decision maker navigating through the events of the story.

Audio Link
Narrative Analysis

In addition to these dominant distinctions, Morrill et al. (2000:534–535) also distinguished the stories by four stylistic dimensions: (1) plot structure (e.g., whether the story unfolds sequentially), (2) dramatic tension (how the central conflict is represented), (3) dramatic resolution (how the central conflict is resolved), and (4) predominant outcomes (how the story ends). Coding reliability was checked through a discussion between the two primary coders, who found that their classifications agreed for a large percentage of the stories.

The excerpt that begins this chapter exemplifies what Morrill et al. (2000) termed an *action tale.* Such tales

unfold in matter-of-fact tones kindled by dramatic tensions that begin with a disruption of the quotidian order of everyday routines. A shove, a bump, a look . . . triggers a response. . . . Authors of action tales typically organize their plots as linear streams of events as they move briskly through the story's scenes. . . . This story's dramatic tension finally resolves through physical fighting, but . . . only after an attempted conciliation. (p. 536)

You can contrast this action tale with the following narrative, which Morrill et al. (2000) classify as a *moral tale,* in which the students "explicitly tell about their moral reasoning, often referring to how normative commitments shape their decisionmaking" (p. 542):

I . . . got into a fight because I wasn't allowed into the basketball game. I was being harassed by the captains that wouldn't pick me and also many of the players. The same type of things had happened almost every day where they called me bad words so I decided to teach the ring leader a lesson. I've never been in a fight before but I realized that sometimes you have to make a stand against the people that constantly hurt you, especially emotionally. I hit him in the face a couple of times and I got [the] respect I finally deserved. (pp. 545–546)

Researcher Interview Link
Narrative Analysis

Morrill et al. (2000:553) summarize their classification of the youth narratives in a simple table that highlights the frequency of each type of narrative and the characteristics associated with each of them (Exhibit 11.8). How does such an analysis contribute to our understanding of youth violence? Morrill et al. (2000) first emphasize that their narratives "suggest that consciousness of conflict among youths—like that among adults—is not a singular entity, but comprises a rich and diverse range of perspectives" (p. 551).

Theorizing inductively, Morrill et al. (2000:553–554) then attempt to explain why action tales were much more common than were the more adult-oriented normative, rational, or emotionally expressive tales. One possibility is Carol Gilligan's (1988) theory of moral development, which suggests that younger students are likely to limit themselves to the simpler action tales that "concentrate on taken-for-granted assumptions of their peer and wider cultures, rather than on more self-consciously reflective interpretation and evaluation" (Morrill et al. 2000:554). More generally, Morrill et al. (2000) argue, "We can begin to think of the building blocks of cultures

Exhibit 11.8	Summary Comparison of Youth Narratives*			
Representation of	**Action Tales (N = 144)**	**Moral Tales (N = 51)**	**Expressive Tales (N = 35)**	**Rational Tales (N = 24)**
Bases of everyday conflict	Disruption of everyday routines & expectations	Normative violation	Emotional provocation	Goal obstruction
Decision making	Intuitive	Principled stand	Sensual	Calculative choice
Conflict handling	Confrontational	Ritualistic	Cathartic	Deliberative
Physical violence†	In 44% (N = 67)	In 27% (N = 16)	In 49% (N = 20)	In 29% (N = 7)
Adults in youth conflict control	Invisible or background	Sources of rules	Agents of repression	Institutions of social control

*Total N = 254.

†Percentages based on the number of stories in each category.

Source: Morrill et al. (2000:553, Table 1). Copyright 2000. Reprinted with permission of Blackwell Publishing Ltd.

as different narrative styles in which various aspects of reality are accentuated, constituted, or challenged, just as others are deemphasized or silenced" (p. 556).

In this way, Morrill et al.'s (2000) narrative analysis allowed an understanding of youth conflict to emerge from the youths' own stories while informing our understanding of broader social theories and processes.

Narrative analysis can also use documents and observations and focus more attention on how stories are constructed, rather than on the resulting narrative (Hyvärinen 2008:452). Narrative analyst Catherine Kohler Riessman (2008:67–73) describes the effective combination of data from documents, interviews, and field observations to learn how members of Alcoholics Anonymous (AA) developed a group identity (Cain 1991). Propositions that Carol Cain (1991:228) identified repeatedly in the documents enter into stories as guidelines for describing the progression of drinking, the desire and inability to stop, the necessity of "hitting bottom" before the program can work, and the changes that take place in one's life after joining AA.

Cain then found that this same narrative was expressed repeatedly in AA meetings. She only interviewed three AA members but found that one who had been sober and in AA for many years told "his story" using this basic narrative, while one who had been sober for only 2 years deviated from the narrative in some ways. One interviewee did not follow this standard narrative at all as he told his story; he had attended AA only sporadically for 20 years and left soon after the interview. Cain (1991) explains,

I argue that as the AA member learns the AA story model, and learns to place the events and experiences of his own life into the model, he learns to tell and to understand his own life as an AA life, and himself as an AA alcoholic. The personal story is a cultural vehicle for identity acquisition. (p. 215)

Grounded Theory

Theory development occurs continually in qualitative data analysis (Coffey & Atkinson 1996:23). Many qualitative researchers use a method of developing theory during their analysis that is termed **grounded theory**, which involves building up inductively a systematic theory that is *grounded* in, or based on, the observations.

> **Grounded theory:** Systematic theory developed inductively, based on observations that are summarized into conceptual categories, reevaluated in the research setting, and gradually refined and linked to other conceptual categories.

The grounded theorist first summarizes observations into conceptual categories and then tests the coherence of these categories directly in the research setting with more observations. Over time, as the researcher refines and links the conceptual categories, a theory evolves (Glaser & Strauss 1967; Huberman & Miles 1994:436). Exhibit 11.9 diagrams the grounded theory of a chronic illness "trajectory" developed by Anselm Strauss and Juliette Corbin (1990:221). Their notes suggested to them that conceptions of self, biography, and body are reintegrated after a process of grieving.

As observation, interviewing, and reflection continue, grounded theory researchers refine their definitions of problems and concepts and select indicators. They can then check the frequency and distribution of phenomena: How many people made a particular type of comment? How often did social interaction lead to arguments? Social system models may then be developed that specify the relationships between different phenomena. These models are modified as researchers gain experience in the setting. For the final analysis, the researchers check their models carefully against their notes and make a concerted attempt to discover negative evidence that might suggest that the model is incorrect.

Heidi Levitt, Rebecca Todd Swanger, and Jenny Butler (2008:435) used a systematic grounded method of analysis to understand the perspective of male perpetrators of violence on female victims. Research participants were recruited from programs the courts used in Memphis to assess and treat perpetrators who admitted to having physically abused a female intimate partner. All program participants were of low socioeconomic status, but in other respects, Levitt and her colleagues (2008:436) sought to recruit a diverse sample.

The researchers (Levitt et al. 2008:437–438) began the analysis of their interview transcripts by dividing them into "meaning units"—"segments of texts that each contain one main idea"—and labeling these units with terms like those used by participants. The researchers then compared these labels and combined them into larger descriptive categories. This process continued until they had combined all the meaning units into seven different clusters. Exhibit 11.10 gives an example of two of their clusters and the four categories of meaning units combined within each (Levitt et al. 2008:439).

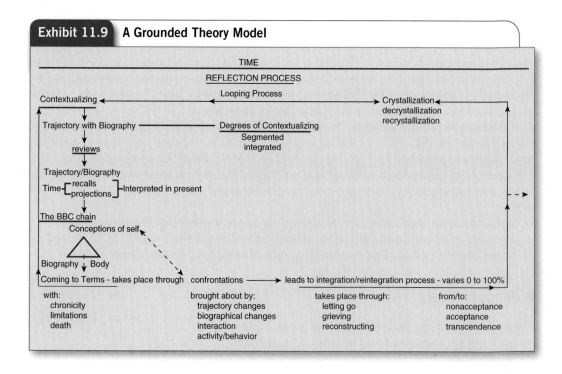

Exhibit 11.9   A Grounded Theory Model

Exhibit 11.10	Clusters and Categories in a Grounded Theory Analysis

Clusters (endorsement)	Categories (endorsement)
1. The arrest incident is a hurdle or a test from god that I alone have to deal with, although the responsibility for the abuse was not all my own. (10)	1. If alcohol or drugs had not been in the picture, we wouldn't have come to blows: Substance use is thought to increase the rate of IPV (2) 2. I don't want to get involved in conflict because I don't want to deal with its consequences (9) 3. Joint responsibility in conflict depends on who did more fighting (8) 4. How women cause IPV: Being treated as a child through nagging and being disrespected (5)
2. Passive avoidance and withdrawal from conflict is the best way to prevent aggression and to please god. (10)	1. DV thought to be "cured" by passively attending classes and learning anger management (6) 2. Religious interventions have been vague or guilt producing, we need explicit advice and aren't getting it (9) 3. Intimate partner violence can be stopped by cutting off relationships, but this can be a painful experience (5) 4. Should resolve conflict to create harmony and avoid depression—but conflict may increase as a result (10)

Source: Levitt, H. M., Todd-Swanger, R., & Butler, J. B. "Male Perpetrators' Perspectives on Intimate Partner Violence, Religion, and Masculinity." *Sex Roles: A Journal of Research*, 58, 435–448. Copyright © 2007, Springer Science + Business Media, LLC. Reprinted with permission.

Here is how Levitt and her colleagues (2008) discuss the comments that were classified in Cluster 2, Category 3:

> Accordingly, when conflicts accumulated that could not be easily resolved, many of the men (5 of 12) thought that ending the relationship was the only way to stop violence from recurring. (p. 440)

> "I don't deal with anybody so I don't have any conflicts. . . . It makes me feel bad because I be lonely sometime, but at the same time, it's the best thing going for me right now. I'm trying to rebuild me. I'm trying to put me on a foundation to where I can be a total leader. Like I teach my sons, 'Be leaders instead of followers.'" (p. 440)

> Although this interviewee's choice to isolate himself was a strategy to avoid relational dependency and conflict, it left him without interpersonal support and it could be difficult for him to model healthy relationships for his children. (p. 440)

With procedures such as these, the grounded theory approach develops general concepts from careful review of text or other qualitative materials and can then suggest plausible relationships between these concepts.

Qualitative Comparative Analysis

Daniel Cress and David Snow (2000) asked a series of very specific questions about social movement outcomes in their study of homeless social movement organizations (SMOs). They collected qualitative data from about 15 SMOs in eight cities. A content analysis of newspaper articles indicated that these cities represented a range of outcomes, and the SMOs within them were also relatively accessible to Cress and Snow because of prior contacts. In each of these cities, Cress and Snow used a snowball sampling strategy to identify the homeless SMOs and the various supporters, antagonists, and significant organizational bystanders with whom they interacted. Cress and Snow then gathered information from representatives of these organizations, including churches, other activist organizations, police departments, mayors' offices, service providers, federal agencies, and, of course, the SMOs themselves.

To answer their research questions, Cress and Snow (2000) needed to operationalize each of the various conditions that they believed might affect movement outcomes, using coding procedures that were much more systematic than those often employed in qualitative research. For example, Cress and Snow defined "sympathetic allies" operationally as

the presence of one or more city council members who were supportive of local homeless mobilization. This was demonstrated by attending homeless SMO meetings and rallies and by taking initiatives to city agencies on behalf of the SMO. (Seven of the 14 SMOs had such allies.) (p. 1078)

> **Qualitative comparative analysis (QCA):** A systematic type of qualitative analysis that identifies the combination of factors that had to be present across multiple cases to produce a particular outcome.

Cress and Snow (2000) also chose a structured method of analysis, **qualitative comparative analysis (QCA)**, to assess how the various conditions influenced SMO outcomes. This procedure identifies the combination of factors that had to be present across multiple cases to produce a particular outcome (Ragin 1987). Cress and Snow (2000) explain why QCA was appropriate for their analysis:

QCA . . . is conjunctural in its logic, examining the various ways in which specified factors interact and combine with one another to yield particular outcomes. This increases the prospect of discerning diversity and identifying different pathways that lead to an outcome of interest and thus makes this mode of analysis especially applicable to situations with complex patterns of interaction among the specified conditions. (p. 1079)

Exhibit 11.11 summarizes the results of much of Cress and Snow's (2000) analysis. It shows that homeless SMOs that were coded as organizationally viable used disruptive tactics, had sympathetic political allies, and

---

Exhibit 11.11   Multiple Pathways to Outcomes and Level of Impact

Pathways	Outcomes	Impact
1. VIABLE * DISRUPT * ALLIES * DIAG * PROG	Representation, Resources, Rights, and Relief	Very strong
2. VIABLE * disrupt * CITY * DIAG * PROG	Representation and Rights	Strong
3. VIABLE * ALLIES * CITY * DIAG * PROG	Resources and Relief	Moderate
4. viable * DISRUPT * allies * diag * PROG.	Relief	Weak
5. viable * allies * city * diag * PROG	Relief	Weak
6. viable * disrupt * ALLIES * CITY * diag * prog	Resources	Weak

Note: Uppercase letters indicate presence of condition and lowercase letters indicate the absence of a condition. Conditions not in the equation are considered irrelevant. Multiplication signs (*) are read as "and."

Source: Cress & Snow (2000:1097, Table 6). Copyright © 2000 University of Chicago Press. Reprinted with permission.

presented a coherent diagnosis and program in response to the problem they were protesting were very likely to achieve all four valued outcomes: (1) representation, (2) resources, (3) protection of basic rights, and (4) some form of tangible relief. Some other combinations of the conditions were associated with increased likelihood of achieving some valued outcomes, but most of these alternatives less frequently had positive effects.

The qualitative textual data on which the codes were based indicate how particular combinations of conditions exerted their influence. For example, one set of conditions that increased the likelihood of achieving increased protection of basic rights for homeless persons included avoiding disruptive tactics in cities that were more responsive to the SMOs. Cress and Snow (2000) use a quote from a local SMO leader to explain this process:

Researcher Interview Link
Comparative Research

> We were going to set up a picket, but then we got calls from two people who were the co-chairs of the Board of Directors. They have like 200 restaurants. And they said, "Hey, we're not bad guys, can we sit down and talk?" We had been set on picketing. . . . Then we got to thinking, wouldn't it be better . . . if they co-drafted those things [rights guidelines] with us? So that's what we asked them to do. We had a work meeting, and we hammered out the guidelines. (p. 1089)

In Chapter 13, you will learn more about qualitative comparative analysis and see how this type of method can be used to understand political processes.

Case-Oriented Understanding

Like many qualitative approaches, a **case-oriented understanding** attempts to understand a phenomenon from the standpoint of the participants. The case-oriented understanding method reflects an interpretive research philosophy that is not geared to identifying causes but provides a different way to explain social phenomena. For example, Constance Fischer and Frederick Wertz (2002) constructed such an explanation of the effect of being criminally victimized. They first recounted crime victims' stories and then identified common themes in these stories.

> **Case-oriented understanding:** An understanding of social processes in a group, formal organization, community, or other collectivity that reflects accurately the standpoint of participants.

> Their explanation began with a description of what they termed the process of "living routinely" *before the crime*: "he/she . . . feels that the defended against crime could never happen to him/her." "I said, 'nah, you've got to be kidding.'" (pp. 288–289, emphasis in original)

> In a second stage, "being disrupted," the victim copes with the discovered crime and fears worse outcomes: "You imagine the worst when it's happening . . . I just kept thinking my baby's upstairs." In a later stage, "reintegrating," the victim begins to assimilate the violation by taking some protective action: "But I clean out my purse now since then and I leave very little of that kind of stuff in there." (p. 289)

> Finally, when the victim is "going on," he or she reflects on the changes the crime produced: "I don't think it made me stronger. It made me smarter." (p. 290)

You can see how Fischer and Wertz (2002:288–290) constructed an explanation of the effect of crime on its victims through this analysis of the process of responding to the experience. This effort to "understand" what happened in these cases gives us a much better sense of why things happened as they did.

Combining Qualitative Methods

Qualitative researchers often combine one or more of these methods within one analysis. Elif Kale-Lostuvali (2007) enriched his research by using a combination of qualitative methodologies—including participant observation and intensive interviewing—to study the citizen–state encounters after the İzmit earthquake.

One important concept that emerged from both the observations and the interviews was the distinction between a *mag˘ dur* (sufferer) and a *depremzade* (son of the earthquake). This was a critical distinction, because a *mag˘ dur* was seen as deserving of government assistance, but a *depremzade* was considered to be taking advantage of the situation for personal gain. Kale-Lostuvali (2007) drew on both interviews and participant observation to develop an understanding of this complex concept:

> A prominent narrative that was told and retold in various versions all the time in the disaster area elaborated the contrast between *mag˘ dur* (sufferer; that is, the truly needy) and *depremzades* (sons of the earthquake) on the other. The *mag˘ dur* (sufferers) were the deserving recipients of the aid that was being distributed. However, they (1) were in great pain and could not pursue what they needed; or (2) were proud and could not speak of their need; or (3) were humble, always grateful for the little they got, and were certainly not after material gains; or (4) were characterized by a combination of the preceding. And because of these characteristics, they had not been receiving their rightful share of the aid and resources. In contrast, *depremzades* (sons of the earthquake) were people who took advantage of the situation. (p. 755)

The qualitative research by Spencer Moore and his colleagues (2004) on the social response to Hurricane Floyd demonstrates the interweaving of data from focus groups and from participant observation with relief workers.

> Reports of heroic acts by rescuers, innumerable accounts of "neighbors helping neighbors," and the comments of HWATF [task force] participants suggest that residents, stranded motorists, relief workers, and rescuers worked and came together in remarkable ways during the relief and response phases of the disaster.

> Like people get along better . . . they can talk to each other. People who hadn't talked before, they talk now, a lot closer. That goes, not only for the neighborhood, job-wise, organization-wise, and all that. . . . [Our] union sent some stuff for some of the families that were flooded out. (Focus Group #4) (pp. 210–211)

Analyses based on combining different qualitative methods in this way can yield a richer understanding of the social context under investigation.

Video Link
Mixed Methods

▣ Visual Sociology

For about 150 years, people have been creating a record of the social world with photography and more recently, with videos. This creates the possibility of "observing" the social world through photographs and films and of interpreting the resulting images as a "text." Some of the earliest U.S. sociologists included photographs in journal articles about social conditions, but the discipline turned away from visual representations by 1916 as part of a general effort to establish more scientific standards of evidence (Emmison, Smith, & Mayall 2012:23–24). Not until the 1970s did qualitative researchers Howard Becker (1974) and Erving Goffman (1979) again draw attention to the value of visual images in understanding social patterns. In more recent years, the availability of photos and videos has exploded because of the ease of taking them with smartphones; already by 2012, almost half of Internet users had posted original photos or videos online (Rainie, Brenner, & Purcell 2012), while by 2013, almost four billion photos had been uploaded and made publicly available at the photo-sharing Flickr site (http://www.flickr.com/photos/franck michel/6855169886/). As a result, increasing numbers of social scientists are collecting and analyzing visual representations of social life and **visual sociology** has become a growth industry.

> **Visual sociology:** Sociological research in which the social world is "observed" and interpreted through photographs, films, and other images.

CAREERS AND RESEARCH

Laurel Person Mecca, MA, Assistant Director and Senior Research Specialist, Qualitative Data Analysis Program

Laurel Person Mecca was uncertain of the exact career she wanted to pursue during her graduate studies at the University of Pittsburgh. Then she happened upon the University Center for Social & Urban Research (UCSUR). It's hard to imagine a better place to launch a research career involving qualitative data analysis. Since 2005, the center has provided services and consultation to investigators in qualitative data analysis. Mecca used UCSUR to recruit participants for her own research and then made it clear to staff that she would love to work there after finishing her degree. Fourteen years later, she enjoys her work there more than ever.

One of the greatest rewards Laurel has found in her work is the excitement of discovering the unexpected when her preconceived notions about what research participants will tell her turn out to be incorrect. She also finds that her interactions with research participants provide a unique view into peoples' lives, thus providing insights in her own life and a richer understanding of the human condition. And in addition to these personal benefits, Laurel has the satisfaction of seeing societal benefits from the projects she consults on: improving technologies designed to enhance independent living about elderly and disabled persons; exploring the barriers to participation in the Supplemental Nutrition Assistance Program (SNAP); evaluating a program to improve parent–adolescent communication about sexual behaviors to reduce sexually transmitted diseases (STDs) and unintended teen pregnancies.

Laurel has some very sound advice for students interested in careers involving doing research or using research results:

Gain on-the-job experience while in college, even if it is an unpaid internship. Find researchers who are conducting studies that interest you, and inquire about working for them. Even if they are not posting an available position, they may bring you on board. Persistence pays off! You are much more likely to be selected for a position if you demonstrate a genuine interest in the work and if you continue to show your enthusiasm by following up.

Definitely check out the National Science Foundation's (NSF) Research Experience for Undergraduates (REU) program. Though most of these internships are in the "hard" sciences, there are plenty of openings in social sciences disciplines. These internships include a stipend and, oftentimes, assistance with travel and housing. They are wonderful opportunities to work directly on a research project and may provide the additional benefit of a conference presentation and/or publication.

You have already seen in this chapter how Stokoe's conversation analysis of "gender talk" (2006) was enriched by her analysis of photographs. You also see later in this chapter how Robert Sampson and Stephen Raudenbush (1999) used systematic coding of videotaped observations to measure the extent of disorder in Chicago neighborhoods. Visual sociologists and other social researchers have been developing methods such as these to learn how others "see" the social world and to create images for further study. Continuous video recordings can help researchers unravel sequences of events and identify nonverbal expressions of feelings (Heath & Luff 2008:501). As in the analysis of written text, however, the visual sociologist must be sensitive to the way in which a photograph or film "constructs" the reality that it depicts.

The International Visual Sociology Association's (IVSA, http://visualsociology.org/about.html) statement of purpose identifies different ways in which visual images can be used in research.

Our Purpose

The purpose of IVSA is to promote the study, production, and use of imagery, visual data, and visually oriented materials in teaching, research, and applied activities. We also foster the use of still photography, film, video, and electronically transmitted images in sociology and other related fields. Together we work to encourage:

- documentary studies of everyday life in contemporary communities

- the interpretive analysis of art and popular visual representations of society

- studies about the social impact of advertising and the commercial use of images

- the analysis of archival images as sources of data on society and culture

- the study of the purpose and the meaning of image-making practices like recreational and family photography

The research by Stokoe and by Sampson and Raudenbush both illustrate the first approach, the use of visual materials to document everyday life in contemporary communities. In both of these projects, the pictures were not the central method used, but they both extended the analysis of the other, quantitative data and gave additional insight into the social processes studied. In an innovative visually based approach to studying interracial friendship patterns, Brent Berry (2006) sampled wedding photos that had been posted on the web. Reasoning that bridesmaids and groomsmen represent who newlyweds consider to be their best friends, Berry compared the rate of different-race members of wedding parties to the prevalence of different-race friends reported in representative surveys. As you can see in Exhibit 11.12, answers to

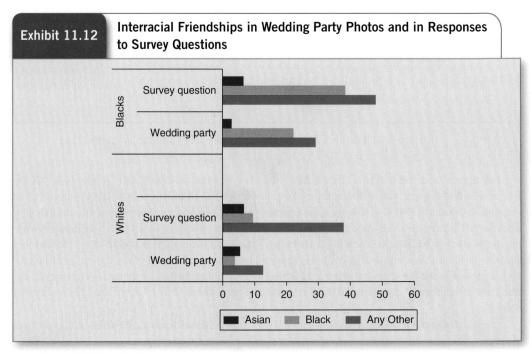

| **Exhibit 11.12** | **Interracial Friendships in Wedding Party Photos and in Responses to Survey Questions** |

Source: Berry (2006:501, Table 3).

survey questions create the impression that interracial friendships are considerably more common than is indicated by the actual wedding party photos.

Alternatively, the researcher can analyze visual materials created by others (Emmison et al. 2012:20–21). Most of the purposes listed by the IVSA reflect this use of visual materials to learn about a society and culture.

An analysis by Eric Margolis (2004) of photographic representations of American Indian boarding schools provides a good example of how the analysis of visual materials created by others can help us understand cultural change (Exhibit 11.13). On the left is a picture taken in 1886 of Chiricahua Apaches who had just arrived at the Carlisle Indian School in Carlisle, Pennsylvania. The school was run by Captain Richard Pratt, who, like many Americans in that period, felt tribal societies were communistic, indolent, dirty, and ignorant, whereas Western civilization was industrious and individualistic. So Pratt set out to acculturate American Indians to the dominant culture. The second picture shows the result: the same group of Apaches looking like Europeans, not Native Americans—dressed in standard uniforms, with standard haircuts, and with more standard posture.

Many other pictures display the same type of transformation. Are these pictures each "worth a thousand words"? They capture the ideology of the school management, but we can be less certain that they document accurately the "before and after" status of the students. Pratt "consciously used photography to represent the boarding school mission as successful" (Margolis 2004:79). Although he clearly tried to ensure a high degree of conformity, there were accusations that the contrasting images were exaggerated to overemphasize the change (Margolis 2004:78). Reality was being constructed, not just depicted, in these photographs. Visual sociologists must always consider the purposes for which pictures were created and the extent to which people consciously posed for the occasion (Tinkler 2013:31). Even more important, visual representations must be analyzed in the context of the associated text and other indications of the social context of the photos.

> It is important that visual researchers make every effort to situate the subject of their research and their specific take on it in its broader context, both visually and verbally. (Pauwels 2010:564)

Darren Newbury (2005:1) cautioned the readers of his journal, *Visual Studies,* "images cannot be simply taken of the world, but have to be made within it." Reflecting this insight (and consistent with the last IVSA purpose), **photo voice** is a method of using photography to engage research participants in explaining how they have made sense of their social worlds. Rather than using images from other sources, the researcher directing a photo voice project distributes cameras to research participants and invites them to take pictures of their surroundings or everyday activities. The participants then meet with the researcher to present their pictures and discuss their meaning. In this way, researchers learn more about the participants' social worlds as they see

> **Photo voice:** A method in which research participants take pictures of their everyday surroundings with cameras the researcher distributes, and then meet in a group with the researcher to discuss the pictures' meaning.

Exhibit 11.13	Pictures of Chiricahua Apache Children Before and After Starting Carlisle Indian School, Carlisle, Pennsylvania, 1886

Source: Margolis (2004:78).

Exhibit 11.14   Picture in Photo Voice Project

Source: Frohmann (2005:1407).

Audio Link
Visual Sociology

it and react to it. The photo voice method also engages participants as part of the research team themselves, thus enriching the researcher's interpretations of the social world.

Lisa Frohmann (2005) recruited 42 Latina and South Asian women from battered women's support groups in Chicago to participate in research about the meaning of violence in their lives. Frohman used photo voice methodology, so she gave each participant a camera. After they received some preliminary instruction, Frohmann invited participants to take about five to seven pictures weekly for 4 to 5 weeks. The photographs were to capture persons, places, and objects that represent the continuums of comfort–discomfort, happiness–sadness, safety–danger, security–vulnerability, serenity–anxiety, protection–exposure, strength–weakness, and love–hate (Exhibit 11.14). Twenty-nine women then returned to discuss the results.

With this very simple picture, one participant, Jenny, described how family violence affected her feelings:

This is the dining room table and I took this picture because the table is empty and I feel that although I am with my children, I feel that it is empty because there is no family harmony, which I think is the most important thing. (Frohmann 2005:1407)

The image and narrative indirectly represent Jenny's concept of family: a husband and wife who love each other and their children. Food and eating together are important family activities. Part of caring for her family, is preparing food. The photo shows that her concept of family is fractured (Frohmann 2005:1407).

Analysis of visual materials can also be used to enrich data collected with other methods. UK researchers Nick Emmel and Andrew Clark (2011) discuss how photographs collected in "walkarounds" enriched their understanding of the social setting they studied.

The research is situated in one geographical location or fieldsite. Periodically we walked through this field along a set pathway taking photographs. . . . The research is conducted in a geographical place covering around 1.5 mile^2 (circa 2.5 km^2) with a mixed population. Relatively affluent students live in close proximity to one of the most deprived populations in England. . . . Within this socially heterogeneous geographical context our research explores, among other aims, the ways different social groups create, maintain, dissemble and experience, social networks over time and across space.

We each use the photographs we take on the walk as an adjunct to the other methods we are using in the research. . . . . They contribute to and facilitate an interpretation of place, which in turn provides a more complete account of the place and space in which we are doing research.

. . . how this analytical process happens. The panorama [see Exhibit 11.15] could be analysed at face value as an empty play area; perhaps supporting ideas about the out-migration of families (a common theme discussed by some resident groups). . . . Subsequent questioning about play spaces in the area however, reveals a range of alternative explanations for under-use. For example, conversational interviews with young people reveal a more nuanced geography of play and socialisation in the area; informal discussion with a local official suggest [*sic*] infrastructural problems with this particular space, while analysis of the recent history of this play space hints at a more political explanation for its existence and apparent under-use. This means that I do not analyse the images alone (that is, as a discrete data set); but rather alongside other

Exhibit 11.15 **A Playground in the Fieldsite of Emmel and Clark**

Source: Emmel and Clark (2011).

methods. . . . Finally, . . . I use the walkaround method as a way of formulating new questions to ask of participants in the other methods. In some respects, it is the making of the photograph (deciding whether, and what, to photograph and why), rather than the image itself, that is more analytically revealing.

Systematic Observation

Observations can be made in a more systematic, quantitative design that allows systematic comparisons and more confident generalizations. A researcher using **systematic observation** develops a standard form on which to record variation within the observed setting in terms of variables of interest. Such variables might include the frequency of some behavior(s), the particular people observed, the weather or other environmental conditions, and the number and state of repair of physical structures. In some systematic observation studies, records will be obtained from a random sample of places or times.

> **Systematic observation:** A strategy that increases the reliability of observational data by using explicit rules that standardize coding practices across observers.

Sampson and Raudenbush's (1999) study of disorder and crime in urban neighborhoods provides an excellent example of systematic observation methods. Although you learned about some features of this pathbreaking research in Chapter 6, in this section I elaborate on their use of systematic social observation to learn about these neighborhoods. A systematic observational strategy increases the reliability of observational data by using explicit rules that standardize coding practices across observers (Reiss 1971b). It is a method particularly well suited to overcome one of the limitations of survey research on crime and disorder: Residents who are fearful of crime perceive more neighborhood disorder than do residents who are less fearful, even though both are observing the same neighborhood (Sampson & Raudenbush 1999:606).

This ambitious multiple-methods investigation combined observational research, survey research, and archival research. The observational component involved a stratified probability (random) sample of

196 Chicago census tracts. A specially equipped sport-utility vehicle was driven down each street in these tracts at the rate of 5 miles per hour. Two video recorders taped the blocks on both sides of the street, while two observers peered out of the vehicle's windows and recorded their observations in the logs. The result was an observational record of 23,816 face blocks (the block on one side of the street is a face block). The observers recorded in their logs codes that indicated land use, traffic, physical conditions, and evidence of physical disorder (see Exhibit 11.16). The videotapes were sampled and then coded for 126 variables, including housing characteristics, businesses, and social interactions. Physical disorder was measured by counting such features as cigarettes or cigars in the street, garbage, empty beer bottles, graffiti, condoms, and syringes. Indicators of social disorder included adults loitering, drinking alcohol in public, fighting, and selling drugs. To check for reliability, a different set of coders recoded the videos for 10% of the blocks. The repeat codes achieved 98% agreement with the original codes.

Sampson and Raudenbush also measured crime levels with data from police records, census tract socioeconomic characteristics with census data, and resident attitudes and behavior with a survey. As you learned in Chapter 6, the combination of data from these sources allowed a test of the relative impact on the crime rate of informal social control efforts by residents and of the appearance of social and physical disorder.

Peter St. Jean (2007) extended the research of Sampson and Raudenbush with a mixed-methods study of high crime areas that used resident surveys, participant observation, in-depth interviews with residents and offenders, and systematic social observation. St. Jean recorded neighborhood physical and social appearances with video cameras mounted in a van that was driven along neighborhood streets. Pictures were then coded for the presence of neighborhood disorder (see Exhibit 11.17 and the Student Study Site for this book).

This study illustrates both the value of multiple methods and the technique of recording observations in a form from which quantitative data can be obtained. The systematic observations give us much greater confidence in the measurement of relative neighborhood disorder than we would have from unstructured descriptive reports or from responses of residents to survey questions. Interviews with residents and participant observation helped identify the reasons that offenders chose particular locations when deciding where to commit crimes.

▥ Participatory Action Research

Participatory action research (PAR):
A type of research in which the researcher involves members of the population to be studied as active participants throughout the research process, from the selection of a research focus to the reporting of research results and efforts to make changes based on the research; also termed *community-based participatory research.*

Whyte (1991) urged social researchers to engage with research participants throughout the research process. He formalized this recommendation into an approach he termed **participatory action research (PAR)**. As the name implies, this approach encourages social researchers to get "out of the academic rut" and bring values into the research process (p. 285). Since Whyte's early call for this type of research, with a focus on research with organizational employees, PAR has become increasingly popular in disciplines ranging from public health to social work, as well as sociology (McIntyre 2008; Minkler 2000). Participatory action research is not itself a qualitative method, but PAR projects tend to use qualitative methods, which are more accessible to members of the lay public and which normally involve some of the same activities as in PAR: engaging with individuals in their natural settings and listening to them in their own words.

In PAR, also termed *community-based participatory research* (CBPR), the researcher involves as active participants some members of the setting studied. "The goal of CBPR is to create an effective translational process that will increase bidirectional connections between academics and the communities that they study" (Hacker 2013:2). Both the members and the researcher are assumed to want to develop valid conclusions, to bring unique insights, and to desire change, but Whyte (1991) believed that these objectives were more likely to be obtained if the researcher collaborates actively with the persons being studied. For example, many academic studies have found that employee participation is associated with job satisfaction but not with employee productivity. After some discussion about this finding with employees and managers, Whyte real-

Exhibit 11.16	Neighborhood Disorder Indicators Used in Systematic Observation Log

Variable	Category	Frequency
Physical Disorder		
Cigarettes, cigars on street or gutter	no	6,815
	yes	16,758
Garbage, litter on street or sidewalk	no	11,680
	yes	11,925
Empty beer bottles visible in street	no	17,653
	yes	5,870
Tagging graffiti	no	12,859
	yes	2,252
Graffiti painted over	no	13,390
	yes	1,721
Gang graffiti	no	14,138
	yes	973
Abandoned cars	no	22,782
	yes	806
Condoms on sidewalk	no	23,331
	yes	231
Needles/syringes on sidewalk	no	23,392
	yes	173
Political message graffiti	no	15,097
	yes	14
Social Disorder		
Adults loitering or congregating	no	14,250
	yes	861
People drinking alcohol	no	15,075
	yes	36
Peer group, gang indicators present	no	15,091
	yes	20
People intoxicated	no	15,093
	yes	18
Adults fighting or hostilely arguing	no	15,099
	yes	12
Prostitutes on street	no	15,100
	yes	11
People selling drugs	no	15,099
	yes	12

Source: Raudenbush and Sampson (1999:15).

| Exhibit 11.17 | One Building in St. Jean's (2007) Study |

Source: © Peter K. B. St. Jean. Reprinted with permission.

Video Link
St. Jean Research

ized that researchers had been using a general concept of employee participation that did not distinguish those aspects of participation that were most likely to influence productivity (pp. 278–279). For example, occasional employee participation in company meetings had not been distinguished from ongoing employee participation in and control of production decisions. When these and other concepts were defined more precisely, it became clear that employee participation in production decisions had substantially increased overall productivity, whereas simple meeting attendance had not. This discovery would not have occurred without the active involvement of company employees in planning the research.

Those who engage in PAR projects are making a commitment "to listen to, learn from, solicit and respect the contributions of, and share power, information, and credit for accomplishments with the groups that they are trying [to] learn about and help" (Horowitz, Robinson, & Seifer 2009:2634). The emphasis on developing a partnership with the community is reflected in the characteristics of the method presented in a leading health journal (see Exhibit 11.18). Each characteristic (with the exception of "emphasis on multiple determinants of health") identifies a feature of the researcher's relationship with community members.

PAR can bring researchers into closer contact with participants in the research setting through groups that discuss and plan research steps and then take steps to implement research findings. For this reason, PAR is "particularly useful for emergent problems for which community partners are in search of solutions but evidence is lacking" (Hacker 2013:8). Stephen Kemmis and Robin McTaggart (2005:563–568) summarize the key steps in the process of conducting a PAR project as creating "a spiral of self-reflecting cycles":

- Planning a change

- Acting and observing the process and consequences of the change

- Reflecting on these processes and consequences

Exhibit 11.18	Characteristics of Community-Based Participatory Research (CBPR)

Community members and researchers contribute equally and in all phases of research.

Trust, collaboration, shared decision making, and shared ownership of the research; findings and knowledge benefit all partners.

Researchers and community members recognize each other's expertise in bidirectional, colearning process.

Balance rigorous research and tangible community action.

Embrace skills, strength, resources, and assets of local individuals and organizations.

Community recognized as a unit of identity.

Emphasis on multiple determinants of health.

Partners commit to long-term research relationships.

Core elements include local capacity building, system development, empowerment, and sustainability.

Source: Horowitz, Carol R., Mimsie Robinson, and Sarena Seifer. 2009. "Community-Based Participatory Research from the Margin to the Mainstream: Are Researchers Prepared?" *Circulation* May 19, 2009. Table 1, Characteristics of CBPR, p. 2634. Reprinted with permission of Wolters Kluwer Health, LWW.

- Replanning

- Acting and observing again

In contrast with the formal reporting of results at the end of a research project, these cycles make research reporting an ongoing part of the research process. "Community partners can deepen the interpretation process once results are available, as they are intimately familiar with the context and meaning" (Hacker 2013:8). Community partners may also work with the academic researchers to make changes in the community reflecting the research findings. Publication of results is only part of the process.

Karen Hacker, while at Harvard University and the Institute for Community Health in Cambridge, Massachusetts, collaborated with community partners in response to a public health emergency in the adjacent town of Somerville (Hacker 2013:8–10; Hacker et al. 2008). After a series of youth suicides and overdoses from 2000 to 2005, a PAR community coalition was formed with members from mental health service providers, school leaders, police, and community parents. After reviewing multiple statistics, the coalition concluded that the deaths represented a considerable increase over previous years. However, when mental health professionals attempted to interview family members of adolescents who had committed suicide to investigate the background to the suicides, they were rebuffed; in contrast, family members were willing to talk at length with PAR members from their community. The PAR team was then able to map the relationships between the suicide victims. The process of using the results of this research to respond to the suicides included a candlelight vigil, a speak-out against substance abuse, the provision of crisis counseling, and programs to support families and educate the community. Subsequently, the suicide rate dropped back to its pre-2000 level.

Computer-Assisted Qualitative Data Analysis

The analysis process can be enhanced in various ways by using a computer. Programs designed for qualitative data can speed up the analysis process, make it easier for researchers to experiment with different codes, test different hypotheses about relationships, and facilitate diagrams of emerging theories and preparation of research reports (Coffey & Atkinson 1996; Richards & Richards 1994). The steps involved in **computer-assisted qualitative data analysis** parallel those used traditionally to

Computer-assisted qualitative data analysis: Uses special computer software to assist qualitative analyses through creating, applying, and refining categories; tracing linkages between concepts; and making comparisons between cases and events.

analyze text such as notes, documents, or interview transcripts: preparation, coding, analysis, and reporting. We use three of the most popular programs to illustrate these steps: HyperRESEARCH, QSR NVivo, and ATLAS.ti. (A free trial version of HyperRESEARCH and tutorials can be downloaded from the ResearchWare site, at http://www.researchware.com.)

Text preparation begins with typing or scanning text in a word processor or, with NVivo, directly into the program's rich text editor. NVivo will create or import a rich text file. HyperRESEARCH requires that your text be saved as a text file (as "ASCII" in most word processors) before you transfer it into the analysis program. HyperRESEARCH expects your text data to be stored in separate files corresponding to each unique case, such as an interview with one subject. These programs now allow multiple types of files, including pictures and videos as well as text. Exhibit 11.19 displays the different file types and how they are connected in the organization of a project (a "hermeneutic unit") with ATLAS.ti.

Coding the text involves categorizing particular text segments. This is the foundation of much qualitative analysis. Each program allows you to assign a code to any segment of text (in NVivo, you drag through the characters to select them; in HyperRESEARCH, you click on the first and last words to select text). You can make up codes as you go through a document and assign codes that you have already developed to text segments. Exhibit 11.20 shows the screens that appear in HyperRESEARCH and NVivo at the coding stage, when a particular text is "autocoded" by identifying a word or phrase that should always receive the same code, or, in NVivo, by coding each section identified by the style of the rich text document—for example, each question or speaker (of course, you should check carefully the results of autocoding). Both programs also let you examine the coded text "in context"—embedded in its place in the original document.

In qualitative data analysis, coding is not a one-time-only or one-code-only procedure. Each program allows you to be inductive and holistic in your coding: You can revise codes as you go along, assign multiple codes to text segments, and link your own comments ("memos") to text segments. You can work "live" with the coded text to alter coding or create new, more subtle categories. You can also place hyperlinks to other documents in the project or to any multimedia files outside it.

| Exhibit 11.19 | File Types and Unit Structure in ATLAS.ti |

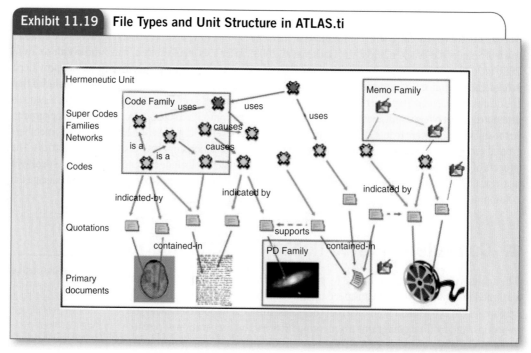

Source: Muhr and Friese (2004:29).

Exhibit 11.20a HyperRESEARCH Coding Stage

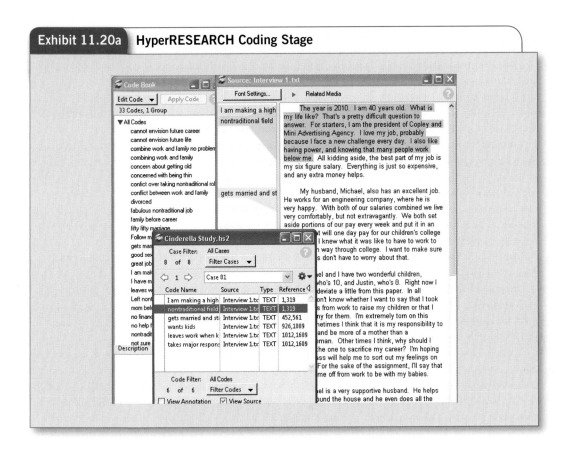

Exhibit 11.20b NVivo Coding Stage

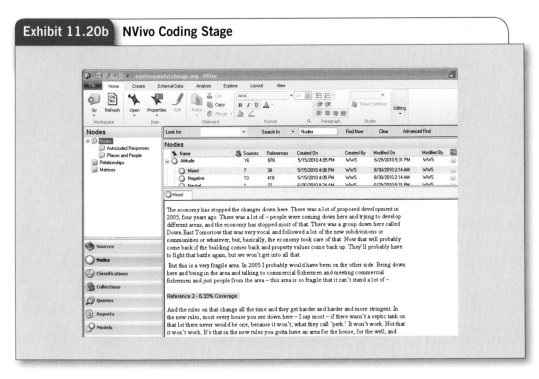

Analysis focuses on reviewing cases or text segments with similar codes and examining relationships between different codes. You may decide to combine codes into larger concepts. You may specify additional codes to capture more fully the variation between cases. You can test hypotheses about relationships between codes and develop more free-form models (see Exhibit 11.21). You can specify combinations of codes that identify cases that you want to examine.

Reports from each program can include text to illustrate the cases, codes, and relationships that you specify. You can also generate counts of code frequencies and then import these counts into a statistical program for quantitative analysis. However, the many types of analyses and reports that can be developed with qualitative analysis software do not lessen the need for a careful evaluation of the quality of the data on which conclusions are based.

In reality, using a qualitative data analysis computer program is not always as straightforward as it appears. Scott Decker and Barrik Van Winkle (1996) describe the difficulty they faced in using a computer program to identify instances of the concept of *drug sales*:

> The software we used is essentially a text retrieval package. . . . One of the dilemmas faced in the use of such software is whether to employ a coding scheme within the interviews or simply to leave them as unmarked text. We chose the first alternative, embedding conceptual tags at the appropriate points in the text. An example illustrates this process. One of the activities we were concerned with was drug sales. Our first chore (after a thorough reading of all the transcripts) was to use the software to "isolate" all of the transcript sections dealing with drug sales. One way to do this would be to search the transcripts for every instance in which the word "drugs" was used. However, such a strategy would have the disadvantages of providing information of too general a character while often missing important statements about drugs. Searching on the word "drugs" would have produced a file including every time the word was used, whether it was in reference to drug sales, drug use, or drug availability, clearly more information than we were interested in. However, such a search would have failed to find all of the slang used to refer to drugs ("boy" for heroin, "Casper" for crack cocaine) as well as the more common descriptions of drugs, especially rock or crack cocaine. (pp. 53–54)

Exhibit 11.21 A Free-Form Model in NVivo

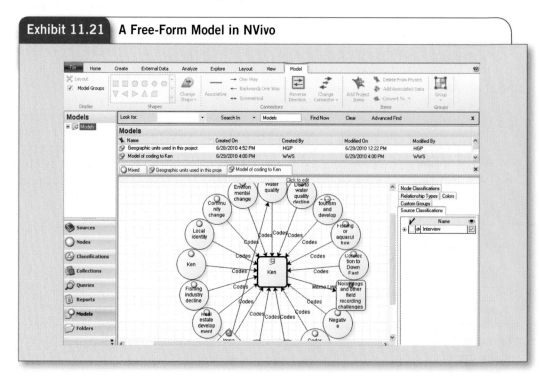

Decker and Van Winkle (1996) solved this problem by parenthetically inserting conceptual tags in the text whenever talk of drug sales was found. This process allowed them to examine all the statements made by gang members about a single concept (drug sales). As you can imagine, however, this still left the researchers with many pages of transcript material to analyze.

Ethics in Qualitative Data Analysis

The qualitative data analyst is never far from ethical issues and dilemmas. Data collection should not begin unless the researcher has a plan that others see as likely to produce useful knowledge. Relations developed with research participants and other stakeholders to facilitate data collection should also be used to keep these groups informed about research progress and findings. Research participants should be encouraged to speak out about emerging study findings (Lincoln 2009:154–155). Decisions to reproduce photos and other visual materials must be considered in light of privacy and copyright issues. Throughout the analytic process, the analyst must consider how the findings will be used and how participants in the setting will react. The need to minimize harm requires attention even after data collection has concluded.

As I noted in the last chapter, some indigenous peoples have established rules for outside researchers to minimize harm to their community and preserve their autonomy. These rules may require collaboration with an indigenous researcher, collective approval of admission to their culture, and review of all research products before publication. The primary ethical commitment is to the welfare of the community as a whole and the preservation of their culture, rather than to the rights of individuals (Lincoln 2009:162–163).

Participatory action research projects create special challenges because the researcher is likely to feel divided loyalties to the community and the university. Even though it may be difficult for researchers to disagree with the interpretations of community members about the implications of research findings, they may feel that a different interpretation is warranted (Sieber & Tolich 2013:94, 102–104). Qualitative researchers need to be sensitive to the potential for these problems and respond flexibly and respectfully to the concerns of research participants (Hacker 2013:109–110). Allowing community leaders and members to comment on the researcher's interpretations is one way to lessen feelings of exclusion. However, it is also important to recognize that "the community" does not refer to a homogeneous singular entity.

> when dealing with human communities; groups are actually made up of individuals, and the interests of the group do not necessarily converge with those of the individuals that constitute it. (Levinson 2010:205)

Qualitative researchers should also take care to consider harm that might occur along all points in the research process. In particular, staff who transcribe interview or focus group transcripts may not seem a part of the formal research process—and may even be independent contractors who are only contacted through the Internet—but they may react emotionally to some of the material in particularly charged interviews. In projects where transcripts contain emotionally charged material, those used as transcriptionists should be given advance warning, and providing connections to counselors should be considered (Sieber & Tolich 2013:175).

Miles and Huberman (1994:293–295) suggest several specific questions that are particularly important during the process of data analysis.

Privacy, confidentiality, and anonymity. "In what ways will the study intrude, come closer to people than they want? How will information be guarded? How identifiable are the individuals and organizations studied?" We have considered this issue already in the context of qualitative data collection, but it also must be a concern during the process of analysis. It can be difficult to present a rich description in a case study while not identifying the setting. It can be easy for participants in the study to identify each other in a qualitative description, even if outsiders cannot.

I confronted the challenge of maintaining confidentiality in my analysis of ethnographic notes collected in the study of housing for homeless persons diagnosed with severe mental illness that I used in the previous chapter to illustrate field notes. I explained the dilemma and the approach I took in the methodological appendix to *Homelessness, Housing, and Mental Illness* (Schutt 2011b:317–318).

> It is not possible to understand what happened in the [six] houses, or to consider possible explanations for particular events, without reading detailed descriptions of what people did and having at least some examples of what people said. But providing such details about specific identified group homes would often reveal who it was who was speaking or acting, at least to former housing staff and participants.
>
> In order to avoid providing intimate and possibly identifiable stories about participants, I have adhered throughout this book to three more specific guidelines. First, I have used arbitrary pseudonyms to refer to everyone whose name appears in the ethnographic notes that I include. Sometimes, I simply refer to individuals by their role, such as "tenant" or "house staff." Second, I have not maintained consistent pseudonyms for individual participants across chapters or even across different incidents that I describe within chapters. This greatly reduces the risk that even a former participant could determine another's identity by gradually being able to imagine the person as I describe different things they said or did. Third, I do not link the activities or statements I report to the individual houses. Since there were only seven different project group homes (six at any one time), it would be much easier for a former participant to link some actions or statements to another participant if the house in which they occurred were identified. However, every group home in our project experienced many of the same types of incidents and interchanges, so by not distinguishing the houses, I left the statements difficult to connect to particular individuals.
>
> Of course this procedure for maintaining participant confidentiality has a cost for the analysis: I cannot "tell the story" of the development of particular houses with the ethnographic details about the houses. However, review of the notes from all the group homes indicates that the similarities in the issues they confronted far outweighed their differences. Moreover, our three ethnographers varied in their styles of observing, interviewing, and even note-taking, so that explicit comparisons of particular houses could be only partial. So maintaining the confidentiality of the individual group homes seems prudent from a methodological standpoint as well as essential from the standpoint of protecting the confidentiality of our research participants.

In ethnographic and other participant studies where initial access is negotiated with community leaders or with groups of participants, qualitative researchers should discuss with participants the approach that will be taken to protect privacy and maintain confidentiality. Selected participants should also be asked to review reports or other products before their public release to gauge the extent to which they feel privacy has been appropriately preserved. Research with photographs that identify individuals raises special ethical concerns. Although legal standards are evolving, it is important not to violate an individual's expectations of privacy in any setting and to seek informed consent for the use of images when privacy is expected (Tinkler 2013:196–198).

Intervention and advocacy. "What do I do when I see harmful, illegal, or wrongful behavior on the part of others during a study? Should I speak for anyone's interests besides my own? If so, whose interests do I advocate?" Maintaining what is called *guilty knowledge* may force the researcher to suppress some parts of the analysis so as not to disclose the wrongful behavior, but presenting "what really happened" in a report may prevent ongoing access and violate understandings with participants. The need for intervention and advocacy is more likely to be anticipated in PAR/CBPR projects because they involve ongoing engagement with community partners who are likely to have an action orientation (Hacker 2013:101–104).

Research integrity and quality. "Is my study being conducted carefully, thoughtfully, and correctly in terms of some reasonable set of standards?" Real analyses have real consequences, so you owe it to yourself and those you study to adhere strictly to the analysis methods that you believe will produce authentic, valid conclusions. Visual images that demean individuals or groups should not be included in publications (Tinkler 2013:197).

Ownership of data and conclusions. "Who owns my field notes and analyses: I, my organization, my funders? And once my reports are written, who controls their diffusion?" Of course, these concerns arise in any social research project, but the intimate involvement of the qualitative researcher with participants in the setting studied makes conflicts of interest between different stakeholders much more difficult to resolve. Working through the issues as they arise is essential. Mitch Duneier (1999:319–330) decided to end *Sidewalk*, his ethnography of New York City sidewalk book vendors, with an afterword by one of his key informants. Such approaches that allow participants access to conclusions in advance and the privilege to comment on them should be considered in relation to qualitative projects. The public availability of visual images on websites does not eliminate concerns about ownership. Copyright law in the United States as well as in the United Kingdom and Australia provides copyright to content on the Internet as soon as it is uploaded, but there are disagreements about the requirement of informed consent before reproducing images from publicly accessible sites (Tinkler 2013:204–205). Researchers leading PAR/CBPR projects must work out data ownership agreements in advance of data collection to ensure there are no misunderstandings about retention of data and maintenance of confidentiality after the project ends (Hacker 2013:99–100).

Use and misuse of results. "Do I have an obligation to help my findings be used appropriately? What if they are used harmfully or wrongly?" It is prudent to develop understandings early in the project with all major stakeholders that specify what actions will be taken to encourage appropriate use of project results and to respond to what is considered misuse of these results. Visual researchers must also consider how participants will feel about their images appearing in publications in the future (Wiles et al. 2012:48).

> People take part in our research, and they don't think in terms of publications arising years and years later. . . . So I think there are lots of problems, even when you have formally and legally the consent they have signed, because it refers to much earlier . . . she might have changed, it's a few years, she might feel very differently, it might remind her now of something very unpleasant. (Youth researcher, focus group 3)

PAR/CBPR projects are designed to help solve local problems, but harm might also occur if results are not what were expected or if some findings cast some elements of the community in an unfavorable light. These possibilities should be addressed as the analysis progresses and resolved before they are publicized (Hacker 2013:114–117).

▣ Conclusions

The variety of approaches to qualitative data analysis makes it difficult to provide a consistent set of criteria for interpreting their quality. Norman Denzin's (2002:362–363) "interpretive criteria" are a good place to start. Denzin suggests that at the conclusion of their analyses, qualitative data analysts ask the following questions about the materials they have produced. Reviewing several of them will serve as a fitting summary for your understanding of the qualitative analysis process.

- *Do they illuminate the phenomenon as lived experience?* In other words, do the materials bring the setting alive in terms of the people in that setting?

Exhibit 12.4   Alameda Family Justice Center Logic Model

Inputs	Activities	Outcomes	Impacts	Goals

• On-site partners
• Intake systems
• Client management process
• Space design
• Site location
	FJC
	• Case management
	• Assistance with restraining orders
	• Assistance with police reports
	• Legal assistance
	• Advocacy
	• Medical care
	• Forensic exams
	• Assessments and referral for treatment
	• Counseling
	• Safety planning
	• Emergency food/cash/transportation
	• Referral for shelter and other ongoing care
	• Assistance with public assistance
	• 24-hour helpline
	• Parenting classes
	• Child care
	• Rape crises services
	• Faith-based services
	• Job training
	• Translation services
		Victims
		• Increase likelihood to access services
		• Increase demand for services
		• Increase usage of services
		• Increase frequency of cross-referrals or use of multiple services
			Victims
			• Reduce tendency to blame oneself for abuse
			• Reduce conditions prevent women from leaving
			• Increase likelihood of reporting incident
			• Increase likelihood of request for temporary/permanent restraining orders
			• Increase likelihood of participating in prosecution
				• Decrease incidents of DV
				  ○ Decreased repeat victimizations
				  ○ Decreased seriousness
				• Hold offenders accountable
				  ○ Decrease repeat offenders
				• Break cycle of violence

	Community • Early intervention and prevention programming • FJC informational materials	**Community** • Increase knowledge of DV/SA/elder abuse • Increase awareness of services available	**Community** • Increase awareness of FJC • Decrease social tolerance for VAW*	

*violence against women

Inputs	Activities	Outcomes	Impacts	Goals
	Systems	**Systems**	**Systems**	
	• Collaboration between government and nongov't providers • Improve access to batterer information	• Improve DV policies and procedures • Increase understanding of each other's services • Increase coordination of services	• Improve institutional response to DV • Decrease secondary trauma • Increase assurance of victim safety • Increase the number of successful criminal legal actions • Increase the number of successful civil legal actions	

Source: From Meg Townsend, Dana Hunt, Caity Baxter, and Peter Finn. 2005. *Interim Report: Evaluability Assessment of the President's Family Justice Center Initiative.* Cambridge, MA: Abt Associates Inc. Reprinted with permission.

Exhibit 12.5	**Components of D.A.R.E. and Other Alcohol and Drug Prevention Programs Rated as Very Satisfactory (%)**

Components	D.A.R.E. Program (N = 222)	Other AOD* Programs (N = 406)
Curriculum	67.5%	34.2%
Teaching	69.7%	29.8%
Administrative Requirements	55.7%	23.1%
Receptivity of Students	76.5%	34.6%
Effects on Students	63.2%	22.8%

*Alcohol and Other Drugs

Source: Ringwalt et al. (1994:58).

Process evaluation also can be used to identify the specific aspects of the service delivery process that have an impact. This, in turn, will help explain why the program has an effect and which conditions are required for these effects. (In Chapter 6, I described this as identifying the causal mechanism.) Implementation problems identified in site visits included insufficient numbers of officers to carry out the program as planned and a lack of Spanish-language D.A.R.E. books in a largely Hispanic school. Classroom observations indicated engaging presentations and active student participation (Ringwalt et al. 1994:58). Sloboda et al.'s (2009) evaluation of the trial *Take Care of Your Life* curriculum found that D.A.R.E. officers delivered all of the lessons and 73% of the

CHAPTER **13**

Historical and Comparative Research and Content Analysis

Although the United States and several European nations have maintained democratic systems of governance for more than 100 years, democratic rule has more often been brief and unstable, when it has occurred at all. What explains the presence of democratic practices in one country and their absence in another? Are democratic politics a realistic option for every nation? What about Libya? Egypt?

Research That Matters, Questions That Count

Is an increase in democratic freedoms in nations associated with greater representation of women in powerful political positions? Prior research indicates that this is not the case; in fact, case studies have shown a drop in women's representation in government in some countries that have adopted democratic forms of governance. However, there are many complicating factors in the histories of particular nations, including whether gender quotas were implemented and the nature of the prior regime. Kathleen Fallon, Liam Swiss, and Jocelyn Viterna designed a historical comparative research project to investigate in more depth this "democracy paradox."

Fallon, Swiss, and Viterna designed a quantitative study of the "democratization process" in 118 developing countries over a 34-year period. The dependent variable in the analysis was the percentage of seats held by women in the national legislature or its equivalent. The researchers distinguished countries transitioning from civil strife, authoritarian regimes, and communist regimes and they accounted for the use of quotas for women as well as the extent of democratic practices and the differences in national culture.

The results indicate that women's legislative representation drops after democratizing changes begin, but then increases with additional elections. However, the strength of this pattern varies with the type of pre-democratic regime and the use of quotas. The nature of the *process* of democratic change is critical to understanding its outcome for women.

1. Would you expect countries that are more democratic to have more representation of women in government? Why or why not? How would you design a research project to test your ideas?

2. Fallon, Swiss, and Viterna review separately the quantitative studies and qualitative studies conducted in the past about democratization and women's political power. What approach do you think would be most likely to improve understanding of this association? Explain your reasoning.

In this chapter, you will learn how researchers use historical and comparative methods to examine social processes over time and between countries or other large units, as well as some of the findings about democratization. By the end of the chapter, you will understand the primary steps involved in the different types of historical and comparative methods and some of the potential pitfalls with such methods. After you finish the chapter, test yourself by reading the 2012 *American Sociological Review* article by Kathleen Fallon, Liam Swiss, and Jocelyn Viterna at the *Investigating the Social World* study site and completing the related interactive exercises for Chapter 13 at edge .sagepub.com/schutt8e.

Fallon, Kathleen M., Liam Swiss, and Jocelyn Viterna. 2012. "Resolving the Democracy Paradox: Democratization and Women's Legislative Representation in Developing Nations, 1975 to 2009." *American Sociological Review* 77(3):380–408.

Iraq? Are there some prerequisites in historical experience, cultural values, or economic resources? (Markoff 2005:384–386). A diverse set of methodological tools allows us to investigate social processes at other times and in other places, when the actual participants in these processes are not available.

Historical and comparative research methods can generate new insights into social processes because of their ability to focus on aspects of the social world beyond recent events in one country. These methods involve several different approaches and a diverse set of techniques, and they may have qualitative or quantitative components. They provide ways to investigate topics that usually cannot be studied with experiments, participant observation, or surveys. However, because this broader focus involves collecting data from records about the past or from other nations, the methods used in historical and comparative investigations present unique challenges to social researchers.

In this chapter, I review the major methods social scientists use to understand historical processes and to compare different societies or regions. I also introduce oral histories, a qualitative tool for historical

Journal Link
Quantitative Research of
Democratization Process

> **Content analysis:** A research method for systematically analyzing and making inferences from recorded human communication, including books, articles, poems, constitutions, speeches, and songs.

investigations, as well as demographic methods, which can strengthen both historical and comparative studies.

Content analysis can be used in historical and comparative research, but is also useful in studies of communication with any type of media. Therefore, like most historical and comparative methods, content analysis can be called an *unobtrusive method* that does not need to involve interacting with live people. Content analysis methods usually begin with text, speech broadcasts, or visual images. The content analyst develops procedures for coding various aspects of the textual, aural (spoken), or visual material and then analyzes this coded content.

Throughout the chapter, I will draw many examples from research on democracy and the process of democratization.

 Overview of Historical and Comparative Research Methods

Encyclopedia Link
Comparative Research

The central insight behind historical and comparative research is that we can improve our understanding of social processes when we make comparisons to other times and places. Max Weber's comparative study of world religions (Bendix 1962) and Émile Durkheim's (1984) historical analysis of the division of labor are two examples of the central role of historical and comparative research during the period sociology emerged as a discipline. Although the popularity of this style of research ebbed with the growth of survey methods and statistical analysis in the 1930s, exemplary works such as Reinhard Bendix's (1956) *Work and Authority in Industry* and Barrington Moore Jr.'s (1966) *Social Origins of Democracy and Dictatorship* helped to fuel a resurgence of historical and comparative methods in the 1970s and 1980s that has continued into the 21st century (Lange 2013:22–33).

Historical and comparative methods are a diverse collection of approaches that can involve combinations of other methods presented in this text (Lange 2013). Research may be historical, comparative, or both historical and comparative. There are no hard-and-fast rules for determining how far in the past the focus of research must be to consider it historical or what types of comparisons are needed to warrant calling research comparative. In practice, research tends to be considered historical when it focuses on a period before the experience of most of those conducting research (Abbott 1994:80). Research involving different nations is usually considered comparative, but so are studies of different regions within one nation if they emphasize interregional comparison. In recent years, the globalization of U.S. economic ties and the internationalization of scholarship have increased the use of unobtrusive methods for comparative research across many different countries (Kotkin 2002). Historical and comparative methods can be quantitative or qualitative, or a mixture of both. Both nomothetic and idiographic approaches to establishing causal effects can be used.

> **Historical events research:** Research in which social events are studied at one past time period.
>
> **Historical process research:** Research in which historical processes are studied over a long time.
>
> **Cross-sectional comparative research:** Research comparing data from one time period between two or more nations.
>
> **Comparative historical research:** Research comparing data from more than one time period in more than one nation.

Distinguishing research with a historical or comparative focus results in four basic types of research: **historical events research**, **historical process research**, **cross-sectional comparative research**, and **comparative historical research**. Research that focuses on events in one short historical period is historical events research, whereas longitudinal research that traces a sequence of events over a number of years is historical process research (see, for example, Skocpol 1984:359). There are also two types of comparative research, the first involving cross-sectional comparisons and the second comparing longitudinal data about historical processes between multiple cases. The resulting four types of research are displayed in Exhibit 13.1.

Historical Social Science Methods

Both historical events research and historical process research investigate questions concerning past times. These methods are used increasingly by social scientists in sociology, anthropology, political science, and economics, as well as by many historians (Monkkonen 1994). The late 20th and early 21st centuries have seen so much change in so many countries that many scholars have felt a need to investigate the background of these changes and to refine their methods of investigation (Hallinan 1997; Robertson 1993). The accumulation of large bodies of data about the past has not only stimulated more historically oriented research but has also led to the development of several different methodologies.

Much historical (and comparative) research is qualitative. This style of historical social science research tends to have several features that are similar to those used in other qualitative methodologies. First, like other qualitative methods, qualitative historical research is inductive: it develops an explanation for what happened from the details discovered about the past. In addition, qualitative historical research is **case-oriented**; it focuses on the nation or other unit as a whole, rather than only on different parts of the whole in isolation from each other (Ragin 2000:68). This could be considered the most distinctive feature of qualitative research on historical processes. The research question is "What was Britain like at the time?" rather than "What did Queen Elizabeth do?" Related to this case orientation, qualitative historical research is **holistic**—concerned with the context in which events occurred and the interrelations between different events and processes: "how different conditions or parts fit together" (Ragin 1987:25–26). For the same reason, qualitative historical research is **conjunctural** because, it is argued, "no cause ever acts except in complex conjunctions with others" (Abbott 1994:101). Charles Ragin (2000:67–68) uses the example of case-oriented research on the changing relationship between income and single parenthood in the United States after World War II:

> In the end, the study is also about the United States in the second half of the twentieth century, not just the many individuals and families included in the analysis. More than likely, the explanation of the changing relation between income and single parenthood would focus on interrelated aspects of the United States over this period, For example, to explain the weakening link between low income and single parenthood the researcher might cite the changing status of women, the decline in the social significance of conventional family forms, the increase in divorce, the decrease in men's job security, and other changes occurring in the United States over this period.

Qualitative historical research is also **temporal** because it looks at the related series of events that unfold over time. It is therefore also likely to be *historically specific*—limited to the specific time(s) and place(s) studied. Qualitative historical research uses **narrative explanations**—idiographic causal reasoning (see Chapter 6)—in which the research tells a story involving specific actors and other events occurring at the same time (Abbott 1994:102) or one that accounts for the position

---

Exhibit 13.1 Types of Historical and Comparative Research

	Cross-Sectional	Longitudinal
Single Case	Historical Events Research	Historical Process Research
Multiple Cases	Cross-Sectional Comparative Research	Comparative Historical Research

---

Case-oriented research: Research that focuses attention on the nation or other unit as a whole.

Holistic research: Research concerned with the context in which events occurred and the interrelations between different events and processes.

Conjunctural research: Research that considers the complex combinations in which causal influences operate.

Temporal research: Research that accounts for the related series of events that unfold over time.

Narrative explanation: An idiographic causal explanation that involves developing a narrative of events and processes that indicate a chain of causes and effects.

of actors and events in time and in a unique historical context (Griffin 1992). Larry Griffin's (1993) research on lynching, in the next section, provides a good example.

The focus on the past presents special methodological challenges:

- Documents and other evidence may have been lost or damaged.

- Available evidence may represent a sample biased toward more newsworthy figures.

- Written records will be biased toward those who were more prone to writing.

- Feelings of individuals involved in past events may be hard, if not impossible, to reconstruct.

Before you judge historical social science research as credible, you should look for convincing evidence that each of these challenges has been addressed.

Historical Events Research

Research on past events that does not follow processes for some long period is historical events research rather than historical process research. Historical events research basically uses a cross-sectional, rather than longitudinal, design. Investigations of past events may be motivated by the belief that they had a critical impact on subsequent developments or because they provide opportunities for testing the implications of a general theory (Kohn 1987).

Event-Structure Analysis

> **Event-structure analysis:** A systematic method of developing a causal diagram showing the structure of action underlying some chronology of events; the result is an idiographic causal explanation.

One technique useful in historical events research, as well as in other types of historical and comparative research, is **event-structure analysis**. Event-structure analysis is a qualitative approach that relies on a systematic coding of key events or national characteristics to identify the underlying structure of action in a chronology of events. The codes are then used to construct event sequences, make comparisons between cases, and develop an idiographic causal explanation for a key event.

An event-structure analysis consists of the following steps:

1. Classifying historical information into discrete events

2. Ordering events into a temporal sequence

3. Identifying prior steps that are prerequisites for subsequent events

4. Representing connections between events in a diagram

5. Eliminating from the diagram connections that are not necessary to explain the focal event

Griffin (1993) used event-structure analysis to explain a unique historical event, a lynching in the 1930s in Mississippi. According to published accounts and legal records, the lynching occurred after David Harris, an African American who sold moonshine from his home, was accused of killing a white tenant farmer. After the killing was reported, the local deputy was called and a citizen search party was formed. The deputy did not intervene as the search party trailed Harris and then captured and killed him. Meanwhile, Harris's friends killed another African American who had revealed Harris's hiding place. This series of events is outlined in Exhibit 13.2.

Which among the numerous events occurring between the time that the tenant farmer confronted Harris and the time that the mob killed Harris had a causal influence on that outcome? To identify these idiographic causal links (see Chapter 6), Griffin identified plausible counterfactual possibilities—events that might have

Exhibit 13.2 Event-Structure Analysis: Lynching Incident in the 1930s

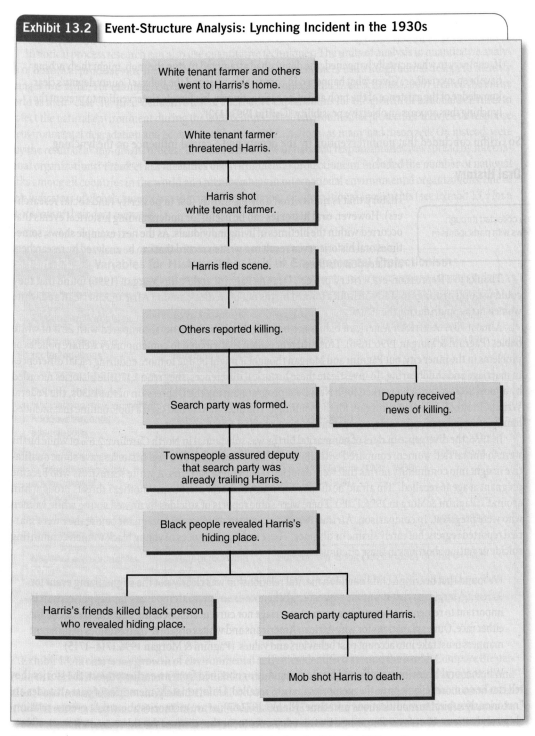

Source: Adapted from Griffin (1993:1110). Reprinted with permission from the University of Chicago Press.

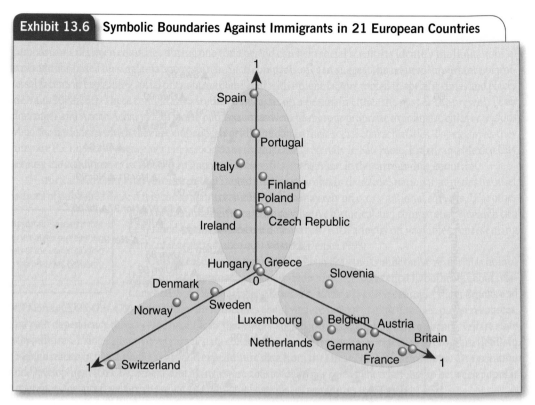

Exhibit 13.6 Symbolic Boundaries Against Immigrants in 21 European Countries

Source: Bail (2008:52).

structural factors generally do not vary within nations, we would never realize their importance if our analysis was limited to data from individuals in one nation.

Despite the unique value of comparative analyses like Franklin's (1996), such cross-national research also confronts unique challenges (de Vaus 2008:255). The meaning of concepts and the operational definitions of variables may differ between nations or regions (Erikson 1966:xi), so the comparative researcher must consider how best to establish measurement equivalence (Markoff 2005:402). For example, the concept of being a *good son or daughter* refers to a much broader range of behaviors in China than in most Western countries (Ho 1996). Rates of physical disability cannot be compared between nations because standard definitions are lacking (Martin & Kinsella 1995:364–365). Individuals in different cultures may respond differently to the same questions (Martin & Kinsella 1995:385). Alternatively, different measures may have been used for the same concepts in different nations, and the equivalence of these measures may be unknown (van de Vijver & Leung 1997:9). The value of statistics for particular geographic units such as counties in the United States may vary over time simply because of changes in the boundaries of these units (Walters et al. 1997). Such possibilities should be considered, and any available opportunity should be taken to test for their effects.

Qualitative data can also be used as a primary tool for comparative research. The Human Relations Area Files (HRAF) Collection of Ethnography provides an extraordinary resource for qualitative comparative cross-sectional research (and, to a lesser extent, for qualitative comparative historical research) (Ember & Ember 2011). The HRAF was founded in 1949 as a corporation designed to facilitate cross-cultural research. The HRAF ethnography collection now contains more than 1,000,000 pages of material from publications and other reports from about 400 different cultural, ethnic, religious, and national groups all over the world. The information is indexed by topic, in 710 categories, and now made available electronically (if your school pays to maintain access to the HRAF). Exhibit 13.8 is an example of a page from an HRAF document that has been indexed for easy retrieval.

Exhibit 13.7	Average Percentage of Voters Who Participated in Presidential or Parliamentary Elections, 1945–1998*		
Country	**Vote %**	**Country**	**Vote %**
Italy	92.5	St. Kitts and Nevis	58.1
Cambodia	90.5	Morocco	57.6
Seychelles	96.1	Cameroon	56.3
Iceland	89.5	Paraguay	56.0
Indonesia	88.3	Bangladesh	56.0
New Zealand	86.2	Estonia	56.0
Uzbekistan	86.2	Gambia	55.8
Albania	85.3	Honduras	55.3
Austria	85.1	Russia	55.0
Belgium	84.9	Panama	53.4
Czech	84.8	Poland	52.3
Netherlands	84.8	Uganda	50.6
Australia	84.4	Antigua and Barbuda	50.2
Denmark	83.6	Burma/Myanmar	50.0
Sweden	83.5	Switzerland	49.3
Mauritius	82.8	USA	48.3
Portugal	82.4	Mexico	48.1
Mongolia	82.3	Peru	48.0
Tuvalu	81.9	Brazil	47.9
Western Samoa	81.9	Nigeria	47.6
Andorra	81.3	Thailand	47.4
Germany	80.9	Sierra Leone	46.8
Slovenia	80.6	Botswana	46.5
Aruba	80.4	Chile	45.9
Namibia	80.4	Senegal	45.6
Greece	80.3	Ecuador	44.7
Guyana	80.3	El Salvador	44.3
Israel	80.0	Haiti	42.9
Kuwait	79.6	Ghana	42.4
Norway	79.5	Pakistan	41.8
San Marino	79.1	Zambia	40.5
Finland	79.0	Burkina Faso	38.3
Suriname	77.7	Nauru	37.3
Malta	77.6	Yemen	36.8
Bulgaria	77.5	Colombia	36.2
Romania	77.2	Niger	35.6

*Based on entire voting-age population in countries that held at least two elections during these years. Only countries with highest and lowest averages are shown.

Source: Reproduced by permission of International IDEA from "Turnout in the World—Country by Country Performance (1945–1998)." From *Voter Turnout: A Global Survey* (http://www.int/vt/survey/voter_turnout_pop2-2.cfm) © International Institute for Democracy and Electoral Assistance.

Exhibit 13.8   HRAF-Indexed Document

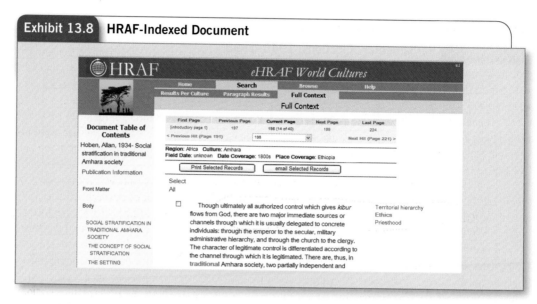

Most of the significant literature published on the chosen groups is included in the HRAF and used to prepare a standard summary about the group. Researchers can use these summaries and systematic searches for specific index terms to answer many questions about other social groups with the HRAF files, such as "What percentage of the world's societies practice polygyny?" and "Does punitive child training affect the frequency of warfare?" (Ember & Ember 2011).

CAREERS AND RESEARCH

Kurt Taylor Gaubatz, PhD, Faculty, Department of Political Science & Geography International Studies Graduate Program

Kurt Taylor Gaubatz is the quintessential comparative researcher whose book *Elections and War* exemplifies the approach. But he started college at the University of California, Berkeley, majoring in music. He became fascinated by the challenge of understanding and modeling human behavior only after he took a required economics class. He realized, "All of the biggest problems we face as a society, indeed as human beings, come down to research questions in the social sciences!"

Driven by his desire to influence public policy, Gaubatz went on to earn one master's degree from the Fletcher School of Law and Diplomacy and another from Princeton Theological Seminary. He then earned his PhD in political science from Stanford University and, several prestigious fellowships later, is now on the faculty in the graduate program in international studies of the Department of Political Science & Geography at Old Dominion University. He describes his career in research as "a life of posing and answering questions, of trying to think about things in new and more interesting ways."

Gaubatz's advice for students interested in research careers focuses on the ongoing revolution in information technology:

We are in the middle of a revolution in data creation and computing power. Just 25 years ago, people could make a career from knowing information. A huge amount of information is now increasingly available to everyone who carries a phone. The critical skill is knowing how to build new ideas from the organization and analysis of that information, and being able to communicate those ideas effectively. Students need to focus on filling their toolboxes with those analytic and communication skills.

Comparative Historical Research

The combination of historical analysis with comparisons between nations or other units often leads to the most interesting results. Historical social scientists may use comparisons between cases "to highlight the particular features of each case" (Skocpol 1984:370) or to identify general historical patterns across nations. A study of processes within one nation may therefore be misleading if important processes within the nation have been influenced by social processes that operate across national boundaries (Markoff 2005:403). For example, comparisons between nations may reveal that differences in political systems are much more important than voluntary decisions by individual political leaders (Rueschemeyer et al. 1992:31–36).

Comparative historical research can also help identify the causal processes at work within the nations or other entities (Lipset 1968:34; Skocpol 1984:374–386). Comparative historical research can result in historically conditional theory, in which the applicability of general theoretical propositions is linked to particular historical circumstances (Paige 1999). For example, James Mahoney (2001) explained the differential success of liberalizing reforms in Central American countries as the result of the particular ways in which liberal elites tried to implement the reforms. As summarized by Lange (2013:77–78), Guatemala and El Salvador tried to implement the reforms quickly by developing a militarized state, whereas Costa Rica used a gradual approach that could be implemented by a democratic regime. In Honduras and Nicaragua, internal pressure and external interventions stopped the liberal reforms entirely. These early events set political processes in these countries on different trajectories for many decades.

Researcher Interview Link
Comparative Ethnographic Research

The comparative historical approach usually focuses on sequences of events rather than on some single past (or current) occurrence that might have influenced an outcome in the present. Comparisons of these sequences may be either quantitative or qualitative. Some studies collect quantitative longitudinal data about a number of nations and then use these data to test hypotheses about influences on national characteristics. (Theda Skocpol [1984:375] terms this *analytic historical sociology*.) Others compare the histories or particular historical experiences of nations in a narrative form, noting similarities and differences and inferring explanations for key national events (*interpretive historical sociology* in Skocpol's terminology [1984:368]).

There are several stages for a systematic, qualitative, comparative historical study (Ragin 1987:44–52; Rueschemeyer et al. 1992:36–39):

1. Specify a theoretical framework and identify key concepts or events that should be examined to explain a phenomenon.

2. Select cases (such as nations) that vary in terms of the key concepts or events.

3. Identify similarities and differences between the cases in these key concepts or events and the outcome to be explained.

4. Propose a causal explanation for the historical outcome and check it against the features of each case. The criterion of success in this method is to explain the outcome for each case, without allowing deviations from the proposed causal pattern.

Dietrich Rueschemeyer et al. (1992) used a comparative historical method to explain why some nations in Latin America (excluding Central America) developed democratic politics, whereas others became authoritarian or bureaucratic–authoritarian states. First, Rueschemeyer et al. developed a theoretical framework that gave key attention to the power of social classes, state (government) power, and the interaction between social classes and the government. The researchers then classified the political regimes in each nation over time (Exhibit 13.9). Next, they noted how each nation varied over time relative to the variables they had identified as potentially important for successful democratization.

[handwritten margin notes: "need to have if anything is same there is no comparison" / "contrast" / "Outcome needs to be same"]

Exhibit 13.10 John Stuart Mill's Method of Agreement (Hypothetical Cases and Variables)

Variable	Case 1	Case 2	Case 3
Importance of peasant agriculture	Different	Different	Different
Expanding industrial base	Different	Same	Same
Rising educational levels	Different	Different	Different
Expanding middle class	Same	Same	Same
Democratization (outcome)	Same	Same	Same

Source: Adapted from Skocpol (1984:379).

[handwritten margin notes: "same/similar except thing you're interested in to explain diffs" / "different outcome"]

Exhibit 13.11 John Stuart Mill's Method of Difference (Hypothetical Cases and Variables)

Country A (Positive Case)	Country B (Negative Case)
Economic development	Economic development
Two-party system begun	Two-party system begun
Proportional representation	Proportional representation
Moderate income disparities	Extreme income disparities
Democratization	No democratization

Source: Adapted from Skocpol and Somers (1979:80).

respect from the country that did democratize. These two countries are similar with respect to other potential influences on democratization. The argument could be improved by adding more positive and negative cases. The focus of the method of difference is actually on identifying a difference between cases that are similar in other respects, so this approach is also called the *most similar case studies* method.

The method of agreement and method of difference approaches can also be combined, "by using at once several positive cases along with suitable negative cases as contrasts" (Skocpol 1979:37). This is the approach that Skocpol (1979) used in her classic book about the French, Russian, and Chinese revolutions, *States and Social Revolutions*. Exhibit 13.12 summarizes part of her argument about the conditions for peasant insurrections, based on a careful historical review. In this exhibit, Skocpol (1979:156) shows how the three countries that experienced revolutions (France, Russia, and China) tended to have more independent peasants and more autonomy in local politics than did three contrasting countries (Prussia/Germany, Japan, and England) that did not experience social revolutions.

Cautions for Comparative Analysis

Of course, ambitious methods that compare different countries face many complications. The features of the cases selected for comparison have a large impact on the researcher's ability to identify influences. Cases should be chosen for their difference on key factors hypothesized to influence the outcome of interest and their similarity on other, possibly confounding, factors (Skocpol 1984:383). For example, to understand how industrialization influences democracy, you would need to select cases for comparison that differ in industrialization, so that you could then see if they differ in democratization (King, Keohane, & Verba 1994:148–152). Nonetheless, relying on just a small number of cases for comparisons introduces uncertainty into the conclusions (de Vaus 2008:256).

And what determines whether cases are similar and different in certain respects? In many comparative analyses, the values of continuous variables are dichotomized. For example, nations may be coded as *democratic* or *not democratic* or as having *experienced revolution* or *not experienced revolution*. The methods of

Exhibit 13.12	Methods of Agreement and Difference Combined: Conditions for Peasant Insurrections

Country	Agrarian Class Structures	Local Politics
France	Peasant smallholders own 30% to 40% of land; work 80% in small plots. Individual property established, but peasant community opposes seigneurs, who collect dues.	Villages relatively autonomous under supervision of royal officials.
Russia	Peasants own 60%+ and rent more; control process of production on small plots; pay rents and redemption payments. Strong community based on collective ownership.	Village sovereign under control of tzarist bureaucracy.
China	Peasants own 50% and work virtually all land in small plots. Pay rents to gentry. No peasant community.	Gentry landlords, usurers, and literati dominate local organizational life; cooperate with Imperial officials.
Contrasts		
Prussia/ Germany	West of Elbe: resembles France. East of Elbe: large estates worked by laborers and peasants with tiny holdings and no strong communities.	Junker landlords are local agents of bureaucratic state; dominate local administration and policing.
Japan	Communities dominated by rich peasants.	Strong bureaucratic controls over local communities.
England	Landed class owns 70%. Peasantry polarizing between yeomen farmers and agricultural laborers. No strong peasant community.	Landlords are local agents of monarchy; dominate administration and policing.

Source: Skocpol (1979:156).

agreement and difference that I have just introduced presume these types of binary (dichotomous) distinctions. However, variation in the social world often involves degrees of difference, rather than all or none distinctions (de Vaus 2008:255). Some countries may be partially democratic and some countries may have experienced a limited revolution. At the individual level, you know that distinctions such as *rich* and *poor* or *religious* and *not religious* reflect differences on underlying continua of wealth and religiosity. So the use of dichotomous distinctions in comparative analyses introduces an imprecise and somewhat arbitrary element into the analysis (Lieberson 1991). For some comparisons, however, qualitative distinctions such as *simple majority rule* or *unanimity required* may capture the important differences between cases better than quantitative distinctions. We don't want to simply ignore important categorical considerations such as this in favor of *degree of majority rule* or some other underlying variable (King et al. 1994:158–163). Careful discussion of the bases for making distinctions is an important first step in any comparative historical research (also see Ragin 2000).

Audio Link
Critiquing Research

The focus on comparisons between nations may itself be a mistake for some analyses. National boundaries often do not correspond to key cultural differences, so comparing subregions within countries or larger cultural units that span multiple countries may make more sense for some analyses (de Vaus 2008:258). Comparing countries that have fractured along cultural or religious divides simply by average characteristics would obscure many important social phenomena.

With cautions such as these in mind, the combination of historical and comparative methods allows for rich descriptions of social and political processes in different nations or regions as well as for causal inferences that reflect a systematic, defensible weighing of the evidence. Data of increasingly good quality are available on a rapidly expanding number of nations, creating many opportunities for comparative research. We cannot expect one study comparing the histories of a few nations to control adequately for every plausible alternative causal influence, but repeated investigations can refine our understanding and lead to increasingly accurate causal conclusions (King et al. 1994:33).

🔲 Demographic Analysis

The social processes that are the focus of historical and comparative research are often reflected in and influenced by changes in the makeup of the population being studied. For example, the plummeting birthrates in European countries will influence the politics of immigration in those countries, their living standards, the character of neighborhoods, and national productivity (Bruni 2002). **Demography** is the field that studies these dynamics. Demography is the statistical and mathematical study of the size, composition, and spatial distribution of human populations and how these features change over time. Demographers explain population change through five processes: (1) fertility, (2) mortality, (3) marriage, (4) migration, and (5) social mobility (Bogue 1969:1).

> **Demography:** The statistical and mathematical study of the size, composition, and spatial distribution of human populations and how these features change over time.

Demographers obtain data from a census of the population (see Chapter 5) and from registries—records of events such as births, deaths, migrations, marriages, divorces, diseases, and employment (Anderton, Barrett, & Bogue 1997:54–79; Baum 1993), then compute various statistics from these data to facilitate description and analysis (Wunsch & Termote 1978). To use these data, you need to understand how they are calculated and the questions they answer. Four concepts are key to understanding and using demographic methods: population change, standardization of population numbers, the demographic bookkeeping equation, and population composition.

Population change is a central concept in demography. The absolute population change is calculated simply as the difference between the population size in one census minus the population size in an earlier census. This measure of absolute change is of little value, however, because it does not consider the total size of the population that was changing (Bogue 1969:32–43). A better measure is the *intercensal percent change,* which is the absolute change in population between two censuses divided by the population size in the earlier census (and multiplied by 100 to obtain a percentage). With the percent change statistic, we can meaningfully compare the growth in two or more nations that differ markedly in size (as long as the intercensal interval does not vary between the nations) (White 1993:1-2).

Standardization of population numbers, as with the calculation of intercensal percent change, is a key concern of demographic methods (Gill, Glazer, & Thernstrom 1992:478–482; Rele 1993). To make meaningful comparisons between nations and over time, numbers that describe most demographic events must be adjusted for the size of the population at risk for the event. For example, the fertility rate is calculated as the ratio of the number of births to women of childbearing age to the total number of women in this age range (multiplied by 1,000). Unless we make such adjustments, we will not know if a nation with a much higher number of births or deaths in relation to its total population size simply has more women in the appropriate age range or has more births per "eligible" woman.

The *demographic bookkeeping* (or *balancing*) *equation* is used to identify the four components of population growth during a time interval ($P_2 P_1$): births (*B*), deaths (*D*), and in-migration (M_i) and out-migration (M_o). The equation is written as follows: $P_2 = P_1 + (B - D) + (M_i - M_o)$. That is, population at a given point in time is equal to the population at an earlier time plus the excess of births over deaths during the interval and the excess of in-migration over out-migration (White 1993:1-4). Whenever you see population size or change statistics used in a comparative analysis, you will want to ask yourself whether it is also important to know which component in the equation was responsible for the change over time or for the difference between countries (White 1993:1-4).

Population composition refers to a description of a population in terms of basic characteristics such as age, race, sex, or marital status (White 1993:1-7). Descriptions of population composition at different times or in different nations can be essential for understanding social dynamics identified in historical and comparative

Research|Social Impact Link
Presenting Conclusions from Research

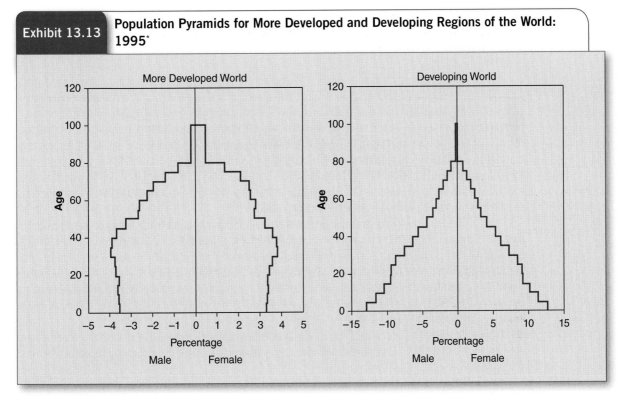

Exhibit 13.13 Population Pyramids for More Developed and Developing Regions of the World: 1995*

*Inconsistent date in original.

Source: Bogue et al. (1993).

research. For example, Exhibit 13.13 compares the composition of the population in more developed and developing regions of the world by age and sex in 1995, using United Nations data. By comparing these *population pyramids,* we see that children constitute a much greater proportion of the population in less developed regions. The more developed regions' population pyramid also shows the greater proportion of women at older ages and the post–World War II baby boom bulge in the population.

Demographic analysis can be an important component of historical research (Bean, Mineau, & Anderton 1990), but problems of data quality must be carefully evaluated (Vaessen 1993). The hard work that can be required to develop demographic data from evidence that is hundreds of years old does not always result in worthwhile information. The numbers of people for which data are available in particular areas may be too small for statistical analysis, data that are easily available (e.g., a list of villages in an area) may not provide the information that is important (e.g., population size), and lack of information on the original data collection procedures may prevent assessment of data quality (Hollingsworth 1972:77).

Content Analysis

How are medical doctors regarded in U.S. culture? Do newspapers use the term *schizophrenia* in a way that reflects what this serious mental illness actually involves? Does the portrayal of men and women in video games reinforce gender stereotypes? Are the body images of male and female college students related to their experiences with romantic love? If you are concerned with understanding culture, attitudes toward mental illness, or gender roles, you'll probably find these to be important research questions. You now know that you could probably find data about each of these issues for a secondary data analysis, but in this section, I would like to introduce procedures for analyzing a different type of data that awaits the enterprising social researcher. Content analysis is "the systematic, objective, quantitative analysis of message characteristics" and is a method particularly well suited to the study of popular culture and many other issues concerning human communication (Neuendorf 2002:1).

The goal of content analysis is to develop inferences from human communication in any of its forms, including books, articles, magazines, songs, films, and speeches (Weber 1990:9). You can think of content analysis as a "survey" of some documents or other records of communication—a survey with fixed-choice responses that produce quantitative data. This method was first applied to the study of newspaper and film content and then developed systematically for the analysis of Nazi propaganda broadcasts in World War II. Since then, content analysis has been used to study historical documents, records of speeches, and other "voices from the past" as well as media of all sorts (Neuendorf 2002:31–37). The same techniques can now be used to analyze blog sites, wikis, and other text posted on the Internet (Gaiser & Schreiner 2009:81–90). Content analysis techniques are also used to analyze responses to open-ended survey questions.

Content analysis bears some similarities to qualitative data analysis because it involves coding and categorizing text and identifying relationships between constructs identified in the text. However, because it usually is conceived as a quantitative procedure, content analysis overlaps with qualitative data analysis only at the margins—the points where qualitative analysis takes on quantitative features or where content analysis focuses on qualitative features of the text. This distinction becomes fuzzy, however, because content analysis techniques can be used with all forms of messages, including visual images, sounds, and interaction patterns, as well as written text (Neuendorf 2002:24–25).

The various steps in a content analysis are represented in the flowchart in Exhibit 13.14. Note that the steps are comparable to the procedures in quantitative survey research. Use this flowchart as a checklist when you design or critique a content analysis project.

Kimberly Neuendorf's (2002:3) analysis of medical prime-time network television programming introduces the potential of content analysis. As Exhibit 13.15 shows, medical programming has been dominated by noncomedy shows, but there have been two significant periods of comedy medical shows—during the 1970s and early 1980s and then again in the early 1990s. It took a qualitative analysis of medical show content to reveal that the 1960s shows represented a very distinct "physician-as-God" era, which shifted to a more human view of the medical profession in the 1970s and 1980s. This era has been followed, in turn, by a mixed period that has had no dominant theme.

Content analysis is useful for investigating many questions about the social world. To illustrate its diverse range of applications, I will use in the next sections Neuendorf's (2002) analysis of TV programming, Matthias A. Gerth and Gabriele Siegert's (2012) analysis of news coverage of an immigrant naturalization campaign, Kenneth Duckworth's, Chris Gillespie's, and my (2003) analysis of newspaper articles, Karen Dill and Kathryn Thill's (2007) analysis of video game characters, and Suman Ambwani and Jaine Strauss's (2007) analysis of student responses to open-ended survey questions. These examples will demonstrate that the units that are "surveyed" in a content analysis can range from newspapers, books, or TV shows to persons referred to in other communications, themes expressed in documents, or propositions made in different statements.

Audio Link
Controversial Research

Identify a Population of Documents or Other Textual Sources

This population should be selected so that it is appropriate to the research question of interest. Perhaps the population will be all newspapers published in the United States, college student newspapers, nomination speeches at political party conventions, or "state of the nation" speeches by national leaders. Books or films are also common sources for content analysis projects. Often, a comprehensive archive can provide the primary data for the analysis (Neuendorf 2002:76–77). For a fee, the LexisNexis service makes a large archive of newspapers available for analysis. For her analysis of prime-time programming since 1951, Neuendorf (2002:3–4) used a published catalog of all TV shows. For my analysis with Duckworth and others (2003:1402) of newspapers' use of the terms *schizophrenia* and *cancer*, I requested a sample of articles from the LexisNexis national newspaper archive.

Exhibit 13.14 **Flowchart for the Typical Process of Content Analysis Research**

1. *Theory and rationale:* What content will be examined, and *why*? Are there certain *theories* or perspectives that indicate that this particular message content is important to study? Library work is needed here to conduct a good literature review. Will you be using an integrative model, linking content analysis with other data to show relationships with source or receiver characteristics? Do you have *research questions? Hypotheses?*

2. *Conceptualizations:* What *variables* will be used in the study, and how do you define them *conceptually* (i.e., with dictionary-type definitions)? Remember, you are the boss! There are many ways to define a given construct, and there is no one right way. You may want to screen some examples of the content you're going to analyze, to make sure you've covered everything you want.

3. *Operationalizations (measures):* Your measures should match your conceptualizations. . . . What *unit of data collection* will you use? You may have more than one unit (e.g., a by-utterance coding scheme and a by-speaker coding scheme). Are the variables measured well (i.e., at a high *level of measurement,* with categories that are *exhaustive and mutually exclusive*)? An *a priori* coding scheme describing all measures must be created. Both face validity and content validity may also be assessed at this point.

Human Coding — Computer Coding

4a. *Coding schemes:* You need to create the following materials:

   a. *Codebook* (with all variable measures *fully* explained)

   b. *Coding form*

4b. *Coding schemes:* With computer text content analysis, you still need a codebook of sorts—a full explanation of your *dictionaries* and method of applying them. You may use standard dictionaries (e.g., those in Hart's program, *Diction*) or originally created dictionaries. When creating custom dictionaries, be sure to first generate a frequencies list from your text sample and examine for key words and phrases.

Human Coding — Computer Coding

(Continued)

and variation, cross-tabulations, and correlation analysis (Weber 1990:58–63). Computer-aided qualitative analysis programs, like those you learned about in Chapter 11 and like the one I selected for the preceding newspaper article analysis, can help, in many cases, develop coding procedures and then carry out the content coding.

The simple chart that Neuendorf (2002:3) used to analyze the frequency of medical programming appears in Exhibit 13.15. My content analysis with Duckworth and others (2003) was simply a comparison of percentages showing that 28% of the articles mentioning schizophrenia used it as a metaphor, compared with only 1% of the articles mentioning cancer. We also presented examples of the text that had been coded into different categories. For example, *the nation's schizophrenic perspective on drugs* was the type of phrase coded as a metaphorical use of the term *schizophrenia* (p. 1403). Dill and Thill (2007:858) presented percentages and other statistics that showed that, among other differences, female characters were much more likely to be portrayed in sexualized ways in video game images than were male characters. Ambwani and Strauss (2007:16) used other statistics that showed that body esteem and romantic love experiences are related, particularly for women. They also examined the original written comments and found further evidence for this relationship. For example, one woman wrote, "[My current boyfriend] taught me to love my body. Now I see myself through his eyes, and I feel beautiful" (p. 17).

Gerth and Siegert (2012:288–295) use both charts and percentage distributions to test the hypotheses they posed about media attention to different political perspectives. Exhibit 13.17 shows how the use of different perspectives (or "frames") varied over the weeks of the campaign, with an emphasis on the "rule of law" being the most common way of framing the issue of naturalization.

The criteria for judging quantitative content analyses of text are the same standards of validity applied to data collected with other quantitative methods. We must review the sampling approach, the reliability and validity of the measures, and the controls used to strengthen any causal conclusions.

Journal Link
Organizing Data

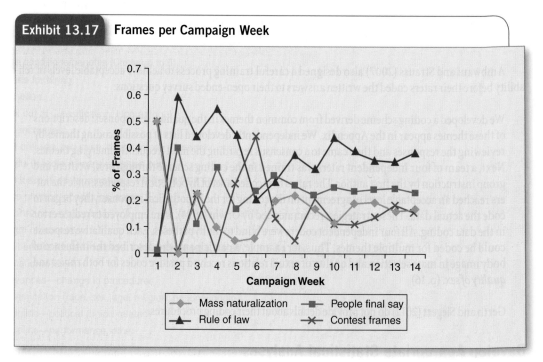

Exhibit 13.17 **Frames per Campaign Week**

Source: Gerth and Siegert (2012:290).

▣ Ethical Issues in Historical and Comparative Research and Content Analysis

Analysis of historical documents, documents from other countries, or content in media does not create the potential for harm to human subjects that can be a concern when collecting primary data. It is still important to be honest and responsible in working out arrangements for data access when data must be obtained from designated officials or data archivists, but many data are available easily in libraries or on the web. Researchers in the United States who conclude that they are being denied access to public records of the federal government may be able to obtain the data by filing a Freedom of Information Act (FOIA) request. The FOIA stipulates that all persons have a right to access all federal agency records unless the records are specifically exempted (Riedel 2000:130–131). Researchers who review historical or government documents must also try to avoid embarrassing or otherwise harming named individuals or their descendants by disclosing sensitive information.

Ethical concerns are multiplied when surveys are conducted or other data are collected in other countries. If the outside researcher lacks much knowledge of local norms, values, and routine activities, the potential for inadvertently harming subjects is substantial. For this reason, cross-cultural researchers should spend time learning about each of the countries in which they plan to collect primary data and strike up collaborations with researchers in those countries (Hantrais & Mangen 1996). Local advisory groups may also be formed in each country so that a broader range of opinion is solicited when key decisions must be made. Such collaboration can also be invaluable when designing instruments, collecting data, and interpreting results.

Cross-cultural researchers who use data from other societies have a particular obligation to try to understand the culture and norms of those societies before they begin secondary data analyses. It is a mistake to assume that questions asked in other languages or cultural contexts will have the same meaning as when asked in the researcher's own language and culture, so a careful, culturally sensitive process of review by knowledgeable experts must precede measurement decisions in these projects. Ethical standards themselves may vary between nations and cultures, so cross-cultural researchers should consider collaborating with others in the places to be compared and take the time to learn about cultural practices, gender norms, and ethical standards (Ayhan 2001; Stake & Rizvi 2009:527).

Video Link
Research Results and Publication

▣ Conclusions

Historical and comparative social science investigations use a variety of techniques that range from narrative histories having much in common with qualitative methods to analyses of secondary data that are in many respects like traditional survey research. Content analysis may also be used in historical and comparative research. Each of these techniques can help the researchers gain new insights into processes such as democratization. They encourage intimate familiarity with the cause of development of the nations studied and thereby stimulate inductive reasoning about the interrelations between different historical events. Systematic historical and comparative techniques can be used to test deductive hypotheses concerning international differences as well as historical events.

Interactive Exercises Link
Historical and Comparative Methods

Most historical and comparative methods encourage causal reasoning. They require the researcher to consider systematically the causal mechanism, or historical sequences of events, by which earlier events influence later outcomes. They also encourage attention to causal context, with a particular focus on the ways in which different cultures and social structures may result in different effects of other variables. Content analysis methods focus attention on key dimensions of variation in news media and other communicative texts. There is much to be gained by learning and continuing to use and develop these methods.

Key Terms

Case-oriented research   477
Comparative historical research   476
Conjunctural research   477
Content analysis   476
Cross-sectional comparative
   research   476
Demography   494
Event-structure analysis   478
Historical events research   476
Historical process research   476
Holistic research   477
Method of agreement   491
Method of difference   491
Narrative explanation   477
Oral history   480
Temporal research   477
Variable-oriented research   484

Highlights

- The central insight behind historical and comparative methods is that we can improve our understanding of social processes when we make comparisons with other times and places.

- There are four basic types of historical and comparative research methods: (1) historical events research, (2) historical process research, (3) cross-sectional comparative research, and (4) comparative historical research. Historical events research and historical process research are likely to be qualitative, whereas comparative studies are often quantitative; however, research of each type may use elements of both.

- Event-structure analysis is a systematic qualitative approach to developing an idiographic causal explanation for a key event.

- Oral history provides a means of reconstructing past events. Data from other sources should be used whenever possible to evaluate the accuracy of memories.

- Qualitative historical process research uses a narrative approach to causal explanation, in which historical events are treated as part of a developing story. Narrative explanations are temporal, holistic, and conjunctural.

- Comparative methods may be cross-sectional, such as when variation between country characteristics is compared, or historical, in which developmental patterns are compared between countries.

- Methodological challenges for comparative and historical research include missing data, variation in the meaning of words and phrases and in the boundaries of geographic units across historical periods and between cultures, bias or inaccuracy of historical documents, lack of measurement equivalence, the need for detailed knowledge of the cases chosen, a limited number of cases, case selection on an availability basis, reliance on dichotomous categorization of cases, and interdependence of cases selected.

- Central concepts for demographic research are population change, standardization of population numbers, the demographic bookkeeping equation, and population composition.

- Content analysis is a tool for systematic quantitative analysis of documents and other textual data. It requires careful testing and control of coding procedures to achieve reliable measures.

STUDENT STUDY SITE

Sharpen your skills with SAGE edge at **edge.sagepub.com/schutt8e. SAGE edge for students** provides a personalized approach to help you accomplish your coursework goals in an easy-to-use learning environment.

Discussion Questions

1. Review the differences between case-oriented, historically specific, inductive explanations and those that are more variable oriented, theoretically general, and deductive. List several arguments for and against each approach. Which is more appealing to you and why?

2. What historical events have had a major influence on social patterns in the nation? The possible answers are too numerous to list, ranging from any of the wars to major internal political conflicts, economic booms and busts, scientific discoveries, and legal changes. Pick one such event in your own nation for this exercise. Find one historical book on this event and list the sources of evidence used. What additional evidence would you suggest for a social science investigation of the event?

3. Consider the comparative historical research by Rueschemeyer et al. (1992) on democratic politics in Latin America. What does comparison between nations add to the researcher's ability to develop causal explanations?

4. Susan Olzak, Suzanne Shanahan, and Elizabeth McEneaney (1996) developed a nomothetic causal explanation of variation in racial rioting in the United States over time, whereas Griffin's (1993) explanation of a lynching can be termed *idiographic*. Discuss the similarities and differences between these types of causal explanation. Use these two studies to illustrate the strengths and weaknesses of each.

5. Select a major historical event or process, such as the Great Depression, World War II, the civil rights movement, or the war in Iraq. Why do you think this event happened? Now, select one of the four major types of historical and comparative methods that you think could be used to test your explanation. Why did you choose this method? What type of evidence would support your proposed explanation? What problems might you face in using this method to test your explanation?

6. Consider the media that you pay attention to in your social world. How could you design a content analysis of the messages conveyed by these media? What research questions could you help to answer by adding a comparison to another region or country to this content analysis?

Practice Exercises

1. The journals *Social Science History* and *Journal of Social History* report many studies of historical processes. Select one article from a recent journal issue about a historical process used to explain some event or other outcome. Summarize the author's explanation. Identify any features of the explanation that are temporal, holistic, and conjunctural. Prepare a chronology of the important historical events in that process. Do you agree with the author's causal conclusions? What additional evidence would strengthen the author's argument?

2. Exhibit 13.18 identifies voting procedures and the level of turnout in one election for 10 countries. Do voting procedures appear to influence turnout in these countries? To answer this question using Mill's methods, you will first have to decide how to dichotomize the values of variables that have more than two values (postal voting, proxy voting, and turnout). You must also decide what to do about missing values. Apply Mill's method of agreement to the pattern in the table. Do any variables emerge as likely causes? What additional information would you like to have for your causal analysis?

3. Using your library's government documents collection or the U.S. Census site on the web, select one report by the U.S. Census Bureau about the population of the United States or some segment of it. Outline the report and list all the tables included in it. Summarize the report in two paragraphs. Suggest a historical or comparative study for which this report would be useful.

4. Find a magazine or newspaper report on a demographic issue, such as population change or migration. Explain how one of the key demographic concepts could be used or was used to improve understanding of this issue.

5. Review the Interactive Exercises on the study site for a lesson that will help you master the terms used in historical and comparative research.

6. Select an article from the book's study site, at edge.sagepub .com/schutt8e, that used a historical/comparative design. Which specific type of design was used? What were the advantages of this design for answering the research question posed?

Exhibit 13.18   Voting Procedures in 10 Countries

	Voting Age	Number of Days Polling Booth Open	Voting Day on Work Day or Rest Day	Postal Voting	Proxy Voting	Constituency Transfer	Advance Voting	Voter Turnout (in %)	Year (P=presidential, L = legislative election)
Switzerland	20	2	Rest day	Automatic for armed forces, otherwise by application 4 days before voting	Varies by canton	No	No	46	1991L
Taiwan	20	1	Rest day					72	1992L
Thailand	20	1	Rest day	No				62	1995L
Turkey	20	1	Rest day	No	No	Special polling stations at border posts for citizens residing abroad	No	80	1991L
Ukraine	18	1	Rest day					71.6	1994P
United Kingdom	18	1	Work day	On application	On application	No	No	77.8	1992L
United States	18	1	Work day	By application; rules vary across states	In some states for blind and disabled	No		51.5	1992P
Uruguay	18	1	Rest day	No	No	No		89.4	1994P
Venezuela	18	1	Rest day	No	Assisted voting for blind and disabled	No	No	60	1993P
Zambia		1	Work day		No			50	1991P

Source: LeDuc et al. (1996:19, Figure 1.3).

Ethics Questions

1. Oral historians can uncover disturbing facts about the past. What if a researcher were conducting an oral history project such as the Depression Writer's Project and learned from an interviewee about his previously undisclosed involvement in a predatory sex crime many years ago? Should the researcher report what he learned to a government attorney who might decide to bring criminal charges? What about informing the victim and/or her surviving relatives? Would it matter if the statute of limitations had expired, so that the offender could not be prosecuted any longer? After Boston College researchers interviewed former participants in "The Troubles," the police in Northern Ireland subsequently demanded ˛ received some of the transcripts and used them in their investigations (Cullen 2014). Should the oral history project not have been conducted?

2. In this chapter's ethics section, I recommended that researchers who conduct research in other cultures form an advisory group of local residents to provide insight into local customs and beliefs. What are some other possible benefits of such a group for cross-cultural researchers? What disadvantages might arise from use of such a group?

Web Exercises

1. The World Bank offers numerous resources that are useful for comparative research. Visit the World Bank website at www.worldbank.org. Click on the "Countries" link at the top of the site and then select one region, such as "Africa." Now, choose a specific country and topic that interests you and write a brief summary of the reported data. Then, compare these data with those for another country in the same region, and summarize the differences and similarities you have identified between the countries.

2. The U.S. Bureau of Labor Statistics (BLS) website provides extensive economic indicator data for regions, states, and cities. Go to the BLS web page that offers statistics by location: http://stats.bls.gov/eag. Now, click on a region and explore the types of data that are available. Write out a description of the steps you would have to take to conduct a comparative analysis using the data available from the BLS website.

3. The U.S. Census Bureau's home page can be found at www.census.gov. This site contains extensive reporting of census data, including population data, economic indicators, and other information acquired through the U.S. Census. This website allows you to collect information on numerous subjects and topics. This information can then be used to make comparisons between different states or cities. Comparative analysis is facilitated by the "State and County Quick Facts" option, which can be accessed directly at http://quickfacts.census.gov/qfd. Now, choose your own state and the county in which you live and copy down several statistics of interest. Repeat this process for other counties in your state. Use the data you have collected to compare your county with other counties in the state. Write a one-page report summarizing your findings.

Video Interview Questions

1. What caused Cinzia Solari's research question to change? What was the comparative element in her research?

2. How did Solari build rapport between her and the migrant workers she was trying to research? Why is this step important when doing qualitative research?

SPSS Exercises

1. In this exercise, you will use Mill's method of agreement to examine international differences in the role of labor unions. For this cross-sectional comparative analysis, you will use the ISSP data set on Work Orientations III 2005. Type in the following URL, http://www.jdsurvey.net/jds/jdsurvey Analisis.jsp?ES_COL=127&Idioma=I&SeccionCol=06&E

SID=453, which contains results of an international survey involving respondents in more than 25 countries.

a. First, go to the Work Orientations III 2005 website and select three countries of interest. State a reason for choosing these three countries. State a hypothesis specifying which countries you expect to be relatively supportive of labor unions and which countries you expect to be relatively unsupportive of labor unions. Explain your reasoning.

b. Once you have selected (checked) the countries you would like to compare, hit "Confirm selection" in the top left corner. Then, scroll down the list of questions and select V25 (Without trade unions the working conditions of employees would be much worse than they are) or some other question of interest.

c. To review your table of similarities and differences between countries click the tab "Cross Tabs." Here you should see a table with the countries represented on the top row and the degree of support in the columns. (It may also be useful to explore the "graphs" tab, which provides a visual comparison.) See if on this basis you can develop a tentative explanation of international variation in support for labor unions using Mill's method of agreement. You might also want to explore the question V24 ("Trade unions are very important for the job security of employees") to further compare international variation.

d. Discuss the possible weaknesses in the type of explanation you have constructed, following John Stuart Mill. Propose a different approach for a comparative historical analysis.

2. How do the attitudes of immigrants to the United States compare with those of people born in the United States? Use the GSS2012x or GSS2012a file and request the cross-tabulations (in percentage form) of POLVIEWS3, BIBLE, SPKATH by BORN (with BORN as the column variable). Inspect the output. Describe the similarities and differences you have found.

3. Because the GSS file is cross-sectional, we cannot use it to conduct historical research. However, we can develop some interesting historical questions by examining differences in the attitudes of Americans in different birth cohorts.

a. Inspect the distributions of the same set of variables. Would you expect any of these attitudes and behaviors to have changed over the 20th century? State your expectations in the form of hypotheses.

b. Request a cross-tabulation of these variables by birth COHORTS. What appear to be the differences between the cohorts? Which differences do you think result from historical change, and which do you think result from the aging process? Which attitudes and behaviors would you expect to still differentiate the baby boom generation and the post-Vietnam generation in 20 years?

Developing a Research Proposal

Add a historical or comparative dimension to your proposed study (Exhibit 3.10, #13 to #17).

1. Consider which of the four types of comparative/historical methods would be most suited to an investigation of your research question. Think of possibilities for qualitative and quantitative research on your topic with the method you prefer. Will you conduct a variable-oriented or case-oriented study? Write a brief statement justifying the approach you choose.

2. Review the possible sources of data for your comparative/historical project. Search the web and relevant government, historical, and international organization sites or publications. Search the social science literature for similar studies and read about the data sources that they used.

3. Specify the hypotheses you will test or the causal sequences you will investigate. Describe what your cases will be (nations, regions, years, etc.). Explain how you will select cases. List the sources of your measures, and describe the specific type of data you expect to obtain for each measure. Discuss how you will evaluate causal influences, and indicate whether you will take a nomothetic or idiographic approach to causality.

4. Review the list of potential problems in comparative/historical research and content analysis, and discuss those that you believe will be most troublesome in your proposed investigation. Explain your reasoning.

CHAPTER 14

Secondary Data Analysis and Big Data

I rish researchers Richard Layte (Economic and Social Research Institute) and Christopher Whelan (University College Dublin) sought to improve understanding of poverty in Europe. Rather than design their own data collection effort, they turned to five waves of data from the European Community Household Panel Survey, which were available to them from Eurostat, the Statistical Office of the European Communities (Eurostat 2003). The data they obtained represented the years from 1994 to 1998, thus allowing Layte and Whelan (2003) to investigate whether poverty tends to persist more in some countries than

Research That Matters, Questions That Count

Robert J. Sampson's 2012 book, *Great American City: Chicago and the Enduring Neighborhood Effect,* was a compelling example of the importance sociologists—particularly those associated with the "Chicago School"—have attached to neighborhoods. But it has not been so easy to distinguish the effects of residential location from the effect of group processes and social characteristics that are not necessarily place-based. Andrew Papachristos, David Hureau, and Anthony Braga (2013:418) designed an analysis to explain variation in gang violence with the different influences inside "this theoretical black box."

For their analysis, the authors combined police records of incidents involving gang violence and detailed geographic maps of gang turf boundaries. The records also identified the size of gangs and their racial composition; the authors were able to add from census records indicators of neighborhood poverty, immigrant concentration, and residential stability. These secondary data sources permitted an analysis designed to distinguish the effect of physical proximity from that of social network patterns.

The analysis revealed that gang violence was highly connected and structured in both cities they investigated, Chicago and Boston, with interaction clustering along racial and ethnic cleavages. The likelihood of violence between gangs was related to their physical proximity and to their having a history of conflicts.

1. The article includes a discussion of the quality of police records about homicide and other violent crimes. What might result in more or less accurate police records about crime? Explain your reasoning.

2. Although this analysis makes a unique contribution to understanding gang violence, it is based on a limited number of measures that were available in the data sources. What would be the advantages and disadvantages of studying these processes using ethnographic methods? Using survey research?

In this chapter, you will learn the basic logic and procedures that guide secondary data analysis, as well as a bit about Big Data research projects. By the end of the chapter, you will understand the appeal of secondary data analysis and Big Data analysis and be able to discuss their strengths and limitations. After you finish the chapter, you can test yourself by reading the 2013 *American Sociological Review* article by Papachristos, Hureau, and Braga at the *Investigating the Social World* study site and by completing the related interactive exercises for Chapter 14 at edge.sagepub.com/schutt8e.

Papachristos, Andrew V., David M. Hureau, and Anthony A. Braga. 2013. "The Corner and the Crew: The Influence of Geography and Social Networks on Gang Violence." *American Sociological Review* 78(3):417–447.

---

in others and what factors influence this persistence in different countries. Their investigation of "poverty dynamics" found a tendency for individuals and households to be "trapped" in poverty, but this phenomenon varied with the extent to which countries provided social welfare supports.

Secondary data analysis is the method of using preexisting data in a different way or to answer a different research question than intended by those who collected the data. The most common sources of **secondary data**—previously collected data that are used in a new analysis—are social science surveys and data collected by government agencies, often with survey research methods. It is also possible to reanalyze data that have been collected in experimental studies or with qualitative methods. Even a researcher's reanalysis of data that he or she collected previously qualifies as secondary analysis if it is employed for a new purpose or in response to a methodological critique.

> **Secondary data analysis:** The method of using preexisting data in a different way or to answer a different research question than intended by those who collected the data.
>
> **Secondary data:** Previously collected data that are used in a new analysis.

Thanks to the data collected by social researchers, governments, and organizations over many years, secondary data analysis has become the research method used by many contemporary social scientists to investigate important research questions. Why consider secondary data? (1) Data collected in previous investigations are available for use by other social researchers on a wide range of topics. (2) Available data sets often include many more measures and cases and reflect more rigorous research procedures than another researcher will have the time or resources to obtain in a new investigation. (3) Much of the groundwork involved in creating and testing measures with the data set has already been done. (4) Most important, most funded social science research projects collect data that can be used to investigate new research questions that the primary researchers who collected the data did not consider. Analyzing secondary data, then, is nothing like buying "used goods"!

I will first review the procedures involved in secondary data analysis, identify many of the sources for secondary data sets and explain how to obtain data from these sources. I will give special attention to some easy-to-overlook problems with the use of secondary data. I then introduce the concept of "Big Data," which involves the analysis of data sets of unprecedented size and has only become possible with the development of very powerful information storage and very fast computing facilities. The chapter concludes with some ethical cautions related to the use of these methods.

Journal Link
Geography and
Social Networks

Secondary Data Sources

Secondary data analysis has been an important social science methodology since the earliest days of social research, whether when Karl Marx (1967) reviewed government statistics in the Reading Room of the British Library during the 1850s to 1870s or Émile Durkheim (1966) analyzed official government cause-of-death data for his study of suicide rates throughout Europe in the late 19th century. With the advent of modern computers and, even more important, the Internet, secondary data analysis has become an increasingly accessible social research method. Literally, thousands of large-scale data sets are now available for the secondary data analyst, often with no more effort than the few commands required to download the data set; a number of important data sets can even be analyzed directly on the web by users who lack their own statistical software.

There are many sources of data for secondary analysis within the United States and internationally. These sources range from data compiled by governmental units and private organizations for administrative purposes, which are subsequently made available for research purposes, to data collected by social researchers for one purpose that are then made available for reanalysis. Many important data sets are collected for the specific purpose of facilitating secondary data analysis. Government units from the Census Bureau to the U.S. Department of Housing and Urban Development; international organizations such as the United Nations, the Organisation for Economic Co-operation and Development (OECD), and the World Bank; and internationally involved organizations such as the Central Intelligence Agency (CIA) sponsor a substantial amount of social research that is intended for use by a broader community of social scientists. The National Opinion Research Center (NORC), with its General Social Survey (GSS), and the University of Michigan, with its Detroit Area Studies, are examples of academically based research efforts that are intended to gather data for social scientists to use in analyzing a range of social science research questions.

Many social scientists who have received funding to study one research question have subsequently made the data they collect available to the broader social science community for investigations of other research questions. Many of these data sets are available from a website maintained by the original research organization, often with some access restrictions. Examples include the Add Health study conducted at the University of North Carolina Population Center, the University of Michigan's Health and Retirement Study as well as its Detroit Area Studies, and the United Nations University's World Income Inequality Database.

What makes secondary data analysis such an exciting and growing option today are the considerable resources being devoted to expanding the amount of secondary data and to making it available to social scientists. For example, the National Data Program for the Social Sciences, funded in part by the National Science Foundation, sponsors the ongoing GSS to make current data on a wide range of research questions available to social scientists. Since 1985, the GSS has participated in an International Social Survey Program that generates comparable data from 47 countries around the world (www.issp.org). Another key initiative is the Data Preservation Alliance for the Social Sciences (Data-PASS), funded by the Library of Congress in 2004

Researcher Interview Link
Secondary Data Analysis

> **ICPSR (Inter-university Consortium for Political and Social Research):** Academic consortium that archives data sets online from major surveys and other social science research and makes them available for analysis by others.

as a part of the National Digital Preservation Program (http://www.icpsr.umich.edu/icpsrweb/content/datamanagement/preservation/policies/index.html). This project is designed to ensure the preservation of digitized social science data. Led by the Inter-university Consortium for Political and Social Research (**ICPSR**) at the University of Michigan, it combines the efforts of other major social research organizations, including the Roper Center for Public Opinion Research at the University of Connecticut; the Howard W. Odum Institute for Research in Social Sciences at the University of North Carolina, Chapel Hill; the Henry A. Murray Research Archive and the Harvard-MIT Data Center at Harvard University; and the Electronic and Special Media Records Service Division of the U.S. National Archives and Records Administration.

Video Link
Secondary Data Resources

Fortunately, you do not have to google your way around the web to find all these sources on your own. Many websites provide extensive collections of secondary data. Chief among these is the ICPSR website at the University of Michigan. The University of California at Berkeley's Survey Documentation and Analysis (SDA) archive provides several data sets from national omnibus surveys, as well as from U.S. Census microdata, from surveys on racial attitudes and prejudice, and from several labor and health surveys. The National Archive of Criminal Justice Data is an excellent source of data in the area of criminal justice, although, like many other data collections, including key data from the U.S. Census, it is also available through the ICPSR. Much of the statistical data collected by U.S. federal government agencies can be accessed through the consolidated FedStats website, www.fedstats.gov.

In this section, I describe several sources of online data in more detail. The decennial population census by the U.S. Census Bureau is the single most important governmental data source, but many other data sets are collected by the U.S. Census and by other government agencies, including the U.S. Census Bureau's *Current Population Survey* (*CPS*) and its Survey of Manufactures or the Bureau of Labor Statistics' Consumer Expenditure Survey. These government data sets typically are quantitative; in fact, the term *statistics*—state-istics—is derived from this type of data.

CAREERS AND RESEARCH

Lee Rainie, Pew Research Center

You already know of Lee Rainie's research from findings presented in Chapter 1 from the Pew Research Center Internet Project. Rainie is a graduate of Harvard University and has an MA in political science from Long Island University. He was for many years managing editor at *U.S. News & World Report*, but since 1999, he has directed the Pew Internet Project, a nonprofit, nonpartisan "fact tank" that studies the social impact of the Internet. Since December 1999, the Washington, D.C., research center has explored how people's Internet use affects their families, communities, health care, education, civic and political life, and workplaces.

The project is funded by the Pew Charitable Trusts and has issued more than 500 reports based on its surveys that examine people's online activities and the Internet's role in their lives. All of its reports and data sets are available online for free at http://www.pewinternet.org. The value of their work is apparent in its wide public impact. Rainie and other project staff have testified before Congress on the new media environment, privacy, and family issues related to Internet use. They have also given briefings and presentations to White House officials; several government commissions; the Federal Communications Commission; the Federal Trade Commission; the U.S. Departments of Commerce, Health and Human Services, and Agriculture; the U.S. Conference of Governors, the National Institutes of Health; the Centers for Disease Control and Prevention; the National Conference of State Legislators; and hundreds of other local, state, and federal officials. Project findings are used by the U.S. Census Bureau, the Organisation for Economic Co-operation and Development (OECD), and the World Economic Forum communications and media group. Many researchers use data collected by the Pew Internet Project as the foundation for secondary data analysis projects.

U.S. Census Bureau

The U.S. government has conducted a census of the population every 10 years since 1790; since 1940, this census has also included a census of housing (see also Chapter 5). This decennial Census of Population and Housing is a rich source of social science data (Lavin 1994). The Census Bureau's monthly *CPS* provides basic data on labor force activity that is then used in U.S. Bureau of Labor Statistics reports. The Census Bureau also collects data on agriculture, manufacturers, construction and other business, foreign countries, and foreign trade.

The U.S. Census of Population and Housing aims to survey one adult in every household in the United States. The basic *complete-count* census contains questions about household composition as well as ethnicity and income. More questions are asked in a longer form of the census that is administered to a sample of the households. A separate census of housing characteristics is conducted at the same time (Rives & Serow 1988:15). Participation in the census is required by law, and confidentiality of the information obtained is mandated by law for 72 years after collection. Census data are reported for geographic units, including states, metropolitan areas, counties, census tracts (small, relatively permanent areas within counties), and even blocks (see Exhibit 14.1). These different units allow units of analysis to be tailored to research questions. Census data are used to apportion seats in the U.S. House of Representatives and to determine federal and state legislative district boundaries, as well as to inform other decisions by government agencies.

Exhibit 14.1	Census Small-Area Geography

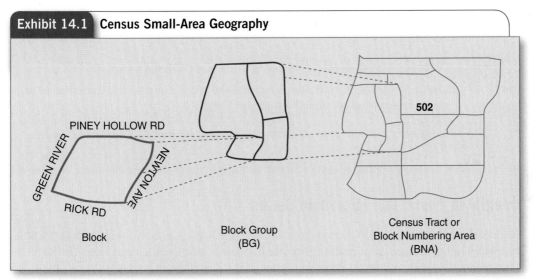

Source: U.S. Census Bureau (1994:8).

The U.S. Census website (www.census.gov) provides much information about the nearly 100 surveys and censuses that the Census Bureau directs each year, including direct access to many statistics for particular geographic units. An interactive data retrieval system, American FactFinder, is the primary means for distributing results from the 2010 Census: You can review its organization and download data at http://factfinder2 .census.gov/main.html. The catalog of the ICPSR (www.icpsr.umich.edu/icpsrweb/ICPSR/) also lists many census reports. Many census files containing microdata—records from persons, households, or housing units— are available online, and others can be purchased on CD-ROM or DVD from the Customer Services Center at (301) 763-INFO (4636); census data can also be inspected online or downloaded for various geographic levels, including counties, cities, census tracts, and even blocks using the DataFerrett application (Federated Electronic Research, Review, Extract, and Tabulation Tool). You can download, install, and use this tool at http://dataferrett.census.gov. This tool also provides access to data sets collected by other federal agencies. An even more accessible way to use U.S. Census data is through the website maintained by the Social Science Data Analysis Network, at www.ssdan.net/. Check out the DataCounts! options.

States also maintain census bureaus and may have additional resources. Some contain the original census data collected in the state 100 or more years ago. The ambitious historical researcher can use these data to conduct detailed comparative studies at the county or state level (Lathrop 1968:79).

Research in the News

LONG-TERM IMPACT; HOW CAN RESEARCH MAKE THE CONNECTION?

Researchers are using quantitative data analysis to determine the long-term effects of Title IX—which required equal treatment for men and women in educational activities—on women's health and overall educational success. By controlling factors such as school size, income, and social differences Betsey Stevenson was able to conclude that Title IX had a direct effect on female achievement. Robert Kaestner found that female athletes have a 7% lower risk of obesity years after participation in high school sports. These researchers compiled data on high school sports participation from the National Federation of State High School Associations and used census data to test their hypotheses.

For Further Thought

1. What are some advantages of using census data to test hypotheses like this?

2. Name one variable that is unlikely to be measured in the Census but that you feel would be useful in an analysis of the long-term effects of Title IX.

News source: Parker-Pope, Tara. 2010. "As Girls Become Women, Sports Pay Dividends." *The New York Times,* February 16:D5.

Integrated Public Use Microdata Series

Individual-level samples from U.S. Census data for the years 1850 to 2000, as well as historical census files from several other countries, are available through the Integrated Public Use Microdata Series (IPUMS) at the University of Minnesota's Minnesota Population Center (MPC). These data are prepared in an easy-to-use format that provides consistent codes and names for all the different samples.

This exceptional resource offers 39 samples of the U.S. population selected from 15 federal censuses, as well as results of the Census Bureau's annual American Community Survey from 2000 to 2006. Each sample is independently selected, so that individuals are not linked between samples. In addition to basic demographic measures, variables in the U.S. samples include educational, occupational, and work indicators; respondent income; disability status; immigration status; veteran status; and various household characteristics, including family composition and dwelling characteristics. The international samples include detailed characteristics from hundreds of thousands of individuals in countries ranging from France and Mexico to Kenya and Vietnam. You can view these resources at www.ipums.umn.edu. You must register to download data, but the registration is free.

Bureau of Labor Statistics (BLS)

Another good source of data is the BLS of the U.S. Department of Labor, which collects and analyzes data on employment, earnings, prices, living conditions, industrial relations, productivity and technology, and occupational safety and health (U.S. Bureau of Labor Statistics 1991, 1997b). Some of these data are collected by the U.S. Census Bureau in the monthly *CPS;* other data are collected through surveys of establishments (U.S. Bureau of Labor Statistics 1997a).

The *CPS* provides a monthly employment and unemployment record for the United States, classified by age, sex, race, and other characteristics. The *CPS* uses a stratified random sample of about 60,000 households (with separate forms for about 120,000 individuals). Detailed questions are included to determine the precise labor force status (whether they are currently working or not) of each household member over the age of 16. Statistical reports are published each month in the BLS's *Monthly Labor Review* and can also be inspected at its website (http://stats.bls.gov). Data sets are available on computer tapes and disks from the BLS and services such as the ICPSR.

Other U.S. Government Sources

Many more data sets useful for historical and comparative research have been collected by federal agencies and other organizations. The National Technical Information Service (NTIS) of the U.S. Department of Commerce maintains a Federal Computer Products Center that collects and catalogs many of these data sets and related reports.

By 2013, more than 3,000,000 data sets and reports were described in the NTIS Database. The NTIS Database is the essential source of information about the data sets and can be searched at www.ntis.gov. Data set summaries can be searched in the database by either subject or agency. Government research reports cataloged by NTIS and other agencies can be searched online at the NTIS website.

Independent Investigator Data Sources

Many researchers who have received funding to investigate a wide range of research topics make their data available on websites where they can be downloaded by other researchers for secondary data analyses. One of the largest, introduced earlier, is the Add Health study, funded at the University of North Carolina by the National Institute of Child Health and Human Development (NICHD) and 23 other agencies and foundations to investigate influences on adolescents' health and risk behaviors (www.cpc.unc.edu/projects/addhealth). The study began in 1994–1995 with a representative sample of more than 90,000 adolescents who completed questionnaires in school and more than 20,000 who were interviewed at home. This first wave of data collection has been followed by three more, resulting in longitudinal data for more than 10 years. Another significant data source, the Health and Retirement Study (HRS), began in 1992 with funding from the National Institute on Aging (NIA) (http://hrsonline.isr.umich.edu/). The University of Michigan oversees HRS interviews every 2 years with more than 22,000 Americans over the age of 50. To investigate family experience change, researchers at the University of Wisconsin designed the National Survey of Families and Households (http://www.ssc.wisc.edu/nsfh/). With funding from both NICHD and NIA, researchers interviewed members of more than 10,000 households in three waves, from 1987 to 2002. Another noteworthy example, among many, is the Detroit Area Studies, with annual surveys between 1951 and 2004 on a wide range of personal, political, and social issues (http://www.icpsr.umich.edu/icpsrweb/ICPSR/series/151).

Inter-university Consortium for Political and Social Research

The University of Michigan's ICPSR is the premier source of secondary data useful to social science researchers. ICPSR was founded in 1962 and now includes more than 640 colleges and universities and other institutions throughout the world. ICPSR archives the most extensive collection of social science data sets in the United States outside the federal government: More than 7,990 studies are represented in more than 500,000 files from 130 countries and from sources that range from U.S. government agencies such as the Census Bureau to international organizations such as the United Nations, social research organizations such as the National Opinion Research Center, and individual social scientists who have completed funded research projects.

The data sets archived by ICPSR are available for downloading directly from the ICPSR website, www.icpsr.umich.edu. ICPSR makes data sets obtained from government sources available directly to the general public, but many other data sets are available only to individuals at the colleges and universities around the world that have paid the fees required to join ICPSR. The availability of some data sets is restricted because of confidentiality issues (see the section later in this chapter on research ethics); to use them, researchers must sign a contract and agree to certain conditions (see http://www.icpsr.umich.edu/icpsrweb/content/ICPSR/access/restricted/index.html).

Survey data sets obtained in the United States and in many other countries that are stored at the ICPSR provide data on topics ranging from elite attitudes to consumer expectations. For example, data collected in the British Social Attitudes Survey in 1998, designated by the University of Chicago's National Opinion Research Center, are available through the ICPSR (go to the ICPSR website, www.icpsr.umich.edu, and search for study no. 3101). Data collected in a monthly survey of Spaniards' attitudes, by the Center for Research on Social Reality (Spain) Survey, are also available (see study no. 6964). Survey data from Russia, Germany, and other countries can also be found in the ICPSR collection.

Do you have an interest in events and interactions between nations, such as threats of military force? A data set collected by Charles McClelland includes characteristics of 91,240 such events (study no. 5211). The history of military interventions in nations around the world between 1946 and 1988 is coded in a data set developed by Frederic Pearson and Robert Baumann (study no. 6035). This data set identifies the intervener and target countries, the starting and ending dates of military intervention, and a range of potential motives (such as foreign policies, related domestic disputes, and pursuit of rebels across borders).

Research|Social Impact Link

Sharing Research

Census data from other nations are also available through the ICPSR, as well as directly through the Internet. In the ICPSR archives, you can find a data set from the Statistical Office of the United Nations on the 1966 to 1974 population of 220 nations throughout the world (study no. 7623). More current international population data are available through data sets available from a variety of sources, such as the study of indicators of globalization from 1975 to 1995 (study no. 4172). (See also the later description of the Eurobarometer Survey Series.) More than 3,000 data sets from countries outside the United States are available through ICPSR's International Data Resource Center.

Obtaining Data From ICPSR

You begin a search for data in the ICPSR archives at http://www.icpsr.umich.edu/icpsrweb/ICPSR/index.jsp. Exhibit 14.2 shows the search screen as I began a search for data from studies involving a subject of domestic violence. You can also see in this screen that you can search the data archives for specific studies, identified by study number or title, as well as for studies by specific investigators (this would be a quick way to find the data set contributed by Lawrence W. Sherman and Richard A. Berk from their research, discussed in Chapter 2, on the police response to domestic violence).

Exhibit 14.3 displays the results of my search: a list of 635 data sets that involved research on domestic violence and that are available through ICPSR. For most data sets, you can obtain a description, the files that are available for downloading, and a list of "related literature"—that is, reports and articles that use the listed data set. Some data sets are made available in collections on a CD-ROM; the CD-ROM's contents are described in detail on the ICPSR site, but you have to place an order to receive the CD-ROM itself.

When you click on the "Download" option, you are first asked to enter your e-mail address and password (ICPSR also has the option that allows sign-in with a Facebook account). What you enter will determine which data sets you can access; if you are not at an ICPSR member institution, you will be able to download only a limited portion of the data sets—mostly those from government sources. If you are a student at a member institution, you will be able to download most of the data sets directly, although you may have to be using a computer that is physically on your campus to do so. Exhibit 14.4 displays the "Terms of Use" ICPSR download screen after I selected files I wanted to download from the study by Lisa Newmark, Adele Harrell, and Bill Adams on victim ratings of police response in New York and Texas. Because I wanted to analyze the data with the SPSS statistical package, I downloaded the data set in the form of an "SPSS Portable File." The files downloaded in a zipped file, so I used the WinZip program to unzip them. After unzipping the SPSS portable file, I was able to start my data analysis with the SPSS program. If you'd like to learn how to analyze data with the SPSS statistical program, review Chapter 9 and Appendix D (on the student study site).

Exhibit 14.2 **Search Screen: Domestic Violence**

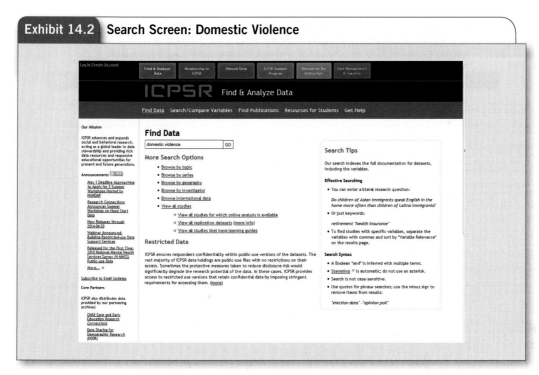

Source: Reprinted with permission from the Inter-university Consortium for Political and Social Research.

Exhibit 14.3 **Search Screen: Domestic Violence Search Results**

Source: Reprinted with permission from the Inter-university Consortium for Political and Social Research.

| Exhibit 14.4 | ICPSR Terms of Use |

Terms of Use

Please read the terms of use below. If you agree to them, click on the "I Agree" button to proceed. If you do not agree, you can click on the "I Do Not Agree" button to return to the home page.

ICPSR adheres to the principles of the Data Seal of Approval ↗, which, in part, require the data consumer to comply with access regulations imposed both by law and by the data repository, and to conform to codes of conduct that are generally accepted in higher education and scientific research for the exchange of knowledge and information.

These data are distributed under the following terms of use, which are governed by ICPSR. By continuing past this point to the data retrieval process, you signify your agreement to comply with the requirements stated below:

Privacy of RESEARCH SUBJECTS

Any intentional identification of a RESEARCH SUBJECT (whether an individual or an organization) or unauthorized disclosure of his or her confidential information violates the PROMISE OF CONFIDENTIALITY given to the providers of the information. Therefore, users of data agree:

- To use these datasets solely for research or statistical purposes and not for investigation of specific RESEARCH SUBJECTS, except when identification is authorized in writing by ICPSR (netmail@icpsr.umich.edu ✉)

- To make no use of the identity of any RESEARCH SUBJECT discovered inadvertently, and to advise ICPSR of any such discovery (netmail@icpsr.umich.edu ✉)

Redistribution of Data

You agree not to redistribute data or other materials without the written agreement of ICPSR, unless:

1. You serve as the OFFICIAL or DESIGNATED REPRESENTATIVE at an ICPSR MEMBER INSTITUTION and are assisting AUTHORIZED USERS with obtaining data, or

2. You are collaborating with other AUTHORIZED USERS to analyze the data for research or instructional purposes.

When sharing data or other materials in these approved ways, you must include all accompanying files with the data, including terms of use. More information on permission to redistribute data can be found on the ICPSR Web site.

Citing Data

You agree to reference the recommended bibliographic citation in any publication that employs resources provided by ICPSR. Authors of publications based on ICPSR data are required to send citations of their published works to ICPSR for inclusion in a database of related publications (bibliography@icpsr.umich.edu ✉) .

Disclaimer

You acknowledge that the original collector of the data, ICPSR, and the relevant funding agency bear no responsibility for use of the data or for interpretations or inferences based upon such uses.

Violations

If ICPSR determines that the terms of this agreement have been violated, ICPSR will act according to our policy on terms of use violations. Sanctions can include:

- ICPSR may revoke the existing agreement, demand the return of the data in question, and deny all future access to ICPSR data.

- The violation may be reported to the Research Integrity Officer, Institutional Review Board, or Human Subjects Review Committee of the user's institution. A range of sanctions are available to institutions including revocation of tenure and termination.

- If the confidentiality of human subjects has been violated, the case may be reported to the Federal Office for Human Research Protections. This may result in an investigation of the user's institution, which can result in institution-wide sanctions including the suspension of all research grants.

- A court may award the payment of damages to any individual(s)/organization(s) harmed by the breach of the agreement.

Source: Reprinted with permission from the Inter-university Consortium for Political and Social Research.

If you prepare your own paper based on an analysis of ICPSR data, be sure to include a proper citation. Here's an example from the ICPSR itself (www.icpsr.umich.edu/icpsrweb/ICPSR/citations/):

> Reif, Karlheinz, and Anna Melich. *Euro-Barometer 39.0: European Community Policies and Family Life, March–April 1993* [Computer file]. Conducted by INRA (Europe), Brussels. ICPSR06195-v4. Ann Arbor, MI: Inter-university Consortium for Political and Social Research [producer], 1995. Koeln, Germany: Zentralarchiv fuer Empirische Sozialforschung/Ann Arbor, MI: Inter-university Consortium for Political and Social Research [distributors], 1997.

You can also search the entire ICPSR database for specific variables and identify the various studies in which they have appeared. Exhibit 14.5 displays one segment of the results of searching for variables related to "victimization." A total of 23,500 names of variables in a multitude of studies were obtained. Reviewing some of these results can suggest additional search strategies and alternative databases to consider.

Some of the data sets are also offered with the option of "Analyze Online." If you have this option, you can immediately inspect the distributions of responses to each question in a survey and examine the relation between variables, without having any special statistical programs of your own. At the bottom of Exhibit 14.6, you'll find the wording reported in the study "codebook" for a question used in the study of police stress and

Exhibit 14.5 ICPSR Variables Related to Victimization

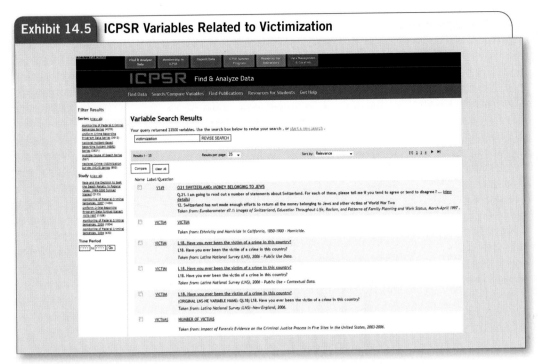

Source: Reprinted with permission from the Inter-university Consortium for Political and Social Research.

Exhibit 14.6 ICPSR Online Analysis: Codebook Information and Statistical Options

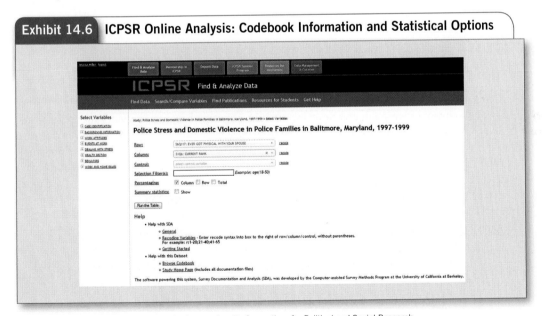

Source: Reprinted with permission from the Inter-university Consortium for Political and Social Research.

domestic violence in Baltimore, as well as, in the top portion, the available statistical options. After choosing one or more variables from the codebook, you can request the analysis.

My analysis involves a cross-tabulation of the relation between likelihood of getting physical with a spouse or partner by officer rank. As you can see in Exhibit 14.7, officer rank is related to likelihood of getting physical with a spouse or partner: 1.1% of the officer trainees report they have done this, compared with 10.4% of the detectives. This approach to analysis with secondary data can jump-start your work (and may jump-start some interesting discussion as well). An online analysis option is also starting to appear at other websites that offer secondary data.

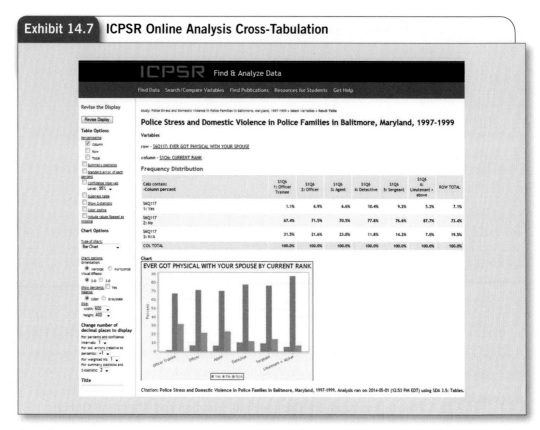

Exhibit 14.7 ICPSR Online Analysis Cross-Tabulation

Source: Reprinted with permission from the Inter-university Consortium for Political and Social Research.

ICPSR also catalogs reports and publications containing analyses that have used ICPSR data sets since 1962—64,498 citations were in this archive on July 10, 2014. This superb resource provides an excellent starting point for the literature search that should precede a secondary data analysis. In most cases, you can learn from detailed study reports a great deal about the study methodology, including the rate of response in a sample survey and the reliability of any indexes constructed. Published articles provide examples of how others have described the study methodology as well as research questions that have already been studied with the data set and issues that remain to be resolved. You can search this literature at the ICPSR site simply by entering the same search terms that you used to find data sets or by entering the specific study number of the data set on which you have focused (see Exhibit 14.8). Don't start a secondary analysis without reviewing such reports and publications.

Even if you are using ICPSR, you shouldn't stop your review of the literature with the sources listed on the ICPSR site. Conduct a search in SocINDEX or another bibliographic database to learn about related studies that used different databases (see Chapter 2).

Institute for Quantitative Social Science

Harvard University's Henry A. Murray Research Archive (www.murray.harvard.edu) has developed a remarkable collection of social science research data sets that are now made available through a larger collaborative secondary data project as part of its Institute for Quantitative Social Science (IQSS) (http://dvn .iq.harvard.edu/dvn). As of July 2014, IQSS provided information on 54,394 studies, cross-referencing many of

Exhibit 14.8   ICPSR Bibliography Search

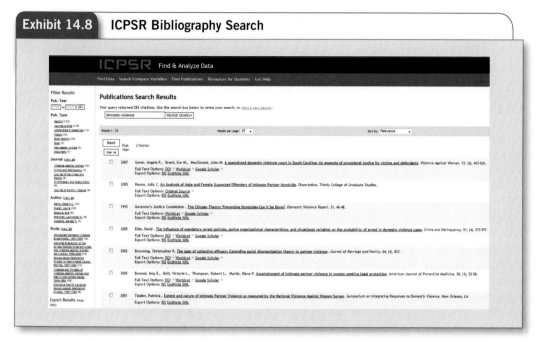

Source: Reprinted with permission from the Inter-university Consortium for Political and Social Research.

those in the ICPSR archives. You can search data sets in the IQSS collection by title, abstract, keywords, and other fields; if you identify a data set that you would like to analyze, you must then submit an application to be given access.

International Data Sources

Comparative researchers and those conducting research in other countries can find data sets on the population characteristics, economic and political features, and political events of many nations. Some of these are available from U.S. government agencies. For example, the Social Security Administration reports on the characteristics of social security throughout the world (Wheeler 1995). This comprehensive source classifies nations by their type of social security program and provides detailed summaries of the characteristics of each nation's programs. Current information is available online at www.ssa.gov/policy/docs/progdesc/ssptw/index.html. More recent data are organized by region. A broader range of data is available in the *World Handbook of Political and Social Indicators,* with political events and political, economic, and social data coded from 1948 to 1982 (www.icpsr.umich.edu, study no. 7761) (Taylor & Jodice 1986).

The European Commission administers the Eurobarometer Survey Series at least twice yearly across all the member states of the European Union. The survey monitors social and political attitudes and reports are published regularly online at www.gesis.org/en/services/data/survey-data/eurobarometer-data-service. Case-level Eurobarometer survey data are stored at the ICPSR. The United Nations University makes available a World Income Inequality Database from ongoing research on income inequality in developed, developing, and transition countries (http://www.wider.unu.edu/research/Database/en_GB/wiid). ICPSR also maintains an International Data Resource Center that provides access to many other data sets from around the world (www.icpsr.umich.edu/icpsrweb/IDRC/index.jsp).

Both the Council of European Social Science Data Archives (CESSDA, www.cessda.org/) and the International Federation of Data Organizations (IFDO, www.ifdo.org/) maintain lists of data archives upheld by a wide range of nations (Dale, Wathan, & Higgins 2008:521). CESSDA makes available more than 9,200 data sets from European countries to European researchers (as of July 2014), and IFDO provides an overview of social science data sets collected throughout the world; access procedures vary, but some data sets can be downloaded directly from the IFDO site.

Qualitative Data Sources

Far fewer qualitative data sets are available for secondary analysis, but the number is growing. European countries, particularly England, have been in the forefront of efforts to promote archiving of qualitative data. The United Kingdom's Economic and Social Research Council established the Qualitative Data Archiving Resource Center at the University of Essex in 1994 (Heaton 2008:507). Now part of the Economic and Social Data Service, UK Data Service QualiBank (2014) provides access to data from 888 qualitative research projects. After registering at the UK Data Service site, interview transcripts and other materials from many qualitative studies can be browsed or searched directly online, but access to many studies is restricted to users in the United Kingdom or according to other criteria.

In the United States, the ICPSR collection includes an expanding number of studies containing at least some qualitative data or measures coded from qualitative data (494 such studies as of May 2011). Studies range from transcriptions of original handwritten and published materials relating to infant and child care from the beginning of the 20th century to World War II (LaRossa 1995) to transcripts of open-ended interviews with high school students involved in violent incidents (Lockwood 1996). Harvard University's Institute for Quantitative Social Science has archived more than 400 studies that contain at least some qualitative data (as of July 2014).

The most unique source of qualitative data available for researchers in the United States is the Human Relations Area Files (HRAF) at Yale University, described in Chapter 13. The HRAF has made anthropological reports available for international cross-cultural research since 1949 and currently contains more than 1,000,000 pages of information on more than 400 different cultural, ethnic, religious, and national groups (Ember & Ember 2011). If you are interested in cross-cultural research, it is well worth checking out the HRAF and exploring access options (reports can be accessed and searched online by those at affiliated institutions).

The University of Southern Maine's Center for the Study of Lives (usm.maine.edu/olli/national/lifestory center/) collects interview transcripts that record the life stories of people of diverse ages and backgrounds. As of July 2014, their collection included transcripts from more than 400 life stories, representing more than 35 different ethnic groups, experiences of historical events ranging from the Great Depression to the Vietnam War, and including reports on dealing with health problems such as HIV/AIDS. These qualitative data are available directly online without any registration or fee.

There are many other readily available sources, including administrative data from hospitals, employers, and other organizations; institutional research data from university offices that collect such data; records of transactions from businesses; and data provided directly by university-based researchers (Hakim 1982:6).

Journal Link
Qualitative Secondary
Data Analysis

Encyclopedia Link
Secondary Data Analysis
With Statistical Review

🔲 Challenges for Secondary Data Analyses

The use of the method of secondary data analysis has the following clear advantages for social researchers (Rew et al. 2000:226):

- It allows analyses of social processes in other inaccessible settings.

- It saves time and money.

- It allows the researcher to avoid data collection problems.

- It facilitates comparison with other samples.

- It may allow inclusion of many more variables and a more diverse sample than otherwise would be feasible.

- It may allow data from multiple studies to be combined.

The secondary data analyst also faces some unique challenges. The easy availability of data for secondary analysis should not obscure the fundamental differences between a secondary and a primary analysis of social science data. In fact, a researcher who can easily acquire secondary data may be tempted to minimize the limitations of the methods used to collect the data as well as insufficient correspondence between the measures in the data set and the research questions that the secondary analyst wants to answer.

So the greatest challenge faced in secondary data analysis results from the researcher's inability to design data collection methods that are best suited to answer his or her research question. The secondary data analyst also cannot test and refine the methods to be used on the basis of preliminary feedback from the population or processes to be studied. Nor is it possible for the secondary data analyst to engage in the iterative process of making observations, developing concepts, or making more observations and refining the concepts. This last problem is a special challenge for those seeking to conduct secondary analyses of qualitative data because an inductive process of developing research questions and refining observation and interview strategies is a hallmark of much qualitative methodology (Heaton 2008:511).

These limitations mean that it may not be possible for a secondary data analyst to focus on the specific research question of original interest or to use the most appropriate sampling or measurement approach for studying that research question. Secondary data analysis inevitably involves a trade-off between the ease with which the research process can be initiated and the specific hypotheses that can be tested and methods that can be used. If the primary study was not designed to measure adequately a concept that is critical to the secondary analyst's hypothesis, the study may have to be abandoned until a more adequate source of data can be found. Alternatively, hypotheses, or even the research question itself, may be modified to match the analytic possibilities presented by the available data (Riedel 2000:53).

Data quality is always a concern with secondary data, even when the data are collected by an official government agency. Government actions result, at least in part, from political processes that may not have as their first priority the design or maintenance of high-quality data for social scientific analysis. For example, political opposition to the British Census's approach to recording ethnic origin led to changes in the 1991 census that rendered its results inconsistent with prior years and that demonstrated the "tenuous relationship between enumeration [Census] categories and possible social realities" (Fenton 1996:155).

It makes sense to use official records to study the treatment of juveniles accused of illegal acts because these records document the critical decisions to arrest, to convict, or to release (Dannefer & Schutt 1982). But research based on official records can be only as good as the records themselves. In contrast to the controlled interview process in a research study, there is little guarantee that the officials' acts and decisions were recorded in a careful and unbiased manner. The same is true for data collected by employees of private and nonprofit organizations. For example, research on the quality of hospital records has created, at best, mixed support for the validity of the key information they contain (Iezzoni 1997:391).

This one example certainly does not question all legal records or all other types of official records. It does, however, highlight the value of using multiple methods, particularly when the primary method of data collection is analysis of records generated by **street-level bureaucrats**—officials who serve clients and have a high degree of discretion (Lipsky 1980). When officials make decisions and record the bases for their decisions without much supervision, records may diverge considerably from the decisions they are supposed to reflect. More generally, it is always important to learn how people make sense of the social world when we want to describe their circumstances and explain their behavior (Needleman 1981).

> **Street-level bureaucrats:** Officials who serve clients and have a high degree of discretion.

The basis for concern is much greater in research across national boundaries because different data collection systems and definitions of key variables may have been used (Glover 1996). Census counts can be distorted by incorrect answers to census questions as well as by inadequate coverage of the entire population

(Rives & Serow 1988:32–35). National differences in the division of labor between genders within households can confuse the picture when comparing household earnings between nations without accounting for these differences (Jarvis 1997:521).

Reanalyzing qualitative data someone else collected also requires setting aside the expectation that qualitative research procedures and interpretations will be informed by intimate familiarity with the context in which the data were collected and with those from whom the data were obtained (Heaton 2008:511). Instead, the secondary analyst of qualitative data must seek opportunities for carrying on a dialogue with the original researchers.

Many of these problems can be lessened by seeking conscientiously to review data features and quality before deciding to develop an analysis of secondary data (Riedel 2000:55–69; Stewart & Kamins 1993:17–31) and then developing analysis plans that maximize the value of the available data. Replicating key analyses with alternative indicators of key concepts, testing for the stability of relationships across theoretically meaningful subsets of the data, and examining findings of comparable studies conducted with other data sets can each strengthen confidence in the findings of a secondary analysis.

Any secondary analysis will improve if the analyst—yourself or the author of the work that you are reviewing—answers several questions before deciding to develop an analysis of secondary data in the first place and then continues to develop these answers as the analysis proceeds (adapted from Riedel 2000:55–69; Stewart & Kamins 1993:17–31):

1. What were the agency's or researcher's goals in collecting the data?

The goals of the researcher, research, or research sponsor influence every step in the process of designing a research project, analyzing the resulting data, and reporting the results. Some of these goals will be stated quite explicitly, but others may only be implicit—reflected in the decisions made but not acknowledged in the research report or other publications. When you consider whether to use a data set for a secondary analysis, you should consider whether your own research goals are similar to those of the original investigator and sponsor. The data collected are more likely to include what is necessary for achieving your own research goals if the original investigator or sponsor had similar goals. When your research question or other goals diverge from those of the original investigator, you should consider how this divergence may have affected the course of the primary research project and whether this affects your ability to use the resulting data for a different purpose.

For example, Pamela Paxton (2002) studied the role of secondary organizations in democratic politics in a sample of 101 countries, but found that she could only measure the prevalence of international nongovernmental associations (INGOs) because comparable figures on purely national associations were not available. She cautioned, "INGOs represent only a specialized subset of all the associations present in a country" (Paxton 2002:261). We need to consider this limitation when interpreting the results of her secondary analysis.

2. What data were collected, and what were they intended to measure?

You should develop a clear description of how data enter the data collection system, for what purpose, and how cases leave the system and why. Try to obtain the guidelines that agency personnel are supposed to follow in processing cases. Have there been any changes in these procedures during the period of investigation (Riedel 2000:57–64)?

3. When was the information collected?

Both historical and comparative analyses can be affected. For example, the percentage of the U.S. population not counted in the United States Census appears to have declined since 1880 from about 7% to 1%, but undercounting continues to be more common among poorer urban dwellers and recent immigrants (King & Magnuson 1995; see also Chapter 5). The relatively successful 2000 U.S. Census reduced undercounting (Forero 2000b) but still suffered from accusations of shoddy data collection procedures in some areas (Forero 2000a).

4. What methods were used for data collection? Who was responsible for data collection, and what were their qualifications? Are they available to answer questions about the data?

Each step in the data collection process should be charted and the involved personnel identified. The need for concern is much greater in research across national boundaries because different data collection systems and definitions of key variables may have been used (Glover 1996). Incorrect answers to census questions as well as inadequate coverage of the entire population can distort census counts (see Chapter 5; Rives & Serow 1988:32–35). Copies of the forms used for data collection should be obtained, specific measures should be inspected, and the ways in which these data are processed by the agency/agencies should be reviewed.

5. How is the information organized (by date, event, etc.)? Are there identifiers that are used to identify the different types of data available (computer tapes, disks, paper files) (Riedel 2000:58–61)?

Answers to these questions can have a major bearing on the work that will be needed to carry out the study.

6. What is known about the success of the data collection effort? How are missing data indicated? What kind of documentation is available? How consistent are the data with data available from other sources?

The U.S. Census Bureau provides extensive documentation about data quality, including missing data, and it documents the efforts it makes to improve data quality. The Census 2000 Testing, Experimentation, and Evaluation Program was designed to improve the decennial census in 2010, as well as other Census Bureau censuses and surveys. This is an ongoing effort, since 1950, with tests of questionnaire design and other issues. You can read more about it at www.census.gov/pred/www/Intro.htm.

Answering these questions helps ensure that the researcher is familiar with the data he or she will analyze and can help identify any problems with it. It is unlikely that you or any secondary data analyst will be able to develop complete answers to all these questions before starting an analysis, but it still is critical to attempt to assess what you know and don't know about data quality before deciding whether to conduct the analysis. If you uncover bases for real concern after checking documents, the other publications with the data, information on websites, and perhaps by making some phone calls, you may have to decide to reject the analytic plan and instead search for another data set. If your initial answers to these six questions give sufficient evidence that the data can reasonably be used to answer your research question, you should still keep seeking to fill in missing gaps in your initial answers to the six questions; through this ongoing process, you will develop the fullest possible understanding of the quality of your data. This understanding can lead you to steer your analysis in the most productive directions and can help you write a convincing description of the data set's advantages and limitations.

This seems like a lot to ask, doesn't it? After all, you can be married for life after answering only one question; here, I'm encouraging you to attempt to answer six questions before committing yourself to a brief relationship with a data set. Fortunately, the task is not normally so daunting. If you acquire a data set for analysis from a trusted source, many of these questions will already have been answered for you. You may need to do no more than read through a description of data available on a website to answer the secondary data questions and consider yourself prepared to use the data for your own purposes. If you are going to be conducting major analyses of a data set, you should take more time to read the complete study documents, review other publications with the data, and learn about the researchers who collected the data.

Exhibit 14.9 contains the description of a data set available from the ICPSR. Read through it and see how many of the secondary data questions it answers.

You will quickly learn that this data set represents one survey conducted as part of the ongoing Detroit Area Studies, so you'll understand the data set better if you also read a general description of that survey project (Exhibit 14.10).

In an environment in which so many important social science data sets are quickly available for reanalysis, the method of secondary data analysis should permit increasingly rapid refinement of social science knowledge,

---

Exhibit 14.9 ICPSR Data Set Description

Description—Study No. 4120

Bibliographic Description

ICPSR Study No.:	4120
Title:	Detroit Area Study, 1997: Social Change in Religion and Child Rearing
Principal Investigator(s):	Duane Alwin, University of Michigan
Series:	*Detroit Area Studies Series*
Bibliographic Citation:	Alwin, Duane. DETROIT AREA STUDY, 1997: SOCIAL CHANGE IN RELIGION AND CHILD REARING [Computer file]. ICPSR04120-v1. Ann Arbor, MI: Detroit Area Studies [producer], 1997. Ann Arbor, MI: Inter-university Consortium for Political and Social Research [distributor], 2005-06-02.
Scope of Study *Summary:*	For this survey, respondents from three counties in the Detroit, Michigan, area were queried about their work, health, marriage and family, finances, political views, religion, and child rearing. With respect to finances, respondent views were elicited on credit card purchases, recording expenditures, and savings and investments. Regarding political views, respondents were. . . .
Subject Term(s):	*abortion, Atheism, Bible, birth control, Catholicism, Catholics, child rearing, children, Christianity, church attendance, communism, Creationism, credit card use, divorce, drinking behavior, economic behavior, educational background, employment, ethnicity, families, . . .*
Geographic Coverage:	Detroit, Michigan, United States
Time Period:	1997
Date(s) of Collection:	1997
Universe:	Residents 21 years and older in the tri-county area (Wayne, Oakland, and Macomb) of Michigan.
Data Type:	survey data
Methodology *Sample:*	A random-digit dialing sample of residential telephone numbers in the Michigan counties of Wayne, Oakland, and Macomb. The sample was restricted to adults 21 years of age and older.
Mode of Data Collection:	telephone interview
Extent of Processing:	CDBK.ICPSR/ DDEF.ICPSR/ REFORM.DATA
Access & Availability *Extent of Collection:*	1 data file + machine-readable documentation (PDF) + SAS setup file + SPSS setup file + Stata setup file
Data Format:	Logical Record Length with SAS, SPSS, and Stata setup files, SPSS portable file, and Stata system file
Original ICPSR Release:	2005-06-02

Source: From *Detroit Area Study, 1997: Social Change in Religion and Child Rearing.* Inter-university Consortium for Political and Social Research. Reprinted with permission.

as new hypotheses can be tested and methodological disputes clarified if not resolved quickly. Both the necessary technology and the supportive ideologies required for this rapid refinement have spread throughout the world. Social science researchers now have the opportunity to take advantage of this methodology as well as the responsibility to carefully and publicly delineate and acknowledge the limitations of the method.

Exhibit 14.10 | **ICPSR Description of Detroit Area Studies**

Detroit Area Studies Series

- View studies in the series
- Related Literature

The Detroit Area Studies series was initiated in 1951 at the University of Michigan and has been carried out nearly every year till the present. The Department of Sociology and the Survey Research Center of the Institute for Social Research are associated with the development of the series. It was initially supported by funds from the Ford Foundation, but since 1988 the University of Michigan has provided primary financial support for the series, with supplemental funding obtained frequently from outside sources. The purpose of these surveys is to provide practical social research training for graduate students and reliable data on the Greater Detroit community. Each survey probes a different aspect of personal and public life, economic and political behavior, political attitudes, professional and family life, and living experiences in the Detroit metropolitan area. The different specific problems investigated each year are selected by the executive committee of the project.

Source: From *Detroit Area Study, 1997: Social Change in Religion and Child Rearing.* Inter-university Consortium for Political and Social Research. Reprinted with permission.

▣ Big Data

When do secondary data become what is now referred to as "Big Data"? After learning that ICPSR offers more than 500,000 files, the reasonable answer may seem to be "it doesn't get much bigger than that!" But there's big and then there's "Big!" **Big Data** refers to data involving an entirely different order of magnitude than what we are used to thinking about as large data sets.

> **Big Data:** Massive datasets produced or accessible in computer-readable form that are produced by people, available to social scientists, and manageable with today's computers.

Overview

Here are some examples of what now qualifies as Big Data (Mayer-Schönberger & Cukier 2013:8–9): Facebook users upload more than 10 million photos every hour and leave a comment or click on a "like" button almost three billion times per day; YouTube users upload more than an hour of video every second; Twitter users were already sending more than 400 million tweets per day in 2012. If all this and other forms of stored information in the world were printed in books, one estimate in 2013 was that these books would cover the face of the Earth 52 layers thick. That's "Big."

All this information would be of no more importance than the number of grains of sand on the beach or of stars in the sky except that these numbers describe information produced by people, available to social scientists, and manageable with today's computers. Already, Big Data analyses are being used to predict the spread of flu, the price of airline tickets, and the behavior of consumers. Access to Big Data also provides another method for investigating the social world, and it is being used increasingly to address important social research questions.

Here's a quick demonstration: What could be more important than interest in sociology and other social sciences? After all, if you have declared sociology or another social science as your major, you probably think that this discipline is having a positive impact in the social world; maybe you want to contribute something to that impact yourself. So would you like to know how popular your discipline is? One way to answer that question is to see how frequently the name of the discipline has appeared in all the books ever written in the world. It may surprise you to learn that it is possible right now to answer that question, although with two key limitations: we can only examine books written in English and in several other languages and as of 2014 we are limited to "only" one quarter of all books ever published—a mere 30 million books (Aiden & Michel 2013:16).

Ngrams: Frequency graphs produced by Google's database of all words printed in more than one third of the world's books over time (with coverage still expanding).

To check this out, go to the Google **Ngrams** site (https://books.google.com/ngrams), type in "sociology, political science, anthropology, criminology, psychology, economics," and check the "case-insensitive" box (and change the ending year to 2010). Exhibit 14.11 shows the resulting screen (if you don't obtain a graph, try using a different browser). Note that the height of a graph line represents the percentage that the term represents of all words in books published in each year, so a rising line means greater relative interest in the word, not simply more books being published. You can see that psychology emerges in the mid-19th century, while sociology, economics, anthropology, and political science appear in the latter part of that century, and criminology arrives in the early 20th century. You can see that interest in sociology soared as the 1960s progressed, but then dropped off sharply in the 1980s. What else can you see in the graph? It's hard to stop checking other ideas by adding in other terms, searching in other languages, or shifting to another topic entirely.

Exhibit 14.11   Ngram of Social Sciences

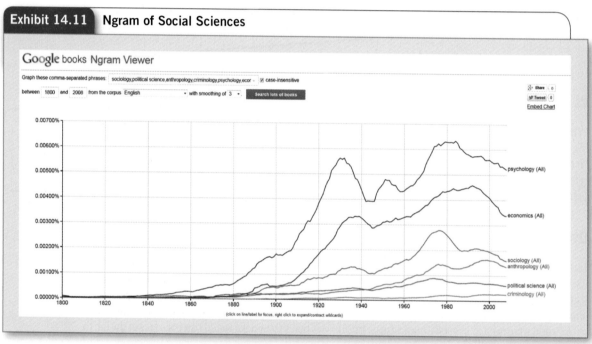

Source: Google Books Ngram Viewer, http://books.google.com/ngrams.

Make no mistake about it: The potential for Big Data is not just of academic interest—Big Data work is already changing lives. For example, Jeremy Ginsberg and some colleagues (2009:1012) at Google realized they could improve the response to the spread of flu around the world by taking advantage of the fact that about 90 million U.S. adults search online for information about specific illnesses each year. Ginsberg et al. started a collaboration with the U.S. Centers for Disease Control and Prevention (CDC), which collects data from about 2,700 health centers about patients' flu symptoms each year (Butler 2013:155). By comparing this official CDC data with information from the Google searches, Ginsberg and his colleagues were able to develop a Big Data–based procedure for predicting the onset of the flu.

Rather than having to wait for patients to visit doctors and for the doctors to file reports—as the CDC does, the Google search approach learns about trends when people first start to experience symptoms and are searching with Google to see what is wrong with them and what to do about it. Google now also compiles trend data on searches for dengue fever, a scourge in tropical countries. You can see the latest trends yourself at http://www.google.org/flutrends.

But there's also a cautionary tale in Google's experience with predicting flu trends. In the 2013 flu season, Google Flu Trends predicted a much higher peak level of flu than actually occurred. The problem seems to have been that widespread media coverage and the declaration of a public health emergency in New York led many more people than usual to search for flu-related information, even though they were not experiencing symptoms themselves. Google has been refining its procedures to account for this problem, and other researchers have shifted their attention to analysis of flu-related "tweets" or to data from networks of thousands of volunteers who report symptoms experienced by family members to a central database (Butler 2013). So having incredible amounts of data does not allow us to forget about the potential for problems in measurement or sampling.

Video Link
Big Data

Issues

Using Big Data is not a research method in itself, but the availability of Big Data and technologies for its analysis mean that researchers can apply standard research methods in exciting new ways. It is not the first time that changes in data availability and technology have altered the use of research methods. For example, the 1880 U.S. Census took 8 years to complete, and it was widely predicted that the 1890 census would take much longer. Fortunately for the future of the U.S. Census, the processing of the 1890 census was shortened to one year after Herman Hollerith invented the punch card and machines for tabulating them (Mayer-Schönberger & Cukier 2013:21–22). But, as you learned in Chapter 5, conducting a census of the U.S. population is still a massive, expensive undertaking; the only way to collect data about the U.S. population more frequently than every 10 years has been to draw random samples. Big Data now permits researchers investigating some issues to forego drawing samples in favor of analyzing data from an entire population (Mayer-Schönberger & Cukier 2013:26–27).

The sources of Big Data are increasing rapidly. One billion people use Facebook, thereby creating digital records that can, with appropriate arrangements, be analyzed to better understand social behavior (Aiden & Michel 2013:12). Big Data are also generated by global positioning system (GPS) users, social media, smartphones, wristband health monitors, student postings, and even student activity in online education programs (Mayer-Schönberger & Cukier 2013:90–96, 115). A new Big Data system records preemies' heart rate, respiration rate, temperature—what amounts to 1,260 data points per second—and can predict the onset of infection 24 hours before the appearance of overt symptoms (Mayer-Schönberger & Cukier 2013:60). Public utilities, government agencies, and private companies can all learn about their customers from analyzing patterns revealed in their records. Although much of these data are inaccessible to those who are not given permission by the organizations that collect the data, and none of it is of value for those who lack the appropriate computing power and statistical skills, it is all creating possibilities for investigation of the social world that could not have been envisioned even 20 years ago.

Audio Link
Big Data

The availability of Big Data allows the transformation of what were previously conducted as small-scale research projects into activities that literally change the social environment. In a striking example, Robert Bond, James Fowler, and others at Facebook and the University of California, San Diego, conducted a randomized experiment with Facebook on the day of the 2010 congressional elections (Bond et al. 2012:295). Here is their description of the research design:

> Users [of Facebook] were randomly assigned to a "social message" group, an "informational message" group, or a control group. The social message group ($n = 60,055,176$) was shown a statement at the top of their "News Feed." This message encouraged the user to vote, provided a link to find local polling places, showed a clickable button reading "I Voted," showed a counter indicating how many other Facebook users had previously reported voting, and displayed up to six small randomly selected "profile pictures" of the user's Facebook friends who had already clicked the I Voted button. . . . The informational message group ($n = 611,044$) was shown the message, poll information, counter, and button, but they were not shown any faces of friends. The control group ($n = 613,096$) did not receive any message at the top of their News Feed.

As indicated in Exhibit 14.12, individuals in the group that received the personalized message about their friends having voted were more likely to vote—and the effect was higher the more closely connected they were to those friends. Bond et al. (2012:297) estimate that receiving this message brought an extra 60,000 voters to the polls in 2010, whereas the effect of friends having seen the message could have increased turnout by 280,000 votes!

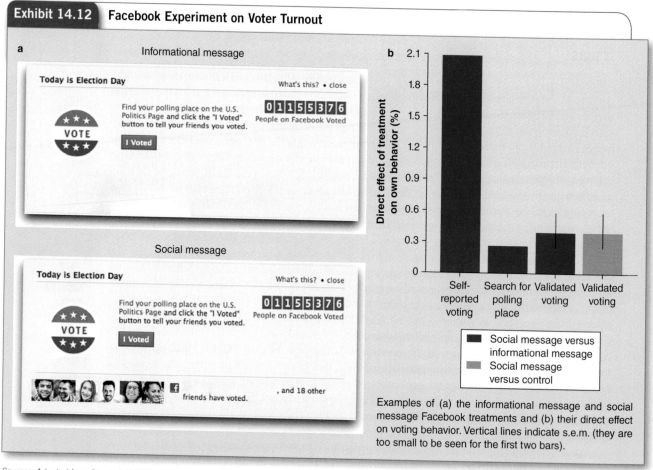

Exhibit 14.12   Facebook Experiment on Voter Turnout

Examples of (a) the informational message and social message Facebook treatments and (b) their direct effect on voting behavior. Vertical lines indicate s.e.m. (they are too small to be seen for the first two bars).

Sources: Adapted from Bond et al. (2012:296); row of photos: © istockpoto.com/franckreporter.

The availability of Big Data also makes possible the analysis of data from samples of a size previously unimaginable—even when limited research resources prevent the analysis of data from an entire population. Angela Bohn, Christian Buchta, Kurt Hornik, and Patrick Mair, in Austria and at Harvard in the United States, analyzed records on 438,851 Facebook users to explore the relation between friendship patterns and access to social capital (Bohn et al. 2014). Bohn et al. (2014:32) started their analysis with data on 1,712 users—they didn't have the computer power to analyze more data—who were selected randomly over a 2-month study period, from about 1.3 million users who had agreed on Facebook to have their data used anonymously for such a study.

Exhibit 14.13 displays one of their findings about social networks: Having more communication partners increased social capital—as indicated by responses received to their postings—up to about 130 partners. Facebook users with more partners than that tended to receive fewer responses to their postings (Bohn et al. 2014:39). Having more partners can definitely lead to too much of what otherwise is a good thing.

As you may have discovered when you started to check out the Google Ngrams site, having enormous sets of data readily available for analysis encourages exploration.

> Rarely does [such a large amount of data] fit into neatly defined categories that are known at the outset. And the questions we want to ask often emerge only when we collect and work with the data we have. (Mayer-Schönberger & Cukier 2013:45)

Patterns discovered in Big Data may then suggest hypotheses that can be tested in causal experiments (Mayer-Schönberger & Cukier 2013:65–66).

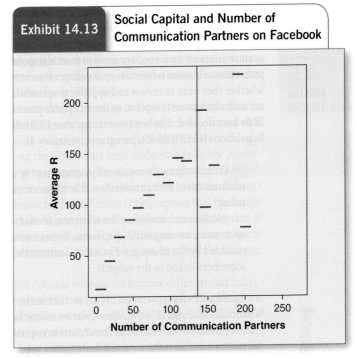

Exhibit 14.13 Social Capital and Number of Communication Partners on Facebook

Source: Bohn et al. (2014).

⊡ Ethical Issues in Secondary Data Analysis and Big Data

Analysis of data collected by others does not create the same potential for immediate harm as does the collection of primary data, but neither ethical nor related political considerations can be ignored. First, because in most cases the secondary researchers did not collect the data, a key ethical obligation is to cite the original, principal investigators, as well as the data source, such as the ICPSR. Researchers who seek access to data sets available through the CESSDA must often submit a request to the national data protection authority in the country (or countries) of interest (Johnson & Bullock 2009:214).

Subject confidentiality is a key concern when original records are analyzed. Whenever possible, all information that could identify individuals should be removed from the records to be analyzed so that no link is possible to the identities of living subjects or the living descendants of subjects (Huston & Naylor 1996:1698). When you use data that have already been archived, you need to find out what procedures were used to preserve subject confidentiality. The work required to ensure subject confidentiality probably will have been done for you by the data archivist. For example, the ICPSR examines carefully all data deposited in the archive for the possibility of disclosure risk. All data that might be used to identify respondents are altered to ensure confidentiality, including removal of information such as birth dates or service dates, specific incomes, or place of residence that could be used to identify subjects indirectly (see http://www.icpsr.umich.edu/icpsrweb/content/ICPSR/access/restricted/index.html). If all information that could be used in any way to identify respondents cannot be removed from a data set without diminishing data set quality (e.g., by preventing links to other essential data records), ICPSR restricts access to the data and requires that investigators agree to conditions of use that preserve subject confidentiality. Those who violate confidentiality may be subject to a scientific misconduct investigation by their home institution at the request of ICPSR (Johnson & Bullock 2009:218). The

Research That Matters, Questions That Count

Violence against women on college campuses is often attributed to excessive drinking and for that reason its seriousness is too often minimized. Maria Testa at the University at Buffalo's Research Institute on Addictions decided that the complex contextual and social factors involved in incidents of violence against women had to be investigated so that we can learn why such violence occurs and how alcohol is involved. Although she had been trained as a quantitative researcher, her experiences had led her to the realization that for such research questions it could help to complement quantitative data with qualitative data.

The resulting research project carried out by Maria Testa, Jennifer Livingston, and Carol VanZile-Tamen used a mixed-methods design to identify women who had been the victims of violence and then develop an in-depth picture of how the violence had occurred. Through analysis of the detailed descriptions that women provided of the incidents when they had been victimized, Testa and her coauthors found that the common assumption that sexual victimization results from women's impaired judgment was simply not correct. Instead, rape occurred after excessive drinking when women were incapacitated and could neither resist nor often even remain fully aware of what was happening to them. Testa termed these incidents *incapacitated rape.*

Testa and her colleagues concluded that insights yielded by the qualitative data analysis fully justified the time-consuming process of reading and re-reading interviews, coding text, and discussing and reinterpreting the codes.

1. What other qualitative methods could be used to study violence against women on college campuses? What would be the advantages and disadvantages of focus groups or observation?

2. If you were asked to design a study of violence against women on a college campus and then develop a comprehensive report about the problem for the student senate, would you put more emphasis on quantitative methods or qualitative methods, or would you attempt to use both equally? Explain your reasoning.

In this chapter, you will learn about the logic and procedures for designing mixed-methods research projects as well as about the research on violence. By the end of the chapter, you will understand why a mixed-methods design can be the most advantageous design for investigating complex social patterns. In addition, you will be able to identify features that distinguish particular mixed-methods designs and evaluate their appropriateness for particular research questions. After you finish the chapter, test yourself by reading Testa et al.'s 2011 article in the journal *Violence Against Women* at the *Investigating the Social World* study site and completing the related interactive exercises for Chapter 15 at edge.sagepub.com/schutt8e.

Testa, Maria, Jennifer A. Livingston, and Carol VanZile-Tamen. 2011. "Advancing the Study of Violence Against Women Using Mixed Methods: Integrating Qualitative Methods Into a Quantitative Research Program." *Violence Against Women* 17(2):236–250.

Journal Link
Mixed Methods

What Needleman learned from her qualitative participant observation surprised her: Probation workers did not regard a referral to court as a harsher sanction than being diverted from court (Needleman 1981:248). In fact, the intake workers believed the court was too lenient in its decisions and instead felt their own "adjustment" effort involving counseling, negotiation, restitution, and social service agencies was harsher and more effective (Needleman 1981:249).

> Considered toothless, useless and counterproductive, the court represents to the intake workers not a harsher sanction, but a dumping ground for the "failures" from the intake's alternative [approach]. (Needleman 1981:253)

In this way, Needleman found that the concepts most researchers believe they are measuring with official records differ markedly from the meaning attached to these records by probation officers. Probation officers often diverted cases from court because they thought the court would be too lenient and that they often based their decisions on juveniles' current social situation (e.g., whether they were living in a stable home), without learning anything about the individual juvenile. Perhaps most troubling for research using case records, Needleman found that probation officers decided how to handle cases first and then created an official record that appeared to justify their decisions. Exhibit 15.1 summarizes the differences Needleman's qualitative interviews identified between researchers' assumptions about juvenile court workers and the juvenile court workers' own assumptions.

This little vignette contains a big lesson: A single method may not represent adequately the social world's complexity that we are trying to understand. The goal of this chapter is to highlight the importance of this lesson and to identify its implications for research practice. I will discuss the historical and philosophical foundation for mixed methods, I will illustrate the different ways that methods can be combined, and I will highlight some of the advantages and challenges of using multiple methods in one study. Although in other chapters I have mentioned some investigations that combined different methods, what is distinctive about this chapter is its focus on research designs that have major qualitative and quantitative components as well as its attention to the challenges of combining methods.

Exhibit 15.1	**Researchers' and Juvenile Court Workers' Discrepant Assumptions**
Researcher Assumptions	**Intake Worker Assumptions**
• Being sent to court is a harsher sanction than diversion from court.	• Being sent to court often results in more lenient and less effective treatment.
• Screening involves judgments about individual juveniles.	• Screening centers on the juvenile's social situation.
• Official records accurately capture case facts.	• Records are manipulated to achieve the desired outcome.

Source: Needleman (1981:248–256).

History of Mixed Methods

Sociologists and other social scientists have long used multiple methods in their research, but only in recent decades have some focused attention on how best to combine qualitative and quantitative methods to better achieve research goals. As an example of the classic tradition, anthropologist W. Lloyd Warner, Marchia Meeker, and Kenneth Eells's (1960) classic *Social Class in America* used both qualitative and quantitative research methods to understand the social complexities of U.S. communities. Based largely on his pioneering field research in the 1930s and 1940s in the New England community of Newburyport—called "Yankee City" in his subsequent books—Warner showed how qualitative data about social position and activities could be converted into a quantitative measure that he termed the "Index of Status Characteristics" (I.S.C.). Here is an example of how Warner et al. (1960) shifted from qualitative description to quantitative assessment.

Video Link
Mixed Methods

> The home of Mr. and Mrs. Henry Adams Breckenridge . . . has three stories and is topped by a captain's walk. . . . Large trees and a tall thick hedge . . . garden stretches one hundred yards . . . many old rose bushes. . . . The life and surroundings of Mrs. Henry Adams Breckenridge, old-family and upper-upper, . . . Her ratings of the characteristics of her I.S.C. give her a final score of 12, or perfect. . . . (pp. 243, 247)

Another classic example of the early use of **mixed methods** is represented in *Union Democracy*, sociologist Seymour Martin Lipset's study of the International Typographical Union (ITU) with Martin Trow and James Coleman (1956). After some preliminary investigations involving reading union literature and interviewing some ITU members, Lipset began systematic qualitative research.

> **Mixed methods:** Research that combines qualitative and quantitative methods in an investigation of the same or related research question(s).

> Aside from long exploratory interviews with key informants in the union, members of the research team that was organized around the study familiarized themselves in every way possible with the actual political life of the union, attending union meetings, party caucuses, and chapel meetings, while paying particular attention to the events preceding the local union election held in May 1951. (Lipset et al. 1956:xiii).

Marcus Weaver-Hightower (2013) explained the basis for his pragmatic rejection of the paradigm wars approach in his report on a mixed-methods study of policy making about boys' education in Australia.

> Both qualitative and quantitative methods do have limitations for studying policy influence; qualitative methods can have difficulty establishing the extent of influence while quantitative methods can have difficulty providing the whys, hows, and so whats. Rather than succumb to paralysis from competing claims for methodological incompleteness, I used mixed methods to ameliorate each approach's limitations. (p. 6)

Does being pragmatic make sense to you? Are you willing to look beyond the opposing philosophical principles of positivism and constructivism and combine different methods to strengthen your investigations of the social world? Are you ready to confront the difficult problems that must be solved before you can integrate different methods effectively? (Morgan 2014:4–5).

Encyclopedia Link
Mixed-Method Research

🔲 Types of Mixed Methods

Qualitative methods may be used before or after quantitative methods; that is, the sequencing of the two approaches can differ. In addition, one method may be given priority in a project or qualitative and quantitative methods may be given equal priority. Distinguishing the sequencing and priority of the qualitative and quantitative methods used in any mixed-methods project results in a number of different types. Before discussing these types, it will help to learn some basic conventions for naming them.

- The primary method used in a mixed-methods project is written in all caps (QUAN or QUAL).

- The secondary method is written in lowercase letters (quan or qual).

- If both methods are given equal priority, they are both written in all caps.

- If one method is used before the other, the sequence is indicated with an arrow (QUAL→ quan, or Qual→QUAN, or QUAN→QUAL, etc.).

- If two methods are used concurrently, but one has priority, the secondary method is said to be "embedded" in the primary method. This is indicated as follows: QUAL(quan) or QUAN(qual).

- If two methods are used concurrently, but they have equal priority, the relation between the two methods is indicated with a +: QUAL+QUAN.

The different types of mixed methods that result from these distinctions in priority and sequence are represented in Exhibit 15.2. Of course, these different types represent only research projects in which each method is used only once; more complex mixed-methods projects may involve combinations of these types, either at the same time or in sequence.

Some examples using the research projects I have already introduced will help to clarify the reasons for using these different types (Creswell & Clark 2011:8; Morgan 2014:20). Needleman (1981) collected quantitative data from case records on dispositions in juvenile cases, but she realized that she might misinterpret the meaning of these numbers unless she also understood the meaning behind the probation officers' dispositions. She therefore embedded a qualitative study of probation officers within her larger quantitative study of case dispositions. This project can be represented as using a QUAN(qual) embedded method.

In their study of the International Typographical Union, Lipset and colleagues (1956) needed to identify the differences in orientations of the union's various social groups and to understand how these differences were expressed in union politics. For this purpose, they used an integrated method (QUAL+QUAN) in which both quantitative methods (a structured survey) and qualitative methods (in-depth interviews) played major roles.

Researcher Interview Link
Mixed Methods

Exhibit 15.2   Types of Mixed Methods

		Priority	
		Prioritized	**Equal**
Sequence	Sequential	Staged Method Qual→QUAN Quan→QUAL QUAL→quan QUAN→qual	Research Program QUAL→QUAN QUAN→QUAL
	Concurrent	Embedded Method QUAL(quan) QUAN(qual)	Integrated Method QUAL+QUAN

You learned in the section on refining and testing questions in Chapter 8 that qualitative methods like focus groups and cognitive interviews can be used to refine questions for a structured quantitative survey: qual→QUAN. In the section on organizing concepts in Chapter 10, you saw that observations may be coded to create systematic quantitative data: QUAL→quan. In these types of staged methods, one method has priority. In addition, the use of one method precedes the other one in time because the data collected with one method shapes the data collected with the other method.

The various studies of the response to domestic violence that I described in Chapter 2 represent a common way of combining methods in an extended **research program**, in which the results of research using one method inform or raise questions about research focused on the same research question that used a different research method. For example, Angela Moe's research (2007) on victim orientation to calling the police after an experience of abuse (Chapter 2's section on exploratory analysis) represented another step in the research program that began with Lawrence Sherman and Richard Berk's (1984) quantitative study of the police response to domestic violence. This would be a QUAN→QUAL research program.

> **Research program with mixed methods:**
> Qualitative and quantitative methods are used in sequence and are given equal priority.

In this section, I will discuss in more depth examples of research projects using staged, embedded, and integrated methods. When qualitative and quantitative methods are combined in these ways, researchers must make key decisions about how best to mix methods to achieve their study purposes. As you see how researchers make these decisions, you will also understand better the strengths and weaknesses of the specific methods. "The more you understand what a set of research methods can and cannot do, the easier it is to match those procedures to your purposes" (Morgan 2014:21).

Integrated Designs

In an **integrated mixed-methods design**, qualitative and quantitative methods are used concurrently and both are given equal importance. Findings produced from these methods are then integrated and compared during the analysis of project data. This is the QUAL+QUAN design. Susan McCarter (2009) extended prior research on juvenile justice processing with an integrated mixed-methods investigation of case processing and participant orientations in Virginia. Her hope was to use the results of the two methods to triangulate the study's findings; that is, to show that different methods lead to similar conclusions and therefore become more credible.

> **Integrated mixed-methods design:**
> Qualitative and quantitative methods are used concurrently and both are given equal importance.

The ethnographic notes recorded in the group homes revealed orientations and processes that helped explain the pronounced association between substance abuse and housing loss (Schutt 2011b):

> The time has come where he has to decide once and for all to drink or not. . . . Tom has been feeling "pinned to the bed" in the morning. He has enjoyed getting high with Sammy and Ben, although the next day is always bad. . . . Since he came back from the hospital Lisandro has been acting like he is taunting them to throw him out by not complying with rules and continuing to drink. . . . (pp. 131, 133)

In this way, my analysis of the quantitative data reveals *what* happened, and my analysis of the ethnographic data helps to understand *why*. The same could be said for the way that qualitative interviews allowed Testa et al. (2011) to develop insights into how excessive alcohol consumption led to the quantitative association they identified between drinking and rape. It proved to be well worth the effort to collect qualitative data that would help interpret the results of the quantitative research.

A mixed-methods design can also improve external validity when a quantitative study is repeated in different contexts. Qualitative comparisons between these different contexts can then help make sense of the similarities and differences between outcomes across these contexts and thus help identify the conditions for the effects.

It was possible to make this type of qualitative comparison of quantitative study outcomes with the five experimental projects funded by the National Institute of Mental Health to identify the value of enhanced housing and services for reducing homelessness among homeless persons diagnosed with serious mental illness (our project in Boston was one of these five) (Schutt et al. 2009). Exhibit 15.7 displays the quantitative comparison for the impact of enhanced housing (the treatment) between these five projects. The results show that enhanced

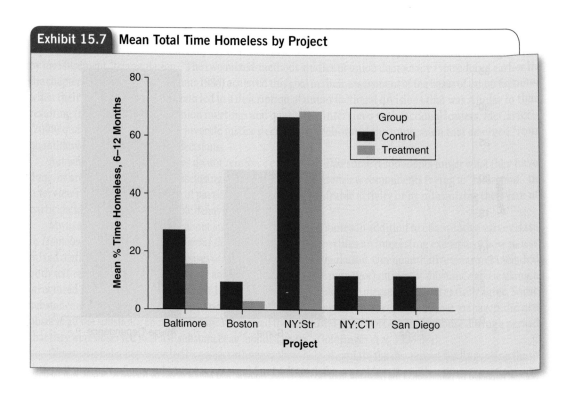

Exhibit 15.7   **Mean Total Time Homeless by Project**

housing reduced the time spent homeless in four of the five projects. The one project that was an exception to this rule was in New York City and involved a focus on moving homeless persons off the streets into a shelter, which is an improvement in residential status but still counts as being homeless (and see Schutt 2011b:250–251). Interpretation of such multisite results must always be considered carefully, given the differences in project design that inevitably occur when the experiment is adapted to the specific conditions of each site.

The generalizability of qualitative findings can also be improved when a representative sample developed with a quantitative design is used to identify cases to study more intensively with qualitative methods. This was the approach used by Zhong and Arnett (2014) when they selected Chinese women for qualitative interviews from among those who had participated in their structured survey. More commonly, the combination of methods to improve generalizability occurs in a research program in which the two studies are conducted sequentially, most often by different researchers.

Mixed methods also facilitate achieving the goal of authenticity within a research project that also seeks to achieve measurement validity, generalizability, or causal validity. Brown et al.'s (2013) complex mixed-method study of homeless men leads to a conclusion that seems much more authentic than would have been the case if they had used just one method. Their analysis moved them away from simplistic assumptions about the men's conceptions of appropriate gender rules to a deeper understanding of their gender role aspirations in the context of limited means for achieving them.

It is naïve to think of mixed methods as simply overcoming problems that can occur when a research design is limited to one method. It is not always clear how best to compare qualitative and quantitative findings or how to interpret the discrepancies that arise after such comparison (Morgan 2014:66–81). We can't be certain that differences in findings mean that deficits have been uncovered in one method—some substance abusers do not disclose their abuse in answer to questions—or that the two methods are really answering different research

CAREERS AND RESEARCH

Amanda Aykanian, Research Associate, Advocates for Human Potential

Amanda Aykanian majored in psychology at Framingham State University and found that she enjoyed the routine and organization of research. She wrote an undergrad thesis to answer the research question: How does the way in which course content is presented affect students' feelings about the content and the rate at which they retain it?

After graduating, Aykanian didn't want to go to graduate school right away; instead she wanted to explore her interests and get a sense of what she could do with research. Advocates for Human Potential (AHP) was the last research assistant (RA) job that Aykanian applied for. Her initial tasks as an RA at AHP ranged from taking notes, writing agendas, and assembling project materials to entering research data, cleaning data, and proofing reports. As she contributed more to project reports, she began to think about data from a more theoretical standpoint.

During 7 years at AHP, Aykanian has helped lead program evaluation research, design surveys and write survey questions, conduct phone and qualitative interviews, and lead focus groups. Her program evaluation research almost always uses a mixed-methods approach, so Aykanian has learned a lot about how qualitative and quantitative methods can complement each other. She has received a lot of on-the-job training in data analysis and has learned how to think about and write a proposal in response to federal funding opportunities.

Aykanian was promoted to research associate and describes her current role as part program evaluation coordinator and part data analyst. She has also returned to graduate school, earning a master's degree in applied sociology and then starting a PhD program in social welfare.

questions—for example, what is the association between drinking and rape on campus compared with how often does drinking result in incapacitation prior to a rape?

Interactive Exercises
Link
Mixed Methods

Mixed methods also create extra challenges for researchers because different types of expertise are required for effective use of quantitative and qualitative methods. Recruiting multiple researchers for a project who then work as a team from conception to execution of the project may be the best way to overcome this limitation. The researchers also have to acknowledge in planning the study timetable that the time required for collection, coding, and analysis of qualitative data can challenge a quantitative researcher's expectation of more rapid progress.

Despite these challenges, the different types of evidence produced in a mixed-methods investigation can strengthen overall confidence in the research findings and result in a more holistic understanding of the social world. Weaver-Hightower (2013) captured these advantages in his methodological reflections on his mixed-method study of influences on public policy in Australia:

> Overall, this mixed-methods process, moving iteratively from qualitative to quantitative back to qualitative, established well the political and ideological influences on the policy makers and their "policy." The quantitative and qualitative methods were highly integrated—that is, the whole of the findings exceeded the sum of the individual quantitative and qualitative parts . . .—because the quantitative procedures in some cases solidified, and in other cases challenged, my qualitative impressions of influence that were hard-won by hanging around, talking to people, and reading about the subject. Indeed, I was surprised by several influentials identified using the embedded quantitative phase. Several groups and individuals, like Canberra Grammar School or Boys in Focus, largely escaped my notice before the mixed-methods approach. Likewise, without the qualitative case descriptions and the negative and positive case analyses, I would have been less able to understand why certain groups and actors were influential. And, regarding negative cases, the qualitative methods were still necessary to identify some influentials not netted by the mixed methods. In the end, then, the methods were integrated because both were necessary to find and evaluate influentials. (p. 17)

▣ Ethics and Mixed Methods

Researchers who combine methods must be aware of the ethical concerns involved in using each of the separate methods, but there are also some ethical challenges that are heightened in mixed-methods projects. One special challenge is defining the researcher's role in relation to the research participants. Every researcher creates an understanding about his or her role with research participants (Mertens 2012). Researchers using quantitative methods often define themselves as outside experts who design a research project and collect research data using objective procedures that are best carried out without participant involvement. By contrast, qualitative researchers often define themselves as engaging in research in some type of collaboration with the community or group they are studying, with much input from their research participants into the research design and the collection and analysis of research data.

Audio Link
Varying Methods

A researcher using mixed methods cannot simply adopt one of these roles: A researcher needs some degree of autonomy when designing quantitative research plans, but a researcher will not be able to collect intensive qualitative data if participants do not accord her or him some degree of trust as an insider. The challenge is compounded by the potential for different reactions of potential participants to the different roles. Authorities who control access to program clients or employees or to community members may be willing to agree to a structured survey but not to a long-term engagement with researchers as participant observers, so that a mixed-methods project that spans programs, communities, or other settings may involve a biased sampling for the qualitative component. Natalia Luxardo, Graciela Colombo, and Gabriela Iglesias (2011) confronted this challenge in their study of Brazilian family violence services and as a result focused their qualitative research on one service that supported the value of giving voice to their service recipients.

Weighing both roles and the best combination of them is critical at the outset of a mixed-methods project, although the dilemma will be lessened if a project uses different researchers to lead the quantitative and qualitative components. In our study of housing alternatives, for example, a team of ethnographers collected data on activities in the group homes while research assistants supervised by a different leader collected the project's quantitative data (Schutt 2011b).

Complex mixed-methods projects in which quantitative surveying is interspersed with observational research or intensive interviews may also require renegotiation of participant consent to the particular research procedures at each stage. As stated by Chih Hoong Sin (2005),

> Different stages and different components of research may require the negotiation of different types of consent, some of which may be more explicit than others. Sampling, contact, re-contact, and fieldwork can be underpinned by different conceptualization and operationalization of "informed consent." This behooves researchers to move away from the position of treating consent-seeking as an exercise that only occurs at certain points in the research process or only for certain types of research. Consent-seeking should not be thought of merely as an event. (p. 290)

In the qualitative component of their study of Brazilian victims of domestic violence, Luxardo and her colleagues (2011) adopted a flexible qualitative interviewing approach to allow participants to avoid topics they did not want to discuss:

> We tried to consider what was important for that adolescent during the interview and, many times, we had to reframe the content of the encounters according to the expectations they had. So, if they were not willing to share during an interview but still had complaints, doubts, or comments to share, we tried to focus on those instead of subtly directing the talk to the arena of the research interests. Moreover, we noticed that some adolescents (most of them migrants from Bolivia) did not feel at ease sharing that kind of information about their lives with a stranger, so we tried not to invade their intimacy by being culturally sensitive; if they did not want to talk, they did not have to do so. (p. 996)

Research|Social Impact Link
Quality of Research

▣ Conclusions

A research project that is designed to answer multiple research questions and investigate a complex social setting often requires a mixed-methods design. Of course, to some extent the complexity of the social world always exceeds what can be captured successfully with one method, but the challenges increase as our questions become more numerous and our social settings more complex. You have learned in this chapter about the different perspectives on combining methods, the different ways of mixing methods, and the challenges that arise when mixing methods. No matter what your methodological preference is at this point, increased understanding of these issues in mixed methods will improve your own research practice and your ability to critique the research of others.

I conclude with my justification for the mixed methods used in the project that was the foundation for my recent book about a very ambitious set of research questions in a complex and changing social setting (Schutt 2011b:284):

> *Homelessness, Housing, and Mental Illness* describes who participated in the Boston McKinney Project, what they wanted, and what they did; it evaluates whether living in group homes or independent apartments influenced participants' desires and actions; it explores how participants interacted with each other and whether they differed in their responses to the same stimuli. For these reasons and more, our project required systematic research methods—not just one method, such as conducting a survey, but multiple methods: different methods to answer different questions and to provide alternative perspectives on similar questions. . . . Even the best and most appropriate research methods do not entirely solve the problem of perspective. When we use social science methods, we see farther and probe deeper than we do in our everyday lives; however, no method—whether used alone or in combination with others—gives us perfect vision or infallible insight. Every method we use for investigating the social world will overlook some processes, distort some realities, and confuse some issues.

Video Interview Questions

Listen to the researcher interview with Dana Hunt for Chapter 15 at edge.sagepub.com/schutt8e.

1. Why was this specific research study challenging?

2. How did the researchers come up with the "counterfactual" component of the study?

SPSS Exercises

Could qualitative data help you understand quantitative associations between variables?

1. Generate the cross-tabulations of CONARMY to CONGOV with EDUCR in the GSS2012x or GSS2012a data set.

2. What do you learn about the relation between education and confidence in social institutions from these crosstabs?

3. What questions would you like to include in a qualitative interview with some GSS respondents in order to improve your understanding of the education-confidence association? Explain.

Developing a Research Proposal

Add a mixed-methods design for your proposed study. Pick the type of mixed method that seems most likely to help answer the research question (see Exhibit 3.10, #13 to #17).

1. Explain why it will be advantageous to give priority to either qualitative or quantitative methods, or to give them equal priority.

2. Explain why you think it advantageous to sequence the methods, or not.

Summarizing and Reporting Research

You learned in Chapter 2 that research is a circular process, so it is appropriate that we end this book where we began. The stage of reporting research results is also the point at which the need for new research is identified. It is the time when, so to speak, "the rubber hits the road"—when we have to make our research make sense to others. To whom will our research be addressed? How should we present our results to them? Should we seek to influence how our research report is used?

The primary goals of this chapter are to guide you in writing worthwhile reports of your own, displaying findings, and communicating with the public about research. This chapter gives particular attention to the writing process itself and points out how that process can differ when writing qualitative versus quantitative research reports. I introduce one new research technique—*meta-analysis*—which is a quantitative method for

Research That Matters, Questions That Count

Cities across the United States have sought to reduce the toll of violent crimes by limiting access to guns. Strategies for controlling gun violence have ranged from gun buy-back programs, background checks, and safe storage laws to enhanced sentences for crimes committed with guns and community-based strategies. But do such strategies have the desired effect? Given the many differences between cities and their populations and criminal justice systems, research projects focused on just one strategy or just one city cannot provide a definitive answer.

Matthew Makarios and Travis Pratt at the University of Cincinnati and Arizona State University, respectively, used meta-analysis to overcome these limitations. They were able to identify 27 research reports that included estimates of 172 effects of gun control programs. When they analyzed these studies together, they found that gun control programs tended to reduce violent crime, but only by a small amount. However, when they distinguished types of gun control programs, they found that some, such as gun buy-back programs, had no effect, whereas several—in particular probation and community-oriented strategies—had substantial effects. However, the strongest effects occurred in studies with weaker research designs.

1. Consider these two research strategies: (1) Studying many aspects of the social world related to a research question in one location. (2) Conducting a meta-analysis of many studies that includes measures of a few variables that each study has in common. Would you be more confident in a study using strategy 1, with more depth, or in a study using strategy 2, with more breadth? Explain your reasoning.

2. Review the research questions in other "Research That Matters" vignettes in this book. Which research question would you most like to see investigated further with a meta-analysis? Explain your preference.

In this chapter, you will learn how meta-analyses are conducted and how research is reported. By the end of the chapter, you will know how to approach different tasks involved in reporting research and how to identify limitations in research reports. After you finish the chapter, test yourself by reading the 2012 *Crime & Delinquency* article by Matthew Makarios and Travis Pratt at the *Investigating the Social World* study site and completing the related interactive exercises for Chapter 16 at edge.sagepub.com/schutt8e.

Makarios, Matthew D. and Travis C. Pratt. 2012. "The Effectiveness of Policies and Programs That Attempt to Reduce Firearm Violence: A Meta-Analysis." *Crime & Delinquency* 58(2):222–244.

statistically evaluating the results of a large body of prior research on a specific topic. I will conclude by considering some of the ethical issues unique to the reporting process, with special attention to the problem of plagiarism.

Journal Link
Meta-Analysis
Publication

▣ Writing Research

The goal of research is not just to discover something but also to communicate that discovery to a larger audience: other social scientists, government officials, your teachers, the general public—perhaps several of these audiences. Whatever the study's particular outcome, if the intended audience for the research comprehends the results and learns from them, the research can be judged a success. If the intended audience does not learn about the study's results, the research should be judged a failure—no matter how expensive the research, how sophisticated its design, or how much you (or others) invested in it.

Successful research reporting requires both good writing and a proper publication outlet. We will first review guidelines for successful writing before we look at particular types of research publications.

Consider the following principles formulated by experienced writers (Booth, Colomb, & Williams 1995:150–151):

- Respect the complexity of the task and don't expect to write a polished draft in a linear fashion. Your thinking will develop as you write, causing you to reorganize and rewrite.

- Leave enough time for dead ends, restarts, revisions, and so on, and accept the fact that you will discard much of what you write.

- Write as fast as you comfortably can. Don't worry about spelling, grammar, and so on until you are polishing things up.

- Ask anyone whom you trust for reactions to what you have written.

- Write as you go along, so you have notes and report segments drafted even before you focus on writing the report.

It is important to outline a report before writing it, but neither the report's organization nor the first written draft should be considered fixed. As you write, you will get new ideas about how to organize the report. Try them out. As you review the first draft, you will see many ways to improve your writing. Focus particularly on how to shorten and clarify your statements. Make sure that each paragraph concerns only one topic. Remember the golden rule of good writing: Writing is revising!

You can ease the burden of report writing in several ways:

Journal Link
Writing for Publication

- Draw on the research proposal and on project notes.

- Use a word processing program on a computer to facilitate reorganizing and editing.

- Seek criticism from friends, teachers, and other research consumers before turning in the final product.

I find it helpful at times to use what I call **reverse outlining**: After you have written a first complete draft, outline it on a paragraph-by-paragraph basis, ignoring the actual section headings you used. See if the paper you wrote actually fits the outline you planned. Consider how the organization could be improved.

> **Reverse outlining:** Outlining the sections in an already written draft of a paper or report to improve its organization in the next draft.

Most important, leave yourself enough time so that you can revise, several times if possible, before turning in the final draft. Here are one student's reflections on writing and revising:

> I found the process of writing and revising my paper longer than I expected. I think it was something I was doing for the first time—working within a committee—that made the process not easy. The overall experience was very good, since I found that I have learned so much. My personal computer also did help greatly.
>
> Revision is essential until complete clarity is achieved. This took most of my time. Because I was so close to the subject matter, it became essential for me to ask for assistance in achieving clarity. My committee members, English editor, and fellow students were extremely helpful. Putting it on disk was also, without question, a timesaver. Time was the major problem.
>
> The process was long, hard, and time-consuming, but it was a great learning experience. I work full time so I learned how to budget my time. I still use my time productively and am very careful of not wasting it. (Graduate Program in Applied Sociology 1990:13)

Encyclopedia Link
Writing

For more suggestions about writing, see Howard Becker (2007), Booth et al. (2008), Lee Cuba (2002), William Strunk Jr. and E. B. White (2000), and Kate Turabian (2007).

Displaying Research

Chapter 9 introduced some conventions for reporting quantitative research results, including tabular displays and graphs. You can improve your displays of quantitative data in research reports by using the *Chart Builder* feature of SPSS (Aldrich & Rodriguez 2013).

Open the chart builder by clicking on "Graphs" and then "Chart Builder" in the SPSS Data Editor screen. Exhibit 16.1 shows the SPSS data editor window as it appears at that point. To build a simple bar chart, click the "Bar" option in the "Choose from" list. Now drag and drop the categorical variable whose distribution you would like to display into the graph window. If you would like to alter the graph or additional elements, double-click on the chart and make changes in the "Properties" window. See Exhibit 16.2.

Chart Builder can also be used to create figures that display the association between two or three variables. Exhibit 16.3 shows the association between political views and race using the General Social Survey (GSS) 2012 data (National Opinion Research Center [NORC] 2014).

Exhibit 16.4 displays a more complex graph that shows the pattern of association between three variables: education, gender, and income. This chart was created with the multiple "Line" option in the Chart Builder. The more time you spend working with the Chart Builder, the more adept you will become at highlighting results in displays that enrich your research reports.

Graphic displays will help draw attention to important aspects of your findings and simplify interpretation of basic patterns. You should use graphic displays judiciously in a report, but use them you must if you want your findings to be accessible to the widest possible audience.

Audio Link
Publishing Controversial
Topics

Exhibit 16.1 Building a Chart With Chart Builder

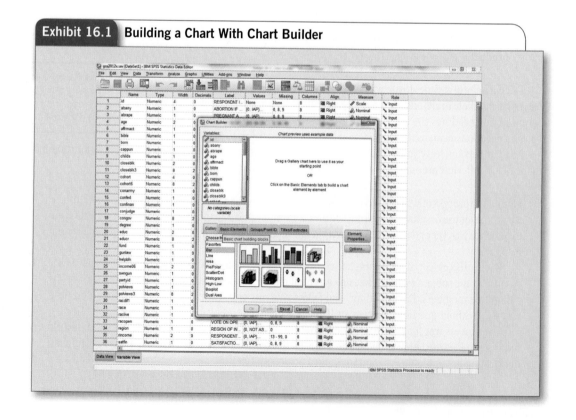

Exhibit 16.2 Adding Chart Features With Properties

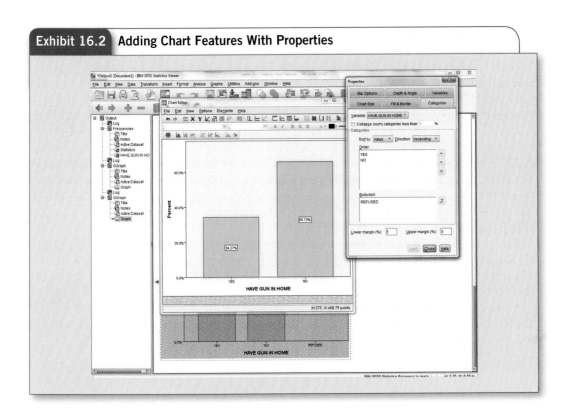

Exhibit 16.3 Displaying a Bivariate Association With Chart Builder

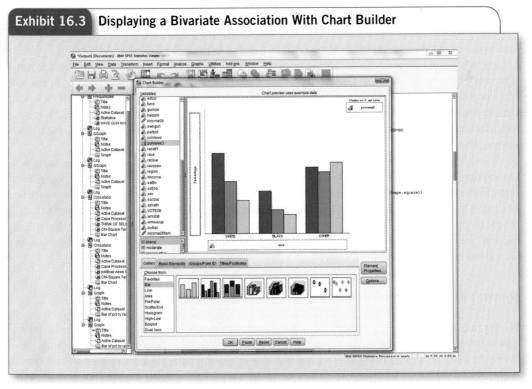

Exhibit 16.4 Creating a Three-Variable Chart With Chart Builder

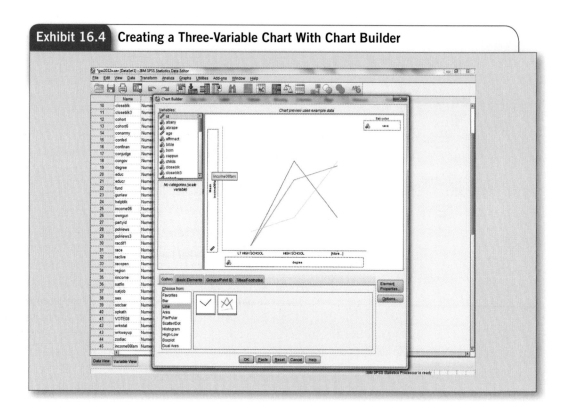

Reporting Research

You begin writing your research report when you are working on the research proposal and writing your literature review (see Chapter 2). You will find that the final report is much easier to write, and more adequate, if you write more material for it as you work out issues during the project. It is very disappointing to discover that something important was left out when it is too late to do anything about it. And I don't need to point out that students (and professional researchers) often leave final papers (and reports) until the last possible minute (often for understandable reasons, including other coursework and job or family responsibilities). But be fore-warned: *The last-minute approach does not work for research reports.*

The organization of your research report will depend to some extent on the audience for which you are writing and the type of research you have conducted. Articles that will be submitted to an academic journal will differ from research reports written for a funding agency or for the general public. Research reports based on qualitative research will differ in some ways from those based on quantitative research. Students writing course papers are often required to structure their research report using the journal article format, and they may be asked to present their results differently if they have used qualitative (or mixed) methods. The following sections outline the major issues to consider.

Journal Articles

Writing for academic journals is perhaps the toughest form of writing because articles are submitted to several experts in your field for careful review—anonymously, with most journals—before acceptance for publication. Perhaps it wouldn't be such an arduous process if so many academic journals did not have rejection rates in excess of 90% and turnaround times for reviews that are usually several months. Even the best articles, in the

Researcher Interview Link
Reporting Research

Research in the News

In the News

HOW MUCH SHOULD SOCIAL SCIENTISTS REPORT?

Marco Bertamini and Marcus Munafo discuss a trend emerging in research that puts a premium on shorter scholarly articles. Although "bite-size" science enables more work to be published and is supposedly easier to read, Bertamini and Munafo raise a number of concerns. They are also uneasy that articles are only written when researchers are successful. Are scientific failures worth reporting?

For Further Thought ?

1. Is shorter better? What are the advantages and disadvantages of compressing research reports into a few pages or even a paragraph or two? Do social scientists need to balance the type of audience and the complexity of the research in deciding how much to report?

2. "Scientific failures" in this sense mean research projects in which no association is found between variables that were hypothesized to be related, or more generally that do not lead to some interesting finding. It is hard to get a paper reporting such null results published because the tendency is to think that the researcher did not "find" anything. Do you see any hazards if social scientists do not publish such "failures"?

News source: Bertamini, Marco and Marcus R. Munafo. 2012. "The Perils of 'Bite Size' Science." *The New York Times,* January 29:SR 12.

judgment of the reviewers, are most often given a "revise and resubmit" after the first review and then are evaluated all over again after the revisions are concluded.

But journal article review procedures have some important benefits. Most important is the identification of areas in need of improvement, as the eyes of the author(s) are replaced by those of previously uninvolved subject-matter experts and methodologists. A good journal editor makes sure that he or she has a list of many different types of experts available for reviewing whatever types of articles the journal is likely to receive. There is a parallel benefit for the author(s): It is always beneficial to review criticisms of your own work by people who know the field well. It can be a painful and time-consuming process, but the entire field moves forward as researchers continually critique and suggest improvements in each other's research reports.

Exhibit 16.5 presents an outline of the sections in an academic journal article, with some illustrative quotes. It is essential to begin with a clear abstract of the article, which summarizes in one paragraph the research question, prior research, study methods and major findings, and key conclusions. Many others who search the literature about the topic of your article will never read the entire article unless they are persuaded by the abstract that the article provides worthwhile and relevant information. The article's introduction highlights the importance of the problem selected—the relationship between marital disruption (divorce) and depression. The introduction, which in this article includes the literature review, also identifies clearly the gap in the research literature that the article is meant to fill: the untested possibility that depression might cause marital disruption rather than, or in addition to, marital disruption causing depression. Literature reviews in journal articles should be integrated reviews that highlight the major relevant findings and identify key methodological lessons from the prior research as a whole, rather than presenting separate summaries of prior research studies (see Chapter 2). The findings section (titled "Results") begins by presenting the basic association between marital disruption and depression. Then it elaborates on this association by examining sex differences, the impact

Video Link
Publishing Your Research

of prior marital quality, and various mediating and modifying effects. Tables and perhaps graphs are used to present the data corresponding to each of the major findings in an easily accessible format. As indicated in the combined Discussion and Conclusions section, the analysis shows that marital disruption does indeed increase depression and specifies the time frame (3 years) during which this effect occurs.

Exhibit 16.5 **Sections in a Journal Article**

Aseltine, Robert H. Jr. and Ronald C. Kessler. 1993. "Marital Disruption and Depression in a Community Sample." Journal of Health and Social Behavior 34(September):237–251.

INTRODUCTION
   Despite 20 years of empirical research, the extent to which marital disruption causes poor mental health remains uncertain. The reason for this uncertainty is that previous research has consistently overlooked the potentially important problems of selection into and out of marriage on the basis of prior mental health. (p. 237)

SAMPLE AND MEASURES
Sample
Measures

RESULTS
The Basic Association Between Marital Disruption and Depression
Sex Differences
The Impact of Prior Marital Quality
The Mediating Effects of Secondary Changes
The Modifying Effects of Transitions to Secondary Roles

DISCUSSION [includes conclusions]
. . . According to the results, marital disruption does in fact cause a significant increase in depression compared to pre-divorce levels within a period of three years after the divorce. (p. 245)

These basic article sections present research results well, but many research articles include subsections tailored to the issues and stages in the specific study being reported. Most journals require a short abstract at the beginning, which summarizes the research question and findings. Most research articles include a general Methodology section that will include subsections on measurement and sampling. A Conclusions section is often used to present the most general conclusions, reflections, and limitations, but some precede that with a general Discussion section.

Applied Research Reports

Applied research reports are written for a different audience from the professional social scientists and students who read academic journals. Typically, an applied report is written with a wide audience of potential users in mind and to serve multiple purposes. Often, both the audience and the purpose are established by the agency or other organization that funded the research project on which the report is based. Sometimes, the researcher may use the report to provide a broad descriptive overview of the study findings, which will be presented more succinctly in a subsequent journal article. In either case, an applied report typically provides much more information about a research project than does a journal article and relies primarily on descriptive statistics rather than only those statistics useful for the specific hypothesis tests that are likely to be the primary focus of a journal article.

Exhibit 16.6 outlines the sections in an applied research report. This particular report was mandated by the California state legislature to review a state-funded program for the homeless mentally disabled. The goals of the report are described as both description and evaluation. Applied reports begin with an Executive Summary that presents the highlights from each section of the report, including major findings, in a brief format, often using bullets. The body of the report presents findings on the number and characteristics of homeless persons and on the operations of the state-funded program in each of 17 counties. This is followed by the Discussion section, which highlights the service needs that are not being met, as well as a Recommendations section, which focuses attention on policy implications of the research findings. Nine appendixes provide details on the study methodology and the counties studied.

Exhibit 16.6   Sections in an Applied Report

Vernez, Georges, M. Audrey Burnam, Elizabeth A. McGlynn, Sally Trude, and Brian S. Mittman. 1988. Review of California's Program for the Homeless Mentally Disabled. *Santa Monica, CA: The RAND Corporation.*

SUMMARY
In 1986, the California State Legislature mandated an independent review of the HMD programs that the counties had established with the state funds. The review was to determine the accountability of funds; describe the demographic and mental disorder characteristics of persons served; and assess the effectiveness of the program. This report describes the results of that review. (p. v)

INTRODUCTION
  Background
  California's Mental Health Services Act of 1985...allocated $20 million annually to the state's 58 counties to support a wide range of services, from basic needs to rehabilitation. (pp. 1–2)
  Study Objectives
  Organization of the Report

HMD PROGRAM DESCRIPTION AND STUDY METHODOLOGY
  The HMD Program
  Study Design and Methods
  Study Limitations

COUNTING AND CHARACTERIZING THE HOMELESS
    Estimating the Number of Homeless People
    Characteristics of the Homeless Population

THE HMD PROGRAM IN 17 COUNTIES
    Service Priorities
    Delivery of Services
    Implementation Progress
    Selected Outcomes
    Effects on the Community and on County Service Agencies
    Service Gaps

(Continued)

(Continued)

> DISCUSSION
>   Underserved Groups of HMD
>   Gaps in Continuity of Care
>   A particularly large gap in the continuum of care is the lack of specialized housing alternatives for the mentally disabled. The nature of chronic mental illness limits the ability of these individuals to live completely independently. But their housing needs may change, and board-and-care facilities that are acceptable during some periods of their lives may become unacceptable at other times. (p. 57)
>
>   Improved Service Delivery
>   Issues for Further Research
> Appendix
> A. SELECTION OF 17 SAMPLED COUNTIES
> B. QUESTIONNAIRE FOR SURVEY OF THE HOMELESS
> C. GUIDELINES FOR CASE STUDIES
> D. INTERVIEW INSTRUMENTS FOR TELEPHONE SURVEY
> E. HOMELESS STUDY SAMPLING DESIGN, ENUMERATION, AND SURVEY WEIGHTS
> F. HOMELESS SURVEY FIELD PROCEDURES
> G. SHORT SCREENER FOR MENTAL AND SUBSTANCE USE DISORDERS
> H. CHARACTERISTICS OF THE COUNTIES AND THEIR HMD-FUNDED PROGRAMS
> I. CASE STUDIES FOR FOUR COUNTIES' HMD PROGRAMS

Source: Vernez et al. (1988). Reprinted with permission.

One of the major differences between an applied research report and a journal article is that a journal article must focus on answering a particular research question, whereas an applied report is likely to have the broader purpose of describing a wide range of study findings and attempting to meet the diverse needs of multiple audiences for the research. But a research report that simply describes "findings" without some larger purpose in mind is unlikely to be effective in reaching any audience. Anticipating the needs of the intended audience(s) and identifying the ways in which the report can be useful to them will result in a product that is less likely to be ignored.

Video Link
Applied Research

Findings From Welfare Reform: What About the Children?

A good example of applied research reporting comes from the Robert Wood Johnson Foundation, which presented an online research report to make widely available the findings from an investigation of the impact of welfare reform (Sunderland 2005). With funding from the Robert Wood Johnson Foundation and 14 other private foundations, the National Institute of Child Health and Human Development, the Social Security Administration, and the National Institute of Mental Health, social scientist P. Lindsay Chase-Lansdale and colleagues (2003) examined the impact of the 1996 federal act mandating changes in welfare requirements—the Personal Responsibility and Work Opportunity Reconciliation Act (PRWORA). Their three-city (Boston, Chicago, San Antonio) research design sought to test the alternative arguments of reform proponents and opponents about the consequences of the reforms for families and children:

> Proponents of welfare reform argued that . . . moving mothers from welfare to work would benefit children because it would increase their families' income, model disciplined work behavior, and better

structure their family routines. Opponents of PRWORA countered that . . . the reforms [would] reduce the time mothers and children spend together, . . . increase parental stress and decrease responsive parenting, and . . . move children into low-quality childcare or unsupervised settings while their parents worked. (p. 1548)

The online report describes the three different components of the research design and refers leaders to sources for details about each (Sunderland 2005:4):

1. A longitudinal survey of adults and children designed to provide information on the health, cognitive, behavioral, and emotional development of the children and on their primary caregivers' work-related behavior, welfare experiences, health, well-being, family lives, and use of social services

2. An "embedded" developmental study of a subsample of children to improve the breadth and depth of the child evaluations

3. Ethnographic studies of low-income families in each city to describe how changes in welfare policy affected their daily lives and influenced neighborhood resources over time

The online report summarizes findings and recommendations that have been reported in various publications and other reports. It also highlights several methodological limitations of the study:

Findings from the March 7, 2003, issue of *Science* [Chase-Lansdale et al. 2003]. Investigators reported findings from the longitudinal survey and embedded developmental study. They looked at how the mothers' employment and welfare transitions were related to outcomes in three areas of the child's development—cognitive achievement, problem behaviors, and psychological well-being. They also analyzed whether employment and welfare transitions meant changes in family income and mothers' time apart from their children, to test whether time and money could explain changes in child outcomes.

- *For preschoolers, neither mothers' employment transitions nor their welfare transitions appear to be problematic or beneficial for cognitive achievement or behavioral problems.* . . . Whether or not a mother left welfare, entered welfare, took a job or left a job between the interviews had no discernable link with preschoolers' development.

- *For adolescents, the dominant pattern was also one of few associations.* But where findings did occur, the most consistent pattern was that mothers' transitions into employment were related to improvements in adolescents' mental health. Adolescents whose mothers began working—whether for one or more hours or 40 hours and whether short- or long-term—reported statistically significant declines in psychological distress. This pattern was strongest for their symptoms of anxiety.

- *Increased income may explain why adolescents' mental health improved when mothers went to work* . . . but the fact that improvements were not seen in other preschool and adolescent outcomes implies that higher family income from maternal employment may not benefit children uniformly and is not the only explanatory factor. In families with either preschoolers or adolescents, mothers' entry into employment was related to a significant increase in family income. . . . For example, teenagers' mothers who went to work had household income-to-needs ratios [i.e., the ratio of their income to the cost of household necessities] that rose from 0.65 to 1.26, on average, bringing the majority of families above the poverty line. In contrast, exits from employment were generally related to decreases in income. However, income did not change when mothers went onto or left the welfare rolls.

- *Adolescents in our study did not experience much additional separation from their mothers due to employment (about 45 minutes each day).* . . . When mothers of adolescents entered the labor force, they compensated for time away from the young teenagers by cutting down on time apart when they were not on the job.

- *Preschoolers . . . experienced a significant decline in time spent with their mothers.* When mothers moved into employment, they decreased total time with their preschoolers by an average of 2.1 hours per day.

- *Time-use data suggest that when mothers went to work, they cut back on personal, social, and educational activities that did not involve their children. . . .* The quality of mothers' parenting (e.g., structured family routines, cognitive stimulation) rarely changed with employment at a statistically significant rate, so parenting may not be an explanatory mechanism. (Sunderland 2005:5–6)

Limitations

The researchers noted two limitations:

1. Researchers conducted the first two waves of the study during an economic boom that lowered unemployment and increased wages for less skilled workers. Their findings might not be replicated during an extended period with different economic conditions.

2. Investigators' findings only pertain to children's development within a 16-month interval; harmful or beneficial effects could arise after a longer interval.

Conclusions

Researchers concluded,

This study suggests that mothers' welfare and employment transitions during this unprecedented era of welfare reform are not associated with negative outcomes for preschoolers or young adolescents. A few positive associations were tenuously indicated for adolescents. . . . The well-being of preschoolers appeared to be unrelated to their mothers' leaving welfare or entering employment, at least as indexed in measures of cognitive achievement and behavior problems. (Sunderland 2005:6)

The Robert Wood Johnson online report also summarized findings about the characteristics of children at the start of the study (Sunderland 2005):

Within a sample of 1,885 low-income children and their families, preschoolers and adolescents show patterns of cognitive achievement and problem behavior that should be of concern to policy makers. The preschoolers and adolescents in [the] sample are more developmentally at risk compared to middle-class children in national samples. In addition, adolescents whose mothers were on welfare in 1999 have lower levels of cognitive achievement and higher levels of behavioral and emotional problems than do adolescents whose mothers had left welfare or whose mothers had never been on welfare. For preschoolers, mothers' current or recent welfare participation is linked with poor cognitive achievement; preschoolers of recent welfare leavers have the most elevated levels of problem behavior. Preschoolers and adolescents in sanctioned families also show problematic cognitive and behavioral outcomes (sanctioning is the withholding of all or part of a family's TANF [Temporary Assistance for Needy Families] benefits for noncompliance with work requirements or other rules). Mothers' marital, educational, mental, and physical health status, as well as their parenting practices, seems to account for most of the welfare group differences. (p. 7)

Because so few families in the sample had reached their time limits, investigators could not tell if families that leave the welfare system after reaching their time limits would show patterns similar to those that leave after sanctions.

Recommendations

The policy brief recommended,

- The intense focus on welfare reform in our country should not impede a general concern and plan of action for all children in poverty, whether on welfare or not. To lessen developmental risks and improve the developmental trajectories of these children, numerous avenues should be pursued for the provision of supportive mental health and educational services.

- State and federal governments should explore options for identifying and reaching out to the most disadvantaged and high-risk families involved in the welfare system—families experiencing welfare sanctions. Sanctioned families have a number of characteristics that serve as markers of concern for the healthy development of children and youth. . . . Possible policy options include assistance to bring families into compliance with rules before they are sanctioned, closer monitoring of sanctioned families and the provision of additional supports, such as mental health services, academic enrichment, after-school programs, and other family support services.

Framing an Applied Report

What can be termed the **front matter** and the **back matter** of an applied report also are important. Applied reports usually begin with an executive summary: a summary list of the study's main findings, often in bullet fashion. Appendixes, the back matter, may present tables containing supporting data that were not discussed in the body of the report. Applied research reports also often append a copy of the research instrument(s).

An important principle for the researcher writing for a nonacademic audience is that the findings and conclusions should be engaging and clear. You can see how I did this in a report from a class research project I designed with my graduate methods students (and in collaboration with several faculty knowledgeable about substance abuse) (Exhibit 16.7). These report excerpts indicate how I summarized key findings in an executive summary (Schutt et al. 1996:iv), emphasized the importance of the research in the introduction (Schutt et al. 1996:1), used formatting and graphing to draw attention to particular findings in the body of the text (Schutt et al. 1996:5), and tailored recommendations to our own university context (Schutt et al. 1996:26).

> **Front matter:** The section of an applied research report that includes an executive summary, abstract, and table of contents.
>
> **Back matter:** The section of an applied research report that may include appendixes, tables, and the research instrument(s).

Exhibit 16.7 | **Student Substance Abuse, Report Excerpts**

Executive Summary

- Rates of substance abuse were somewhat lower at UMass–Boston than among nationally selected samples of college students.
- Two-thirds of the respondents reported at least one close family member whose drinking or drug use had ever been of concern to them—one-third reported a high level of concern.
- Most students perceived substantial risk of harm due to illicit drug use, but just one-quarter thought alcohol use posed a great risk of harm.

Introduction

Binge drinking, other forms of alcohol abuse, and illicit drug use create numerous problems on college campuses. Deaths from binge drinking are too common and substance abuse is a factor in as many as two-thirds of on-campus sexual assaults (Finn 1997; National Institute of Alcohol Abuse and Alcoholism 1995). College presidents now rate alcohol abuse as the number one campus problem (Wechsler, Davenport,

(Continued)

(Continued)

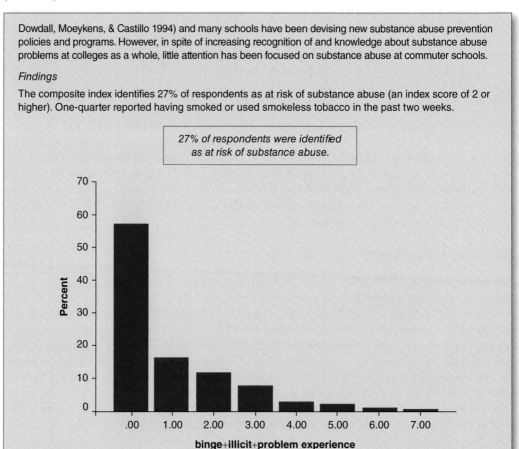

Dowdall, Moeykens, & Castillo 1994) and many schools have been devising new substance abuse prevention policies and programs. However, in spite of increasing recognition of and knowledge about substance abuse problems at colleges as a whole, little attention has been focused on substance abuse at commuter schools.

Findings

The composite index identifies 27% of respondents as at risk of substance abuse (an index score of 2 or higher). One-quarter reported having smoked or used smokeless tobacco in the past two weeks.

> 27% of respondents were identified
> as at risk of substance abuse.

Source: Schutt et al. (1996).

CAREERS AND RESEARCH

Ruth Westby, MA

For Ruth Westby, research—particularly public health research—means the chance to make new discoveries that affect people's lives by improving community health. She has studied how programs for disadvantaged and underserved groups are implemented and whether they have meaningful health impacts.

Westby was inspired to pursue a career in clinical research after her father died from cancer shortly after she received her BA from Emory University. After a few years of working with sick individuals on clinical trials, she decided to focus on public health so that she could look toward *preventing* disease. She sought out skill-based research courses and then internships that would help her use those skills as a graduate student. One such internship, at the Centers for Disease Control and Prevention, led to coauthored journal articles and a presentation at a large conference. In this way, Westby was exposed to opportunities that cemented her passion for public health research and provided a job in which every day at work is different and evokes a sense of pride.

Westby's research job also has kept her learning new research methods. She has already been exposed to systematic literature reviews, secondary data analyses, quantitative and qualitative data collection and analyses, and program evaluation. She finds program evaluation particularly rewarding, as she studies how programs are implemented and whether they have meaningful health impacts on disadvantaged populations.

If she could give current students advice, it would be to take advantage of mentors, faculty members, and anyone who is willing to help you learn:

I've seen first-hand the advantages of getting to know faculty members on a personal level, networking and interning at institutions where I might want to work later, and using new research skills outside of class. Doing all of these things taught me so much more than if I had just attended lectures and read my textbooks. By the time I graduated from graduate school, I felt much more competent and set up for success than after college. In the long run, those relationships and experiences will mean just as much, if not more, than your GPA or course schedule.

Reporting Quantitative and Qualitative Research

The requirements for good research reports are similar in many respects for quantitative and qualitative research projects. Every research report should include good writing, a clear statement of the research question, an integrated literature and presentation of key findings with related discussion, conclusions, and limitations. The outline used in Robert Aseltine and Ronald Kessler's (1993) report of a quantitative project may also be used by some authors of qualitative research reports. The Robert Wood Johnson research report also provides an example of how a research report of a mixed-methods study can integrate the results of analyses of both types of data. However, the differences between qualitative and quantitative research approaches mean that it is often desirable for research reports based on qualitative research to diverge in some respects from those reflecting quantitative research.

Journal Link
Writing Journal Articles

Reports based on qualitative research should be enriched in each section with elements that reflect the more holistic and reflexive approach of qualitative projects. The introduction should include background about the development of the researcher's interest in the topic, whereas the literature review should include some attention to the types of particular qualitative methods used in prior research. The methodology section should describe how the researcher gained access to the setting or individuals studied and the approach used to managing relations with research participants. The presentation of findings in qualitative studies may be organized into sections reflecting different themes identified in interviews or observational sessions. Quotes from participants or from observational notes should be selected to illustrate these themes, although qualitative research reports differ in the extent to which the researcher presents findings in summary form or uses direct quotes to identify key issues. The findings sections in a qualitative report may alternate between presentations of quotes or observations about the research participants, the researcher's interpretations of this material, and some commentary on how the researcher reacted in the setting, although some qualitative researchers will limit their discussion of their reactions to the discussion section.

Reports on mixed-methods projects should include subsections in the methods section that introduce each method, and then distinguish findings from qualitative and quantitative analyses in the findings section. Some mixed-methods research reports may present analyses that use both qualitative and quantitative data in yet another subsection, but others may just discuss implications of analyses of each type for the overall conclusions in the discussions and conclusions sections (Dahlberg, Wittink, & Gallo 2010:785–791). When findings based on each method are presented, it is important to consider explicitly both the ways in which the specific methods influenced findings obtained with those methods and to discuss the implications of findings obtained using both methods for the overall study conclusions.

🔲 Performing Meta-Analyses

Meta-analysis: The quantitative analysis of findings from multiple studies.

A **meta-analysis** is a quantitative method for identifying patterns in findings across multiple studies of the same research question (Cooper & Hedges 1994). Unlike a traditional literature review, which describes previous research studies verbally, meta-analyses treat previous studies as cases, whose features are measured as variables and then analyzed statistically. It is like conducting a survey in which the "respondents" are previous studies. Meta-analysis shows how evidence about social processes varies across research studies. If the methods used in these studies varied, then meta-analysis can describe how this variation affected the study findings. If social contexts varied across the studies, then meta-analysis will indicate how social context affected the study findings.

Meta-analysis can be used when a number of studies have attempted to answer the same research question with similar quantitative methods, most often experiments. Meta-analysis is not appropriate for evaluating results from qualitative studies or from multiple studies that used different methods or measured different dependent variables. It is also not very sensible to use meta-analysis to combine study results when the original case data from these studies are available and can actually be combined and analyzed together (Lipsey & Wilson 2001). Meta-analysis is a technique for combination and statistical analysis of published research reports.

After a research problem is formulated based on the findings of prior research, the literature must be searched systematically to identify the entire population of relevant studies. Typically, multiple bibliographic databases are used; some researchers also search for relevant dissertations and conference papers. Once the studies are identified, their findings, methods, and other features are coded (e.g., sample size, location of sample, and strength of the association between the independent and dependent variables). Eligibility criteria must be specified carefully to determine which studies to include and which to omit as too different. Mark Lipsey and David Wilson (2001:16–21) suggested that eligibility criteria include the following:

- *Distinguishing features:* This includes the specific intervention tested and perhaps the groups compared.

- *Research respondents:* The pertinent characteristics of the research respondents (subject sample) who provided study data must be similar to those of the population about which generalization is sought.

- *Key variables:* These must be sufficient to allow tests of the hypotheses of concern and controls for likely additional influences.

- *Research methods:* Apples and oranges cannot be directly compared, but some trade-off must be made between including the range of studies about a research question and excluding those that are so different in their methods as not to yield comparable data.

- *Cultural and linguistic range:* If the study population is going to be limited to English-language publications, or limited in some other way, this must be acknowledged, and the size of the population of relevant studies in other languages should be estimated.

- *Time frame:* Social processes relevant to the research question may have changed for reasons such as historical events or the advent of new technologies, so temporal boundaries around the study population must be considered.

- *Publication type:* It must be determined whether the analysis will focus only on published reports in professional journals, or include dissertations and unpublished reports.

Statistics are then calculated to identify the average effect of the independent variable on the dependent variable, as well as the effect of methodological and other features of the studies (Cooper & Hedges

1994). The **effect size** statistic is the key to capturing the association between the independent and dependent variables across multiple studies. The effect size statistic is a standardized measure of association—often the difference between the mean of the experimental group and the mean of the control group on the dependent variable, adjusted for the average variability in the two groups (Lipsey & Wilson 2001).

> **Effect size:** A standardized measure of association—often the difference between the mean of the experimental group and the mean of the control group on the dependent variable, adjusted for the average variability in the two groups.

The meta-analytic approach to synthesizing research findings can result in much more generalizable findings than those obtained with just one study. Methodological weaknesses in the studies included in the meta-analysis are still a problem, however; only when other studies without particular methodological weaknesses are included can we estimate effects with some confidence. In addition, before we can place any confidence in the results of a meta-analysis, we must be confident that all (or almost all) relevant studies were included and that the information we need to analyze was included in all (or most) of the studies (Matt & Cook 1994).

Case Study: Patient–Provider Race Concordance and Minority Health Outcomes

Do minority patients have better health outcomes when they receive treatment from a provider of the same race or ethnicity? Salimah Meghani and other researchers in nursing at the University of Pennsylvania and other Pennsylvania institutions sought to answer this question with a meta-analysis of published research. Their research report illustrates the key steps in a meta-analysis (Meghani et al. 2009).

They began their analysis with a comprehensive review of published research that could be located in three health-related bibliographic databases with searches for English-language research articles linked to the key words *race, ethnicity, concordance,* or *race concordance.* This search identified 159 articles; after reading the abstracts of these articles, 27 were identified that had investigated a research question about the effect of patient–provider race concordance on minority patients' health outcomes (see Exhibit 16.8).

Meghani and her coauthors then summarized the characteristics and major findings of the selected studies (see Exhibit 16.9). Finally, each study was classified according to the health outcome(s) examined and its findings about the effect of race concordance on each outcome (see Exhibit 16.10). Because only 9 of the 27 studies provided support for a positive effect of race concordance on outcomes, and in many of these studies the effects were modest, Meghani and her coauthors concluded that patient–provider racial concordance had little relevance to health care outcomes.

Case Study: Broken Homes and Delinquency

Many studies have tested the hypothesis that juveniles from broken homes have higher rates of delinquency than those from homes with intact families, but findings have been inconclusive. L. Edward Wells and Joseph Rankin (1991) were able to find 50 studies that tested this hypothesis, with estimates of the increase in delinquency among juveniles from broken homes ranging from 1% to 50%. To explain this variation, Wells and Rankin coded key characteristics of the research studies, such as the population sampled—the general population? a specific age range?—and the measures used: Did researchers consider stepparents? Did they measure juveniles' relations with the absent parent? Was delinquency measured with official records or by self-report? What types of delinquency were measured? Unlike Meghani et al.'s (2009) meta-analysis, Wells and Rankin conducted a statistical analysis of effects across the studies.

The average effect of broken homes across the studies was an increase in the likelihood of delinquency by about 10% to 15% (see Exhibit 16.11). Effects varied with the studies' substantive features and their methods, however. Juveniles from broken homes were more likely to be involved in status offenses (such as truancy and running away) and drug offenses but were no more likely to commit crimes involving theft or violence than

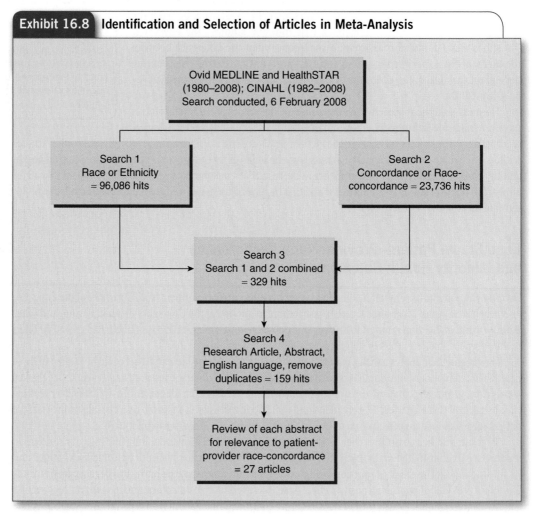

Exhibit 16.8 Identification and Selection of Articles in Meta-Analysis

Ovid MEDLINE and HealthSTAR
(1980–2008); CINAHL (1982–2008)
Search conducted, 6 February 2008

Search 1
Race or Ethnicity
= 96,086 hits

Search 2
Concordance or Race-
concordance = 23,736 hits

Search 3
Search 1 and 2 combined
= 329 hits

Search 4
Research Article, Abstract,
English language, remove
duplicates = 159 hits

Review of each abstract
for relevance to patient-
provider race-concordance
= 27 articles

Source: Meghani et al. (2009:109).

were juveniles from intact homes. Juveniles' race, sex, and age and whether a stepparent was present did not have consistent effects. Conversely, differences in methods accounted for much of the variation between the studies in the estimated effect of broken homes. The effect of broken homes on delinquency tended to be greater in studies using official records rather than those using surveys and in studies of smaller special populations rather than of the general population. In general, the differences in estimates of the association between broken homes and delinquency primarily resulted from differences in study methods and only secondarily to differences in the social characteristics of the people studied.

Meta-analyses such as the Meghani et al. (2009) and Wells and Rankin (1991) studies make us aware of how hazardous it is to base understanding of social processes on single studies that are limited in time, location, and measurement. Although one study may not support the hypothesis that we deduced from what seemed to be a compelling theory, this is not a sufficient basis for discarding the theory itself or even for assuming that the hypothesis is no longer worthy of consideration in future research. You can see that a meta-analysis combining the results of many studies may identify the conditions for which the hypothesis is supported and others for which it is not.

Of course, we need to have our wits about us when we read reports of meta-analytic studies. It is not a good idea to assume that a meta-analysis is the definitive word on a research question just because it cumulates the

Exhibit 16.9 Summary of Studies in Meta-Analysis

Citation	Aims	Sample Characteristics	Design/Setting	Major Findings	Limitations
Studies supporting race-concordance hypothesis (n = 9)					
Cooper et al. (2003)	Does race-concordance affect patient-physician communication and patients' ratings of physicians' participatory decision making?	Patients (N = 252) • Whites = 110 (44%) • African Americans = 142 (56%) Physicians (N = 31) • Whites = 13 (42%) • African Americans = 18 (58%)	Cohort study of pre and post-visit follow-up surveys and audiotaped analysis from 16 urban primary care practices in the Baltimore, MD, and Washington, D.C., area.	Patients in ethnic-concordant encounters had longer and more meaningful visits, had higher coder rating for positive affect, and had higher patient ratings for satisfaction and positive judgments of their physician's participatory decision-making style.	– Small physician sample. – Limited statistical power to detect differences in speech speed, patient centered interviewing and physicians' positive affect.
Cooper-Patrick et al. (1999)	What is the association between race and gender concordance or discordance in the patient-physician relationship and participatory decision making?	Patients (N = 1816) • Whites = 784 (43%) • African Americans = 814 (45%) • Hispanics = 218 (12%) Physicians (N = 64) • Whites = 36 (56%) • African Americans = 16 (25%) • Hispanics = 2 (3%) • Asians = 10 (15%)	Telephone survey conducted between 1996 and 1998 of adults who had attended one of the 32 primary care practices in an urban, primary care setting in Washington, DC area.	Patients in race-concordant relationships with their physicians rated their visits as significantly more participatory than patients in race-discordant relationships.	– Small sample of minority physicians. – Data based on patient self-report. – Data may be confounded by physician or practice-related variables not included in the study.
King et al. (2004)	Does race-concordance explain why African Americans are less likely than Whites to receive antiretroviral treatment?	Patients (N = 1241) • White–White = 803 (61%) • African American patients–White providers = 341 (32%) • African American–African American = 86 (6%)	Secondary analysis of data from 1996 HIV Cost and Service Utilization Study—a national probability, prospective cohort study of adults receiving HIV-related medical care and their providers.	African–American patients with White providers received protease inhibitors significantly later than African Americans with African American providers and White patients with White providers.	– Relied on self-reported dates for the receipt of protease inhibitor. – Not enough patients to allow both races cared for by same provider. – Small sample for African American providers.

Source: Meghani et al. (2009:111).

Exhibit 16.10	Classification of Outcomes in Meta-Analysis

Category	Specific Race-Concordance Outcome Studied	Support for Race-Concordance?
Provision of health care (*n* = 8)		
King et al. (2004)	Time to receipt of protease inhibitor in HIV-positive patients	+
Malat (2001)	Rating of time spent during last medical visit	−
McKinlay et al. (2002)	Diagnosis of depression and polymyalgia rheumatica, level of certainty, and test ordering	−
Modi et al. (2007)	Recommendations for percutaneous endoscopic gastrostomy in patients with advanced dementia	+
Stevens et al. (2003)	Parents' report of primary care experiences of their children	−
Stevens et al. (2005)	Receipt of basic preventative services or family centered care	−
Tai-Seale et al. (2005)	Assessment of depression in elderly	−
Zayas et al. (2005)	Diagnoses of psychiatric illness	−
Utilization of health care (*n* = 7)		
Konrad et al. (2005)	Use of antihypertensive medications	+/−
Lasser et al. (2005)	Missed appointment rates in primary care	+
LaVeist et al. (2003)	Failure to use needed care and delay in using needed care	+/−
Murray-Garcia et al. (2001)	Visits made to race-concordant residents	+
Saha et al. (1999)	Use of preventive care and needed health services	+/−
Saha et al. (2003)	Use of basic health-care services	−
Sterling et al. (2001)	Retention in outpatient substance abuse treatment	−
Patient–provider communication (*n* = 5)		
Brown et al. (2007)	Pediatrician-parent communication patterns in medical encounters	+/−
Clark et al. (2004)	Physician-patient agreement on change in behavior (diet, exercise, medication, smoking, stress, and weight)	−
Cooper-Patrick et al. (1999)	Patient-provider participatory decision-making	+
Cooper et al. (2003)	Patient-centered communication	+
Gordon et al. (2006)	Doctors' information-giving in lung cancer consultations	+/−
Patient satisfaction (*n* = 5)		
Cooper et al. (2003)	Satisfaction and rating of care	+
LaVeist & Nuru-Jeter (2002)	Patient satisfaction with provider of same race	+
LaVeist & Carroll (2002)	Patient satisfaction with provider of same race	+
Saha et al. (1999)	Patient satisfaction with provider of same race	+/−
Saha et al. (2003)	Patient satisfaction with health care	−

Source: Meghani et al. (2009:123).

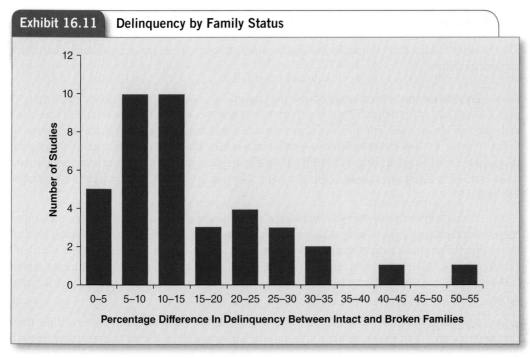

Exhibit 16.11 **Delinquency by Family Status**

Source: Wells, L. Edward and Joseph H. Rankin. "Families and Delinquency: A Meta-Analysis of the Impact of Broken Homes." *Social Problems* 38 (February):71–93. Copyright © 1991, The Society for the Study of Social Problems. Reprinted with permission.

results of multiple studies. Arlene Fink (2005:202–215) suggests evaluating meta-analytic studies by the following seven criteria:

1. *A clear statement of the analytic objectives:* The study's methods cannot be evaluated without knowledge of the objectives they were intended to achieve. Meta-analyses are most appropriate for summarizing research conducted to identify the effect of some type of treatment or some other readily identifiable individual characteristic.

2. *Explicit inclusion and exclusion criteria:* On what basis were research reports included in the analysis? Were high-quality studies—those that used a rigorous research design—distinguished from low-quality studies? When high-quality and low-quality studies are distinguished, their results should be summarized separately so that it is clear whether better research designs led to different results.

3. *Satisfactory search strategies:* Both electronic and written reference sources should be searched. Was some method used to find studies that were conducted but not published? It may be necessary to write directly to researchers in the field and to consult lists of papers presented at conferences.

4. *A standardized protocol for screening the literature:* Screening involves rating the quality of the study and its relevance to the research question. This screening should be carried out with a simple rating form.

5. *A standardized protocol for collecting data:* It is best to have two reviewers use a standard form for coding the characteristics of the reported research. The level of agreement between these reviewers should be assessed.

6. *Complete explanation of the method of combining results:* Some checks should be conducted to determine where particular study features influenced the size of the treatment effect.

7. *Report of results, conclusions, and limitations:* This seems obvious, but it's easy for a researcher to skirt over study limitations or some aspects of the findings.

▣ Ethics, Politics, and Research Reports

The researcher's ethical duty to be honest and open becomes paramount when reporting research results. Here are some guidelines:

- *Provide an honest accounting of how the research was carried out and where the initial research design had to be changed.* Readers do not have to know about every change you made in your plans and each new idea you had, but they should be informed about major changes in hypotheses or research design. If important hypotheses were not supported, acknowledge this, rather than conveniently forgetting to mention them (Brown & Hedges 2009:383). If a different approach to collecting or analyzing the data could have led to different conclusions, this should be acknowledged in the limitations section (Bergman 2008:588–590).

- *Evaluate honestly the strengths and weaknesses of your research design.* Systematic evaluations suggest that the stronger the research design from the standpoint of establishing internal (causal) validity, the weaker the empirical support that is likely to be found for hypothesized effects (compare Weisburd, Lum, & Petrosino 2001:64). Finding support for a hypothesis tested with a randomized experimental design is stronger evidence than support based on correlations between variables measured in a cross-sectional survey.

- *Refer to prior research and interpret your findings within the body of literature resulting from that prior research.* Your results are likely to be only the latest research conducted to investigate a research question that others have studied. It borders on unethical practice to present your findings as if they are the only empirical information with which to answer your research question, yet many researchers commit this fundamental mistake (Bergman 2008:599). For example, a systematic evaluation of citation frequency in articles reporting clinical trial results in medical journals found that, on average, just 21% of the available prior research was cited (for trials with at least three prior articles that could have been cited) (Robinson & Goodman 2011:53). The result of such omission is that readers may have no idea whether your own research supports a larger body of evidence or differs from it—and so should be subject to even greater scrutiny.

- *Maintain a full record of the research project so that questions can be answered if they arise.* Many details will have to be omitted from all but the most comprehensive reports, but these omissions should not make it impossible to track down answers to specific questions about research procedures that may arise during data analysis or presentation. Tests of relationships that were conducted but not included in the report should be acknowledged.

- *Avoid "lying with statistics" or using graphs to mislead.* (See Chapter 9 for more on this topic.) There is a more subtle problem to be avoided, which is "cherry-picking" results to present. Although some studies are designed to test only one hypothesis involving variables that each are measured in only one way, many studies collect data that can be used to test many hypotheses, often with alternative measures. If many possible relationships have been examined with the data collected and only those found to yield a statistically significant result are reported, the odds of capitalizing on chance findings are multiplied. This is a major temptation in research practice and has the unfortunate result that most published findings are not replicated or do not stand up to repeated tests over time (Lehrer 2010:57). Every statistical test presented can only be adequately understood in light of the entire body of statistical analyses that led to that particular result.

- *Acknowledge the sponsors of the research.* This is important partly so that others can consider whether this sponsorship may have tempted you to bias your results in some way. Whether you conducted your research for a sponsor, or together with members of an underserved community, give research participants an opportunity to comment on your main findings before you release them to the public. Consider revising your report based on their suggestions or, if you disagree with their suggestions, include their comments in footnotes at relevant points in your report or as an appendix to it (Bledsoe & Hopson 2009:392).

- *Thank staff who made major contributions.* This is an ethical as well as a political necessity. Let's maintain our social relations!

- *Be sure that the order of authorship for coauthored reports is discussed in advance and reflects agreed-on principles.* Be sensitive to coauthors' needs and concerns.

Ethical research reporting should not mean ineffective reporting. You need to tell a coherent story in the report and avoid losing track of the story in a thicket of minuscule details. You do not need to report every twist and turn in the conceptualization of the research problem or the conduct of the research. But be suspicious of reports that don't seem to admit to the possibility of any room for improvement. Social science is an ongoing enterprise in which one research report makes its most valuable contribution by laying the groundwork for another, more sophisticated, research project. Highlight important findings in the research report but also use the research report to point out what are likely to be the most productive directions for future researchers.

Research|Social Impact Link
Bad Research

Communicating With the Public

Even following appropriate guidelines such as these, however, will not prevent controversy and conflict over research on sensitive issues. The sociologist Peter Rossi (1999) recounts the controversy that arose when he released a summary of findings conducted in his 1989 study of homeless persons in Chicago (see Chapter 5). Despite important findings about the causes and effects of homelessness, media attention focused on Rossi's markedly smaller estimate of the numbers of homeless persons in Chicago compared with the "guesstimates" that had been publicized by local advocacy groups. "Moral of the story: Controversy is news, to which careful empirical findings cannot be compared" (Rossi 1999:2).

Does this mean that ethical researchers should avoid political controversy by sidestepping media outlets for their work? Many social scientists argue that the media offers one of the best ways to communicate the practical application of sociological knowledge and that when we avoid these opportunities, "some of the best sociological insights never reach policy makers because sociologists seldom take advantage of useful mechanisms to get their ideas out" (Wilson 1998:435).

The sociologist William Julius Wilson (1998:438) urges the following principles for engaging the public through the media:

1. Focus on issues of national concern, issues that are high on the public agenda.

2. Develop creative and thoughtful arguments that are clearly presented and devoid of technical language.

3. Present the big picture whereby the arguments are organized and presented so that the readers can see how the various parts are interrelated.

Ultimately each researcher must make a decision about the most appropriate and important outlets for his or her work.

Plagiarism

It may seem depressing to end a book on research methods with a section on **plagiarism**, but it would be irresponsible to avoid the topic. Of course, you may have a course syllabus detailing instructor or university policies about plagiarism and specifying the penalties for violating that policy, so I'm not simply going to repeat that kind of warning. You probably realize that the practice of selling term papers is revoltingly widespread (my search of "term papers" on Google returned 2,230,000 websites on June 1, 2014), so I'm not going to just repeat that academic dishonesty is widespread. Instead, I will use this section to review the concept of

> **Plagiarism:** Presenting as one's own the ideas or words of another person or persons for academic evaluation without proper acknowledgment.

plagiarism and to show how that problem connects to the larger issue of the integrity of social research. When you understand the dimensions of the problem and the way it affects research, you should be better able to detect plagiarism in other work and avoid it in your own.

You learned in Chapter 3 that maintaining professional integrity—honesty and openness in research procedures and results—is the foundation for ethical research practice. When it comes to research publications and reports, being honest and open means above all else avoiding plagiarism—that is, presenting as one's own the ideas or words of another person or persons for academic evaluation without proper acknowledgment (Hard, Conway, & Moran 2006:1059).

An increasing body of research suggests that plagiarism is a growing problem on college campuses. Jason Stephen, Michael Young, and Thomas Calabrese (2007:243) found in a web survey of self-selected students at two universities that one quarter acknowledged having plagiarized a few sentences (24.7%) or a complete paper (0.3%) in coursework within the past year (many others admitted to other forms of academic dishonesty, such as copying homework). Hard et al. (2006) conducted an anonymous survey in selected classes in one university, with almost all students participating, and found much higher plagiarism rates: 60.6% reported that they had copied "sentences, phrases, paragraphs, tables, figures, or data directly or in slightly modified form from a book, article, or other academic source without using quotation marks or giving proper acknowledgment to the original author or source" (p. 1069) and 39.4% reported that they had "copied information from Internet websites and submitted it as [their] work" (p. 1069).

So the plagiarism problem is not just about purchasing term papers—although that is really about as bad as it gets (Broskoske 2005:1); plagiarism is also about what you do with the information you obtain from a literature review or inspection of research reports. And rest assured that this is not only about student papers; it also is about the work of established scholars and social researchers who publish reports that you want to rely on for accurate information. Several noted researchers have been accused of plagiarizing passages that they used in popular books or academic articles; some have admitted to not checking the work of their research assistants, to not keeping track of their sources, or to being unable to retrieve the data they claimed they had analyzed. Whether the cause is cutting corners to meet deadlines or consciously fudging facts, the effect is to undermine the trustworthiness of social research.

Now that you are completing this course in research methods, it's time to think about how to do your part to reduce the prevalence of plagiarism. Of course, the first step is to maintain careful procedures for documenting the sources that you rely on for your own research and papers, but you should also think about how best to reduce temptations among others. After all, what people believe about what others do is a strong influence on their own behavior (Hard et al. 2006:1058).

Reviewing the definition of plagiarism and how your discipline's professional association enforces it is an important first step. These definitions and procedures reflect a collective effort to help social scientists maintain standards throughout the discipline. Awareness is the first step (American Sociological Association 1999:19).

Sociologists have an obligation to be familiar with their Code of Ethics, other applicable ethics codes, and their application to sociologists' work. Lack of awareness or misunderstanding of an ethical standard is not, in itself, a defense to a charge of unethical conduct.

The American Sociological Association (ASA)'s (1999) *Code of Ethics* includes an explicit prohibition of plagiarism:

14. Plagiarism

(a) In publications, presentations, teaching, practice, and service, sociologists explicitly identify, credit, and reference the author when they take data or material verbatim from another person's written work, whether it is published, unpublished, or electronically available.

(b) In their publications, presentations, teaching, practice, and service, sociologists provide acknowledgment of and reference to the use of others' work, even if the work is not quoted verbatim or paraphrased, and they do not present others' work as their own whether it is published, unpublished, or electronically available. (p. 16)

The next step toward combating the problem and temptation of plagiarism is to keep focused on the goal of social research methods: investigating the social world. If researchers are motivated by a desire to learn about social relations, to understand how people understand society, and to discover why conflicts arise and how they can be prevented, they will be as concerned with the integrity of their research methods as are those, like yourself, who read and use the results of their research. Throughout *Investigating the Social World,* you have been learning how to use research processes and practices that yield valid findings and trustworthy conclusions. Failing to report honestly and openly on the methods used or sources consulted derails progress toward that goal.

It works the same as with cheating in school. When students are motivated only by the desire to "ace" their tests and receive better grades than others, they are more likely to plagiarize and use other illicit means to achieve that goal. Students who seek first to improve their understanding of the subject matter and to engage in the process of learning are less likely to plagiarize sources or cheat on exams (Kohn 2008:6–7). They are also building the foundation for becoming successful researchers who help others understand our social world.

Audio Link
Ghost Authors

Conclusions

A well-written research article or report requires (to be just a bit melodramatic) blood, sweat, and tears and more time than you will, at first, anticipate. But the process of writing one will help you write the next. And the issues you consider, if you approach your writing critically, will be sure to improve your subsequent research projects and sharpen your evaluations of other investigators' research projects.

Good critical skills are essential when evaluating research reports, whether your own or those produced by others. There are *always* weak points in any research, even published research. It is an indication of strength, not weakness, to recognize areas where one's own research needs to be, or could have been, improved. And it is really not just a question of sharpening your knives and going for the jugular. You need to be able to weigh the strengths and weaknesses of particular research results and to evaluate a study for its contribution to understanding the social world—not whether it gives a definitive answer for all time.

But this is not to say that anything goes. Much research lacks one or more of the three legs of validity—measurement validity, causal validity, or generalizability—and contributes more confusion than understanding about the social world. Top journals generally maintain very high standards, partly because they have good critics in the review process and distinguished editors who make the final acceptance decisions. But some daily newspapers do a poor job of screening, and research-reporting standards in many popular magazines, TV shows, and books are often abysmally poor. Keep your standards high and your views critical when reading research reports, but not so high or so critical that you turn away from studies that make tangible contributions to understanding the social world—even if they don't provide definitive answers. And don't be so intimidated by the need to maintain high standards that you shrink from taking advantage of opportunities to conduct research yourself.

The growth of social science methods from its infancy to adolescence, perhaps to young adulthood, ranks as a key intellectual accomplishment of the 20th century. Opinions about the causes and consequences of homelessness no longer need to depend on the scattered impressions of individuals; criminal justice policies can be shaped by systematic evidence of their effectiveness; and changes in the distribution of poverty and wealth in populations can be identified and charted. Employee productivity, neighborhood cohesion, and societal conflict may each be linked to individual psychological processes and to international economic strains.

Interactive Exercises Link
Reporting Research

Of course, social research methods are no more useful than the commitment of researchers to their proper application. Research methods, like all knowledge, can be used poorly or well, for good purposes or bad, when appropriate or not. A claim that a belief is based on social science research in itself provides no extra credibility. As you have learned throughout this book, we must first learn which methods were used, how they were applied, and whether interpretations square with the evidence. To investigate the social world, we must keep in mind the lessons of research methods. Doing so will help us build a better social world in the 21st century.

Key Terms

Back matter 573
Effect size 577
Front matter 573
Meta-analysis 576
Plagiarism 583
Reverse outlining 56

Highlights

- Research reports should be evaluated systematically, using the review guide in Appendix A and considering the interrelations between the design elements.

- All write-ups of research should be revised several times and critiqued by others before being presented in final form. "Reverse outlining" can help in this process.

- Different types of reports typically pose different problems. Authors of student papers must be guided in part by the expectations of their professor. Thesis writers have to meet the requirements of different committee members but can benefit greatly from the areas of expertise represented on a typical thesis committee. Applied research reports are constrained by the expectations of the research sponsor; an advisory committee from the applied setting can help avoid problems. Journal articles must pass a peer review by other social scientists and are often much improved in the process.

- Research reports should include an introductory statement of the research problem, a literature review, a methodology section, a findings section with pertinent data displays, and a conclusions section that identifies any weaknesses in the

research design and points out implications for future research and theorizing. This basic report format should be modified according to the needs of a particular audience.

- The central ethical concern in research reporting is to be honest. This honesty should include providing a truthful accounting of how the research was carried out, maintaining a full record about the project, using appropriate statistics and graphs, acknowledging the research sponsors, and being sensitive to the perspectives of coauthors.

- Credit must be given where credit is due. The contributions of persons and organizations to a research project must be acknowledged in research reports.

- Meta-analysis provides a quantitative test of key findings across multiple similar studies.

- Plagiarism is a grievous violation of scholarly ethics. All direct quotes or paraphrased material from another author's work must be appropriately cited.

- Social scientists are obligated to evaluate the credibility of information obtained from any source before using it in their research reports.

STUDENT STUDY SITE

Sharpen your skills with SAGE edge at **edge.sagepub.com/schutt8e. SAGE edge for students** provides a personalized approach to help you accomplish your coursework goals in an easy-to-use learning environment.

Discussion Questions

1. A good place to start developing your critical skills would be with one of the articles reviewed in this chapter. Try reading one, and fill in the answers to the article review questions that I did not cover (Appendix A). Do you agree with my answers to the other questions? Could you add some points to my critique or to the lessons on research design that I drew from these critiques?

2. Read the journal article "Marital Disruption and Depression in a Community Sample," by Aseltine and Kessler, in the September 1993 issue of *Journal of Health and Social Behavior.* How effective is the article in conveying the design and findings of the research? Could the article's organization be improved at all? Are there bases for disagreement about the interpretation of the findings? Did reading the full article increase your opinion of its value?

3. Rate four journal articles on the study site for the overall quality of the research and for the effectiveness of the writing and data displays. Discuss how each could have been improved.

Practice Exercises

1. Call a local social or health service administrator or a criminal justice official, and arrange for an interview. Ask the official about his or her experience with applied research reports and conclusions about the value of social research and the best techniques for reporting to practitioners.

2. Interview a student who has written an independent paper or thesis based on original data. Ask your subject to describe his or her experiences while writing the thesis. Review the decisions made in designing the research, and ask about the stages of research design, data collection and analysis, and report writing that proved to be difficult.

3. Complete the interactive exercises on reporting research on the ISW8 study site.

Ethics Questions

1. Plagiarism is no joke. What are the regulations on plagiarism in class papers at your school? What do you think the ideal policy would be? Should this policy account for cultural differences in teaching practices and learning styles? Do you think this ideal policy is likely to be implemented? Why or why not? Based on your experiences, do you believe that most student plagiarism is the result of misunderstanding about proper citation practices, or is it the result of dishonesty? Do you think that students who plagiarize while in school are less likely to be honest as social researchers?

2. Full disclosure of funding sources and paid consulting and other business relationships is now required by most journals. Should researchers publishing in social science journals also be required to fully disclose all sources of funding, including receipt of payment for research done as a consultant? Should full disclosure of all previous funding sources be required in each published article? Write a short justification of the regulations you propose.

Web Exercises

1. Go to the National Science Foundation's (NSF) Sociology Program website at www.nsf.gov/funding/pgm_summ .jsp?pims_id=5369. What are the components that the NSF's Sociology Program looks for in a proposed piece of research? Examine the Table of Contents for an NSF proposal at http:// www.nsf.gov/pubs/policydocs/grantsgovguide0113.pdf. Now outline a research proposal to the NSF to investigate a research question of your choice.

2. The National Academy of Sciences wrote a lengthy report on ethics issues in scientific research. Visit the site and read the free executive summary. Go to www.nap.edu/catalog .php?record_id=10430 and click on "Download." Summarize the information and guidelines in the report.

3. Using the web, find five different examples of social science research projects that have been completed. Briefly describe each. How does each differ in its approach to reporting the research results? To whom do you think the author(s) of each are "reporting" (i.e., who is the audience)? How do you think the predicted audience has helped shape the author's approach to reporting the results? Be sure to note the websites at which you located each of your five examples.

Video Interview Questions

Listen to my interview for Chapter 16 at edge.sagepub.com/schutt8e.

1. What were our primary research findings?

2. What changes did the Women's Health Network implement in light of the research findings?

SPSS Exercises

1. Review the output you have generated in previous SPSS exercises. Select the distributions, statistics, and crosstabs that you believe provide a coherent and interesting picture of support for capital punishment in the United States. Prepare these data displays using the graphic techniques presented in this chapter and number them (Figure 1, Figure 2, etc.).

2. Write a short report based on the analyses you conducted for the SPSS exercises throughout this book, including the data displays you have just prepared. Include in your report a brief introduction and literature review (you might use the articles I referred to in the SPSS exercises for Chapter 2). In a short methods section, review the basic methods used in the GSS 2012, and list the variables you have used for the analysis.

3. In your conclusions section, include some suggestions for additional research on support for capital punishment.

Developing a Research Proposal

Now it's time to bring all the elements of your proposal together (Exhibit 3.10, #19 to #23).

1. Organize the proposal material you wrote for previous chapters in a logical order. Select what you feel is the strongest research method (Chapters 7, 8, 10, 12–14) as your primary method.

2. Add a multiple-method component to your research design (Chapter 15).

3. Rewrite the entire proposal, adding an introduction. Also add sections that outline a budget, and state the limitations of your study.

4. Review the proposal with the "Decisions in Research" checklist (Exhibit 3.10). Answer each question (or edit your previous answers), and justify your decision at each checkpoint.

Appendix A

Questions to Ask About a Research Article

1. What is the basic research question, or problem? Try to state it in just one sentence. (Chapter 2)

2. Is the purpose of the study explanatory, evaluative, exploratory, or descriptive? Did the study have more than one purpose? (Chapter 1)

3. Was a theoretical framework presented? What was it? Did it seem appropriate for the research question addressed? Can you think of a different theoretical perspective that might have been used? What philosophy guides the research? Is this philosophy appropriate to the research question? (Chapters 1, 2)

4. What prior literature was reviewed? Was it relevant to the research problem? Was it relevant to the theoretical framework? Does the literature review appear to be adequate? Are you aware of (or can you locate) any important studies that have been omitted? (Chapter 2)

5. What features identified the study as deductive or inductive? Do you need additional information in any areas to evaluate the study or to replicate it? (Chapters 1, 2)

6. Did the study seem consistent with current ethical standards? Were any trade-offs made between different ethical guidelines? Was an appropriate balance struck between adherence to ethical standards and use of the most rigorous scientific practices? (Chapter 3)

7. Were any hypotheses stated? Were these hypotheses justified adequately in terms of the theoretical framework and in terms of prior research? (Chapter 2)

8. What were the independent and dependent variables in the hypothesis or hypotheses? Did these variables reflect the theoretical concepts as intended? What direction of association was hypothesized? Were any other variables identified as potentially important? (Chapter 2)

9. What were the major concepts in the research? How, and how clearly, were they defined? Were some concepts treated as unidimensional that you think might best be thought of as multidimensional? (Chapter 4)

10. Did the instruments used, the measures of the variables, seem valid and reliable? How did the authors attempt to establish this? Could any more have been done in the study to establish measurement validity? (Chapter 4)

11. Was a sample or the entire population of elements used in the study? What type of sample was selected? Was a probability sampling method used? Did the authors think the sample was generally representative of the population from which it was drawn? Do you? How would you evaluate the likely generalizability of the findings to other populations? (Chapter 5)

12. Was the response rate or participation rate reported? Does it appear likely that those who did not respond or participate were markedly different from those who did participate? Why or why not? Did the author(s) adequately discuss this issue? (Chapter 5)

13. What were the units of analysis? Were they appropriate for the research question? If groups were the units of analysis, were any statements made at any point that are open to the ecological fallacy? If individuals were the units of analysis, were any statements made at any point that suggest reductionist reasoning? (Chapter 6)

14. Was the study design cross-sectional or longitudinal, or did it use both types of data? If the design was longitudinal, what type of longitudinal design was it? Could the longitudinal design have been improved in any way, as by collecting panel data rather than trend data, or by decreasing the dropout rate in a panel design? If cross-sectional data were used, could the research question have been addressed more effectively with longitudinal data? (Chapter 6)

15. Were any causal assertions made or implied in the hypotheses or in subsequent discussions? What approach was used to demonstrate the existence of causal effects? Were all three criteria and two cautions for establishing causal relationships addressed? What, if any, variables were controlled in the analysis to reduce the risk of spurious relationships? Should any other variables have been measured and controlled? How satisfied are you with the internal validity of the conclusions? What about external validity? (Chapter 6)

16. Which type of research design was used: experimental, survey, participant observation, historical comparative, or some other? How well was this design suited to the research question posed and the specific hypotheses tested, if any? Why do you suppose the author(s) chose this particular design? How was the design modified in response to research constraints? How was it modified to take advantage of research opportunities? (Chapters 7, 8, 10, 12, 13, 14)

17. Was this an evaluation research project? If so, which type of evaluation was it? Which design alternatives did it use? (Chapter 12)

18. Was a historical comparative design or a content analysis used? Which type was it? Were problems resulting from using historical or cross-national data addressed? (Chapter 13)

19. Was a secondary data analysis design used? If so, what were the advantages and disadvantages of using data collected in another project? Were Big Data analyzed? If so, did the methods raise any ethical alarms? (Chapter 14)

20. Were mixed methods used? What methods were combined and how can they be distinguished in priority and sequence? In what ways did the combination of qualitative and quantitative data enrich the study's value? (Chapter 15)

21. Was any attention given to social context and subjective meanings? If so, what did this add? If not, would it have improved the study? Explain. (Chapter 10)

22. Summarize the findings. How clearly were statistical or qualitative data presented and discussed? Were the results substantively important? (Chapters 9, 11)

23. Did the author(s) adequately represent the findings in the discussion and/or conclusions sections? Were conclusions well grounded in the findings? Are any other interpretations possible? (Chapter 16)

24. Compare the study to others addressing the same research question. Did the study yield additional insights? In what ways was the study design more or less adequate than the design of previous research? Would a meta-analysis be useful? (Chapters 2, 16)

25. What additional research questions and hypotheses are suggested by the study's results? What light did the study shed on the theoretical framework used? On social policy questions? (Chapters 2, 12, 16)

Appendix B

How to Read a Research Article

The discussions of research articles throughout the text may provide all the guidance you need to read and critique research on your own. But reading about an article in bits and pieces to learn about particular methodologies is not quite the same as reading an article in its entirety to learn what the researcher found out. The goal of this appendix is to walk you through an entire research article, answering the review questions introduced in Appendix A. Of course, this is only one article and our "walk" will take different turns than would a review of other articles, but after this review you should feel more confident when reading other research articles on your own.

We will use for this example an article by Seth Abrutyn and Anna S. Mueller (2014) on suicidal behavior among adolescents, reprinted on pages 596 to 612 of this appendix. It focuses on a topic of great social concern and of key importance in social theory. Moreover, it is a solid piece of research published by a top SAGE journal, the American Sociological Association's *American Sociological Review*.

I have reproduced below each of the article review questions from Appendix A, followed by my answers to them. After each question, I indicate the chapter where the question was discussed and after each answer, I cite the article page or pages that I am referring to. You can also follow my review by reading through the article itself and noting my comments.

1. *What is the basic research question, or problem? Try to state it in just one sentence.* (Chapter 2)

Abrutyn and Mueller present an overall research problem and then four specific research questions. They define their research problem by stating, "We investigate the role suicide suggestion plays in the suicide process, independent of other measures of social integration and psychological well-being" (p. 212). They summarize their research questions as being "the critical questions of how, when, and for whom does suggestion matter?" The four specific research questions highlight

Four major gaps in the literature: (1) whether suicide suggestion is associated with the development of suicidal thoughts among individuals who reported no suicidal thoughts at the

time a role model attempted suicide; (2) whether the effects of suicide suggestion fade with time; (3) whether the relationship between the role model and respondent matters; and (4) whether there are differences between boys and girls. (p. 212)

Before this point, the authors focus on this research question by highlighting the apparent paradox that the social integration that Émile Durkheim assumed helped protect individuals from suicide can instead spread suicidality.

2. *Is the purpose of the study explanatory, evaluative, exploratory, or descriptive? Did the study have more than one purpose?* (Chapter 1)

The study's primary purpose is explanatory because the authors conclude each section of their literature review with an expectation for influences on risk of suicidality. For example, the section on "gender differences" concludes with a summary statement that highlights the goal of explanation:

These findings suggest girls may be more susceptible than boys to role models' suicide attempts. (p. 215)

There is also a descriptive element in the authors' framing of the research because they indicate their strategy includes,

examining the development of suicidal behaviors in a sample of youth with no suicidal behaviors at Time I. (p. 215)

Of course, the authors also present descriptive statistics for their key variables (Table 1, p. 217).

3. *Was a theoretical framework presented? What was it? Did it seem appropriate for the research question addressed? Can you think of a different theoretical perspective that might have been used? What philosophy guides the research? Is this philosophy appropriate to the research question?* (Chapters 1, 2)

Abrutyn and Mueller's overarching theoretical framework for this research is Durkheim's classic theory of suicide and its emphasis on the protective value of social integration (pp. 212–215). The article begins and ends by discussing Durkheim's theory and it introduces the concept of suicide suggestion as important for sociologists because of the "apparent contradiction" it involves with Durkheim's theory. The literature review is focused on theorizing and research about suicide suggestion and so is very appropriate for the research questions addressed. Some connections are made to identity theory, which provides a somewhat different theoretical perspective that is more appropriate for some of the influences tested. The researchers follow a positivist research philosophy as they seek to understand social processes in the social world, rather than how people make sense of their experiences. In this study, the focus on suicide "suggestion" certainly raises a question about meaning, but their methods use standard measures to identify variation in this phenomenon, rather than intensive interviews or observations to discover how adolescents construct the experience of a friend's suicide. We can conclude that the positivist philosophy guiding the research is appropriate to the research question, while realizing that a researcher guided by a constructivist philosophy could have studied the same phenomenon but with different research methods and a somewhat different research question.

4. *What prior literature was reviewed? Was it relevant to the research problem? Was it relevant to the theoretical framework? Does the literature review appear to be adequate? Are you aware of (or can you locate) any important studies that have been omitted?* (Chapter 2)

Abrutyn and Mueller review literature from the article's first page until the "Methods" section (pp. 212–215). It is all very relevant to the general theoretical framework problem, and there is a section focused on each of the four specific research questions. In the first few paragraphs, several studies are mentioned that draw attention to the importance of suicide suggestion and thus the potential negative effects of social ties on suicidality (pp. 211–212). Subsequent sections in the literature review focus on prior research about suicidality and the effects of media, role models, recency ("temporal limitations"), family versus friends, and gender. The review provides an adequate foundation for expecting these effects. I leave it to you to find out whether any important studies were omitted.

5. *What features identified the study as deductive or inductive?* (Chapters 1,2)

The study clearly involves a test of ideas against empirical reality as much as that reality could be measured; it was carried out systematically and with a deductive design. Because the authors used an available data set, others can easily obtain the complete documentation for the study and try to replicate the authors' findings. The authors explicitly note and challenge assumptions made by many other researchers using Durkheim's theory of social integration and suicide (p. 211). They aim clearly to build social theory and encourage others to build on their findings: "this study is not without its limitations" (p. 224). The study thus seems to exemplify adherence to the logic of deductive research and to be very replicable.

6. *Did the study seem consistent with current ethical standards? Were any trade-offs made between different ethical guidelines? Was an appropriate balance struck between adherence to ethical standards and use of the most rigorous scientific practices?* (Chapter 3)

Abrutyn and Mueller use survey data collected by others and so encounter no ethical problems in their treatment of human subjects. The reporting seems honest and open. Although the research should help inform social policy, the authors' explicit focus is on how their research can inform social theory. This is quite appropriate for research reported in a scientific journal, so there are no particular ethical problems raised about the uses to which the research is put. The original survey used by the authors does not appear at all likely to have violated any ethical guidelines concerning the treatment of human subjects, although it would be necessary to inspect the original research report to evaluate this.

7. *Were any hypotheses stated? Were these hypotheses justified adequately in terms of the theoretical framework and in terms of prior research?* (Chapter 2)

Although they do not explicitly label their predictions as hypotheses, Abrutyn and Mueller carefully specify their independent and dependent variables and link them to their five specific research questions. Each one is justified and related to prior research in the "theoretical background" section (pp. 212–215).

8. *What were the independent and dependent variables in the hypothesis or hypotheses? Did these variables reflect the theoretical concepts as intended? What direction of association was hypothesized? Were any other variables identified as potentially important?* (Chapter 2)

Independent and dependent variables are identified explicitly in the measurement section and several control variables are specified as important (pp. 216–218). Independent variables are friend suicide attempt, family suicide attempt, family integration scale, friends care, and religious attendance. Although it is not stated explicitly as an independent variable, the authors identify another independent variable, recency of others' suicide, by distinguishing the survey follow-up wave at which that event occurred and the wave at which the dependent variable is measured. Additional variables controlled as known risk factors for suicide are same-sex attraction and emotional distress. Several demographic and personal characteristics are also used as controls: grade point average, family structure, race/ethnicity, parents' education, and age.

9. *What were the major concepts in the research? How, and how clearly, were they defined? Were some concepts treated as unidimensional that you think might best be thought of as multidimensional?* (Chapter 4)

The key concept in the research is that of "suicide suggestion"; it is defined in the article's second sentence and distinguished from the parallel concept of "social integration" that Durkheim emphasized

(p. 211). Two dimensions of this key concept are then distinguished (emotional—suicidality and behavioral—suicides) and the concept of suicidality is discussed at length in a section on the spread of suicide (p. 212). Other important concepts in the research are personal role models, similarity between individuals and role models, type of role model (family versus friends), temporal limits, and gender. They are each elaborated in the separate sections of the literature review. Several related concepts are mentioned in the course of discussing others, including significant others, reality of role model (p. 212), media exposure, depression, social similarity of friends (p. 214), suggestibility and network diffusion (p. 215), family integration and care by others (p. 216), and religious attendance (p. 217).

10. *Did the instruments used, the measures of the variables, seem valid and reliable? How did the authors attempt to establish this? Could any more have been done in the study to establish measurement validity?* (Chapter 4)

The measures of the dependent variables, suicidal ideation and suicide attempts, were based on answers to single questions (p. 216). The wording of these questions is quite straightforward, but no information is provided about their reliability or validity. This can be seen as a weakness of the article, although Abrutyn and Miller do note in the "limitations" section that they do not know how stated thoughts or intentions were related to actual suicidal behavior (p. 225). The same single-question approach was used to measure the independent variables, friend suicide attempt and family suicide attempt (p. 216), again without any information on reliability or validity. The authors report that family integration was measured with a four-item scale, for which they report interitem reliability, and relations with friends, religious attendance, and same-sex attraction were assessed with just single questions (pp. 216–217). Abrutyn and Mueller measured emotional distress with an abridged version of the widely used Center for Epidemiological Studies Depression (CES-D) scale (pp. 217–218). They mention the interitem reliability of the CES-D in their data ("Cronbach's alpha = .873") but do not discuss its validity; because the scale has been used in so many other studies and has been evaluated so many times for its reliability and validity, and because it does not play a central role in this new research, it is reasonable that the authors do not discuss it further. Overall, the study can be described as relatively weak in information provided on measurement reliability and validity.

11. *Was a sample or the entire population of elements used in the study? What type of sample was selected? Was a probability sampling method used? Did the authors think the sample was generally representative of the population from which it was drawn? Do you? How would you evaluate the likely generalizability of the findings to other populations?* (Chapter 5)

The sample was a national random (probability) sample of adolescents at three time points. Called the "Add Health" study, the original researchers used a two-stage cluster sampling design, in which first all schools in the United States containing an 11th grade were sampled, with stratification by region, urbanicity, school type, ethnic composition, and size. A nationally representative subsample of students was then interviewed from these schools ($n = 20,745$). Students (and graduates) from the subsample were then reinterviewed in two more waves, with Wave II 1 to 2 years after Wave I and Wave III another 5 to 6 years after Wave II. A total of 10,828 respondents were interviewed in all three waves (p. 215). Abrutyn and Mueller attempt to determine whether suicidality is influenced among adolescents who have not previously thought of suicide by processes of contagion, so they limit their sample further to those who reported no suicidal thoughts or attempts in Wave I (p. 216). The authors identify their sample explicitly as representative of the national population of adolescents in school in this age range. Do you think the findings could be generalized to adolescents who had dropped out of school, or to other countries with different cultural values about suicide?

12. *Was the response rate or participation rate reported? Does it appear likely that those who did not respond or participate were markedly different from those who did participate? Why or why not? Did the author(s) adequately discuss this issue?* (Chapter 5)

The number of cases is identified at each wave, and the consequences of exclusion criteria applied are specified, but the response rate is not stated. Readers are referred for details to the original research report on the Add Health survey (p. 215). The authors do evaluate the possibility that the exclusion of adolescents who reported suicidal ideation in Wave I could have biased their sample, but they suggest this is unlikely because average levels of emotional distress and demographic variables are similar whether these cases are excluded or not (p. 216). There does not seem to be a serious problem here, but it would have been helpful to have had details about the response rate in the article, instead of just in a separate report (albeit one that is available online). More consideration of possibilities for sample bias could also have led to greater confidence in generalizations from this sample.

13. *What were the units of analysis? Were they appropriate for the research question? If groups were the units of analysis, were any statements made at any point that are open to the ecological fallacy? If individuals were the units of analysis, were any statements made at any point that suggest reductionist reasoning?* (Chapter 6)

The survey sampled adolescents within schools, so individuals were the units of analysis (pp. 215–216). The focus was on the behavior of individuals, so this is certainly appropriate. However, it is possible that the process of suicide contagion could differ between different schools, so the authors could have added a great deal to their study by also using schools as the units of analysis and determining whether there were some distinctive characteristics of schools in which contagion was more likely. Therefore, the individual-level analysis could obscure some group-level processes and thus lead to some reductionist reasoning.

14. *Was the study design cross-sectional or longitudinal, or did it use both types of data? If the design was longitudinal, what type of longitudinal design was it? Could the longitudinal design have been improved in any way, as by collecting panel data rather than trend data, or by decreasing the dropout rate*

in a panel design? If cross-sectional data were used, could the research question have been addressed more effectively with longitudinal data? (Chapter 6)

The study used a longitudinal panel design, although the sample at Wave II was limited to those adolescents who had not already graduated (p. 215). The reduction in the sample size by about half from the first wave to the third follow-up 5 to 6 years later is typical for a panel design; it is not possible to consider whether procedures could have been improved without knowing more about the details contained in the original research report.

15. *Were any causal assertions made or implied in the hypotheses or in subsequent discussions? What approach was used to demonstrate the existence of causal effects? Were all three criteria and two cautions for establishing causal relationships addressed? What, if any, variables were controlled in the analysis to reduce the risk of spurious relationships? Should any other variables have been measured and controlled? How satisfied are you with the internal validity of the conclusions? What about external validity?* (Chapter 6)

Causal assertions are implied in the predictions about "how exposure to suicidal behaviors shapes adolescent suicidality" (p. 215). A nomothetic approach to causation is used and each of the criteria for establishing causal effects is addressed: association (by checking for an association between the independent and dependent variables), time order (by using a longitudinal design that establishes clearly that the precipitating cause occurred before the "contagion"), and nonspuriousness (by controlling for variables that could have created a spurious association). The variables controlled included family integration, closeness to friends, religious attendance, same-sex attraction, and emotional distress, as well as several personal and demographic characteristics. The combination of the longitudinal design and the breadth of the variables controlled increases confidence in the internal validity of the conclusions, but because there was not random assignment to experiencing a friend or family member's suicide (an ethical and practical impossibility), we cannot be completely confident that adolescents exposed to suicide did not differ from their peers in some unmeasured risk factor. There is little basis for evaluating external validity.

16. *Which type of research design was used: experimental, survey, participant observation, historical comparative, or some other? How well was this design suited to the research question posed and the specific hypotheses tested, if any? Why do you suppose the author(s) chose this particular design? How was the design modified in response to research constraints? How was it modified to take advantage of research opportunities?* (Chapters 7, 8, 10, 12, 13, 14)

Survey research was the method used in the Add Health study, which generated the data set used in this secondary data analysis project. Survey research seems appropriate for the research questions posed, although only because Add Health used a longitudinal panel design. The survey design was somewhat modified after the fact for this

analysis by eliminating respondents who had already experienced a suicide of a friend or family member at Wave I (p. 215).

17. *Was this an evaluation research project? If so, which type of evaluation was it? Which design alternatives did it use?* (Chapter 12)

This study did not use an evaluation research design. The issues on which it focused might profitably be studied in some evaluations of adolescent suicide prevention programs.

18. *Was a historical comparative design or a content analysis used? Which type was it? Were problems resulting from using historical or cross-national data addressed?* (Chapter 13)

This study did not use any type of historical or comparative design. It is interesting to consider how the findings might have differed if comparisons with other cultures or to earlier times had been made. The authors include in their literature review content analyses of the reporting of suicide as part of investigating media effects on suicide, but they did not take this approach themselves (p. 213).

19. *Was a secondary data analysis design used? If so, what were the advantages and disadvantages of using data collected in another project? Were Big Data analyzed? If so, did the methods raise any ethical alarms?* (Chapter 14)

This article reported a secondary analysis of the Add Health survey data (p. 215). This analysis of the previously collected data allowed the authors to conduct a very careful and fruitful analysis of a research question that had not previously been answered with these data, without having to secure funds for conducting such an ambitious longitudinal survey themselves. However, the result was that they could not include more extensive questions about suicidality and friends' and family members' suicides as they probably would have done if they had designed the primary data collection themselves. This standard survey data set would not qualify as Big Data.

20. *Were mixed methods used? What methods were combined and how can they be distinguished in terms of priority and sequence? In what ways did the combination of qualitative and quantitative data enrich the study's value?* (Chapter 15)

Mixed methods were not used. The analysis is entirely of quantitative data. The original study could have been enriched for the purposes of addressing suicide contagion by adding qualitative interviews of students who had been exposed to a suicide, as the authors note (p. 223).

21. *Was any attention given to social context and subjective meanings? If so, what did this add? If not, would it have improved the study? Explain.* (Chapter 10)

Social context and subjective meanings are really at the heart of the phenomenon of suicide contagion, but the Add Health researchers did not add a qualitative component to their research or adopt a constructivist philosophy to focus more attention on these issues. A participant observation study of suicide contagion in high schools could yield great insights, and a researcher with a constructivist philosophy who focused on how adolescents make sense of others' suicides would add another dimension to understanding this phenomenon.

22. *Summarize the findings. How clearly were statistical or qualitative data presented and discussed? Were the results substantively important?* (Chapters 9, 11)

Statistical data are presented clearly in two tables. The first table describes the sample at each wave in terms of the key variables for the study. The second table presents the results of a multivariate analysis of the data using a technique called "logistic regression." The authors use this technique to test for the associations between their dependent and independent variables over time, while controlling for other variables. The results seem substantively important. In the authors' own words,

> For adolescents, ties do bind, but whether these ties integrate adolescents into society, with positive repercussions for their emotional well-being, or whether they promote feelings of alienation, depends in part on the qualities embedded in those ties. (p. 225)

23. *Did the author(s) adequately represent the findings in the discussion or conclusions sections? Were conclusions well grounded in the findings? Are any other interpretations possible?* (Chapter 16)

The findings are well represented in the discussion and conclusions section, with a limitations section that strikes an appropriate note of caution (pp. 222–225). Interesting conjectures are presented in the discussion of gender differences and differences in the apparent effects of different types of role model. The conclusions section makes explicit connections to the initial questions posed about Durkheim's theorizing. You might want to consider what other interpretations of the findings might be possible. Remember that other interpretations always are possible for particular findings—it is a question of the weight of the evidence, the persuasiveness of the theory used, and the consistency of the findings with other research.

24. *Compare the study to others addressing the same research question. Did the study yield additional insights? In what ways was the study design more or less adequate than the design of previous research?* (Chapters 2, 16)

Summaries of prior research in the literature review suggest that Abrutyn and Mueller have added new insights to the literature on suicide contagion by overcoming limitations in previous research designs. The use of a longitudinal panel design was more adequate than much previous research using cross-sectional designs.

25. *What additional research questions and hypotheses are suggested by the study's results? What light did the study shed on the theoretical framework used? On social policy questions? Would a meta-analysis be useful?* (Chapters 2, 12, 16)

Perhaps the most obvious research question suggested by the study's results is that of whether social integration of some type can have protective effects as predicted by Durkheim even at the same time that other social connections heighten the risk of suicide due to a process of social contagion. Research designed to answer this question could lead to an overarching theoretical framework encompassing both the protective benefits of social ties that Durkheim identified and the risk that social ties create a process of social contagion. If the focus is on understanding the process of social contagion, it is clear that Abrutyn and Mueller's research has made an important contribution. The authors highlight some policy implications in their conclusions (p. 225). It is not clear that there are sufficient other studies like this to attempt a meta-analysis.

Are Suicidal Behaviors Contagious in Adolescence? Using Longitudinal Data to Examine Suicide Suggestion

American Sociological Review
2014, Vol. 79(2) 211–227
© American Sociological
Association 2014
DOI: 10.1177/0003122413519445
http://asr.sagepub.com
⑤SAGE

Seth Abrutyn[a] and Anna S. Mueller[a]

Abstract

Durkheim argued that strong social relationships protect individuals from suicide. We posit, however, that strong social relationships also have the potential to increase individuals' vulnerability when they expose people to suicidality. Using three waves of data from the National Longitudinal Study of Adolescent Health, we evaluate whether new suicidal thoughts and attempts are in part responses to exposure to role models' suicide attempts, specifically friends and family. We find that role models' suicide attempts do in fact trigger new suicidal thoughts, and in some cases attempts, even after significant controls are introduced. Moreover, we find these effects fade with time, girls are more vulnerable to them than boys, and the relationship to the role model—for teenagers at least—matters. Friends appear to be more salient role models for both boys and girls. Our findings suggest that exposure to suicidal behaviors in significant others may teach individuals new ways to deal with emotional distress, namely by becoming suicidal. This reinforces the idea that the structure—and content—of social networks conditions their role in preventing suicidality. Social ties can be conduits of not just social support, but also antisocial behaviors, like suicidality.

Keywords

suicide, social networks, suicide suggestion, Durkheim, gender, Add Health

Understanding suicide has been essential to the sociological enterprise since Durkheim ([1897] 1951) wrote his famous monograph, arguing that groups that integrated and (morally) regulated their members offered protective benefits against suicide. Durkheimian mechanisms remain highly relevant (cf. Maimon and Kuhl 2008; Pescosolido and Georgianna 1989; Thorlindsson and Bjarnason 1998), but emphasis on *suicide suggestion,* or the effect a role model's suicidal behavior has on an observer's suicidality, has become increasingly essential to the sociological understanding of suicide (e.g., Gould 2001; Phillips 1974; Stack 2003, 2009).

Whereas Durkheim assumed that social integration protected individuals, suicide suggestion demonstrates that suicidality can spread through the very ties that Durkheim theorized as protective. This apparent contradiction is not such a problem for modern interpretations of Durkheim's theory that focus on the structure

[a]The University of Memphis

Corresponding Authors:
Seth Abrutyn and Anna Mueller, Department of Sociology, Clement Hall 231, The University of Memphis, Memphis, TN 38152-3530
E-mail: seth.abrutyn@memphis.edu;
anna.mueller@memphis.edu

Downloaded from asr.sagepub.com at UNIV MASSACHUSETTS BOSTON on April 12, 2014

of social ties themselves, and how the networks individuals are embedded within produce the protective benefits Durkheim observed (Bearman 1991; Pescosolido 1990; Wray, Colen, and Pescosolido 2011). It is possible to imagine social ties as capable of both social support and social harm (Baller and Richardson 2009; Haynie 2001; Pescosolido 1990). Durkheim was right that collective solidarity is often protective, but we argue that the behaviors, values, and emotions embedded in network ties must be elaborated to truly understand how social relationships shape individuals' life chances.[1] This subtle shift provides an opportunity to integrate two equally important, but often unnecessarily separate, realms in the sociology of suicide: the literature on suicide suggestion and the literature on social integration.

The existing literature on suicide suggestion demonstrates that concern over the emotions (suicidality) and behaviors (suicides) embedded in social networks is warranted. Suicides often occur in clusters, with spikes in suicide rates following media coverage of suicides (Stack 2003, 2005, 2009), so much so that a group of public health agencies (including the National Institute of Mental Health [NIMH]) issued guidelines for how the media should report on suicides so as to limit their spread (Suicide Prevention Resource Center [SPRC] 2013). Less research has examined how suicides spread through personal role models, but studies show a robust association between a friend's (and sometimes family member's) suicidal behavior and that of the person exposed to it (Bearman and Moody 2004; Bjarnason 1994; Liu 2006; Niederkrotenthaler et al. 2012; Thorlindsson and Bjarnason 1998). However, these studies often fail to address the critical questions of how, when, and for whom does suggestion matter?

With this study, we employ three waves of data from the National Longitudinal Study of Adolescent Health to examine these questions. By using longitudinal data rich in measures of adolescent life, we investigate the role suicide suggestion plays in the suicide process, independent of other measures of social

integration and psychological well-being. We tease out nuances related to the harmful side of social integration by shedding light on four major gaps in the literature: (1) whether suicide suggestion is associated with the development of suicidal thoughts among individuals who reported no suicidal thoughts at the time a role model attempted suicide; (2) whether the effects of suicide suggestion fade with time; (3) whether the relationship between the role model and respondent matters; and (4) whether there are differences between boys and girls.

THEORETICAL BACKGROUND

The Spread of Suicide

Beginning with Phillips's (1974) groundbreaking work, suicide suggestion studies typically examine (1) the association between celebrity suicides and national and local suicide rates (Gould 2001; Stack 2003, 2005), (2) the association between fictionalized media suicides and national and local rates (e.g., Stack 2009), and (3) the apparent geographic and temporal clustering of suicides (e.g., Baller and Richardson 2002; Gould, Wallenstein, and Kleinman 1990). A few studies have also investigated the effect a role model's suicidal behavior has on friends or family members exposed to it. The logic of these studies is predicated on social psychological assumptions. Significant others or persons labeled as members of a reference group with whom we identify are far more likely to influence and shape behavior than are nonsignificant others or outsiders (Turner 2010). Additionally, direct ties infused with socioemotional meanings can act as conduits for the spread of behavioral norms (Goffman 1959) and positive *and* negative affect, which motivate the reproduction of these behavioral norms (Lawler 2006).

Suicide suggestion and the media. In a comprehensive review of the suicide suggestion literature, Stack (2005:121) estimates that about one-third of suicide cases in the

Downloaded from asr.sagepub.com at UNIV MASSACHUSETTS BOSTON on April 12, 2014

United States involve "suicidal behavior following the dissemination of a suicidal model in the media." Models may be real celebrities like Marilyn Monroe or fictionalized characters such as those found in popular novels or television shows. The length of exposure and the status of the role model appear to matter: on average, publicized celebrity suicides produce a 2.51 percent spike in aggregate rates, whereas Marilyn Monroe's suicide, a high status and highly publicized suicide, was followed by a 13 percent spike in the U.S. suicide rate (Phillips 1974; Stack 2003). The evidence concerning effects of fictionalized suicides, such as those found occasionally in television series (Schmidtke and Hafner 1988), is less consistent (e.g., Niederkrontenthaler and Sonneck 2007), but a recent meta-analysis found youths are particularly at risk of suicide suggestion via fictional suicides (Stack 2009).

Spikes following celebrity suicides are confined geographically to the subpopulation exposed to the suicide—for example, local newspapers should only affect their readership, whereas nationally televised shows should reach more people. Furthermore, research shows that temporal effects of media exposure vary to some degree, typically ranging from two weeks to a month (Phillips 1974; Stack 1987). To date, these studies have had a difficult time determining whether suggestion plays a role above and beyond individuals' personal circumstances: finding an association between media and suicide rates "does not necessarily identify [suggestion] as the underlying mechanism" (Gould et al. 1990:76). If suicide suggestion plays a role in the suicide process, the question is: does it have an effect above and beyond other risk factors for suicide, such as suicidal thoughts or depression prior to exposure to media coverage of a suicide?

Suicide suggestion via personal role models. Like media exposure suggestion studies, studies of personal role models focus on demonstrating a link between a role model's and the exposed individual's suicidal

behaviors. The majority of these studies focus on adolescent suicide, perhaps because adolescent suicide has tripled since the 1950s and thus represents a serious public health problem (NIMH 2003). Adolescents may also be particularly vulnerable to suicide suggestion: adolescents are particularly socially conscious—social status and social relationships are a major focus of their daily lives. Moreover, teenagers are greatly influenced by their peers' values and behaviors (Giordano 2003), which may increase their vulnerability to suicide epidemics. Finally, adolescents are unique in that their sense of self is still forming, so they are more malleable than adults (Crosnoe 2000; Crosnoe and Johnson 2011). Any insights into factors contributing to the development of suicidality are thus crucial to teen suicide prevention.

Generally, studies of personal role models show that having a friend or family member exhibit suicidal behavior is positively associated with an exposed adolescent's own suicidality (Bjarnason and Thorlindsson 1994; Bridge, Goldstein, and Brent 2006; Evans, Hawton, and Rodham 2004), even after controlling for other measures of social integration, regulation, and psychological distress (e.g., Bearman and Moody 2004; Bjarnason 1994). A few studies also demonstrate a positive association between exposure to suicidal behavior in role models and an individual's likelihood of attempting suicide (Bearman and Moody 2004). These studies add to our understanding of sociological influences on suicide, but they fail to examine who is most vulnerable to suggestion and how long effects may linger, and they are often limited by the use of cross-sectional data.

Three studies employ longitudinal data and thus shed further light on suicide suggestion within the adolescent suicide process. Brent and colleagues (1989) had the rare opportunity to collect data immediately following a suicide at a high school. Although they were unable to measure students' predispositions to suicide prior to a peer's suicide, their findings suggest that suicide suggestion can spread rapidly and then gradually lose some

Downloaded from asr.sagepub.com at UNIV MASSACHUSETTS BOSTON on April 12, 2014

of its effect. More recently, Niederkrotenthaler and colleagues (2012) found that young children exposed to a parent's suicidal behavior were far more likely to develop suicidal behaviors over time than were their counterparts. This work, however, is primarily epidemiological and fails to control for potentially significant confounding factors, such as social integration. Finally, Thompson and Light (2011) examined which factors are associated with adolescent nonfatal suicide attempts and found that role models' attempts significantly increase adolescents' likelihood of attempting suicide, net of respondents' histories of suicidal thoughts and many other factors. These studies provide insights into exposure to a role model's suicidal behavior, but questions of who is most vulnerable and how long that vulnerability lasts remain open, and the role suggestion plays as an aspect of social integration remains unacknowledged.

Similarity between individuals and role models. A primary limitation in the existing literature on suicide suggestion is its failure to determine whether the similarity between friends' or family members' suicidal behaviors is due to the tendency for individuals to form friendships with people they are similar to. This proverbial "birds of a feather" is often the case for teens, who select friends and peer groups based on how similar potential friends are to themselves (Crosnoe, Frank, and Mueller 2008; Joyner and Kao 2000). Research shows that adolescent friendships tend to be homophilous in terms of depression levels (Schaefer, Kornienko, and Fox 2011) and aggression (Cairns et al. 1988). The effect of suicide suggestion on an adolescent's suicidal behaviors may thus be due to unobserved preexisting similarities between friends. To address this limitation, we focus on the development of suicidal behaviors in a sample of adolescents with no documented history of suicidality, to avoid (to the extent possible with survey data) confounding the observed effect of suicide suggestion with selection into friendships. Answering this crucial question, whether suicide suggestion

contributes to the development of suicidal behaviors, is a central goal of this study.

Temporal limits. In the process of discerning how suggestion shapes adolescent suicidality, it is useful to consider whether effects of suggestion via personal role models linger as time passes, and for whom. Given past research, suggestive effects likely have temporal limitations. Previous studies on effects of media exposure generally find that spikes in suicide rates last between two and four weeks (Phillips 1974; Stack 1987). Significant others tend to have a greater impact on individuals than do nonsignificant others (Turner 2010), so it is reasonable to expect effects of personal role models will last longer than suicides publicized in the media. We thus utilize the Add Health survey to test whether the impact of a role model's suicide attempt is observable after approximately one year and six years.

Family versus friends. Generally, studies of suicide suggestion do not distinguish between effects of a family member's versus a friend's suicide attempt on those exposed. Given that past research demonstrates that "the influence of friends surpasses that of parents" by mid-adolescence (Crosnoe 2000:378), and friends' influence is strongly linked with teen delinquency, health behaviors, and pro-social behaviors (Frank et al. 2008; Giordano 2003; Haynie 2001; Mueller et al. 2010), we would expect to see differences based on an individual's relationship to the role model. It is plausible, given the extant research on adolescents and peer influence, that a friend's suicidal behavior provides a more salient model for imitating than would family. We thus analyze the two types of role models separately.

Gender differences. The final aspect deserving greater attention is potential gender differences in suggestion and suicidality. Little research emphasizes potential gender differences in how adolescents develop suicidal behaviors, despite the fact that key differences exist in suicidal behaviors between

Downloaded from asr.sagepub.com at UNIV MASSACHUSETTS BOSTON on April 12, 2014

adolescent boys and girls (Baca-Garcia et al. 2008); for example, girls are more likely than boys to report nonfatal suicide attempts, whereas boys are more likely to experience fatal suicides. Another important reason to consider how suicide suggestion affects boys and girls stems from differences in boys' and girls' friendships. Girls tend to have fewer, but more intimate, emotionally laden friendships, whereas boys tend to maintain less emotional and more diffuse networks focused around shared activities (Crosnoe 2000). Moreover, girls tend to be more sensitive to others' opinions (Gilligan 1982) and are more easily influenced by peers than are boys (Maccoby 2002). These findings suggest girls may be more susceptible than boys to role models' suicide attempts.

In summary, this study shifts the sociological focus away from the protective nature of social ties toward the potential harm these ties can have on individuals. Specifically, we elaborate how exposure to suicidal behaviors shapes adolescent suicidality by identifying how, when, and for whom suicide suggestion matters. Our strategy includes (1) examining the development of suicidal behaviors in a sample of youth with no suicidal behaviors at Time I; (2) determining how long the effect of suggestion lasts; and if (3) the type of role model or (4) gender makes a difference in the process. Answers to these questions will help us understand how social relationships work in daily life to both protect and, sometimes, put individuals at risk of suicidality, thereby moving us closer to a robust sociological theory of suicide.

METHODS

Data

This study employs data from Waves I, II, and III of the National Longitudinal Study of Adolescent Health (Add Health). Add Health contains a nationally representative sample of U.S. adolescents in grades 7 through 12 in 132 middle and high schools in 80 different communities. From a list of all schools containing an 11th grade in the United States,

Add Health selected a nationally representative sample of schools using a school-based, cluster sampling design, with the sample stratified by region, urbanicity, school type, ethnic composition, and size.

The preliminary in-school survey collected data from all students in all Add Health high schools ($n = 90,118$ students) in 1994 to 1995; from this sample, a nationally representative subsample was interviewed at Wave I ($n = 20,745$), shortly after the in-school survey. Wave II followed in 1996 and collected information from 14,738 Wave I participants. Some groups of respondents were generally not followed up at Wave II; the largest of these were Wave I 12th graders, who had generally graduated high school by Wave II. Wave III was collected in 2001 to 2002 and followed up the Wave I in-home respondents (including respondents excluded from Wave II) who were then approximately age 18 to 23 years. Additional information about Add Health can be found in Harris and colleagues (2009).

Sample Selection

We used several sample selection filters to produce analytic samples that allow us to assess suicide suggestion in adolescence. First, we selected respondents with valid sample weights so we could properly account for the complex sampling frame of the Add Health data. Second, we used longitudinal data analysis; as such, we restricted our sample to adolescents who participated in Waves I and II of Add Health for our analyses of Wave II outcomes, and Waves I, II, and III for our analyses of Wave III outcomes. Among respondents, 10,828 had valid sample weights and participated in all three waves of Add Health. Our third selection filter selected only adolescents with no suicidal thoughts or attempts at Wave I, so the time order of events is preserved such that we can determine whether suicide suggestion plays a role above and beyond preexisting vulnerabilities to suicidality. This restriction reduced our analytic sample to 9,309 respondents. With this sample restriction, our models are not estimating the

Downloaded from asr.sagepub.com at UNIV MASSACHUSETTS BOSTON on April 12, 2014

potential for role models to maintain or dissolve an adolescent's suicidal thoughts. Instead, our models estimate whether role models' behaviors at Wave I are associated with the development of previously undocumented suicidal thoughts and attempts at later waves. This also allows us to control for potential unmeasured factors that may shape both who adolescents choose as friends and their vulnerability to suicide (following the logic of classic ANCOVA; cf. Shadish, Campbell, and Cook 2002). Our final selection filter excluded adolescents missing any key independent variables.

These restrictions have the potential to bias our sample, but they also enable our analysis of critical aspects of suicidal behaviors in adolescence. To assess any potential bias, Table 1 presents descriptive statistics for the entire Wave I sample and our Wave II and Wave III analytic samples. The only substantial difference between the Wave I Add Health sample and our analytic sample is the lower incidence of suicidal thoughts and attempts at Waves II and III due to our restricting our analyses to adolescents with no suicidal thoughts at Wave I. Our analytic samples do not vary substantially from the entire Wave I sample in terms of average levels of emotional distress or demographic variables.

Measures

Dependent variables. We analyze two dependent variables: *suicidal ideation* and *suicide attempts* at Wave II and Wave III. *Suicidal ideation* is based on adolescents' responses to the question: "During the past 12 months, did you ever seriously think about committing suicide?" Adolescents who answered "yes" were coded 1 on a dichotomous outcome indicating suicidal ideation. Adolescents who reported having suicidal thoughts were then asked, "During the past 12 months, how many times did you actually attempt suicide?" Answers ranged from 0 (0 times) to four (six or more times). We recoded these responses into a dichotomous variable where 1 indicates a report of at least one suicide

attempt in the past 12 months and 0 indicates no attempts. Adolescents who reported no suicidal thoughts were also coded 0 on *suicide attempts*. These variables were asked at all three waves.

Independent variables. Our first key independent variable, one of two ways we measure suicide suggestion, is *friend suicide attempt* and is based on adolescents' responses to the question: "Have any of your friends tried to kill themselves during the past 12 months?" Adolescents who responded "yes" were coded 1 on a dichotomous variable. This question was asked at all waves. For models predicting suicidal thoughts and attempts at Wave II, we rely on adolescents' responses at Wave I to preserve time order in these data. For models predicting Wave III dependent variables, we use adolescents' responses to this question at Wave II. Our second key independent measure of suicide suggestion is *family suicide attempt*. The treatment of this variable is identical to *friend suicide attempt* and is based on adolescents' responses to the question: "Have any of your family tried to kill themselves during the past 12 months?"

Our models also control for protective factors for suicide suggested by prior research. Following Durkheim's ideas about the importance of social integration as a protective factor for suicide, we measure adolescents' family integration, how close they feel to their friends, and their religious attendance. Our *family integration scale* (Cronbach's alpha = .769) is based on four items that measure how integrated adolescents are in their families (Bjarnason 1994). Adolescents were asked how much they feel their parents care about them, how much people in their family understand them, whether they have fun with their family, and whether their family pays attention to them. Responses were coded so that a higher value on the scale indicates a higher feeling of family caring. Our measure of adolescents' relationships with their friends, *friends care,* is based on adolescents' responses to the question, "How much do you feel that your friends care about you?" Higher

Downloaded from asr.sagepub.com at UNIV MASSACHUSETTS BOSTON on April 12, 2014

analyses that fail to correct for Add Health's oversampled populations.

RESULTS

To begin our investigation of suicide suggestion, we first examine the roles of family members' and friends' suicide attempts in adolescent girls' and boys' suicidal behaviors at Wave II, before turning to boys' and girls' behaviors at Wave III. Among boys, reports of a new suicidal attempt were extremely rare; only 1 percent of boys reported a suicide attempt at Wave II after reporting no suicidal thoughts at Wave 1. For this reason, we focus most heavily on suicidal thoughts and examine suicide attempts only among adolescent girls. The models for boys' suicidal attempts are available from the authors by request.

Suicidal Behaviors at Wave II

Table 2 presents odds ratios from logistic regressions predicting suicide ideation and suicide attempts for girls and boys. As a first step, we estimate the bivariate relationship between family members' suicide attempts (Wave I) and adolescents' suicidal thoughts and attempts a year later (Wave II) (see Models 1, 4, and 7 in Table 2). A family member's attempted suicide (Model 1) significantly increases the likelihood that adolescent girls report suicidal thoughts at Wave II; however, it is not associated with suicide attempts at Wave II (Model 4). On average, girls who reported that a family member attempted suicide at Wave I are 2.994 times more likely to report suicidal thoughts at Wave II than are girls who did not experience a family member's suicide attempt. This pattern is not found among boys. For boys, we find no significant relationship between a family member's suicide attempt and boys' likelihood of reporting suicidal thoughts. This is our first piece of evidence for gender differences in suicide suggestion.

Next we turn to friends as role models for suicide suggestion. For girls, a friend's suicide attempt significantly increases their likelihood of reporting suicidal thoughts (Model 2) and attempts (Model 5). For boys,

experiencing a friend's suicide attempt has a significant and positive relationship to boys' likelihood of reporting suicidal thoughts (Model 8). These significant bivariate relationships indicate that *who* the role model is may condition the likelihood that suicides spread through social relationships in gendered ways. Our next step is to evaluate whether these relationships maintain their significance once potential risk and protective factors are held constant in our models.

Substantively, our findings do not change after the addition of important controls.[3] On average, adolescent girls are 2.129 times more likely to report suicidal *thoughts* after experiencing a family member's attempted suicide, and 1.561 times more likely after experiencing a friend's suicide attempt, net of all other variables (Model 3). Girls' reports of suicide *attempts,* on average, are significantly related to friends' suicide attempts, but not family members' attempts, net of all other variables, confirming in Model 6 the bivariate relationships observed in Models 4 and 5. For girls, the relationship between suicide suggestion, via family or friend role models, is robust to many vital risk and protective factors for suicide.

For boys, the story is similar. The bivariate relationships observed in Models 7 and 8 are robust to the addition of control variables. Boys remain affected by a friend's suicide attempt at Wave I. Specifically, a friend's suicide attempt renders boys 1.649 times more likely to report suicidal thoughts at Wave II. The suicide attempt of a family member remains insignificant (confirming associations found in Model 7).

Overall, these findings suggest that suicide suggestion is associated with the development of suicidal behaviors within a year or so of a role model's suicide attempt, particularly when the role model is a friend. Significant gender differences do emerge: girls appear more sensitive than boys to familial role models.

Suicidal Behaviors at Wave III

In the analyses presented in Table 3, we investigate the impact a role model's suicide attempt at Wave II has on respondents' suicidal thoughts and attempts at Wave III, as

Downloaded from asr.sagepub.com at UNIV MASSACHUSETTS BOSTON on April 12, 2014

Table 2. Odds Ratios from Models Predicting Suicidal Thoughts and Attempts among Adolescents at Wave II

| | Girls | | | | | | Boys | | |
| | Suicide Ideation | | | Suicide Attempt | | | Suicide Ideation | | |
	Model 1	Model 2	Model 3	Model 4	Model 5	Model 6	Model 7	Model 8	Model 9
Suicide Suggestion									
Family Suicide Attempt	2.994***		2.129**	1.069		.535	1.263		.947
Friend Suicide Attempt		2.054***	1.561**		3.214***	2.577***		1.935**	1.649*
Background									
Age			.733***			.679***			.979
African American			.625*			1.041			.809
Asian American			.966			1.580			.741
Latino\a			.811			1.082			.863
Other Race or Ethnicity			.692			1.332			1.019
Parents' Education Level			.967			.865			1.060
Same-Sex Attraction			1.660			1.281			1.499
GPA			.870			.967			.796
Social Integration									
Religious Attendance			.996			.900			.969
Single-Parent Family			1.499*			1.145			.943
Step-Parent Family			1.295			1.868			.866
Other Family Structure			1.050			1.578			1.817
Family Integration Scale			.877			.681			.770
Friends Care			1.204			1.216			1.404**
Psychological Factors									
Emotional Distress			1.067***			1.067***			1.038**
−2 Log Likelihood	2708.714	2698.139	2499.105	1073.977	1039.891	947.583	1729.374	1717.750	1672.626
Response Profile (n=1/n=0)	351/4172	351/4172	351/4172	100/4423	100/4423	100/4423	222/4079	222/4079	222/4079
N	4,523	4,523	4,523	4,523	4,523	4,523	4,301	4,301	4,301

Note: All independent variables measured at Wave I.
Source: The National Longitudinal Study of Adolescent Health.
$*p < .05; **p < .01; ***p < .001$ (two-tailed tests).

220

Downloaded from asr.sagepub.com at UNIV MASSACHUSETTS BOSTON on April 12, 2014

Table 3. Odds Ratios from Models Predicting Suicidal Thoughts and Attempts among Adolescents at Wave III

	Girls						Boys		
	Suicide Ideation			Suicide Attempt			Suicide Ideation		
	Model 1	Model 2	Model 3	Model 4	Model 5	Model 6	Model 7	Model 8	Model 9
Suicide Suggestion									
Family Suicide Attempt	.725		.466	1.298		.779	1.782		1.572
Friend Suicide Attempt		1.978***	1.546		1.794	1.254		1.665	1.168
Background									
Age			.811***			.824			.861*
African American			.535*			.693			.477*
Asian American			1.286			4.808***			.551
Latino\a			.804			.698			.900
Other Race or Ethnicity			.678			<.001***			.683
Parents' Education Level			1.220*			1.173			1.248*
Gay, Lesbian, Bisexual Identity (W3)			2.879**			2.917			3.042**
GPA			.840			.645			.823
High School Dropout (W3)			1.557			2.688*			1.555
Some College (W3)			1.063			1.264			.881
Social Integration									
Religious Attendance			.845			.883			.964
Single-Parent Family			1.200			2.796*			1.184
Step-Parent Family			.995			2.560*			1.049
Other Family Structure			1.447			1.939			1.894
Not Currently Married or Cohabiting (W3)			1.309			1.173			2.751***
Family Integration Scale			.871			1.015			1.083
Friends Care			1.014			1.481			.799
Psychological Factors									
Emotional Distress			1.041**			1.026			1.055***
–2 Log Likelihood	1841.515	1821.903	1709.455	794.630	789.706	709.774	1660.011	1656.320	1547.991
Response Profile (n=1/n=0)	202/3873	202/3873	202/3873	59/4016	59/4016	59/4016	197/3658	197/3658	197/3658
N	4,075	4,075	4,075	4,075	4,075	4,075	3,855	3,855	3,855

Note: All independent variables measured at Wave II unless otherwise noted.
Source: The National Longitudinal Study of Adolescent Health.
p < .05; **p* < .01; ***p* < .001 (two-tailed tests).

221

Downloaded from asr.sagepub.com at UNIV MASSACHUSETTS BOSTON on April 12, 2014

respondents are entering early adulthood. These models help us understand the temporality of suicide suggestion, while also allowing us to establish a clear time order between an adolescent's history of suicidal thoughts (Wave I), the experience of a friend's or family member's suicide attempt (Wave II), and subsequent suicidal behaviors (Wave III).

Overall, models presented in Table 3 demonstrate a significantly different pattern from those presented in Table 2. For boys and girls, the impact of a role model's suicide attempt, whether a family member or a friend, appears to fade with time. By Wave III, we find only one significant relationship between a measure of suicide suggestion and suicidal thoughts. Model 2 in Table 3 indicates a significant bivariate relationship between the experience of a friend's suicide attempt at Wave II and girls' reports of suicidal thoughts at Wave III. This finding, however, does not hold in full models, although the odds ratio is in the expected direction (OR = 1.546) and the *p*-value is very close to the threshold for statistical significance ($p > .055$) (Model 3 in Table 3). We further investigated the change in statistical significance between the bivariate and saturated models in analyses not presented here (but available from the authors by request). We found that adolescent girls' emotional distress at Wave II explains the impact of a friend's suicide attempt on girls' likelihood of reporting suicidal thoughts at Wave III, net of other key controls. The significant effect of a friend's suicide attempt on girls' likelihood of suicidal thoughts remains until emotional distress is included in the model. This suggests that emotional distress may serve as an important mechanism through which suicide suggestion operates, particularly for girls.

Our models from Wave III suggest that the increased risk of suicide suggestion found over the short run (in Table 2) fades with time. Six years later, we find little evidence that experiencing a role model's suicide attempt, whether friend or family member, has a long-term effect, except perhaps for girls for whom it is mediated by emotional distress.

DISCUSSION

Within the sociology of suicide, social integration and regulation are often emphasized as the primary social forces that protect or put individuals at risk of suicide. These Durkheimian mechanisms are undoubtedly important (Bearman 1991; Pescosolido 1990; Pescosolido and Georgianna 1989; Wray et al. 2011), but much research on the spread of health behaviors implicates social ties as not just mechanisms for social support, but also potential conduits for the spread of suicidal behaviors via suicide suggestion, illuminating another side to social integration. We find that suicide attempts of role models—primarily friends—are in fact associated with adolescents' development of suicidal thoughts and, in some cases, attempts. Effects of suicide suggestion appear to fade with time, girls are more vulnerable to suicide suggestion than boys, and the type of role model—for teenagers at least—matters. Our findings suggest that social relationships, contra Durkheim, are not always protective against suicide, at least not when significant others exhibit suicidal tendencies. This reinforces the idea that the structure—and content—of social networks conditions their role in preventing suicidality. Specifically, social ties can be conduits of not just social support but also antisocial behaviors, like suicidality.

Our study has four primary implications for advancing the sociological understanding of suicide. Our most essential contribution to the literature on suicide suggestion via personal role models is the evidence we provide indicating that being aware of a role model's suicide attempt is associated with the development of suicidal thoughts and sometimes attempts. This relationship is robust to many measures of risk and protective factors. Experiencing the suicide attempt of a significant other may serve as a vehicle for learning a way to deal with distressing life events—by becoming suicidal (Jamison 1999). Future research should continue to probe the question of how suicide suggestion contributes to the development of suicidality. Many potential mechanisms—social learning, imitation,

Downloaded from asr.sagepub.com at UNIV MASSACHUSETTS BOSTON on April 12, 2014

and emotional contagion—may underlay the observed association between role models and those exposed to their suicidality. Qualitative research, in particular, may provide valuable insights into which potential mechanisms promote the spread of suicidality via social ties. Understanding how and when suicide suggestion becomes salient to youths' suicidality would greatly help practitioners prevent suicides. Our study provides a first step toward this larger goal.

In addition to providing insights into suicide suggestion as an important mechanism in the adolescent suicide process, our study has implications for understanding the temporality of suicide suggestion via individuals' role models. Previous research on suicide rates and media exposure found effects of suicide suggestion tend to last two to four weeks (Phillips 1974; Stack 1987). Considering the potential differences in connectedness derived from face-to-face relationships and direct contact versus mediated sources, we hypothesized that personal role models would have a stronger, or longer lasting, effect on adolescents exposed to their behavior. In fact, our findings suggest that having a friend attempt suicide has a longer lasting effect than reading about a suicide in the paper or seeing a fictive suicide on television. We find that effects of a friend's or family member's suicide attempt last at least one year, if not more—considerably longer than the effect of exposure via the media documented in prior research. By six years, however, the effect of a friend's or family member's suicide attempt appears to fade in significance. Among adolescent girls, however, a friend's suicide attempt may continue to shape suicidal thoughts even six years later; notably, this effect is explained by girls' emotional distress levels. Future research should examine this pattern in more detail, as this finding suggests an indirect, but potentially important, long-term impact of suicide suggestion via girls' emotional distress.

Perhaps it is not shocking that we do not find strong evidence that effects of role models' suicide attempts last over the long run. Teens who survive the first year (or so) following a friend's suicide attempt may be, or

become, emotionally resilient. By early adulthood, a role model's suicide attempt in adolescence may no longer be central to one's daily life, a life no longer constrained within the bounds of high school. Research on contagion generally focuses on relatively bounded social spaces—like Native American reservations, mental wards, or high schools—and finds these spaces are at higher risk of geographic-temporal suicide clustering (e.g., Gould et al. 1990). Outside of relatively bounded social environments, do effects of role models' suicides spread via social ties? Investigating the role of exposure to suicides inside and out of bounded social contexts would add more depth to our understanding of how suicides—and potentially other behaviors—become socially contagious.

Our third major contribution to the literature comes from our emphasis on the role of gender in the suicide suggestion process. Given that boys and girls experience peer relationships differently (Crosnoe 2000), understanding how a social mechanism, such as suicide suggestion, differs for boys and girls is crucial to arriving at a full understanding of the development of adolescent suicidality. In fact, we find significant gender differences in the role of suicide suggestion: suggestion appears more salient to girls. Among boys, friends are the only relevant personal role models for triggering the development of suicidal thoughts; girls' suicidal behaviors, on the other hand, are influenced by both family and friends. Moreover, among girls, suicidal thoughts *and attempts* are associated with suicide suggestion. Finally, effects of a friend's or family member's suicide attempt may last longer for girls.

Although we found girls were more vulnerable, absent an observed history of suicidal thoughts, boys were not immune to suicide suggestion. Note that Thompson and Light (2011), who analyzed suicide attempts net of prior suicidal thoughts, found that boys and girls responded similarly to a role model's suicide attempt. This suggests the role of gender may change at different points in the suicidal process and that a predisposition toward suicidality may be particularly important for understanding those differences.

Downloaded from asr.sagepub.com at UNIV MASSACHUSETTS BOSTON on April 12, 2014

Why would girls be more vulnerable than boys to suicide suggestion? A definitive answer to this question is beyond the scope of this article, but we can suggest some theoretical considerations that may help explain this variation and offer paths for future research. Because girls develop and maintain more intense intimate relationships (Crosnoe 2000), they may be more primed to "take the role of the other" and hence may be more vulnerable to suggestive mechanisms, including developing emotional distress that sustains the original suggestive triggers. For boys, having relationships that are far less emotionally anchored may reduce or mitigate the effects of suggestion, which raises vital questions about which mechanisms are more salient in the development of boys' suicidal thoughts. Future research should continue to examine the complex role gender plays in the adolescent suicide process, as this may help determine different strategies for preventing suicides.

Our fourth and final major contribution to the sociology of suicide stems from our examination of how different role models—friends and family members—vary in terms of their importance in the suicide suggestion process. Our findings indicate that peers may be more meaningful than family to adolescents, for both boys and girls. Social psychology has long shown that behavior is more strongly shaped by members of reference groups central to the formation and maintenance of one's identity (Stryker 1980). To be sure, a teen's family consists of similar individuals whom the teen may identify with, but research on adolescents clearly demonstrates that purposive efforts to differentiate oneself from one's family are accompanied by concomitant identification with peers. This is not to say that a family member's suicidal tendencies are not distressing in adolescence. For example, we find that for adolescent girls, over the short run, a family member's suicide attempt increases their likelihood of reporting suicidal thoughts (but not attempts) one year later. Yet taken as a whole, our findings indicate that friends' suicide attempts are more influential than family members' suicide

attempts in adolescents' lives, at least once adolescents' Wave I suicidality is controlled.

Limitations

Although our findings provide new and important insights into the sociology of suicide, this study is not without its limitations. First, and perhaps most obvious, we are limited to analyzing respondents' suicidal behaviors because we have no information on Add Health respondents who commit suicide. Individuals who report suicidal thoughts or have a history of nonfatal suicide attempts are significantly more likely to commit suicide, but fatal suicide attempts are most common among individuals with no history of nonfatal suicide attempts. Generalizing these findings to the spread of suicide deaths should thus be done with caution. Furthermore, there is attrition in the Add Health sample between waves, and given the higher completion rate among male suicide attempters, more boys than girls may be missing from our analyses due to a completed suicide. Additionally, respondents who actually commit suicide may have been the most likely to be affected by suicide suggestion. Unfortunately, we could find no information from Add Health on whether suicide, or even death, played a significant role in sample attrition. Fortunately, the rarity of suicide among adolescents reduces the risk of this substantially biasing our findings. However, this discussion highlights the significance of finding a way to compare the "lethality" of all types of role models, from the personal to the media-based. Future data collection efforts should note this key gap in the literature.

Our second limitation is related. We chose to focus on friends' and family members' suicide attempts, rather than actual suicides, for practical reasons. Very few respondents reported having a friend or family member complete suicide. This fact may affect our findings on the importance of suicide suggestion. The power of suicide suggestion in the case of a suicide may be greater than the power of suggestion based on a nonfatal suicide attempt. If anything, our findings may thus underrepresent the

Downloaded from asr.sagepub.com at UNIV MASSACHUSETTS BOSTON on April 12, 2014

potential salience of suicide suggestion as a social mechanism in suicidal behaviors.

Finally, although we did our best to account for adolescents' vulnerability to suicide, we are limited by available data. Specifically, we analyzed a sample of adolescents who reported no suicidal thoughts at Wave I in an attempt to parse out effects of selection into friendships from the influence those friendships may have on an individual. Some adolescents with a history of suicidality, perhaps prior to Wave I, may have been included in our sample. Our study provides one of the best efforts to date to isolate selection from the effect of suicide suggestion, but further investigation of these issues is needed before we can be confident that suggestion affects the development of suicidality.

CONCLUSIONS

Sociologists commonly turn to Durkheimian measures of social integration and regulation when searching for sociological explanations for suicide, but our findings indicate that suicides, like other behaviors, can spread through social relationships via suicide suggestion. Friends' and family members' suicide attempts may trigger the development of suicidal behaviors, suggesting that exposure to role models is a powerful way that drastic and deviant behaviors, like suicide, become normalized. Notably, the relationship to the role model conditions the experience of suicide suggestion. Furthermore, adolescent girls appear more susceptible than boys to adopting the suicidal behaviors they observe through social relationships. This study provides important information for the evolution of the sociology of suicide, but our findings also have vital policy implications for public health officials attempting to prevent adolescent suicide. Namely, policies and practitioners need to be sensitive to the importance of suicide attempts (and not simply suicides), particularly among peers and for girls. Additionally, the increased risk of suicidality associated with friends' suicide attempts may last a year or more, which is longer than previously thought.

For adolescents, ties do bind, but whether these ties integrate adolescents into society, with positive repercussions for their emotional well-being, or whether they promote feelings of alienation, depends in part on the qualities embedded in those ties. On the surface, these findings may appear to contradict Durkheim's sociology, given his focus on solidarity through collective effervescence. Yet, Durkheim argued that solidarity was a product of a shared, collective conscience that spreads through ritualized, emotion-laden interaction. Why should we expect deviant behavior like suicide to be precluded from the types of norms that can spread across actors? Instead, we posit that for a full understanding of how social integration works in individuals' lives to shape their life chances, we must consider not only the social support social ties provide, but also the emotions, behaviors, and values that inhere in those social relations.

Acknowledgments

Seth Abrutyn and Anna Mueller contributed equally to this work. This article is a revision of a paper presented at the 2012 annual meetings of the American Sociological Association. The authors would like to thank Marty Levin, Chandra Muller, Ken Frank, Sarah Blanchard, and six anonymous reviewers for their insightful comments and suggestions. The authors acknowledge the helpful research assistance of Cynthia Stockton.

Data and Funding

This research uses data from Add Health (http://www.cpc.unc.edu/addhealth), a program project directed by Kathleen Mullan Harris and designed by J. Richard Udry, Peter S. Bearman, and Kathleen Mullan Harris at the University of North Carolina at Chapel Hill, and funded by grant P01-HD31921 from the Eunice Kennedy Shriver National Institute of Child Health and Human Development, with cooperative funding from 23 other federal agencies and foundations. Special acknowledgment is due Ronald R. Rindfuss and Barbara Entwisle for assistance in the original design. No direct support was received from grant P01-HD31921 for this analysis. Opinions reflect those of the authors and do not necessarily reflect those of the granting agencies.

Notes

1. We are particularly grateful to an anonymous reviewer for suggesting this formulation.
2. The SAS programs used to recode and analyze all data are available from the authors by request.
3. Tables presenting odds ratios and confidence intervals are available from the authors by request.

Downloaded from asr.sagepub.com at UNIV MASSACHUSETTS BOSTON on April 12, 2014

References

An, Anthony. 2002. "Performing Logistic Regression on Survey Data with the New SURVEYLOGISTIC Procedure." Paper 258-27, pp. 1–9. Proceedings of the 27th Annual SAS Users Group International Conference (SUGI 27), Orlando, FL, April 14–17.

Baca-Garcia, Enrique, M. Mercedes Perez-Rodriguez, J. John Mann, and Maria A. Oquendo. 2008. "Suicidal Behavior in Young Women." *Psychiatric Clinics of North America* 31:317–31.

Baller, Robert D. and Kelly K. Richardson. 2002. "Social Integration, Imitation, and the Geographic Patterning of Suicide." *American Sociological Review* 67:873–88.

Baller, Robert D. and Kelly K. Richardson. 2009. "The 'Dark Side' of the Strength of Weak Ties: The Diffusion of Suicidal Thoughts." *Journal of Health and Social Behavior* 50:261–76.

Bearman, Peter S. 1991. "The Social Structure of Suicide." *Sociological Forum* 6:501–524.

Bearman, Peter S. and James Moody. 2004. "Suicide and Friendships among American Adolescents." *American Journal of Public Health* 94:89–95.

Bell, Bethany A., Anthony J. Onwuegbuzie, John M. Ferron, Qun G. Jiao, Susan T. Hibbard, and Jeffrey D. Kromrey. 2012. "Use of Design Effects and Sample Weights in Complex Health Survey Data: A Review of Published Articles Using Data From 3 Commonly Used Adolescent Health Surveys." *American Journal of Public Health* 102:1399–1405.

Bjarnason, Thoroddur. 1994. "The Influence of Social Support, Suggestion and Depression on Suicidal Behavior among Icelandic Youth." *Acta Sociologica* 37:195–206.

Bjarnason, Thoroddur and Thorolfur Thorlindsson. 1994. "Manifest Predictors of Past Suicide Attempts in a Population of Icelandic Adolescents." *Suicide and Life Threatening Behavior* 24:350–58.

Brent, David A., Mary M. Kerr, Charles Goldstein, James Bozigar, Marty Wartella, and Marjorie J. Allan. 1989. "An Outbreak of Suicide and Suicidal Behavior in a High School." *American Academy of Child and Adolescent Psychiatry* 28:918–24.

Bridge, Jeffrey A., Tina R. Goldstein, and David A. Brent. 2006. "Adolescent Suicide and Suicidal Behavior." *Journal of Child Psychology and Psychiatry* 47:372–94.

Cairns, Robert B., Beverly D. Cairns, Holly J. Neckerman, Scott D. Gest, and Jean-Louis Gariepy. 1988. "Social Networks and Aggressive Behavior: Peer Support or Peer Rejection?" *Developmental Psychology* 61:157–68.

Crosnoe, Robert. 2000. "Friendships in Childhood and Adolescence: The Life Course and New Directions." *Social Psychology Quarterly* 63:377–91.

Crosnoe, Robert, Kenneth Frank, and Anna Strassmann Mueller. 2008. "Gender, Body Size, and Social Relations in American High Schools." *Social Forces* 86:1189–1216.

Crosnoe, Robert and Monica Kirkpatrick Johnson. 2011. "Research on Adolescence in the Twenty-First Century." *Annual Review of Sociology* 37:479–60.

Durkheim, Emile. [1897]1951. *Suicide: A Study in Sociology*. Glencoe, IL: Free Press.

Evans, Emma, Keith Hawton, and Karen Rodham. 2004. "Factors Associated with Suicidal Phenomena in Adolescents: A Systematic Review of Population-Based Studies." *Clinical Psychology Review* 24:957–79.

Frank, Kenneth, Chandra Muller, Catherine Riegle-Crumb, Anna Strassmann Mueller, and Jennifer Pearson. 2008. "The Social Dynamics of Mathematics Coursetaking in High Schools." *American Journal of Sociology* 113:1645–96.

Gilligan, Carol. 1982. *In A Different Voice: Psychological Theory and Women's Development*. Cambridge, MA: Harvard Press.

Giordano, Peggy C. 2003. "Relationships in Adolescence." *Annual Review of Sociology* 29:252–81.

Goffman, Erving. 1959. *The Presentation of Self in Everyday Life*. New York: Anchor Books.

Gould, Madelyn S. 2001. "Suicide and the Media." Pp. 200–224 in *Suicide Prevention: Clinical and Scientific Aspects,* edited by H. Hendin and J. J. Mann. New York: New York Academy of Science.

Gould, Madelyn S., Sylvan Wallenstein, and Marjorie Kleinman. 1990. "Time-Space Clustering of Teenage Suicide." *American Journal of Epidemiology* 131:71–78.

Harris, Kathleen M., C. T. Halpern, E. Whitsel, J. Hussey, J. Tabor, P. Entzel, and J. Richard Udry. 2009. "The National Longitudinal Study of Adolescent Health: Research Design." (http://www.cpc.unc.edu/projects/addhealth/design).

Haynie, Dana L. 2001. "Delinquent Peers Revisited: Does Network Structure Matter?" *American Journal of Sociology* 106:1013–57.

Jamison, Kay Redfield. 1999. *Night Falls Fast: Understanding Suicide*. New York: Vintage Books.

Joyner, Kara and Grace Kao. 2000. "School Racial Composition and Adolescent Racial Homophily." *Social Science Quarterly* 81:810–25.

Lawler, Edward J. 2006. "The Affect Theory of Social Exchange." Pp. 248–67 in *Contemporary Social Psychological Theories,* edited by P. J. Burke. Stanford, CA: Stanford University Press.

Liu, Ruth X. 2006. "Vulnerability to Friends' Suicide Influence: The Moderating Effects of Gender and Adolescent Depression." *Journal of Youth and Adolescence* 35:479–89.

Maccoby, Eleanor E. 2002. "Gender and Group Process: A Developmental Perspective." *Current Directions in Psychological Science* 11:54–58.

Maimon, David and Danielle C. Kuhl. 2008. "Social Control and Youth Suicidality: Situating Durkheim's Ideas in a Multilevel Framework." *American Sociological Review* 73:921–43.

Mueller, Anna S., Jennifer Person, Chandra Muller, Kenneth Frank, and Alan Turner. 2010. "Sizing Up Peers:

Downloaded from asr.sagepub.com at UNIV MASSACHUSETTS BOSTON on April 12, 2014

Adolescent Girls' Weight Control and Social Comparison in the School Context." *Journal of Health and Social Behavior* 51:64–78.

National Institute of Mental Health (NIMH). 2003. *In Harm's Way: Suicide in America*. U.S. Department of Mental and Human Services. NIH Publication no. 03-4594.

Niederkrotenthaler, Thomas, Brigitta Roderus, Kristina Alexanderson, Finn Rasmussen, and Ellenor Mittendorfer-Rutz. 2012. "Exposure to Parental Mortality and Markers of Morbidity, and the Risks of Attempted and Completed Suicide in Offspring: An Analysis of Sensitive Life Periods." *Journal of Epidemiology and Community Health* 66:232–39.

Niederkrotenthaler, Thomas and Gernot Sonneck. 2007. "Assessing the Impact of Media Guidelines for Reporting Suicides in Austria: Interrupted Time Series Analysis." *Australian and New Zealand Journal of Psychiatry* 41:419–28.

Pearson, Jennifer, Chandra Muller, and Lindsey Wilkinson. 2007. "Adolescent Same-Sex Attraction and Academic Outcomes: The Role of School Attachment and Engagement." *Social Problems* 54:523–42.

Pescosolido, Bernice A. 1990. "The Social Context of Religious Integration and Suicide: Pursuing Network Explanation." *Sociological Quarterly* 31:337–57.

Pescosolido, Bernice and Sharon Georgianna. 1989. "Durkheim, Suicide, and Religion: Toward a Network Theory of Suicide." *American Sociological Review* 54:33–48.

Phillips, David P. 1974. "The Influence of Suggestion on Suicide: Substantive and Theoretical Implications of the Werther Effect." *American Sociological Review* 39:340–54.

Schaefer, David R., Olga Kornienko, and Andrew M. Fox. 2011. "Misery Does Not Love Company: Network Selection Mechanisms and Depression Homophily." *American Sociological Review* 76:764–85.

Schmidtke, Armin and H. Hafner. 1988. "The Werther Effect after Television Films: New Evidence for an Old Hypothesis." *Psychological Medicine* 18:665–76.

Shadish, William R., Donald T. Campbell, and Thomas D. Cook. 2002. *Experimental and Quasi-Experimental Designs for Generalized Causal Inference*. New York: Houghton Mifflin.

Stack, Steven. 1987. "Celebrities and Suicide: A Taxonomy and Analysis, 1948–1983." *American Sociological Review* 52:401–412.

Stack, Steven. 2003. "Media Coverage as a Risk Factor in Suicide." *Journal of Epidemiology and Community Health* 57:238–40.

Stack, Steven. 2005. "Suicide in the Media: A Quantitative Review of Studies Based on Nonfictional Stories." *Suicide and Life Threatening Behavior* 35:121–33.

Stack, Steven. 2009. "Copycat Effects on Fictional Suicide: A Meta-Analysis." Pp. 231–44 in *Suicide and the Creative Arts,* edited by S. Stack and D. Lester. New York: Nova Science Publishers.

Stryker, Sheldon. 1980. *Symbolic Interactionism: A Social Structural Version*. Menlo Park, CA: The Benjamin Cummings Publishing Company.

Suicide Prevention Resource Center (SPRC). 2013. *Reporting on Suicide: Recommendations for the Media*. Washington, DC: Suicide Prevention Resource Center. Retrieved April 24, 2013 (http://www.sprc.org/sites/sprc.org/files/library/sreporting.pdf).

Thompson, Martie P. and Laney S. Light. 2011. "Examining Gender Differences in Risk Factors for Suicide Attempts Made 1 and 7 Years Later in a Nationally Representative Sample." *Journal of Adolescent Health* 48:391–97.

Thorlindsson, Thorolfur and Thoroddur Bjarnason. 1998. "Modeling Durkheim on the Micro Level: A Study of Youth Suicidality." *American Sociological Review* 63:94–110.

Turner, Jonathan H. 2010. *Theoretical Principles of Sociology*. Vol. 2, *Microdynamics*. New York: Springer.

Wray, Mary, Cynthia Colen, and Bernice Pescosolido. 2011. "The Sociology of Suicide." *Annual Review of Sociology* 37:505–528.

Seth Abrutyn is Assistant Professor of Sociology at the University of Memphis. As a general sociological theorist, he has long been interested in macrosociology and institutions, which has culminated in a recently published book, *Revisiting Institutionalism in Sociology*. Recently, his research interests have moved toward the sociology of suicide, including examining the processes by which suicides can spread as well as how these processes relate to and expand Durkheim's classic thesis.

Anna S. Mueller is Assistant Professor of Sociology at the University of Memphis. Her research examines how peers shape adolescent health and well-being over the transition to adulthood, with a focus on weight-control behaviors, body weight, and suicide. Her research emphasizes why and how behaviors and values spread between individuals generally using insights from social psychology. She recently published a study, with Kenneth A. Frank and Chandra Muller (*American Journal of Sociology* 2013), that investigates how schools shape adolescent friendship formation in ways that have implications for adolescent status hierarchies.

Downloaded from asr.sagepub.com at UNIV MASSACHUSETTS BOSTON on April 12, 2014

Appendix C

Table of Random Numbers

Line/Col.	(1)	(2)	(3)	(4)	(5)	(6)	(7)	(8)	(9)	(10)	(11)	(12)	(13)	(14)
1	10480	15011	01536	02011	81647	91646	69179	14194	62590	36207	20969	99570	91291	90700
2	22368	46573	25595	85393	30995	89198	27982	53402	93965	34095	52666	19174	39615	99505
3	24130	48360	22527	97265	76393	64809	15179	24830	49340	32081	30680	19655	63348	58629
4	42167	93093	06243	61680	07856	16376	39440	53537	71341	57004	00849	74917	97758	16379
5	37570	39975	81837	16656	06121	91782	60468	81305	49684	60672	14110	06927	01263	54613
6	77921	06907	11008	42751	27756	53498	18602	70659	90655	15053	21916	81825	44394	42880
7	99562	72905	56420	69994	98872	31016	71194	18738	44013	48840	63213	21069	10634	12952
8	96301	91977	05463	07972	18876	20922	94595	56869	69014	60045	18425	84903	42508	32307
9	89579	14342	63661	10281	17453	18103	57740	84378	25331	12566	58678	44947	05585	56941
10	85475	36857	43342	53988	53060	59533	38867	62300	08158	17983	16439	11458	18593	64952
11	28918	69578	88231	33276	70997	79936	56865	05859	90106	31595	01547	85590	91610	78188
12	63553	40961	48235	03427	49626	69445	18663	72695	52180	20847	12234	90511	33703	90322
13	09429	93969	52636	92737	88974	33488	36320	17617	30015	08272	84115	27156	30613	74952
14	10365	61129	87529	85689	48237	52267	67689	93394	01511	26358	85104	20285	29975	89868
15	07119	97336	71048	08178	77233	13916	47564	81056	97735	85977	29372	74461	28551	90707
16	51085	12765	51821	51259	77452	16308	60756	92144	49442	53900	70960	63990	75601	40719
17	02368	21382	52404	60268	89368	19885	55322	44819	01188	65255	64835	44919	05944	55157
18	01011	54092	33362	94904	31273	04146	18594	29852	71585	85030	51132	01915	92747	64951
19	52162	53916	46369	58586	23216	14513	83149	98736	23495	64350	94738	17752	35156	35749
20	07056	97628	33787	09998	42698	06691	76988	13602	51851	46104	88916	19509	25625	58104
21	48663	91245	85828	14346	09172	30168	90229	04734	59193	22178	30421	61666	99904	32812
22	54164	58492	22421	74103	47070	25306	76468	26384	58151	06646	21524	15227	96909	44592
23	32639	32363	05597	24200	13363	38005	94342	28728	35806	06912	17012	64161	18296	22851
24	29334	27001	87637	87308	58731	00256	45834	15398	46557	41135	10367	07684	36188	18510
25	02488	33062	28834	07351	19731	92420	60952	61280	50001	67658	32586	86679	50720	94953

Line/Col.	(1)	(2)	(3)	(4)	(5)	(6)	(7)	(8)	(9)	(10)	(11)	(12)	(13)	(14)
26	81525	72295	04839	96423	24878	82651	66566	14778	76797	14780	13300	87074	79666	95725
27	29676	20591	68086	26432	46901	20849	89768	81536	86645	12659	92259	57102	80428	25280
28	00742	57392	39064	66432	84673	40027	32832	61362	98947	96067	64760	64584	96096	98253
29	05366	04213	25669	26422	44407	44048	37937	63904	45766	66134	75470	66520	34693	90449
30	91921	26418	64117	94305	26766	25940	39972	22209	71500	64568	91402	42416	07844	69618
31	00582	04711	87917	77341	42206	35126	74087	99547	81817	42607	43808	76655	62028	76630
32	00725	69884	62797	56170	86324	88072	76222	36086	84637	93161	76038	65855	77919	88006
33	69011	65797	95876	55293	18988	27354	26575	08625	40801	59920	29841	80150	12777	48501
34	25976	57948	29888	88604	67917	48708	18912	82271	65424	69774	33611	54262	85963	03547
35	09763	83473	73577	12908	30883	18317	28290	35797	05998	41688	34952	37888	38917	88050
36	91567	42595	27958	30134	04024	86385	29880	99730	55536	84855	29080	09250	79656	73211
37	17955	56349	90999	49127	20044	59931	06115	20542	18059	02008	73708	83317	36103	42791
38	46503	18584	18845	49618	02304	51038	20655	58727	28168	15475	56942	53389	20562	87338
39	92157	89634	94824	78171	84610	82834	09922	25417	44137	48413	25555	21246	35509	20468
40	14577	62765	35605	81263	39667	47358	56873	56307	61607	49518	89656	20103	77490	18062
41	98427	07523	33362	64270	01638	92477	66969	98420	04880	45585	46565	04102	46880	45709
42	34914	63976	88720	82765	34476	17032	87589	40836	32427	70002	70663	88863	77775	69348
43	70060	28277	39475	46473	23219	53416	94970	25832	69975	94884	19661	72828	00102	66794
44	53976	54914	06990	67245	68350	82948	11398	42878	80287	88267	47363	46634	06541	97809
45	76072	29515	40980	07391	58745	25774	22987	80059	39911	96189	41151	14222	60697	59583
46	90725	52210	83974	29992	65831	38857	50490	83765	55657	14361	31720	57375	56228	41546
47	64364	67412	33339	31926	14883	24413	59744	92351	97473	89286	35931	04110	23726	51900
48	08962	00358	31662	25388	61642	34072	81249	35648	56891	69352	48373	45578	78547	81788
49	95012	68379	93526	70765	10593	04542	76463	54328	02349	17247	28865	14777	62730	92277
50	15664	10493	20492	38391	91132	21999	59516	81652	27195	48223	46751	22923	32261	85653

(Continued)

(Continued)

Line/Col.	(1)	(2)	(3)	(4)	(5)	(6)	(7)	(8)	(9)	(10)	(11)	(12)	(13)	(14)
51	16408	81899	04153	53381	79401	21438	83035	92350	36693	31238	59649	91754	72772	02338
52	18629	81953	05520	91962	04739	13092	97662	24822	94730	06496	35090	04822	86772	98289
53	73115	35101	47498	87637	99016	71060	88824	71013	18735	20286	23153	72924	35165	43040
54	57491	16703	23167	49323	45021	33132	12544	41035	80780	45393	44812	12515	98931	91202
55	30405	83946	23792	14422	15059	45799	22716	19792	09983	74353	68668	30429	70735	25499
56	16631	35006	85900	98275	32388	52390	16815	69298	82732	38480	73817	32523	41961	44437
57	96773	20206	42559	78985	05300	22164	24369	54224	35083	19687	11052	91491	60383	19746
58	38935	64202	14349	82674	66523	44133	00697	35552	35970	19124	63318	29686	03387	59846
59	31624	76384	17403	53363	44167	64486	64758	75366	76554	31601	12614	33072	60332	92325
60	78919	19474	23632	27889	47914	02584	37680	20801	72152	39339	34806	08930	85001	87820
61	03931	33309	57047	74211	63445	17361	62825	39908	05607	91284	68833	25570	38818	46920
62	74426	33278	43972	10119	89917	15665	52872	73823	73144	88662	88970	74492	51805	99378
63	09066	00903	20795	95452	92648	45454	09552	88815	16553	51125	79375	97596	16296	66092
64	42238	12426	87025	14267	20979	04508	64535	31355	86064	29472	47689	05974	52468	16834
65	16153	08002	26504	41744	81959	65642	74240	56302	00033	67107	77510	70625	28725	34191
66	21457	40742	29820	96783	29400	21840	15035	34537	33310	06116	95240	15957	16572	06004
67	21581	57802	02050	89728	17937	37621	47075	42080	97403	48626	68995	43805	33386	21597
68	55612	78095	83197	33732	05810	24813	86902	60397	16489	03264	88525	42786	05269	92532
69	44657	66999	99324	51281	84463	60563	79312	93454	68876	25471	93911	25650	12682	73572
70	91340	84979	46949	81973	37949	61023	43997	15263	80644	43942	89203	71795	99533	50501
71	91227	21199	31935	27022	84067	05462	35216	14486	29891	68607	41867	14951	91696	85065
72	50001	38140	66321	19924	72163	09538	12151	06878	91903	18749	34405	56087	82790	70925
73	65390	05224	72958	28609	81406	39147	25549	48542	42627	45233	57202	94617	23772	07896
74	27504	96131	83944	41575	10573	08619	64482	73923	36152	05184	94142	25299	84387	34925
75	37169	94851	39117	89632	00959	16487	65536	49071	39782	17095	02330	74301	00275	48280

Line/Col.	(1)	(2)	(3)	(4)	(5)	(6)	(7)	(8)	(9)	(10)	(11)	(12)	(13)	(14)
76	11508	70225	51111	38351	19444	66499	71945	05422	13442	78675	84081	66938	93654	59894
77	37449	30362	06694	54690	04052	53115	62757	95348	78662	11163	81651	50245	34971	52924
78	46515	70331	85922	38329	57015	15765	97161	17869	45349	61796	66345	81073	49106	79860
79	30986	81223	42416	58353	21532	30502	32305	86482	05174	07901	54339	58861	74818	46942
80	63798	64995	46583	09765	44160	78128	83991	42865	92520	83531	80377	35909	81250	54238
81	82486	84846	99254	67632	43218	50076	21361	64816	51202	88124	41870	52689	51275	83556
82	21885	32906	92431	09060	64297	51674	64126	62570	26123	05155	59194	52799	28225	85762
83	60336	98782	07408	53458	13564	59089	26445	29789	85205	41001	12535	12133	14645	23541
84	43937	46891	24010	25560	86355	33941	25786	54990	71899	15475	95434	98227	21824	19585
85	97656	63175	89303	16275	07100	92063	21942	18611	47348	20203	18534	03862	78095	50136
86	03299	01221	05418	38982	55758	92237	26759	86367	21216	98442	08303	56613	91511	75928
87	79626	06486	03574	17668	07785	76020	79924	25651	83325	88428	85076	72811	22717	50585
88	85636	68335	47539	03129	65651	11977	02510	26113	99447	68645	34327	15152	55230	93448
89	18039	14367	61337	06177	12143	46609	32989	74014	64708	00533	35398	58408	13261	47908
90	08362	15656	60627	36478	65648	16764	53412	09013	07832	41574	17639	82163	60859	75567
91	79556	29068	04142	16268	15387	12856	66227	38358	22478	73373	88732	09443	82558	05250
92	92608	82674	27072	32534	17075	27698	98204	63863	11951	34648	88022	56148	34925	57031
93	23982	25835	40055	67006	12293	02753	14827	22235	35071	99704	37543	11601	35503	85171
94	09915	96306	05908	97901	28395	14186	00821	80703	70426	75647	76310	88717	37890	40129
95	50937	33300	26695	62247	69927	76123	50842	43834	86654	70959	79725	93872	28117	19233
96	42488	78077	69882	61657	34136	79180	97526	43092	04098	73571	80799	76536	71255	64239
97	46764	86273	63003	93017	31204	36692	40202	35275	57306	55543	53203	18098	47625	88684
98	03237	45430	55417	63282	90816	17349	88298	90183	36600	78406	06216	95787	42579	90730
99	86591	81482	52667	61583	14972	90053	89534	76036	49199	43716	97548	04379	46370	28672
100	38534	01715	94964	87288	65680	43772	39560	12918	86537	62738	19636	51132	25739	56947

Glossary

Adaptive research design A research design that develops as the research progresses.

Alternate-forms reliability A procedure for testing the reliability of responses to survey questions in which subjects' answers are compared after the subjects have been asked slightly different versions of the questions or when randomly selected halves of the sample have been administered slightly different versions of the questions.

Anomalous findings Unexpected findings in data.

Anonymity Provided by research in which no identifying information is recorded that could be used to link respondents to their responses.

Applied research Research conducted using the scientific method that addresses immediate, practical concerns, such as determining whether one program or policy has a more desirable impact than another.

Assignment variable The variable used to specify a cutoff score for eligibility in some treatment in a regression–discontinuity design.

Association A criterion for establishing a nomothetic causal relationship between two variables: Variation in one variable is related to variation in another variable.

Authenticity When the understanding of a social process or social setting is one that reflects fairly the various perspectives of participants in that setting.

Availability sampling Sampling in which elements are selected on the basis of convenience.

Back matter The section of an applied research report that may include appendixes, tables, and the research instrument(s).

Balanced response choices An equal number of responses to a fixed-choice survey question express positive and negative choices in comparable language.

Bar chart A graphic for qualitative variables in which the variable's distribution is displayed with solid bars separated by spaces.

Base number *(N)* The total number of cases in a distribution.

Basic science Research conducted using the scientific method that has the goals of figuring out what the world is like and why it works as it does

Before-and-after design A quasi-experimental design consisting of several before-after comparisons involving the same variables but no comparison group.

Behavior coding Observation in which the researcher categorizes, according to strict rules, the number of times certain behaviors occur.

Belmont Report Guidelines developed by the U.S. National Commission for the Protection of Human Subjects of Biomedical and Behavioral Research in 1979 for the protection of human subjects.

Beneficence The ethical requirement of minimizing possible harms and maximizing benefits in research involving human subjects that was included in the *Belmont Report*.

Big Data Massive datasets produced or accessible in computer-readable form that are produced by people, available to social scientists, and manageable with today's computers.

Bimodal A distribution that has two nonadjacent categories with about the same number of cases, and these categories have more cases than any others.

Bipolar response options Response choices to a survey question that include a middle category and parallel responses with positive and negative valence.

Black box evaluation This type of evaluation occurs when an evaluation of program outcomes ignores, and does not identify, the process by which the program produced the effect.

Case-oriented research Research that focuses attention on the nation or other unit as a whole.

Case-oriented understanding An understanding of social processes in a group, formal organization, community, or other collectivity that reflects accurately the standpoint of participants.

Case study A setting or group that the analyst treats as an integrated social unit that must be studied holistically and in its particularity.

Causal effect (idiographic perspective) When a series of concrete events, thoughts, or actions results in a particular event or individual outcome.

Causal effect (nomothetic perspective) When variation in one phenomenon, an independent variable, leads to or results, on average, in variation in another phenomenon, the dependent variable.

Causal validity (internal validity) Exists when a conclusion that A leads to or results in B is correct.

Census Research in which information is obtained through responses from or information about all available members of an entire population.

Central tendency The most common value (for variables measured at the nominal level) or the value around which cases tend to center (for a quantitative variable).

Certificate of Confidentiality A certificate issued to a researcher by the National Institutes of Health that ensures the right to protect information obtained about high-risk populations or behaviors—except child abuse or neglect—from legal subpoenas.

Ceteris paribus Latin phrase meaning "other things being equal."

Chi-square An inferential statistic used to test hypotheses about relationships between two or more variables in a cross-tabulation.

Closed-ended (fixed-choice) question   A survey question that provides preformatted response choices for the respondent to circle or check.

Cluster   A naturally occurring, mixed aggregate of elements of the population.

Cluster sampling   Sampling in which elements are selected in two or more stages, with the first stage being the random selection of naturally occurring clusters and the last stage being the random selection of elements within clusters.

Code of Ethics   Professional code of the American Sociological Association for the treatment of human subjects by members, employees, and students, designed to comply with federal policy and revised in 1997.

Coding   The process of assigning a unique numerical code to each response to survey questions.

Cognitive interview   A technique for evaluating questions in which researchers ask people test questions and then probe with follow-up questions to learn how they understood the question and what their answers mean.

Cohort   Individuals or groups with a common starting point. Examples include college class of 1997, people who graduated from high school in the 1980s, General Motors employees who started work between the years 1990 and 2000, and people who were born in the late 1940s or the 1950s (the baby boom generation).

Cohort study   See **event-based design.**

Combined frequency display   A table that presents together the distributions for a set of conceptually similar variables having the same response categories; common headings are used for the responses.

Comparative historical research   Research comparing data from more than one time period in more than one nation.

Comparison group   In an experiment, a group that has been exposed to a different treatment (or value of the independent variable) than the experimental group.

Compensatory rivalry (John Henry effect)   A type of contamination in experimental and quasi-experimental designs that occurs when control group members are aware that they are being denied some advantage and increase their efforts by way of compensation.

Complete (or covert) participant   A role in field research in which the researcher does not reveal his or her identity as a researcher to those who are observed while participating.

Complete (or overt) observer   A role in participant observation in which the researcher does not participate in group activities and is publicly defined as a researcher.

Complex mixed-methods research design   Qualitative and quantitative methods are combined in a research project that uses more than one of the four basic types of mixed-methods designs or that repeats at least one of those basic types.

Compressed frequency display   A table that presents cross-classification data efficiently by eliminating unnecessary percentages, such as the percentage corresponding to the second value of a dichotomous variable.

Computer-assisted personal interview (CAPI)   A personal interview in which the laptop computer is used to display interview questions and to process responses that the interviewer types in, as well as to check that these responses fall within allowed ranges.

Computer-assisted qualitative data analysis   Uses special computer software to assist qualitative analyses through creating, applying, and refining categories; tracing linkages between concepts; and making comparisons between cases and events.

Computer-assisted telephone interview (CATI)   A telephone interview in which a questionnaire is programmed into a computer, along with relevant skip patterns, and only valid entries are allowed; incorporates the tasks of interviewing, data entry, and some data cleaning.

Concept   A mental image that summarizes a set of similar observations, feelings, or ideas.

Conceptualization   The process of specifying what we mean by a term. In deductive research, conceptualization helps to translate portions of an abstract theory into specific variables that can be used in testable hypotheses. In inductive research, conceptualization is an important part of the process used to make sense of related observations.

Concurrent validity   The type of validity that exists when scores on a measure are closely related to scores on a criterion measured at the same time.

Confidentiality   Provided by research in which identifying information that could be used to link respondents to their responses is available only to designated research personnel for specific research needs.

Conflict of interest   When a researcher has a significant stake in the design or outcome of his or her own research.

Conflict theory   Identifies conflict between social groups as the primary force in society; understanding the bases and consequences of the conflict is key to understanding social processes.

Conjunctural research   Research that considers the complex combinations in which causal influences operate.

Constant   A number that has a fixed value in a given situation; a characteristic or value that does not change.

Construct validity   The type of validity that is established by showing that a measure is related to other measures as specified in a theory.

Constructivism   Methodology based on questioning belief in an external reality; emphasizes the importance of exploring the way in which different stakeholders in a social setting construct their beliefs.

Contamination   A source of causal invalidity that occurs when either the experimental or the comparison group is aware of the other group and is influenced in the posttest as a result.

Content analysis   A research method for systematically analyzing and making inferences from recorded human communication, including books, articles, poems, constitutions, speeches, and songs.

Content validity   The type of validity that exists when the full range of a concept's meaning is covered by the measure.

Context   A set of interrelated circumstances that alters a relationship between other variables or social processes.

Context effects   Occur in a survey when one or more questions influence how subsequent questions are interpreted.

Contextual effects   Variation in relationships of dependent with independent variables between geographic units or other social settings.

Contingency table   In the simplest case, a bivariate (two-variable) distribution, showing the distribution of one variable for each category of another variable; can be elaborated using three or more variables. Also called *cross-tabulation.*

Contingent question   A question that is asked of only a subset of survey respondents.

Continuous measure   A measure with numbers indicating the values of variables as points on a continuum.

Control group   A comparison group that receives no treatment.

Convergent validity   The type of validity achieved when one measure of a concept is associated with different types of measures of the same concept.

Correlational analysis A statistical technique that summarizes the strength of a relationship between two quantitative variables in terms of its adherence to a linear pattern.

Correlation coefficient A summary statistic that varies from 0 to 1 or −1, with 0 indicating the absence of a linear relationship between two quantitative variables and 1 or −1 indicating that the relationship is completely described by the line representing the regression of the dependent variable on the independent variable.

Cost–benefit analysis A type of evaluation research that compares program costs with the economic value of program benefits.

Cost–effectiveness analysis A type of evaluation research that compares program costs with actual program outcomes.

Counterfactual The situation that would have occurred if the subjects who were exposed to the treatment actually were not exposed, but otherwise had had identical experiences to those they underwent during the experiment.

Cover letter The letter sent with a mailed questionnaire that explains the survey's purpose and auspices and encourages the respondent to participate.

Covert observer A role in participant observation in which the researcher does not participate in group activities and is not publicly defined as a researcher.

Covert participant A role in field research in which the researcher does not reveal his or her identity as a researcher to those who are observed while participating.

Criterion validity The type of validity that is established by comparing the scores obtained on the measure being validated with those obtained with a more direct or already validated measure of the same phenomenon (the criterion).

Cronbach's alpha A statistic commonly used to measure interitem reliability.

Cross-population generalizability (external validity) Exists when findings about one group, population, or setting hold true for other groups, populations, or settings.

Cross-sectional comparative research Research comparing data from one time period between two or more nations.

Cross-sectional research design A study in which data are collected at only one point in time.

Cross-tabulation (crosstab) In the simplest case, a bivariate (two-variable) distribution, showing the distribution of one variable for each category of another variable; can be elaborated using three or more variables. Also called *contingency table.*

Curvilinear Any pattern of association between two quantitative variables that does not involve a regular increase or decrease.

Data cleaning The process of checking data for errors after the data have been entered in a computer file.

Data entry The process of typing (word processing) or otherwise transferring data on survey or other instruments into a computer file.

Debriefing A researcher's informing subjects after an experiment about the experiment's purposes and methods and evaluating subjects' personal reactions to the experiment.

Deception Used in social experiments to create more "realistic" treatments in which the true purpose of the research is not disclosed to participants, often within the confines of a laboratory.

Deductive research The type of research in which a specific expectation is deduced from a general premise and is then tested.

Demography The statistical and mathematical study of the size, composition, and spatial distribution of human populations and how these features change over time.

Demoralization A type of contamination in experimental and quasi-experimental designs that occurs when control group members feel they have been left out of some valuable treatment and perform worse as a result.

Dependent variable A variable that is hypothesized to vary depending on, or under the influence of, another variable.

Descriptive research Research in which social phenomena are defined and described.

Descriptive statistics Statistics used to describe the distribution of and relationship between variables.

Dichotomy Variable having only two values.

Differential attrition (mortality) A problem that occurs in experiments when comparison groups become different because subjects are more likely to drop out of one of the groups for various reasons.

Direction of association A pattern in a relationship between two variables—the values of variables tend to change consistently in relation to change on the other variable; the direction of association can be either positive or negative.

Discrete measure A measure that classifies cases in distinct categories.

Discriminant validity An approach to construct validation; the scores on the measure to be validated are compared with scores on another measure of the same variable and to scores on variables that measure different but related concepts. Discriminant validity is achieved if the measure to be validated is related most strongly to its comparison measure and less so to the measures of other concepts.

Disproportionate stratified sampling Sampling in which elements are selected from strata in different proportions from those that appear in the population.

Double-barreled question A single survey question that actually asks two questions but allows only one answer.

Double-blind procedure An experimental method in which neither the subjects nor the staff delivering experimental treatments know which subjects are getting the treatment and which are receiving a placebo.

Double negative A question or statement that contains two negatives, which can muddy the meaning of the question.

Ecological fallacy An error in reasoning in which incorrect conclusions about individual-level processes are drawn from group-level data.

Effect size A standardized measure of association—often the difference between the mean of the experimental group and the mean of the control group on the dependent variable, adjusted for the average variability in the two groups.

Efficiency analysis A type of evaluation research that compares program costs with program effects. It can be either a cost–benefit analysis or a cost–effectiveness analysis.

Elaboration analysis The process of introducing a third variable into an analysis to better understand—to elaborate—the bivariate (two-variable) relationship under consideration. Additional control variables also can be introduced.

Electronic survey A survey that is sent and answered by computer, either through e-mail or on the web.

Elements The individual members of the population whose characteristics are to be measured.

Embedded mixed-methods design Qualitative and quantitative methods are used concurrently in the research but one is given priority.

Emergence The appearance of phenomena at a group level that cannot be explained by the properties of individuals within the group; emergence implies phenomena that are more than "the sum of their parts."

Emic focus Representing a setting with the participants' terms and from their viewpoint.

Empirical generalization A statement that describes patterns found in data.

Enumeration units Units that contain one or more elements and that are listed in a sampling frame.

Ethnography The study of a culture or cultures that some group of people shares, using participant observation over an extended period.

Ethnomethodology A qualitative research method focused on the way that participants in a social setting create and sustain a sense of reality.

Etic focus Representing a setting with the researchers' terms and from their viewpoint.

Evaluability assessment A type of evaluation research conducted to determine whether it is feasible to evaluate a program's effects within the available time and resources.

Evaluation research Research that describes or identifies the effects of social policies and programs.

Event-based design (cohort study) A type of longitudinal study in which data are collected at two or more points in time from individuals in a cohort.

Event-structure analysis A systematic method of developing a causal diagram showing the structure of action underlying some chronology of events; the result is an idiographic causal explanation.

Exhaustive Every case can be classified as having at least one attribute (or value) for the variable.

Expectancies of experimental staff A source of treatment misidentification in experiments and quasi-experiments that occurs when change among experimental subjects results from the positive expectancies of the staff who are delivering the treatment rather than from the treatment itself; also called a *self-fulfilling prophecy*.

Experience sampling method (ESM) A technique for drawing a representative sample of everyday activities, thoughts, and experiences. Participants carry a pager and are beeped at random times over several days or weeks; on hearing the beep, participants complete a report designed by the researcher.

Experimental group In an experiment, the group of subjects that receives the treatment or experimental manipulation.

Explanatory research Seeks to identify causes and effects of social phenomena and to predict how one phenomenon will change or vary in response to variation in some other phenomenon.

Exploratory research Seeks to find out how people get along in the setting under question, what meanings they give to their actions, and what issues concern them.

Ex post facto control group design A nonexperimental design in which comparison groups are selected after the treatment, program, or other variation in the independent variable has occurred, but when the participants were able to choose the group in which they participated. Often confused with a quasi-experimental design.

External events A source of causal invalidity that occurs when events external to the study influence posttest scores; also called a *history effect*.

External validity (cross-population generalizability) Exists when findings about one group, population, or setting hold true for other groups, populations, or settings.

Extraneous variable A variable that influences both the independent and dependent variables, creating a spurious association between them that disappears when the extraneous variable is controlled.

Face validity The type of validity that exists when an inspection of items used to measure a concept suggests that they are appropriate "on their face."

Factorial survey A survey in which randomly selected subsets of respondents are asked different questions, or are asked to respond to different vignettes, to determine the causal effect of the variables represented by these differences.

Federal Policy for the Protection of Human Subjects Specific regulations adopted in 1991 by the Department of Health and Human Services and the Food and Drug Administration that were based on the principles of the *Belmont Report*.

Feedback Information about service delivery system outputs, outcomes, or operations that can guide program input.

Feminist research Research with a focus on women's lives that often includes an orientation to personal experience, subjective orientations, the researcher's standpoint, and emotions.

Fence-sitters Survey respondents who see themselves as being neutral on an issue and choose a middle (neutral) response that is offered.

Field experiment A study using an experimental design that is conducted in a real-world setting.

Field notes Notes that describe what has been observed, heard, or otherwise experienced in a participant observation study. These notes usually are written after the observational session.

Field research Research in which natural social processes are studied as they happen and left relatively undisturbed.

Field researcher A researcher who uses qualitative methods to conduct research in the field.

Filter question A survey question used to identify a subset of respondents who then are asked other questions.

Fixed-choice question See **closed-ended question.**

Fixed-sample panel design (panel study) A type of longitudinal study in which data are collected from the same individuals—the panel—at two or more points in time. In another type of panel design, panel members who leave are replaced with new members.

Floaters Survey respondents who provide an opinion on a topic in response to a closed-ended question that does not include a "Don't know" option, but who will choose "Don't know" if it is available.

Focus groups A qualitative method that involves unstructured group interviews in which the focus group leader actively encourages discussion among participants on the topics of interest.

Forced-choice questions Closed-ended survey questions that do not include "Don't know" as an explicit response choice.

Formative evaluation Process evaluation that is used to shape and refine program operations.

Frequency distribution Numerical display showing the number of cases, and usually the percentage of cases (the relative frequencies), corresponding to each value or group of values of a variable.

Frequency polygon A graphic for quantitative variables in which a continuous line connects data points representing the variable's distribution.

Front matter The section of an applied research report that includes an executive summary, abstract, and table of contents.

Functional theory   A social theory that explains social patterns in terms of their consequences for society as a whole and emphasizes the interdependence of social institutions and their common interest in maintaining the social order.

Gamma   A measure of association that is sometimes used in cross-tabular analysis.

Gatekeeper   A person in a field setting who can grant researchers access to the setting.

Generalizability   Exists when a conclusion holds true for the population, group, setting, or event that we say it does, given the conditions that we specify.

Grand tour question   A broad question at the start of an interview that seeks to engage the respondent in the topic of interest.

Grounded theory   Systematic theory developed inductively, based on observations that are summarized into conceptual categories, reevaluated in the research setting, and gradually refined and linked to other conceptual categories.

Group-administered survey   A survey that is completed by individual respondents who are assembled in a group.

Hawthorne effect   A type of contamination in research designs that occurs when members of the treatment group change relative to the dependent variable because their participation in the study makes them feel special.

Health Insurance Portability and Accountability Act (HIPAA)   A congressional act passed in 1996 that creates stringent regulations for the protection of health care data.

Hermeneutic circle   Represents the dialectical process in which the researcher obtains information from multiple stakeholders in a setting, refines his or her understanding of the setting, and then tests that understanding with successive respondents.

Histogram   A graphic for quantitative variables in which the variable's distribution is displayed with adjacent bars.

Historical events research   Research in which social events are studied at one past time period.

Historical process research   Research in which historical processes are studied over a long time.

History effect   A source of causal invalidity that occurs when events external to the study influence posttest scores; also called an effect of *external events.*

Holistic research   Research concerned with the context in which events occurred and the interrelations between different events and processes.

Hypothesis   A tentative statement about empirical reality, involving a relationship between two or more variables.

ICPSR (Inter-university Consortium for Political and Social Research)   Academic consortium that archives data sets online from major surveys and other social science research and makes them available for analysis by others.

Idiographic causal explanation   An explanation that identifies the concrete, individual sequence of events, thoughts, or actions that resulted in a particular outcome for a particular individual or that led to a particular event; may be termed an *individualist* or *historicist* explanation.

Idiosyncratic, or random, errors   Errors that affect individuals or other cases in unique ways that are unlikely to be repeated in just the same way.

Idiosyncratic variation   Variation in responses to questions that is caused by individuals' reactions to particular words or ideas in the question instead of by variation in the concept that the question is intended to measure.

Illogical reasoning   When we prematurely jump to conclusions or argue on the basis of invalid assumptions.

Impact evaluation (or analysis)   Analysis of the extent to which a treatment or other service has an effect; also known as *summative evaluation.*

Inaccurate observation   An observation based on faulty perceptions of empirical reality.

Independent variable   A variable that is hypothesized to cause, or lead to, variation in another variable.

Index   The sum or average of responses to a set of questions about a concept.

Indicator   The question or other operation used to indicate the value of cases on a variable.

Inductive research   The type of research in which general conclusions are drawn from specific data.

Inferential statistics   A mathematical tool for estimating how likely it is that a statistical result based on data from a random sample is representative of the population from which the sample is assumed to have been selected.

In-person interview   A survey in which an interviewer questions respondents face-to-face and records their answers.

Inputs   The resources, raw materials, clients, and staff that go into a program.

Institutional review board (IRB)   A group of organizational and community representatives required by federal law to review the ethical issues in all proposed research that is federally funded, involves human subjects, or has any potential for harm to human subjects.

Integrated mixed-methods design   Qualitative and quantitative methods are used concurrently and both are given equal importance.

Integrative approach   An orientation to evaluation research that expects researchers to respond to the concerns of people involved with the program—stakeholders—as well as to the standards and goals of the social scientific community.

Intensive (in-depth) interviewing   A qualitative method that involves open-ended, relatively unstructured questioning in which the interviewer seeks in-depth information on the interviewee's feelings, experiences, and perceptions.

Intent-to-treat analysis   When analysis of the effect of a treatment on outcomes in an experimental design compares outcomes for all those who were assigned to the treatment group with outcomes for all those who were assigned to the control group, whether or not participants remained in the treatment group.

Interactive voice response (IVR)   A survey in which respondents receive automated calls and answer questions by pressing numbers on their touch-tone phones or speaking numbers that are interpreted by computerized voice recognition software.

Intercoder reliability   When the same codes are entered by different coders who are recording the same data.

Interitem reliability   An approach that calculates reliability based on the correlation among multiple items used to measure a single concept; also known as internal consistency.

Internal validity (causal validity)   Exists when a conclusion that A leads to or results in B is correct.

Interobserver reliability   When similar measurements are obtained by different observers rating the same persons, events, or places.

Interpretive questions   Questions included in a questionnaire or interview schedule to help explain answers to other important questions.

Interpretivism   The belief that the subjective meanings people give to their experiences is a key focus for social science research without believing that reality itself is socially constructed.

Interquartile range The range in a distribution between the end of the first quartile and the beginning of the third quartile.

Intersubjective agreement Agreement between scientists about the nature of reality; often upheld as a more reasonable goal for science than certainty about an objective reality.

Interval level of measurement A measurement of a variable in which the numbers indicating a variable's values represent fixed measurement units but have no absolute, or fixed, zero point.

Interval–ratio level of measurement A measurement of a variable in which the numbers indicating a variable's values represent fixed measurement units but may not have an absolute, or fixed, zero point.

Intervening variable See **mediator.**

Interview schedule The survey instrument containing the questions asked by the interviewer in an in-person or phone survey.

Intrarater (or intraobserver) reliability Consistency of ratings by an observer of an unchanging phenomenon at two or more points in time.

John Dewey (1859–1952) Major figure in development of philosophy of pragmatism and proponent of progressive education.

Jottings Brief notes written in the field about highlights of an observation period.

Justice The ethical principle of distributing benefits and risks of research in research involving human subjects fairly that was included in the *Belmont Report.*

Key informant An insider who is willing and able to provide a field researcher with superior access and information, including answers to questions that arise in the course of the research.

Labeled unipolar response options Response choices for a survey question that use words to identify categories ranging from low to high (or vv).

Level of measurement The mathematical precision with which the values of a variable can be expressed. The nominal level of measurement, which is qualitative, has no mathematical interpretation; the quantitative levels of measurement—ordinal, interval, and ratio—are progressively more precise mathematically.

Likert item A statement followed by response choices ranging from "strongly agree" to "strongly disagree."

Longitudinal research design A study in which data are collected that can be ordered in time; also defined as research in which data are collected at two or more points in time.

Mailed survey A survey involving a mailed questionnaire to be completed by the respondent.

Marginal distribution The summary distributions in the margins of a cross-tabulation that correspond to the frequency distribution of the row variable and of the column variable.

Matching A procedure for equating the characteristics of individuals in different comparison groups in an experiment. Matching can be done on either an individual or an aggregate basis. For individual matching, individuals who are similar in key characteristics are paired before assignment, and then the two members of each pair are assigned to the two groups. For aggregate matching, also termed *blocking*, groups are chosen for comparison that are similar in the distribution of key characteristics.

Matrix A form on which can be recorded systematically particular features of multiple cases or instances that a qualitative data analyst needs to examine.

Matrix questions A series of questions that concern a common theme and that have the same response choices.

Mean The arithmetic, or weighted, average, computed by adding the value of all the cases and dividing by the total number of cases.

Measurement The process of linking abstract concepts to empirical indicants.

Measurement validity Exists when a measure measures what we think it measures.

Measure of association A type of descriptive statistic that summarizes the strength of an association.

Mechanism A discernible process that creates a causal connection between two variables.

Median The position average, or the point that divides a distribution in half (the 50th percentile).

Mediator A variable involved in a causal mechanism (intervening variable).

Meta-analysis The quantitative analysis of findings from multiple studies.

Method of agreement A method proposed by John Stuart Mill for establishing a causal relation, in which the values of cases that agree on an outcome variable also agree on the value of the variable hypothesized to have a causal effect, although they differ on other variables.

Method of difference A method proposed by John Stuart Mill for establishing a causal relation, in which the values of cases that differ on an outcome variable also differ on the value of the variable hypothesized to have a causal effect, although they agree on other variables.

Milgram's obedience experiments Experiments begun in 1960 at Yale University by psychologist Stanley Milgram to determine the likelihood of people following orders from an authority despite their own sentiments; widely cited as helping to understand the emergence of phenomena such as Nazism and mass cults.

Mixed methods Research that combines qualitative and quantitative methods in an investigation of the same or related research question(s).

Mixed-mode survey A survey that is conducted by more than one method, allowing the strengths of one survey design to compensate for the weaknesses of another and maximizing the likelihood of securing data from different types of respondents; for example, nonrespondents in a mailed survey may be interviewed in person or over the phone.

Mode The most frequent value in a distribution; also termed the **probability average**.

Moderator A variable that identifies a context for the effect of other variables.

Monotonic A pattern of association in which the value of cases on one variable increases or decreases fairly regularly across the categories of another variable.

Multiple group before-and-after design A type of quasi-experimental design in which several before-and-after comparisons are made involving the same independent and dependent variables but different groups.

Multitrait–multimethod matrix A method of evaluating the validity of measures by determining whether measuring the same phenomenon with different methods leads to convergent results and measuring different phenomena with the same method leads to divergent results.

Mutually exclusive A variable's attributes (or values) are mutually exclusive when every case can be classified as having only one attribute (or value).

Narrative analysis A form of qualitative analysis in which the analyst focuses on how respondents impose order on the flow of experience in their lives and thus make sense of events and actions in which they have participated.

Narrative explanations An idiographic causal explanation that involves developing a narrative of events and processes that indicate a chain of causes and effects.

Needs assessment A type of evaluation research that attempts to determine the needs of some population that might be met with a social program.

Netnography The use of ethnographic methods to study online communities; also termed *cyberethnography* and *virtual ethnography*.

Ngrams Frequency graphs produced by Google's database of all words printed in more than one third of the world's books over time (with coverage still expanding).

Nominal level of measurement Variables whose values have no mathematical interpretation; they vary in kind or quality, but not in amount.

Nomothetic causal explanation An explanation that identifies common influences on a number of cases or events.

Nonequivalent control group design A quasi-experimental design in which experimental and comparison groups are designated before the treatment occurs but are not created by random assignment.

Nonprobability sampling method Sampling method in which the probability of selection of population elements is unknown.

Nonrespondents People or other entities who do not participate in a study although they are selected for the sample.

Nonspuriousness A criterion for establishing a causal relation between two variables; when a relationship between two variables is not caused by variation in a third variable.

Normal distribution A symmetric, bell-shaped distribution that results from chance variation around a central value.

Normal science The gradual, incremental research conducted by scientists within the prevailing scientific paradigm.

Nuremberg War Crime Trials The International Military Tribunal held by the victorious Allies after World War II in Nuremberg, Germany, that exposed the horrific medical experiments conducted by Nazi doctors and others in the name of "science."

Office for Protection From Research Risks, National Institutes of Health The office in the U.S. Department of Health and Human Services (DHHS) that provides leadership and supervision about the protection of the rights, welfare, and well-being of subjects involved in research conducted or supported by HHS, including monitoring IRBs.

Omnibus survey A survey that covers a range of topics of interest to different social scientists.

Open-ended question A survey question to which the respondent replies in his or her own words, either by writing or by talking.

Operationalization The process of specifying the measures that will indicate the value of cases on a variable.

Oral history Data collected through intensive interviews with participants in past events.

Ordinal level of measurement A measurement of a variable in which the numbers indicating a variable's values specify only the order of the cases, permitting *greater than* and *less than* distinctions.

Outcomes The impact of the program process on the cases processed.

Outlier An exceptionally high or low value in a distribution.

Outputs The services delivered or new products produced by the program process.

Overgeneralization Occurs when we unjustifiably conclude that what is true for some cases is true for all cases.

Panel study See **fixed-sample panel design.**

Paradigm wars The intense debate from the 1970s to the 1990s between social scientists over the value of positivist and interpretivist/constructivist research philosophies; also see *scientific paradigm.*

Participant observation A qualitative method for gathering data that involves developing a sustained relationship with people while they go about their normal activities.

Participant observer A researcher who gathers data through participating and observing in a setting where he or she develops a sustained relationship with people while they go about their normal activities. The term *participant observer* is often used to refer to a continuum of possible roles, from complete observation, in which the researcher does not participate along with others in group activities, to complete participation, in which the researcher participates without publicly acknowledging being an observer.

Participatory action research (PAR) A type of research in which the researcher involves members of the population to be studied as active participants throughout the research process, from the selection of a research focus to the reporting of research results and efforts to make changes based on the research; also termed *community-based participatory research.*

Part–whole question effects These occur when responses to a general or summary question about a topic are influenced by responses to an earlier, more specific question about that topic.

Percentages Relative frequencies, computed by dividing the frequency of cases in a particular category by the total number of cases and then multiplying by 100.

Periodicity A sequence of elements (in a list to be sampled) that varies in some regular, periodic pattern.

Phone survey A survey in which interviewers question respondents over the phone and then record their answers.

Photo voice A method in which research participants take pictures of their everyday surroundings with cameras the researcher distributes, and then meet in a group with the researcher to discuss the pictures' meaning.

Placebo effect A source of treatment misidentification that can occur when subjects receive a fake "treatment" they think is beneficial and improve because of that expectation even though they did not receive the actual treatment or received a treatment that had no real effect.

Plagiarism Presenting as one's own the ideas or words of another person or persons for academic evaluation without proper acknowledgment.

Policy research A process in which research results are used to provide policy actors with recommendations for action that are based on empirical evidence and careful reasoning.

Population The entire set of individuals or other entities to which study findings are to be generalized.

Population parameter The value of a statistic, such as a mean, computed using the data for the entire population; a sample statistic is an estimate of a population parameter.

Positivism The belief, shared by most scientists, that there is a reality that exists quite apart from our own perception of it, that it can be understood through observation, and that it follows general laws.

Postpositivism A philosophical view that modifies the positivist premise of an external, objective reality by recognizing its complexity, the limitations of human observers, and therefore the impossibility of developing more than a partial understanding of reality.

Posttest In experimental research, the measurement of an outcome (dependent) variable after an experimental intervention or after a presumed independent variable has changed for some other reason.

Pragmatism A philosophy developed by John Dewey and others that emphasized the importance of taking action and learning from the outcomes to generate knowledge.

Precoding A number represents every response choice to a survey question, and respondents are instructed to indicate their response to a question by checking a number.

Predictive validity The type of validity that exists when a measure predicts scores on a criterion measured in the future.

Pretest   In experimental research, the measurement of an outcome (dependent) variable before an experimental intervention or change in a presumed independent variable for some other reason. The pretest is exactly the same "test" as the posttest, but it is administered at a different time.

Pretest–posttest control group design
See **randomized comparative change design.**

Probability average   The most frequent value in a distribution; also termed the **mode.**

Probability of selection   The likelihood that an element will be selected from the population for inclusion in the sample. In a census of all elements of a population, the probability that any particular element will be selected is 1.0. If half the elements in the population are sampled on the basis of chance (say, by tossing a coin), the probability of selection for each element is one half, or .5. As the size of the sample as a proportion of the population decreases, so does the probability of selection.

Probability sampling method   A sampling method that relies on a random, or chance, selection method so that the probability of selection of population elements is known.

Procedural justice theory   A theory that predicts that people will obey the law from a sense of obligation that flows from seeing legal authorities as moral and legitimate.

Process consent   An interpretation of the ethical standard of voluntary consent that allows participants to change their decision about participating at any point by requiring that the researcher check with participants at each stage of the project about their willingness to continue in the project.

Process evaluation   Evaluation research that investigates the process of service delivery.

Program process   The complete treatment or service delivered by the program.

Program theory   A descriptive or prescriptive model of how a program operates and produces effects.

Progressive focusing   The process by which a qualitative analyst interacts with the data and gradually refines his or her focus.

Proportionate stratified sampling   Sampling method in which elements are selected from strata in exact proportion to their representation in the population.

Pseudoscience   Claims presented so that they appear scientific even though they lack supporting evidence and plausibility.

Purposive sampling   A nonprobability sampling method in which elements are selected for a purpose, usually because of their unique position.

Qualitative comparative analysis (QCA)   A systematic type of qualitative analysis that identifies the combination of factors that had to be present across multiple cases to produce a particular outcome.

Qualitative methods   Methods such as participant observation, intensive interviewing, and focus groups that are designed to capture social life as participants experience it rather than in categories predetermined by the researcher. These methods rely on written or spoken words or observations that do not often have a direct numerical interpretation and typically involve exploratory research questions, inductive reasoning, an orientation to social context and human subjectivity, and the meanings attached by participants to events and to their lives.

Quantitative methods   Methods such as surveys and experiments that record variation in social life in terms of categories that vary in amount. Data that are treated as quantitative are either numbers or attributes that can be ordered by magnitude.

Quartiles   The points in a distribution corresponding to the first 25% of the cases, the first 50% of the cases, and the first 75% of the cases.

Quasi-experimental design   A research design in which there is a comparison group that is comparable with the experimental group in critical ways, but subjects are not randomly assigned to the comparison and experimental groups.

Questionnaire   The survey instrument containing the questions in a self-administered survey.

Quota sampling   A nonprobability sampling method in which elements are selected to ensure that the sample represents certain characteristics in proportion to their prevalence in the population.

Random assignment   A procedure by which each experimental subject is placed in a group randomly.

Random digit dialing   The random dialing by a machine of numbers within designated phone prefixes, which creates a random sample for phone surveys.

Randomization   The random assignment of cases, as by the toss of a coin.

Randomized comparative change design   The classic true experimental design in which subjects are assigned randomly to two groups; both these groups receive a pretest, then one group receives the experimental intervention, and then both groups receive a posttest. Also known as a *pretest–posttest control group design.*

Randomized comparative posttest design   A true experimental design in which subjects are assigned randomly to two groups—one group then receives the experimental intervention and both groups receive a posttest; there is no pretest. Also known as *posttest-only control group design.*

Random number table   A table containing lists of numbers that are ordered solely on the basis of chance; it is used for drawing a random sample.

Random sampling   A method of sampling that relies on a random, or chance, selection method so that every element of the sampling frame has a known probability of being selected.

Random sampling error (chance sampling error)   Differences between the population and the sample that are due only to chance factors (random error), not to systematic sampling error. Random sampling error may or may not result in an unrepresentative sample. The magnitude of sampling error resulting from chance factors can be estimated statistically.

Random variation   See **idiosyncratic variation.**

Range   The true upper limit in a distribution minus the true lower limit (or the highest rounded value minus the lowest rounded value, plus one).

Ratio level of measurement   A measurement of a variable in which the numbers indicating a variable's values represent fixed measuring units and an absolute zero point.

Rational choice theory   A social theory that explains individual action with the principle that actors choose actions that maximize their gains from taking that action.

Reactive effects   The changes in individual or group behavior that result from being observed or otherwise studied.

Reductionist fallacy (reductionism)   An error in reasoning that occurs when incorrect conclusions about group-level processes are based on individual-level data; also known as individualist fallacy.

Reflexivity   Sensitivity of and adaptation by the researcher to his or her influence in the research setting.

Regression analysis   A statistical technique for characterizing the pattern of a relationship between two quantitative variables in terms of a linear equation and for summarizing the strength of this relationship in terms of its deviation from that linear pattern.

Regression–discontinuity design   A quasi-experimental design in which individuals are assigned to a treatment and a comparison group solely on the basis of a cutoff score on some assignment variable and then treatment effects are identified by a discontinuity in the regression line that displays the relation between the outcome and the assignment variable at the cutoff score.

Regression effect   A source of causal invalidity that occurs when subjects who are chosen for a study because of their extreme scores on the dependent variable become less extreme on the posttest because of natural cyclical or episodic change in the variable.

Reliability   A measurement procedure yields consistent scores when the phenomenon being measured is not changing.

Reliability measure   Statistics that summarize the consistency among a set of measures; Cronbach's alpha is the most common measure of the reliability of a set of items included in an index.

Repeated cross-sectional design (trend study)   A type of longitudinal study in which data are collected at two or more points in time from different samples of the same population.

Repeated measures panel design   A quasi-experimental design consisting of several pretest and posttest observations of the same group.

Replacement sampling   A method of sampling in which sample elements are returned to the sampling frame after being selected, so they may be sampled again. Random samples may be selected with or without replacement.

Replications   Repetitions of a study using the same research methods to answer the same research question.

Representative sample   A sample that "looks like" the population from which it was selected in all respects that are potentially relevant to the study. The distribution of characteristics among the elements of a representative sample is the same as the distribution of those characteristics among the total population. In an unrepresentative sample, some characteristics are overrepresented or underrepresented.

Research circle   A diagram of the elements of the research process, including theories, hypotheses, data collection, and data analysis.

Research program with mixed methods   Qualitative and quantitative methods are used in sequence and are given equal priority.

Resistance to change   The reluctance to change our ideas in light of new information.

Respect for persons   The ethical principle of treating persons as autonomous agents and protecting those with diminished autonomy in research involving human subjects that was included in the *Belmont Report.*

Responsive evaluation   An orientation to evaluation research that expects researchers to be responsive primarily to the people involved with the program. See **stakeholder approach.**

Reverse outlining   Outlining the sections in an already written draft of a paper or report to improve its organization in the next draft.

Sample   A subset of a population that is used to study the population as a whole.

Sample generalizability   Exists when a conclusion based on a sample, or subset, of a larger population holds true for that population.

Sample statistic   The value of a statistic, such as a mean, computed from sample data.

Sampling error   Any difference between the characteristics of a sample and the characteristics of a population; the larger the sampling error, the less representative the sample.

Sampling frame   A list of all elements or other units containing the elements in a population.

Sampling interval   The number of cases from one sampled case to another in a systematic random sample.

Sampling units   Units listed at each stage of a multistage sampling design.

Saturation point   The point at which subject selection is ended in intensive interviewing, when new interviews seem to yield little additional information.

Science   A set of logical, systematic, documented methods for investigating nature and natural processes; the knowledge produced by these investigations.

Scientific paradigm   A set of beliefs that guide scientific work in an area, including unquestioned presuppositions, accepted theories, and exemplary research findings.

Scientific revolution   The abrupt shift from one dominant scientific paradigm to an alternative paradigm that may be developed after accumulation of a large body of evidence that contradicts the prevailing paradigm.

Secondary data   Previously collected data that are used in a new analysis.

Secondary data analysis   The method of using preexisting data in a different way or to answer a different research question than intended by those who collected the data.

Selection bias   A source of internal (causal) invalidity that occurs when characteristics of experimental and comparison group subjects differ in any way that influences the outcome.

Selective distribution of benefits   An ethical issue about how much researchers can influence the benefits subjects receive as part of the treatment being studied in a field experiment.

Selective observation   Choosing to look only at things that are in line with our preferences or beliefs.

Serendipitous findings   Unexpected patterns in data, which stimulate new ideas or theoretical approaches.

Simple random sampling   A method of sampling in which every sample element is selected only on the basis of chance, through a random process.

Skewness   The extent to which cases are clustered more at one or the other end of the distribution of a quantitative variable rather than in a symmetric pattern around its center. Skew can be positive (a right skew), with the number of cases tapering off in the positive direction, or negative (a left skew), with the number of cases tapering off in the negative direction.

Skip pattern   The unique combination of questions created in a survey by filter questions and contingent questions.

Snowball sampling   A method of sampling in which sample elements are selected as they are identified by successive informants or interviewees.

Social desirability bias   The tendency to "agree" with a statement just to avoid seeming disagreeable.

Social research question   A question about the social world that is answered through the collection and analysis of firsthand, verifiable, empirical data.

Social science   The use of scientific methods to investigate individuals, societies, and social processes; the knowledge produced by these investigations.

Social science approach   An orientation to evaluation research that expects researchers to emphasize the importance of researcher expertise and maintenance of autonomy from program stakeholders.

Solomon four-group design A type of experimental design that combines a randomized pretest–posttest control group design with a randomized posttest-only design, resulting in two experimental groups and two comparison groups.

Specification A type of relationship involving three or more variables in which the association between the independent and dependent variables varies across the categories of one or more other control variables.

Split-ballot design Unique questions or other modifications in a survey administered to randomly selected subsets of the total survey sample, so that more questions can be included in the entire survey or so that responses to different question versions can be compared.

Split-half reliability Reliability achieved when responses to the same questions by two randomly selected halves of a sample are about the same.

Spurious relationship A relationship between two variables that is caused by variation in a third variable.

Staged mixed-methods design Qualitative and quantitative methods are used in sequence in the research and one is given priority.

Stakeholder approach An orientation to evaluation research that expects researchers to be responsive primarily to the people involved with the program; also termed **responsive evaluation**.

Stakeholders Individuals and groups who have some basis of concern with the program.

Standard deviation The square root of the average squared deviation of each case from the mean.

Statistical control A method in which one variable is held constant so that the relationship between two (or more) other variables can be assessed without the influence of variation in the control variable.

Statistical significance The mathematical likelihood that an association is due to chance, judged by a criterion set by the analyst (often that the probability is less than 5 out of 100 or $p < .05$).

Stratified random sampling A method of sampling in which sample elements are selected separately from population strata that are identified in advance by the researcher.

Street-level bureaucrats Officials who serve clients and have a high degree of discretion.

Subject fatigue Problems caused by panel members growing weary of repeated interviews

and dropping out of a study or becoming so used to answering the standard questions in the survey that they start giving stock or thoughtless answers.

Subtables Tables describing the relationship between two variables within the discrete categories of one or more other control variables.

Summative evaluation See **impact evaluation (or analysis).**

Survey pretest A method of evaluating survey questions and procedures by testing them on a small sample of individuals like those to be included in the actual survey and then reviewing responses to the questions and reactions to the survey procedures.

Survey research Research in which information is obtained from a sample of individuals through their responses to questions about themselves or others.

Symbolic interaction theory Focuses on the symbolic nature of social interaction—how social interaction conveys meaning and promotes socialization.

Systematic bias Overrepresentation or underrepresentation of some population characteristics in a sample resulting from the method used to select the sample; a sample shaped by systematic sampling error is a biased sample.

Systematic observation A strategy that increases the reliability of observational data by using explicit rules that standardize coding practices across observers.

Systematic random sampling A method of sampling in which sample elements are selected from a list or from sequential files, with every nth element being selected after the first element is selected randomly within the first interval.

Tacit knowledge In field research, a credible sense of understanding of social processes that reflects the researcher's awareness of participants' actions as well as their words, and of what they fail to state, feel deeply, and take for granted.

Target population A set of elements larger than or different from the population sampled and to which the researcher would like to generalize study findings.

Tearoom Trade Study by sociologist Laud Humphreys of men who engage in homosexual behavior in public facilities, including subsequent later interviews in their homes after recording their license plate numbers; widely cited in discussions of the need for informed consent to research.

Temporal research Research that accounts for the related series of events that unfold over time.

Test–retest reliability A measurement showing that measures of a phenomenon at two points in time are highly correlated, if the phenomenon has not changed, or has changed only as much as the phenomenon itself.

Theoretical sampling A sampling method recommended for field researchers by Glaser and Strauss (1967). A theoretical sample is drawn in a sequential fashion, with settings or individuals selected for study as earlier observations or interviews indicate that these settings or individuals are influential.

Theory A logically interrelated set of propositions about empirical reality.

Theory-driven evaluation A program evaluation that is guided by a theory that specifies the process by which the program has an effect.

Thick description A rich description that conveys a sense of what it is like from the standpoint of the natural actors in that setting.

Time order A criterion for establishing a causal relation between two variables; the variation in the presumed cause (the independent variable) must occur before the variation in the presumed effect (the dependent variable).

Time series design A quasi-experimental design consisting of many pretest and posttest observations of the same group over an extended period.

Trend study See **repeated cross-sectional design.**

Triangulation The use of multiple methods to study one research question; also used to mean the use of two or more different measures of the same variable.

True experiment Experiment in which subjects are assigned randomly to an experimental group that receives a treatment or other manipulation of the independent variable and a comparison group that does not receive the treatment or receives some other manipulation; outcomes are measured in a posttest.

Tuskegee Study of Untreated Syphilis in the Negro Male U.S. Public Health Service study of the "natural" course of syphilis that followed 399 low-income African American men from the 1930s to 1972, without providing them with penicillin after this was discovered as treating the illness. The study was stopped after it was exposed in 1972, resulting in an out-of-court settlement and then, in 1997, an official public apology by President Bill Clinton.

Unbalanced response choices A fixed-choice survey question has a different number of positive and negative response choices.

Unimodal   A distribution of a variable in which there is only one value that is the most frequent.

Units of analysis   The level of social life on which a research question is focused, such as individuals, groups, towns, or nations.

Units of observation   The cases about which measures actually are obtained in a sample.

Unlabeled unipolar response options   Response choices for a survey question that use numbers to identify categories ranging from low to high (or vv).

Unobtrusive measures   A measurement based on physical traces or other data that are collected without the knowledge or participation of the individuals or groups that generated the data.

Validity   The state that exists when statements or conclusions about empirical reality are correct.

Variability   The extent to which cases are spread out through the distribution or clustered in just one location.

Variable   A characteristic or property that can vary (take on different values or attributes).

Variable-oriented research   Research that focuses attention on variables representing particular aspects of the cases studied and then examines the relations between these variables across sets of cases.

Variance   A statistic that measures the variability of a distribution as the average squared deviation of each case from the mean.

Visual sociology   Sociological research in which the social world is "observed" and interpreted through photographs, films, and other images.

Web survey   A survey that is accessed and responded to on the World Wide Web.

Zimbardo's prison simulation study   Famous prison simulation study at Stanford University by psychologist Philip Zimbardo designed to investigate the impact of social position on behavior—specifically, the impact of being either a guard or a prisoner in a "total institution"; widely cited as demonstrating the likelihood of emergence of sadistic behavior in guards.

Bibliography

Abbey, Antonia. 2002. "Alcohol-Related Sexual Assault: A Common Problem Among College Students." *Journal of Studies on Alcohol,* Suppl. 14:118–128.

Abbott, Andrew. 1992. "From Causes to Events: Notes on Narrative Positivism." *Sociological Methods and Research* 20(May): 428–455.

Abbott, Andrew. 1994. "History and Sociology: The Lost Synthesis." Pp. 77–112 in *Engaging the Past: The Uses of History Across the Social Sciences,* edited by Eric H. Monkkonen. Durham, NC: Duke University Press.

Abel, David. 2000. "Census May Fall Short at Colleges." *The Boston Sunday Globe,* March 26, pp. B1, B4.

Abma, Tineke A. 2005. "Responsive Evaluation: Its Meaning and Special Contribution to Health Promotion." *Evaluation and Program Planning* 28:279–289.

Abrutyn, Seth and Anna S. Mueller. 2014. "Are Suicidal Behaviors Contagious in Adolescence? Using Longitudinal Data to Examine Suicide Suggestion." *American Sociological Review* 79:211–227.

Adair, G., T. W. Dushenko, and R. C. L. Lindsay. 1985. "Ethical Regulations and Their Impact on Research Practice." *American Psychologist* 40:59–72.

Aguirre, Adalberto Jr. and David V. Baker. 1993. "Racial Prejudice and the Death Penalty: A Research Note." *Social Justice* 20:150–155.

Aiden, Erez and Jean-Baptiste Michel. 2013. *Uncharted: Big Data as a Lens on Human Culture.* New York: Riverhead Books.

Akyüz, Aygül, Tülay Yavan, Gönül Şahiner, and Ayşe Kılıç. 2012. "Domestic Violence and Woman's Reproductive Health: A Review of the Literature." *Aggression and Violent Behavior* 17:514–518.

Aldrich, James O. and Hilda M. Rodriguez. 2013. *Building SPSS Graphs to Understand Data.* Thousand Oaks, CA: Sage.

Alfred, Randall. 1976. "The Church of Satan." Pp. 180–202 in *The New Religious Consciousness,* edited by Charles Glock and Robert Bellah. Berkeley: University of California Press.

Alise, Mark A. and Charles Teddlie. 2010. "A Continuation of the Paradigm Wars? Prevalence Rates of Methodological Approaches Across the Social/Behavioral Sciences." *Journal of Mixed Methods Research* 4:103–126.

Alkire, Sabina, José Manuel Roche, Maria Emma Santos, and Suman Seth. 2011. "Multidimensional Poverty Index 2011: Brief Methodological Note." Oxford, England: Oxford Poverty & Human Development Initiative (OPHI), Oxford Department of International Development. Retrieved May 11, 2014, from www.ophi.org.uk/wp-content/uploads/MPI_2011_Methodology_Note_4-11-2011_1500.pdf?79d835

Allport, Gordon. 1954. *The Nature of Prejudice.* Cambridge, MA: Addison-Wesley.

Altheide, David L. and John M. Johnson. 1994. "Criteria for Assessing Interpretive Validity in Qualitative Research." Pp. 485–499 in *Handbook of Qualitative Research,* edited by Norman K. Denzin and Yvonna S. Lincoln. Thousand Oaks, CA: Sage.

Altman, Lawrence K. 1987. "U.S. and France End Rift on AIDS." *The New York Times,* April 1. Retrieved May 28, 2007, from www.nytimes.com

Altman, Lawrence K. 1998. "Getting It Right on the Facts of Death." *The New York Times,* December 22, p. D7.

Alwin, Duane F. and Jon A. Krosnick. 1991. "The Reliability of Survey Attitude Measurement: The Influence of Question and Respondent Attributes." *Sociological Methods & Research* 20:139–181.

Ambwani, Suman and Jaine Strauss. 2007. "Love Thyself Before Loving Others? A Qualitative and Quantitative Analysis of Gender Differences in Body Image and Romantic Love." *Sex Roles* 56:13–21.

American Association for Public Opinion Research (AAPOR). 2014. "Nonresponse in RDD Cell Phone Surveys." Retrieved May 25, 2014, from www.aapor.org/AM/Template.cfm?Section=Cell_Phone_Task_Force_Report&Template=/CM/ContentDisplay.cfm&ContentID=3176#.U4JzqPldXTo

American Medical Association (AMA). 2011. *AMA Code of Medical Ethics.* Retrieved August 31, 2011, from www.ama-assn.org/ama/physician-resources/medical-ethics/code-medical-ethics.page?

American Psychiatric Association. 1994. *Diagnostic Criteria From DSM-IV.* Washington, DC: American Psychiatric Association.

American Psychiatric Association. 2000. *Diagnostic and Statistical Manual of Mental Disorders,* 4th ed. *(DSM-IV-TR),* Version 6.1.10/2005.3.29. Arlington, VA: American Psychiatric Publishing.

American Sociological Association (ASA). 1999. *Code of Ethics and Policies and Procedures of the ASA Committee on Professional Ethics.* Washington, DC: American Sociological Association.

Anderson, Elijah. 1990. *Streetwise: Race, Class, and Change in an Urban Community.* Chicago: University of Chicago Press.

Anderson, Elijah. 1999. *Code of the Street: Decency, Violence, and the Moral Life of the Inner City.* New York: Norton.

Anderson, Elijah. 2003. "Jelly's Place: An Ethnographic Memoir." *Symbolic Interaction* 26:217–237.

Anderton, Douglas L., Richard E. Barrett, and Donald J. Bogue. 1997. *The Population of the United States.* New York: Free Press.

Andresen E., T. K. Malmstrom, F. D. Wolinsky, M. Schootman, J. P. Miller, and D. K. Miller. 2008. "Rating Neighborhoods for Older Adult Health: Results From the African American Health Study." *BMC Public Health* 8:35. doi:10.1186/1471-2458-8-35

Aneshensel, Carol S. 2002. *Theory-Based Data Analysis for the Social Sciences.* Thousand Oaks, CA: Sage.

Anspach, Renee R. 1991. "Everyday Methods for Assessing Organizational Effectiveness." *Social Problems* 38(February):1–19.

Antaki, Charles. 2008. "Discourse Analysis and Conversation Analysis." Pp. 431–446 in *The SAGE Handbook of Social Research Methods,* edited by Pertti Alasuutari, Leonard Bickman, and Julia Brannen. Thousand Oaks, CA: Sage.

Applebaum, Robert, Valerie Wellin, Cary Kart, J. Scott Brown, Heather Menne, Farida Ejaz, and Keren Brown Wilson. 2007. *Evaluation of Ohio's Assisted Living Medicaid Waiver Program: Final Summary Report.* Oxford, OH: Scripps Gerontology Center and Miami University.

Archibold, Randal C. 2010. "On Border Violence, Truth Pales Compared to Ideas." *The New York Times,* June 19. Retrieved March 17, 2011, from www.nytimes.com

Armas, Genaro C. 2002. "Government Won't File Appeal in Census Case." *The Boston Globe,* November 23, p. A1.

Armstrong, Karen. 2008. "Ethnography and Audience." Pp. 54–63 in *The SAGE Handbook of Social Research Methods,* edited by Pertti Alasuutari, Leonard Bickman, and Julia Brannen. Thousand Oaks, CA: Sage.

Aronson, Elliot and Judson Mills. 1959. "The Effect of Severity of Initiation on Liking for a Group." *Journal of Abnormal and Social Psychology* 59(September):177–181.

Arthur, Michael W., John S. Briney, J. David Hawkins, Robert D. Abbott, Blair L. Brooke-Weiss, and Richard F. Catalano. 2007. "Measuring Risk and Protection in Communities Using the Communities That Care Youth Survey." *Evaluation and Program Planning* 30:197–211.

Arwood, Tracy and Sangeeta Panicker. 2007. "Assessing Risk in Social and Behavioral Sciences." *Collaborative Institutional Training Initiative.* Retrieved June 5, 2008, from https://www.citi program.org/members/learners

Asch, Solomon E. 1958. "Interpersonal Influence." Pp. 174–183 in *Readings in Social Psychology,* 3rd ed., edited by Eleanor Maccoby, Theodore Newcomb, and Eugene Hartley. New York: Holt, Rinehart & Winston.

Aseltine, Robert H. Jr. and Ronald C. Kessler. 1993. "Marital Disruption and Depression in a Community Sample." *Journal of Health and Social Behavior* 34(September):237–251.

Ayhan, H. Öztaş. 2001. "Gender Bias in Agricultural Surveys Statistics by Gender: Measures to Reduce Gender Bias in Agricultural Surveys." *International Statistical Review* 69:447–460.

Babor, Thomas F., Robert S. Stephens, and G. Alan Marlatt. 1987. "Verbal Report Methods in Clinical Research on Alcoholism: Response Bias and Its Minimization." *Journal of Studies on Alcohol* 48(5):410–424.

Bail, Christopher A. 2008. "The Configuration of Symbolic Boundaries Against Immigrants in Europe." *American Sociological Review* 73:37–59.

Bainbridge, William Sims. 1989. *Survey Research: A Computer-Assisted Introduction.* Belmont, CA: Wadsworth.

Bakalar, Nicholas. 2010. "Child Abuse Investigations Didn't Reduce Risk, a Study Finds." *The New York Times,* October 12, p. D3.

Ball, Richard A. and G. David. Curry. 1995. "The Logic of Definition in Criminology: Purposes and Methods for Defining 'Gangs.'" *Criminology* 33:225–245.

Banks, J. A. 1972. "Historical Sociology and the Study of Population." Pp. 55–70 in *Population and Social Change,* edited by D. V. Glass and Roger Revelle. London: Edward Arnold.

Bargh, John A., Mark Chen, and Lara Burrows. 1996. "Automaticity of Social Behavior: Direct Effects of Trait Construct and Stereotype Activation on Action." *Journal of Personality and Social Psychology* 71:230–244.

Bargh, John A., Katelyn Y. A. McKenna, and Grainne M. Fitzsimons. 2002. "Can You See Me? Activation and Expression of the 'True Self' on the Internet." *Journal of Social Issues* 58:33–48.

Barkan, Steven B. and Steven F. Cohn. 1994. "Racial Prejudice and Support for the Death Penalty by Whites." *Journal of Research in Crime and Delinquency* 31:202–209.

Barrera, Davide and Brent Simpson. 2012. "Much Ado About Deception: Consequences of Deceiving Research Participants in the Social Sciences." *Sociological Methods & Research* 41:383–413.

Barringer, Felicity. 1993. "Majority in Poll Back Ban on Handguns." *The New York Times,* June 4, p. A14.

Bartholomew, David J. 2010. "Indirect Measurement." Pp. 455–468 in *The SAGE Handbook of Measurement,* edited by Geoffrey Walford, Eric Tucker, and Madhu Viswanathan. Thousand Oaks, CA: Sage.

Baum, Samuel. 1993. "Sources of Demographic Data." Pp. 3-1–3-50 in *Readings in Population Research Methodology. Vol. 1, Basic Tools,* edited by Donald J. Bogue, Eduardo E. Arriaga, and Douglas L. Anderton. Chicago: Social Development Center, for the United Nations Population Fund.

Baumrind, Diana. 1964. "Some Thoughts on Ethics of Research: After Reading Milgram's 'Behavioral Study of Obedience.'" *American Psychologist* 19:421–423.

Baumrind, Diana. 1985. "Research Using Intentional Deception: Ethical Issues Revisited." *American Psychologist* 40:165–174.

Bean, Lee L., Geraldine P. Mineau, and Douglas L. Anderton. 1990. *Fertility Change on the American Frontier: Adaptation and Innovation.* Berkeley: University of California Press.

Becker, Howard S. 1958. "Problems of Inference and Proof in Participant Observation." *American Sociological Review* 23:652–660.

Becker, Howard S. 1963. *The Outsiders: Studies in the Sociology of Deviance.* New York: Free Press.

Becker, Howard S. 1974. "Photography and Sociology." *Studies in the Anthropology of Visual Communication* 1:3–26.

Becker, Howard S. 2007. *Writing for Social Scientists,* 2nd ed. Chicago: University of Chicago Press.

Bell, Joyce M. and Douglas Hartmann. 2007. "Diversity in Everyday Discourse: The Cultural Ambiguities and Consequences of 'Happy Talk.'" *American Sociological Review* 72:895–914.

Bellah, Robert N., Richard Madsen, William M. Sullivan, Ann Swidler, and Steven M. Tipton. 1985. *Habits of the Heart: Individualism and Commitment in American Life.* New York: Harper & Row.

Belousov, Konstantin, Tom Horlick-Jones, Michael Bloor, Yakov Gilinskiy, Valentin Golbert, Yakov Kostikovsky, Michael Levi, and Dmitri Pentsov. 2007. "Any Port in a Storm: Fieldwork Difficulties in Dangerous and Crisis-Ridden Settings." *Qualitative Research* 7:155–175.

Bendix, Reinhard. 1956. *Work and Authority in Industry: Ideologies of Management in the course of Industrialization.* Berkeley: University of California Press.

Bendix, Reinhard. 1962. *Max Weber: An Intellectual Portrait.* Garden City, NY: Doubleday/Anchor.

Benkler, Yochai. 2006. *The Wealth of Networks: How Social Production Transforms Markets and Freedom.* New Haven, CT: Yale University Press.

Benwell, Bethan and Elizabeth Stokoe. 2006. *Discourse and Identity.* Edinburgh, Scotland: Edinburgh University Press.

Berger, Joseph, Bernard P. Cohen, and Morris Zelditch Jr. 1972. "Status Characteristics and Social Interaction." *American Sociological Review* 37:241–255.

Bergman, Manfred Max. 2008. "Combining Different Types of Data for Quantitative Analysis." Pp. 585–601 in *The SAGE Handbook of Social Research Methods,* edited by Pertti Alasuutari, Leonard Bickman, and Julia Brannen. Thousand Oaks, CA: Sage.

Berk, Richard A., Alec Campbell, Ruth Klap, and Bruce Western. 1992. "The Deterrent Effect of Arrest: A Bayesian Analysis of Four Field Experiments." *American Sociological Review* 57 (October):698–708.

Berk, Richard A., Kenneth J. Lenihan, and Peter H. Rossi. 1980. "Crime and Poverty: Some Experimental Evidence From Ex-Offenders." *American Sociological Review* 45:766–786.

Berman, Greg and Aubrey Fox. 2009. *Lessons From the Battle Over D.A.R.E.: The Complicated Relationship Between Research and Practice.* Washington, DC: Center for Court Innovation and Bureau of Justice Assistance, U.S. Department of Justice.

Berry, Brent. 2006. "Friends for Better or for Worse: Interracial Friendship in the United States as Seen Through Wedding Party Photos." *Demography* 43:491–510.

Bertamini, Marco and Marcus R. Munafo. 2012. "The Perils of 'Bite Size' Science." *The New York Times,* January 29, p. SR 12.

Bierman, Alex. 2012. "Functional Limitations and Psychological Distress: Marital Status as Moderator." *Society and Mental Health* 2(1):35–52.

Binder, Arnold and James W. Meeker. 1993. "Implications of the Failure to Replicate the Minneapolis Experimental Findings." *American Sociological Review* 58(December):886–888.

Birkeland, Sarah, Erin Murphy-Graham, and Carol Weiss. 2005. "Good Reasons for Ignoring Good Evaluation: The Case of the Drug Abuse Resistance Education (D.A.R.E.) Program." *Evaluation and Program Planning* 28:247–256.

Black, Donald J. (Ed.). 1984. *Toward a General Theory of Social Control.* Orlando, FL: Academic Press.

Black, M. C., K. C. Basile, M. J. Breiding, S. G. Smith, M. L. Walters, M. T. Merrick, J. Chen, & M. R. Stevens. 2011. *The National Intimate Partner and Sexual Violence Survey (NISVS): 2010 Summary Report.* Atlanta, GA: National Center for Injury Prevention and Control, Centers for Disease Control and Prevention.

Blau, Peter M. 1964. *Exchange and Power in Social Life.* New York: Wiley.

Bledsoe, Katrina L. and Rodney K. Hopson. 2009. "Conducting Ethical Research and Evaluation in Underserved Communities." Pp. 391–406 in *The Handbook of Social Research Ethics,* edited by Donna M. Mertens and Pauline E. Ginsberg. Thousand Oaks, CA: Sage.

Bloom, Howard S. 2008. "The Core Analytics of Randomized Experiments for Social Research." Pp. 115–133 in *The SAGE Handbook of Social Research Methods,* edited by Pertti Alasuutari, Leonard Bickman, and Julia Brannen. Thousand Oaks, CA: Sage.

Boase, Jeffrey, John B. Horrigan, Barry Wellman, and Lee Rainie. 2006. *The Strength of Internet Ties: The Internet and Email Aid Users in Maintaining Their Social Networks and Provide Pathways to Help When People Face Big Decisions.* Washington, DC: Pew Internet & American Life Project.

Bogdewic, Stephan P. 1999. "Participant Observation." Pp. 47–70 in *Doing Qualitative Research,* 2nd ed., edited by Benjamin F. Crabtree and William L. Miller. Thousand Oaks, CA: Sage.

Bogue, Donald J. 1969. *Principles of Demography.* New York: Wiley.

Bogue, Donald J., Eduardo E. Arriaga, and Douglas L. Anderton. 1993. *Readings in Population Research Methodology. Vol. 1, Basic Tools.* Chicago: Social Development Center, for the United Nations Population Fund.

Bohn, Angela, Christian Buchta, Kurt Hornik, and Patrick Mair. 2014. "Making Friends and Communicating on Facebook: Implications for the Access to Social Capital." *Social Networks* 37:29–41.

Bollen, Kenneth A., Barbara Entwisle, and Arthur S. Alderson. 1993. "Macrocomparative Research Methods." *Annual Review of Sociology* 19:321–351.

Bond, Robert M., Christopher J. Fariss, Jason J. Jones, Adam D. I. Kramer, Cameron Marlow, Jaime E. Settle, and James H. Fowler. 2012. "A 61-Million-Person Experiment in Social Influence and Political Mobilization." *Nature* 489:295–298.

Booth, Brenda M., Greer Sullivan, Paul Koegel, and Audrey Burnam. 2002. "Vulnerability Factors for Homelessness Associated With Substance Dependence in a Community Sample of Homeless Adults." *American Journal of Drug and Alcohol Abuse* 28:429–452.

Booth, Wayne C., Gregory G. Colomb, and Joseph M. Williams. 1995. *The Craft of Research.* Chicago: University of Chicago Press.

Booth, Wayne C., Gregory G. Colomb, and Joseph M. Williams. 2008. *The Craft of Research,* 3rd ed. Chicago: University of Chicago Press.

Borg, Marian J. 1997. "The Southern Subculture of Punitiveness? Regional Variation in Support for Capital Punishment." *Journal of Research in Crime and Delinquency* 34:25–45.

Borg, Marian J. 1998. "Vicarious Homicide Victimization and Support for Capital Punishment: A Test of Black's Theory of Law." *Criminology* 36:537–567.

Boruch, Robert F. 1997. *Randomized Experiments for Planning and Evaluation: A Practical Guide.* Thousand Oaks, CA: Sage.

Bos, Johannes, Aletha Huston, Robert Granger, Greg Duncan, Thomas Brock, and Vonnie McLoyd. 1999. *New Hope for People With Low Incomes: Two-Year Results of a Program to Reduce Poverty and Reform Welfare.* MRDC Report. Retrieved June 19, 2014, from www.mdrc.org/publication/new-hope-people-low-incomes

Bosk, Charles L. and Raymond G. De Vries. 2004. "Bureaucracies of Mass Deception: Institutional Review Boards and the Ethics of Ethnographic Research." *Annals of the American Academy of Political and Social Science* 595:249–263.

Bourgois, Philippe, Mark Lettiere, and James Quesada. 1997. "Social Misery and the Sanctions of Substance Abuse: Confronting HIV Risk Among Homeless Heroin Addicts in San Francisco." *Social Problems* 44:155–173.

Braga, Anthony A., Andrew V. Papachristos, and David M. Hureau. 2012. "Hot Spots Policing Effects on Crime." *Campbell Systematic Reviews* 2012:8. doi:10.4073/csr.2012.8

Bray, Hiawatha. 1999. "Plugging in to the Electronic Campus." *The Boston Globe Magazine,* April 11, pp. 20–30.

Brenner, Philip S. 2012. "Investigating the Effect of Bias in Survey Measures of Church Attendance." *Sociology of Religion* 73:361–383.

Brewer, John and Albert Hunter. 1989. *Multimethod Research: A Synthesis of Styles.* Newbury Park, CA: Sage.

Bridges, George S. and Joseph G. Weis. 1989. "Measuring Violent Behavior: Effects of Study Design on Reported Correlates of Violence." Pp. 14–34 in *Violent Crime, Violent Criminals,* edited by Neil Alan Weiner and Marvin E. Wolfgang. Newbury Park, CA: Sage.

Brooks, Clem and Jeff Manza. 2006. "Social Policy Responsiveness in Developed Democracies." *American Sociological Review* 71:474–494.

Broskoske, Steve. 2005. "How to Prevent Paper Recycling." *The Teaching Professor* 19:1, 4.

Brown, Bruce L. and Dawson Hedges. 2009. "Use and Misuse of Quantitative Methods: Data Collection, Calculation, and Presentation." Pp. 373–386 in *The Handbook of Social Research Ethics,* edited by Donna M. Mertens and Pauline E. Ginsberg. Thousand Oaks, CA: Sage.

Brown, Judith Belle. 1999. "The Use of Focus Groups in Clinical Research." Pp. 109–124 in *Doing Qualitative Research,* 2nd ed., edited by Benjamin F. Crabtree and William L. Miller. Thousand Oaks, CA: Sage.

Brown, Ryan A., David P. Kennedy, Joan S. Tucker, Daniela Golinelli, and Suzanne L. Wenzel. 2013. "Monogamy on the Street: A Mixed Methods Study of Homeless Men." *Journal of Mixed Methods Research* 7:328–346.

Bruni, Frank. 2002. "Persistent Drop in Fertility Reshapes Europe's Future." *The New York Times,* December 26, pp. A1, A10.

Bureau of Justice Statistics. 2011. "Key Facts at a Glance: Drug Arrests by Age, 1970–2007." Washington, DC: Bureau of Justice Statistics, U.S. Department of Justice. Retrieved March 17, 2011, from http://bjs.ojp.usdoj.gov/content/glance/drug.cfm

Burke, Garance. 2000. "Mexico's Census Battles Perception of Corruption." *The Boston Globe,* March 2, p. A2.

Burt, Martha R. 1996. "Homelessness: Definitions and Counts." Pp. 15–23 in *Homelessness in America,* edited by Jim Baumohl. Phoenix, AZ: Oryx.

Bushman, Brad J., Roy F. Baumeister, and Angela D. Stack. 1999. "Catharsis, Aggression, and Persuasive Influence: Self-Fulfilling or Self-Defeating Prophecies?" *Journal of Personality and Social Psychology* 76:367–376.

Butler, Declan. 2013. "When Google Got Flu Wrong." *Nature* 494(February 14):155–156.

Butler, Dore and Florence Geis. 1990. "Nonverbal Affect Responses to Male and Female Leaders: Implications for Leadership Evaluations." *Journal of Personality and Social Psychology* 58(January):48–59.

Buttel, Frederick H. 2000. "World Society, the Nation-State, and Environmental Protection: Comment on Frank, Hironaka, and Schofer." *American Sociological Review* 65:117–121.

Buzawa, Eve S. and Carl G. Buzawa (Eds.). 1996. *Do Arrests and Restraining Orders Work?* Thousand Oaks, CA: Sage.

Cain, Carol. 1991. "Personal Stories: Identity Acquisition and Self-Understanding in Alcoholics Anonymous." *Ethos* 19: 210–253.

Campbell, Donald T. and Donald W. Fiske. 1959. "Convergent and Discriminant Validation by the Multitrait–Multimethod Matrix." *Psychological Bulletin* 56:81–105.

Campbell, Donald T. and M. Jean Russo. 1999. *Social Experimentation.* Thousand Oaks, CA: Sage.

Campbell, Donald T. and Julian C. Stanley. 1966. *Experimental and Quasi-Experimental Designs for Research.* Chicago: Rand McNally.

Campbell, Richard T. 1992. "Longitudinal Research." Pp. 1146–1158 in *Encyclopedia of Sociology,* edited by Edgar F. Borgatta and Marie L. Borgatta. New York: Macmillan.

Campbell, Wilson. 2002. "A Statement From the Governmental Accounting Standards Board and Performance Measurement Staff." American Society for Public Administration. Retrieved July 20, 2002, from www.aspanet.org/cap/forum_statement.html#top

Cannell, C. F., L. Oksenberg, G. Kalton, K. Bischoping, and Floyd J. Fowler. 1989. *New Techniques for Pretesting Survey Questions.* Final Report. Grant No. HS05616. National Center for Health Service Research, Health Care Technology Assessment. Retrieved from www.psc.isr.umich.edu/dis/infoserv/isrpub/pdf/NewTechniquesPretestingSurveyQuestions_OCR.pdf

Caplan, Brina, Russell K. Schutt, Winston M. Turner, Stephen M. Goldfinger, and Larry J. Seidman. 2006. "Change in Neurocognition by Housing Type and Substance Abuse Among Formerly Homeless Seriously Mentally Ill Individuals." *Schizophrenia Research* 83:77–86.

Carmines, Edward G. and Richard A. Zeller. 1979. *Reliability and Validity Assessment,* no. 17, Quantitative Applications in the Social Sciences. Beverly Hills, CA: Sage.

Carr, Patrick J. and Maria Kefalas. 2009. *Hollowing Out the Middle: The Rural Brain Drain and What It Means for America.* Boston: Beacon Press.

Cava, Anita, Reid Cushman, and Kenneth Goodman. 2007. "HIPAA and Human Subjects Research." *Collaborative Institutional Training Initiative.* Retrieved June 5, 2008, from https://www.citiprogram.org/members/learners

Cave, Emma and Soren Holm. 2003. "Milgram and Tuskegee—Paradigm Research Projects in Bioethics." *Health Care Analysis* 11:27–40.

Ceglowski, Deborah. 2002. "Research as Relationship." Pp. 5–27 in *The Qualitative Inquiry Reader,* edited by Norman Denzin and Yvonna S. Lincoln. Thousand Oaks, CA: Sage.

Center for Survey Research, University of Massachusetts at Boston. 1987. "Methodology: Designing Good Survey Questions." *Newsletter,* April, p. 3.

Centers for Disease Control and Prevention (CDC). 2009. "The Tuskegee Timeline." Atlanta, GA: National Center for HIV/AIDS, Viral Hepatitis, STD, and TB Prevention, Centers for Disease Control and Prevention. Retrieved March 16, 2011, from www.cdc.gov/tuskegee/timeline.htm

Chabris, Christopher and Daniel Simons. 2013. "Does This Ad Make Me Fat?" *The New York Times,* March 10, p. SR12.

Chase-Dunn, Christopher and Thomas D. Hall. 1993. "Comparing World-Systems: Concepts and Working Hypotheses." *Social Forces* 71:851–886.

Chase-Lansdale, P. Lindsay, Robert A. Moffitt, Brenda J. Lohman, Andrew J. Cherlin, Rebekah Levine Coley, Laura D. Pittman, Jennifer Roff, and Elizabeth Votruba-Drzal. 2003. "Mothers' Transitions From Welfare to Work and the Well-Being of Preschoolers and Adolescents." *Science* 299:1548–1552.

Chen, Huey-Tsyh. 1990. *Theory-Driven Evaluations.* Newbury Park, CA: Sage.

Chen, Huey-Tsyh and Peter H. Rossi. 1987. "The Theory-Driven Approach to Validity." *Evaluation and Program Planning* 10:95–103.

Christian, Leah, Scott Keeter, Kristen Purcell, and Aaron Smith. 2010. "Assessing the Cell Phone Challenge to Survey Research in 2010." Washington, DC: Pew Research Center for the People & the Press and Pew Internet & American Life Project.

Church, Allan H. 1993. "Estimating the Effects of Incentives on Mail Survey Response Rates: A Meta-Analysis." *Public Opinion Quarterly* 57:62–79.

Church, A. Timothy. 2010. "Measurement Issues in Cross-Cultural Research." Pp. 151–175 in *The SAGE Handbook of Measurement,* edited by Geoffrey Walford, Eric Tucker, and Madhu Viswanathan. Thousand Oaks, CA: Sage.

CIRCLE. 2013. "Fact Sheet: Voter Turnout Among Young Women and Men in the 2012 Presidential Election." Medford, MA: The Center for Information & Research on Civil Learning & Engagement, Jonathan M. Tisch College of Citizenship and Public Service, Tufts University. Retrieved May 26, 2014, from www.civicyouth.org/wp-content/uploads/2013/05/fs_gender_13_final.pdf

Clark, Herbert H. and Michael F. Schober. 1994. "Asking Questions and Influencing Answers." Pp. 15–48 in *Questions About Questions: Inquiries Into the Cognitive Bases of Surveys,* edited by Judith M. Tanur. New York: Russell Sage Foundation.

Code of Federal Regulations. 2009. Title 45, Public Welfare. Department of Health and Human Services, Part 46, Protection of Human Subjects. Retrieved September 1, 2011, from www.hhs.gov/ohrp/humansubjects/guidance/45cfr46.html#46.101

Coffey, Amanda and Paul Atkinson. 1996. *Making Sense of Qualitative Data: Complementary Research Strategies.* Thousand Oaks, CA: Sage.

Cohen, Alison K. and Benjamin W. Chaffee. 2012. "The Relationship Between Adolescents' Civic Knowledge, Civic Attitude, and Civic Behavior and Their Self-Reported Future Likelihood of Voting." *Education, Citizenship and Social Justice* 8(1):43–57.

Cohen, Sheldon, Robin Mermelstein, Tom Kamarck, and Harry M. Hoberman. 1985. "Measuring the Functional Components of Social Support." Pp. 73–94 in *Social Support: Theory, Research and Applications,* edited by Irwin G. Sarason and Barbara R. Sarason. The Hague, The Netherlands: Martinus Nijhoff.

Cohen, Susan G. and Gerald E. Ledford Jr. 1994. "The Effectiveness of Self-Managing

Teams: A Quasi-Experiment." *Human Relations* 47:13–43.

Coleman, James S. 1990. *Foundations of Social Theory*. Cambridge, MA: Harvard University Press.

Coleman, James S. and Thomas Hoffer. 1987. *Public and Private High Schools: The Impact of Communities*. New York: Basic Books.

Coleman, James S., Thomas Hoffer, and Sally Kilgore. 1982. *High School Achievement: Public, Catholic, and Private Schools Compared*. New York: Basic Books.

College Alcohol Study. 2008. "College Alcohol Study News." *Harvard School of Public Health*. Retrieved May 5, 2008, from www.hsph.harvard.edu/cas/Home.html

Collins, Patricia Hill. 1991. "Learning From the Outsider Within: The Sociological Significance of Black Feminist Thought." Pp. 35–59 in *Beyond Methodology*, edited by Mary Margaret Fonow and Judith A. Cook. Bloomington: Indiana University Press.

Collins, Randall. 1994. *Four Sociological Traditions*. New York: Oxford University Press.

Connolly, Francis J. and Charley Manning. 2001. "What 'Push Polling' Is and What It Isn't." *The Boston Globe*, August 16, p. A21.

Connor, Jennie, Andrew Gray, and Kypros Kypri. 2010. "Drinking History, Current Drinking and Problematic Sexual Experiences Among University Students." *Australian and New Zealand Journal of Public Health* 34:487–494.

Connors, Gerard J. and Robert J. Volk. 2004. "Self-Report Screening for Alcohol Problems Among Adults." Pp. 21–35 in *Assessing Alcohol Problems: A Guide for Clinicians and Researchers*, 2nd ed., edited by John P. Allen and Veronica B. Wilson. NIH Publication No. 03–3745, revised 2003. Bethesda, MD: National Institute on Alcohol Abuse and Alcoholism, National Institutes of Health. Retrieved October 6, 2005, from http://pubs.niaaa.nih.gov/publications/Assesing%20Alcohol/index.htm#contents

Converse, Jean M. 1984. "Attitude Measurement in Psychology and Sociology: The Early Years." Pp. 3–40 in *Surveying Subjective Phenomena*, vol. 2, edited by Charles F. Turner and Elizabeth Martin. New York: Russell Sage Foundation.

Cook, Gareth. 2005. "Face It: Appearances Sway Voters." *The Boston Globe*, June 14, pp. E1, E4.

Cook, Gareth. 2011. "TV's Sleeper Effect." *The Boston Globe*, October 30.

Cook, Thomas D. and Donald T. Campbell. 1979. *Quasi-Experimentation: Design and Analysis Issues for Field Settings*. Chicago: Rand McNally.

Cook, Thomas D. and Vivian C. Wong. 2008. "Better Quasi-Experimental Practice."

Pp. 134–165 in *The SAGE Handbook of Social Research Methods*, edited by Pertti Alasuutari, Leonard Bickman, and Julia Brannen. Thousand Oaks, CA: Sage.

Cooper, Harris and Larry V. Hedges. 1994. "Research Synthesis as a Scientific Enterprise." Pp. 3–14 in *The Handbook of Research Synthesis*, edited by Harris Cooper and Larry V. Hedges. New York: Russell Sage Foundation.

Cooper, Kathleen B. and Michael D. Gallagher. 2004. *A Nation Online: Entering the Broadband Age*. Washington, DC: Economics and Statistics Administration and National Telecommunications and Information Administration, U.S. Department of Commerce. Retrieved June 15, 2005, from www.ntia.doc.gov/reports/anol/index.html

Cooper, Kathleen B. and Nancy J. Victory. 2002. "Foreword." P. iv in *A Nation Online: How Americans Are Expanding Their Use of the Internet*. Washington, DC: National Telecommunications and Information Administration, Economics and Statistics Administration, U.S. Department of Commerce.

Core Institute. 1994. "Core Alcohol and Drug Survey: Long Form." Carbondale, IL: FIPSE Core Analysis Grantee Group, Core Institute, Student Health Programs, Southern Illinois University.

Correll, Joshua, Bernadette Park, Charles M. Judd, and Bernd Wittenbrink. 2002. "The Police Officer's Dilemma: Using Ethnicity to Disambiguate Potentially Threatening Individuals." *Journal of Personality and Social Psychology* 83:1314–1329.

Corse, Sara J., Nancy B. Hirschinger, and David Zanis. 1995. "The Use of the Addiction Severity Index With People With Severe Mental Illness." *Psychiatric Rehabilitation Journal* 19(1):9–18.

Costner, Herbert L. 1989. "The Validity of Conclusions in Evaluation Research: A Further Development of Chen and Rossi's Theory-Driven Approach." *Evaluation and Program Planning* 12:345–353.

Couper, Mick P. 2000. "Web Surveys: A Review of Issues and Approaches." *Public Opinion Quarterly* 64:464–494.

Couper, Mick P., Reginald P. Baker, Jelke Bethlehem, Cynthia Z. F. Clark, Jean Martin, William L. Nicholls II, and James M. O'Reilly (Eds.). 1998. *Computer-Assisted Survey Information Collection*. New York: Wiley.

Couper, Mick P. and Peter V. Miller. 2008. "Web Survey Methods: Introduction." *Public Opinion Quarterly* 72:831–835.

Couper, Mick P., Michael W. Traugott, and Mark J. Lamias. 2001. "Web Survey Design and Administration." *Public Opinion Quarterly* 65:230–253.

Cowan, Gloria. 2002. "Content Analysis of Visual Materials." Pp. 345–368 in

Handbook for Conducting Research on Human Sexuality, edited by Michael W. Wiederman and Bernard E. Whitley Jr. London: Lawrence Erlbaum.

Crawford, Susan P. 2011. "The New Digital Divide." *The New York Times*, December 4, p. A1.

Cress, Daniel M. and David A. Snow. 2000. "The Outcomes of Homeless Mobilization: The Influence of Organization, Disruption, Political Mediation, and Framing." *American Journal of Sociology* 4:1063–1104.

Creswell, John W. and Vicki L. Plano Clark. 2011. *Designing and Conducting Mixed Methods Research*, 2nd ed. Thousand Oaks, CA: Sage.

Cuba, Lee J. 2002. *A Short Guide to Writing About Social Science*, 4th ed. New York: Addison-Wesley.

Cullen, Kevin. 2014. "The Gunmen, the Shadows, and the Damage Done." *Boston Sunday Globe*, July 6, pp. A1, A6, A7.

Currie, Janet and Duncan Thomas. 1995. "Does Head Start Make a Difference?" *American Economic Review* 85:341–365.

Curtin, Richard, Stanley Presser, and Eleanor Singer. "Changes in Telephone Survey Nonresponse Over the Past Quarter Century." *Public Opinion Quarterly*, 69:87–98.

Czopp, Alexander M., Margo J. Monteith, and Aimee Y. Mark. 2006. "Standing Up for a Change: Reducing Bias Through Interpersonal Confrontation." *Journal of Personality and Social Psychology* 90:784–803.

Dahlberg, Britt, Marsha N. Wittink, and Joseph J. Gallo. 2010. "Funding and Publishing Integrated Studies: Writing Effective Mixed Methods Manuscripts and Grant Proposals." Pp. 775–802 in *SAGE Handbook of Mixed Methods in Social & Behavioral Research*, 2nd ed., edited by Abbas Tashakkori and Charles Teddlie. Thousand Oaks, CA: Sage.

Dale, Angela, Jo Wathan, and Vanessa Higgins. 2008. "Secondary Analysis of Quantitative Data Sources." Pp. 520–535 in *The SAGE Handbook of Social Research Methods*, edited by Pertti Alasuutari, Leonard Bickman, and Julia Brannen. Thousand Oaks, CA: Sage.

D'Amico, Elizabeth J. and Kim Fromme. 2002. "Brief Prevention for Adolescent Risk-Taking Behavior." *Addiction* 97:563–574.

Dannefer, W. Dale and Russell K. Schutt. 1982. "Race and Juvenile Justice Processing in Court and Police Agencies." *American Journal of Sociology* 87(March):1113–1132.

D.A.R.E. 2008. *The "New" D.A.R.E. Program*. Retrieved May 31, 2008, from www.dare.com/newdare.asp

D.A.R.E. 2014. "Drug Abuse Resistance Education." Retrieved February 15, 2014, from www.dare.org/starting-a-dare-program

Davidoff, Steven M. 2012. "Seeking Critical Mass of Gender Equality in the Boardroom." *The New York Times,* September 12, p. B5.

Davies, Philip, Anthony Petrosino, and Iain Chalmers. 1999. *Report and Papers From the Exploratory Meeting for the Campbell Collaboration.* London: School of Public Policy, University College.

Davis, James A. 1985. *The Logic of Causal Order.* Sage University Paper Series on Quantitative Applications in the Social Sciences, series No. 07–055. Beverly Hills, CA: Sage.

Davis, James A. and Tom W. Smith. 1992. *The NORC General Social Survey: A User's Guide.* Newbury Park, CA: Sage.

Davis, Ophera A. and Marie Land. 2007. "Southern Women Survivors Speak About Hurricane Katrina, the Children and What Needs to Happen Next." *Race, Gender & Class* 14:69–86.

Dawes, Robyn. 1995. "How Do You Formulate a Testable Exciting Hypothesis?" Pp. 93–96 in *How to Write a Successful Research Grant Application: A Guide for Social and Behavioral Scientists,* edited by Willo Pequegnat and Ellen Stover. New York: Plenum Press.

de Leeuw, Edith. 2008. "Self-Administered Questionnaires and Standardized Interviews." Pp. 311–327 in *The SAGE Handbook of Social Research Methods,* edited by Pertti Alasuutari, Leonard Bickman, and Julia Brannen. Thousand Oaks, CA: Sage.

de Vaus, David. 2008. "Comparative and Cross-National Designs." Pp. 248–264 in *The SAGE Handbook of Social Research Methods,* edited by Pertti Alasuutari, Leonard Bickman, and Julia Brannen. Thousand Oaks, CA: Sage.

Decker, Scott H. and Barrik Van Winkle. 1996. *Life in the Gang: Family, Friends, and Violence.* Cambridge: Cambridge University Press.

Deegan, Allison. 2012. "Stranger in a Strange Land: The Challenges and Benefits of Online Interviews in the Social Networking Space." Pp. 69–99 in *Cases in Online Interview Research,* edited by Janet Salmons. Thousand Oaks, CA: Sage.

Demos, John. 1998. "History Beyond Data Bits." *The New York Times,* December 30, p. A23.

Dentler, Robert A. 2002. *Practicing Sociology: Selected Fields.* Westport, CT: Praeger.

Denzin, Norman K. 2002. "The Interpretive Process." Pp. 349–368 in *The Qualitative Researcher's Companion,* edited by A. Michael Huberman and Matthew B. Miles. Thousand Oaks, CA: Sage.

Denzin, Norman and Yvonna S. Lincoln. 1994. "Introduction: Entering the Field of Qualitative Research." Pp. 1–28 in *The Handbook of Qualitative Research,* edited by Norman Denzin and Yvonna S. Lincoln. Thousand Oaks, CA: Sage.

Denzin, Norman and Yvonna S. Lincoln. 2000. "Introduction: The Discipline and Practice of Qualitative Research." Pp. 1–28 in *The Handbook of Qualitative Research,* 2nd ed., edited by Norman Denzin and Yvonna S. Lincoln. Thousand Oaks, CA: Sage.

Denzin, Norman K. and Yvonna S. Lincoln. 2008. *Strategies of Qualitative Inquiry,* 3rd ed. Thousand Oaks, CA: Sage.

DeParle, Jason. 1999. "Project to Rescue Needy Stumbles Against the Persistence of Poverty." *The New York Times,* May 15, pp. A1, A10.

Department of Health and Human Services (DHHS). 2009. Code of Federal Regulations, Title 45: Public Welfare. Department of Health and Human Services, Part 46, Protection of Human Subjects. Retrieved December 31, 2013, from hhs.gov/ohrp/policy/ohrpregulations.pdf

Department of Health, Education, and Welfare. 1979. *The Belmont Report: Ethical Principles and Guidelines for the Protection of Human Subjects of Research.* Washington, DC: The National Commission for the Protection of Human Subjects of Biomedical and Behavioral Research, Office of the Secretary, Department of Health, Education, and Welfare. Retrieved June 20, 2005, from www.hss.gov/ohrp/humansubjects/guidance/belmont.htm

Dewan, Shaila K. 2004a. "As Murders Fall, New Tactics Are Tried Against Remainder." *The New York Times,* December 31, pp. A24–A25.

Dewan, Shaila K. 2004b. "New York's Gospel of Policing by Data Spreads Across U.S." *The New York Times,* April 26, pp. A1, C16.

Dewey, John. [1933] 1986. *How We Think: A Restatement of the Relation of Reflective Thinking to the Educative Process* (rev. ed.). In *John Dewey: The Later Works, 1925–1953,* vol. 8. Carbondale: Southern Illinois University Press.

Diamond, Timothy. 1992. *Making Gray Gold: Narratives of Nursing Home Care.* Chicago: University of Chicago Press.

Dickson-Swift, Virginia, Erica L. James, Sandra Kippen, and Pranee Liamputtong. 2008. "Risk to Researchers in Qualitative Research on Sensitive Topics: Issues and Strategies." *Qualitative Health Research* 18:133–144.

DiClemente, C. C., J. P. Carbonari, R. P. G. Montgomery, and S. O. Hughes. 1994. "The Alcohol Abstinence Self-Efficacy Scale." *Journal of Studies on Alcohol* 55:141–148.

Dill, Karen E. and Kathryn P. Thill. 2007. "Video Game Characters and the Socialization of Gender Roles: Young People's Perceptions Mirror Sexist Media Depictions." *Sex Roles* 57:851–864.

Dillman, Don A. 1978. *Mail and Telephone Surveys: The Total Design Method.* New York: Wiley.

Dillman, Don A. 1982. "Mail and Other Self-Administered Questionnaires." Chapter 12 in *Handbook of Survey Research,* edited by Peter Rossi, James Wright, and Andy Anderson. New York: Academic Press. As reprinted on pp. 637–638 in Delbert C. Miller, 1991. *Handbook of Research Design and Social Measurement,* 5th ed. Beverly Hills, CA: Sage.

Dillman, Don A. 2000. *Mail and Internet Surveys: The Tailored Design Method,* 2nd ed. New York: Wiley.

Dillman, Don A. 2007. *Mail and Internet Surveys: The Tailored Design Method,* 2nd ed. Updated With New Internet, Visual, and Mixed-Mode Guide. Hoboken, NJ: Wiley.

Dillman, Don A., James A. Christenson, Edwin H. Carpenter, and Ralph M. Brooks. 1974. "Increasing Mail Questionnaire Response: A Four-State Comparison." *American Sociological Review* 39(October):744–756.

Dillman, Don A. and Leah Melani Christian. 2005. "Survey Mode as a Source of Instability in Responses Across Surveys." *Field Methods* 17:30–52.

Doucet, Andrea and Natasha Mauthner. 2008. "Qualitative Interviewing and Feminist Research." Pp. 328–343 in *The SAGE Handbook of Social Research Methods,* edited by Pertti Alasuutari, Leonard Bickman, and Julia Brannen. Thousand Oaks, CA: Sage.

Douglas, Jack D. 1985. *Creative Interviewing.* Beverly Hills, CA: Sage.

Drake, Robert E., Gregory J. McHugo, and Jeremy C. Biesanz. 1995. "The Test-Retest Reliability of Standardized Instruments Among Homeless Persons With Substance Use Disorders." *Journal of Studies on Alcohol* 56(2):161–167.

Drew, Paul. 2005. "Conversation Analysis." Pp. 71–102 in *Handbook of Language and Social Interaction,* edited by Kristine L. Fitch and Robert E. Sanders. Mahwah, NJ: Lawrence Erlbaum.

Duckworth, Kenneth, John H. Halpern, Russell K. Schutt, and Christopher Gillespie. 2003. "Use of Schizophrenia as a Metaphor in U.S. Newspapers." *Psychiatric Services* 54:1402–1404.

Duncombe, Jean and Julie Jessop. 2002. "'Doing Rapport' and the Ethics of 'Faking Friendship.'" Pp. 107–122 in *Ethics in Qualitative Research,* edited by Melanie Mauthner, Maxine Birch, Julie Jessop, and Tina Miller. Thousand Oaks, CA: Sage.

Duneier, Mitchell. 1999. *Sidewalk.* New York: Farrar, Strauss, and Giroux.

Durkheim, Émile. 1951. *Suicide.* New York: Free Press.

Durkheim, Émile. 1966. *Suicide: A Study in Sociology.* Translated by John A. Spaulding and George Simpson. New York: Free Press.

Durkheim, Émile. 1984. *The Division of Labor in Society.* Translated by W. D. Halls. New York: Free Press.

Dykema, Jennifer and Nora Cate Schaeffer. 2000. "Events, Instruments, and Reporting Errors." *American Sociological Review* 65:619–629.

Eckholm, Erik. 2006. "Report on Impact of Federal Benefits on Curbing Poverty Reignites a Debate." *The New York Times,* February 18, p. A8.

Egan, Patrick. 2012. "The Declining Culture of Guns and Violence in the United States." The Monkey Cage Blog, posted July 21. Retrieved May 26, 2014, from http://themonkeycage. org/2012/07/21/the-declining-culture-of-guns-and-violence-in-the-united-states/

Elder, Keith, Sudha Xirasagar, Nancy Miller, Shelly Ann Bowen, Saundra Glover, and Crystal Piper. 2007. "African Americans' Decisions Not to Evacuate New Orleans Before Hurricane Katrina: A Qualitative Study." *American Journal of Public Health* 97(Suppl. 1):S124–S129.

Elliott, Jane, Janet Holland, and Rachel Thomson. 2008. "Longitudinal and Panel Studies." Pp. 228–248 in *The SAGE Handbook of Social Research Methods,* edited by Pertti Alasuutari, Leonard Bickman, and Julia Brannen. Thousand Oaks, CA: Sage.

Ellis, Carolyn. 1995. "Emotional and Ethical Quagmires in Returning to the Field." *Journal of Contemporary Ethnography* 24:68–98.

Ember, Carol R. and Melvin Ember. 2011. *A Basic Guide to Cross-Cultural Research. New Haven, CT: Human Relations Area Files, Yale University.* Retrieved August 31, 2011, from www.yale.edu/hraf/guides.htm

Emmel, Nick and Andrew Clark. 2011. "Learning to Use Visual Methodologies in Our Research: A Dialogue Between Two Researchers." *Forum: Qualitative Social Research* 12(1): Article 36, http://nbn-resolving.de/urn:nbn:de:0114-fqs1101360

Emerson, Robert M. (Ed.). 1983. *Contemporary Field Research.* Prospect Heights, IL: Waveland.

Emerson, Robert M., Rachel I. Fretz, and Linda L. Shaw. 1995. *Writing Ethnographic Fieldnotes.* Chicago: University of Chicago Press.

Emmison, Michael, Philip Smith, and Margery Mayall. 2012. *Researching the Visual,* 2nd ed. Thousand Oaks, CA: Sage.

Ennett, Susan T., Karl E. Bauman, Andrea Hussong, Robert Faris, Vangie A. Foshee, and Li Cai. 2006. "The Peer Context of Adolescent Substance Use: Findings From Social Network Analysis." *Journal of Research on Adolescence* 16:159–186.

Ennett, Susan T., Nancy S. Tobler, Christopher L. Ringwalt, and Robert L. Flewelling. 1994.

"How Effective Is Drug Abuse Resistance Education? A Meta-Analysis of Project DARE Outcome Evaluations." *American Journal of Public Health* 84(9):1394–1401.

Erikson, Kai T. 1966. *Wayward Puritans: A Study in the Sociology of Deviance.* New York: Wiley.

Erikson, Kai T. 1967. "A Comment on Disguised Observation in Sociology." *Social Problems* 12: 366–373.

Ettelt, Stefanie, Nicholas Mays, and Ellen Nolte. 2013. "Policy–Research Linkage: What We Have Learned From Providing a Rapid Response Facility for International Healthcare Comparisons to the Department of Health in England." *Evidence & Policy* 9:245–254.

Eurostat. 2003. *ECHP UDB Manual: European Community Household Panel Longitudinal Users' Database.* Brussels, Belgium: European Commission.

Exum, M. Lyn. 2002. "The Application and Robustness of the Rational Choice Perspective in the Study of Intoxicated and Angry Intentions to Aggress." *Criminology* 40:933–966.

Exum, M. Lyn, Jennifer L. Hartman, Paul C. Friday, and Vivian B. Lord. 2010. "Policing Domestic Violence in the Post-SARP Era: The Impact of a Domestic Violence Police Unit." *Crime & Delinquency* 20(10):1–34.

Facebook. 2013. Retrieved December 26, 2013, from http://newsroom.fb.com/Key-Facts

Fallon, Kathleen M., Liam Swiss, and Jocelyn Viterna. 2012. "Resolving the Democracy Paradox: Democratization and Women's Legislative Representation in Developing Nations, 1975 to 2009." *American Sociological Review* 77(3):380–408.

Fears, Darryl. 2002. "For Latinos in U.S., Race Not Just Black or White." *The Boston Globe,* December 30, p. A3.

Fedyuk, Olena. 2012. "Images of Transnational Motherhood: The Role of Photographs in Measuring Time and Maintaining Connections Between Ukraine and Italy." *Journal of Ethnic and Migration Studies* 38:279–300.

Fenno, Richard F. Jr. 1978. *Home Style: House Members in Their Districts.* Boston: Little, Brown.

Fenton, Steve. 1996. "Counting Ethnicity: Social Groups and Official Categories." Pp. 143–165 in *Interpreting Official Statistics,* edited by Ruth Levitas and Will Guy. New York: Routledge.

Ferguson, Kristin M., Kimberly Bender, Sanna J. Thompson, Elaine M. Maccio, and David Pollio. 2012. "Employment Status and Income Generation Among Homeless Young Adults: Results From a Five-City, Mixed-Methods Study." *Youth & Society* 44:385–407.

Fergusson, Ross. 2013. "Risk, Responsibilities and Rights: Reassessing the 'Economic Causes of Crime' Thesis in a Recession." *Youth Justice* 13(1):31–56.

File, Thom. 2013a. "Computer and Internet Use in the United States." Pp. 20–569 in *Current Population Survey Reports.* Washington, DC: U.S. Census Bureau

File, Thom. 2013b. "The Diversifying Electorate—Voting Rates by Race and Hispanic Origin in 2012 (and Other Recent Elections)." *Population Characteristics, Current Population Survey.* Washington, DC: U.S. Census Bureau.

Fink, Arlene. 2005. *Conducting Research Literature Reviews: From the Internet to Paper,* 2nd ed. Thousand Oaks, CA: Sage.

Fischer, Claude. 2009. "The 2004 GSS Finding of Shrunken Social Networks: An Artifact?" *American Sociological Review* 74(4):657–669.

Fischer, Constance T. and Frederick J. Wertz. 2002. "Empirical Phenomenological Analyses of Being Criminally Victimized." Pp. 275–304 in *The Qualitative Researcher's Companion,* edited by A. Michael Huberman and Matthew B. Miles. Thousand Oaks, CA: Sage.

Fisher, Celia B. and Andrea E. Anushko. 2008. "Research Ethics in Social Science." Pp. 94–109 in *The SAGE Handbook of Social Research Methods,* edited by Pertti Alasuutari, Leonard Bickman, and Julia Brannen. Thousand Oaks, CA: Sage.

Forero, Juan. 2000a. "Census Takers Say Supervisors Fostered Filing of False Data." *The New York Times,* July 28, p. A21.

Forero, Juan. 2000b. "Census Takers Top '90 Efforts in New York City, With More to Go." *The New York Times,* June 12, p. A29.

Fowler, Floyd J. 1988. *Survey Research Methods,* Rev. ed. Newbury Park, CA: Sage.

Fowler, Floyd J. 1995. *Improving Survey Questions: Design and Evaluation.* Thousand Oaks, CA: Sage.

Fox, Nick and Chris Roberts. 1999. "GPs in Cyberspace: The Sociology of a 'Virtual Community.'" *The Sociological Review* 47:643–669.

Frank, David John, Ann Hironaka, and Evan Schofer. 2000. "The Nation-State and the Natural Environment Over the Twentieth Century." *American Sociological Review* 65:96–116.

Frankfort-Nachmias, Chava and Anna Leon-Guerrero. 2006. *Social Statistics for a Diverse Society,* 4th ed. Thousand Oaks, CA: Sage.

Franklin, Mark N. 1996. "Electoral Participation." Pp. 216–235 in *Comparing Democracies: Elections and Voting in Global Perspective,* edited by Lawrence LeDuc, Richard G. Niemi, and Pippa Norris. Thousand Oaks, CA: Sage.

Freshman, Audrey. 2012. "Financial Disaster as a Risk Factor for Posttraumatic Stress Disorder: Internet Survey of Trauma in Victims of the Madoff Ponzi Scheme." *Health & Social Work* 37:39–48.

Frohmann, Lisa. 2005. "The Framing Safety Project: Photographs and Narratives by Battered Women." *Violence Against Women* 11:1396–1419.

Frone, Michael R. 2008. "Are Work Stressors Related to Employee Substance Use? The Importance of Temporal Context in Assessments of Alcohol and Illicit Drug Use." *Journal of Applied Psychology* 93:199–206.

Gaiser, Ted J. and Anthony E. Schreiner. 2009. *A Guide to Conducting Online Research.* Thousand Oaks, CA: Sage.

Gall, Carlotta. 2003. "Armed With Pencils, Army of Census Workers Fans Out Into Afghan Outback." *The New York Times,* July 15, p. A4.

Gallup. 2011. *Election Polls—Accuracy Record in Presidential Elections.* Retrieved March 17, 2011, from http://www.gallup.com/poll/9442/Election-Polls-Accuracy-Record-Presidential-Elections.aspx?version=print

Gallup. 2012. *Gender Gap in 2012 Vote Is Largest in Gallup's History.* Retrieved June 4, 2014, from www.gallup.com/poll/158588/gender-gap-2012-vote-largest-gallup-history.aspx

Gans, Curtis. 2008. "2008 Primary Turnout Falls Just Short of Record Nationally, Breaks Records in Most States." *AU News,* May 19. Washington, DC: Center for the Study of the American Electorate, American University. Retrieved June 2, 2008, from www.american.edu/media

Garfinkel, Harold. 1967. *Studies in Ethnomethodology.* Englewood Cliffs, NJ: Prentice Hall.

Gartrell, C. David and John W. Gartrell. 2002. "Positivism in Sociological Research: USA and UK (1966–1990)." *British Journal of Sociology* 53:639–657.

Geertz, Clifford. 1973. "Thick Description: Toward an Interpretive Theory of Culture." Pp. 3–30 in *The Interpretation of Cultures,* edited by Clifford Geertz. New York: Basic Books.

Gerth, Matthias A. and Gabriele Siegert. 2012. "Patterns of Consistence and Constriction: How News Media Frame the Coverage of Direct Democratic Campaigns." *American Behavioral Scientist* 56:279–299.

"'Get Tough' Youth Programs Are Ineffective, Panel Says." 2004. *The New York Times,* October 17, p. 25.

Gilchrist, Valerie J. and Robert L. Williams. 1999. "Key Informant Interviews." Pp. 71–88 in *Doing Qualitative Research,* 2nd ed., edited by Benjamin F. Crabtree and William L. Miller. Thousand Oaks, CA: Sage.

Gill, Hannah E. 2004. "Finding a Middle Ground Between Extremes: Notes on Researching Transnational Crime and Violence." *Anthropology Matters Journal* 6:1–9.

Gill, Richard T., Nathan Glazer, and Stephan A. Thernstrom. 1992. *Our Changing Population.* Englewood Cliffs, NJ: Prentice Hall.

Gilligan, Carol. 1988. "Adolescent Development Reconsidered." Pp. vii–xxxix in *Mapping the Moral Domain,* edited by Carol Gilligan, Janie Victoria Ward, and Jill McLean Taylor. Cambridge, MA: Harvard University Press.

Ginsberg, Jeremy, Matthew H. Mohebbi, Rajan S. Patel, Lynnette Brammer, Mark S. Smolinski, and Larry Brilliant. 2009. "Detecting Influenza Epidemics Using Search Engine Query Data." *Nature* 457(February 19):1012–1015.

Glaser, Barney G. and Anselm L. Strauss. 1967. *The Discovery of Grounded Theory: Strategies for Qualitative Research.* London: Weidenfeld and Nicholson.

Glover, Judith. 1996. "Epistemological and Methodological Considerations in Secondary Analysis." Pp. 28–38 in *Cross-National Research Methods in the Social Sciences,* edited by Linda Hantrais and Steen Mangen. New York: Pinter.

Glueck, Sheldon and Eleanor Glueck. 1950. *Unraveling Juvenile Delinquency.* New York: Commonwealth Fund.

Gobo, Giampietro. 2008. "Re-Conceptualizing Generalization: Old Issues in a New Frame." Pp. 193–213 in *The SAGE Handbook of Social Research Methods,* edited by Pertti Alasuutari, Leonard Bickman, and Julia Brannen. Thousand Oaks, CA: Sage.

Goertz, Gary. 2006. *Social Science Concepts: A User's Guide.* Princeton, NJ: Princeton University Press.

Goffman, Erving. 1961. *Asylums: Essays on the Social Situation of Mental Patients and Other Inmates.* Garden City, NY: Doubleday.

Goffman, Erving. 1963. *Stigma: Notes on the Management of Spoiled Identity.* Englewood, NJ: Prentice Hall/Spectrum.

Goffman, Erving. 1979. *Gender Advertisements.* London: Macmillan.

Goldfinger, Stephen M. and Russell K. Schutt. 1996. "Comparison of Clinicians' Housing Recommendations and Preferences of Homeless Mentally Ill Persons." *Psychiatric Services,* 47:413–415.

Goldfinger, Stephen M., Russell K. Schutt, Larry J. Seidman, Winston M. Turner, Walter E. Penk, and George S. Tolomiczenko. 1996. "Self-Report and Observer Measures of Substance Abuse Among Homeless Mentally Ill Persons in the Cross-Section and Over Time." *The Journal of Nervous and Mental Disease* 184(11):667–672.

Goleman, Daniel. 1993a. "Placebo Effect Is Shown to Be Twice as Powerful as Expected." *The New York Times,* August 17, p. C3.

Goleman, Daniel. 1993b. "Pollsters Enlist Psychologists in Quest for Unbiased Results." *The New York Times,* September 7, pp. C1, C11.

Goode, Erich. 2002. "Sexual Involvement and Social Research in a Fat Civil Rights Organization." *Qualitative Sociology* 25:501–534.

Goodnough, Abby. 2010. "A Wave of Addiction and Crime, With the Medicine Cabinet to Blame." *The New York Times,* September 22. Retrieved March 17, 2011, from www.nytimes.com

Gordon, Raymond. 1992. *Basic Interviewing Skills.* Itasca, IL: Peacock.

Graduate Program in Applied Sociology. 1990. *Handbook for Thesis Writers.* Boston: University of Massachusetts.

Grady, John. 1996. "The Scope of Visual Sociology." *Visual Sociology* 11:10–24.

Grant, Bridget F., Deborah A. Dawson, Frederick S. Stinson, S. Patricia Chou, Mary C. Dufour, and Roger P. Pickering. 2004. "The 12-Month Prevalence and Trends in DSM-IV Alcohol Abuse and Dependence: United States, 1991–1992 and 2001–2002." *Drug and Alcohol Dependence* 74:223–234.

Greenberg, David, Mark Shroder, and Mathew Onstott. 1999. *The Digest of Social Experiments.* 2nd ed. Washington, DC: Urban Institute Press.

Grey, Robert J. Jr. 2005. "Jury Service: It's a Privilege." Retrieved June 18, 2005, from American Bar Association website, www.abanet.org/media/releases/opedjuror2.html

Grieco, Elizabeth M., Yesenia D. Acosta, G. Patricia de la Cruz, Christine Gambino, Thomas Gryn, Luke J. Larsen, Edward N. Trevelyan, and Nathan P. Walters. 2012. *The Foreign-Born Population in the United States: 2010.* Washington, DC: U.S. Census Bureau.

Griffin, Larry J. 1992. "Temporality, Events, and Explanation in Historical Sociology: An Introduction." *Sociological Methods & Research* 20:403–427.

Griffin, Larry J. 1993. "Narrative, Event-Structure Analysis, and Causal Interpretation in Historical Sociology." *American Journal of Sociology* 98(March):1094–1133.

Grissom, Brandi. 2011. "Proposals Could Make It Harder to Leave Prison." *The New York Times,* March 12. Retrieved March 17, 2011, from www.nytimes.com

Groves, Robert M. 1989. *Survey Errors and Survey Costs.* New York: Wiley.

Groves, Robert M. and Mick P. Couper. 1998. *Nonresponse in Household Interview Surveys.* New York: Wiley.

Groves, Robert M. and Robert L. Kahn. 1979. *Surveys by Telephone: A National Comparison With Personal Interviews.* New York: Academic Press. As adapted in Delbert C. Miller, 1991. *Handbook of Research Design and Social Measurement,* 5th ed. Newbury Park, CA: Sage.

Groves, Robert M., Eleanor Singer, and Amy Corning. 2000. "Leverage-Salience Theory of Survey Participation: Description and an Illustration." *Public Opinion Quarterly* 64:299–308.

Gruenewald, Paul J., Andrew J. Treno, Gail Taff, and Michael Klitzner. 1997. *Measuring Community Indicators: A Systems Approach to Drug and Alcohol Problems.* Thousand Oaks, CA: Sage.

Guba, Egon G. and Yvonna S. Lincoln. 1989. *Fourth Generation Evaluation.* Newbury Park, CA: Sage.

Guba, Egon G. and Yvonna S. Lincoln. 1994. "Competing Paradigms in Qualitative Research." Pp. 105–117 in *Handbook of Qualitative Research,* edited by Norman K. Denzin and Yvonna S. Lincoln. Thousand Oaks, CA: Sage.

Gubrium, Jaber F. and James A. Holstein. 1997. *The New Language of Qualitative Method.* New York: Oxford University Press.

Gubrium, Jaber F. and James A. Holstein. 2000. "Analyzing Interpretive Practice." Pp. 487–508 in *The Handbook of Qualitative Research,* 2nd ed., edited by Norman Denzin and Yvonna S. Lincoln. Thousand Oaks, CA: Sage.

Guterbock, Thomas M. 2008. *Strategies and Standards for Reaching Respondents in an Age of New Technology.* Presentation to the Harvard Program on Survey Research Spring Conference, New Technologies and Survey Research. Cambridge, MA: Institute of Quantitative Social Science, Harvard University, May 9.

Hacker, Karen. 2013. *Community-Based Participatory Research.* Thousand Oaks, CA: Sage.

Hacker, Karen, Jessica Collins, Leni Gross-Young, Stephanie Almeida, and Noreen Burke. 2008. "Coping With Youth Suicide and Overdose: One Community's Efforts to Investigate, Intervene, and Prevent Suicide Contagion." *Crisis* 29:86–95.

Hadaway, C. Kirk, Penny Long Marler, and Mark Chaves. 1993. "What the Polls Don't Show: A Closer Look at U.S. Church Attendance." *American Sociological Review* 58(6): 741–752.

Hafner, Katie. 2004. "For Some, the Blogging Never Stops." *The New York Times,* May 27, pp. E1, E7.

Hage, Jerald and Barbara Foley Meeker. 1988. *Social Causality.* Boston: Unwin Hyman.

Hakim, Catherine. 1982. *Secondary Analysis in Social Research: A Guide to Data Sources and Methods With Examples.* London: George Allen & Unwin.

Hakimzadeh, Shirin and D'Vera Cohn. 2007. *English Usage Among Hispanics in the United States.* Washington, DC: Pew Hispanic Center. Retrieved May 24, 2008, from http://pewhispanic.org/files/reports/82 .pdf

Halcón, Linda L. and Alan R. Lifson. 2004. "Prevalence and Predictors of Sexual Risks Among Homeless Youth." *Journal of Youth and Adolescence* 33:71–80.

Hallinan, Maureen T. 1997. "The Sociological Study of Social Change." *American Sociological Review* 62:1–11.

Hammersley, Martyn. 2008. "Assessing Validity in Social Research." Pp. 42–53 in *The SAGE Handbook of Social Research Methods,* edited by Pertti Alasuutari, Leonard Bickman, and Julia Brannen. Thousand Oaks, CA: Sage.

Hammersley, Martyn and Anna Traianou. 2012. *Ethics in Qualitative Research: Controversies and Contexts.* Thousand Oaks, CA: Sage.

Hampton, Keith N. 2003. "Grieving for a Lost Network: Collective Action in a Wired Suburb." *The Information Society* 19:417–428.

Hampton, Keith N., Lauren Sessions Goulet, Eun Ja Her, and Lee Rainie. 2009. "Social Isolation and New Technology: How the Internet and Mobile Phones Impact Americans' Social Networks.' Washington, DC: Pew Internet & American Life Project. Retrieved December 27, 2013, from http://www.pewinternet.org/2009/11/04/social-isolation-and-new-technology/

Hampton, Keith N., Lauren Sessions Goulet, Lee Rainie, and Kristen Purcell. 2011. "Social Networking Sites and Our Lives: How People's Trust, Personal Relationships, and Civic and Political Involvement Are Connected to Their Use of Social Networking Sites and Other Technologies." Washington, DC: Pew Internet & American Life Project. Retrieved December 27, 2013, from http://pewinternet.org/Reports/2011/Technology-and-social-networks.aspx

Hampton, Keith N. and Neeti Gupta. 2008. "Community and Social Interaction in the Wireless City: Wi-Fi Use in Public and Semi-Public Spaces." *New Media & Society* 10(6):831–850.

Hampton, Keith N. and Barry Wellman. 1999. "Netville On-line and Off-Line: Observing and Surveying a Wired Suburb." *American Behavioral Scientist* 43:475–492.

Hampton, Keith N. and Barry Wellman. 2000. "Examining Community in the Digital Neighborhood: Early Results From Canada's Wired Suburb." Pp. 475–492 in *Digital Cities: Technologies, Experiences, and Future Perspectives,* edited by Toru Ishida and Katherine Isbister. Berlin, Germany: Springer-Verlag.

Hampton, Keith N. and Barry Wellman. 2001. "Long Distance Community in the Network Society." *American Behavioral Scientist* 45:476–495.

Haney, C., C. Banks, and Philip G. Zimbardo. 1973. "Interpersonal Dynamics in a Simulated Prison." *International Journal of Criminology and Penology* 1:69–97.

Hantrais, Linda and Steen Mangen. 1996. "Method and Management of Cross-National Social Research." Pp. 1–12 in *Cross-National Research Methods in the Social Sciences,* edited by Linda Hantrais and Steen Mangen. New York: Pinter.

Hard, Stephen F., James M. Conway, and Antonia C. Moran. 2006. "Faculty and College Student Beliefs About the Frequency of Student Academic Misconduct." *The Journal of Higher Education* 77:1058–1080.

Harding, David J. 2007. "Cultural Context, Sexual Behavior, and Romantic Relationships in Disadvantaged Neighborhoods." *American Sociological Review* 72:341–364.

Harris, David R. and Jeremiah Joseph Sim. 2002. "Who Is Multiracial? Assessing the Complexity of Lived Race." *American Sociological Review* 67:614–627.

Hart, Chris. 1998. *Doing a Literature Review: Releasing the Social Science Research Imagination.* London: Sage.

Hasin, Deborah S., Frederick S. Stinson, Elizabeth Ogburn, and Bridget F. Grant. 2007. "Prevalence, Correlates, Disability, and Comorbidity of *DSM-IV* Alcohol Abuse and Dependence in the United States: Results From the National Epidemiologic Survey on Alcohol and Related Conditions." *Archives of General Psychiatry* 64:830–842.

Hawkins, Donald N., Paul R. Amato, and Valarie King. 2007. "Nonresident Father Involvement and Adolescent Well-Being: Father Effects or Child Effects?" *American Sociological Review* 72: 990–1010.

Heath, Christian and Paul Luff. 2008. "Video and the Analysis of Work and Interaction." Pp. 493–505 in *The SAGE Handbook of Social Research Methods,* edited by Pertti Alasuutari, Leonard Bickman, and Julia Brannen. Thousand Oaks, CA: Sage.

Heaton, Janet. 2008. "Secondary Analysis of Qualitative Data." Pp. 506–535 in *The SAGE Handbook of Social Research Methods,* edited by Pertti Alasuutari, Leonard Bickman, and Julia Brannen. Thousand Oaks, CA: Sage.

Heckathorn, Douglas D. 1997. "Respondent-Driven Sampling: A New Approach to the Study of Hidden Populations." *Social Problems* 44:174–199.

Heckathorn, Douglas D. 2002. "Respondent-Driven Sampling II: Deriving Valid

Population Estimates From Chain-Referral Samples of Hidden Populations." *Social Problems* 49:11–34.

Heckman, James, Neil Hohmann, and Jeffrey Smith. 2000. "Substitution and Dropout Bias in Social Experiments: A Study of an Influential Social Experiment." *The Quarterly Journal of Economics* 115:651–694.

Hedström, Peter and Richard Swedberg (Eds.). 1998. *Social Mechanisms: An Analytical Approach to Social Theory*. Cambridge: Cambridge University Press.

Heise, David R. 2010. *Surveying Cultures: Discovering Shared Conceptions and Sentiments*. Hoboken, NJ: Wiley.

Herek, Gregory. 1995. "Developing a Theoretical Framework and Rationale for a Research Proposal." Pp. 85–91 in *How to Write a Successful Research Grant Application: A Guide for Social and Behavioral Scientists*, edited by Willo Pequegnat and Ellen Stover. New York: Plenum Press.

Heritage, John. n.d. *Conversation Analysis. Chapter in E-Source, Social and Behavioral Sciences Research*. Washington, DC: Office of Behavioral and Social Sciences Research, National Institutes of Health. Retrieved May 13, 2014, from www.esourceresearch.org/eSourceBook/ConversationAnalysis/10TranscriptionSymbols/tabid/531/Default.aspx

Hesse-Biber, Sharlene. 1989. "Eating Problems and Disorders in a College Population: Are College Women's Eating Problems a New Phenomenon?" *Sex Roles* 20:71–89.

Hesse-Biber, Sharlene Nagy and Patricia Lina Leavy. 2007. *Feminist Research Practice: A Primer*. Thousand Oaks, CA: Sage.

Hicks, Lorna. 2013. *The Regulations—SBE*. Miami, FL: Collaborative Institutional Training Initiative at the University of Miami. Retrieved December 31, 2013, from https://www.citiprogram.org/

The Hippocratic Oath. n.d. Charlottesville: University of Virginia, Historica Medicina. Retrieved May 10, 2014, from http://exhibits.hsl.virginia.edu/antiqua/hippocrates/

Hirsch, Kathleen. 1989. *Songs From the Alley*. New York: Doubleday.

Hirschel, David, Eve Buzawa, April Pattavina, and Don Faggiani. 2008. "Domestic Violence and Mandatory Arrest Laws: To What Extent Do They Influence Police Arrest Decisions?" *Journal of Criminal Law & Criminology* 98(1):255–298.

Ho, D. Y. F. 1996. "Filial Piety and Its Psychological Consequences." Pp. 155–165 in *Handbook of Chinese Psychology*, edited by M. H. Bond. Hong Kong: Oxford University Press.

Hoffman, Stephen. 2014. "Zero Benefit: Estimating the Effect of Zero Tolerance Discipline Polices on Racial Disparities in School Discipline." *Educational Policy* 28(1):69–95.

Holbrook, Allyson L., Melanie C. Green, and Jon A. Krosnick. 2003. "Telephone Versus Face-to-Face Interviewing of National Probability Samples With Long Questionnaires: Comparisons of Respondent Satisficing and Social Desirability Response Bias." *Public Opinion Quarterly* 60:58–88.

Hollingsworth, T. H. 1972. "The Importance of the Quality of Data in Historical Demography." Pp. 71–86 in *Population and Social Change*, edited by D. V. Glass and Roger Revelle. London: Edward Arnold.

Holmes, Steven A. 2000. "Stronger Response by Minorities Helps Improve Census Reply Rate." *The New York Times*, May 4, pp. A1, A22.

Holmes, Steven A. 2001a. "Census Officials Ponder Adjustments Crucial to Redistricting." *The New York Times*, February 12, p. A17.

Holmes, Steven A. 2001b. "The Confusion Over Who We Are." *The New York Times*, June 3, p. WK 1.

Horney, Julie, D. Wayne Osgood, and Ineke Haen Marshall. 1995. "Criminal Careers in the Short-Term: Intra-Individual Variability in Crime and Its Relation to Local Life Circumstances." *American Sociological Review* 60:655–673.

Horowitz, Carol R., Mimsie Robinson, and Sarena Seifer. 2009. "Community-Based Participatory Research From the Margin to the Mainstream: Are Researchers Prepared?" *Circulation* 119:2633–2642.

Houtzager, Peter P. and Arnab K. Acharya. 2011. "Associations, Active Citizenship, and the Quality of Democracy in Brazil and Mexico." *Theory and Society* 40:1–36.

Howell, James C. 2003. *Preventing and Reducing Juvenile Delinquency: A Comprehensive Framework*. Thousand Oaks, CA: Sage.

Hoyle, Carolyn and Andrew Sanders. 2000. "Police Response to Domestic Violence: From Victim Choice to Victim Empowerment." *British Journal of Criminology* 40:14–26.

Hrobjartsson, Asbjorn and Peter C. Gotzsche. 2001. "Is the Placebo Powerless? An Analysis of Clinical Trials Comparing Placebo With No Treatment." *New England Journal of Medicine* 344:1594–1602.

Hu, Winnie. 2014. "Severe Cold Moves New York's Homeless to Seek Help." *The New York Times*, January 28, p. A19. Retrieved May 18, 2014, from www.nytimes.com

Huberman, A. Michael and Matthew B. Miles. 1994. "Data Management and Analysis Methods." Pp. 428–444 in *Handbook of Qualitative Research*, edited by Norman K. Denzin and Yvonna S. Lincoln. Thousand Oaks, CA: Sage.

Huff, Darrell. 1954. *How to Lie With Statistics*. New York: Norton.

Humes, Karen R., Nicholas A. Jones, and Roberto R. Ramirez. 2011. *Overview of Race and Hispanic Origin: 2010*. C2010BR-02. Washington, DC: U.S. Census Bureau.

Humphrey, Nicholas. 1992. *A History of the Mind: Evolution and the Birth of Consciousness*. New York: Simon & Schuster.

Humphreys, Laud. 1970. *Tearoom Trade: Impersonal Sex in Public Places*. Chicago: Aldine de Gruyter.

Humphries, Courtney. 2011. "Deeply Conflicted: How Can We Insulate Ourselves From Conflicts of Interest? The Most Popular Solution—Disclosing Them—Turns Out Not to Help." *Boston Globe*, May 15, pp. K1, K3.

Hunt, Morton. 1985. *Profiles of Social Research: The Scientific Study of Human Interactions*. New York: Russell Sage Foundation.

Huston, Patricia and C. David Naylor. 1996. "Health Services Research: Reporting on Studies Using Secondary Data Sources." *Canadian Medical Association Journal* 155:1697–1702.

Hyvärinen, Matti. 2008. "Analyzing Narratives and Story-Telling." Pp. 447–460 in *The SAGE Handbook of Social Research Methods*, edited by Pertti Alasuutari, Leonard Bickman, and Julia Brannen. Thousand Oaks, CA: Sage.

Iezzoni, Lisa I. 1997. "How Much Are We Willing to Pay for Information About Quality of Care?" *Annals of Internal Medicine* 126:391–393.

Innstrand, Siw Tone, Geir Arild Espries, and Reidar Mykletun. 2004. "Job Stress, Burnout and Job Satisfaction: An Intervention Study of Staff Working With People With Intellectual Disabilities." *Journal of Applied Research in Intellectual Disabilities* 17:119–126.

Internet World Statistics. 2012. Retrieved December 26, 2013, from http://www.internetworldstats.com/stats.htm

Irvine, Leslie. 1998. "Organizational Ethics and Fieldwork Realities: Negotiating Ethical Boundaries in Codependents Anonymous." Pp. 167–183 in *Doing Ethnographic Research: Fieldwork Settings*. Thousand Oaks, CA: Sage.

Jalbert, Sarah Kuck, William Rhodes, Christopher Flygare, and Michael Kane. 2010. "Testing Probation Outcomes in an Evidence-Based Practice Setting: Reduced Caseload Size and Intensive Supervision Effectiveness." *Journal of Offender Rehabilitation*, 49:233–253

James, Nalita and Hugh Busher. 2009. *Online Interviewing*. Thousand Oaks, CA: Sage.

Jarvis, Helen. 1997. "Housing, Labour Markets and Household Structure: Questioning the Role of Secondary Data Analysis in Sustaining the Polarization Debate." *Regional Studies* 31:521–531.

Jervis, Robert. 1996. "Counterfactuals, Causation, and Complexity." Pp. 309–316 in *Counterfactual Thought Experiments in World Politics: Logical, Methodological, and Psychological Perspectives,* edited by Philip E. Tetlock and Aaron Belkin. Princeton, NJ: Princeton University Press.

Jesnadum, Anick. 2000. "Researchers Fear Privacy Breaches With Online Research." *Digital Mass.* Retrieved September 15, 2000, from www.digitalmass.com/news/daily/09/15/researchers.html

Johnson, David and Merry Bullock. 2009. "The Ethics of Data Archiving: Issues From Four Perspectives." Pp. 214–228 in *The Handbook of Social Research Ethics,* edited by Donna M. Mertens and Pauline E. Ginsberg. Thousand Oaks, CA: Sage.

Jones, Jeffrey M. 2012. "Gender Gap in 2012 Vote Is Largest in Gallup's History." November 9. Retrieved from www.gallup.com/poll/158588/gender-gap-2012-vote-largest-gallup-history.aspx

Jones, Stephen R. G. 1992. "Was There a Hawthorne Effect?" *American Journal of Sociology* 98:451–468.

Kagay, Michael R. with Janet Elder. 1992. "Numbers Are No Problem for Pollsters. Words Are." *The New York Times,* October 9, p. E5.

Kale-Lostuvali, Elif. 2007. "Negotiating State Provision: State-Citizen Encounters in the Aftermath of the İzmit Earthquake." *The Sociological Quarterly* 48:745–767.

Kaplan, Fred. 2002. "NY Continues to See Plunge in Number of Felonies." *The Boston Globe,* April 15, p. A3.

Kato, Yuki, Catarina Passidomo, and Daina Harvey. 2013. "Political Gardening in Post-Disaster City: Lessons From New Orleans." *Urban Studies* 51:1833–1849.

Kaufman, Sharon R. 1986. *The Ageless Self: Sources of Meaning in Late Life.* Madison: University of Wisconsin Press.

Keeter, Scott. 2008. *Survey Research and Cell Phones: Is There a Problem?* Presentation to the Harvard Program on Survey Research Spring Conference, New Technologies and Survey Research. Cambridge, MA: Institute of Quantitative Social Science, Harvard University, May 9.

Keeter, Scott, Michael Dimock, and Leah Christian. 2008. "Cell Phones and the 2008 Vote: An Update." Pew Center for the People & the Press, September 23. Retrieved from www.pewresearch.org/2008/09/23/cell-phones-and-the-2008-vote-an-update-2/

Kemmis, Stephen and Robin McTaggart. 2005. "Participatory Action Research: Communicative Action and the Public Sphere." Pp. 559–603 in *The SAGE Handbook of Qualitative Research,* 3rd ed., edited by Norman K. Denzin and Yvonna S. Lincoln. Thousand Oaks, CA: Sage.

Kennedy, David M., Anthony M. Piehl and Anne A. Braga. 1996. "Youth Violence in Boston: Gun Markets, Serious Youth Offenders, and a Use-Reduction Strategy." *Law and Contemporary Problems* 59:147–196.

Kenney, Charles. 1987. "They've Got Your Number." *The Boston Globe Magazine,* August 30, pp. 12, 46–56, 60.

Kershaw, David and Jerilyn Fair. 1976. *The New Jersey Income-Maintenance Experiment,* vol. 1. New York: Academic Press.

Kershaw, Sarah. 2000. "In a Black Community, Mistrust of Government Hinders Census." *The New York Times,* May 16, p. A20.

Kifner, John. 1994. "Pollster Finds Error on Holocaust Doubts." *The New York Times,* May 20, p. A12.

King, Gary, Robert O. Keohane, and Sidney Verba. 1994. *Scientific Inference in Qualitative Research.* Princeton, NJ: Princeton University Press.

King, Miriam L. and Diana L. Magnuson. 1995. "Perspectives on Historical U.S. Census Undercounts." *Social Science History* 19:455–466.

King, Nigel and Christine Horrocks. 2010. *Interviews in Qualitative Research.* Thousand Oaks, CA: Sage.

Kiser, Edgar and Michael Hechter. 1991. "The Role of General Theory in Comparative-Historical Sociology." *American Journal of Sociology* 97:1–30.

Kitchener, Karen Strohm and Richard F. Kitchener. 2009. "Social Science Research Ethics: Historical and Philosophical Issues." Pp. 5–22 in *The Handbook of Social Research Ethics,* edited by Donna M. Mertens and Pauline E. Ginsberg. Thousand Oaks, CA: Sage.

Klein, Malcolm W. 1971. *Street Gangs and Street Workers.* Englewood Cliffs, NJ: Prentice Hall.

Klinenberg, Eric. 2002. *Heat Wave: A Social Autopsy of Disaster in Chicago.* Chicago: University of Chicago Press.

Klinenberg, Eric. 2012. "One's a Crowd." *The New York Times,* February 5, p. SR4.

Knight, John R., Henry Wechsler, Meichun Kuo, Mark Seibring, E. R. Weitzman, and M. A. Schuckit. 2002. "Alcohol Abuse and Dependence Among U.S. College Students." *Journal of Studies on Alcohol* 63:263–270.

Koegel, Paul. 1987. *Ethnographic Perspectives on Homeless and Homeless Mentally Ill Women.* Washington, DC: Alcohol, Drug Abuse, and Mental Health Administration,

Public Health Service, U.S. Department of Health and Human Services.

Kohn, Alfie. 2008. "Who's Cheating Whom?" *The Education Digest* 73:4–11.

Kohn, Melvin L. 1987. "Cross-National Research as an Analytic Strategy." *American Sociological Review* 52:713–731.

Kohut, Andrew. 1988. "Polling: Does More Information Lead to Better Understanding?" *The Boston Globe,* November 7, p. 25.

Kohut, Andrew. 2008. "Getting It Wrong." *The New York Times,* January 10, p. A27.

Kohut, Andrew, Scott Keeter, Carroll Doherty, Michael Dimock, and Leah Christian. 2012. *Assessing the Representativeness of Public Opinion Surveys.* Washington, DC: Pew Research Center. Retrieved May 25, 2014, from www.people-press.org/2012/05/15/assessing-the-representativeness-of-public-opinion-surveys

Kolata, Gina. 2013. "Decades Later, Condemnation for a Skid Row Cancer Study." *The New York Times,* October 18, p. A1.

Kolbert, Elizabeth. 1992. "Test-Marketing a President." *The New York Times Magazine,* August 30, pp. 18–21, 60, 68, 72.

Kollock, Peter and Marc A. Smith. 1999. "Communities in Cyberspace." Pp. 3–25 in *Communities in Cyberspace,* edited by Peter Kollock and Marc A. Smith. New York: Routledge.

Koppel, Ross. 2008. "The Utility of Sociology." *Sociological Viewpoints* (Fall): 5–16.

Korn, James H. 1997. *Illusions of Reality: A History of Deception in Social Psychology.* Albany: State University of New York Press.

Kotkin, Stephen. 2002. "A World War Among Professors." *The New York Times,* September 7, Arts pp. 1, 17.

Kozinets, Robert V. 2010. *Netnography: Doing Ethnographic Research Online.* Thousand Oaks, CA: Sage.

Kraemer, Helena Chmura and Sue Thiemann. 1987. *How Many Subjects? Statistical Power Analysis in Research.* Newbury Park, CA: Sage.

Kramer, Adam D. I., Jamie E. Guillory, and Jeffrey T. Hancock. 2014. "Experimental Evidence of Massive-Scale Emotional Contagion Through Social Networks." *Proceedings of the National Academy of Sciences (PNAS),* 111:8788–8790.

Kraut, Robert, Sara Kiesler, Bonka Boneva, Jonathon Cummings, Vicki Helgeson, and Anne Crawford. 2002. "Internet Paradox Revisited." *Journal of Social Issues* 58:49–74.

Kreuter, Frauke, Stanley Presser, and Roger Tourangeau. 2008. "Social Desirability Bias in CATI, IVR, and Web Surveys: The Effects of Mode and Question Sensitivity." *Public Opinion Quarterly* 72:847–865.

Krosnick, Jon A. 1999. "Survey Research." *Annual Review of Psychology* 50:537–567.

Krosnick, Jon A. 2006. *The Handbook of Questionnaire Design: Insights From Social and Cognitive Psychology.* Eric M. Mindich Encounters With Authors Symposium at Institute for Quantitative Social Science, Harvard University, Cambridge MA, January 19–21.

Krueger, Richard A. and Mary Anne Casey. 2009. *Focus Groups: A Practical Guide for Applied Research,* 4th ed. Thousand Oaks, CA: Sage.

Kubey, Robert. 1990. "Television and the Quality of Family Life." *Communication Quarterly* 38(Fall):312–324.

Kuhn, Thomas S. 1970. *The Structure of Scientific Revolutions,* 2nd ed. Chicago: University of Chicago Press.

Kuzel, Anton J. 1999. "Sampling in Qualitative Inquiry." Pp. 33–45 in *Doing Qualitative Research,* 2nd ed., edited by Benjamin F. Crabtree and William L. Miller. Thousand Oaks, CA: Sage.

Kvale, Steinar. 1996. *Interviews: An Introduction to Qualitative Research Interviewing.* Thousand Oaks, CA: Sage.

Kvale, Steinar. 2002. "The Social Construction of Validity." Pp. 299–325 in *The Qualitative Inquiry Reader,* edited by Norman K. Denzin and Yvonna S. Lincoln. Thousand Oaks, CA: Sage.

Labaw, Patricia J. 1980. *Advanced Questionnaire Design.* Cambridge, MA: ABT Books.

Lacey, John H., Tara Kelley-Baker, Robert B. Voas, Eduardo Romano, C. Debra Furr-Holden, Pedro Torres, and Amy Berning. 2011. "Alcohol- and Drug-Involved Driving in the United States: Methodology for the 2007 National Roadside Survey." *Evaluation Review* 35:319–353.

Lange, Matthew. 2013. *Comparative-Historical Methods.* Thousand Oaks, CA: Sage.

Langford, Terri. 2000. "Census Workers in Dallas Find the Well-Off Hard to Count." *The Boston Globe,* June 1, p. A24.

Larence, Eileen Regan. 2006. *Prevalence of Domestic Violence, Sexual Assault, Dating Violence, and Stalking. Letter to Congressional Committees.* Washington, DC: U.S. Government Accountability Office.

LaRossa, Ralph. 1995. "Parenthood in Early Twentieth- Century America Project (PETCAP), 1900–1944" [Computer file]. Atlanta, GA: Georgia State University [producer], 1995. Ann Arbor, MI: Interuniversity Consortium for Political and Social Research [distributor], 1997.

Larson, Calvin J. 1993. *Pure and Applied Sociological Theory: Problems and Issues.* New York: Harcourt Brace Jovanovich.

Lathrop, Barnes F. 1968. "History From the Census Returns." Pp. 79–101 in *Sociology and History: Methods,* edited by Seymour Martin Lipset and Richard Hofstadter. New York: Basic Books.

Latour, Francie. 2002. "Marching Orders: After 10 Years, State Closes Prison Boot Camp." *Boston Sunday Globe,* June 16, pp. B1, B7.

Laub, John H. 2012. "Presidential Plenary Address—Strengthening Science to Promote Justice and Public Safety." ACJS Annual Conference, March 15. Retrieved June 11, 2014, from www.nij.gov/about/speeches/pages/acjs-march-2012.aspx

Lavin, Michael R. 1994. *Understanding the 1990 Census: A Guide for Marketers, Planners, Grant Writers and Other Data Users.* Kenmore, NY: Epoch Books.

Lavrakas, Paul J. 1987. *Telephone Survey Methods: Sampling, Selection, and Supervision.* Newbury Park, CA: Sage.

Layte, Richard and Christopher T. Whelan. 2003. "Moving In and Out of Poverty: The Impact of Welfare Regimes on Poverty Dynamics in the EU." *European Societies* 5:167–191.

Leakey, Tricia, Kevin B. Lunde, Karin Koga, and Karen Glanz. 2004. "Written Parental Consent and the Use of Incentives in a Youth Smoking Prevention Trial: A Case Study From Project SPLASH." *American Journal of Evaluation* 25:509–523.

LeDuc, Lawrence, Richard G. Niemi, and Pippa Norris (Eds.). 1996. *Comparing Democracies: Elections and Voting in Global Perspective.* Thousand Oaks, CA: Sage.

Lehrer, Jonah. 2010. "The Truth Wears Off: Is There Something Wrong With the Scientific Method?" *The New Yorker,* December 13:52–57.

Lempert, Richard. 1989. "Humility Is a Virtue: On the Publicization of Policy-Relevant Research." *Law & Society Review* 23:146–161.

Lempert, Richard and Joseph Sanders. 1986. *An Invitation to Law and Social Science: Desert, Disputes, and Distribution.* New York: Longman.

Levine, James P. 1976. "The Potential for Crime Overreporting in Criminal Victimization Surveys." *Criminology* 14:307–330.

Levinson, Martin P. 2010. "Accountability to Research Participants: Unresolved Dilemmas and Unravelling Ethics." *Ethnography and Education* 5:193–207.

Levitas, Ruth and Will Guy. 1996. "Introduction." Pp. 1–6 in *Interpreting Official Statistics,* edited by Ruth Levitas and Will Guy. New York: Routledge.

Levitt, Heidi M., Rebecca Todd Swanger, and Jenny B. Butler. 2008. "Male Perpetrators' Perspectives on Intimate Partner Violence, Religion, and Masculinity." *Sex Roles* 58:435–448.

Levy, Paul S. and Stanley Lemeshow. 1999. *Sampling of Populations: Methods and Applications,* 3rd ed. New York: Wiley.

Lewin, Tamar. 2001a. "Income Education Is Found to Lower Risk of New Arrest." *The New York Times,* November 16, p. A18.

Lewin, Tamar. 2001b. "Surprising Result in Welfare-to-Work Studies." *The New York Times,* July 31, p. A16.

Lewis, Chandra, Gwen Hyatt, Keith Lafortune, and Jennifer Lembach. 2010. *History of the Use of Risk and Protective Factors in Washington State's Healthy Youth Survey.* Portland, OR: RMC Research Corporation. Retrieved May 11, 2014, from https://www.askhys.net/library/Old/RPHistory.pdf, page 26.

Lewis, Kevin, Nicholas Christakis, Marco Gonzalez, Jason Kaufman, and Andreas Wimmer. 2008. "Tastes, Ties, and Time: A New Social Network Dataset Using Facebook.com." *Social Networks* 30(4):330–342.

Lewis-Beck, Michael S., Alan Bryman, and Tim Futing Liao (Eds.). 2004. *The SAGE Encyclopedia of Social Science Research Methods,* vol. 1. Thousand Oaks, CA: Sage.

Lieberson, Stanley. 1985. *Making It Count: The Improvement of Social Research and Theory.* Berkeley: University of California Press.

Lieberson, Stanley. 1991. "Small N's and Big Conclusions: An Examination of the Reasoning in Comparative Studies Based on a Small Number of Cases." *Social Forces* 70:307–320.

Lillard, Lee A. and Constantijn W. A. Panis. 1998. "Panel Attrition From the Panel Study of Income Dynamics: Household Income, Marital Status, and Mortality." *The Journal of Human Resources* 33:437–457.

Lincoln, Yvonna S. 2009. "Ethical Practices in Qualitative Research." Pp. 150–169 in *The Handbook of Social Research Ethics,* edited by Donna M. Mertens and Pauline E. Ginsberg. Thousand Oaks, CA: Sage.

Lindsay, Sally, Simon Smith, Frances Bell, and Paul Bellaby. 2007. "Tackling the Digital Divide: Exploring the Impact of ICT on Managing Heart Conditions in a Deprived Area." *Information, Communication & Society* 10:95–114.

Ling, Rich and Gitte Stald. 2010. "Mobile Communities: Are We Talking About a Village, a Clan, or a Small Group?" *American Behavioral Scientist* 53(8):113–1147.

Link, Bruce G., Jo C. Phelan, Ann Stueve, Robert E. Moore, Michaeline Brenahan, and Elmer L. Struening. 1996. "Public Attitudes and Beliefs About Homeless People." Pp. 143–148 in *Homelessness in America,* edited by Jim Baumohl. Phoenix, AZ: Oryx.

Link, Michael. 2008. "Solving the Problems Cell Phone Create for Survey Research." Presentation to the Harvard Program on Survey Research Spring Conference, New Technologies and Survey Research. Cambridge, MA: Institute of Quantitative Social Science, Harvard University, May 9.

Lipset, Seymour Martin. 1968. *Revolution and Counterrevolution.* New York: Basic Books.

Lipset, Seymour Martin, Martin Trow, and James Coleman. 1956. *Union Democracy: The Internal Politics of the International Typographical Union.* New York: Doubleday Anchor.

Lipsey, Mark W. and David B. Wilson. 2001. *Practical Meta-Analysis.* Thousand Oaks, CA: Sage.

Lipsky, Michael. 1980. *Street-Level Bureaucracy.* New York: Russell Sage Foundation.

Liptak, Kevin. 2012. "Report Shows Turnout Lower Than 2008 and 2004." CNN. Retrieved May 26, 2014, from http://politicalticker.blogs.cnn.com/2012/11/08/report-shows-turnout-lower-than-2008-and-2004

Litwin, Mark S. 1995. *How to Measure Survey Reliability and Validity.* Thousand Oaks, CA: Sage.

Loader, Brian D., Steve Muncer, Roger Burrows, Nicolas Pleace, and Sarah Nettleton. 2002. "Medicine on the Line? Computer-Mediated Social Support and Advice for People With Diabetes." *International Journal of Social Welfare* 11:53–65.

Locke, Lawrence F., Stephen J. Silverman, and Waneen Wyrick Spirduso. 1998. *Reading and Understanding Research.* Thousand Oaks, CA: Sage.

Locke, Lawrence F., Waneen Wyrick Spirduso, and Stephen J. Silverman. 2000. *Proposals That Work: A Guide for Planning Dissertations and Grant Proposals,* 4th ed. Thousand Oaks, CA: Sage.

Lockwood, Daniel. 1996. *Violent Incidents Among Selected Public School Students in Two Large Cities of the South and the Southern Midwest, 1995:* [United States] [Computer file]. ICPSR version. Atlanta, GA: Clark Atlantic University [producer], 1996. Ann Arbor, MI: Inter-university Consortium for Political and Social Research [distributor], 1998.

Lofland, John and Lyn H. Lofland. 1984. *Analyzing Social Settings: A Guide to Qualitative Observation and Analysis,* 2nd ed. Belmont, CA: Wadsworth.

Lund, Laura and William E. Wright. 1994. "Mitofsky–Waksberg vs. Screened Random Digit Dial: Report on a Comparison of the Sample Characteristics of Two RDD Survey Designs." Presented at the Center for Disease Control's 11th Annual Behavioral Risk Factor Survey Conference, Atlanta, GA, June.

Luxardo, Natalia, Graciela Colombo, and Gabriela Iglesias. 2011. "Methodological and Ethical Dilemmas Encountered During Field Research of Family Violence Experienced by Adolescent Women in Buenos Aires." *The Qualitative Report* 16: 984–1000.

Lyall, Sarah. 2004. "Does Queen Get Her Mail on Time? You've Got to Wonder." *The New York Times,* May 28, p. A4.

Lyberg, Lars, and Patricia Dean. 1992. "Methods for Reducing Nonresponse Rates: A Review." Annual Meeting of the American Association for Public Opinion Research. St. Petersburg, Florida.

Lynch, Michael and David Bogen. 1997. "Sociology's Asociological 'Core': An Examination of Textbook Sociology in Light of the Sociology of Scientific Knowledge." *American Sociological Review* 62:481–493.

Mabry, Linda. 2008. "Case Study in Social Research." Pp. 214–227 in *The SAGE Handbook of Social Research Methods,* edited by Pertti Alasuutari, Leonard Bickman, and Julia Brannen. Thousand Oaks, CA: Sage.

Madden, Raymond. 2010. *Being Ethnographic: A Guide to the Theory and Practice of Ethnography.* Thousand Oaks, CA: Sage.

Mahoney, James. 2001. *The Legacies of Liberalism: Path Dependence and Political Regimes in Central America.* New York: Cambridge University Press.

Majchrzak, Ann and M. Lynne Markus. 2014. *Methods for Policy Research: Taking Socially Responsible Action,* 2nd ed. Thousand Oaks, CA: Sage.

Makarios, Matthew D. and Travis C. Pratt. 2012. "The Effectiveness of Policies and Programs That Attempt to Reduce Firearm Violence: A Meta-Analysis." *Crime & Delinquency* 58(2):222–244.

Mangione, Thomas W. 1995. *Mail Surveys: Improving the Quality.* Thousand Oaks, CA: Sage.

Manza, Jeff, Clem Brooks, and Michael Sauder. 2005. "Money, Participation, and Votes: Social Cleavages and Electoral Politics." Pp. 201–226 in *The Handbook of Political Sociology: States, Civil Societies, and Globalization,* edited by Thomas Janoski, Robert R. Alford, Alexander M. Hicks, and Mildred A. Schwartz. New York: Cambridge University Press.

Margolis, Eric. 2004. "Looking at Discipline, Looking at Labour: Photographic Representations of Indian Boarding Schools." *Visual Studies* 19:72–96.

Marini, Margaret Mooney and Burton Singer. 1988. "Causality in the Social Sciences." Pp. 347–409 in *Sociological Methodology,* vol. 18, edited by Clifford C. Clogg. Washington, DC: American Sociological Association.

Mark, Melvin M. and Chris Gamble. 2009. "Experiments, Quasi-Experiments, and Ethics." Pp. 198–213 in *The Handbook of Social Research Ethics,* edited by Donna M. Mertens and Pauline E. Ginsberg. Thousand Oaks, CA: Sage.

Markham, Annette N. 2008. "The Methods, Politics, and Ethics of Representation in Online Ethnography." Pp. 247–284 in *Collecting and Interpreting Qualitative Materials,* 3rd ed., edited by Norman Denzin and Yvonna S. Lincoln. Thousand Oaks, CA: Sage.

Markoff, John. 2005. "Transitions to Democracy." Pp. 384–403 in *The Handbook of Political Sociology: States, Civil Societies, and Globalization,* edited by Thomas Janoski, Robert R. Alford, Alexander M. Hicks, and Mildred A. Schwartz. New York: Cambridge University Press.

Marsden, Peter V. 1987. "Core Discussion Networks of Americans." *American Sociological Review* 52:122–131.

Marshall, Catherine and Gretchen B. Rossman. 2011. *Designing Qualitative Research,* 5th ed. Thousand Oaks, CA: Sage.

Marshall, Gary D. and Philip G. Zimbardo. 1979. "Affective Consequences of Inadequately Explained Physiological Arousal." *Journal of Personality and Social Psychology* 37:970–988.

Martin, Lawrence L. and Peter M. Kettner. 1996. *Measuring the Performance of Human Service Programs.* Thousand Oaks, CA: Sage.

Martin, Linda G. and Kevin Kinsella. 1995. "Research on the Demography of Aging in Developing Countries." Pp. 356–403 in *Demography of Aging,* edited by Linda G. Martin and Samuel H. Preston. Washington, DC: National Academy Press.

Marx, Karl. 1967. *Capital: A Critique of Political Economy.* New York: International Publishers.

Marx, Karl and Friedrich Engels. 1961. "The Communist Manifesto." Pp. 13–44 in *Essential Works of Marxism,* edited by Arthur P. Mendel. New York: Bantam.

Matt, Georg E. and Thomas D. Cook. 1994. "Threats to the Validity of Research Syntheses." Pp. 503–520 in *The Handbook of Research Synthesis,* edited by Harris Cooper and Larry V. Hedges. New York: Russell Sage Foundation.

Maxwell, Joseph A. 2005. *Qualitative Research Design: An Interactive Approach,* 2nd ed. Thousand Oaks, CA: Sage.

Mayer-Schönberger, Viktor and Kenneth Cukier. 2013. *Big Data: A Revolution That Will Transform How We Live, Work, and Think.* Boston: Houghton Mifflin Harcourt.

Maynard, Douglas W., Jeremy Freese, and Nora Cate Schaeffer. 2010. "Calling for Participation: Requests, Blocking Moves, and Rational (Inter)action in Survey Introductions." *American Sociological Review* 75:791–814.

Mayrl, Damon, Ben Moodie, Jon Norman, Jodi Short, Sarah Staveteig, and Cinzia Solari. 2004. "A Theory of Relativity." *Contexts* 3:10.

McCarter, Susan A. 2009. "Legal and Extralegal Factors Affecting Minority Overrepresentation in Virginia's Juvenile Justice System: A Mixed-Method Study." *Child and Adolescent Social Work Journal* 26:533–544.

McGeeney, Kyley and Scott Keeter. 2014. "Pew Research Increases Share of Interviews Conducted by Cellphone." Pew Research Center, January 15. Retrieved July 2, 2014, from www.pewresearch .org/fact-tank/2014/01/15/pew-research-increases-share-of-interviews-conducted-by-cellphone

McIntyre, Alice. 2008. *Participatory Action Research.* Thousand Oaks, CA: Sage.

McLellan, A. Thomas, Lester Luborsky, John Cacciola, Jeffrey Griffith, Frederick Evans, Harriet L. Barr, and Charles P. O'Brien. 1985. "New Data From the Addiction Severity Index: Reliability and Validity in Three Centers." *The Journal of Nervous and Mental Disease* 173(7):412–423.

McPhail, Clark and John McCarthy. 2004. "Who Counts and How: Estimating the Size of Protests." *Contexts* 3:12–18.

McPherson, Miller, Lynn Smith-Lovin, and Matthew E. Brashears. 2006. "Social Isolation in America: Changes in Core Discussion Networks Over Two Decades." *American Sociological Review* 71:353–375.

Medway, Rebecca L. and Jenna Fulton. 2012. "When More Gets You Less: A Meta-Analysis of the Effect of Concurrent Web Options on Mail Survey Response Rates." *Public Opinion Quarterly* 76:733–746.

Meghani, S. H., Brooks, J., Gipson-Jones, T., Waite, R., Whitefield-Harris, L., Deatrick, J. 2009. "Patient–Provider Race-Concordance: Does it Matter in Improving Minority Patients' Health Outcomes?" *Ethnicity & Health* 14(1):107–130.

Mertens, Donna M. 2012. "Transformative Mixed Methods: Addressing Inequities." *American Behavioral Scientist* 56:802–813.

Merton, Robert K., Marjorie Fiske, and Patricia L. Kendall. 1956. *The Focused Interview.* Glencoe, IL: Free Press.

Mieczkowski, Tom. 1997. "Hair Assays and Urinalysis Results for Juvenile Drug Offenders." *National Institute of Justice Research Preview.* Washington, DC: U.S. Department of Justice.

Milbrath, Lester and M. L. Goel. 1977. *Political Participation,* 2nd ed. Chicago: Rand McNally.

Miles, Matthew B. and A. Michael Huberman. 1994. *Qualitative Data Analysis,* 2nd ed. Thousand Oaks, CA: Sage.

Miles, Matthew B., A. Michael Huberman, and Johnny Soldaña. 2014. *Qualitative Data Analysis: A Methods Sourcebook,* 3rd ed. Thousand Oaks: Sage.

Milgram, Stanley. 1963. "Behavioral Study of Obedience." *Journal of Abnormal and Social Psychology* 67:371–478.

Milgram, Stanley. 1964. "Issues in the Study of Obedience: A Reply to Baumrind." *American Psychologist* 19:848–852.

Milgram, Stanley. 1965. "Some Conditions of Obedience and Disobedience to Authority." *Human Relations* 18:57–76.

Milgram, Stanley. 1974. *Obedience to Authority: An Experimental View.* New York: Harper & Row.

Milgram, Stanley. 1977. "Subject Reaction: The Neglected Factor in the Ethics of Experimentation." *Hastings Law Review,* October, pp. 19–23 (as cited in Cave, Emma and Soren Holm. 2003. "Milgram and Tuskegee—Paradigm Research Projects in Bioethics." *Health Care Analysis* 11:27–40).

Milgram, Stanley. 1992. *The Individual in a Social World: Essays and Experiments,* 2nd ed. New York: McGraw-Hill.

Mill, John Stuart. 1872. *A System of Logic: Ratiocinative and Inductive,* 8th ed., vol. 2. London: Longmans, Green, Reader, & Dyer.

Miller, Arthur G. 1986. *The Obedience Experiments: A Case Study of Controversy in Social Science.* New York: Praeger.

Miller, Delbert C. and Neil J. Salkind. 2002. *Handbook of Research Design and Social Measurement,* 6th ed. Thousand Oaks, CA: Sage.

Miller, JoAnn. 2003. "An Arresting Experiment: Domestic Violence Victim Experiences and Perceptions." *Journal of Interpersonal Violence* 18:695–716.

Miller, Susan. 1999. *Gender and Community Policing: Walking the Talk.* Boston: Northeastern University Press.

Miller, Ted R. and Delia Hendrie. 2008. *Substance Abuse Prevention Dollars and Cents: A Cost-Benefit Analysis,* DHHS Pub. No. (SMA) 07-4298. Rockville, MD: Center for Substance Abuse Prevention, Substance Abuse and Mental Health Services Administration.

Miller, Walter B. 1992. *Crime by Youth Gangs and Groups in the United States.* Washington, DC: Office of Juvenile Justice and Delinquency Prevention.

Miller, William L. and Benjamin F. Crabtree. 1999a. "Clinical Research: A Multimethod Typology and Qualitative Roadmap." Pp. 3–30 in *Doing Qualitative Research,* 2nd ed., edited by Benjamin F. Crabtree and William L. Miller. Thousand Oaks, CA: Sage.

Miller, William L. and Benjamin F. Crabtree. 1999b. "The Dance of Interpretation." Pp. 127–143 in *Doing Qualitative Research,* edited by Benjamin F. Crabtree and William L. Miller. Thousand Oaks, CA: Sage.

Miller, William L. and Benjamin F. Crabtree. 1999c. "Depth Interviewing." Pp. 89–107 in *Doing Qualitative Research,* 2nd ed., edited by Benjamin F. Crabtree and William L. Miller. Thousand Oaks, CA: Sage.

Mills, C. Wright. 1959. *The Sociological Imagination.* New York: Oxford University Press.

Minkler, Meredith. 2000. "Using Participatory Action Research to Build Healthy Communities." *Public Health Reports* 115:191–197.

Mirowsky, John. 1999. *Aging, Status, and the Sense of Control: Competing Continuation* (Proposal to the National Institute of Aging). Urbana: University of Illinois Press.

Mirowsky, John and Catherine E. Ross. 1999. "Economic Hardship Across the Life Course." *American Sociological Review* 64:548–569.

Mirowsky, John and Catherine E. Ross. 2001. *Aging, Status, and the Sense of Control (ASOC), 1995, 1998, 2001 [United States] Questionnaire* (ICPSR 3334). Ann Arbor, MI: Inter-university Consortium for Political and Social Research.

Mirowsky, John and Catherine E. Ross. 2003. *Education, Social Status, and Health.* New York: Aldine de Gruyter.

Mitchell, Richard G. Jr. 1993. *Secrecy and Fieldwork.* Newbury Park, CA: Sage.

Moe, Angela M. 2007. "Silenced Voices and Structural Survival—Battered Women's Help Seeking." *Violence Against Women* 13(7):676–699.

Mohr, Lawrence B. 1992. *Impact Analysis for Program Evaluation.* Newbury Park, CA: Sage.

Monkkonen, Eric H. 1994. "Introduction." Pp. 1–8 in *Engaging the Past: The Uses of History Across the Social Sciences.* Durham, NC: Duke University Press.

Mooney, Christopher Z. and Mei Hsien Lee. 1995. "Legislating Morality in the American States: The Case of Abortion Regulation Reform." *American Journal of Political Science* 39:599–627.

Moore, Barrington Jr. 1966. *Social Origins of Democracy and Dictatorship: Lord and Peasant in the Making of the Modern World.* Boston: Beacon Press.

Moore, Spencer, Mark Daniel, Laura Linnan, Marci Campbell, Salli Benedict, and Andrea Meier. 2004. "After Hurricane Floyd Passed: Investigating the Social Determinants of Disaster Preparedness and Recovery." *Family and Community Health* 27:204–217.

Morgan, David L. 2014. *Integrating Qualitative & Quantitative Methods: A*

Pragmatic Approach. Thousand Oaks, CA: Sage.

Morrill, Calvin, Christine Yalda, Madeleine Adelman, Michael Musheno, and Cindy Bejarano. 2000. "Telling Tales in School: Youth Culture and Conflict Narratives." *Law & Society Review* 34:521–565.

Mosher, Clayton J., Terance D. Miethe, and Dretha M. Phillips. 2002. *The Mismeasure of Crime.* Thousand Oaks, CA: Sage.

Muhr, Thomas and Susanne Friese. 2004. *User's Manual for ATLAS.ti 5.0,* 2nd ed. Berlin: Scientific Software Development.

Myers, Steven Lee. 2002. "Russia Takes Stock of a Nation's Transformation." *The New York Times,* September 29, p. 3.

Myers, Steven Lee. 2010. "Delays in a Head Count Keep Crucial Numbers a Matter of Guesswork." *The New York Times,* December 7, p. A10.

Nagourney, Adam. 2002. "Cellphones and Caller ID Are Making It Harder for Pollsters to Pick a Winner." *The New York Times,* November 5, p. A20.

Nakonezny, Paul A., Rebecca Reddick, and Joseph Lee Rodgers. 2004. "Did Divorces Decline After the Oklahoma City Bombing?" *Journal of Marriage and Family* 66:90–100.

Narayan, Sowmya and Jon A. Krosnick. 1996. "Education Moderates Some Response Effects in Attitude Measurement." *Public Opinion Quarterly* 60:58–88.

National Center for Health Statistics (NCHS). 2013. *Health, United States, 2012: With Special Feature on Emergency Care.* Hyattsville, MD: U.S. Department of Health and Human Services, Centers for Disease Control and Prevention.

National Geographic Society. 2000. *Survey 2000.* Retrieved from http://survey2000.nationalgeographic.com

National Institute on Alcohol Abuse and Alcoholism (NIAAA). 1994. "Alcohol-Related Impairment." *Alcohol Alert* 25 (July):1–5.

National Institute on Alcohol Abuse and Alcoholism (NIAAA). 1997. "Alcohol Metabolism." *Alcohol Alert* 35(January):1–4.

National Institute on Alcohol Abuse and Alcoholism (NIAAA). 2013. *NIAAA Recognizes Alcohol Awareness Month.* Retrieved March 20, 2014, from www.niaaa.nih.gov/news-events/alcohol-awareness-month-2013

National Oceanic and Atmospheric Administration (NOAA). 2005. *Hurricane Katrina.* Washington, DC: U.S. Department of Commerce. Retrieved June 4, 2014 from www.ncdc.noaa.gov/extre meevents/specialreports/Hurricane-Katrina.pdf

National Opinion Research Center (NORC). 2011. General Social Survey (GSS).

Chicago: NORC at the University of Chicago. Retrieved August 31, 2011, from www.norc.org/Research/Projects/Pages/general-social-survey.aspx

National Opinion Research Center (NORC). 2013. Release Notes for the GSS 2012 Merged Data, Release 1. Retrieved May 25, 2014, from http://publicdata.norc.org:41000/gss/documents//OTHR/Release%20Notes%20for%20the%20GSS%202012%20Merged%20R1.pdf

National Opinion Research Center (NORC). 2014. General Social Survey. Retrieved May 25, 2014, from www3.norc.org/GSS+Website/Publications/GSS+Questionnaires

Navarro, Mireya. 2012. "For Many Latinos, Racial Identity Is More Culture Than Color." *The New York Times,* January 14, p. A9.

Needleman, Carolyn. 1981. "Discrepant Assumptions in Empirical Research: The Case of Juvenile Court Screening." *Social Problems* 28 (February):247–262.

Neuendorf, Kimberly A. 2002. *The Content Analysis Guidebook.* Thousand Oaks, CA: Sage.

Newbury, Darren. 2005. "Editorial: The Challenge of Visual Studies." *Visual Studies* 20:1–3.

Newport, Frank. 1992. "Look at Polls as a Fever Chart of the Electorate." Letter to the Editor, *The New York Times,* November 6, p. A28.

Nie, Norman H. and Lutz Erbring. 2000. *Internet and Society: A Preliminary Report.* Palo Alto, CA: Stanford Institute for the Quantitative Study of Society.

Nordanger, Dag. 2007. "Discourses of Loss and Bereavement in Tigray, Ethiopia." *Culture, Medicine and Psychiatry* 31:173–194.

Norris, Pippa. 2004. "The Bridging and Bonding Role of Online Communities." Pp. 31–41 in *Society Online: The Internet in Context,* edited by Philip N. Howard and Steve Jones. Thousand Oaks, CA: Sage.

Nunberg, Geoffrey. 2002. "The Shifting Lexicon of Race." *The New York Times,* December 22, p. WK3.

Ogburn, William F. 1930. "The Folkways of a Scientific Sociology," *Scientific Monthly* 30:300–306.

Olson, Kristen, Jolene D. Smyth, and Heather M. Wood. 2012. "Does Giving People Their Preferred Survey Mode Actually Increase Survey Participation Rates? An Experimental Examination." *Public Opinion Quarterly* 76:611–635.

Olzak, Susan, Suzanne Shanahan, and Elizabeth H. McEneaney. 1996. "Poverty, Segregation, and Race Riots: 1960 to 1993." *American Sociological Review* 61:590–613.

Onishi, Norimitsu. 2003. "Crime Rattles Japanese Calm, Attracting Politicians' Notice." *The New York Times,* September 7, pp. A1, A4.

Onoye, Jane M., Deborah A. Goebert, and Stephanie T. Nishimura. 2012. "Use of Incentives and Web-Based Administration for Surveying Student Alcohol and Substance Use in an Ethnically Diverse Sample." *Journal of Substance Use* 17(1):61–71.

Orcutt, James D. and J. Blake Turner. 1993. "Shocking Numbers and Graphic Accounts: Quantified Images of Drug Problems in the Print Media." *Social Problems* 49(May):190–206.

Orr, Larry L. 1999. *Social Experiments: Evaluating Public Programs With Experimental Methods.* Thousand Oaks, CA: Sage.

Orshansky, Mollie. 1977. "Memorandum for Daniel P. Moynihan. Subject: History of the Poverty Line." Pp. 232–237 in *The Measure of Poverty. Technical Paper I: Documentation of Background Information and Rationale for Current Poverty Matrix,* edited by Mollie Orshansky. Washington, DC: U.S. Department of Health, Education, and Welfare.

Orwin, Robert G. 1994. "Evaluating Coding Decisions." Pp. 138–162 in *The Handbook of Research Synthesis,* edited by Harris Cooper and Larry V. Hodges. New York: Russell Sage Foundation.

Ousey, Graham C. and Matthew R. Lee. 2004. "Investigating the Connections Between Race, Illicit Drug Markets, and Legal Violence, 1984–1997." *Journal of Research in Crime and Delinquency* 41:352–383.

Pagnini, Deanna L. and S. Philip Morgan. 1996. "Racial Differences in Marriage and Childbearing: Oral History Evidence From the South in the Early Twentieth Century." *American Journal of Sociology* 101:1694–1715.

Paige, Jeffery M. 1999. "Conjuncture, Comparison, and Conditional Theory in Macrosocial Inquiry." *American Journal of Sociology* 105:781–800.

Paika, Anthony and Kenneth Sanchagrina. 2013. "Social Isolation in America: An Artifact." *American Sociological Review* 78(3):339–360.

Pan, Yuling and Manuel de la Puente. 2005. *Census Bureau Guideline for the Translation of Data Collection Instruments and Supporting Materials: Documentation on How the Guideline Was Developed* (Research Report Series, Survey Methodology #2005-06). Washington, DC: Statistical Research Division, U.S. Census Bureau.

Panagopoulos, Costas. 2008. "Poll Accuracy in the 2008 Presidential Election." Retrieved March 17, 2011, from www.fordham.edu/images/academics/gradu ate_ schools/gsas/elections_and_cam paign_/poll%20accuracy%20in%20 the%202008%20presidential%20elec tion.pdf

Papachristos, Andrew V., David M. Hureau, and Anthony A. Braga. 2013. "The Corner and the Crew: The Influence of Geography and Social Networks on Gang Violence." *American Sociological Review* 78(3):417–447.

Papineau, David. 1978. *For Science in the Social Sciences.* London: Macmillan.

Parker-Pope, Tara. 2008. "Love, Sex, and the Changing Landscape of Infidelity." *The New York Times,* October 28, p. D1.

Parker-Pope, Tara. 2010. "As Girls Become Women, Sports Pay Dividends." *The New York Times,* February 16, p. D5.

Parks, Kathleen A., Ann M. Pardi, and Clara M. Bradizza. 2006. "Collecting Data on Alcohol Use and Alcohol-Related Victimization: A Comparison of Telephone and Web-Based Survey Methods." *Journal of Studies on Alcohol* 67:318–323.

Parlett, Malcolm and David Hamilton. 1976. "Evaluation as Illumination: A New Approach to the Study of Innovative Programmes." Pp. 140–157 in *Evaluation Studies Review Annual,* vol. 1, edited by G. Glass. Beverly Hills, CA: Sage.

Pate, Antony M. and Edwin E. Hamilton. 1992. "Formal and Informal Deterrents to Domestic Violence: The Dade County Spouse Assault Experiment." *American Sociological Review* 57(October):691–697.

Paternoster, Raymond, Robert Brame, Ronet Bachman, and Lawrence W. Sherman. 1997. "Do Fair Procedures Matter? The Effect of Procedural Justice on Spouse Assault." *Law & Society Review* 31(1):163–204.

Patterson, Orlando. 1997. "The Race Trap." *The New York Times,* July 11, p. A25.

Patton, Michael Quinn. 2002. *Qualitative Research & Evaluation Methods,* 3rd ed. Thousand Oaks, CA: Sage.

Pauwels, Luc. 2010. "Visual Sociology Reframed: An Analytical Synthesis and Discussion of Visual Methods in Social and Cultural Research." *Sociological Methods & Research* 38:545–581.

Paxton, Pamela. 2002. "Social Capital and Democracy: An Interdependent Relationship." *American Sociological Review* 67:254–277.

Paxton, Pamela. 2005. "Trust in Decline?" *Contexts* 4:40–46.

Pearson, Michael, Helen Sweeting, Patrick West, Robert Young, Jacki Gordon, and Katrina Turner. 2006. "Adolescent Substance Use in Different Social and Peer Contexts: A Social Network Analysis." *Drugs: Education, Prevention and Policy* 13:519–536.

Pepinsky, Harold E. 1980. "A Sociologist on Police Patrol." Pp. 223–234 in *Fieldwork Experience: Qualitative Approaches to Social Research,* edited by William B. Shaffir, Robert A. Stebbins, and Allan Turowetz. New York: St. Martin's Press.

Perry, Gina. 2013. *Behind the Shock Machine: The Untold Story of the Notorious Milgram Psychology Experiments.* New York: New Press.

Peterson, Robert A. 2000. *Constructing Effective Questionnaires.* Thousand Oaks, CA: Sage.

Pew Hispanic Center. 2008. *Statistical Portrait of the Foreign-Born Population in the United States, 2006.* Statistical tables from 2000 Census and 2006 American Community Survey, Retrieved May 24, 2008, from http://pewhispanic.org/factsheets/factsheet.php?FactsheetID=36

Pew Research Center. 2013. "Social Networking Use." Retrieved December 26, 2013, www.pewresearch.org/data-trend/media-and-technology/social-networking-use/

Pew Research Center. 2014. "Pew Research Internet Project: Internet User Demographics." Retrieved May 25, 2014, from www.pewinternet.org/data-trend/internet-use/latest-stats/

Phillips, David P. 1982. "The Impact of Fictional Television Stories on U.S. Adult Fatalities: New Evidence on the Effect of the Mass Media on Violence." *American Journal of Sociology* 87:1340–1359.

Piliavin, Jane Allyn and Irving M. Piliavin. 1972. "Effect of Blood on Reactions to a Victim." *Journal of Personality and Social Psychology* 23:353–361.

Plessy v. Ferguson, 163 U.S. 537 (1896).

Pollner, Melvin and Richard E. Adams. 1994. "The Interpersonal Context of Mental Health Interviews." *Journal of Health and Social Behavior* 35:283–290.

Porter, Stephen R. and Michael E. Whitcomb. 2003. "The Impact of Contact Type on Web Survey Response Rates." *Public Opinion Quarterly* 67:579–588.

Posavac, Emil J. and Raymond G. Carey. 1997. *Program Evaluation: Methods and Case Studies,* 5th ed. Upper Saddle River, NJ: Prentice Hall.

Presley, Cheryl A., Philip W. Meilman, and Rob Lyerla. 1994. "Development of the Core Alcohol and Drug Survey: Initial Findings and Future Directions." *Journal of American College Health* 42:248–255.

Presser, Stanley and Johnny Blair. 1994. "Survey Pretesting: Do Different Methods Produce Different Results?" *Sociological Methodology* 24:73–104.

Presser, Stanley, Mick P. Couper, Judith T. Lessler, Elizabeth Martin, Jean Martin, Jennifer M. Rothgeb, and Eleanor Singer. 2004. "Methods for Testing and Evaluating Survey Questions." *Public Opinion Quarterly* 68:109–130.

Price, Richard H., Michelle Van Ryn, and Amiram D. Vinokur. 1992. "Impact of a Preventive Job Search Intervention on the Likelihood of Depression Among the Unemployed." *Journal of Health and Social Behavior* 33 (June):158–167.

Princeton Survey Research Associates International. 2010. *SNS and Facebook Survey.* Retrieved December 27, 2013, from www.pewinternet.org/~/media//Files/Reports/2011/PIP%20-%20Social%20networking%20sites%20and%20our%20lives.pdf

Punch, Maurice. 1994. "Politics and Ethics in Qualitative Research." Pp. 83–97 in *Handbook of Qualitative Research,* edited by Norman K. Denzin and Yvonna S. Lincoln. Thousand Oaks, CA: Sage.

Purdy, Matthew. 1994. "Bronx Mystery: 3rd-Rate Service for 1st-Class Mail." *The New York Times,* March 12, pp. 1, 3.

Putnam, Israel. 1977. "Poverty Thresholds: Their History and Future Development." Pp. 272–283 in *The Measure of Poverty. Technical Paper I: Documentation of Background Information and Rationale for Current Poverty Matrix,* edited by Mollie Orshansky. Washington, DC: U.S. Department of Health, Education, and Welfare.

Pyrczak, Fred. 2005. *Evaluating Research in Academic Journals: A Practical Guide to Realistic Evaluation,* 3rd ed. Glendale, CA: Pyrczak.

Radloff, Lenore. 1977. "The CES-D Scale: A Self-Report Depression Scale for Research in the General Population." *Applied Psychological Measurement* 1:385–401.

Ragin, Charles C. 1987. *The Comparative Method: Moving Beyond Qualitative and Quantitative Strategies.* Berkeley: University of California Press.

Ragin, Charles C. 1994. *Constructing Social Research.* Thousand Oaks, CA: Sage.

Ragin, Charles C. 2000. *Fuzzy-Set Social Science.* Chicago: University of Chicago Press.

Rainie, Lee, Joanna Brenner, and Kristen Purcell. 2012. *Photos and Videos as Social Currency Online.* Washington, DC: Pew Internet & American Life Project. Retrieved June 4, 2014, from http://pewinternet.org/Reports/2012/Online-Pictures.aspx

Rainie, Lee and John Horrigan. 2005. *A Decade of Adoption: How the Internet Has Woven Itself Into American Life.* Pew Internet & American Life Project. Retrieved June 18, 2005, from the Pew Internet & American Life Project, www.pewinternet.org/PPF/r/148/report_display.asp (PDF version).

Rainie, Lee, Aaron Smith, and Maeve Duggan. 2013. *Coming and Going on Facebook.* Washington, DC: Pew Internet & American Life Project.

Randall, Ann. 2012. "Beneficial Interview Effects in Virtual Worlds: A Case Study." Pp. 131–149 in *Cases in Online Interview Research,* edited by Janet Salmons. Thousand Oaks, CA: Sage.

Raphael, Dennis. 2013. "The Politics of Poverty: Definitions and Explanations." *Social Alternatives* 32:5–11.

Rashbaum, William K. 2002. "Reasons for Crime Drop in New York Elude Many." *The New York Times,* November 29, p. A28.

Raudenbush, Stephen W. and Robert J. Sampson. 1999. "Ecometrics: Toward a Science of Assessing Ecological Settings, With Application to the Systematic Social Observation of Neighborhoods." *Sociological Methodology* 29:1–41.

Reinharz, Shulamit. 1992. *Feminist Methods in Social Research.* New York: Oxford University Press.

Reisman, David. [1950] 1969. *The Lonely Crowd: A Study of the Changing American Character.* New Haven, CT: Yale University Press.

Reiss, Albert J. Jr. 1971a. *The Police and the Public.* New Haven, CT: Yale University Press.

Reiss, Albert J. Jr. 1971b. "Systematic Observations of Natural Social Phenomena." Pp. 3–33 in *Sociological Methodology,* vol. 3, edited by Herbert Costner. San Francisco: Jossey-Bass.

Rele, J. R. 1993. "Demographic Rates: Birth, Death, Marital, and Migration." Pp. 2–1–2–26 in *Readings in Population Research Methodology. Vol. 1, Basic Tools,* edited by Donald J. Bogue, Eduardo E. Arriaga, and Douglas L. Anderton. Chicago: Social Development Center, for the United National Population Fund.

Reuter, Peter, Rosalie Liccardo Pacula, and Jonathan P. Caulkins. 2010. "Addiction Research Centres and the Nurturing of Creativity: RAND's Drug Policy Research Center." *Addiction* 106:253–259.

Rew, Lynn, Deborah Koniak-Griffin, Mary Ann Lewis, Margaret Miles, and Ann O'Sullivan. 2000. "Secondary Data Analysis: New Perspective for Adolescent Research." *Nursing Outlook* 48:223–229.

Reynolds, Paul Davidson. 1979. *Ethical Dilemmas and Social Science Research.* San Francisco: Jossey-Bass.

Richards, Thomas J. and Lyn Richards. 1994. "Using Computers in Qualitative Research." Pp. 445–462 in *Handbook of Qualitative Research,* edited by Norman K. Denzin and Yvonna S. Lincoln. Thousand Oaks, CA: Sage.

Richardson, Laurel. 1995. "Narrative and Sociology." Pp. 198–221 in *Representation in Ethnography,* edited by John Van Maanen. Thousand Oaks, CA: Sage.

Riedel, Marc. 2000. *Research Strategies for Secondary Data: A Perspective for Criminology and Criminal Justice.* Thousand Oaks, CA: Sage.

Riessman, Catherine Kohler. 2008. *Narrative Methods for the Human Sciences.* Thousand Oaks, CA: Sage.

Rinehart, Jenny K. and Elizabeth A. Yeater. 2011. "A Qualitative Analysis of Sexual Victimization Narratives." *Violence Against Women* 17(7):925–943.

Ringwalt, Christopher L., Jody M. Greene, Susan T. Ennett, Ronaldo Iachan, Richard R. Clayton, and Carl G. Leukefeld. 1994. *Past and Future Directions of the D.A.R.E. Program: An Evaluation Review.* Research Triangle, NC: Research Triangle Institute.

Rives, Norfleet W. Jr. and William J. Serow. 1988. *Introduction to Applied Demography: Data Sources and Estimation Techniques.* SAGE University Paper Series on Quantitative Applications in the Social Sciences, series No. 07–039. Thousand Oaks, CA: Sage.

Robertson, David Brian. 1993. "The Return to History and the New Institutionalism in American Political Science." *Social Science History* 17:1–36.

Robinson, Karen A. and Steven N. Goodman. 2011. "A Systematic Examination of the Citation of Prior Research in Reports of Randomized, Controlled Trials." *Annals of Internal Medicine* 154:50–55.

Rodríguez, Havidán, Joseph Trainor, and Enrico L. Quarantelli. 2006. "Rising to the Challenges of a Catastrophe: The Emergent and Prosocial Behavior Following Hurricane Katrina." *The Annals of the American Academy of Political and Social Science* 604:82–101.

Roman, Anthony. 2005. *Women's Health Network Client Survey: Field Report.* Unpublished report. Boston: Center for Survey Research, University of Massachusetts.

Rookey, Bryan D., Steve Hanway, and Don A. Dillman. 2008. "Does a Probability-Based Household Panel Benefit From Assignment to Postal Response as an Alternative to Internet-Only?" *Public Opinion Quarterly* 72:962–984.

Rosen, Lawrence. 1995. "The Creation of the Uniform Crime Report: The Role of Social Science." *Social Science History* 19:215–238.

Rosenbach, Margo, Carol Irvin, Angela Merrill, Shanna Shulman, John Czajka, Christopher Trenholm, Susan Williams, So Sasigant Limpa-Amara, and Anna Katz. 2007. *National Evaluation of the State Children's Health Insurance Program: A Decade of Expanding Coverage and Improving Access: Final Report.* Cambridge, MA: Mathematica Policy Research.

Rosenbaum, Dennis P. 2007. "Just Say No to D.A.R.E." *Criminology & Public Policy* 6:815–824.

Rosenbaum, Dennis P. and Gordon S. Hanson.1998. "Assessing the Effects of School-Based Drug Education: A Six-Year Multi-Level Analysis of Project D.A.R.E." *Journal of Research in Crime and Delinquency* 35:381–412.

Rosenberg, Morris. 1968. *The Logic of Survey Analysis.* New York: Basic Books.

Rosenfeld, Richard. 2004. "The Case of the Unsolved Crime Decline." *Scientific American* 290:82–89.

Rosenthal, Elisabeth. 2000. "Rural Flouting of One-Child Policy Undercuts China's Census." *The New York Times,* April 14, p. A10.

Rosenthal, Rob. 1994. *Homeless in Paradise: A Map of the Terrain.* Philadelphia: Temple University Press.

Ross, Catherine E. 1990. *Work, Family, and the Sense of Control: Implications for the Psychological Well-Being of Women and Men.* Proposal submitted to the National Science Foundation. Urbana: University of Illinois.

Rossi, Peter H. 1989. *Down and Out in America: The Origins of Homelessness.* Chicago: University of Chicago Press.

Rossi, Peter H. 1999. "Half Truths With Real Consequences: Journalism, Research, and Public Policy. Three Encounters." *Contemporary Sociology* 28:1–5.

Rossi, Peter H. and Howard E. Freeman. 1989. *Evaluation: A Systematic Approach,* 4th ed. Newbury Park, CA: Sage.

Rossman, Gretchen B. and Sharon F. Rallis. 1998. *Learning in the Field: An Introduction to Qualitative Research.* Thousand Oaks, CA: Sage.

Roth, Dee. 1990. "Homelessness in Ohio: A Statewide Epidemiological Study." Pp. 145–163 in *Homeless in the United States, Vol. 1: State Surveys,* edited by Jamshid Momeni. New York: Greenwood.

Rotolo, Thomas and Charles R. Tittle. 2006. "Population Size, Change, and Crime in U.S. Cities." *Journal of Quantitative Criminology* 22:341–367.

Rubin, Herbert J. and Irene S. Rubin. 1995. *Qualitative Interviewing: The Art of Hearing Data.* Thousand Oaks, CA: Sage.

Ruderman, Wendy. 2012. "Crime Report Manipulation Is Common Among New York Police, Study Finds." *The New York Times,* June 29, p. A17.

Rueschemeyer, Dietrich, Evelyne Huber Stephens, and John D. Stephens. 1992. *Capitalist Development and Democracy.* Chicago: University of Chicago Press.

Ruggles, Patricia. 1990. *Drawing the Line: Alternative Poverty Measures and Their Implications for Public Policy.* Washington, DC: Urban Institute Press.

Sacks, Stanley, Karen McKendrick, George DeLeon, Michael T. French, and Kathryn E. McCollister. 2002. "Benefit-Cost Analysis of a Modified Therapeutic Community for Mentally Ill Chemical Abusers." *Evaluation and Program Planning* 25:137–148.

Salisbury, Robert H. 1975. "Research on Political Participation." *American Journal of Political Science* 19(May):323–341.

Salmons, Janet. 2012. "Designing and Conducting Research With Online Interviews." Pp. 1–35 in *Cases in Online Interview Research,* edited by Janet Salmons. Thousand Oaks, CA: Sage.

Sampson, Robert J. 1987. "Urban Black Violence: The Effect of Male Joblessness and Family Disruption." *American Journal of Sociology* 93(September):348–382.

Sampson, Robert J. 2008. "Rethinking Crime and Immigration." *Contexts* 7:28–33.

Sampson, Robert J. 2012. *Great American City: Chicago and the Enduring Neighborhood Effect.* Chicago: University of Chicago Press.

Sampson, Robert J. and John H. Laub. 1990. "Crime and Deviance Over the Life Course: The Salience of Adult Social Bonds." *American Sociological Review* 55(October):609–627.

Sampson, Robert J. and John H. Laub. 1993. "Structural Variations in Juvenile Court Processing: Inequality, the Underclass, and Social Control." *Law & Society Review* 27(2):285–311.

Sampson, Robert J. and John H. Laub. 1994. "Urban Poverty and the Family Context of Delinquency: A New Look at Structure and Process in a Classic Study." *Child Development* 65:523–540.

Sampson, Robert J. and Stephen W. Raudenbush. 1999. "Systematic Social Observation of Public Spaces: A New Look at Disorder in Urban Neighborhoods." *American Journal of Sociology* 105:603–651.

Sampson, Robert J. and Stephen W. Raudenbush. 2001. "Disorder in Urban Neighborhoods—Does It Lead to Crime?" In *Research in Brief.* Washington, DC: National Institute of Justice, U.S. Department of Justice.

Sampson, Robert J., Stephen W. Raudenbush, and Felton Earls. 1997. "Neighborhoods and Violent Crime: A Multilevel Study of Collective Efficacy." *Science* 277:918–924.

Savage, Charlie. 2011. "Trend to Lighten Harsh Sentences Catches on in Conservative States." *The New York Times,* August 13, p. A12.

Sayer, Andrew. 2003. "Reductionism in Social Science." Lancaster, England: Department of Sociology, Lancaster University. Retrieved February 1, 2014, from www.lancaster.ac.uk/fass/sociology/research/publications/papers/sayer-paris1.pdf

Schaeffer, Nora Cate and Stanley Presser. 2003. "The Science of Asking Questions." *Annual Review of Sociology* 29:65–88.

Schegloff, Emanuel A. 1996. "Issues of Relevance for Discourse Analysis: Contingency in Action, Interaction and Coparticipant Context." Pp. 3–35 in *Computational and Conversational Discourse: Burning Issues—An Interdisciplinary Account,* edited by Eduard H. Hovy and Donia R. Scott. New York: Springer.

Schleyer, Titus K. L. and Jane L. Forrest. 2000. "Methods for the Design and Administration of Web-Based Surveys." *Journal of the American Medical Informatics Association* 7:418–425.

Schober, Michael F. 1999. "Making Sense of Survey Questions." Pp. 77–94 in *Cognition and Survey Research,* edited by Monroe G. Sirken, Douglas J. Herrmann, Susan Schechter, Norbert Schwartz, Judith M. Tanur, and Roger Tourangeau. New York: Wiley.

Schofield, Janet Ward. 2002. "Increasing the Generalizability of Qualitative Research." Pp. 171–203 in *The Qualitative Researcher's Companion,* edited by A. Michael Huberman and Matthew B. Miles. Thousand Oaks, CA: Sage.

Schorr, Lisbeth B. and Daniel Yankelovich. 2000. "In Search of a Gold Standard for Social Programs." *The Boston Globe,* February 18, p. A19.

Schreck, Christopher J., Eric A. Steward, and Bonnie S. Fisher. 2006. "Self-Control, Victimization, and Their Influence on Risky Lifestyles: A Longitudinal Analysis Using Panel Data." *Journal of Quantitative Criminology* 22:319–340.

Schuck, Amie M. 2013. "A Life-Course Perspective on Adolescents' Attitudes to Police: DARE, Delinquency, and Residential Segregation." *Journal of Research in Crime and Delinquency* 50(4):579–607.

Schuman, Howard and Stanley Presser. 1981. *Questions and Answers in Attitude Surveys: Experiments on Question Form, Wording, and Context.* New York: Academic Press.

Schutt, Russell K. 1986. *Organization in a Changing Environment.* Albany: State University of New York Press.

Schutt, Russell K. (with the assistance of Tatjana Meschede). 1992. *The Perspectives of DMH Shelter Staff: Their Clients, Their Jobs, Their Shelters and the Service System.* Unpublished report to the Metro Boston Region of the Massachusetts Department of Mental Health. Boston: Department of Sociology, University of Massachusetts.

Schutt, Russell K. 2011a. "Evaluation of the Coordinated Care Program." Proposal to Institutional Review Board for the Protection of Human Subjects, University of Massachusetts Boston.

Schutt, Russell K. 2011b. *Homelessness, Housing, and Mental Illness.* Cambridge, MA: Harvard University Press.

Schutt, Russell K. and W. Dale Dannefer. 1988. "Detention Decisions in Juvenile Cases: JINS, JDs and Gender." *Law & Society Review* 22(3):509–520.

Schutt, Russell K., Xiaogang Deng, Gerald R. Garrett, Stephanie Hartwell, Sylvia Mignon, Joseph Bebo, Matthew O'Neill, Mary Aruda, Pat Duynstee, Pam DiNapoli, and Helen Reiskin. 1996. *Substance Use and Abuse Among UMass Boston Students.* Boston: Department of Sociology, University of Massachusetts. Unpublished report.

Schutt, Russell K. and Jacqueline Fawcett. 2005. *Case Management in the Women's Health Network.* Boston: University of Massachusetts. Unpublished report.

Schutt, Russell K. and M. L. Fennell. 1992. "Shelter Staff Satisfaction With Services, the Service Network and Their Jobs." *Current Research on Occupations and Professions* 7:177–200.

Schutt, Russell K. and Stephen M. Goldfinger. 1996. "Housing Preferences and Perceptions of Health and Functioning Among Homeless Mentally Ill Persons." *Psychiatric Services* 47:381–386.

Schutt, Russell K., Stephen M. Goldfinger, and Walter E. Penk. 1997. "Satisfaction With Residence and With Life: When Homeless Mentally Ill Persons Are Housed." *Evaluation and Program Planning* 20(2):185–194.

Schutt, Russell K., Suzanne Gunston, and John O'Brien. 1992. "The Impact of AIDS Prevention Efforts on AIDS Knowledge and Behavior Among Sheltered Homeless Adults." *Sociological Practice Review* 3(1):1–7.

Schutt, Russell K., Richard L. Hough, Stephen M. Goldfinger, Anthony F. Lehman, David L. Shern, Elie S. Valencia, and Patricia A. Wood. 2009. "Lessening Homelessness Among Persons With Mental Illness: A Comparison of Five Randomized Treatment Trials." *Asian Journal of Psychiatry* 2:100–105. www.ncbi.nlm.nih.gov/pmc/articles/PMC2788308/pdf/nihms147743.pdf

Schwandt, Thomas A. 1994. "Constructivist, Interpretivist Approaches to Human Inquiry." Pp. 118–137 in *Handbook of Qualitative Research,* edited by Norman K. Denzin and Yvonna S. Lincoln. Thousand Oaks, CA: Sage.

Schwartz, John. 2005. "Myths Run Wild in Blog Tsunami Debate." *The New York Times,* January 3, p. A9.

Schwarz, Norbert. 2010. "Measurement as Cooperative Communication: What Research Participants Learn From Questionnaires." Pp. 43–59 in *The SAGE Handbook of Measurement,* edited by Geoffrey Walford, Eric Tucker, and Madhu Viswanathan. Thousand Oaks, CA: Sage.

Scott, Janny. 2001. "A Nation by the Numbers, Smudged." *The New York Times,* July 1, pp. 21, 22.

Scott, John. 2013. *Social Network Analysis,* 3rd ed. Thousand Oaks, CA: Sage.

Scriven, Michael. 1972a. "The Methodology of Evaluation." Pp. 123–136 in *Evaluating Action Programs: Readings in Social Action and Education,* edited by Carol H. Weiss. Boston: Allyn & Bacon.

Scriven, Michael. 1972b. "Prose and Cons About Goal-Free Evaluation." *Evaluation Comment* 3:1–7.

Scull, Andrew T. 1988. "Deviance and Social Control." Pp. 667–693 in *Handbook of Sociology*, edited by Neil J. Smelser. Newbury Park, CA: Sage.

Sechrest, Lee and Souraya Sidani. 1995. "Quantitative and Qualitative Methods: Is There an Alternative?" *Evaluation and Program Planning* 18:77–87.

Selm, Martine Van and Nicholas W. Jankowski. 2006. "Conducting Online Surveys." *Quality & Quantity* 40:435–456.

Selwitz, Ada Sue, Norma Epley, and Janelle Erickson. 2013. "Basic Institutional Review Board (IRB): Regulations and Review Process." Miami: Collaborative Institutional Training Initiative at the University of Miami. Retrieved December 31, 2013, from https://www.citiprogram.org/

Shadish, William R., Thomas D. Cook, and Laura C. Leviton (Eds.). 1991. *Foundations of Program Evaluation: Theories of Practice*. Thousand Oaks, CA: Sage.

Sharma, Divya. 2009. "Research Ethics and Sensitive Behaviors: Underground Economy." Pp. 426–441 in *The Handbook of Social Research Ethics*, edited by Donna M. Mertens and Pauline E. Ginsberg. Thousand Oaks, CA: Sage.

Shepherd, Jane, David Hill, Joel Bristor, and Pat Montalvan. 1996. "Converting an Ongoing Health Study to CAPI: Findings From the National Health and Nutrition Study." Pp. 159–164 in *Health Survey Research Methods Conference Proceedings*, edited by Richard B. Warnecke. Hyattsville, MD: U.S. Department of Health and Human Services.

Sherman, Lawrence W. 1992. *Policing Domestic Violence: Experiments and Dilemmas*. New York: Free Press.

Sherman, Lawrence W. 1993. "Implications of a Failure to Read the Literature." *American Sociological Review* 58:888–889.

Sherman, Lawrence W. and Richard A. Berk. 1984. "The Specific Deterrent Effects of Arrest for Domestic Assault." *American Sociological Review* 49:261–272.

Sherman, Lawrence W. and Heather M. Harris. 2013. "Increased Homicide Victimization of Suspects Arrested for Domestic Assault: A 23-Year Follow-Up of the Milwaukee Domestic Violence Experiment (MilDVE)." *Journal of Experimental Criminology* 9:491–514.

Sherman, Lawrence W. and Douglas A. Smith, with Janell D. Schmidt and Dennis P. Rogan. 1992. "Crime, Punishment, and Stake in Conformity: Legal and Informal Control of Domestic Violence." *American Sociological Review* 57:680–690.

Shermer, Michael. 1997. *Why People Believe Weird Things: Pseudoscience, Superstition, and Other Confusions of Our Time*. New York: W. H. Freeman.

Shrout, Patrick E. 2011. "Integrating Causal Analysis into Psychopathology Research." Pp. 3–24 in *Causality and Psychopathology: Finding the Determinants of Disorders and Their Cures*, edited by Patrick E. Shrout, Katherine M. Keyes, and Katherine Ornstein. New York: Oxford University Press.

Sieber, Joan E. 1992. *Planning Ethically Responsible Research: A Guide for Students and Internal Review Boards*. Thousand Oaks, CA: Sage.

Sieber, Joan E. and Martin B. Tolich. 2013. *Planning Ethically Responsible Research*, 2nd ed. Thousand Oaks, CA: Sage.

Sin, Chih Hoong. 2005. "Seeking Informed Consent: Reflections on Research Practice." *Sociology* 39:277–294.

Sjoberg, Gideon (Ed.). 1967. *Ethics, Politics, and Social Research*. Cambridge, MA: Schenkman.

Skinner, Harvey A. and Wen-Jenn Sheu. 1982. "Reliability of Alcohol Use Indices: The Lifetime Drinking History and the MAST." *Journal of Studies on Alcohol* 43(11):1157–1170.

Skocpol, Theda. 1979. *States and Social Revolutions: A Comparative Analysis of France, Russia, and China*. New York: Cambridge University Press.

Skocpol, Theda. 1984. "Emerging Agendas and Recurrent Strategies in Historical Sociology." Pp. 356–391 in *Vision and Method in Historical Sociology*, edited by Theda Skocpol. New York: Cambridge University Press.

Skocpol, Theda and Margaret Somers. 1979. "The Uses of Comparative History in Macrosocial Inquiry." Pp. 72–95 in *Social Revolutions in the Modern World*, edited by Theda Skocpol. New York: Cambridge University Press.

Sloboda, Zili, Richard C. Stephens, Peggy C. Stephens, Scott F. Grey, Brent Teasdale, Richard D. Hawthorne, Joseph Williams, and Jesse F. Marquette. 2009. "The Adolescent Substance Abuse Prevention Study: A Randomized Field Trial of a Universal Substance Abuse Prevention Program." *Drug and Alcohol Dependence* 102(1–3):1–10.

Smith, Erica L. and Alexia Cooper. 2013. *Homicide in the U.S. Known to Law Enforcement, 2011*. Washington, DC: Bureau of Justice Statistics, U.S. Department of Justice.

Smith, Tom W. 1984. "Nonattitudes: A Review and Evaluation." Pp. 215–255 in *Surveying Subjective Phenomena*, vol. 2, edited by Charles F. Turner and Elizabeth Martin. New York: Russell Sage Foundation.

Smith, Tom W. 1995. "Trends in Nonresponse Rates." *International Journal of Public Opinion Research* 7: 157–171.

Smith-Lovin, Lynn. 2007. "Do We Need a Public Sociology? It Depends on What You Mean by 'Sociology.'" Pp. 124–134 in *Public Sociology: Fifteen Eminent Sociologists Debate Politics and the Profession in the Twenty-First Century*, edited by Dan Clawson, Robert Zussman, Joya Misra, Naomi Gerstel, and Randall Stokes. Berkeley: University of California Press.

Smithson, Janet. 2008. "Focus Groups." Pp. 357–370 in *The SAGE Handbook of Social Research Methods*, edited by Pertti Alasuutari, Leonard Bickman, and Julia Brannen. Thousand Oaks, CA: Sage.

Smyth, Jolene D., Don A. Dillman, Leah Melani Christian, and Michael J. Stern. 2004. *How Visual Grouping Influences Answers to Internet Surveys*. Extended version of paper presented at the Annual Meeting of the American Association for Public Opinion Research, Phoenix, AZ, May 13. Retrieved July 5, 2005, from http://survey.sesrc.wsu.edu/dillman/papers.htm

Snipp, C. Matthew. 2003. "Racial Measurement in the American Census: Past Practices and Implications for the Future." *Annual Review of Sociology* 29:563–588.

Snow, David L., Jacob Kraemer Tebes, and Michael W. Arthur. 1992. "Panel Attrition and External Validity in Adolescent Substance Use Research." *Journal of Consulting and Clinical Psychology* 60:804–807.

Sobell, Linda C., Mark B. Sobell, Diane M. Riley, Reinhard Schuller, D. Sigfrido Pavan, Anthony Cancilla, Felix Klajner, and Gloria I. Leo. 1988. "The Reliability of Alcohol Abusers' Self-Reports of Drinking and Life Events That Occurred in the Distant Past." *Journal of Studies on Alcohol* 49(2):225–232.

Sosin, Michael R., Paul Colson, and Susan Grossman. 1988. *Homelessness in Chicago: Poverty and Pathology, Social Institutions and Social Change*. Chicago: Chicago Community Trust.

Speiglman, Richard and Patricia Spear. 2009. "The Role of Institutional Review Boards: Ethics: Now You See Them, Now You Don't." Pp. 121–134 in *The Handbook of Social Research Ethics*, edited by Donna M. Mertens and Pauline E. Ginsberg. Thousand Oaks, CA: Sage.

Spretnak, Charlene. 1991. *States of Grace: The Recovery of Meaning in the Postmodern Age*. New York: HarperCollins.

St. Jean, Peter K. B. 2007. *Pockets of Crime: Broken Windows, Collective Efficacy, and the Criminal Point of View*. Chicago: University of Chicago Press.

St. Pierre, Robert G. and Peter H. Rossi. 2006. "Randomize Groups, Not Individuals: A Strategy for Improving Early Childhood Programs." *Evaluation Review* 30:656–685.

Stake, Robert E. 1995. *The Art of Case Study Research.* Thousand Oaks, CA: Sage.

Stake, Robert and Fazal Rizvi. 2009. "Research Ethics in Transnational Spaces." Pp. 521–536 in *The Handbook of Social Research Ethics,* edited by Donna M. Mertens and Pauline E. Ginsberg. Thousand Oaks, CA: Sage.

Statistic Brain. 2013. "Social Networking Statistics." Retrieved December 27, 2013, from www.statisticbrain.com/social-networking-statistics/

Stephen, Jason M., Michael F. Young, and Thomas Calabrese. 2007. "Does Moral Judgment Go Offline When Students Are Online? A Comparative Analysis of Undergraduates' Beliefs and Behaviors Related to Conventional and Digital Cheating." *Ethics & Behavior* 17:233–254.

Stern, Michael J. and Don A. Dillman. 2006. "Community Participation, Social Ties, and Use of the Internet." *City & Community* 5:409–424.

Stewart, David W. and Michael A. Kamins. 1993. *Secondary Research: Information Sources and Methods,* 2nd ed. Newbury Park, CA: Sage.

Stewart, James K. 2011. "John Laub and Robert Sampson Awarded Stockholm Prize." Retrieved June 11, 2014, from www.nij.gov/about/director/Pages/stockholm-prize.aspx

Stille, Alexander. 2000. "A Happiness Index With a Long Reach: Beyond G.N.P. to Subtler Measures." *The New York Times,* May 20, pp. A17, A19.

Stokoe, Elizabeth. 2006. "On Ethnomethodology, Feminism, and the Analysis of Categorical Reference to Gender in Talk-in-Interaction." *The Sociological Review* 54:467–494.

Strauss, Anselm L. and Juliette Corbin. 1990. *The Basics of Qualitative Research: Grounded Theory Procedures and Techniques.* Newbury Park, CA: Sage.

Strickling, Lawrence E. 2010. *Digital Nation: 21st Century America's Progress Toward Universal Broadband Internet Access. An NTIA Research Preview.* Washington, DC: National Telecommunications and Information Administration, U.S. Department of Commerce.

Strunk, William Jr. and E. B. White. 2000. *The Elements of Style,* 4th ed. New York: Allyn & Bacon.

Sudman, Seymour. 1976. *Applied Sampling.* New York: Academic Press.

Sue, Valerie M. and Lois A. Ritter. 2012. *Conducting Online Surveys,* 2nd ed. Thousand Oaks, CA: Sage.

Sulkunen, Pekka. 2008. "Social Research and Social Practice in Post-Positivist Society." Pp. 68–80 in *The SAGE Handbook of Social Research Methods,* edited by Pertti Alasuutari, Leonard Bickman, and Julia Brannen. Thousand Oaks, CA: Sage.

Sunderland, Antonia. 2005. *Children, Families and Welfare Reform: A Three-City Study.* Princeton, NJ: The Robert Wood Johnson Foundation. Retrieved October 5, 2005, from www.rwjf.org/reports/grr/037218.htm

"Survey on Adultery: 'I Do' Means 'I Don't.'" 1993. *The New York Times,* October 19, p. A20.

Survey Research Laboratory. 2008. *List of Academic and Not-for-Profit Survey Research Organizations (LANSRO).* Chicago: College of Urban Planning and Public Affairs, University of Illinois at Chicago. Retrieved May 17, 2008, from www.srl.uic.edu/LANSRO.doc

Swarns, Rachel L. 2004. "Hispanics Debate Racial Grouping by Census." *The New York Times,* October 24, pp. A1, A18.

Tavernise, Sabrina. 2002. "How Many Russians? Let Us Weigh the Count, Cooperation or No." *The New York Times,* October 10, p. A13.

Taylor, Charles Lewis and David A. Jodice. 1986. *World Handbook of Political and Social Indicators III: 1948–1982.* File available from the Inter-university Consortium for Political and Social Research (ICPSR), Study #7761.

Taylor, Jerry. 1999. "DARE Gets Updated in Some Area Schools, Others Drop Program." *The Boston Sunday Globe,* May 16, pp. 1, 11.

Taylor, Paul, Rick Fry, and Paul Oates. 2014. *The Rising Cost of Not Going to College.* Washington, DC: Pew Research Center, February.

Testa, Maria, Jennifer A. Livingston, and Carol VanZile-Tamsen. 2011. "Advancing the Study of Violence Against Women Using Mixed Methods: Integrating Qualitative Methods Into a Quantitative Research Program." *Violence Against Women* 17(2): 236–250.

Thomas, Neil. 2005. "Disaster Center Researchers to Study Katrina Response." *UDaily,* September 15. Retrieved May 26, 2008, from www.udel.edu/PR/UDaily/2005/mar/DRC091505.html

Thorne, Barrie. 1993. *Gender Play: Girls and Boys in School.* New Brunswick, NJ: Rutgers University Press.

Thrasher, Frederic M. 1927. *The Gang: A Study of 1,313 Gangs in Chicago.* Chicago: University of Chicago Press.

Tierney, John. 2009. "Public Policy That Makes Test Subjects of Us All." *The New York Times,* April 7, p. D1.

Tierney, John. 2013. "Prison Population Can Shrink When Police Crowd the Streets." *The New York Times,* January 26, p. A1.

Tigges, Beth Baldwin. 2003. "Parental Consent and Adolescent Risk Behavior Research." *Journal of Nursing Scholarship* 35:283–289.

Timmer, Doug A., D. Stanley Eitzen, and Kathryn D. Talley. 1993. *Paths to Homelessness: Extreme Poverty and the Urban Housing Crisis.* Boulder, CO: Westview Press.

Tinkler, Penny. 2013. *Using Photographs in Social and Historical Research.* Thousand Oaks, CA: Sage.

Tjaden, Patricia and Nancy Thoennes. 2000. *Extent, Nature, and Consequences of Intimate Partner Violence: Findings From the National Violence Against Women Survey, NCJ 181867.* Washington, DC: Office of Justice Programs, National Institute of Justice and the Centers for Disease Control and Prevention.

Toby, Jackson. 1957. "Social Disorganization and Stake in Conformity: Complementary Factors in the Predatory Behavior of Hoodlums." *Journal of Criminal Law, Criminology and Police Science* 48:12–17.

Toppo, Greg. 2002. "Antidrug Program Backed by Study." *The Boston Globe,* October 29, p. A10.

Tourangeau, Roger. 1999. "Context Effects." Pp. 111–132 in *Cognition and Survey Research,* edited by Monroe G. Sirken, Douglas J. Herrmann, Susan Schechter, Norbert Schwartz, Judith M. Tanur, and Roger Tourangeau. New York: Wiley.

Tourangeau, Roger. 2004. "Survey Research and Societal Change." *Annual Review of Psychology* 55:775–801.

Tourangeau, Roger, Frederick G. Conrad, and Mick P. Couper. 2012. *The Science of Web Surveys.* Oxford: Oxford University Press.

Townsend, Meg, Dana Hunt, Caity Baxter, and Peter Finn. 2005. *Interim Report: Evaluability Assessment of the President's Family Justice Center Initiative.* Cambridge, MA: Abt Associates. Retrieved March 20, 2011, from www.ncjrs.gov/pdffiles1/nij/grants/212278.pdf

Tufte, Edward R. 1983. *The Visual Display of Quantitative Information.* Cheshire, CT: Graphics Press.

Turabian, Kate L. 2007. *A Manual for Writers of Term Papers, Theses, and Dissertations.* 7th ed. Chicago: University of Chicago Press.

Turkle, Sherry. 2011. *Alone Together: Why We Expect More From Technology and Less From Each Other.* New York: Basic Books.

Turner, Charles F. and Elizabeth Martin (Eds.). 1984. *Surveying Subjective Phenomena,* vols. 1 and 2. New York: Russell Sage Foundation.

Turner, Jonathan H., Leonard Beeghley, and Charles H. Powers. 1995. *The Emergence of*

Sociological Theory, 3rd ed. Belmont, CA: Wadsworth.

Tyler, Tom R. 1990. "The Social Psychology of Authority: Why Do People Obey an Order to Harm Others?" *Law & Society Review* 24:1089–1102.

Uchitelle, Louis. 1997. "Measuring Inflation: Can't Do It, Can't Stop Trying." *The New York Times,* March 16, p. 4.

Uchitelle, Louis. 1999. "Devising New Math to Define Poverty." *The New York Times,* October 16, pp. A1, A14.

UCLA Center for Communication Policy. 2001. *The UCLA Internet Report 2001: Surveying the Digital Future.* Los Angeles: UCLA Center for Communication Policy.

UCLA Center for Communication Policy. 2003. *The UCLA Internet Report: Surveying the Digital Future, Year Three.* Los Angeles: UCLA Center for Communication Policy. Retrieved June 15, 2005, from www.digitalcenter.org/pdf/InternetReport-YearThree.pdf

UK Data Service. 2014. "Key Data." Retrieved July 10, 2014, from http://ukdataservice.ac.uk/get-data/key-data.aspx

U.S. Bureau of Economic Analysis. 2004. *Customer Satisfaction Survey Report, FY 2004.* Washington, DC: U.S Department of Commerce.

U.S. Bureau of Labor Statistics, Department of Labor. 1991. *Major Programs of the Bureau of Labor Statistics.* Washington, DC: U.S. Bureau of Labor Statistics, Department of Labor.

U.S. Bureau of Labor Statistics, Department of Labor. 1997a. *Employment and Earnings.* Washington, DC: U.S. Bureau of Labor Statistics, Department of Labor.

U.S. Bureau of Labor Statistics, Department of Labor. 1997b. *Handbook of Methods.* Washington, DC: U.S. Bureau of Labor Statistics, Department of Labor.

U.S. Census Bureau. 1981. *Section 1, Vital Statistics. Statistical Abstract of the United States, 1981,* 102nd ed. Washington, DC: U.S. Department of Commerce, Census Bureau.

U.S. Census Bureau. 1994. *Census Catalog and Guide, 1994.* Washington, DC: U.S. Bureau of the Census.

U.S. Census Bureau. 1999. *United States Census 2000, Updated Summary: Census 2000 Operational Plan.* Washington, DC: U.S. Department of Commerce, Bureau of the Census, February.

U.S. Census Bureau. 2001. "Statement by William G. Barron Jr. on the Current Status of Results of Census 2000 Accuracy and Coverage Evaluation Survey." *United States Department of Commerce News,* July 13. Retrieved January 19, 2003, from www.census.gov/PressRelease/www/2001/cb01cs06.html

U.S. Census Bureau. 2006. *Census Bureau Guideline: Language Translation of Data Collection Instruments and Supporting Materials.* Washington, DC: U.S. Census Bureau, Census Advisory Committees. Retrieved May 24, 2008, from www.census.gov/cac/www/007585.html

U.S. Census Bureau. 2010a. "$1.6 Billion in 2010 Census Savings Returned." *United States Department of Commerce News,* August 10. Retrieved March 17, 2011, from http://2010.census.gov/news/releases/operations/

U.S. Census Bureau. 2010b. "Door-to-Door Visits Begin for 2010 Census." *United States Department of Commerce News,* April 30. Retrieved March 17, 2011, from http://2010.census.gov/news/releases/operations/

U.S. Census Bureau. 2010c. "2010 Census Forms Arrive in 120 Million Mailboxes Across Nation." *United States Department of Commerce News,* March 15. Retrieved March 17, 2011, from http://2010.census.gov/news/releases/operations/

U.S. Census Bureau. 2010d. *Questions and Answers: Real People, Real Questions, Real Answers.* Washington, DC: U.S. Department of Commerce, Bureau of the Census. Retrieved March 17, 2011, from http://2010.census.gov/2010census/about/answers.php

U.S. Census Bureau. 2013a. "U.S. and World Population Clock." Retrieved December 27, 2013, from www.census.gov/popclock

U.S. Census Bureau. 2013b. "Census Bureau News—Extended Measures of Well-Being: Living Conditions in the United States: 2011." Washington, DC: U.S. Census Bureau. Retrieved May 5, 2014, from www.prnewswire.com/news-releases/census-bureau-news----extended-measures-of-well-being-living-conditions-in-the-united-states-2011-222530671.html

U.S. Department of Health and Human Services, Substance Abuse and Mental Health Services Administration, Center for Mental Health Services. 1995. *Client- Level Evaluation Procedure Manual.* Washington, DC: U.S. Department of Health and Human Services.

U.S. Government Accountability Office (GAO). 2006. *Prevalence of Domestic Violence, Sexual Assault, Dating Violence, and Stalking: Briefing to Congressional Committees.* GAO 07–148R Washington, DC: GAO.

U.S. Office of Management and Budget. 2002. *Government and Performance Results Act of 1993.* Washington, DC: U.S. Office of Management and Budget, Executive Office of the President.

Vaessen, Martin. 1993. "Evaluation of Population Data: Errors and Deficiencies." Pp. 4-1–4-69 in *Readings in Population Research Methodology, Vol. 1, Basic Tools,* edited by Donald J. Bogue, Eduardo E. Arriaga, and Douglas L. Anderton. Chicago: Social Development Center, for the United Nations Population Fund.

Vaillant, George E. 1995. *The Natural History of Alcoholism Revisited.* Cambridge, MA: Harvard University Press.

van de Vijver, Fons and Kwok Leung. 1997. *Methods and Data Analysis for Cross-Cultural Research.* Thousand Oaks, CA: Sage.

Van Hoye, Greet and Filip Lievens. 2003. "The Effects of Sexual Orientation on Hirability Ratings: An Experimental Study." *Journal of Business and Psychology* 18:15–30.

Van Maanen, John. 1982. "Fieldwork on the Beat." Pp. 103–151 in *Varieties of Qualitative Research,* edited by John Van Maanen, James M. Dabbs Jr., and Robert R. Faulkner. Beverly Hills, CA: Sage.

Van Maanen, John. 1995. "An End to Innocence: The Ethnography of Ethnography." Pp. 1–35 in *Representation in Ethnography,* edited by John Van Maanen. Thousand Oaks, CA: Sage.

Vega, Tanzina. 2014. "To Measure More Diverse America, Solution May Be in Census Questions." *The New York Times,* July 2, pp. A12, A16.

Venkatapuram, Sridhar. 2013. "Subjective Wellbeing: A Primer for Poverty Analysts." *Journal of Poverty and Social Justice* 21:5–17.

Venkatesh, Sudhir. 2008. *Gang Leader for a Day: A Rogue Sociologist Takes to the Streets.* New York: Penguin.

Verba, Sidney and Norman Nie. 1972. *Political Participation: Political Democracy and Social Equality.* New York: Harper & Row.

Verba, Sidney, Norman Nie, and Jae-On Kim. 1978. *Participation and Political Equality: A Seven-Nation Comparison.* New York: Cambridge University Press.

Vernez, Georges, M. Audrey Burnam, Elizabeth A. McGlynn, Sally Trude, and Brian S. Mittman. 1988. *Review of California's Program for the Homeless Mentally Disabled.* Santa Monica, CA: RAND.

Vidich, Arthur J. and Stanford M. Lyman. 2004. "Qualitative Methods: Their History in Sociology and Anthropology." Pp. 27–84 in *The Handbook of Qualitative Research,* 2nd ed., edited by Norman Denzin and Yvonna S. Lincoln. Thousand Oaks, CA: Sage.

Villarreal, Andrés. 2010. "Stratification by Skin Color in Contemporary Mexico." *American Sociological Review* 75:652–678.

Vincus, Amy A., Chris Ringwalt, Melissa S. Harris, Stephen R. Shamblen. 2010. "A Short-Term, Quasi-Experimental Evaluation of D.A.R.E.'s Revised Elementary School Curriculum." *Journal of Drug Education* 40:37–49.

Viswanathan, Madhu. 2005. *Measurement Error and Research Design.* Thousand Oaks, CA: Sage.

Index

Exhibits are indicated by "e" following the page number.

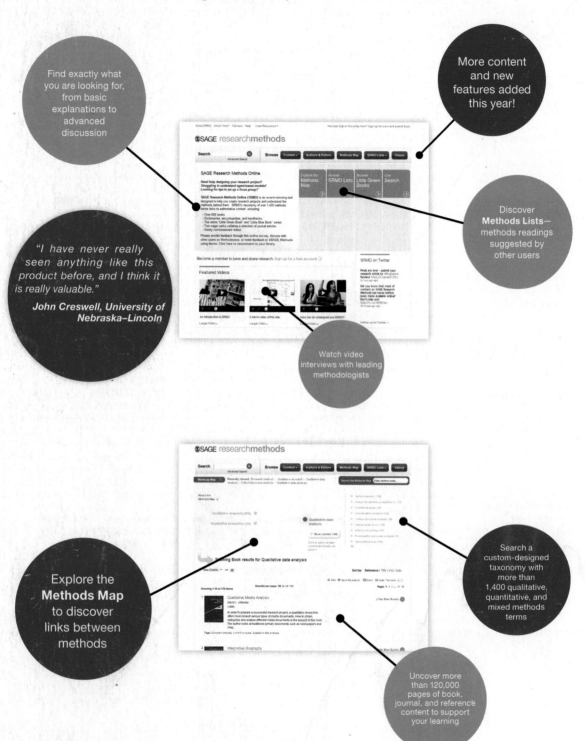

SAGE researchmethods

The essential online tool for researchers from the world's leading methods publisher

Find exactly what you are looking for, from basic explanations to advanced discussion

More content and new features added this year!

"I have never really seen anything like this product before, and I think it is really valuable."

John Creswell, University of Nebraska–Lincoln

Discover **Methods Lists**—methods readings suggested by other users

Watch video interviews with leading methodologists

Explore the **Methods Map** to discover links between methods

Search a custom-designed taxonomy with more than 1,400 qualitative, quantitative, and mixed methods terms

Uncover more than 120,000 pages of book, journal, and reference content to support your learning

Find out more at
www.sageresearchmethods.com